D0742233

Contributions to Insurance Economics

Huebner International Series on Risk, Insurance, and Economic Security

J. David Cummins, Editor
The Wharton School
University of Pennsylvania
Philadelphia, Pennsylvania, USA

Series Advisors:

Dr. Phelim P. Boyle
University of Waterloo, Canada
Dr. Jean Lemaire
University of Pennsylvania, USA
Professor Akihiko Tsubol
Kagawa University, Japan
Dr. Richard Zeckhauser
Harvard University, USA

OTHER books in the series:

Cummins, J. David; Smith, Barry D.; Vance, R. Neil; VanDerhei, Jack L.: *Risk Classification in Life Insurance*
Mintel, Judith: *Insurance Rate Litigation*
Cummins, J. David: *Strategic Planning and Modeling in Property-Liability Insurance*
Lemaire, Jean: *Automobile Insurance: Actuarial Models*
Rushing, William.: *Social Functions and Economic Aspects of Health Insurance*
Cummins, J. David and Harrington, Scott E.: *Fair Rate of Return in Property-Liability Insurance*
Appel, David and Borba, Philip S.: *Workers Compensation Insurance Pricing*
Cummins, J. David and Derrig, Richard A.: *Classical Insurance Solvency Theory*
Borba, Philip S. and Appel, David: *Benefits, Costs, and Cycles in Workers Compensation*
Cummins, J. David and Derrig, Richard A.: *Financial Models of Insurance Solvency*
Williams, C. Arthur: *An International Comparison of Workers' Compensation*
Cummins, J. David and Derrig, Richard A.: Managing the Insolvency Risk of Insurance Companies

The objective of the series is to publish original research and advanced textbooks dealing with all major aspects of risk bearing and economic security. The emphasis is on books that will be of interest to an international audience. Interdisciplinary topics as well as those from traditional disciplines such as economics, risk and insurance, and actuarial science are within the scope of the series. The goal is to provide an outlet for imaginative approaches to problems in both the theory and practice of risk and economic security.

Contributions to Insurance Economics

edited by

Georges Dionne
Université de Montréal

Kluwer Academic Publishers
Boston/Dordrecht/London

Distributors for North America:
Kluwer Academic Publishers
101 Philip Drive
Assinippi Park
Norwell, Massachusetts 02061 USA

Distributors for all other countries:
Kluwer Academic Publishers Group
Distribution Centre
Post Office Box 322
3300 AH Dordrecht, THE NETHERLANDS

Library of Congress Cataloging-in-Publication Data

Contributions to insurance economics/edited by Georges Dionne.
        p.   cm. — (Huebner international series on risk, insurance,
and economic security)
    Includes bibliographical references and index.
    ISBN 0-7923-9175-6
    1. Insurance.   2. Risk (Insurance)   I. Dionne, Georges.
II. Series.
HG8052.C66   1991
368 — dc20   91-19773
                                                        CIP

Printed on acid-free paper.

Printed in the United States of America

à Danielle,
Jean-François
et André-Pierre

Contents

Preface

For a number of years, I have been teaching and doing research in the economics of uncertainty, information, and insurance. Although it is now possible to find textbooks and books of essays on uncertainty and information in economics and finance for graduate students and researchers, there is no equivalent material that covers advanced research in insurance.

The purpose of this book is to fill this gap in literature. It provides original surveys and essays in the field of insurance economics. The contributions offer basic reference, new material, and teaching supplements to graduate students and researchers in economics, finance, and insurance. It represents a complement to the book of readings entitled *Foundations of Insurance Economics — Readings in Economics and Finance*, recently published by the S.S. Huebner Foundation of Insurance Education. In that book, the editors (G. Dionne and S. Harrington) disseminate key papers in the literature and publish an original survey of major contributions in the field.

This book is divided into two main parts. Part I contains six survey articles on subjects that represent significant developments over the past years: optimality of insurance contracting, liability insurance, moral hazard, adverse selection, insurance pricing, and econometric estimation of accident distributions. Part II extends the recent literature by presenting fourteen essays on subjects of current research in a) the theory of insurance economics covering nonlinear expected utility, prudence, deviant beliefs, incomplete markets, increases in risk, ambiguity, b) problems of information including moral hazard and competitive markets, adverse selection and probationary periods, incomplete information and risk categorization, and c) empirical studies on workers' compensation, adverse selection, and the effects of no-fault automobile insurance. Each paper is presented with an abstract and key words, and can be read independently of the other contributions in the volume. All of the submitted papers were reviewed by at least one anonymous referee.

I wish to acknowledge the S.S. Huebner Foundation for Insurance Education at the University of Pennsylvania, the Université de Montréal, and the Geneva Association for providing financial support to the preparation and publication of this book. Many thanks are also addressed to all authors and referees for their significant collaboration and, more important, for their respect for the academic standards of quality established at the beginning of the project. This book would not have been possible without the generosity of many collaborators at the Economics Department and the Centre for Research on Transportation of the Université de Montréal who spent many hours on all stages of the production process. I would like to emphasize the collaboration of Anne Lacaille, Carole Laflamme, Josée Lafontaine, and Andrée Mathieu. Finally, I would like to thank the people with whom I have discussed the content and the form of this book and, particularly, R. Arnott, M. Boyer, E. Briys, D. Cummins, P. Danzon, N. Doherty, L. Eeckhoudt, C. Fluet, C. Gollier, M. Gaudry, R. Grimes, S. Harrington, R. Lacroix, H. Loubergé, C. Montmarquette, B. Ryder, Z. Rolnik, C. Vanasse, and P. Viala.

— Georges Dionne
Université de Montréal

List of Contributors

Y. Alarie
Université de Montréal

R. Arnott
Boston College

M. Boyer
Université de Montréal

J. D. Cummins
University of Pennsylvania

B. Dahlby
University of Alberta

P. Danzon
University of Pennsylvania

R. A. Devlin
University of Ottawa

G. Dionne
Université de Montréal

N. Doherty
University of Pennsylvania

R. M. Hogarth
University of Chicago

E. Karni
Johns Hopkins University

M. Kimball
University of Michigan

H. Kunreuther
University of Pennsylvania

J. M. Marshall
University of California at Santa Barbara

M. Moore
Duke University

S. Rea
University of Toronto

B. Ramaswami
University of Minnesota

T. L. Roe
University of Minnesota

L. Eeckhoudt
*Universités Catholiques de Mons
    et de Lille*

C. Fluet
Université du Québec à Montréal

M. Gaudry
Université de Montréal

C. Gollier
H.E.C., Paris

S. Harrington
University of South Carolina

C. Vanasse
Université de Montréal

K. Viscusi
Duke University

M. Weiss
Temple University

R. Winter
University of Toronto

List of Referees

R. Arnott
Boston College

L. Bauwens
Core, Belgium

U. Berkok
Université du Québec à Montréal

G. Blazenko
Simon Fraser University

D. Bolduc
Université Laval

E. Briys
H.E.C., Paris

K. J. Crocker
Pennsylvania State University

J. D. Cummins
University of Pennsylvania

B. Dahlby
University of Alberta

M. Demers
Carleton University

N. Doherty
University of Pennsylvania

L. Eeckhoudt
Universités Catholiques de Mons et de Lille

L. Epstein
University of Toronto

C. Fluet
Université du Québec à Montréal

N. Fortin
Université de Montréal

M. Gaudry
Université de Montréal

C. Gollier
H.E.C., Paris

C. Gouriéroux
C.E.P.R.E.M.A.P., Paris

S. Harrington
University of South Carolina

S. Klugman
Drake University

A. Krueger
Princeton University

R. Lacroix
Université de Montréal

P. Lefebvre
Université du Québec à Montréal

J. Lemaire
University of Pennsylvania

L. Lévy-Garboua
Université de Paris I

H. Loubergé
Université de Genève

J. M. Marshall
University of California at Santa Barbara

S. Rea
University of Toronto

J. Ruser
U.S. Department of Labor

H. Schlesinger
University of Alabama

P. St-Michel
C.S.S.T. (Québec)

C. Vanasse
Université de Montréal

P. Viala
H.E.C., Paris

M. Weiss
Temple University

R. Winter
University of Toronto

Introduction

In the Arrow-Debreu economy, different market arrangements are introduced to obtain efficient risk shifting. The role of insurance is to transfer individual risks to parties with comparative advantage in risk bearing. For example, risk-averse individuals pay a fixed price to a more diversified insurer who offers to bear the risk at that price. Under well known assumptions of basic insurance models, an equilibrium is characterized by full insurance coverage. The two standard theorems of welfare economics hold and market prices of insurance are equal to social opportunity costs.

However, risk is not completely shifted in any market. The contributions published in this book discuss many of the reasons that explain incomplete insurance coverage. C. Gollier's article is concerned with transaction costs and insurers' risk aversion. Coinsurance is explained by either insurers' risk aversion or convexity of transaction costs. Transaction costs are also shown to be a motivation for deductibles. The role of the technical constraint that coverage must be nonnegative is also discussed. Another assumption in the standard models of optimum insurance concerns the implicit agreement of both parties on the probabilities of loss. J. M. Marshall relaxes that assumption and considers the case where the insured is more optimistic than the insurer. The results are functions of how *optimism* is defined. When optimism is defined broadly, the optimum risk bearing contracts can have almost any form and may not resemble insurance contracts. However, under a condition that restricts disagreement, the optimum contracts are insurance arrangements.

Externalities between individuals' losses are sufficient to justify the emergence of liability rules for injuries caused to third parties and risk aversion can explain the presence of liability insurance. P. Danzon and S.

Harrington introduce the literature on the demand for and the supply of liability insurance. Emphasis is put on the relationships between liability law, liability insurance, and risk reduction. Asymmetric information on individuals' actions that affect other parties' welfare results in a tradeoff between care and risk bearing in liability insurance as in any form of insurance contracts. R. Winter synthesizes and extends the general theory of optimal insurance under moral hazard. He distinguishes ex-ante moral hazard on the probability of an accident from ex-ante moral hazard on the size of the loss. The distinction generates predictions as to when deductibles, coinsurance, and coverage limits are observed. Moral hazard, however, does not only affect the nature of insurance contracts but also alters the positive and normative properties of competitive equilibrium. R. Arnott shows how moral hazard may give rise to nonconvex indifference curves, for example, and may alter the definition of competitive equilibrium. At one extreme, competitive equilibrium may not exist, while, at the other, there may be an infinity of equilibria. With moral hazard, neither the first nor the second theorem of welfare economics holds, and market prices do not correspond to social opportunity costs.

From the above theoretical contributions, we retain that insurance is not only an income transfer between different agents in the economy. Under moral hazard, it is predicted that insurance alters incentives for care. This prediction is empirically investigated by four papers in this volume. Moore and Viscusi analyze the net effect of job safety insurance programs where, on one hand, there are positive incentives for safety when the costs of the program are tied to the firm's safety records and, on the other hand, there are disincentives to maintain both safety (ex-ante moral hazard) and recovery periods (ex-post moral hazard) at levels corresponding to full information. From their data set, they found that net workers' compensation insurance provides incentives for safety to firms that outweigh the moral hazard effects. They also obtained that the insurance provided to workers on unsafe jobs reduces the net compensation paid to these workers.

The other three empirical contributions on moral hazard investigate the effects of no-fault automobile insurance. The main finding of D. Cummins and M. Weiss is that no-fault insurance induces drivers to shift property claims from property damage liability coverage into collision coverage. However, the effect of no-fault on total claims is less conclusive. Their results were obtained by using data from the United States. M. Gaudry and R. A. Devlin analyze the effects of the introduction of a pure no-fault system for all bodily-injury accidents in Quebec (1978). Although they used different methodologies and data, they obtained similar results concerning the increases of accidents in the new system. However, their interpretations of the results differ. While R. A. Devlin attributes significant variations to the reduction in liability, M. Gaudry argues that very little significance is explained by that factor.

Adverse selection is another problem of information that explains partial insurance. G. Dionne and N. Doherty review some of the significant results in the literature. Particularly, they discuss the issues that multi-period contracting raises: time horizon, discounting, commitment of the parties, contract renegotiation, and underreporting of accidents. They also show that different predictions on the evolution of insurer profits over time can be obtained from different assumptions concerning the sharing of information between insurers in competitive markets. Commitment between the parties to the contract is another important factor. The role of risk categorization to improve resource allocation is also discussed and the last section of the paper presents models that consider moral hazard and adverse selection simultaneously. One of the predicted results from the literature on adverse selection is tested by B. Dalhby with data on collision insurance in Canada: if the market is subject to adverse selection, an increase in an insurance policy's premium holding the coverage constant should increase the average claim frequency. He obtains that, in general, the statistical results are consistent with the presence of adverse selection.

In the literature on adverse selection, partial coverage is generally interpreted as a monetary deductible. However, as pointed out by C. Fluet, in many insurance markets the insurance coverage is excluded during a probationary period, which can be interpreted as a sorting device. In fact, he demonstrates that contracts with time-dependent coverage provide a desirable screening mechanism. The presence of adverse selection is also a sufficient condition for risk categorization. In particular, costless imperfect categorization is known to enhance efficiency. However, when categorization entails some costs, the results are ambiguous. S. Rea shows that the gains from separation may be small and the market may give overinvestment in information. The author also obtains that it may be efficient to determine the individual's risk even when neither the insurer nor the insured knows the expected loss ex-ante.

In his survey, D. Cummins reviews the theory of financial pricing of insurance and proposes some extensions that include an option model of the insurance firm and an analysis of insurance company equity as a down-and-out option. By using a model of financial insurance pricing, H. Kunreuther and R. Hogarth show evidence of the importance of ambiguity on the insurance premium setting process. Their analysis is based on recently completed national surveys of both actuaries and underwriters. The paper also explores whether new institutional arrangements are required to replace traditional insurance mechanisms for providing protection that is currently unavailable.

The last survey article (Boyer, Dionne, Vanasse) deals with the econometrics of accident distributions with an application of the different models to automobile accidents. The authors have estimated four categorical models (linear probability, probit, logit, and multinomial logit) and four count data models (Poisson and negative binomial models with and without individual characteristics in the regression component). It is shown that the negative binomial model with a regression component produces a reasonable approximation of the true distribution of accidents. In the last section of this article, they apply the statistical results to a model of insurance rating in presence of moral hazard.

The linear expected utility model has been a very useful tool in the study of optimal insurance decisions. Until recently, it was the standard paradigm used to analyze economic behavior under uncertainty. The linearity in probabilities is directly associated with the independence axiom. This axiom has been challenged by many researchers and some of them have proposed alternative models. E. Karni reviews some of the recent developments in the theory of decision making under uncertainty and apply them to the choice of optimal insurance coverage and the associated comparative statics analysis with respect to the insured's risk aversion. The contribution highlights the methodology of local expected utility analysis.

However, for many contributors in this volume, the classical expected utility model remains a useful approach for applications in insurance. L. Eeckhoudt and M. Kimball show how the concept of absolute prudence can be useful to derive comparative statics results of optimal insurance in presence of uninsurable background risk. In particular, they show that background independent risk may raise the optimal coinsurance rate and reduce the optimal level of the deductible. Generally, the presence of multiple risks is associated with incomplete markets. B. Ramaswami and T. Roe consider the effect of price risk on the crop insurance decision. They show that increasing demand uncertainty reduces optimal crop insurance whenever risk aversion is constant or decreasing. They also consider the special cases when either output risk or demand uncertainty is the sole cause of price risk. The optimal insurance coverage can also be affected by increases in the risk of the insurable asset. Intuitively, one may anticipate that a risk-averse agent faced with an exogenous mean preserving spread in the loss distribution will demand more insurance.

Y. Alarie, G. Dionne and L. Eeckhoudt show that this widespread belief does not always turn out to be true. They then present subclasses of mean preserving increases in risk that make it possible to obtain intuitively acceptable results and apply their analysis to the coinsurance coverage.

One of the common conclusions of these contributions is the absence of perfect risk shifting in any market. Many limiting elements have been identified and analyzed in different chapters: transaction costs, moral hazard, adverse selection, imperfect information, ambiguity, externalities, deviant beliefs, absence of perfect diversification on the supply side, and nonindependence of individual risks. A next important step in the understanding of the functioning of different markets is to propose a general framework that would integrate these elements. As indicated by some authors, a promising way is the integration of economics and financial models of insurance decisions.

PART I SURVEY ARTICLES

ECONOMIC THEORY OF RISK EXCHANGES: A REVIEW

Christian Gollier

CORE and Groupe HEC

Abstract

This paper reviews the economic theory of risk-sharing. We focus on the link between models with a complete set of markets for contingent claims and the theory of optimal insurance. Accordingly, an insurance contract can be viewed as a bundle of contingent goods. Transaction costs are shown to be the driving force for deductibles. Coinsurance can be due to either insurers' risk aversion or nonlinearity in administrative costs. We conclude that insurance markets seem to be inefficient in that they do not satisfy the mutuality principle, a property of efficient contingent allocations.

Key words: Insurance, risk-sharing, mutuality principle, deductible, coinsurance

Uncertainty is present in most human activities. Deterministic outcomes are definitely exceptional in the real world. This explains the growing role of the economic theory of uncertainty in the evolution of this science. Many economists have recognized that uncertainty is central in economic analysis, but early attempts to formalize this dimension were unsuccessful because of the inability to develop a theory for economic decisions under uncertainty. Daniel Bernoulli (1738), Adam Smith (1775), and Bohm-Bawerk (1881) are usually cited for their initial contribution.

3

A central problem is to determine an efficient allocation of risks in an economy as a whole. A similar problem is to characterize market mechanisms that would lead to one of these efficient allocations. This is, of course, a central question when some economic activities generate considerable risks. Without the existence of channels to share these risks, it is likely that these activities would never be initiated, therefore drastically reducing the economic growth we actually observe. A decisive step in the direction of developing a framework in which these problems can be analyzed has been made by Arrow (1953) and Debreu (1959), who introduced uncertainty in the model of Theory of Value. In this pioneering paper, risks were traded through markets for contingent goods. This view deeply influenced the development of the economic theory of uncertainty.

Insurance markets are special markets for contingent goods. Borch (1962) used the framework developed by Arrow to build an economic theory of insurance. It is fair to state that the blossoming of research in this area in the last thirty years springs from the work of these two authors. Their analysis has been extended to include transaction costs and institutional regulations. Optimal forms of insurance policies have been derived depending upon these characteristics of insurance markets. The goal of this paper is to review this research. According to initial researches on the subject, we will assume that there is a unique source of insurable risk. We recognize that this is an extreme assumption. Some authors, e.g., Doherty and Schlesinger (1983), proposed models in which this assumption is relaxed, but reviewing this part of the literature would probably be premature.

There are many areas of economic theory that use optimal insurance results as the main input of the analysis. The theory of so-called "implicit" labor contracts, initiated by Baily (1974) and Azariadis (1975), is a striking example of this fatherhood. Similarly, we could consider the analysis of Fried and Howitt (1980) and Lefebvre (1986) relative to efficient risk-sharing on the credit market. Another well-known application of efficient risk exchanges is the Capital Asset Pricing Model.

The properties of efficient allocation of risks with contingent goods are reviewed in the next section, without reference to insurance markets. Section 2 considers the particular case of insurance. The impact of transaction costs on the optimal allocation of risk is analyzed. The first part of section 2 is devoted to the historically important case of a risk-neutral insurer with linear transaction costs; alternative models are considered in section 2.2. Conclusions are contained in the last section.

1. The Mutuality Principle

Consider a model with n persons, $i = 1, \cdots, n$, and a continuum of possible future states of nature. The state θ, which will prevail in the future is unknown, but there is an agreed-upon probability distribution $F(\theta)$ attached to the random variable $\tilde{\theta}$. For each state θ, $x_i(\theta)$ denotes the initial endowment of individual i. The randomness of the initial endowment signifies that agents face uncertainty related to their future wealth, providing room for insurance. Except for socially diversifiable risks, the group also faces risks prior to the realization of $\tilde{\theta}$, since the aggregate wealth $X(\tilde{\theta}) = \Sigma_{i=1}^{n} x_i(\tilde{\theta})$ is a random variable.

It is assumed that agents have a consistent preference ordering over the set of probability distributions of wealth. As we make specific assumptions, the existence of a cardinal utility function over wealth follows, and the ojective of rational agents is to maximize expected utility. However, some would question the appropriateness of that representation.[1] Following the classical model, each individual i has a cardinal utility function $u_i(y)$. This function is increasing and concave, i.e., individuals are risk-averse. An allocation of risks is a set of n random variables $y_i(\tilde{\theta})$, $i = 1, \cdots, n$, which describe the individuals' net wealth depending upon the prevailing state. This corresponds to risk-sharing arrangements — or insurance treaties — $z_i(\tilde{\theta}) = x_i(\tilde{\theta}) - y_i(\tilde{\theta})$, $i = 1, \cdots, n$, which stipulate the participation of person i in a *mutual* fund. The problem is to determine allocations of risks and their corresponding risk-sharing arrangements which are *ex-ante Pareto efficient*.

Definition: *An allocation of risks is ex-ante Pareto efficient if and only if:*
1. it is feasible: $\Sigma_{i=1}^{n} y_i(\tilde{\theta}) = X(\tilde{\theta})$;
2. there is no alternative feasible allocation of risks providing a larger expected utility to some players without reducing the expected utility of any other member.

The first condition, which is by the way equivalent to $\Sigma_{i=1}^{n} z_i(\tilde{\theta}) = 0$, expresses the fact that there is no opportunity to insure the aggregate risk or, equivalently, that the group's wealth is unaffected by the arrangement. In addition, this implies that the mutual fund operates at no (transaction) costs, an assumption that will be relaxed in section 3. The second condition is the well-known Pareto-efficiency condition adapted for uncertainty. So, the problem raised by this definition is to describe operational rules for a mutual fund to spread specific risks efficiently in the group of underwriters, knowing individuals' attitudes towards risks and risk distributions.

Wilson (1968) uses a simple procedure to solve this problem. It is well-known that the Pareto-frontier, i.e., the locus of the players' expected utilities obtainable by all possible choices of risk allocation, is a convex set. This implies that all risk allocations belonging to the frontier of that set are ex-ante Pareto efficient. The determination of a particular efficient allocation of risks depends upon an assignment of weights $\{\lambda_i | i = 1, \cdots, n\}$. Thus, to every assignment $\{\lambda_i\}$, there corresponds an efficient allocation of risks, which is obtained as the solution to the following problem:

$$\max_{y_1(\cdot), \cdots y_n(\cdot)} \sum_{i=1}^{n} \lambda_i E[u_i(y_i(\tilde{\theta}))] \tag{1}$$

$$\text{s.t.} \sum_{i=1}^{n} y_i(\tilde{\theta}) = X(\tilde{\theta}) \quad \text{for all } \tilde{\theta}, \tag{2}$$

where $E[h]$ denotes the expected value of random variable h, i.e., $E[h] = \int h(\theta) dF(\theta)$. Solving this variational problem leads to the following straightforward result, which is due to Borch (1960) and Wilson (1968).

Proposition 1: *A necessary and sufficient condition for the feasible allocation of risk $\{y_i(\tilde{\theta})\}$ to be ex ante Pareto efficient is that there exist nonnegative weights $\{\lambda_i\}$ such that for each couple (i, j) and almost every θ such that $dF(\theta) > 0$:*

$$\lambda_i u_i'(y_i(\theta)) = \lambda_j u_j'(y_j(\theta)). \tag{3}$$

Condition 3 is often called the Borch condition. It states that the group will always allocate wealth so as to equate the weighted marginal utilities of its members. Taking state $\theta = 0$ as a reference, we can rewrite the Borch condition as

$$\frac{u_i'(y_i(\tilde{\theta}))}{u_i'(y_i(0))} = \frac{u_j'(y_j(\tilde{\theta}))}{u_j'(y_j(0))}. \tag{4}$$

This condition states that the marginal rate of substitution of any couple of state-contingent commodities is uniform in the population. It is worthwhile to sketch an intuitive proof of the Proposition 1. In a two-state model, the uniformity of the MRS between the two contingent goods can be verified by drawing an Edgeworth box. This was done, for example, by Hirshleifer and Riley (1979). Mathematically, define $\Pi_i(\theta)$ as the shadow price of the state-contingent good $y_i(\theta)$ in terms of $y_i(0)$, for individual i. In other words, $\Pi_i(\theta)$ is the maximum amount of the state-contingent commodity $y_i(\theta)$ individual i is willing to pay for one unit of the state-contingent commodity in state θ. The shadow price of the contingent good in state θ is the marginal rate of substitution between these two state-contingent goods:

$$\Pi_i(\theta) = -\frac{dy_i(0)}{dy_i(\theta)}\bigg|_{Eu_i} = \frac{u_i'(y_i(\theta))dF(\theta)}{u_i'(y_i(0))dF(0)}.$$

(5)

The Borch condition can now be restated as follows: risk-sharing efficiency requires that any contingent good in the economy be charged the same shadow price by all agents: $\Pi_i(\tilde{\theta}) = \pi(\tilde{\theta})$. Otherwise, suppose without loss of generality that there exists a state θ such that $\Pi_i(\theta) > \Pi_j(\theta)$. Then, it clearly appears that there exists a better allocation of risks in the sense that both i and j can be better off by trading the contingent good of state θ against the contingent good of state 0. Specifically, agent j can give up a small amount ε in state θ. In return, agent i can give up an amount $\delta \in [\varepsilon\Pi_j(\theta), \varepsilon\Pi_i(\theta)]$ of commodity in state 0. It follows that

$$dE[u_i] = -\delta u_i'(y_i(0))dF(0) + \varepsilon u_i'(y_i(\theta))dF(\theta)$$
$$= u_i'(y_i(0))dF(0)[\varepsilon\Pi_i(\theta) - \delta] > 0$$

and

$$dE[u_j] = \delta u_j'(y_j(0))dF(0) - \varepsilon u_j'(y_j(\theta))dF(\theta)$$
$$= u_j'(y_j(0))dF(0)[\delta - \varepsilon\Pi_i(\theta)] > 0$$

Therefore, the new allocation of risks dominates the previous one.

One can solve the system of n equations (2), (3) for every θ, given $\{\lambda_i\}$. Since the state of the world may be described by a vector of individual initial endowment $\theta = (x_1, \cdots, x_n)$, an allocation of risks may be described by a set of n functions, $g_i(x_1, \cdots, x_n)$ which stipulate individual actual wealth y_i as a function of the vector of initial endowments. By totally differentiating (3) with respect to $(x_1, \cdots, x_n)$, it follows that $\partial g_i/\partial x_1 = \cdots = \partial g_i/\partial x_n$ for efficient allocations. Therefore, y_i depends only upon the one-dimensional variable $X = \sum_{i=1}^n x_i$, the aggregate wealth. This is called the *mutuality principle*. Any efficient risk-sharing arrangement contains a pooling rule: before determining specific levels of indemnity, all members give their initial endowment up to a pool. Then, after observing the aggregate wealth, a specific rule is used to share it. In an insurance context, indemnities only depend upon the aggregate loss incurred by the mutual fund. At the optimum, specific risks are diversified through the mutualization: the member's final wealth depends upon his/her initial wealth only through its impact on the aggregate outcome X. A limit case arises when the Law of Large Numbers may be applied. When there is a large number of members with stochastically independent risks, individual risks can be fully diversified through the mutual agreement: final wealths are nonstochastic. Otherwise, with correlated risks or with relatively few participants in the pool, it remains to find a rule to allocate the undiversifiable risk.

Our goal now is to characterize efficient sharing rules. In general there will exist an infinite number of such rules, since the assignment $\{\lambda_i\}$ can be arbitrarily chosen. However, Wilson (1968) and Eliasbherg and Winkler (1981) obtained a simple characterization of efficient risks allocations. Denoting

$$t_i(y) = -\frac{u_i'(y)}{u_i''(y)},$$

the Arrow-Pratt absolute index of risk tolerance measured at wealth y, a necessary and sufficient condition for an allocation of risks to be ex ante Pareto efficient is

$$\frac{dy_i}{dX} = \frac{t_i(y_i(X))}{\Sigma_{j=1}^n t_j(y_j(X))} \tag{6}$$

This condition is easily obtained from differentiating the Borch condition. It states that *any increment in the group's wealth should be shared in proportion to individual risk tolerances*. This specific sharing rule is the one that minimizes the sum of individual risk premia due to the share of an infinitesimal increase in aggregate risk. Indeed, as observed by Pratt (1964), the risk premium of agent i facing an infinitesimal risk with variance σ_i^2 equals $P_i = \sigma_i^2/2t_i$. Consider an infinitesimal aggregate risk with variance σ^2. The optimal sharing rule for this risk is a vector $(\alpha_1, \cdots, \alpha_n)$ of share rates ($y_i = \alpha_i X$) that is the solution to the following program:

$$\min_{(\alpha_1, \cdots, \alpha_n)} \sum_{i=1}^n P_i = \sum_{i=1}^n \frac{\alpha_i^2 \sigma^2}{2t_i}$$

$$\text{s.t.} \quad \sum_{i=1}^n \alpha_i = 1.$$

It is straightforward to verify that the solution to this program is $\alpha_i = t_i/\Sigma_j t_j$.

For small risks, it is an acceptable approximation to consider linear sharing rules. However efficient sharing rules for larger risks will not be linear since the RHS of equation (6) depends upon X via variations of members' attitude towards risk when the level of final wealth is not constant. There are four exceptions to this observation:

(i) $u_i(y) = 1 - e^{-y/T_i}$;
(ii) $u_i(y) = sign(\beta)(y - c_i)^\beta, \beta \leq 1$ or $u_i(y) = c_i y - 0.5y^2; y \leq c_i$;
(iii) $u_i(y) = log(y - c_i); y \geq c_i$;
(iv) an agent is risk neutral.

Case i is a straightforward application of condition 6, since exponential utility functions entail constant absolute risk tolerances $t_i = T_i$. The two next cases are proved by solving the system (6) of n differential equations. Observing that case iii is the limit case of ii when β tends towards zero, the reader will verify that equation (6) can be rewritten in these cases as

$$\frac{dy_i}{dX} = \frac{y_i - c_i}{X - \Sigma_{j=1}^n c_j} \tag{6'}$$

since $t_i = sign(\beta)(1 - \beta)^{-1}(y_i - c_i)$. Notice that it is important here — contrary to case (i) — to verify that all agents have the same β. The linearity of the sharing rule comes from the fact that

$$\frac{d^2y_i}{dX^2} = \left[X - \sum_{j=1}^n c_j \right]^{-1} \frac{dy_i}{dX} - \frac{y_i - c_i}{(X - \Sigma_{j=1} c_j)^2} = 0.$$

Indeed, solving system 6' yields $dy_i/dX = c_i/\Sigma_{j=1}^n c_j$. In case (iv), the RHS of equation 6 vanishes for all risk averse agents $i \neq k$, when t_k tends towards infinity. It is always efficient to transfer all risks to risk neutral agents in the group. Buhlmann and Jewell (1979) propose an algorithm to calculate nonlinear efficient allocations of risks and get numerical solutions for different utility functions.

The group evaluation of risks is obtained by considering the group's utility function $V(X) = \Sigma \lambda_i u_i(y_i(X))$. Indeed, $V'(X)$ evaluates the welfare increase for a marginal increase in the group's wealth. Following Wilson (1968), a "syndicate" risk tolerance index is then defined as $t_0(X) = -V'(X)/V''(X)$. Using (3) and (6), we verify that

$$t_0(X) = \sum_{i=1}^n t_i(y_i(X)). \tag{7}$$

The absolute risk tolerance of the group is the sum of the members' absolute risk tolerances. We can now interpret equation 6 as follows: a member's incremental sharing of the aggregate risk equals his/her proportion of the group risk tolerance. As a conclusion, the efficiency of the allocations of risks presented comes from either the mutualization of risks (specific risks are diversified) and the way undiversifiable risks are distributed (the most risk tolerant people bear a larger proportion of the aggregate risk).

Up to this point, we only wanted to characterize Pareto-efficient contracts. Thus, we have defined the "contract curve." There exists an infinity
of efficient allocations of risks belonging to this "curve". Parameters λ_i,
or equivalently the initial conditions of system 6, are arbitrary. There
exist several models that deal with that difficulty. The problem is to
predict the *equilibrium* allocation of risks. If the equilibrium solution has
the Paretian property, we want to predict the vector of λ_i that will
correspond to this equilibrium. Equivalently, we would like to determine
how the members divide the surplus resulting from the efficient spread of
risks. Borch (1960) has suggested the use of the Nash bargaining solution,
or other equilibrium concept of n-person games (Borch (1962)). Buhlmann
and Jewell (1979) consider a "fair" solution that is such that, over the long-
run, no single agent shall profit from another in the sense of modifying
the premium of contributed and assumed loss. Finally, a competitive
model is analyzed by Borch (1962). It is an application of the famous
contingent claim model of Arrow (1953), and it is connected to the model
of Allais (1953). In this model, it is assumed that there exists a complete
set of markets for state-contingent commodities. Prior to the realization
of the state, there is trade in contracts for consumption contingent to each
θ. The price of the contingent-good in state θ is denoted $p(\theta)$. Markets
are competitive, so the equilibrium price $p(\theta)$ clears the market for the
corresponding contingent-commodity. Each individual maximizes his
expected utility subject to a budget constraint (8).

$$\max_{y_i(\cdot)} E[u_i(y_i(\tilde{\theta}))]$$

$$\text{s.t.} \quad \int p(\theta)[y_i(\theta) - x_i(\theta)]d\theta = 0, \tag{8}$$

The direct application of the first theorem of welfare economics yields
that the competitive price function supports an allocation of risks that is
Pareto efficient. If we take the contingent-good in state $\theta = 0$ as the
numeraire, it results that, at equilibrium, $\Pi_i(\theta) = \pi(\theta) = p(\theta)$, i.e.,
shadow prices equal actual prices. This is the first-order condition of
the above program. It is equivalent to the efficiency condition (4), therefore proving that the competitive allocation of risks is ex-ante Pareto-
efficient. The prevailing vector of λs is such that budget constraints (8)
are satisfied.

A problem arises when competitive contingent markets are incomplete
(when there is no market for some contingent-commodities). In such a
situation, the competitive allocation of risks is in general inefficient.
Gollier (1990) proves that some forms of spot price rigidity is a second-

best strategy to limit the inefficiency of the allocation of risks, even at the expense of some inefficiencies of the allocation of resources. A well-known exception is the so-called Capital Asset Pricing Model (CAPM). Indeed, despite the fact that markets are not assumed to be complete (capital markets do not span the contingent claims space), an efficient sharing of risks is obtained. This is due to the fact that utility functions are assumed to be quadratic, a particular case for which it is known that efficient sharing rules are linear (case ii). This is precisely what stock markets provide: dividends are proportional to (random) profits. Both the complete contingent markets model and the CAPM provide guiding rules for insurance companies to price risks, as stressed by D'Arcy and Doherty (1988). In particular, specific risks that are highly negatively correlated to the aggregate risk (or market risk) should be more valuable because they can be fully diversified. Basically, this is due to the fact that $p(\tilde{\theta})$ is negatively correlated to aggregate supply, $X(\tilde{\theta})$.

The theory of efficient risk sharing has numerous applications in economic theory. The analysis of financial markets is probably the most obvious application. The theory of so-called implicit labor contracts is another typical example (for a recent survey, see Rosen (1985)). Fried and Howitt (1980) have initiated a theory of risk sharing on credit markets. Drèze and Gollier (1989) propose to index wages to GNP for considerations of risk-sharing efficiency. But the theory has been historically devoted to the analysis of insurance markets. Borch bases his analysis on reinsurance markets, which are well suited for the above model. The functioning of Lloyd's in London is a striking illustration of efficient risk-sharing treaties.

In contrast the overwhelming majority of insurance contracts does not fit the mutuality principle in which each person's indemnity depends upon others' losses through dependence upon the aggregate loss in the economy. In theory, a globally efficient risk bearing arrangement in the economy could be achieved by a set of decentralized risk trading between pairs of persons. Risk-sharing arrangements are created between customers of an insurance company. If the company has shareholders, they will participate in the arrangement. It may be extended through chains of reinsurance/coinsurances until risk sharing becomes virtually universal. In this idealized world, insurance companies play the role of brokerage firms[2] buying and selling risks to attain an efficient allocation of risks. However, it is definitely exceptional that insurance indemnities depend upon GNP or, say, upon an index of worldwide economic growth. There exists several reasons for this. Gerber (1978) and Buhlmann and Jewell (1979) prove that when side payments are limited, it is efficient f~r the most risk tolerant members of the pool not to participate in the pooling of relatively small risks. Marshall (1974a, b) points out the existence of transaction costs that limit the desirable spread of risks in the economy. He estimates the magnitude of efficiency gains available from using mutual contracts. Taking into account transaction costs, the structure of insurance markets is predicted by that author. The impact of transaction costs on individual insurance choices is analyzed in the next section.

Some forms of insurance, however, are close to the mutuality principle. Participating policies, as they prevail in life insurance, are representatives of this class of insurance: the premium is subject to a retroactive adjustment, which is a known function of the aggregate loss experience. Such a clause is sometimes encountered in workers' compensation insurance. As observed by Doherty and Dionne (1989), the Risk Retention Act (1986) is an example of the evolution of insurance towards mutualization. Indeed, it allowed some insurers to issue inalienable stock of the insurance company to their policyholders. Thereby, the net indemnity, including the dividend, resembles the indemnity schedule of an efficient mutual contract. Finally, these authors observe that policyholders can, in principle, duplicate the efficient risk-sharing by buying insurance plus a certain number of equity of the insurer. This is labeled "homemade mutualization." All limitations due to taxes, contracting costs, and agency costs apply.

2. Optimal insurance policies

In this section, we examine the problem of a rational consumer who is willing to insure a risk on the insurance market. The problem can be stated as follows: the consumer's initial wealth is denoted W_1, but he faces the risk of a loss $\tilde{\theta}$, which is a random variable with probability distribution $F(\tilde{\theta})$. An insurance contract is a couple $(P, I(\tilde{\theta}))$, where $I(\tilde{\theta})$ is the indemnity paid by an insurance company for each possible loss θ, namely, $I(\tilde{\theta})$ denotes the coverage function. P is the premium paid by the insured. The actuarial value of policy $(P, I(\tilde{\theta}))$ is $E[I(\tilde{\theta})]$. If the consumer buys policy $(P, I(\tilde{\theta}))$, his/her state-dependent wealth equals $y_1(\tilde{\theta}) = W_1 - \tilde{\theta} + I(\tilde{\theta}) - P$, whereas his initial endowment was $x_1(\tilde{\theta}) = W_1 - \tilde{\theta}$.

On the supply side, the insurance company has a reserve $x_2 = W_2$ prior to the occurrence of a claim. The processing of a claim I generates a deadweight loss $C(I)$ that covers general overhead costs of the company and costs of adjusting and paying claims. If the insurance company sells policy $(P, I(\tilde{\theta}))$, the stochastic insurer's reserve will equal $y_2(\tilde{\theta}) = W_2 +$

$P - I(\tilde{\theta}) - C(I(\tilde{\theta}))$. The problem can be represented as the determination of the form of Pareto efficient insurance contracts among the set of feasible contracts. An insurance contract is feasible if the coverage function is nonnegative, i.e., $I(\tilde{\theta}) \geq 0 \ \forall \ \tilde{\theta}$. This constraint was considered as institutional by Arrow (1971), without comment.[3] $(P, I(\cdot))$ is ex ante Pareto efficient if there exists a $\lambda > 0$ such that it is the solution to the following program:

$$\max_{(P, I.)} E[u_1(y_1(\tilde{\theta}))] + \lambda E[u_2(y_2(\tilde{\theta}))] \tag{9}$$

$$\text{s.t.} \quad z_1(\tilde{\theta}) = P - I(\tilde{\theta}) \leq P. \tag{10}$$

This program is equivalent to program (1) with $n = 2$ except for the existence of transaction costs and the institutional constraint (10). This problem was initially treated by Arrow (1971) but in a different context. The formulation of Arrow is described by program (11).

$$\max E[u_1(y_1(\tilde{\theta}))] \tag{11}$$

s.t. *(i)* P satisfies $E[u_2(W_2 - I(\tilde{\theta}) - C(I(\tilde{\theta})) + P)] = u_2(W_2 + \pi)$;
    (ii) $I(\tilde{\theta}) \geq 0$.

The functional constraint implicitly stipulates the insurance premium P as a function of the coverage, the structure of costs, the distribution of claims, and a mark-up expected profit π. In other terms, program (11) is the program of a rational insurance purchaser who faces a specified insurance pricing. Using the theory of Lagrangian multipliers, it clearly appears that programs (9) and (11) are equivalent.[4] The first-order condition for these problems may be written as

$$u_1'(y_1(\tilde{\theta})) - \lambda(1 + C'(I(\tilde{\theta})))u_2'(y_2(\tilde{\theta})) \leq 0 \tag{12}$$

with equality when $I(\tilde{\theta}) > 0$.

Different forms of coverage functions are provided by insurance markets. The simplest from is full insurance, i.e., $I(\tilde{\theta}) = \tilde{\theta}$. The most common form of insurance is the deductible type in which the insurer provides 100 percent coverage above some specified deductible amount D: $I(\tilde{\theta}) = max(0, \tilde{\theta} - D)$. A policy with a franchise — or "disappearing deductible" — is described by the function $I(\theta) = 0$ if $\theta < D$, but $I(\theta) = \theta$ if $\theta \geq D$. The function $I(\tilde{\theta}) = \alpha\tilde{\theta}$ describes an insurance policy with a proportional deductible, also called coinsurance. Numerous other forms of insurance exist on the market, like policies with an upper limit on coverage or with a combination of a straight deductible and a proportional deductible. Depending upon the characteristics of the market, we now determine which of type of insurance, if any, is optimal.

2.1. The model of Arrow

The first theorem on the topic is due to Arrow (1971).

> **Proposition 2** *(Arrow 1971): If an insurance company is willing to offer an insurance policy against loss desired by a buyer at a premium which depends only on the policy's actuarial value, then the policy chosen by a risk-averting buyer will take the form of 100 percent coverage above a deductible minimum: $I(\tilde{\theta}) = max(0, \tilde{\theta} - D)$.*

According to our model, the insurance tariff will be a function of the policy's actuarial value only if *the insurer is risk neutral ($u_2'(y) = constant$)* and if *the cost function is linear*: $C(I) = c_0 + kI$. The constant k is the loading factor of the policy. Arrow solved program (11) using a relatively sophisticated argument. In his next paper on the topic, Arrow (1974) solved a discrete version of the problem using the Kuhn-Tucker conditions. Raviv (1979) used the well-suited tool of the theory of optimal control, or variational calculus. Since then, all papers on the topic followed that way.[5] However, it is interesting to outline an intuitive proof of Proposition 2, as proposed by Marshall (1991). Consider the insurance contract as an exchange of the certainty commodity (the premium) against a bundle of state-contingent goods. This bundle is described by the coverage function $I(\tilde{\theta})$. Since the only allowed exchanges are transfers of contingent goods from the insured in exchange for the certainty commodity, we have to adapt our definition of shadow prices. To fit this institutional constraint, the shadow price of the goods in state θ, $\Pi_i(\theta)$, is expressed in terms of the certainty good P. For the insurance purchaser, we obtain

$$\Pi_1(\theta) = \left.\frac{dP}{dI(\theta)}\right|_{Eu_1} = \frac{u_1'(W_1 - \theta)}{E_{\tilde{\theta}}[u_1'(W1 - \tilde{\theta})]}dF(\theta) \qquad (13)$$

if there is no insurance. Since the insurer is assumed to be risk neutral and to face variable costs, the reader will verify that

$$\Pi_2(\theta) = \left.\frac{dP}{dI(\theta)}\right|_{Eu_2} = (1 + k)dF(\theta) \qquad (14)$$

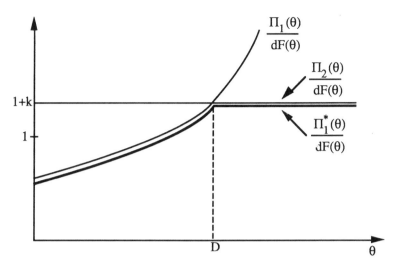

Figure 1. Shadow contingent prices with optimal insurance.

The shadow price of the insurer, adjusted for probability density, is constant and equals the probability loading (the 1) plus the marginal transaction cost loading, k.

At this stage, notice that the ratio in the right-hand side of equation (13) — the shadow price adjusted for probability density — is less than unity when $\theta = 0$ and increases with θ. Since the insured is risk-averse, his valuation of a one-dollar claim, adjusted for probability density, is an increasing function of his actual loss. In figure 1, both sets of adjusted shadow prices are drawn before exchanges take place. For losses θ less than a critical value D, $\Pi_1(\theta) < \Pi_2(\theta)$: the demand price is below the insurer's supply price. In those states, it would be mutually beneficial to transfer contingent goods from consumers to insurer. The nonnegativity constraint on claims prohibits that possibility.[6] At the optimum, no indemnity is paid for these small losses. There is simply no trade on contingent markets $\theta < D$. But once the loss exceeds D, the price that the insurance purchaser is willing to pay for coverage in state θ exceeds the market price $\Pi_2(\theta)$. As a result, exchange is possible and $\Pi_1^*(\theta) = \Pi_2^*(\theta)$ at the optimum. This signifies that

$$\frac{\Pi_1^*(\theta)}{dF(\theta)} = \frac{u_1'(W_1 - \theta + I(\theta) - P)}{E_{\tilde{\theta}}[u_1'(W_1 - \tilde{\theta} + I(\tilde{\theta}) - P)]} = 1 + k \ \forall \theta > D. \quad (15)$$

Equation (15) directly implies that $(W_1 - \theta + I(\theta) - P)$ is independent of θ in that range of losses, implying $I(\theta) = \theta - D$.

In short, the existence of transaction costs prevents the insured to buy contingent goods for small losses. The improvement in the efficiency of the allocation of risks would simply be overbalanced by deadweight costs. This is not the case for larger risks, which are fully transferred to the risk-neutral insurer. It corresponds to an efficient allocation of risks in the subset $\{\theta | \theta > D\}$ (see case iv in section 1). The deductible regulates the division of risk-bearing so that the insurer's obligations are restricted to large losses, i.e., when the shadow price for consumption is large.

It remains to determine the level of deductibility so as to maximize expected utility. Solutions to this problem have been developed by Pashigian, Schkade, and Menefee (1966), Mossin (1968), Gould (1969), Moffet (1977), and Schlesinger (1981). Smith (1968) explores the condition under which full coverage ($D = 0$) may be optimal. Stuart (1983) estimates the optimal level of deductibility for the Swedish Homeowner Insurance, with a Paretian distribution of losses. Schlesinger (1981) proves under various assumptions that an individual with higher degree of risk aversion, a higher loss probability, or a lower level of initial wealth will purchase more insurance, i.e., a lower deductible.

The optimal deductible can be obtained by solving equation (15) where $\theta - I(\theta)$ is replaced by $min\ (\theta, D)$. There is no analytical solution due to nonlinearities. Drèze (1981) gives a simplified formula that is exact for quadratic utility function. Equivalently, let us use first-order Taylor expansions of $u_1'(W_1 - \theta - P)$ around $u_1'(W_1 - D - P)$ for all $\theta < D$. This procedure generates the following approximation:

$$E[u_1'(W_1 - \theta + I(\theta) - P)]$$
$$= u_1'(W_1 - D - P) + u_1''(W_1 - D - P) \int_0^D (D - \theta)dF(\theta)$$

Equation 15 may then be rewritten as

$$kt_1 = (1 + k) \int_0^D (D - \theta)dF(\theta), \qquad (16)$$

where $t_1 = -u_1'(W_1 - D - P)/u_1''(W_1 - D - P)$ is the risk tolerance coefficient measured at the minimum wealth level. To get a simplified guiding rule to determine the optimal deductible, observe that

$$DF(0) \leq \int_0^D (D - \theta)dF(\theta) \leq D(F(D) - F(0)) \leq D,$$

It results that equation 16 yields:

$$\frac{kt_1}{1 + k} \leq D \leq \frac{kt_1}{F(0)(1 + k)} \qquad (17)$$

The lower bound has been found by Drèze (1981) to infer risk aversion from the choice of deductibles in insurance contracts. From (17), this approximation will be reliable when the no-loss probability $F(0)$ is close to unity. If the no-loss probability tends to unity as it is the case for a large number of insurable risks, the two bounds tend to coincide and we get the useful approximation (18):

$$D = t_1 \frac{k}{1 + k} \tag{18}$$

Notice that it is in general easier to work with the *relative* risk tolerance index, which has no dimension. It is defined as $t_1^r = t_1 / W_1 - P - D$. Using this definition, we can rewrite condition (18) as follows:

$$\frac{D}{W_1 - P - D} = t_1^r \frac{k}{1 + k} \tag{19}$$

The figure $t_1^r = 1$, sometimes found in the literature, and a loading k of 50% would imply deductibles as high as one-third of the consumer's minimal wealth, or equivalently one-fourth of the consumer's initial wealth, if P is small with respect to W. As shown by Drèze (1981), the observation of actual levels of deductibility selected by consumers seems to suggest an order of magnitude for the relative risk tolerance index that is substantially less than commonly recognized. This is consistent with findings by Friend and Blume (1975) and Farber (1978). The coefficient of relative risk tolerance is likely to be less than 0.5.

Arrow's results imply that efficient insurance companies have to offer a large choice of deductibles. Nevertheless, this result holds only if the insurance premium is unambiguously determined by the policy's actuarial value. We will now review other formulations proposed in the literature in which this assumption is violated. Indeed, the premium will be a function of the actuarial value only if equilibrium contingent prices $p(\tilde{\theta})$ are proportional to $F'(\tilde{\theta})$, an exceptional case.

2.2. Other forms of coverage

The first extension to Arrow's original model is due to Arrow (1971) himself and Raviv (1979) who analyzed the case of risk-averse insurers. Raviv solved program 9 for $C(I) = c_0 + kI$ and $u_2''(\cdot) \le 0$. He proved that a policy involving coinsurance of losses above a deductible is ex ante Pareto efficient. This is a combination of the deductible result — to limit deadweight transaction cost — and the efficient sharing of risks between two risk-averse persons as presented in section 1. As a matter of fact, the efficient (marginal) coinsurance rate can be obtained by differentiating condition 12. It yields

$$I'(\theta) = \frac{\dfrac{t_2}{1 + k}}{t_1 + \dfrac{t_2}{1 + k}} \qquad \forall \theta: I(\theta) > 0. \tag{20}$$

This property can be derived directly from condition 6, which characterizes the efficient spread of risk. Indeed, the aggregate loss X is the sum of the loss incurred by the customer *and* the deadweight cost generated by insurance: $X = \theta + C(I(\theta))$. Therefore $dX = (1 + kI'(\theta))d\theta$. Using equation 6, we derive that the efficient sharing of risk is such that

$$\frac{dy_1}{d\theta} = \frac{dX}{d\theta}\frac{dy_1}{dX} = (1 + kI'(\theta)) \frac{t_1}{t_1 + t_2}.$$

Since the LHS of this equality is $1 - I'(\theta)$, the reader will verify that this is compatible with equation 20. Notice that $I'(\theta)$ equals unity when the insurer is risk neutral. Otherwise, the coinsurance rate is less than 1. Because of the risk aversion of insurers, the equilibrium level of shadow prices will increase with θ. Therefore the premium will not be a function of the actuarial value, and insurance purchasers will prefer to reduce the level of coverage for high losses (to reduce costs charged in the premium). This gives a logic to coinsurance. The deductible is used to deal with transaction costs, as before. Indeed, Blazenko (1985) proves that a necessary and sufficient condition for the Pareto optimal deductible to equal zero is that the cost function be constant.

Risk aversion, however, is not the only reason for coinsurance. Raviv (1979) also proved that coinsurance above a deductible is optimal provided the insurance costs are a strictly convex function of the coverage. Solving program 9 with $u_2''(.) = 0$ yields

$$\frac{d(\theta - I(\theta))}{d\theta} = \frac{t_1}{t_1 + \dfrac{1 + C'(I(\theta))}{C''(I(\theta))}}, \qquad \forall \theta: I(\theta) > 0. \tag{21}$$

It results that the coinsurance rate is less than unity, since $C''(I) > 0$. As before, equilibrium shadow prices are rising with θ, but it is due to increasing transaction costs.

Huberman, Mayers, and Smith (1983) argued that transactions costs are neither proportional nor convex but rather are strictly concave. They considered costs structure with economies of scale. It is a direct consequence of equation 21 that the net wealth of the insured becomes an increasing function of the loss, i.e., $dI/d\theta > 1$, when $C''(I) < 0$. Shadow prices are now decreasing with θ, inciting insurance purchasers to buy more coverage for large losses. The resulting optimal policy contains a disappearing deductible. However, this type of policy generates an ex-post moral hazard: once damage has occurred, this policy encourages the insured to create further damage. The authors then show that it is efficient to offer full coverage above a deductible to escape this hazard.

Gollier (1987) considers the case of a noncontinuous cost function at $I = 0$. This formulation is introduced to deal with nuisance claims, i.e., claims that are small relative to the administrative adjustment expenses they generate. The proposed cost function is

$$C(I) = \begin{cases} c_0, & \text{if } I = 0; \\ c_0 + c_1 + kI, & \text{if } I > 0; \end{cases} \qquad (22)$$

where c_1 is a per-claim fixed cost covering costs to estimate damage and related costs. It is shown that a policy with a partially disappearing deductible is optimal in this case:

$$I(\theta) = \begin{cases} 0, & \text{if } \theta \leq L; \\ x - D, & \text{if } \theta > L, \end{cases} \qquad (23)$$

with $L > D$. With this policy, nuisance claims less than $L - D$ are not paid simply because the equilibrium contingent prices for these $\theta \in [D, L]$ — which include fixed costs — exceed the shadow prices charged by consumers. The author also estimates optimal values for L and D.

Finally, some attempts have been made to explain the prevalence of upper limits on coverage. Raviv (1979) obtained such an optimal policy by considering some regulatory constraints on the supply risk. Huberman, Mayers, and Smith (1983) recognize that bankruptcy rules provide insurers with a form of limited liability for high losses, leading to an inefficient undercoverage for this range of losses.

3. Conclusion

Insurance markets can be viewed as a special case of markets for contingent claims. Indeed, an insurance policy should be analyzed as a bundle of contingent goods. To be efficient, insurers should provide bundles that are likely to correspond to equilibrium transactions observed if consumers were able to trade in complete contingent markets. With complete information, two features preclude markets for insurance contracts from organizing efficient sharings of risks. First, insurers are not allowed to buy contingent claims, i.e., insureds are not allowed to "go short" in θ. They may only sell contingent claims against the certainty commodity. Second, the existence of transaction costs is recognized. These two limitations explain the prevalence of deductible clauses. The coinsurance arrangement is due to two sources: the risk aversion of the insurer and the nonlinearity of insurance costs. This coinsurance clause is consistent with the view that insurance companies play the role of efficient brokerage in contingent markets. However, it was shown that the only efficient insurance policies are those that satisfy the mutuality principle, i.e., policies that stipulate individual indemnities as a function of the aggregate loss incurred by customers of the insurance company. The reason such mutual agreements are not provided by the market remains an open question.

Notes

1. See Machina (1982) with his valuable source of references on the question.
2. Cf., Marshall (1974b)
3. Marshall (1991) argues that prohibitive transaction costs prevent the consumer to *sell* state-contingent commodities. This is proved by Gollier (1987a) for some types of risks. When costs are a function of the *absolute value* of the volume of transactions, the non-negativity constraint on claims is never binding when the loss probability is less than 0.5, as in homeowner insurance and automobile insurance. For other types of risks, we should recognize the insurance markets are incomplete.
4. Since program (9) is convex, there is a one-to-one correspondence between λ and π.
5. There is an exception to that evolution: Schlesinger (1988) uses the second-degree stochastic dominance principle to prove Proposition 2.
6. For more detail, see Gollier (1987a). Basically, the model is mispecified to analyze negative claims. In fact, a dollar transferred from the insured to the insurer should be evaluated $1 - k'$ dollar, rather than $1 + k$ as in equation (14), by the insurer where k' denotes the (proportional) costs incurred for this type of transaction. If $\Pi_1(0) > (1 - k')dF(0)$, $I(0) < 0$ is inefficient.

References

Allais, M. (1953). "Généralisation des Théories de l'Equilibre Economique Général et du Rendement Social au cas du Risque," *Econometrie*, 81–110. Paris: CNRS.

Arrow, K. J. (1953). "Le Rôle des Valeurs Boursières pour la Répartition la Meilleure des Risques," *Econometrie*, 41–47. Paris: CNRS. Translated (1964) as "The Role of Securities in the Optimal Allocation of Risk-Bearing", *Review of Economic Studies* 31, 31–36.

Arrow, K. J. (1971). *Essays in the Theory of Risk Bearing*. Chicago: Markham Publishing Co.

Arrow, K. J. (1974). "Optimal Insurance and Generalized Deductibles," *Scandinavian Actuarial Journal* 1, 1–42.

Azariadis, C. (1975). "Implicit Contracts and Underemployment Equilibria," *Journal of Political Economy* 83, 1183–1202.

Baily, M. N. (1974). "Wages and Employment Under Uncertain Demand," *Review of Economic Studies* 41, 37–50.

Bernoulli, D. (1738). "Specimen Theoriae Novae de Mesura Sortis," Translated (1954) in *Econometrica* 22, 23–46.

Blazenko, G. (1985). "The Design of an Optimal Insurance Policy: Note," *American Economic Review* 75, 253–255.

Bohm-Bawerk, E. (1881). *Rechte und Verhaltnisse von Standpunkte der Volkswirtschaftlichen Guterlehre*, Innsbruck.

Borch, K. (1960). "The Safety Loading of Reinsurance Premiums," *Skandinavisk Aktuarietskrift* 153–184.

Borch, K. (1962). "Equilibrium in a Reinsurance Market," *Econometrica* 30, 424–444.

Borch, K. (1979). "Problems in the Economic Theory of Insurance," *Astin Bulletin* 10, 1–11.

Buhlmann, H., and W. S. Jewell. (1979). "Optimal Risk Exchange," *Astin Bulletin* 10, 243–262.

D'Arcy, S. P., and N. A. Doherty. (1988). *The Financial Theory of Pricing Property-Liability Insurance Contract*, Huebner Foundation Monograph 15, R.D. Irwin, Homewood.

Debreu, G. (1959). *Theory of Value*, New York: Wiley.

Doherty, N. A., and H. Schlesinger. (1983). "Optimal Insurance in Incomplete Markets," *Journal of Political Economy* 91, 1045–1054.

Doherty, N. A., and G. Dionne. (1989). "Risk Pooling, Contract Structure and Organizational Form of Insurance Firms," Département de sciences économiques, Université de Montréal, Cahier 8935, 1–31.

Drèze, J. H. (1981). "Inferring Risk Tolerance from Deductibles in Insurance Contracts," *The Geneva Papers* 6, 48–52.

Drèze, J. H. (1987). *Essays on Economic Decision Under Uncertainty*, Cambridge: Cambridge University Press.

Drèze, J. H., and C. Gollier. (1989). "Risk Sharing on the Labor Market," mimeo, CORE, Louvain La-Neuve, Belgium.

Eliashberg, J., and R. Winkler. (1981). "Risk Sharing and Group Decision Making," *Management Science* 27, 1221–1235.

Farber, H. S. (1978). "Individual Preferences and Union Wage Determination: The Case of the United Mine Workers." *Journal of Political Economy* 86, 923–942.

Fried, J., and P. Howitt. (1980). "Credit Rationing and Implicit Contract Theory," *Journal of Money, Credit and Banking* 12, 471–487.

Friend, I., and M. E. Blume. (1975). "The Demand for Risky Assets," *American*

Economic Review 65, 900–922.

Gerber, H. U. (1978). "Pareto-Optimal Risk Exchanges and Related Decision Problems," *Astin Bulletin* 10,155–179.

Gollier, C. (1987a). "The Design of Optimal Insurance without the Nonnegativity Constraint on Claims," *Journal of Risk and Insurance* 54, 312–324.

Gollier, C. (1987b). "Pareto-Optimal Risk Sharing with Fixed Costs per Claim," *Scandinavian Actuarial Journal* 13, 62–73.

Gollier, C. (1990). "On the Efficiency of Credit Rationing," Groupe HEC, Paris, mimeo.

Gould, J. P. (1969). "The Expected Utility Hypothesis and the Selection of Optimal Deductibles for a Given Insurance Policy," *Journal of Business* 42, 143–151.

Hirshleifer, J., and J. G. Riley. (1979). "The Analytics of Uncertainty and Information — An Expository Survey," *Journal of Economic Literature* 17, 1375–1421.

Huberman, G., D. Mayers and C. W. Smith. (1983). "Optimal Insurance Policy Indemnity Schedules," *The Bell Journal of Economics* 14, 415–426.

Kahane, Y., H. Schlesinger and N. Yanai. (1988). "Rudiments of Insurance Purchasing: A Graphical State-Claims Analysis, *Insurance: Mathematics and Economics* 7, 211–217.

Lefebvre, O. (1979). "Risk Sharing in the Banking Deposit Contract," *Journal of Business Finance and Accounting* 13, 547–559.

Machina, M. (1982). "Expected Utility Analysis without the Independence Axiom," *Econometrica* 50, 277–323.

Marshall, J. M. (1974a). "Insurance Theory: Reserves Versus Mutuality," *Economic Inquiry* 12, 476–492.

Marshall, J. M. (1974b) . "Insurance as a Market in Contingent Claims: Structure and Performance," *The Bell Journal of Economics* 5, 670–681.

Marshall, J. M. (1991). "Optimum Insurance with Deviant Beliefs," in G. Dionne (ed.), *Contributions to Insurance Economics*. Boston: Kluwer Academic Publishers.

Moffet, D. (1977). "Optimal Deductible and Consumption Theory," *Journal of Risk and Insurance* 44, 669–682.

Mossin, J. (1968). "Aspects of Rational Insurance Purchasing," *Journal of Political Economy* 76, 533–568.

Pashigian, B. P., L. Schkade and G. Menefee. (1966). "The Selection of an Optimal Deductible for a Given Insurance Policy," *Journal of Business* 39, 35–44.

Pratt, J. W. (1964). "Risk Aversion in the Small and in the Large," *Econometrica* 32, 122–136.

Raviv, A. (1979). "The Design of an Optimal Insurance Policy," *American Economic Review* 69, 84–96.

Rosen, S. (1985). "Implicit Contracts: A Survey," *Journal of Economic Literature* 23, 1144–1175.

Schlesinger, H. (1981). "The Optimal Level of Deductibility in Insurance Contracts," *Journal of Risk and Insurance* 48, 465–481.

Schlesinger, H. (1988). "The Nonoptimality of Optimal Insurance," mimeo, University of Alahama.

Smith, A. (1775). *The Wealth of Nations*, Reprint 1976. Chicago: University of Chicago Press.

Smith, V. (1968). "Optimal Insurance Coverage," *Journal of Political Economy* 76, 68–77.

Stuart, C. (1983). "Pareto-Optimal Deductibles in Property-Liability Insurance: The Case of Homeowner Insurance in Sweden," *Scandinavian Actuarial Journal* 9, 227–238.

Wilson, R. (1968). "The Theory of Syndicates," *Econometrica* 36, 113–132.

THE DEMAND FOR AND SUPPLY OF LIABILITY INSURANCE

Patricia M. Danzon

University of Pennsylvania

Scott E. Harrington

University of South Carolina

Abstract

The demand for and supply of liability insurance arise from the legal liability of individuals and corporations for injuries caused to third parties. Tort liability rules and liability insurance markets have attracted substantial attention in recent years. This paper introduces the literature on the demand for and supply of liability insurance. The focus is on issues that distinguish liability from first-party insurance. Particular emphasis is given to the relationships between liability law, liability insurance, and risk reduction.

Key words: liability law, liability insurance, deterrence, compensation, experience rating, undiversifiable risk, underwriting cycle, default risk, regulation

The demand for and supply of liability insurance arise from the legal liability of individuals and corporations for personal injuries and financial losses caused to third parties, as distinct from first-party insurance that covers losses suffered directly by the policyholder. Automobile liability and workers' compensation have the largest volume (table 1). However, the lines that have grown most rapidly and attracted the most attention in recent years are medical malpractice and comprehensive general liability (GL), which includes product liability, municipal liability, and other general liability coverages.

25

This paper introduces the literature on the demand for and supply of liability insurance.[1] The focus is on issues that distinguish liability from first-party insurance, except to the extent that much of the work on supply deals with the overall property-liability insurance market. Particular attention is given to the relationships between liability law, liability insurance, and risk reduction.

1. The Demand for Liability Insurance

1.1. General Issues

1.1.1. The Role of Liability Rules in Controlling Risk. Since the pioneering work by Coase (1960), Calabresi (1970), and Posner (1972, 1973), the burgeoning field of law and economics has applied standard tools of positive and normative economics to analyze the structure of common law, including the law of tort liability. A major focus of this analysis has been to show that appropriately designed liability rules can be used to achieve a Pareto optimal allocation of resources to risk reduction in contexts where market forces alone would fail because of imperfect information or transactions costs. This extensive literature on optimal liability rules is only briefly summarized here.[2] We focus on the derivative questions: Under what conditions does liability give rise to a demand for liability insurance? How does the optimal liability insurance contract differ from the optimal first-party insurance contract? Can the structure of competitively determined liability insurance contracts be socially non-optimal in the sense that insurance interferes with the deterrent function of liability?

Accidents involving third parties can arise in many circumstances, including the use of automobiles and other consumer products, professional services such as medical care, and workplace and environmental hazards. The production of safety (risk reduction) can be modeled either in a standard production framework (Brown, 1973) or as a joint product or spillover associated with other beneficial activities (Shavell, 1980; Polinsky, 1980). Formally, the activity of one party, the "injurer," can result in risk of injury to another party, the "victim." The probability or size of loss may depend on both the level of the activity and the amount of care per unit of activity exercised by the injurer (unilateral accidents), and possibly also on activity level and care per unit taken by the victim (bilateral accidents).

In the general case of bilateral accidents where both injurers and victims choose levels of care and activity levels, the social optimum is defined as the solution to the problem of maximizing the sum of injurers' and victims' utilities from engaging in their activities, net of their costs of care, and expected accident losses (using the notation in Shavell, 1987, pp. 43–44):

$$\text{Max}[u(s) - sx] + [v(t) - ty - stl(x, y)]$$

where

$$s = \text{injurer's activity level,}$$
$$u(s) = \text{injurer's gross dollar benefits from the activity,}$$
$$t = \text{victim's activity level}$$
$$v(t) = \text{victim's gross dollar benefits from the activity,}$$
$$x = \text{injurer's level of care, measured in unit costs,}$$
$$y = \text{victim's level of care, measured in unit costs,}$$
$$l(x, y) = \text{expected accident loss per unit of activity, and}$$
$$stl(x, y) = \text{expected accident losses.}$$

The optimal values x^*, y^*, s^*, and t^* are defined by the first-order conditions

$$tl_x(x, y) = -1$$
$$sl_y(x, y) = -1$$
$$u'(s) = x + tl(x, y)$$
$$v'(t) = y + sl(x, y)$$

These conditions imply that the marginal cost of taking care must equal the marginal benefit in terms of reduction in expected accident costs, and that the marginal utility of increasing the level of activity must equal the sum of the marginal cost of taking optimal care and the increase in expected accident costs.

The standard results of the Coase theorem apply. Optimal investment in all dimensions of risk reduction will be achieved, regardless of the liability rule, if both parties are informed about the risks and if the costs of negotiation are low. An important corollary is that if risks are obvious and if the parties are in an ongoing contractual relation, as employer/employee or producer/consumer, then market prices will reflect the potential victim's demand for safety and induce optimal levels of safety. Market contracts will also generate an optimal allocation of risk between the parties and optimal levels of compensation in the event of injury.[3]

In the case of accidents involving strangers, transactions costs may prevent the achievement of a first best solution by voluntary contract. And even in buyer-seller situations where contracting costs are low, Spence (1977) shows that if consumers misperceive risk, producers have nonoptimal incentives for care and consumers will be nonoptimally insured.

Liability rules are one among several possible policy tools for achieving efficient levels of loss prevention and risk allocation where voluntary contracting in private markets fails.[4] The two benchmark liability rules are negligence and strict liability. Under a negligence rule, the injurer is liable for failure to take due care that is the cause of injury to the victim. Under a simple strict liability rule, the injurer is liable for activities that cause an injury to the victim, regardless of the injurer's level of care. In the United States, negligence is the prevailing rule for personal and professional liability (including medical malpractice) and for automobile injuries except in states that have explicitly adopted first-party no-fault statutes that limit tort liability for minor injuries. Strict liability is exemplified by workers' compensation statutes whereby employers are strictly liable for work-related injuries, regardless of who is negligent. For product-related injuries, manufacturers can be sued under theories of negligence and strict liability, but liability is strict only for injuries caused by *defective* products.[5] Important variants of these benchmark rules are the application of a contributory negligence defense (which shifts liability to a victim who fails to take due care, regardless of the defendant's care), and comparative negligence, whereby damages are apportioned between the parties in proportion to their degree of negligence.

Brown (1973) first formally modeled the effects of these alternative liability rules on levels of care. He assumed noncooperative (Nash) behavior in a context of bilateral accidents with level of care the only determinant of risk, risk neutrality of both parties, costless administration, and perfect information, in the sense that courts know the level of care actually taken and the parties know safety production functions and the due standard of care. Under these assumptions, three liability rules are potentially efficient: negligence, with or without a contributory negligence defense, and strict liability with a contributory negligence defense. Strict (no) liability is potentially efficient only in the context of unilateral accidents where victim (defendant) care is irrelevant. Haddock and Curran (1985), Cooter and Ulen (1987), and Rubinfeld (1987) show that it is possible to define an efficient comparative negligence rule.[6]

Shavell (1980) generalized Brown's model to allow both levels of activity and levels of care as determinants of risk. The conclusions now depend critically on the potential victim's information about accident risk. If average risk is misperceived, no liability rule is fully efficient. If victims know at least the average risk, a negligence rule is potentially efficient provided that the formulation of the due care standard includes both the level of care and the level of risky activities (see also Polinsky, 1980). More generally, the due care standard must include all relevant dimensions of care-taking to achieve optimal investment in all dimensions of safety.

1.1.2. The Demand for Liability Insurance.   The early models of effects of liability on levels of care ignored the role of liability in allocating risk by assuming that losses are purely financial and either risk neutrality or the availability of actuarially fair insurance to both parties. Shavell (1982) first formally examined the demand for liability insurance, introducing risk aversion of victims and injurers and the availability of first-party and liability insurance into a model of unilateral accidents with pecuniary losses only.[7] A first best solution now requires a) a level of care that minimizes expected accident losses plus the cost of care, and b) an optimal allocation of risk for both parties.[8] The demand for liability insurance and its effect on social welfare depend critically on the information available to courts and to insurers.

Perfect information.   Under a negligence rule with the standard of care optimally defined and perfectly implemented, there is no demand for liability insurance since it is cheaper for defendants to be nonnegligent than to be negligent and insure against the resulting liability. Since defendants are not liable, they bear no risk.[9]

Under strict liability, if injurers are risk averse and liability insurance is not available, a first best outcome is not attainable. Optimal risk spreading requires setting damage awards at less than full compensation, which leaves both victims and injurers bearing risk. Injurers may take excessive care or engage suboptimally in risky activities. When liability insurance is available and insurers can observe defendant care (perfect experience rating), injurers can be fully protected against risk while preserving optimal incentives for care, and optimal damage awards provide full compensation to victims. Thus liability insurance unambiguously improves social welfare and permits a first-best solution for level of care and allocation of risk.

Imperfect information.   Demand for liability insurance under a negligence rule derives from imperfect information of claimants, courts, and insurers. If victims or courts systematically commit Type 1 errors, failing to file and award liability in all instances of negligence, then with actuarial insurance it is cheaper for defendants to be negligent and to insure against the resulting liability than to always be nonnegligent. Conversely, if claimants or courts commit Type 2 errors, making erroneous filings or findings of negligence, then defendants are exposed to a risk akin to strict liability and will demand liability insurance (Shavell, 1982, 1987; Danzon, 1985a). Even if the level of care is correctly defined on average, random errors can generate a demand for liability insurance.[10] If the insured's level of care is observable to the insurer, the optimal contract would exclude coverage if the defendant acted negligently. But obviously if insurers had the information necessary to implement such a policy, the courts could use the information and eliminate the errors that generated the demand for insurance in the first place.[11]

Under strict liability, if insurers cannot observe defendants' care, defendants will choose less than full coverage and the outcome for both level of care and allocation of risk is not first best. Thus in the single period context moral hazard induced by asymmetric information results in a tradeoff between loss prevention and risk spreading in the context of liability insurance, as for first-party insurance (Zeckhauser, 1970; Shavell, 1979). But Shavell (1982) concludes that even with imperfect experience rating, government intervention in liability insurance markets is not warranted.[12]

1.1.3. The Judgment Proof Problem and Compulsory Liability. If injurers lack sufficient assets to fully satisfy a judgment, deterrence and incentives to purchase liability insurance are diminished, because part of the premium would cover losses they would not expect to bear (e.g., Calabresi, 1970; Keeton and Kwerel, 1984; Shavell, 1986). The effects of limited liability depend on the level of injurers' assets relative to expected losses.

Under a negligence rule, if the injurer's wealth is less than a critical level that is less than the potential loss, incentives for care are suboptimal. Under strict liability, if insurance is perfectly experience rated, full coverage is purchased and the level of care is efficient if injurers' wealth exceeds some critical level; at lower levels of wealth, injurers do not buy insurance and the level of care is suboptimal. If insurers cannot observe care, above some (higher) critical level of wealth, injurers buy partial coverage but the level of care is nonoptimal. Making liability insurance compulsory can restore efficient incentives for care under both negligence and strict liability, provided that enforcement is complete and that insurers can observe defendants' care and rate premiums appropriately.[13] But if injurers' care is unobservable, compulsory coverage that fully protects injurers' assets is counterproductive, whereas prohibiting coverage could improve the level of care (see Shavell, 1986).

In the United States, liability insurance (or ex ante proof of financial responsibility) is compulsory for workers' compensation in all states and in most states for automobile liability. Two arguments can be made for compulsory coverage even in the absence of individual experience rating. First, with experience rating at the level of the group but not the individual, compulsory coverage still internalizes accident costs to the responsible activity or class of individuals. The cost of insurance operates like a tax on the activity and achieves general but not specific deterrence (optimal level of the activity, conditional on nonoptimal care per unit of activity). Second, compulsory insurance assures the compensation function of tort liability. Concern with compensation and the resulting distributive effects between classes of injurers and victims may influence the political demand for compulsory insurance.[14]

1.1.4. Optimal Damage Awards.   Tort awards simultaneously provide deterrence to injurers and compensation to victims. Viewing tort liability as a system of (conditional) compulsory insurance (Oi, 1973; Danzon, 1984b), it is unique among systems of social and private insurance in that the amount of compensation is determined after the injury, traditionally by jury and without contractual or statutory limits, and is intended to provide full compensation of monetary and nonmonetary loss. This reflects the dual function of tort awards, as compensation to victims and penalties to defendants.

A single award is optimal for both deterrence and compensation only in a restricted set of circumstances. If the victim suffers only a monetary loss (utility is not state-dependent) and if the injurer is either risk neutral or can fully insure at actuarial rates, an award equal to the loss simultaneously provides optimal insurance to the victim and optimal deterrence to the injurer.

When the victim suffers a nonfinancial loss (utility is state dependent), optimal compensation still requires equalization of marginal utility of wealth across states of the world, but the size of award necessary to achieve this result depends on whether the injury raises or lowers the marginal utility of wealth (Cook and Graham, 1977). Since this optimal compensatory award is no longer identical to the optimal deterrence penalty on the injurer, a first best result requires supplementing compensatory awards with a system of fines, paid initially to the state and refunded as subsidies to the risky activity (Spence, 1977). Danzon (1984b) shows that the optimal compensatory award to the victim is inversely related to the load on the defendant's liability insurance.[15] Rea (1981) demonstrates that lump sum awards are more efficient than periodic payments contingent on losses actually incurred. Contingent periodic payment overinsures the victim and encourages ex post moral hazard.[16]

1.2. Optimal Form of Liability Insurance Contracts

The optimal form of insurance contracts has been extensively studied in the context of first-party insurance. Since the policyholder insures against a loss to himself, there is a presumption that the contractual form that emerges in competitive insurance markets maximizes policyholder utility and is also socially optimal even under conditions of moral hazard.[17] But for liability insurance against loss caused by the policyholder to a third party, control of moral hazard is more complex and there is a much weaker presumption that the policy that is privately optimal to the policyholder/defendant is also socially optimal. The liability insurance loss depends not only on the policyholder's effort at injury prevention but also on his cooperation in legal defense and the liability insurer's legal defense effort; the incentives of the victim to pursue a claim and to mitigate the amount of loss in the event of injury; the propensities of judge and jury, given the constraints of statutory and common law; and the structure of statutory and common law constraints. In addition to the influence of moral hazard, the optimal form of liability insurance contract can be affected by undiversifiable risk. The presence of liability insurance also might affect the endogenous choice of legal rules.

1.2.1. Optimal Copayment When Claim Outcome Is Exogenous. If the probability and size of injury depend only on the defendant's level of care and there is a proportional loading, theorems of optimal first-party insurance imply that optimal copayment would include a deductible, a coinsurance rate, or both in the single period case. In the multiperiod case, the optimal policy is experience rated. In the liability context, socially optimal coverage if the insurer could observe the insured's care would provide full coverage of losses if care is efficient $(x \geq x^*)$ and zero coverage if care is suboptimal $(x < x^*)$. But if there are Type 1 errors (failure to file or find liability for all injuries caused by $x < x^*$), then defendants may prefer a policy that provides coverage even if $x < x^*$ (Danzon, 1985a).

When care is not observable, policyholders may prefer a policy that requires insurers to invest in information, rather than levy copayments automatically for all claims or all paid claims. Paid claims do not convey perfect information about whether negligence occurred even if courts are unbiased because over 90% of paid claims are settled out of court. The decision to settle and amount of settlement may be influenced by many factors other than the defendant's level of care and plaintiff's true damages, including the parties' misperceptions of the expected verdict, costs of litigation, risk aversion, concerns over precedent, and other factors (see Cooter and Rubinfeld, 1989, for a survey). The private and socially optimal policy would attempt to protect the insured from these exogenous risks and relate copayment only to losses caused by suboptimal care. Thus in the case of Type 2 errors, competitive liability insurance markets will tend to devise contract terms that do not interfere with efficient deterrence.

1.2.2. Optimal Copayment When Claim Outcomes Depend on Legal Defense. When the courts lack perfect information about the defendant's care, the victim's damages, or the injury production function, both parties have incentives to invest in legal effort to influence the outcome.[18] This generates a demand for legal defense insurance. Combining legal defense and damages insurance in a single policy avoids duplicative monitoring of the actions of defense attorneys and policyholders.

But when both the insurer and the policyholder can affect the magnitude of loss, no simple loss sharing contract can simultaneously provide both with optimal marginal incentives. In general, if it is costly for policyholders to monitor the insurer's legal defense effort, the privately optimal copayment is lower than first-party coverage with comparable policyholder moral hazard and even lower if defense effort reduces plaintiff's incentives to file claims (Danzon, 1985a).[19] When claim outcomes depend on legal defense effort, defendants may choose policies with too little copayment: from a social standpoint, too many resources may be devoted to fighting claims and too few to preventing injuries. Private and social optima diverge unless potential victims are in a contractual relationship with defendants and accurately perceive the nature of the defendant's insurance coverage and its likely effects on claim outcomes — but in that case the liability rule is irrelevant.

1.2.3. Empirical Evidence on Copayments. Deductibles are common for product liability and professional liability policies for attorneys, accountants, and corporate directors and officers, but not for medical malpractice. Medical malpractice insurance is typically rated on the basis of limits of coverage, medical specialty, and geographic location. Individual rating on the basis of exposure (performance of high-risk procedures), volume of business, and individual claim record is relatively limited.[20] Several studies have shown that the actual distribution of claims and awards is inconsistent with a purely random distribution, after controlling for specialty (Rolph, 1981; Nye and Hofflander, 1988; Ellis, Gallup, and McGuire, 1990; Sloan, et al., 1989).

If more experience rating is statistically feasible than in fact occurs for medical malpractice insurance, this suggests a lack of demand. The apparent lack of copayment may be deceptive if physicians face significant copayment in the form of uninsurable time and disutility of being sued, or higher premium costs if they are denied coverage by more selective, lower-cost insurers (Danzon, 1985a). To the extent copayment and experience rating exist, it is usually based on additional information to distinguish Type 2 errors from valid claims, rather than automatic copayment for all paid claims, consistent with the hypothesis that the risk of judicial error contributes to the lack of demand for experience-rated policies.[21] Ellis, Gallup, and McGuire (1990) show that automatic experience rating based on Bayesian conditional means would impose significant risk on physicians and create inequities in premiums across physicians with identical true risks. Thus the lack of experience rating of medical malpractice may reflect a rational demand for protection against the risk of judicial error and being erroneously rated.

1.2.4. Effects of Undiversifiable Risk on Optimal Contractual Form. Positive correlation of liability losses among policyholders can affect the optimal form of liability insurance contract.[22] Positive correlation derives from the dependence of number of claims and size of awards on unanticipated changes in law and social norms. By the operation of legal precedent, a ruling by one court can influence the outcome of related cases, but given the multiplicity of courts and jurisdictions, it may be many years before new majority standards become firmly established.

The undiversifiable risk associated with common factors increases with the duration of insurer liability, which is typically longer for liability insurance than for first-party insurance. Delay between the writing of the policy and the ultimate disposition of all claims is caused partly by delay in the legal process of settling claims. More significant time lapse derives from discovery-based statutes of limitations that do not begin to run until the injury and its cause have been (or with reasonable diligence should have been) discovered, which could be twenty years for some cancers or birth defects. The longer the duration of liability, the greater the risk that unanticipated information about hazards or new legal standards will shift the distribution of expected loss for all outstanding policies. Socio-legal risk has become more significant with the expansion of liability for defects in product design and warnings, where a single ruling can render all units of a product line defective and hence lay the grounds for hundreds or thousands of claims (e.g., asbestosis claims). Even if courts admit a state-of-the-art defense in principle, some degree of retroactivity is implicit in basic common law rules of procedure and damages, and some courts have explicitly disallowed a state-of-the-art defense.[23]

Doherty and Dionne (1989) show that contracts that allow policy-holders to bear undiversifiable risk through premium adjustments, dividends, or other features (e.g., claims-made coverage) may have a comparative advantage over occurrence contracts with fixed premiums.[24] The intuitive reason is that insureds can share diversifiable idiosyncratic risk without paying a risk premium. Of course, if undiversifiable insurance risk can be costlessly diversified through capital markets, the risk-bearing advantage of such contracts disappears.

A limitation of contracts that provide for retroactive premium adjustments through dividends or assessments on policyholders is that they are costly to enforce when there is asymmetric information between insurer and policyholder in observing the true loss or when the realized loss depends in part on the insurer's incentive for legal defense (Danzon, 1985a). A mutual organizational form that eliminates possible conflicts between owners and policyholders may thus have an advantage in assuring optimal investment in legal defense and in offering contracts with retroactive adjustment or multiperiod policies.

The effect of undiversifiable risk on the optimal structure of damage awards and duration of liability (statutes of limitations) is discussed in Danzon (1984b) and Rubinfeld (1984) but has not been analyzed rigorously in formal models. More generally, the effect of the current structure of liability rules on the risk faced by liability insurers has played a major role in the debate over tort reform and liability insurance crises.

1.2.5. Endogeneity of Legal Standards. A smaller literature adopts a positive approach to explain why certain liability rules have been adopted in particular circumstances (for example, Landes and Posner, 1981, 1987). This literature is not immediately relevant to a survey of liability insurance, except to the extent that the existence of liability insurance influences the evolution of legal rules.

It is often argued anecdotally that jury decisions, in particular the size of awards, are influenced by knowledge of the defendant's liability insurance coverage, although in principle this is not admissable evidence. Consistent with this hypothesis, Chin and Peterson (1985) find that jury verdicts are significantly higher for the same type of injury if the defendant is a corporation or physician, rather than an individual. Danzon (1980) estimated an elasticity of award size with respect to limits of the defendants' insurance coverage of 0.14. More generally, it is often argued that one factor underlying the shift towards strict product liability in recent years has been the perception of courts that corporate defendants can obtain and pass on the costs of liability insurance more readily than individuals can obtain first-party insurance.

1.3. Liability Rules and Accident Rates: Empirical Evidence

Despite the policy interest in the effect of liability rules on resource allocation to risk reduction and the possible dulling effect of liability insurance, empirical evidence is so far limited and inconclusive. One fundamental problem is the unobservability of relevant rules of common law and of injury rates as opposed to claim rates. Moreover, as discussed above, the rate of injuries, claim frequency and severity, legal expenditures, and even legal rules are simultaneously determined. Data necessary to identify the structural equations of this system are generally not available.

Several studies have estimated the effects of liability on resource allocation in medical care, but without a measure of injury rates have been unable to distinguish cost-justified improvements in prevention that liability is intended to induce from wasteful defensive medicine (Greenwald and Mueller, 1978; Reynolds, Rizzo, and Gonzalez, 1985; Danzon, 1990b).[25] Several studies have estimated the impact of a limited set of legal rules on the frequency and severity of claims (for medical malpractice, see Danzon, 1984a, 1986; Danzon and Lillard, 1983; Sloan, Mergenhagen, and Bovbjerg, 1989; for product liability, see Viscusi, 1989). None of these studies have attempted to measure whether liability insurance with imperfect experience rating undermines the incentive effects of liability rules.

Measurement of the relevant law and insurance parameters is generally easier if liability is governed by statute rather than common law, as in workers' compensation and no-fault automobile regimes. Data on accident rates as opposed to claim rates are also available, although subject to reporting error. The evidence for work-related injuries is reviewed here.[26]

The effect of liability rules on workplace injuries is ambiguous a priori. Since the setting is one of repeated or multiperiod contracting with enduring production technologies, transactions costs may be sufficiently low and information sufficiently symmetric for the rule of liability to be irrelevant (Coase, 1960), except possibly for risks of long-latent diseases such as cancer caused by toxic exposures. Differences across states in timing of adoption of workers' compensation statutes (which replaced traditional common-law employer liability for negligence with strict employer lability) and in statutory benefit provisions have provided the empirical variation necessary to test whether the liability rule matters. However there remains a difficulty of distinguishing injury rates from claim rates.

Several empirical studies have analyzed the effects of workers' compensation statutes or benefit levels on claim rates (e.g., Fenn, 1981; Chelius, 1982; Worrall and Appel, 1982; Butler and Worrall, 1983; Ruser, 1986; Dionne and St-Michel, 1991). Butler and Worrall (1983) use a time-series and cross-section of 35 states for 1972 to 1978 and estimate a simultaneous system in which claim rates, hours of work, and wages are treated as endogenous. They estimate an own benefit elasticity of 0.37 for temporary total injuries, and generally positive elasticities for major and minor permanent partial injuries.[27]

Ruser (1986) shows formally that the safety response to higher benefit levels depends on the degree of experience rating. Since large firms are either self-rated or self-insured, whereas experience rating is imperfect for medium and small firms, large firms are expected to be more responsive, in addition to having economies of scale in providing safety. Using claim rates and injury rates for 25 industries in 41 states for 1972–1979, Ruser finds some evidence that higher benefit levels have a greater (more negative) effect on injury rates in large firms, consistent with the theoretical prediction from experience rating.

1.4. Relative Efficiency of First- and Third-Party Coverage

It is popular to compare liability insurance to first-party insurance and to note that, from the standpoint of delivering compensation to the victim, transactions costs are much greater for liability insurance. Roughly 40 cents of the product liability or medical malpractice insurance dollar reaches the victim as compensation; of the remainder, roughly 40 cents is litigation expense, divided evenly between plaintiff and defense, and the remainder is insurance overhead (Munch, 1977; Kakalik and Pace, 1986).

By contrast, the load on large group first-party health insurance may be less than 10 cents of the insurance dollar, although higher for small groups and individual policies.

A simple comparison of loading charges is an inappropriate measure of overall efficiency since part of the purpose of the litigation expense component of liability insurance is enforcement of liability rules that in principle serve a deterrent as well as a compensation function. Liability insurance provides the joint products of compensation of the victim, insurance of the defendant, and deterrence, in contexts that intrinsically involve asymmetric information and multiple agency problems. Thus from a social perspective, liability and first-party insurance perform different functions and are used in contexts that make them noncomparable. About all that can be said is that the administrative costs of tort liability are not justified if the impact of legal rules on deterrence is less than some critical level (see Shavell, 1987, ch. 11), and, as previously noted, that optimal compensatory awards are inversely related to liability insurance load factors (Danzon, 1984b).

Epstein (1985) and Priest (1987) examine product liability as an insurance market and argue that it is much less efficient than first-party insurance for purposes of controlling moral hazard and adverse selection. But in the context of two-party accidents such as consumer product injuries, first-party insurance is relatively inefficient at controlling moral hazard on the part of producers, just as liability insurance does little to control moral hazard on the part of consumers. There is parallel here between liability insurance and liability rules: just as one-sided liability rules such as caveat emptor and strict liability without a contributory negligence defense are inefficient for controlling bilateral accidents, the associated insurance arrangements similarly fail to provide efficient incentives for care to the party that is immune from liability. It is not obvious a priori that for bilateral accidents, first-party insurance is more efficient than liability insurance.

2. The Supply of Liability Insurance

The effects of liability rules and insurance on resources allocated to risk reduction and the total cost of risk depend on the structure, performance, and regulation of liability insurance markets. Major issues include the degree of competition in the market, determinants of fair premiums and the nature and causes of fluctuations in price and in the availability of coverage, and the effects of insurance regulation. Much of the work in these areas has dealt with the overall property-liability insurance market.

2.1. Market Structure

2.1.1. Marketing Methods and Organizational Form. The U.S. liability insurance market is characterized by two principal methods of product distribution (independent agency and direct writers) and two principal organizational forms (stocks and mutuals).[28] Insurers that use independent agents (and brokers) to distribute their products account for the bulk of premiums for commercial liability insurance and workers' compensation (see table 1). Direct writers generally have significantly lower operating expenses as a proportion of premiums than agency insurers. Whether higher operating expenses for agency companies are associated with greater service to policyholders has been subject to considerable debate, especially for private passenger auto and homeowners' coverage (see the following).

A large majority of premiums in most commercial liability lines is written by stock companies, but mutuals account for over a third of private passenger auto liability premiums.[29] Mayers and Smith (1981, 1988) argue that the tradeoff between the ability of mutual organization to eliminate potential incentive conflicts between owners and policyholders and the possibly greater cost of controlling manager-policyholder conflicts with mutuals than with stock companies is likely to make mutual organization advantageous in markets where managerial discretion is limited. Hansmann (1985) suggests that mutual organization may involve less conflict with policyholders over the choice of default risk and that it may have facilitated improved risk selection during the formative years of insurance markets.[30]

2.1.2. Concentration and Barriers to Entry. The structure of the market for most property-liability insurance lines generally has been regarded as competitive (e.g., Danzon, 1983; Clarke, et al., 1988; Winter, 1988; also see Joskow, 1973). Market concentration generally is low whether measured at the state or national level, especially for commercial lines.[31] Most studies conclude that there are no substantial barriers to entry.[32]

Institutional arrangements for the pooling and analysis of claim cost data and cooperative development of policy forms facilitate entry (e.g., Danzon, 1983; Eisenach, 1985). Absent these arrangements, large insurers would have an advantage over small insurers in forecasting future

Table 1. Liability Insurance Premiums — 1987

	Net Premiums Written ($ millions)	Market Shares				
		Largest 4 Groups	Stock Co.	Mutual Co.	Independent Agency	Direct Writers
Private Passenger Auto Liability	$ 37,449	42%	52%	35%	36%	64%
Workers' Compensation	23,429	28	72	26	73	27
General Liability	20,874	28	88	11	82	18
Commercial Multiperil	17,231	24	84	13	81	19
Commerical Auto Liability	11,755	21	77	21	79	21
Medical Malpractice	4,004	38	59	20	45	55
All Property-Liability	193,246	23	70	24	58	42

Source: *Best's Aggregates and Averages*, A.M. Best Co., 1988 ed.

claims and in bearing fixed costs of ratemaking and complying with rate regulation. Since many small firms exist, it is unlikely that either greater variability in average claim costs for small insurers due to their smaller number of exposures or minimum capital and licensing requirements for insurers constitute significant entry barriers.

No substantive entry barriers would appear to be associated with use of independent agents and brokers. Fixed costs associated with risk selection can be reduced by firms that anticipate little volume in a given market by using managing general agents.[33] Joskow (1973) argued that differences in operating costs between direct writers and independent agency insurers could not be explained by differences in service (also see Cummins and VanDerhei, 1979). To explain why direct writers had not grown more rapidly, he suggests that prior approval rate regulation had discouraged price cuts by direct writers, that difficulty in raising capital and obtaining consumer recognition slowed their expansion, and that it would be costly for independent agency insurers to become direct writers (also see Smallwood, 1975). More recently, Pauly, Kleindorfer, and Kunreuther (1986) argue that significant barriers to raising capital for growth are unlikely, and they suggest that direct writers and independent agency insurers produce different levels and types of services.

Numerous studies have estimated property-liability insurer cost functions using cross-firm data on operating expenses and some proxy for output. While the results often suggest increasing returns to scale (e.g., Cummins and VanDerhei, 1979; Doherty, 1981), the use of accounting data to infer returns to scale is problematic. Among other limitations, data on operating expenses aggregate capital (e.g., product and market development) expenditures and current costs. Firm output also cannot be measured accurately (e.g., Doherty, 1981; also see Braeutigam and Pauly, 1986). Appel, Worrall, and Butler (1985) analyze changes in the size distribution of insurers over time. Their results are inconsistent with increasing returns for small insurers and thus more in line with evidence on entry and concentration.[34]

2.2. Prices, Profits, and Market Volatility

2.2.1. Determinants of Fair Premiums. What level of premiums is needed to produce a fair return to suppliers of capital? Biger and Kahane (1978), Fairley (1979), and Hill (1979) derive fair underwriting margins implied by the Capital Asset Pricing Model (CAPM) (also see Cummins and Harrington, 1985). Myers and Cohn (1986) develop a simple discounted cash flow model of insurance prices. Kraus and Ross (1982) consider a continuous time model and apply arbitrage pricing theory. Option pricing models are applied to premium determination by Doherty and Garven (1986) and Cummins (1988).

The essence of this research is that fair premiums equal the (risk-adjusted) discounted value of all expected costs associated with writing coverage including the expected cost of claim payments, underwriting expenses, and income taxes. Higher levels of capital lead to higher premiums and lower default risk.[35] An important implication is that variability in claim costs that cannot be eliminated by insurer diversification increases fair premiums for a given level of default risk and thus reduces gains from trade. A number of studies emphasize that uncertainty associated with liability law and jury awards can be very costly for this reason (e.g., Danzon, 1984b, 1985b; Clarke, et al., 1988; Abraham, 1988; also see Doherty and Dionne, 1989).

2.2.2. Profitability. Property-liability insurer profitability has been examined using a variety of profitability measures, time periods, and benchmarks for fair profits. Some studies (e.g., Insurance Services Office, 1987) compare accounting returns on net worth (surplus) for property-liability insurers to those of other industries after adjusting for differences in the variability of returns. Other studies compare underwriting profit margins to levels implied by theoretical models (e.g., Fairley, 1979; D'Arcy and Garven, 1990). As discussed further below, insurer financial results during and following the so-called liability insurance crisis of the mid-1980s also have been examined (e.g., Harrington, 1988; also see Lacey, 1988).

Studies of average accounting returns on surplus over time generally suggest that property-liability insurer returns are low to moderate compared to other industries with comparable variability in returns, but the interpretation of these studies is problematic (see Venezian, 1984). In addition to a weak theoretical basis for assuming a positive tradeoff between returns and variability, accounting returns at best are only rough approximations of economic returns.[36] Attempts to assess profitability by line (or by line and by state) also are plagued by the lack of a rigorous basis for allocating insurer operating expenses, investment income, and most important, surplus. These and other problems also affect comparisons of reported underwriting margins with levels implied by financial models of insurance prices. Hence, while the results of this literature generally suggest only normal profits, they have not prevented allegations of excessive profits in the policy debate over the cost and availability of liability insurance.

2.2.3. Market Volatility and the Underwriting Cycle. Many lines of insurance appear to be characterized by soft markets, in which prices are stable or falling and coverage is readily available, followed by hard markets, in which prices rise rapidly and the number of insurers offering coverage for some risks declines substantially. Popular wisdom holds that soft and hard markets occur in six-year cycles. Reported underwriting and total operating profit margins for insurers follow a second-order autoregressive process that is consistent with a cycle (see Venezian, 1985; Cummins and Outreville, 1987; Doherty and Kang, 1988; also see Smith, 1989).

According to the traditional view of cycles by industry analysts, which assumes an inelastic supply of capital, competition drives prices down until capital is depleted, insurers ultimately constrain supply to prevent default, and attendant increases in prices and retained earnings replenish capital until price-cutting ensues again.[37] Academic researchers have frequently questioned this scenario and whether prices are in fact cyclical. For example, Cummins and Outreville (1987) consider whether cycles in reported underwriting results could simply reflect insurer financial reporting procedures in conjunction with information, policy renewal, and regulatory lags.[38]

The most controversial episode of volatility in insurance markets was the liability insurance crisis of the mid-1980s, which was characterized by dramatic increases in premiums for many commercial liability risks and reductions in the availability of coverage. Industry financial results surrounding this period suggest that rapid premium growth in general liability insurance during 1985–1986 was associated with upward revisions in insurer loss reserves for prior years' business and rapid growth in reported losses for new business (Harrington, 1988; Harrington and Litan, 1988). Much of the total growth in premiums during 1980–1986 probably can be explained by growth in expected losses and changes in interest rates (i.e., by determinants of fair premiums). However, premiums grew slower than discounted reported losses during the early 1980s and much faster than discounted reported losses during 1985–1986, a result that is consistent with cyclical effects.

The underlying causes of cycles are not well understood. Conventional descriptions suggest a persistent tendency towards destructive price cutting and inelasticity in the supply of capital to the industry. Two possible causes of excessive price cutting in soft markets are overly optimistic forecasts of future claim costs by some insurers and the possibility of aggressive behavior by firms with little to lose in the event of default (McGee, 1986; Harrington, 1988; also see Harrington and Danzon, 1990).[39]

Winter (1988, 1989) develops a model in which undiversifiable risk and constraints on external capital flows (such as those that might arise from asymmetric information between insurer managers and investors or from income tax treatment of shareholder dividends) and solvency (which could be imposed by regulators or reflect policyholder preferences) could lead to periods of soft markets followed by sharp increases in prices.[40] Cummins and Danzon (1990) analyze conditions in which costly external capital and exogenous shocks that reduce surplus (such as increases in the liability for unpaid claims) can lead to premium increases in excess of changes in expected costs of providing coverage.[41]

Other studies argue that increased uncertainty about the level of future claim costs is likely to have contributed to rapid premium growth and availability problems in commercial liability insurance during the mid-1980s (e.g., Clarke, et al., 1988; also see Danzon, 1984b).[42] Priest (1987) suggests that an expansion in tort law aggravated adverse selection to the point where some coverage became unavailable at any price. Abraham (1988) argues that expansive court decisions concerning contract language contributed to availability problems in the market for environmental impairment liability coverage in the mid-1980s. As noted earlier, undiversifiable risk associated with the legal system also can make claims-made contracts with premium adjustments attractive relative to fixed premium, occurrence coverage.

2.3. Regulation

Most economic analyses of insurance regulation have focused on solvency regulation and regulation of premium rates and the availability of coverage.[43]

2.3.1. Default Risk and Solvency Regulation. The traditional rationale for solvency regulation is that consumers are unable to monitor the risk of insurer default. In the United States, solvency regulation has three major facets: 1) direct controls on certain activities and financial reporting, 2) monitoring of insurer behavior, and 3) a system for paying claims of insolvent insurers (see Harrington and Danzon, 1986, for details). Direct controls include minimum capital requirements and limitations on investment activities. The principal monitoring system is administered by the National Association of Insurance Commissioners. Guaranty funds exist to pay claims of insolvent property-liability insurers in all states.[44]

The default rate for property-liability insurers increased substantially in 1984 and has continued at historically high levels since that time. During 1984–1989, the number of failures requiring guaranty fund assessments averaged about 20 per year and assessments totaled $3 billion (NCIGF, 1990).

Economic analysis of insurer default risk has focused on factors that influence insurer capital decisions.[45] Munch and Smallwood (1982) and Finsinger and Pauly (1984) model the capital decision assuming that insurers maximize value to shareholders, that demand is inelastic with respect to default risk, and that investing financial capital to support insurance operations is costly. The principal implication is that optimal capital is positively related to the amount of loss that shareholders would suffer if claim costs were to exceed the firm's financial assets. Munch and Smallwood (1982) consider possible loss of goodwill in the event of default; Finsinger and Pauly (1984) assume that an entry cost would be forfeited that otherwise would allow the firm to continue operating. If shareholders have nothing to lose, they will not commit any capital. If they are exposed to loss and it is assumed that firms cannot add capital after claims are realized, firms will commit some capital ex ante.[46]

Default risk for insurers that specialize in liability coverage could be expected to exceed risk for insurers that specialize in first-party coverage if liability policyholders would be judgment proof in the absence of coverage and the demand for first-party coverage depends on default risk (see Harrington and Danzon, 1986). Specifically, compulsory liability requirements could lead judgment proof consumers to seek coverage from firms with high default risk and correspondingly low premiums. As a result, there could be a need for solvency regulation of liability insurance even if policyholders were fully informed about default risk.

In an empirical analysis of the effects of solvency regulation, Munch and Smallwood (1980) provide evidence that minimum capital requirements reduced insolvencies by reducing the number of small domestic insurers in the market. Other empirical studies generally have focused on predicting insurer defaults using financial data without relating the variables chosen to the theory of default risk (e.g., Harrington and Nelson, 1986; McDonald, 1988). Not much is known empirically about the magnitude of the effects of regulatory monitoring and guaranty funds on default risk, or about the extent to which unpredictable growth in claim costs for commercial liability or other lines of insurance contributed to the increased default rate in recent years, as opposed to excessive price cutting due to overly optimistic forecasts or aggressive or fraudulent behavior.

2.3.2. Rate Regulation. Regulation of property-liability insurance rates can affect an insurer's average rate level or overall percentage change in its rates during a given period. It also can affect rate differentials between groups of consumers by imposing limits on voluntary or involuntary market rates or by restricting risk classification.[47]

Voluntary market rates for most property-liability lines presently are subject to prior approval regulation in about half of the states. Most states had prior approval regulation during the 1950s and 1960s, and rate regulation probably encouraged insurers to use rates developed by rating bureaus (Joskow, 1973; Harrington, 1984). A trend towards deregulation began in the late 1960s and continued until the early 1980s. A number of states reregulated commercial liability insurance rates following the liability insurance crisis of 1985–1986. California adopted prior approval regulation for property-liability insurance with the enactment of Proposition 103 in 1988. Several additional states either have reenacted or are considering reenactment of prior approval regulation.[48]

Most studies of rate regulation estimate the impact of voluntary market rate regulation in auto insurance on average rate levels for the overall (voluntary and involuntary) market. Major hypotheses are that regulation raises rates due to capture by industry, that regulation has short-run effects due to regulatory lag, and that regulation persistently reduces rates due to consumer pressure. The results of studies using data from the late 1970s and early 1980s (e.g., Pauly, Kleindorfer, and Kunreuther, 1986; Harrington, 1987; Grabowski, Viscusi, and Evans, 1989) suggest that on average prior approval regulation reduced the ratio of premiums to losses, a result that is consistent with consumer pressure for low rates.[49]

Involuntary markets in auto insurance are significantly larger in states with prior approval regulation of voluntary market rates (e.g., Ippolito, 1979; Grabowski, Viscusi, and Evans, 1989). States that have significantly limited involuntary market rates, adopted restrictions on rate classification (e.g., unisex rating), or both generally have large involuntary markets, but the relative effects of these influences and of voluntary market rate regulation would be difficult to sort out. Voluntary and involuntary market regulation of auto liability insurance rates could possibly reduce the number of uninsured drivers by lowering rates to drivers who otherwise would fail to buy coverage (Kunreuther, Kleindorfer, and Pauly, 1983; Keeton and Kwerel, 1984). If so, the efficiency loss from rate regulation that otherwise would be expected from any cross-subsidies would be mitigated.

Several studies have attempted to estimate the impact of prior approval regulation in commercial lines of business without firm conclusions (e.g., Stewart, 1987; Cummins and Harrington, 1987; Rizzo, 1988; also see Hunt, Krueger, and Burton, 1988). It is very difficult to control for factors that will influence premiums (or the ratio of premiums to losses) for commercial lines in the absence of rate regulation. A priori, rate regulation is likely to have little or no impact in most years for some commercial lines (such as general liability) due to widespread use of individual risk rating (Stewart, 1987).

There has been little formal analysis to date of the wide variation in involuntary market size in workers' compensation, of cross-state variation in the size of joint underwriting associations in medical malpractice insurance and other commercial liability lines, and, in general, of economic and political factors that lead to government intervention in the rate-setting process. A large amount of anecdotal evidence suggests that substantial regulatory intervention in insurance pricing tends to occur in states where the unregulated cost of coverage would be relatively high, that rate regulation tends to favor high-risk groups, and that exits eventually have occurred in response to restrictive regulation. The implication is that high costs lead to effective political pressure for limits on rates. Any tendency for regulation to hold down liability insurance rates for high risks would be likely to dull the incentive affects of tort liability and increase the cost of risk, but it would probably be very difficult to estimate the effects of such policies on levels of activity and care.

2.3.3. The McCarran-Ferguson Act. The McCarran-Ferguson Act (enacted by the U.S. Congress in 1945) establishes the primacy of state insurance regulation and provides the insurance industry with an exemption from federal antitrust law that allows cooperative activities to the extent that they are regulated by the states or unless boycott, coercion, and intimidation are involved.[50] Two forms of cooperative activity have been subject to substantial controversy in recent years: the development of advisory rates or prospective loss costs by advisory organizations such as the Insurance Services Office (ISO), and the cooperative development of policy forms.[51]

Several groups claim that the ISO advisory rate system aggravated rate increases during the liability insurance crisis. For example, Angoff (1988) argues that advisory rates or loss costs stimulate price-cutting during soft markets and permit collusion to raise rates above costs during hard markets. These effects are difficult to reconcile with the industry's competitive structure and with the modern operation of advisory organizations (e.g., Clarke, et al., 1988; Winter, 1988; Harrington and Litan, 1988).

Danzon (1983) concludes that current activities of advisory organizations in auto insurance are inconsistent with cartel behavior and likely to be procompetitive (also see Eisenach, 1985). In commercial liability insurance, independent rate filings, percentage deviations from ISO advisory rates or loss costs, and individual risk rating provide substantial flexibility in pricing. Winter (1988), Harrington (1988), and others also argue that cooperative ratemaking activities allowed under the McCarran-Ferguson Act are likely to enhance efficiency.

3. Conclusions

A major focus of economic analysis of tort liability has been on the design of liability rules to minimize the cost of risk in society. When moral hazard, transactions costs, limited liability, and nonmonetary losses are introduced, the relation between liability law, liability insurance, and risk reduction becomes extremely complex. Unobservability of policyholder care and imperfect experience rating in liability insurance markets undermine the deterrent effects of tort liability and, as in the case of first-party coverage, can produce a tradeoff between risk sharing and loss prevention. Limited liability and the resultant judgment proof problem also reduce incentives for care. Compulsory coverage might produce an efficient reduction in risky activity, but it cannot restore efficient incentives for care when care is unobservable. Nonmonetary losses make it impossible to achieve both efficient deterrence and optimal compensation with a single award for victims.

Undiversifiable risk associated with changes in liability rules is likely to increase premium rates necessary to achieve a given probability of insurer default, alter the optimal form of liability insurance contracts for some risks, aggravate volatility in the price and availability of liability insurance, and increase default risk for some insurers. Increases in expected liability claim costs also are likely to increase pressure on regulators to limit rate increases, especially for high-risk insureds, and thus to further dull the incentive effects of liability law.

Notes

1. Our treatment is not exhaustive; space limitations prevented us from discussing or citing many good papers on these subjects.

2. For reviews of this literature, see Polinsky (1983), Posner (1986), Shavell (1987), Landes and Posner (1987), Cooter and Ulen (1988), and references cited therein.

3. For formal models and empirical estimates of the wage premium for risk-bearing in risky employments and use of such estimates to infer a willingness-to-pay for safety or "value of life," see, for example, Thaler and Rosen (1976), Viscusi (1983), and Viscusi and Moore (1987).

4. Other possible corrective policies, such as regulatory standard setting, taxes and subsidies, and fines and injunctions, are not addressed in this survey since any resulting losses are generally not covered by liability insurance. Liability rules differ from regulatory standard setting in that they do not proscribe a specific course of action ex ante. Rather, liability rules define general conditions for allocating the cost of accidents and determining the amount of damages payable.

5. This notion of product defect reintroduces an issue of reasonable care, defined by some weighing of risks and benefits of additional care, analogous to a due care standard under a negligence rule. Thus strict liability for products is not the absolute liability used in simple theoretical models.

6. Cooter and Ulen (1987) argue that a comparative negligence rule is superior to a negligence rule when injurers and victims bear risk and there is evidentiary uncertainty. Rubinfeld (1987) reinforces this conclusion when injurers and victims are heterogeneous.

7. Corporate demand for liability insurance may be explained by risk aversion of customers, suppliers, managers, or employees (Mayers and Smith, 1982).

8. Formally, the problem is to maximize expected utility of the victim, subject to constraints of a) a reservation utility level for the defendant, b) an overall resource constraint, c) victims and injurers choose first-party and liability insurance to maximize their respective utilities, and d) insurers break even. If insurance is not available, then the choice between liability rules depends on which party is better able to bear risk. In particular, strict liability is preferable to negligence if injurers are risk neutral or better able to bear risk.

9. A first best outcome is achieved only if victims can eliminate risk by buying actuarially fair first-party insurance.

10. Calfee and Craswell (1984) analyze effects of uncertain legal standards on compliance under a negligence regime in the absence of liability insurance.

11. In the context of automobile accidents with externalities, Boyer and Dionne (1987) show that multiperiod no-fault insurance contracts (with an infinite horizon and no discounting) using experience rating based on past driving record can induce optimal levels of care.

12. This assumes that government has no information advantage, that damage awards are optimally set, and that defendants are not judgment proof.

13. Other possible remedies are vicarious liability and imposing asset requirements for participating in the activity. Shavell (1986) shows that imposing asset requirements equal to the maximum possible loss may overdeter, because it is socially efficient for parties to participate in an activity if their assets equal the expected loss, which is less than the maximum possible loss.

14. Obviously if compulsory coverage leads to a political demand for rate regulation that guarantees availability of coverage for high risks at subsidized rates, incentives for care are undermined. For further discussion, see Harrington (1989).

15. These conclusions follow from the standard assumption that the optimal damage award is chosen to maximize the utility of the victim, subject to a reservation level of utility for the defendant. Thus by assumption, the incidence of costs of liability is on victims. This is reasonable assuming a perfectly elastic long-run supply of the products or services that are subject to strict liability. But with imperfectly elastic supply in the short run, the incidence of unanticipated changes in liability costs is partly on defendants (Danzon, 1990a).

16. Noncontingent periodic payment of awards, where the amount is determined at time of trial or settlement (also called structured settlements) are potentially more efficient than lump sum awards if the defendant is permitted to provide for the payment of these future damages by the purchase of an annuity or other financial instrument. This transfers from the jury to financial markets the issue of determining expected rates of interest (Danzon, 1984b).

17. The convergence of private and social optima may not hold with adverse selection.

18. For product liability and medical malpractice, plaintiff and defense legal expenditures each average about one half of the net compensation received by plaintiffs (Danzon 1985b; Kakalik and Pace, 1986). For the effects of costly litigation on the efficiency of liability rules see, for example, Polinsky and Rubinfeld (1988) and Cooter and Rubinfeld (1989).

19. For example, a deductible undermines the insurer's incentives to fight claims that can be settled for less than the deductible. For medical malpractice claims closed during 1975–78, 64% of claims closed for under $3,000 but with mean legal expense in excess of mean damages paid (NAIC, 1980, p. 34). Incurring legal expense in excess of damages may be a privately optimal strategy if it deters other potential claims.

20. Some companies also apply surcharges or exclusions for certain high-risk procedures, such as shock therapy; a crude adjustment for part-time practice; and surcharges of limits on coverage for multiple paid claims.

21. Professional liability policies explicitly exclude coverage of intentional acts. The existence of a demand for and supply of coverage for punitive damages in states where this is permitted suggests a significant risk of Type 2 errors, despite the higher standard of proof (gross negligence or willful misconduct) for punitive awards.

22. The effect of undiversifiable risk on prices, "crises", and cycles in the supply of insurance is discussed in section 2.2.

23. In *Beshada v. Johns-Manville Products Corp.*, 90, New Jersey Supreme Court, 191,447 A2nd 539 (1982) the New Jersey Supreme Court held asbestos manufacturers liable even if the risks were unknowable at the time of manufacture. But in 1984 the same court held that manufacturers are not liable for defects they did not or could not know about when their products were sold (see *Feldman v. Lederle*, cited in *Business Insurance*, August 6, 1984). Retroactivity in tort is discussed by Schwartz (1983) and Danzon (1984b).

24. Danzon (1984b, 1985a,b) makes similar arguments in explaining the switch from claims-made to occurrence coverage and the growth of physician-owned mutuals following the medical malpractice crisis of the 1970s. Also see Marshall (1974).

25. *Defensive medicine* should be defined as practice patterns that would not have been chosen by a fully informed patient, given his or her first-party insurance coverage, and that would not have been taken in the absence of liability. This definition excludes resource misallocations that may be induced by moral hazard on first-party health insurance or asymmetric information in the physician/patient relationship.

26. Studies of automobile injuries (e.g., Landes, 1982; Zador and Lund, 1986; and Cummins and Weiss, 1988) are briefly discussed by Cummins and Weiss elsewhere in this volume (also see Bruce, 1984).

27. Some of the estimated elasticities are implausibly large for major permanent partial injuries.

28. Direct writers use exclusive agents or employees to market their products. Independent agents and brokers have access to more than one insurer.

29. Most large mutuals are direct writers. Reciprocal insurance exchanges and Lloyds associations also account for a small percentage of premiums. For detailed discussion of

alternative organizational forms, see Mayers and Smith (1988).

30. As noted in Section 1, mutual-type insurance schemes also may be advantageous with undiversifiable risk.

31. For medical malpractice, the most highly concentrated of the major property-liability lines, the four-firm concentration ratio exceeds 60% in most states. Danzon (1985b) discusses how higher concentration in medical malpractice is influenced by the prevalence of group coverage sponsored by state medical associations. Joskow (1973) argues that national concentration measures are more appropriate than state measures since most large insurers operate in all states and could readily expand writings in any state.

32. Regulatory prohibitions on the sale and underwriting of insurance by banks, which appear to be eroding, may prevent entry by entities that would employ alternative modes of distribution for some lines of business.

33. Managing general agents have considerable authority to make underwriting and pricing decisions for insurers that they represent. Regulators have recently examined the possible role of managing general agents in insurance company insolvencies. Managing general agents often make risk selection decisions for a fixed percentage of premium revenue. The incentives under these arrangements could be associated with increased default risk for insurers in some instances.

34. Joskow (1973) and others (e.g., Kunreuther, Kleindorfer, and Pauly, 1983) argue that it is difficult for consumers to compare prices, primarily because information from friends and neighbors is unlikely to be useful in view of the dependence of price on differences in risk across consumers. Dahlby and West (1986) (also see Berger, Kleindorfer, and Kunreuther, 1989) provide evidence that suggests that premium variation in auto insurance is influenced by costly search. Costly search for information on premium rates is likely to be less consequential for the commercial market, especially if independent agents are used. In fact, the major problem confronting most consumers may be quality assessment. Costly consumer search has been used to justify solvency regulation for insurers (see below). Costly search associated with the timing and magnitude of claim payments in the absence of insurer default also has received attention (e.g., Smallwood, 1975). The implications of moral hazard and imperfect information for experience rating in liability insurance were briefly discussed in Section 1. Some implications of imperfect information on future claim costs for insurance pricing, price cycles, and pooling of data are discussed below. Work on adverse selection in insurance markets is reviewed elsewhere in this volume.

35. Fair premiums depend on the amount of invested capital in these models because selling insurance (as opposed to operating an investment fund) exposes owners to income tax on investment earnings on capital.

36. For property-liability insurers, accounting returns do not reflect unrealized capital gains on bonds, realized capital gains reflect changes in bond values that occurred in periods prior to the year in which the gain or loss is recognized, and incurred losses are not discounted under either statutory or generally accepted accounting principles. Accounting returns also may be affected by nonrandom reserve errors (Weiss, 1985; also see Harrington, 1988).

37. Berger (1988) provides a simple model of this scenario.

38. Doherty and Kang (1988) argue that cycles in insurer operating results reflect slow adjustment of premiums to changes in the present value of expected future costs. Their analysis seems to imply that cyclical changes in factors such as interest rates cause cycles in operating results, but the relative roles of such changes and slow adjustment are not clear.

39. Venezian (1985) argues that industrywide use of suboptimal forecasting methods could produce cycles.

40. Winter's model predicts a negative relation between price and capital. He reports (1989) some evidence consistent with this prediction using (aggregate) industry data prior to the crisis of 1985–1986, at which time the relationship became positive.

41. Evidence of cycles and experience in the commercial liability insurance market during the 1980s has led to a number of other recent working papers (several of which only contain preliminary analysis and results). See, for example, Gron (1989), Tennyson (1989), and Doherty and Garven (1990).

42. This result would be expected if increased uncertainty raises the amount of capital needed to achieve a given default probability.

43. See Kunreuther, Kleindorfer, and Pauly (1983) for an overview of insurance regulation that also discusses compulsory insurance requirements. Possible conflicts between regulatory goals of reducing rates and promoting solvency have been discussed in many studies.

44. Almost all guaranty funds are financed by post-insolvency assessments on surviving insurers. The scope of coverage is limited. For example, the maximum property-liability claim payable commonly is $300,000 or less except for workers' compensation claims, which generally are fully covered.

45. A large actuarial literature also analyzes default risk. Portfolio models of property-liability insurance company behavior (e.g., Kahane and Nye, 1975) either treat default risk as exogenously determined or subject to insurer choice, but economic factors that could influence this choice are not emphasized.

46. Doherty (1989) and Tapiero, Kahane, and Jacques (1986) consider insurer capital decisions when demand for coverage depends on default risk. Following Mayers and Smith (1981, 1988), Garven (1987) analyzes default risk within an agency cost framework in which shareholders, managers, sales personnel, and policyholders have different incentives regarding default risk.

47. For background information on insurance rate regulation, see Harrington (1984). Involuntary markets, which are important mainly in auto, workers' compensation, and medical malpractice insurance, include mechanisms such as assigned risk plans and joint underwriting associations. They require joint provision of coverage by insurers at a regulated rate.

48. California and a few other states also enacted rate rollbacks during the last few years.

49. Some evidence of variation in the impact of prior approval regulation across states is provided in several studies, but causes of such variation generally are not analyzed. Pauly, Kleindorfer, and Kunreuther (1986) provide evidence that direct writer market share was significantly lower in states with prior approval regulation and that restrictive rate regulation was associated with lower operating expenses (and presumably lower quality; also see Ippolito, 1979, and Braeutigam and Pauly, 1986).

50. Many states have similar exemptions from state antitrust statutes.

51. Recent policy developments include the filing and subsequent dismissal (based on the McCarran exemption, the state action doctrine, and other grounds) of a federal antitrust suit by a group of state attorneys general, congressional proposals to repeal the industry's antitrust exemption, and a decision by the ISO to cease distributing advisory rates including expense and profit loadings and instead to disseminate developed and trended loss costs. The antitrust suit alleged that the ISO, the Reinsurance Association of America, and a number of insurers and brokers engaged in collusion and boycott when making changes in the standard form of general liability coverage during 1984–1985. The major charges dealt with the inclusion of an optional claims-made form, the inclusion of the retroactive date in

the claims-made form, the exclusion of all coverage for pollution liability, and a proposal (not adopted) to include insurer defense costs within policy limits.

References

Abraham, Kenneth S. (1988). "Environmental Liability and the Limits of Insurance," *Columbia Law Review* 88, 942–988.

Angoff, A. (1988). "Insurance Against Competition: How the McCarran-Ferguson Act Raises Prices and Profits in the Property-Casualty Insurance Industry, *Yale J. on Regulation* 5, 397–415.

Appel, David, Jack D. Worrall, and Richard J. Butler. (1985). "Survivorship and the Size Distribution of the Property-Liability Insurance Industry," *J. of Risk and Insurance* 52, 424–440.

Berger, Lawrence A. (1988). "A Model of Underwriting Cycles in the Property-Liability Insurance Industry," *J. of Risk and Insurance* 55, 298–306.

Berger, Lawrence A., Paul R. Kleindorfer, and Howard Kunreuther. (1989). "A Dynamic Model of Price Information in Auto Insurance Markets," *J. of Risk and Insurance* 56, 17–33.

Biger, Nahum, and Yehuda Kahane. (1978). "Risk Considerations in Insurance Ratemaking," *J. of Risk and Insurance* 45, 121–132.

Boyer, Marcel, and Georges Dionne. (1987). "The Economics of Road Safety," *Transportation Research* 21B, 413–431.

Braeutigam, Ronald R., and Mark V. Pauly. (1986). "Cost Function Estimation and Quality Bias: The Regulated Automobile Insurance Industry," *Rand J. of Economics* 17, 606–617.

Brown, John. (1973). "Toward an Economic Theory of Liability." *J. of Legal Studies* 2, 323–350.

Bruce, Christopher. (1984). "The Deterrent Effects of Automobile Insurance and Tort Law: A Survey of the Empirical Literature," *Law and Policy* 6, 67–100.

Butler, Richard J., and Jack D. Worrall. (1983). "Workers' Compensation: Benefit and Injury Claim Rates in the Seventies," *Review of Economics and Statistics* 65, 580–589.

Calabresi, Guido. (1970). *The Costs of Accidents*. New Haven, Conn.: Yale University Press.

Calfee, John, and Richard Craswell. (1984). "Some Effects of Uncertainty on Compliance with Legal Standards," *Virginia Law Review* 70, 965–1003.

Chelius, J. R. (1982). "The Influence of Workers' Compensation on Safety Incentives," *Industrial and Labor Relations Review* 35, 235–242.

Chin, Audrey, and Mark A. Peterson. (1985). "Deep Pockets, Empty Pockets: Who Wins in Cook County Jury Trials." R-3249-ICJ. Santa Monica, Calif.: The RAND Corporation.

Clarke, Richard N., Frederick Warren-Boulton, David K. Smith, and Marilyn J. Simon (1988). "Sources of the Crisis in Liability Insurance: An Empirical Analysis," *Yale J. on Regulation* 5, 367–395.

Coase, Ronald. (1960). "The Problem of Social Cost," *Journal of Law and Economics* 3, 1–44.

Cook, Philip, and Donald Graham. (1977). "The Demand for Insurance and Protection: The Case of Irreplaceable Commodities," *Quarterly J. of Economics* 91, 143–156.

Cooter, Robert, and Thomas Ulen. (1987). "The Economic Case for Comparative Negligence," *New York University Law Review* 61, 1067–1110.

Cooter, Robert. (1988). *Law and Economics*. Glenview, Ill.: Scott Foresman and Co.

Cooter, Robert, and Daniel L. Rubinfeld. (1989). "Economic Analysis of Legal Disputes and Their Resolution," *J. of Economic Literature* 27, 1067–1097.

Cummins, J. David. (1988). "Risk-Based Premiums for Insurance Guaranty Funds," *J. of Finance* 43, 823–839.

Cummins, J. David, and Patricia M. Danzon. (1990). "Price Shocks and Capital Flows in Property-Liability Insurance," Mimeo. University of Pennsylvania.

Cummins, J. David, and Scott E. Harrington. (1985). "Property-Liability Insurance Rate Regulation: Estimation of Underwriting Betas Using Quarterly Profit Data," *J. of Risk and Insurance* 52, 16–43.

Cummins, J. David, and Scott E. Harrington. (1987). "The Impact of Rate Regulation on Property-Liability Insurance Loss Ratios: A Cross-Sectional Analysis with Individual Firm Data," *Geneva Papers on Risk and Insurance* 12, 50–62.

Cummins, J. David, and Francois Outreville. (1987). "An International Analysis of Underwriting Cycles in Property-Liability Insurance," *J. of Risk and Insurance* 54, 246–262.

Cummins, J. David, and Jack VanDerhei. (1979). "A Note on the Relative Efficiency of Property-Liability Insurance Distribution Systems," *Bell J. of Economics* 10, 709–719.

Cummins, J. David, and Mary Weiss. (1988) "An Economic Analysis of No-Fault Auto Insurance," Mimeo. University of Pennsylvania.

Dahlby, Bev, and Douglas S. West. (1986). "Price Dispersion in An Automobile Insurance Market," *J. of Political Economy* 94, 418–438.

Danzon, Patricia. (1980). "The Disposition of Medical Malpractice Claims," R-2622-HCFA. Santa Monica, Calif.: The RAND Corporation.

Danzon, Patricia. (1983). "Rating Bureaus in U.S. Property-Liability Insurance Markets: Anti or Pro-Competitive?" *Geneva Papers on Risk and Insurance* 8, 371–402.

Danzon, Patricia. (1984a). "The Frequency and Severity of Medical Malpractice Claims," *J. of Law and Economics* 27, 115–147.

Danzon, Patricia. (1984b). "Tort Reform and the Role of Government in Private Insurance Markets," *J. of Legal Studies* 13, 517–549.

Danzon, Patricia. (1985a). "Liability and Liability Insurance for Medical Malpractice," *J. of Health Economics* 4, 309–331.

Danzon, Patricia. (1985b). *Medical Malpractice: Theory, Evidence and Public Policy*. Cambridge, Mass.: Harvard University Press.

Danzon, Patricia. (1986). "New Evidence on the Frequency and Severity of Medical Malpractice Claims," *Law and Contemporary Problems* 49, 57–84.

Danzon, Patricia. (1990a). "Alternative Liability Regimes for Medical Injuries." *Geneva Papers on Risk and Insurance* 54, 3–21.

Danzon, Patricia. (1990b). "Liability for Medical Malpractice: Incidence and Incentive Effects." Paper presented at the Rand Conference on Health Economics, March 1990.

Danzon, Patricia, and Lee Lillard. (1983). "Settlement out of Court: The Disposition of Medical Malpractice Claims," *J. of Legal Studies* 12, 345–378.

D'Arcy, Stephen, and James R. Garven. (1990). "Property-Liability Insurance Pricing Models: An Empirical Evaluation," *J. of Risk and Insurance* 57, 391–430.

Dionne, Georges, and Pierre St-Michel. (1991). "Workers' Compensation and Moral Hazard," *Review of Economics and Statistics*, 73, 236–244.

Doherty, Neil. (1981). "The Measurement of Output and Economies of Scale in Property-Liability Insurance," *J. of Risk and Insurance* 48, 390–402.

Doherty, Neil. (1989). "On the Capital Structure of Insurance Firms," *Financial Models of Insurer Solvency*. Norwell, MA: Kluwer Academic Publishers.

Doherty, Neil, and Georges Dionne. (1989). "Risk Pooling, Contract Structure and Organizational Form of Insurance Firms." Mimeo. University of Pennsylvania and University of Montreal.

Doherty, Neil, and James R. Garven. (1986). "Price Regulation in Property-Liability Insurance: A Contingent Claims Analysis," *J. of Finance* 41, 1031–1050.

Doherty, Neil, and James R. Garven (1990). "Capacity and the Cyclicality of Insurance Markets." Mimeo. University of Pennsylvania and University of Texas.

Doherty, Neil, and Han Bin Kang. (1988). "Price Instability for a Financial Intermediary: Interest Rates and Insurance Price Cycles," *J. of Banking and Finance* 12, 199–214.

Eisenach, Jeffrey A. (1985). "The Role of Collective Pricing in Auto Insurance," Staff Report, Bureau of Economics, U.S. Federal Trade Commission.

Ellis, Randall P., Cynthia L. Gallup, and Thomas G. McGuire. (1990). "Should Medical Professional Liability Insurance be Experience Rated?" *J. of Risk and Insurance* 57, 66–78.

Epstein, Richard A. (1986). "Product Liability as an Insurance Market," *J. of Legal Studies* 14, 645–669.

Fairley, William. (1979). "Investment Income and Profit Margins in Property-Liability Insurance: Theory and Empirical Results," *Bell J. of Economics* 10, 192–210.

Fenn, Paul. (1981). "Sickness Duration, Residual Disability and Income Replacement: An Empirical Analysis," *The Economic Journal* 91, 158–173.

Finsinger, Jorg, and Mark V. Pauly. (1984). "Reserve Levels and Reserve Requirements for Profit-Maximizing Insurance Firms," *Risk and Capital*. Berlin: Springer-Verlag.

Garven, James R. (1987). "On the Application of Finance Theory to the Insurance Firm," *J. of Financial Services Research* 1, 57–76.

Grabowski, Henry, W. Kip Viscusi, and William N. Evans. (1989). "Price and Availability Tradeoffs of Automobile Insurance Regulation," *J. of Risk and Insurance* 56, 275–299.

Greenwald, Bruce C., and Marnie W. Mueller. (1978). "Medical Malpractice and Medical Costs," *The Economics of Medical Malpractice*. Washington, D.C.: American Enterprise Institute.

Gron, Anne. (1989). "Capacity Constraints and Cycles in Property-Casualty Insurance Markets." Mimeo. Massachusetts Institute of Technology.

Haddock, David, and Christopher Curran. (1985). "An Economic Theory of Comparative Negligence," *J. of Legal Studies* 14, 49–72.

Hansmann, Henry. (1985). "The Organization of Insurance Companies: Mutual versus Stock," *J. of Law, Economics, and Organization* 1, 125–153.

Harrington, Scott E. (1984). "The Impact of Rate Regulation on Prices and Underwriting Results in the Property-Liability Insurance Industry: A Survey," *J. of Risk and Insurance* 51, 577–617.

Harrington, Scott E. (1987). "A Note on the Impact of Auto Insurance Rate Regulation," *Review of Economics and Statistics* 69, 737–741.

Harrington, Scott E. (1988). "Prices and Profits in the Liability Insurance Market," *Liability: Perspectives and Policy*. Washington, D.C.: The Brookings Institution.

Harrington, Scott E. (1989). "The Efficiency and Equity of Compulsory Automobile Insurance Laws." Mimeo. University of South Carolina.

Harrington, Scott E., and Patricia M. Danzon. (1986). "An Evaluation of Solvency Surveillance in the Property-Liability Insurance Industry." Schaumburg, Ill.: Alliance of American Insurers.

Harrington, Scott E., and Patricia M. Danzon. (1990). "Price-Cutting in Liability Insurance Markets." Mimeo. University of Pennsylvania and University of South Carolina.

Harrington, Scott E., and Robert E. Litan. (1988). "Causes of the Liability Insurance Crisis," *Science* 239, 737–741.

Harrington, Scott E., and Jack M. Nelson. (1986). "A Regression-Based Methodology for Solvency Surveillance in the Property-Liability Insurance Industry," *J. of Risk and Insurance* 53, 583–605.

Hill, Raymond D. (1979). "Profit Regulation in Property-Liability Insurance," *Bell J. of Economics* 10, 172–191.

Hunt, H. Allen, Alan B. Krueger, and John F. Burton, Jr. (1988). "The Impact of Open Competition in Michigan on the Employer's Cost of Worker's Compensation," *Worker's Compensation Insurance Pricing*. Boston: Kluwer.

Insurance Services Office. (1987). *Insurer Profitability: A Long-Term Perspective*. New York, N.Y.: Insurance Services Office.

Ippolito, Richard. (1979). "The Effects of Price Regulation in the Automobile Insurance Industry," *J. of Law and Economics* 22, 55–89.

Joskow, Paul. (1973). "Cartels, Competition, and Regulation in the Property-

Liability Insurance Industry," *Bell J. of Economics and Managment Science* 4, 375–427.

Kahane, Yehuda, and David J. Nye. "A Portfolio Approach to the Property Liability Insurance Industry," *J. of Risk and Insurance* 42, 579–598.

Kakalik, James S., and Nicholas M. Pace. (1986). "Costs and Compensation Paid in Tort Litigation," R-3391-ICJ. Santa Monica, Cal.: The RAND Corporation.

Keeton, William R., and Evan Kwerel. (1984). "Externalities in Automobile Insurance and the Uninsured Driver Problem," *J. of Law and Economics* 27, 149–180.

Kraus, Alan, and Stephen A. Ross. (1982). "The Determinants of Fair Profits for the Property-Liability Insurance Firm," *J. of Finance* 37, 1015–1030.

Kunreuther, Howard, Paul R. Kleindorfer, and Mark V. Pauly. (1983). "Insurance Regulation and Consumer Behavior in the United States," *J. of Institutional and Theoretical Economics* 139, 452–472.

Lacey, Nelson J. (1988). "Recent Evidence on the Liability Crisis," *J. of Risk and Insurance* 55, 499–508.

Landes, Elizabeth M. (1982). "Insurance, Liability, and Accidents: A Theoretical and Empirical Investigation of the Effects of No-Fault Accidents," *J. of Law and Economics* 25, 49–65.

Landes, William M., and Richard Posner. (1981). "The Positive Economic Theory of Tort Law," *Georgia Law Review* 15, 851–924.

Landes, William M. (1987). *The Economic Structure of Tort Law*. Cambridge, Mass.: Harvard University Press.

McDonald, James B. (1988). "Predicting Insurance Insolvency Using Generalized Qualitative Response Models." Mimeo. Brigham Young University.

McGee, Robert T. (1986). "The Cycle in Property/Casualty Insurance," *Federal Reserve Bank of New York Quarterly Review* 22–30.

Marshall, John M. (1974). "Insurance Theory: Reserves versus Mutuality," *Economic Inquiry* 12, 476–492.

Mayers, David, and Clifford W. Smith, Jr. (1981). "Contractual Provisions, Organizational Structure, and Conflict Control in Insurance Markets," *J. of Business* 54, 407–434.

Mayers, David, and Clifford W. Smith, Jr. (1982). "On the Corporate Demand for Insurance," *J. of Business* 55, 281–296.

Mayers, David, and Clifford W. Smith, Jr. (1988). "Ownership Structure Across Lines of Property-Casualty Insurance," *J. of Law and Economics* 31, 351–378.

Munch, Patricia. (1977). "The Costs and Benefits of the Tort System if Viewed as a Compensation System," P-5921. Santa Monica, Cal.: The RAND Corporation.

Munch, Patricia, and Dennis Smallwood. (1980). "Solvency Regulation in the Property-Liability Insurance Industry: Empirical Evidence," *Bell J. of Economics* 11, 261–282.

Munch, Patricia, and Dennis Smallwood. (1982). "Theory of Solvency Regulation in the Property and Casualty Insurance Industry," *Studies in Public Regulation*. Cambridge, Mass.: MIT Press.

Myers, Stewart C., and Richard A. Cohn. (1986). "A Discounted Cash Flow Approach to Property-Liability Insurance Rate Regulation," *Fair Rate of Return in Property-Liability Insurance.* Boston, Mass.: Kluwer.

National Association of Insurance Commissioners (NAIC). (1980). *Malpractice Claims.* Brookfield, Wis.: NAIC.

National Conference of Insurance Guaranty Funds (NCIGF). (1990). *State Insurance Guaranty Funds and Insurance Company Insolvency Assessment Information* 1969–89. Columbus, Oh.: NCIGF.

Nye, Blain F., and Alfred E. Hofflander. (1988). "Experience Rating in Medical Professional Liability Insurance," *J. of Risk and Insurance* 60, 150–157.

Oi, Walter. (1973). "The Economics of Product Safey," *Bell J. of Economics* 4, 3–28.

Pauly, Mark V., Paul R. Kleindorfer, and Howard Kunreuther. (1986). "Regulation and Quality Competition in the U.S. Insurance Industry," *The Economics of Insurance Regulation.* London: MacMillan Press.

Polinsky, A. Mitchell. (1980). "Strict Liability vs. Negligence in a Market Setting," *American Economic Review* 70, 363–370.

Polinsky, A. Mitchell. (1983) *An Introduction to Law and Economics.* Boston, Mass.: Little-Brown.

Polinsky, A. Mitchell, and Daniel L. Rubinfeld. (1988). "The Welfare Implications of Costly Litigation," *J. of Legal Studies* 17, 151–164.

Posner, Richard. (1972) "A Theory of Negligence," *J. of Legal Studies* 2, 205–221.

Posner, Richard. (1973). *Economic Analysis of Law.* Boston, Mass.: Little-Brown.

Posner, Richard. (1986). *Economic Analysis of Law,* 3rd ed. Boston, Mass.: Little-Brown.

Priest, George. (1987). "The Current Insurance Crisis and Modern Tort Law," *Yale Law J.* 96, 1521–1590.

Rea, Samuel. (1981). "Lump Sum versus Periodic Damage Awards," *J. of Legal Studies* 10, 131–154.

Reynolds, Roger A., John A. Rizzo, and Martin L. Gonzalez. (1987). "The Cost of Medical Professional Liability," *J. of the American Medical Association* 257, 2776–2781.

Rizzo, John A. (1989). "The Impact of Medical Malpractice Insurance Rate Regulation," *J. of Risk and Insurance* 56, 482–500.

Rolph, John E. (1981). "Some Statistical Evidence on Merit Rating in Medical Malpractice Insurance," *J. of Risk and Insurance* 48, 247–260.

Rubinfeld, Daniel L. (1984). "On the Optimal Magnitude and Length of Liability in Torts," *J. of Legal Studies* 15, 551–563.

Rubinfeld, Daniel L. (1987). "The Efficiency of Comparative Negligence," *J. of Legal Studies* 16, 375–394.

Ruser, John H. (1986). "Workers' Compensation Insurance, Experience Rating and Occupational Injuries," *Rand J. of Economics* 16, 487–503.

Schwartz, Gary. (1983). "New Products, Old Products, Evolving Law, Retroactive Law," *New York University Law Review*. 58, 796–840.

Shavell, Steven. (1979). "On Moral Hazard and Insurance," *Quarterly J. of Economics* 93, 541–562.

Shavell, Steven. (1980). "Strict Liability versus Negligence," *J. of Legal Studies* 9, 1–25.

Shavell, Steven. (1982). "On Liability and Insurance," *Bell J. of Economics* 13, 120–132.

Shavell, Steven. (1986). "The Judgment Proof Problem," *International Review of Law and Economics* 6, 45–58.

Shavell, Steven. (1987) *Economic Analysis of Accident Law*. Cambridge, Mass.: Harvard University Press.

Sloan, Frank A., Paula M. Mergenhagen, and Randall R. Bovbjerg. (1989). "Effects of Tort Reforms on the Value of Closed Medical Malpractice Claims: A Microanalysis," *J. of Health Politics, Policy, and Law* 14, 663–689.

Sloan, Frank A., Paula M. Mergenhagen, W. Bradley Burfield, Randall R. Bovbjerg, and Mahmud Hassan. (1989). "Medical Malpractice Experience of Physicians," *J. of American Medical Association* 262, 3291–3297.

Smallwood, Dennis. (1975). "Competition, Regulation, and Product Quality in the Automobile Insurance Industry." In Almarin Phillips, ed., *Promoting Competition in Regulated Markets*. Washington, D.C.: The Brookings Institution. 241–299.

Smith, Michael L. (1989). "Investment Returns and Yields to Holders of Insurance," *J. of Business* 62, 81–98.

Spence, Michael. (1977). "Consumer Misperceptions, Product Failure and Product Liability," *Review of Economic Studies* 64, 561–572.

Stewart, Richard E. (1987). *Remembering a Stable Future: Why Flex Rating Cannot Work*. New York: Insurance Services Office and Insurance Information Institute.

Tapiero, Charles S., Yehuda Kahane, and Laurent Jacques. (1986). "Insurance Premiums and Default Risk in Mutual Insurance," *Scandinavian Actuarial J.* 82–97.

Tennyson, Sharon. (1989). "Capacity Constraints and Cycles in Property-Casualty Insurance Markets." Mimeo. Northwestern University.

Thaler, Richard, and Sherwin Rosen. (1976). "The Value of Saving a Life: Evidence from the Labor Market." In N. Terleckyz, ed. *Household Production and Consumption*. NBER Studies in Income and Wealth no. 40. New York: Columbia University Press.

Venezian, Emilio. (1984). "Are Insurers Under-Earning?" *J. of Risk and Insurance* 51, 150–156.

Venezian, Emilio. (1985). "Ratemaking Methods and Profit Cycles in Property and Liability Insurance," *J. of Risk and Insurance* 52, 477–500.

Viscusi, W. Kip. (1983). *Risk by Choice: Regulating Health and Safety in the Workplace*. Cambridge, Mass.: Harvard University Press.

Viscusi, W. Kip. (1989). "The Interaction between Product Liability and Workers' Compensation as Ex Post Remedies for Workplace Injuries," *J. of Law, Economics, and Organization* 5, 185–209.

Viscusi, W. Kip, and Michael J. Moore. (1987). "Workers' Compensation: Wage Effects, Benefit Inadequacies and the Value of Health Losses," *Review of Economics and Statistics* 69, 249–261.

Weiss, Mary. (1985). "A Multivariate Analysis of Loss Reserving Estimates in Property-Liability Insurers," *J. of Risk and Insurance* 52, 199–221.

Winter, Ralph A. (1988). "The Liability Crisis and the Dynamics of Competitive Insurance Markets," *Yale J. on Regulation* 5, 455–499.

Winter, Ralph A. (1989). "The Dynamics of Competitive Insurance Markets." Mimeo. University of Toronto.

Worrall, John D., and David Appel. (1982). "The Wage Replacement Rate and Benefit Utilization in Workers' Compensation Insurance," *J. of Risk and Insurance* 49, 361–371.

Zador, Paul, and Adrian Lund. (1986). "Re-Analysis of the Effects of No-Fault Auto Insurance on Fatal Crashes," *J. of Risk and Insurance* 50, 631–669.

Zeckhauser, Richard. (1970). "Medical Insurance: A Case Study of the Tradeoff Between Risk Spreading and Appropriate Incentives," *J. of Economic Theory* 2, 10–26.

MORAL HAZARD AND INSURANCE CONTRACTS

Ralph A. Winter

University of Toronto

Abstract

This essay synthesizes and extends the theory of optimal insurance under moral hazard, with a focus on the form of insurance contracts. The simplest model illustrates the most fundamental result: that the market responds to moral hazard with partial insurance coverage. But this model is not general enough to predict the contractual form of this response. The most general model, the Principal-Agent model, yields mostly negative results. In extending the theory, I adopt an intermediate approach, distinguishing between moral hazard on the probability of an accident and moral hazard on the size of the loss. This approach generates predictions as to when deductibles, coinsurance and coverage limits will be observed. The essay reviews as well moral hazard with a partially informed insurer and dynamic models of moral hazard. It concludes with a discussion of open questions in the theory of moral hazard and insurance.

Key words: moral hazard, insurance, principal-agent, contracts

Moral hazard refers to the detrimental effect that insurance has on an individual's incentives to avoid losses. A car theft, an accident, or a house fire may not be completely avoidable, but the probability or size of the loss involved is almost always influenced by an individual's actions.

I am grateful to Richard Arnott, Georges Dionne, Cheng-hu Ma, Pascale Viala and three referees for valuable comments.

61

Anyone who is insured against a risk will not capture the full benefits of efforts to reduce the risk. The incentives to avoid or to mitigate losses are therefore compromised by insurance, unless an individual can somehow commit to undertaking optimal precautions at the time that an insurance contract is struck. Insurers anticipate this effect, of course, and one consequence of moral hazard is a higher insurance premium.

Moral hazard arises in insurance contracts under two conditions. The first is that the insured risk be influenced by decisions taken by the insured individual after the insurance contract is signed. The expenditure or effort taken to reduce risks or mitigate losses is referred to as the individual's care. In fire insurance, for example, care refers to expediture on the maintenance of buildings, fire sprinklers, or extinguishers. Care even includes the decision to refrain from arson. In fire insurance as in theft insurance, most care is taken ex ante or before the realized loss. In medical insurance, care can similarly refer to costly precautions taken against accident or illness; but the main moral hazard problem in this line of insurance is excessive expenditure on medical services ex post, or after an illness has occured. Here care refers to a reduction in these expenditures. The moral hazard problem arises because medical insurance provides for reimbursement of expenses rather than lump sum payments conditional upon accidents or illnesses of precisely specified types.

The law and economics literature often distinguishes between care and activity levels (Shavell (1987)). In automobile insurance, for example, care refers to driving at lower speeds and with greater diligence; the level of activity refers to the amount of driving. In products liability insurance, activity could refer to to the number of new products offered and care defined as the extent to which safety features are incorporated in new products. Decisions on ex ante care, ex post care and activity levels are all potentially distorted by insurance.

For moral hazard to arise, however, it is not enough that these decisions affect the insured risk. The second necessary condition is that the care and activity levels cannot be costlessly specified in the insurance contract and enforced by the insurer. The requirement that an adequate number of fire sprinklers be installed in any new building would not give rise to moral hazard because it could be easily enforced in a general fire insurance policy. But the maintenance of buildings, precautions taken against automobile or bicycle theft, or whether a particular visit to the doctor is really warranted, are not easily monitored by an insurer.[1] Any decision taken after an insurance contract is signed that affects the chance or size of the insured loss and that cannot be costlessly specified in the insurance contract is subject to moral hazard inefficiencies.

The problem of moral hazard was historically discussed mainly in the context of insurance contracts. More recently, the principal-agent literature in economics has analyzed the design of a vast number of contracts or institutions as attempts to reconcile individual and collective interests. In that moral hazard can be defined broadly as a conflict in interests between an individual in an organization (that is, a party to a set of contracts) and the collective interest of the organization, this entire literature is concerned with the problem of moral hazard. The importance of moral hazard extends beyond the context of insurance to the entire paradigm of agency theory.[2]

The scope of this essay, however, is the moral hazard problem within insurance contracts. The purpose of the essay is to review systematically the economic analysis of optimal insurance under moral hazard. Its central focus is the nature of optimal insurance contracts. The essay is pitched at a level that assumes familiarity with microeconomics, but not with the theory of agency, of which moral hazard in insurance contracts is a special case. I begin in section 1 of the essay with the simplest model, and then in subsequent sections review the various extensions of the model.

In the simplest model, an individual faces a known loss with a probability that is a function of subsequent effort or care invested by the individual. This model is sufficient to illustrate some basic results on optimal insurance under moral hazard. The most important result is that the market response to moral hazard is partial insurance coverage. Optimal insurance with moral hazard involves a tradeoff between the goal of efficient risk bearing, which is met by allocating the risk to the insurer, and the goal of efficient incentives, which requires leaving the consequences of decisions about care with the decision maker.

This simple model, however, is not rich enough to address the characterization of optimal insurance contracts. For example, with a single possible value for a loss, the contractual features of a deductible, coinsurance, and coverage limits are all equivalent. The simple model offers no predictions about the *form* of optimal insurance contracts under moral hazard.

Section 2 analyzes the simplest extension of the model that can offer such predictions. This is the extension to the case of uncertain losses. In this section we retain the assumption that only the probability of a loss is affected by care. Section 3 of the essay considers a second kind of moral hazard problem: that the size of loss at risk is affected by noncontractable decisions by the individual.

The distinction between care that affects the probability of a loss and care that affects the size of a loss is illustrated with a number of examples. This distinction was originally made in the economics literature by Ehrlich and Becker (1972).[3] These authors, however, assume that care is contracted for by the insurer and monitored at zero cost or incurred by the insured prior to the insurance contract. This assumption precludes any consideration of the moral hazard problem.[4]

Section 4 of this essay formulates the moral hazard problem under a general assumption on the distribution of losses, using the standard Principal-Agent model. Section 5 reviews the extensions of the moral hazard problem to the case in which the insurer has at least some information on the insured's care level. This information may be exogenous or endogenous. Section 6 reviews the results from models of repeated moral hazard, which investigate the extent to which the moral hazard problem is resolved through a long-term relationship. The concluding section identifies some open questions in the theory of insurance under moral hazard.

1. The Basic Moral Hazard Problem[5]

The simplest model of moral hazard is the following: an individual faces a known loss with a probability that depends on the individual's care. We represent care as a pecuniary expense, i.e., an expenditure of money or time. Most examples of care in insurance — security systems, locks, product safety decisions, fire sprinklers — fit this assumption. But care could also include diligence, e.g., the mental concentration of an automobile driver, or intensity of effort rather than expenditure; in the case of medical insurance, loss-avoidance costs would include physical discomfort from cutting back on medical care. The individual maximizes the expected utility of final wealth net of the expenditure on care.

Information between the insurer and the insured at the time of contracting is symmetric, in our formulation of the moral hazard problem. In particular, the distribution of the random loss as it depends upon care is known to both the insured and the insurer. The central assumption in any model of moral hazard is that the level of care is chosen by the individual after the contract is signed, rather than specified in the contract.

The assumption of symmetric information at the time of contracting means that we are abstracting from the problem of *adverse selection* in insurance markets (Akerlof (1970), Rothschild and Stiglitz (1976)). Adverse selection in insurance markets refers to the implications of insurers' inability to identify the risk types of individuals. Some of the contractual implications of adverse selection and moral hazard are identical; for example, under both moral hazard and adverse selection partial coverage for at least some individuals is optimal. Other implications (for example, the self-selection of lower risk individuals into contracts with less coverage) distinguish adverse selection from moral hazard situations. Of course, in reality, both problems occur together, and the simultaneous treatment of the two is an important, relatively unexplored area.

While care cannot enter into the contract, we assume that the total coverage purchased by an individual *can* enter into the contract. (It is then assumed without loss of generality that the individual purchase all coverage from the same insurer.) This assumption, which avoids the possible moral hazard of duplicate insurance, is relaxed at the end of this section.

The following notation is used throughout this essay. Let $U(\cdot)$ be a utility function over wealth. U is twice-differentiable, increasing and strictly concave. U is event-independent.[6]

Let

W be initial wealth;
e be the care, or resources invested to avoid the loss;
r be the cost of care (in dollars per unit of care);
l be the loss, or cost of an accident; and
$p(e)$ be the probability of the accident.

The function $p(e)$ satisfies $p' < 0$ and $p'' > 0$. That is, $p(e)$ is decreasing at a decreasing rate.

Throughout the essay, we adopt the assumption that insurance markets are competitive and that insurers are risk-neutral.[7] This assumption implies that the equilibrium insurance contract maximizes an individual's expected utility subject to the constraint that expected profits be nonnegative.

With the assumption that e cannot enter the insurance contract, the feasible contracts in this simple model consist of pairs $[\pi, q]$ where π is the premium paid by the individual to the insurer and q is the amount of coverage paid by the insurer in the event of an accident. While e cannot enter the insurance contract, one can pose the optimal insurance problem as the choice among all contracts $[\pi, q, e]$, i.e., *as if* the choice of e could enter the contract, subject to the *incentive compatibility constraint* that the e specified in the contract be consistent with the individual's incentives given the rest of the contract $[\pi, q]$. This method of formulating the problem follows the standard approach of the principal–agent theory. We adopt the method for the pedagogic purpose of illustrating the explicit incentive compatibility constraint; in more complicated problems this approach leads to easier characterizations of the solution.

The following problem characterizes the optimal insurance contract in this model:

(P1) $\max_{\pi,q,e} (1 - p(e))U(W - \pi - re) + p(e)U(W - \pi - re - l + q)$

subject to

$$\pi \geq p(e)q \tag{1}$$

$$e = \arg \max_{z} (1 - p(z))U(W - \pi - rz)$$
$$+ p(z)U(W - \pi - rz - l + q) \tag{2}$$

In this problem, (1) is the break-even constraint. Equation 2 is the incentive-compatibility constraint. Any other level of e "promised" by the individual in the contract would not be credible. The first-best optimal insurance contract corresponding to the problem, as with the problems analyzed later, is characterized by the same maximization problem, with the incentive compatibility constraint deleted. The effect of the incomplete contracting or moral hazard problem is to constrain the set of available contracts to those for which promises on noninforceable dimensions of the contracts are credible.

In characterizing the solution to the problem, as with more general principal-agent problems, three technical issues arise. The first issue is, when can the incentive compatibility constraint be replaced by the Kuhn-Tucker condition of the agent's maximization problem? As Mirrlees (1975) first noted, because expected utility is often nonconcave in care or effort, the set of care levels satisfying a first-order condition is different from the set satisfying the incentive compatibility constraint. The first-order conditions are satisfied at saddle points, local minima and local-but-not-global maxima as well as interior global maxima; on the other hand, the conditions are not satisfied at corner solutions. For the current problem, however, our assumption that $p(e)$ is convex is sufficient for the second-order conditions on the problem expressed by (2). This assumption is therefore enough to justify the first-order approach to the characterization of any interior solution to (P1), i.e., a solution involving positive care. (The first-order conditions do not characterize corner solutions).

Lemma 1: Under the assumptions of concave U and convex p, the constraint (2) is equivalent to the following Kuhn-Tucker condition:

$$(1/r)p'(e)[U(W - \pi - r \cdot e - l + q) - U(W - \pi - r \cdot e)]$$
$$= [1 - p(e)]U'(W - \pi - r \cdot e) + p(e)U'(W - \pi - r \cdot e - l + q)$$
and $\quad e > 0 \qquad\qquad\qquad\qquad\qquad\qquad\qquad\qquad\qquad (3)$

or

$$(1/r)p'(0)[U(W - \pi - l + q) - U(W - \pi)]$$
$$< [1 - p(0)]U'((W - \pi) + p(0)U'(W - \pi - l + q) \text{ and } \quad e = 0$$
$$\qquad\qquad\qquad\qquad\qquad\qquad\qquad\qquad\qquad\qquad\qquad (4)$$

Proof: Follows from direct verification of the second-order condition for (2).

The second technical issue presented by the (P1) is that, in general, a breakeven contract with the highest expected utility may involve *random* coverage. This possibility was demonstrated by Gjesdal (1982).[8] A sufficient condition for the solution to be nonrandom is that the utility be separable in income and effort; for the context of insurance; however, this separability is unrealistic as most forms of care involve pecuniary cost. Following Shavel (1979b) and almost all of the literature on moral hazard in insurance, we simply ignore the possibility of random contracts.

Consider the expected utility of the insured and the expected profits of the insurer as functions of the insurance contract, (π, q). A contract solving (P1) must be Pareto optimal between the two parties to the contract, and can therefore be represented on the space of contracts by a tangency of an indifference and the zero expected profits curve. The third technical issue presented by the problem (P1) is that the indifference curves and the expected profit curves on this space may be *nonconvex*. The nonconvexity is in contrast to the standard consumer theory, and to the theory of optimal insurance in the absence of moral hazard.

The implications of the moral hazard nonconvexities are investigated by Helpman and Laffont (1975) and Arnott and Stiglitz (1983a,b) and reviewed in Richard Arnott's essay in this volume. The main implications are for the case in which insurers are constrained to offer *uniform price contracts*, i.e., unlimited amounts of insurance at any premium. This constraint would arise if insurers could not observe the amount of insurance that an individual purchased from other insurers. The implications for moral hazard under uniform pricing are discussed briefly at the end of this section. In the meantime, we retain the assumption that contracts limiting the amount of coverage purchased by the individual are enforceable. This assumption does not eliminate the nonconvexities, of course, and their implications are discussed below.

Our exposition of the solution to P1 is based on Shavell (1979), which is a clear investigation of this basic moral hazard problem.[9] The most important characterization of the solution to the optimal insurance contract is the level of insurance coverage offered. A critical determinant of the level of care is, in turn, the cost of care.

We can illustrate at the outset the basic result. Figure 1 shows the level of coverage as a function of the cost of care, denoted by r. At low cost levels, insurance coverage is less than full: the benefits of insurance are traded off against the incentive or moral hazard costs of insurance and providing that care is costly, less-than-full coverage is optimal.

Above some cost of care, $\hat{r}$, care would be zero under the fully optimal or complete contracting solution, because the benefits of even the first unit of care would not cover the cost of care. At another level of care, r^*, care becomes zero under the moral hazard problem (P1) because (4) holds rather than (3). I show below that $r^* < \hat{r}$, i.e., that as the cost of care rises, the corner solution is reached for the incomplete contracting solution before it is reached for the complete contracting solution.

Now if care is zero, then full insurance coverage is optimal even under the incomplete contract, because additional insurance has no marginal disincentive costs. This implies, as Figure 1 illustrates, that there are three possible outcomes, depending on the cost of care: The level of care is positive and coverage is partial (Region A in the Figure); the level of care is zero and the moral hazard problem is reflected only in a higher premium in the contract (Region B); and the level of care is zero as it would be with a complete contract (Region C). In Region C, there is effectively no moral hazard problem.

The solution to (P1) is described by its first-order conditions when the incentive compatibility constraint has an interior solution (3). To save on notation, we substitute the break-even constraint into the objective, and define $e(q)$ as the solution in e to the incentive compatibility constraint.[10] This yields expected utility as a function of q alone. Differentiating this function, and substitution in (3) yields the condition (5) below for the optimal coverage. Let W_L and W_N be shorthand for the realized wealth given an accident and no accident, respectively; that is, $W_L \equiv W - \pi - r \cdot e - l + q$ and $W_N \equiv W - \pi - r \cdot e$.

$$
\begin{aligned}
EU'(q) = &- e'p'q[(1 - p)U'(W_N) + pU'(W_L)] \\
&- p[(1 - p)U'(W_N) + pU'(W_L)] \\
&+ pU'(W_L)
\end{aligned} \tag{5}
$$

optimal coverage

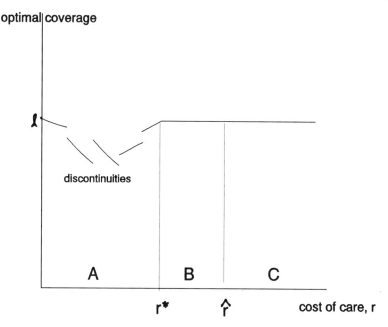

Figure 1. Optimal coverage as a function of *r*.

Following Shavell (1979), the three terms in this expression reflect the marginal expected utility, with an additional dollar of coverage, from a) a change in the premium due to a change in the premium *rate* per dollar of coverage, b) a change in the premium due to an increased *level* of coverage, and c) a change in the level of coverage.

The latter two terms would be present even without the second constraint in problem (P1). That is, these terms reflect the marginal benefits and costs of increased insurance even without moral hazard. Moral hazard is reflected only in the first term of the expression.

Proposition 1 formalizes the results depicted in figure 1.

Proposition 1: The optimal insurance contract solving (P1) satisfies the following conditions:
a) For a sufficiently small but positive cost of care, the optimal coverage is positive but less than full coverage.
b) For a cost of care greater or equal to some value r^* in the incomplete contract and $\hat{r}$ in the complete contract, the optimal coverage is full and care is zero. The value r^* is not greater than $\hat{r}$, and if coverage is a continuous function of r at $\hat{r}$, then r^* is strictly less than $\hat{r}$.

Proof: see Appendix.

1.1. Implications of nonconvexities

Nothing in the proof of Proposition I assumed that expected utility was a concave function of the contract (π, q) or that the break-even constraint described a convex feasible set of these contracts.

In fact, expected utility may be non-concave, and the feasible set of contracts under the incentive compatibility constraint is *never* convex. To prove the latter, it is easy to show that the value of

$$\frac{d\pi}{dq}\bigg| \quad (1)$$

is *increasing* in q. This is because a higher value of q induces a lower care, hence a higher value of p. The higher value of p necessitates a greater change in premium to offset any marginal change in coverage. The implications for this analysis are that the optimal contract, the optimal effort, and the expected utility are, in general, all discontinuous functions of any exogenous parameters, such as the level of care (Arnott and Stiglitz (1983)). The reader is referred to Richard Arnott's essay in this volume for an excellent discussion of the nonconvexities in moral hazard problems.

1.2. Equilibrium under Uniform Pricing

A substantial part of the moral hazard literature analyzes competitive equilibria under the assumption that insurers offer uniform pricing contracts, i.e., allow as much insurance to be purchased as the buyer chooses at the posted premium (Helpman and Laffont (1975), Arnott and Stiglitz (1983)). This assumption is critical in these models, because at the equilibrium premium *rate*, i.e., premium paid per dollar of coverage, the buyer of insurance in the model that we are analyzing would want to purchase additional insurance (Pauly (1974)). Buyers are rationed at the equilibrium premium rate in our model.

The assumption of uniform pricing, while the basis for Marshallian competitive market analysis and Walrasian general equilibrium analysis in economics, is justified in the insurance market only by the special assumption that insurers cannot observe how much insurance an individual purchases from other insurers on a given loss. Individuals are typically constrained legally against collecting on more than one insurance policy in North American jurisdictions, and the penalties for violating this law are criminal penalties for fraud (not just the cancellation of coverage). Obviously the incentive to overinsure: If I could insure my car with each of a thousand different insurers, I would profit by destroying it. In contexts other than insurance markets, however, the assumption that sellers cannot observe quantities may be more reasonable. Helpman and Laffont (1975) and Arnott and Stiglitz (1983) investigate the general equilibrium implications of moral hazard under the uniform pricing assumption.

2. Self-Protection and Uncertain Losses[11]

In the basic moral hazard model of Section 1 we assumed that the cost of an accident is nonrandom. This framework is restrictive in that it allows one to address essentially only one question: How much insurance coverage is optimal under moral hazard? There are only two outcomes in the model: accident or no accident.

This section and the next introduce the simplest extension that allows one to inquire into the *form* that insurance contracts take under moral hazard. Clearly moral hazard should lead to less insurance coverage — but does this reduction in insurance take the form of deductibles, coinsurance, or upper limits on coverage? All three of these contractual features are observed in practice.

Following Ehrlich and Becker (1972), I distinguish between expenditure to reduce the probability of an accident and expenditure to reduce the size of the contingent loss. In Ehrlich and Becker's terminology, the former is *self-protection*. The latter these authors call *self-insurance*, although I will use the term *loss-reduction*[12] because *self-insurance* has more than one meaning in the insurance literature.

Expenditures on fire sprinklers reduce the size of a loss, but not the probability of an accident. Expenditures on a burglar alarm reduce the probability of a theft, whereas the decision not to buy expensive silverware reduces the loss if there is a theft. In the case of earthquake insurance, all precaution is loss-reducing; it cannot with current technology change the probability of a loss. Driving an automobile more slowly and carefully, however, reduces both the probability of an accident and the costs of an accident should it occur.

While many other expenditures lead to reductions in both the chance of an accident and the cost of an accident, it is instructive to consider separately the consequences of moral hazard in each type of expenditure. Posing the moral hazard or agency problem in the most general way yields few specific predictions as we argue in Section 3. Insight is gained by dissecting moral hazard into two types and investigating separately their implications for insurance contracts.

As it turns out, the consequences of each type of moral hazard for insurance contracts are quite different. For example, moral hazard on self-protection leads to a deductible under reasonable assumptions, and low losses would have negative payout were it not for the contracting or monitoring constraint that such losses would then go unreported by the individual.[13] Moral hazard on loss-reduction on the other hand leads to overinsurance or more than full coverage of low losses.

In some contexts it is reasonable to assume that insurance payments cannot exceed losses. With this constraint and the constraint against negative payouts, we find that the two types of moral hazard give rise to a simple insurance contract: a deductible in one case, and full coverage up to a limit with coinsurance thereafter, in the other case.

To analyze the moral hazard on expenditures for self-protection, we retain most of the notation of Section 1. The function $p(e)$ represents the probability of an accident, as before, with $p' < 0$ and $p'' > 0$. We assume that the cost of care is one dollar per unit, and also assume an interior solution on the optimal care. The event of an accident in this section refers to a random loss, with distribution function $F(l)$ and density $f(l)$. That is, F is the conditional distribution of l given $l > 0$. Self-protection then refers to an increase in the probability of a zero loss, with no change in the conditional distribution F. Loss-reduction refers to a first-order stochastic reduction in the random loss with no change in the probability of a loss.

A general insurance contract in this case consists of a premium π and a payment function or sharing rule $q(l)$ specifying how much the insurer promises to pay with each loss, l. Thus the insurer is assumed to be able to verify the size of the loss.[14] As before, the optimal insurance contract maximizes expected utility subject to a break-even constraint for the insurer and an incentive-compatibility constraint for the individual.

In addition, we impose the constraint that the specified insurance payment can never be negative. The contract cannot specify a transfer from the insured to the insurer that is contingent upon particular realizations of the random loss. This "limited liability" constraint reflects an assumption that the insurer is aware of losses only when the insured reports them.

The following problem characterizes the optimal contract with moral hazard on self-protection:

(P2)
$$\max_{\pi,q(l)} (1 - p(e))U(W - \pi - e)$$
$$+ p(e)\int U(W - \pi - e - l + q(l))f(l)dl$$

subject to

$$\pi - p(e)\int q(l)f(l)dl \geq 0 \tag{10}$$

$$e = \arg\max_{z} [1 - p(z)]U(W - \pi - z)$$
$$+ p(z)\int [U(W - \pi - z - l + q(l)]f(l)dl \tag{11}$$
$$q(l) \geq 0 \tag{12}$$

For any interior solution to this problem, the incentive-compatibility constraint can be replaced by a first-order condition in an interior solution, because of the convexity of $p(\cdot)$. That is, the constraint (11) can be replaced by

$$-[1 - p(e)]U'(W - \pi - e) - p(e)\int U'(W - \pi - e - l + q(l))f(l)\,dl$$
$$-p'(e)\left[U(W - \pi - e) - \int U(W - \pi - e - l + q(l))f(l)dl\right] = 0 \tag{13}$$

The problem is a problem of Lagrange, and an interior solution to this problem must satisfy a set of first-order conditions corresponding to the choice of each $q(l)$, as well as a first-order condition on e, the level of care.[15] Let W_l be shorthand for the wealth level given a loss of l, and W_0 be the wealth level with no accident ($W_0 = W - \pi - e$ and $W_1 = W - \pi - e - l + q(l)$). Let the shadow prices on the first two constraints be λ_1 and λ_2 as before:

At each l:

$$q(l) = 0$$

or

$$p(e)U'(W_l)f(l) - \lambda_1 p(e)f(l) - \lambda_2[-p(e)f(l)U''(W_l) + p'(e)f(l)U'(W_l)] = 0 \tag{14}$$

which implies that for all positive W_l,

$$\lambda_2 U''(W_l) + \left[1 - \lambda_2 \frac{p'(e)}{p(e)}\right]U'(W_l) - \lambda_1 = 0 \tag{15}$$

If equation 15 is solved at a particular loss, $\hat{l}$, by a wealth level $\hat{W}$, then obviously $\hat{W}$ also solves the equation at any other loss. That is, (15) implies that at the optimum, W_l is constant (independent of l) wherever it is positive. From $W_l \equiv W - \pi - e - l + q(l)$, this implies that $q(l) = \max(0, l - D)$ for some constant D. It is easy to verify that D must be positive. In sum, we have proved:

> **Proposition 2:** The optimal contract $[\pi^*, q^* (\cdot)]$ solving (P2), optimal insurance under moral hazard on self-protection, satisfies, for some constant D,

$$q^*(l) = \max (0, l - D)$$

That is, the optimal contract is a deductible.

The intuition for this result is clear. Suppose that negative payouts were feasible. Because there is no moral hazard on the magnitude of the loss, large losses should be fully insured relative to small losses. The equalization of final wealth in all states with a positive loss is efficient. On the other hand, the moral hazard with respect to a loss dictates that the individual face some penalty (reduction in wealth) in the event of the loss. This reduction in wealth will exceed the loss for small-loss states; i.e., the payout will be negative.

If we extend this analysis to incorporate a variable cost of care, then from arguments parallel to Section 1 (Figure 1), the optimal deductible approaches zero as the cost of care approaches zero, but is positive for a small cost of care. If the cost of care is sufficiently high, then the optimal deductible is zero.

2.1. Limited insurer knowledge

In the above analysis, we assume that both the insurer and the insured can observe the size of the loss, l, although only the insured can observe the care or effort. In many insurance contracts, however, the insurer is able to verify an accident but unable to verify the size of the loss. Accordingly, the insurance contract will specify a fixed amount of coverage contingent upon an accident, in spite of the randomness of the loss. For example, jewelry or artwork is typically insured against theft or destruction for a fixed sum of money even though the replacement cost of the item is uncertain. Only for goods where markets are thick, such as automobiles, can the size of the loss be determined with accuracy.

The analysis of moral hazard in this case is very similar to the model in the introduction, since the contract is again a premium and an amount of coverage. As a remark on the underlying theory of optimal insurance purchase, however, I note that the optimal purchase of insurance in this case (in the absence of moral hazard) exceeds the expected value of the loss:

Proposition 3: Consider the problem of optimal insurance where the loss is random but unobservable by the insurer, and where there is no moral hazard problem. Suppose that utility U satisfies decreasing absolute risk aversion. Then the optimal insurance policy (π, q) that specifies payment of q in an accident, satisfies $q > El$ if the loss l is random.

Proof: The proof follows directly from the application of Jensen's inequality to the convexity of U' (implied by decreasing absolute risk aversion) in the first-order condition for this problem.

The assumption of decreasing absolute risk aversion is standard in the theory of insurance (Arrow (1970)). Individuals exhibit decreasing absolute risk aversion if their demand for insurance, for a given risk, is decreasing with wealth. An optimal insurance policy under the assumptions of Proposition 3 leaves the individual's marginal utility of wealth in the event of no accident equal to the expected marginal utility of wealth in the event of an accident. Since $U''' > 0$ for decreasing absolute risk aversion utility functions, U' is convex and the expected marginal utility of wealth is therefore greater than the marginal utility of expected wealth. To offset this inequality, the individual allocates more wealth to the event of a loss. The implication for the context of this essay is that if the moral hazard problem is not too severe, the individual may still insure an object for more than its expected value.

3. Loss Reduction and Moral Hazard

The moral hazard problem under self-protection, or the reduction of the chance of an accident, was analyzed above given uncertainty about the size of the loss. In the case of moral hazard on loss reduction, the motivation for considering uncertain losses is even stronger: this moral hazard problem does not even exist unless the losses are random. For suppose that the loss conditional upon an accident is a deterministic function of unobservable expenditure by the individual. An insurance contract that covered only the loss associated with the first-best level of expenditure would leave the marginal cost of additional loss entirely on the insured, and would therefore elicit the first-best expenditure. The moral hazard problem would disappear.

Accordingly, we consider the moral hazard problem under the assumption that an additional unit of expenditure yields a reduction in the random loss in the sense of first-order stochastic dominance. To avoid complexity, we assume that conditional upon an accident, there are finite possible loss values, $l_1, l_2, \cdots, l_n$. These losses occur with probability $p_i(e)$, $i = 1, \cdots, n$ conditional upon an accident, i.e., conditional upon $l > 0$, given expenditure e, loss-reduction refers to a first-order stochastic drop in the conditional distribution of losses, with no change in the probability of an accident.[16]

We consider here the constraint that insurance coverage given any loss cannot exceed the loss. This is based on the assumption that the individual could effect (without being observed by the insurer) a loss of any particular size. For example, if an item such as a bicycle is insured for more than its worth, it would purposely be lost. To avoid this moral hazard problem, the wealth of the individual in any state cannot be higher than the wealth in the event of no accident. In some contexts, this constraint is unrealistic since it may require positive effort to cause a loss; we consider this case as well.)

The probability of a positive loss is p, and the remaining notation is as in the previous section. The optimal insurance contract $(\pi^*; q_1, q_2, \cdots, q_n)$ solves the following problem

(P3)
$$\max_{\pi, q_1, \cdots; e} (1 - \mathbf{p})U(W - \pi - e)$$
$$+ \mathbf{p} \sum_{i=1}^{n} p_i(e)U(W - \pi - e - l_i + q_i)$$

subject to

$$\mathbf{p} \sum_{i=1}^{n} p_i(e)q_i - \pi \leq 0 \tag{16}$$

$$e = \arg \max_{z} (1 - \mathbf{p})U(W - \pi - z)$$
$$+ \mathbf{p} \sum_{i=1}^{n} p_1(z)U(W - \pi - z - l_i + q_i) \tag{17}$$

$$q_i - l_i \leq 0 \tag{18}$$

In this problem (16) is the break-even constraint and (17) the incentive compatibility constraint. The constraint (18) reflects an assumption that an insurance policy that promised to pay out more than the loss in any state i would lead an individual to cause an accident (assuming this is costless). A constraint that the insurance payment is positive is also justified as before, but is never binding in this problem.

The first assumption that we impose on the problem is that every loss have positive probability when the first-best care level, e^*, is taken. If this did not hold, then the insurance contract could impose a penalty of zero coverage in outcomes that signalled a suboptimal level of effort.

We adopt the assumption here that the incentive-compatibility condition can be represented by the first-order condition to the individual's maximization problem. (This assumption is discussed below.) With this assumption, the constraint becomes[17]

$$(1 - \mathbf{p})U'(W - \pi - e) + \mathbf{p} \sum_{i=1,\cdots,n} \{p_i(e)U'(W - \pi - e - l_i + q_i)$$
$$- p_i'(e)U(W - \pi - e - l_i + q_i)\} = 0 \tag{19}$$

The following proposition characterizes the insurance market reaction to moral hazard on loss-reduction activities. The technical condition of a monotone likelihood ratio is discussed in Rogerson (1985) and Arnott (in this volume).

Proposition 4: If U exhibits nonincreasing absolute risk aversion, and the distribution of losses satisfies the condition of monotone likelihood ratio, then the solution to (P3) satisfies:
a) $(l_i - q_i)$ is nondecreasing in i. That is, the amount of the risk borne by the individual is a nondecreasing function of the size of the loss.
b) There is some m such that:
For $i \le m$, $q_i = l_i$ and the constraint (18) is binding.
For $i > m$, $q_i < l_i$.

Proof: see Appendix.

Part a of the proposition states that the amount of the loss borne by the individual is a nondecreasing function of the realized loss. Part b states that sufficiently small losses are fully covered by the optimal policy with moral hazard in loss-reduction activities, and that the constraint against over-insurance is binding for these losses. In contrast to the case of self-protection, optimal insurance contracts with moral hazard on loss-reduction activities involve full coverage of small losses (more than full coverage if possible) and on average, less than full coverage of the marginal dollar of high losses.[18]

The intuition for this result is as follows. Ignore for the moment the constraint (18). Because there is no moral hazard problem on the *event* of an accident, efficient risk-bearing dictates that the individual's marginal utility of wealth in the event of no accident be equated to the expected marginal utility of wealth conditional upon the event of an accident.

Wealth will be transferred, through insurance, between these two events to achieve this condition. But within the event of an accident, wealth will be transferred from high-loss states to low-loss states relative to the full insurance solution, to enhance incentives for loss-reduction, because of moral hazard. This leaves wealth in the low-loss states greater than in the event of no accident (that is, the insurance payment for a low loss exceeds the loss). With the constraint (18) binding, low losses are fully insured.

4. More General Assumptions on the Distribution of Losses: The Principal-Agent Model

When we generalize the models of Sections 1 and 2 to allow for an arbitrary distribution of losses, with care affecting both the probability of a loss and the size of the loss, the resulting model is the Principal-Agent model. This model is at the heart of a recent and still emerging paradigm in economics.

The interpretation of this optimal insurance contract under moral hazard is only one of many interpretations. The economic modeling of virtually any organization involves incentives, the allocations of risk-bearing, and incomplete contracting. The most popular applications of the Principal-Agent model are to the contractual relationship between managers of corporations and the owners in corporations, an employer and an employee when the actions or effort of the employee are not perfectly monitored by the employer, a manufacturer and a franchisee, and so on. Almost every economic relationship is influenced by risk and a tradeoff between the efficient allocation of risk-bearing and the minimization of incentive distortions is fundamental.

Moral hazard arises in any contractual setting whenever an individual is not assigned the full costs and benefits, at the margin, of a decision that affects other parties to the contract. Moral hazard therefore arises in a contractual setting where the full residual claim (the total output or profit from the enterprise, minus a lump sum) is not assigned to each party making a decision after the contract. The manager of firm that purchases the firm from its shareholders for a lump sum of money or an issue of riskless debt has resolved the moral hazard or agency problem, but a manager who has only partial equity in the firm has not.

There are three reasons why an individual would not be assigned the full consequences of his decisions and, correspondlingly, three types of principal-agent problems. First, the agent (a manager of a firm, for example) may not have the wealth to purchase the enterprise for its value to the principal or principals. A wealth constraint gives rise to the limited liability class of principal-agent models (e.g., Sappington (1983)). Second, there may be more than one agent or individual whose actions affect the return to the enterprise. With only one residual claim to divide among many agents, each agent cannot receive the full benefits of additional effort at the margin (Alchian and Demsetz (1963), Holmström (1982), Carmichael (1983)).[19] In either of these two agency models, moral hazard exists even if all parties are risk-neutral. Finally, in the class of principal agent models that are of interest here, it is possible but not optimal to allocate the full residual claim to the agent. The agent's risk aversion implies that the principal should bear at least some part of the uncertainty that is tied to ownership of the residual claim. The actual contract is second-best in that it compromises between the goal of efficient risk allocation and the achievement of efficient incentives. This is the essence of optimal insurance contracts under moral hazard.

The following is the basic set of assumptions defining the Principal-Agent problem. Adopting standard notation,[20] we consider a principal and an agent who have property rights to an uncertain income stream. The random income stream depends on an input such as care or effort on the part of the agent, to be taken in the future. The income stream may represent a firm or project that is initially owned by the principal, the management of which is delegated to the agent; it may represent a project owned by the agent who must raise capital by promising some share of the income stream to the principal; or, it may represent a possible loss from current wealth if the agent insures with the principal.

Let e represent the effort of the agent, and θ the random state of the world. The principal and agent establish a sharing rule or contract to share the random income stream. In the insurance example, this contract describes the insurance payment to the agent., $I(L)$, as a function of the loss incurred by the agent. The loss $L(e, \theta)$ depends on the effort input by the agent as well as the state of the world. The critical assumption is that that neither e nor θ can enter the contract. For example, neither is observable to the principal; alternatively, neither is observable to a third party enforcer of the contract (the courts).

The utility of the agent is represented by $U(W_a, e)$ which is increasing and concave in the agent's wealth, W_a, and decreasing in effort. The set of possible effort levels is denoted by A. The objective of the principal and agent is to choose a Pareto optimal sharing rule. If the principal owns the project, this is represented as maximizing the principal's utility subject to achieving a reservation level for the agent.

In the case of an optimal insurance contract with a competitive insurance market, however, the most natural formulation is the dual problem: maximize U subject to a break-even constraint on the part of the insurer. Furthermore, in the insurance context, the usual assumption is that the principal (the insurer) is risk-neutral because a large number of independent risks are insured. Finally, in most formulations, the effort on the part of the agent is assumed to be decided before the state θ is realized. The optimal contract under these assumptions is characterized by the maximization of agent's expected utility subject to two constraints: the break-even constraint and the incentive-compatiblity constraint:

(P4) $$\max_{\pi, I(L), e} E\{U(W - \pi - L(e, \theta) + I[L(e, \theta)])\}$$

subject to

$$\pi - EI[L(e, \theta)] \geq 0 \tag{26}$$

$$e \in \arg \max_{x \in A} E\{U(W - \pi - L(x, \theta) + I[L(x, \theta)])\} \tag{27}$$

This problem is formally identical to the formal Principal-Agent model that is reviewed in Richard Arnott's essay in this volume. I refer the reader to that essay for an exceptionally clear exposition of the model.

The Principal-Agent model is too general in the sense that it yields few specific propositions. Even the intuitive proposition that the agent's wealth is nondecreasing with output — in our context, that the insured does not contract for more than full coverage of the marginal loss — does not follow directly.[21] Grossman and Hart (1983) and Rogerson (1985), however, prove this monotonicity condition under reasonable restrictions on the distribution of losses. A general result that is relevant for insurance contracts is proved by Shavell (1979): While moral hazard reduces the expected utility achieved with an insurance contract, under the assumptions of this section it never eliminates the gains to trade from insurance (Shavell (1979)). There is always some gain from the first dollar of insurance coverage.[22]

5. Moral Hazard with a Partially Informed Insurer

To this point, we have assumed that the insurer has no information whatsoever about the level of care taken by the insured, or is for some other reason completely prevented from contracting on the level of care. In reality, the moral hazard problem may be mitigated by partial information about the insured's actions, even if this information is imperfect or costly for the insurer.

The analysis of partial information in moral hazard problems falls into two classes. In the first the principal observes an exogenous signal that is correlated with the effort of the agent (Holmström (1979), Shavell (1979)). The set of available contracts is expanded to include sharing rules that depend on the realized signal as well as the realized output from the enterprise (or the loss in an insurance policy).

The main implication of this class of models for insurance contracts under moral hazard is that the random signal *will* enter the contract if and only if the signal conveys some information about the individual's care or effort beyond what can be inferred from the realized loss. That is, if the random loss is not a sufficient statistic for the effort within the set of variables consisting of the loss and the signal, then the signal will enter the contract (Holmstom (1979)). This intuitive proposition is elegantly proved in Holmström, and I refer the reader to that paper for the details. An equivalent statement is that if the signal has, for at least some realizations, an effect on a posterior distribution of the agent's effort conditional upon the observed output, then it will be used (Shavell (1979)).[23]

In the second class of models, the insurer or principal chooses to invest in information about the insured's level of care. The state of the insurer's knowledge is endogenous in these models. This is an important class of models to examine, since investment in information about the insured's care is, along with partial coverage, one of two market responses to the moral hazard problem.

The main attempt at endogenizing the insurer's information in a moral hazard problem is Shavell (1979a: Section IV). This attempt is not entirely successful. Shavell allows the insurer to observe (at some cost) the care undertaken by the insured and considers two cases: an ex ante observation of care (at the time the policy is written) and an ex post observation of care, taken in the event of a claim. In both cases, the insurer may observe the care with error.

The ex ante model corresponds implicitly to the following game. The insurer and insured enter a contract; the care level of the insured is taken; the care is observed (in general, with error) by the insurer; the premium, which depends upon the observation, is paid by the insured; the random loss is realized; and the claim is paid. The initial contract specifies the premium as a function of the observed signal as well as the insurance coverage as a function of the observed signal. After entering the contract, both the insured and the insurer are committed to its terms and cannot leave the contract even before the premium is paid. The insurer faces a break-even constraint that its expected profits be nonnegative, with the expectation taken over the observation error. If the error has a symmetric distribution, then half the time the insurer will, once it observes the signal, regret having entered the contract. The insured may also regret having entered the contract.

I know of no insurance contracting that corresponds to the sequence of events described. In particular, in actual insurance contracts the current premium is known when the policy is purchased; if the premium were random, either party would be legally able to exit before the premium (the legal "consideration") were paid. The expenditure by insurers on information at the time of contracting, which Shavell calls the ex ante case, is related more closely to the determination of the characteristics of the prospective client — that is, to the problem of adverse selection — than to moral hazard. I will turn therefore to the model of ex post observation.

In this model, Shavell assumes that the insurer can (at a cost) observe the agent's care after the realization of an accident. For example, tests of the alcohol content of drivers are most often taken after accidents (and affect the claims paid by the insurer). Evidence of care, if not destroyed by an accident, can be gathered after a claim. Ex post observation, as Shavell points out, requires only that those filing claims be investigated. This is the role, for example, of the claims adjuster in automobile insurance companies.

Two results are obtained for the case of ex post observation: First, if the observation is without error, then for a sufficiently small cost of information the insurance contract calls for full insurance with the premium compensating the insurer for the expected cost of the information as well as the expected claim. In this case, the care of the insured is always observed and the moral hazard problem is therefore resolved (at the cost of observing the information). Second, if the observation is a noisy signal of care, then providing it has a sufficiently low cost and any information value at all is nonetheless incorporated in the optimal contract. The logic behind this result is similar to the case of incorporating an exogenous information signal, which was discussed previously.

Shavell assumes in the ex post model that once the insurer and the insured enter the contract, the insurer is committed to making the observation of care. In fact, taking the case of zero observation error as an example, the insurer has no incentive to carry out the announced plan of spending the resources on information ex post, once the insured has determined the care levels. The insurer knows that the optimal care levels have been undertaken and that the full insurance claim will therefore have to be paid. The insurer would pay this claim and not bother verifying the care level.[24] Of course, if an insurer attracted a reputation of not verifying care levels, then policyholders would exploit the insurer's strategy by not taking adequate care. In a market where insurers are repeat players and reputations are easily formed, it is reasonable to assume that the insurer can commit itself to the strategy of verifying care ex post.

But if we accept the ability of the insurer to commit to a plan of verifying ex post the care taken by an policyholder, then there is no reason why the insurer could not commit to verifying the claim with some probability less than one. The economic analysis of the enforcement of crimes (Becker (1968), Polinsky and Shavell (1979)) shows that there is a tradeoff between higher penalties and higher probabilities of detection in enforcing the law. The same tradeoff should exist in private contracts. In the present context, it may, in general, pay the insurer to verify only some proportion of claims and attach a relatively high penalty to those cases where the observation indicated (with high probability) that there was inadequate care. Mookerjee and Png (1989) examine random auditing in insurance contracts.

If we assume that the insurer hasn't the ability to commit to a plan of verifying ex post the care taken by a policyholder, then the appropriate model involves an equilibrium in mixed strategies. In this model, the insured decides with some probability whether or not to take care; the insurer decides whether or not to observe the care, at a cost; and the contract calls for coverage that may be limited by the observation of inadequate care.[25] This model has not been investigated in the literature on moral hazard in insurance. In general, more research is needed to understand the mix of the two market responses, partial coverage and expenditure on information to the moral hazard problem. The insights of the literature on Principle-Agent problems with auditing (e.g., Mookerjee and Png (1989)) will undoubtedly be useful in this research.

6. The Dynamics of Moral Hazard

Part of the conventional wisdom in insurance economics is that moral hazard problems are likely to be less severe under a repeated relationship between the insurer and the insured. Increased frequency of accidents because of failure on the part of an individual to take adequate care, the argument goes, will be met with increases in premiums. That is, the incentives to take adequate care are enhanced with experience rating of premiums. The central question in multiperiod moral hazard models has been the extent to which this conjecture is valid.

A basic starting point for this discussion is that with finite repetitions, this conventional wisdom is wrong. Suppose that the individual's utility exhibits constant absolute risk aversion, so that there are no income effects in the demand for insurance. Then when the relationship between the Principal and Agent is as modeled in Section 3 (i.e., with no observation of information signals by the Principal), and the repetition of the relationship occurs a finite number of times,[26] the contract and effort of the agent is identical to the single period case. Repetition has no impact on the moral hazard problem. Where measure of absolute risk aversion varies with wealth, contracts vary from period to period only because of the effect of changes in the individual's wealth on the demand for insurance.

The logic of this proposition is clear.[27] Suppose that the principal and agent have access to the same interest rate for borrowing or lending in the capital market. Then a penalty for an accident in the current period, in the form of a higher premium in next period's contract, offers no additional degrees of freedom as compared with the static model. Such a penalty, contingent upon an accident the current period, is identical to a reduction in coverage for the current period equal to the present value of the increased future premium. The tradeoff between optimal insurance and adequate incentives is unchanged by the repetition of the simplest moral hazard game.

The theory of repeated moral hazard proceeds by relaxing various of the assumptions in this "irrelevance" proposition. The assumptions to be discarded have been the assumptions of finite numbers of periods, zero information on the part of the Principal, and equal access to capital markets.

Rogerson (1985) relaxes the assumption that the principal and agent have equal access to capital markets. The long-term contract between the agent and the principal is governed by the goal of realizing the gains to trade arising from this difference in access (effectively, the gains from intermediation by the principal) and the usual goal of achieving the right mix of incentives and insurance. Regerson shows that the expected wealth allocated to the agent by the contract may increase or decrease over time, depending on how quickly risk aversion decreases with wealth.

In another approach to long-term contracts under moral hazard, Becker and Stigler (1974) show that a strategy of increasing wages over time (relative to marginal product), together with a rule that shirking agents be fired if detected, can improve efficiency under moral hazard.

The analysis of long-term contracts, however, is less relevant to the insurance context than to the context of long-term labor contracts. Life insurance contracts appear to be the only insurance contracts in which premiums are guaranteed for long periods, and for this type of insurance moral hazard is surely not a major issue.

A different branch of the literature on repeated moral hazard examines the extent to which the moral hazard problem can be resolved through punishment strategies by the principal when the principal infers that the agent has shirked care (Radner (1981), Rubinstein and Yaari (1983). Expressed differently, this literature offers an explanation of experience rating, i.e., discounts on premiums offered to clients who possess a favorable record of part claims. It argues that experience rating provides a mechanism that enables the parties to the contract to mitigate or eliminate the moral hazard inefficiency.

The Rubinstein and Yaari (1983) analysis, in particular, is framed in the context of insurance markets. These authors show that if there are infinite periods and no discounting (the insured and the insurer are interested in the average payoff in each period), then the insurer can eliminate the moral hazard problem by choosing an appropriate no-claims-discount (NCD) strategy. An NCD involves giving a discount for coverage in any period if the history of claims up to that period leads to an inference that the level of care is sufficiently high. Facing this announced strategy, it pays the insured to choose the first best care level in each period.

The insurer's problem is to determine exactly which claims histories should warrant a discount on the premium. If the definition of excessive claims is too strict, then the owner of the asset would end up paying a high premium too often, even when due care is exercised. If the definition is too lax, then the optimal care is not elicited. Rubinstein and Yaari show that the two types of possible errors in inferring a deviation from optimal care are both minimized with a particular class of insurance premium strategies.[28]

Radner (1981) has a similar model, although his equilibrium strategies do not satisfy the property of "perfection" as Rubinstein and Yaari point out. Both of these papers can be thought of as extensions of the Folk Theorem of repeated games to the case in which a player makes a move in each period without full knowledge of the previous moves of the other player. Whatever the theoretical interest of these models, their implications for actual insurance contracts is limited by the assumptions of no discounting and infinite periods. A zero discount rate is simply counter-factual, and it is very difficult to determine the deviation from first best that arises when there is a discount rate. The assumption of infinite periods is also unrealistic.

In a finite period model, it is possible that an individual's incentive to take adequate care is enhanced by a desire to achieve a reputation as one who is careful. This, however, becomes a model of adverse selection (hidden types) rather than a model of moral hazard alone. A conjecture is that the resolution of adverse selection via revelation of information about types, can reduce welfare in a combined adverse selection — moral hazard model, because it eliminates the possibility of taking care to acquire a reputation with finite repetitions. In general, the literature on repeated moral hazard does not offer an implication for experience rating in actual contracts that is testable against the alternative hypothesis of adverse selection. Adverse selection clearly leads to experience rating (e.g., Hosios and Peters (1989)). There is no reason not to think that experience-rating in actual insurance contracts is entirely explained by adverse selection.

An interesting case that has not been investigated in the repeated moral hazard literature is the case of long-lived, capital investments in care. In the case of product liability insurance, for example, *care* refers to the investment in safety in product design and the decision not to market excessively dangerous products. A decision to invest in care affects not just the immediate rate of accidents but the future rate as well. In a finitely repeated contract, when there is common knowledge at the beginning of the relationship (so that the problem is one of moral hazard), the incentive to take care is enhanced by the dependence of future premiums on past claims records: the future insurers infer the care decision from past claims.[29] A conjecture is that (even with a finite number of periods) in the case of long-lived care decisions, repetition, and the ability of premiums to respond to claims' histories do mitigate the moral hazard problem.

7. Conclusion

This essay reviews and extends the theory of insurance contracts under moral hazard. The main results of this theory are easily summarized. The inability to contract over an individual's level of care reduces the benefits of insurance, but not to zero. Some gains to trade remain under moral hazard, so that (in contrast to adverse selection) the market cannot disappear when the set of feasible contracts is large enough. The market responds to moral hazard with a reduction of coverage as well as a linkage of claims paid to any informational signal (endogenous or exogenous) of the insured's level of care. The cutback on coverage is greatest for intermediate costs of care; at either extreme, coverage tends towards full insurance.

Even for the simplest model of insurance contracting under moral hazard, many results are negative. Indifference curves need not be convex, and the set of feasible, breakeven contracts virtually never is. This leads to discontinuities in the market contractual responses to moral hazard as exogenous parameters change, and potential difficulty in empirical testing. The coverage offered by the market, for example, need not be a monotonic function of the severity of the moral hazard problem.

Where the moral hazard problem is in efforts to reduce the probability of an accident, i.e., the self-protection decision, the market response is to offer contracts with deductibles. Negative insurance of small losses would be optimal, if feasible, and higher losses are, at the margin, fully insured. Moral hazard on the loss-reduction decisions, in contrast, leads to full insurance of small losses. Overinsurance of small losses would be optimal in this case, if it were feasible. Higher losses are less than fully covered at the margin.

While the distinction between self-protection and loss-reduction activities is somewhat forced, I argue that there are examples where one or the other is more important, and that it is necessary to dissect the aspects of moral hazard to generate testable predictions. In the general case, which is the canonical principal-agent model, few results obtain. Substantial assumptions and machinery are needed in this literature to prove even the simple result that coverage will be nondecreasing in the size of a loss, and will not increase more than one-for-one with the loss. The general model does predict, however, that insurance will be less than full, with some risk borne by the insured, and that gains to trade between the insured and insurer exist in spite of moral hazard. Finally, under some conditions, repetition of the insured-insurer contract may resolve the moral hazard problem to some extent. The extent of this resolution under realistic assumptions, however, is not clear at this stage of the theoretical development. Apart from income effects in the demand for insurance (i.e., departures from constant absolute risk aversion), finite repetitions do not affect insurance contracts under moral hazard.

At least five areas of the theory of moral hazard in insurance contracts remain fertile ground for further research. First, I suggested that an dynamic model of moral hazard in investment in safety capital would yield important insights as well as a set of circumstances in which finite repetition of the insurance contracting does affect the nature of the contract.[30] Second, I was critical of the attempts to endogenize the insured's information (i.e., the observation of care in insurance contracts) and conjectured that the appropriate model would always yield a mixed strategy on the information acquisition decision by the insurer.

The theory of moral hazard in insurance, indeed the theory of optimal insurance in general, has not been fully developed for the case of liability insurance purchased by a corporation with limited liability.[31] The presence of limited liability means that even prior to the insurance purchase, moral hazard is potentially a problem, as creditors bear some of the costs of lax effort on the part of equity holders.

The two remaining areas for further research in moral hazard concern the market reaction to moral hazard, which is the fundamental unifying question in the area. The basic assumption of moral hazard models is that some decisions about care on the part of the insured cannot be contracted for. But there are often both substitute or complementary inputs by the individual that are observable. The mental concentration of an automobile driver cannot be contractually specified, but the attendance in an advanced driving class or the choice by the driver of a car model, can be specified. The literature has not considered the contractual requirement of extra expenditure on contractible, substitute loss-reducing activities as a response to moral hazard. Finally, insurers often engage in loss-reducing and accident-avoiding activities themselves (Schlesinger and Venezian (1986)). The interaction of these decisions with moral hazard on the part of consumers is worth investigating.

Appendix

Proof of Proposition 1: To prove the proposition, we first note the following lemma.

Lemma 2: $e(q)$, defined by (3), is decreasing in q for all $q \leq l$.

Lemma 2 is demonstrated by totally differentiating (3) and relying on the second-order conditions for the agent's maximization problem (Lemma 1).

To show that e is positive for sufficiently low r, it suffices to show that the inequality (4) cannot hold for sufficiently low r. This follows directly from the fact that the right-hand side of (4) is bounded and the left-hand side is unbounded as $r \to 0$. To show that when $e > 0$, $q < l$, consider the expression in (5) evaluated at $q = l$. When $q = l$, then $W_N = W_L$ and the last two terms of (5) sum to zero. Since $e' < 0$ by Lemma 2 and $p' < 0$ by assumption, the first term is negative. This shows that expected utility can be increased by lowering q below l.

To prove that r^*, as defined in b, exists, let r increase without limit. The left-hand side of (3) approaches zero, and the right-hand side is bounded below by $U'(W)$, so (3) cannot hold for sufficiently large r. Defining r^* as the minimum r for which the incentive compatibility constraint is defined by (4) rather than (3), it is straightforward to show that for any r above r^*, (4) continues to hold. Similarly, the existence of $\hat{r}$ is easily established.

To show that $\hat{r} \geq r^*$, let $V(r)$ represent the maximum expected utility under (P1) at r and let $v(r; e)$ represent the maximum expected utility with the additional constraint that effort equal e. Let $\hat{V}$ and $\hat{v}$ be the corresponding functions for the complete contract (without the incentive compatibility constraint). Then $\hat{V}(\hat{r}) = \hat{v}(\hat{r}; 0)$ since the optimal e is 0 at $\hat{r}$. Furthermore, $\hat{v}(\hat{r}; 0) = v(\hat{r}; 0)$ since the incentive compatibility constraint is not binding if $e = 0$. Next, $v(\hat{r}; 0) \leq V(\hat{r}) \equiv \max_e v(\hat{r}, e)$. In short, $V(\hat{r}) \geq \hat{V}(\hat{r})$. But the opposite inequality holds because the complete contract problem is less constrained. This shows that $V(\hat{r}) = \hat{V}(\hat{r}) = v(\hat{r}, 0)$ and therefore that the optimal effort under (P1) at $\hat{r}$ is 0. Hence $\hat{r} \geq r^*$.

To show that $\hat{r} > r^*$ if coverage is a continuous function of r at $\hat{r}$, we consider expected utility as a function of effort (with abuse of notation, $EU(e)$), obtained by substituting the break-even constraint (1) into the objective function of (P1). Note that at $\hat{r}$,[32]

$$\frac{dEU}{de} = 0$$

We show that at $\hat{r}$,

$$\frac{dEU}{de} > \frac{dEU}{de}\bigg|_{(2)} \tag{6}$$

The left-hand side of (6) refers to the marginal utility of an additional unit of care specified in the complete contract; the right-hand side refers to the marginal utility of an additional unit of care when q must be reduced to preserve the incentive compatiblity constraint, (2). The inequality (6) directly implies the second statement in b of the proposition.

To prove (6), the left-hand side is calculated as

$$0 = \frac{dEU}{de} = U'(W_N) \cdot [-p'(0)l - r] \tag{7}$$

In expressing the right-hand side of (b), let $q(e)$ represent the solution to the incentive compatibility constraint in q, given e; that is, $q(e)$ is the inverse of the function described in Lemma 2. Substituting $q(e)$ into the objective function of (P1) and differentiating, yields

$$
\left.\frac{dEU}{de}\right|_{(2)} = [-p'q(e) - r]\{[1 - p(e)]U'(W_N) + p(e)U'(W_L)\}
$$
$$
p'[U'(W_L) - U''(W_N)]
$$
$$
+ pq'(e)\{(1 - p)[U'(W_L) - U'(W_N)]\} \tag{8}
$$

Only the last term of (8), and the fact that W_N and W_L differ, reflect the moral hazard. Because $q'(e) < 0$ by Lermma 2 and $p' < 0$ by assumption, the last two terms of (8) are negative. This implies:

$$
\left.\frac{dEU}{de}\right|_{(2)} < [-p'q(e) - r] \cdot EU' < [-p'l - r] \cdot EU' \tag{9}
$$

Now the expression $[-p'l - r]$ in (9) equals zero at $\hat{r}$, from (7). This proves (6). QED

Proof of Proposition 4: Let w_i denote $W - \pi - e - l_i + q_i$, the individual's wealth in state i. The first-order conditions for this problem, corresponding to q_i, π and e are as follows:

$$
(\forall i)\ pp_iU'(w_i) - \lambda_1pp_i - \lambda_2pp_iU''(w_i) + \lambda_2pp_i'U'(w_i) - \lambda_{3i} = 0 \tag{20}
$$

$$
-(1 - p)U'(w_o) - p\sum_i p_iU'(w_i) + \lambda_1 + \lambda_2((1 - p)U''(w_o)
$$
$$
+ p\sum_i[p_iU''(w_i) - p_i'U'(w_i)]) = 0 \tag{21}
$$

$$
-(1 - p)U'(w_o) - p\sum_i p_iU'(w_i) + p\sum_i p_i'U(w_i) - \lambda_1p\sum_i p_i'q_i
$$
$$
-\lambda_2\left[-(1 - p)U''(w_o) - p\sum_i\{p_iU''(w_i) - p_i'U'(w_i)\right.
$$
$$
\left. - p_i'U'(w_i) + p_i''U(w_i)\}\right] = 0 \tag{22}
$$

To prove (a) of the proposition, we must show that $w_{j+1} \le w_j$, for all $j = 1, n - 1$. If the constraint (18) is binding for both j and $j + 1$, or only for j this is trivial. Consider the case where (18) is binding for neither j nor $j + 1$. Equation (20) and $\lambda_i = 0$, for $i = j, j + 1$ imply that

$$
1 - \frac{\lambda_1}{U'(w_i)} + \lambda_2 \cdot \frac{-U''(w_i)}{U'(w_i)} = -\lambda_2\frac{p_i'}{p_i} \tag{23}
$$

As a function of w_i, the left-hand side of (23) is strictly decreasing (the second term is strictly decreasing by the concavity of U and the third is nonincreasing by the assumption of nonincreasing absolute risk aversion). It follows from Milgrom (1981: Proposition 5) that under the monotone likelihood ratio condition, the right-hand side of (23) is nondecreasing in i. To maintain the equality (23) for all i, therefore, it must be that w_i is decreasing in i. The case where (18) is binding only for $j + 1$ is similar. This proves part (a) of the proposition.

To prove part b), suppose that $\lambda_{3i} = 0$ for all i. Then equation (23) implies

$$U'(w_i) - \lambda_1 - \lambda_2 U''(w_i) + \lambda_2 \frac{P'_i}{p_i} U'(w_i) = 0 \qquad (24)$$

Adding up all n first-order constraints represented by equation (20), subtracting (21) and simplifying yields

$$U'(w_0) - \lambda_1 - \lambda_2 U''(w_0) = 0 \qquad (25)$$

Next, note that $\Sigma_i p_i = 1$ implies $\Sigma_i p'_i = 0$. This and the fact that not all p'_i are zero implies p'_i are neither all negative nor all positive. The monotonicity decreasing in i of p'_i/p_i (see proof of a) above) then implies that there exists j, $j \geq 1$ such that that the last term of (24) is positive for all $i \leq j$, and negative for all $i > j$. Comparing with (25) and using the fact that the left hand side of (25) is decreasing in w_0 because $U''' > 0$ for nonincreasing absolute risk aversion utility functions, shows that $w_i > w_0$ for $i \leq j$. From the definitions of w_0 and w_i, this contradicts the constraint (18). Thus the supposition that $\lambda_{3i} = 0$ for all i is contradicted, and the constraint (18) must therefore be binding for some i. Part (a) of the proposition implies that (18) is binding for small i. QED

Notes

1. Note that even some individual decisions that could be contractually protected for may not be. Life insurance policies generally cover death from suicide after the first two years, so that they may include insurance against the future event of a state-of-mind (or a loss in wealth) that would lead to suicide. This decision may be influenced by the existence of insurance but is nonetheless covered by the typical policy.

2. In agency theory, the definition of moral hazard is correspondingly broader than in the specific context of insurance contracts. The broad definition of moral hazard includes any inefficiency in the decisions of a contractual party that results from the incompleteness of the contracts and externalities among the contractual parties. One source of such a moral hazard or agency problem is team production where individual outputs cannot be identified or perhaps even defined (Alchian and Demsetz (1972), Holmström (1982), Carmichael (1983)). This type of moral hazard can arise even if agents are risk-neutral. Insurance, therefore, is not necessary for moral hazard in general.

3. See also Boyer and Dionne (1983 and 1989) and Chang and Ehrlich (1985).

4. The assumption of complete contracting in Ehrlich and Becker accounts for the conclusion that their analysis "challenges the notion that 'moral hazard' is an inevitable consequence of market insurance, by showing that under 'certain conditions the latter may lead to a reduction in the probabilities of hazardous events." (Ehrlich and Becker (1972: 623). In fact, there is no tension between their result and the conventional moral hazard results.

5. The model described in this section, or very similar models, have been analyzed by many authors. See Shavell (1979b), Arnott and Stiglitz (1983a,b), Spence and Zeckhauser (1971).

6. An implication of event-independence is that the only risks involved are pecuniary.

7. Risk-neutrality of insurers can be deduced from the law of large numbers and an assumption of independence of risks in the insurance market or an assumption that risks are independent of aggregate wealth or factors in the equity market.

8. The possibility of random contracts arises because of the following nonconvexity. Consider the function $V(R)$ that gives the highest expected utility to the individual from any contract, subject to the constraint that insurer profits be at least R. Let $(\pi(R), q(R))$ be the corresponding contract. The function $V(R)$ may be locally convex at 0. In this case, for sufficiently small ε, randomizing between the contracts $(\pi(\varepsilon), q(\varepsilon))$ and $(\pi(-\varepsilon), q(-\varepsilon))$ yields higher expected utility than $(\pi(0), q(0))$. Randomness in insurance contracts is analyzed in detail in Arnott and Stiglitz (1988b).

9. The analysis here is a modest extension of Shavell's treatment, in that I provide sufficient conditions for the first-order approach (lemma 1) rather than just assuming it; prove the second part of the Proposition 1; and simplify the proof of the first part of the proposition.

10. That is, $e(q)$ is the care under coverage q.

11. Sections 2 and 3 are based on Winter (1990).

12. Where the loss is random, loss-reduction refers to expenditures that decrease the loss in the sense of first-order stochastic dominance.

13. The optimality of deductibles under moral hazard on self-protection was proved by Holmström (1979), Proposition 2, for the case of separable preferences. Separability of preferences is unrealistic for most insurance problems.

14. At the end of this section, I briefly consider the case in which the insurer cannot verify the size of the loss.

15. That is, the problem can be viewed as a standard Kuhn-Tucker maximization problem under constraints, with a continuum of choice variables.

16. Self-protection analyzed in the previous section, referred to an increase in the probability of a zero loss, with no change in the conditional distribution of a positive loss.

17. I have multiplied the individual's first-order condition by -1 so that the shadow price in the maximization problem be positive. (The left-hand side of (19) is increasing in e.)

18. In this proposition, I adopted the first-order approach without formal justification. Sufficient technical conditions for the first-order approach to principal-agent problems have been established by Rogerson (1985) and Jewett (1988) but only for the case of utility that is separable in wealth and effort. These conditions for the first-order approach are discussed in Arnott's essay in this volume. With some reasonable alternative assumptions (on observability), the first-order approach can be justified for our context. The key is that in reality insurers most often do not observe the size of the loss directly but rely to some extent on the file claimed by the insured. The first assumption is that $q(l)$ is nondecreasing in l. For if $q(x_2) < q(x_1)$ for $x_2 > x_1$, then the individual would report only x_1 when x_2 were incurred

(repairing the loss of $x_2 - x_1$ if necessary). Second, dq/dl is assumed to be bounded by 1, since if $q(x_2) - q(x_1) > x_2 - x_1$, then an individual who incurred x_1 could (at, we suppose, zero cost) cause the damage to increase to x_2. The individual would then be better off. Under the assumption that $0 \leq dq/dl \leq 1$, together with the assumptions of monotone likelihood ratio and convexity of distribution (Rogerson (1985)), the replacement of the incentive compatibility with the corresponding first-order condition can be formally justified. The boundedness of dq/dl seems like a weak condition, but is in fact the crux of justifying the first-order approach.

19. The same budget constraint problem plagues the design of efficient liability rules in tort law. Holmström interprets the role of equity in the modern corporation as breaking the budget constraint.

20. I change the notation to be consistent with the literature, but the only change in assumptions from the previous section is that the probability of an accident and the distribution of the loss may now depend on the care level.

21. This is because for some distributions, the realization of a particular, intermediate loss may signal that the agent has, with high probability, exerted low effort. Such a loss would be associated with very low coverage, so as to discourage low effort, possbility to the extent that the coverage of a slightly higher loss is much higher.

22. This result contrasts with the case where insurers cannot observe the amount of coverage an individual has purchased from other insurers (Arnott and Stiglitz (1983a,b).

23. The introduction into the Principle-Agent model of an informative signal leads to yet another nonconvexity in moral hazard problems: The marginal value of the information is zero at the point of zero information (Singh (1985) as in standard single-agent decision problems (Radner and Stiglitz (1984)). Singh explores the consequences of this nonconvexity for optimal organizations.

24. If the information signal is noisy, the insurer's threat to observe care ex post may or may not be credible.

25. The equilibrium in this model cannot be in pure strategies: If the insured decides to take care, then the optimal action for the insurer is not to observe; but if the insurer does not observe, then the optimal action for the individual is to take no care.

26. Alternatively, assume a finite upper bound on the possibly random length of the relationship. In insurance contracts such an upper bound is the only realistic possibility.

27. The point is essentially the same as the chain-store paradox that equilibrium in a static noncooperative game unaffected by a finite number of repetitions. In repeated moral hazard models, however, the past actions of other players are not observable.

28. In the tth contract, a high-penalty premium is charged if the average of past claims exceeds the expected claim (given optimal care) plus α^t where $\{\alpha^t\}$ is any sequence converging to zero more slowly than $(2\lambda\sigma^2 \log \log t/t)^{1/2}$ for some $\lambda > 1$. Otherwise, the insurer charges a lower premium. Like Radner (1981), these authors invoke the Law of Iterated Logarithm from probability theory.

29. Although, as in the basic principal-agent model, insurers with knowledge of the model can actually deduce exactly the optimal decision of the insured, if that decision is a pure strategy.

30. This model would parallel a model in the context of labor markets on unobserved personal investment in human capital.

31. An exception is Huberman, Mayers, and Smith (1983).

32. All derivatives in the following are left-hand derivatives. The left-hand derivatives exist at $\hat{r}$ by the supposition of continuity at $\hat{r}$.

References

Alchian, A., and H. Demsetz. (1972). "Production, information costs, and economic organization," *American Economic Review* 5, 777–795.

Arnott R., (1991) "Moral Hazard in Competitive Insurance Markets" in G. Dionne (ed) Contributions to Insurance Economics Kluwer Academic Publishers, in this volume.

Arnott, R., and J. Stiglitz. (1983a). "Equilibrium in Competitive Insurance Markets: The Welfare Economics of Moral Hazard," Working Paper, Queen's University.

Arnott, R., and J. Stiglitz. (1983b). "The Basic Analytics of Moral Hazard: Ill-behaved Consumers with Well-behaved Utility Functions," Working Paper, Queen's University.

Arnott, R., and J. Stiglitz. (1988a). "The Basic Analytics of Moral Hazard," *Scandinavian Journal of Economics* 90, 383–413.

Arnott, R., and J. Stiglitz. (1988b). "Randomization with Asymmetric Information," *Rand Journal of Economics* 19, 344–362.

Arrow, K. (1970). "Uncertainty and the Welfare Economics of Medical Care," *Essays in the Theory of Risk-Bearing*. North-Holland.

Becker, G. (1968). "Crime and Punishment," *Journal of Political Economy* March-April: 169–217.

Becker, G., and G. Stigler. (1974). "Law Enforcement, Malfeasance, and Compensation of Enforcers," *Journal of Legal Studies* 3, 1–18.

Boyer, M., and G. Dionne. (1983). "Variations in the Probability and Magnitude of Loss: Their Impact on Risk," *Canadian Journal of Economics* 16, 411–419.

Boyer, M., and G. Dionne. (1989). "More on Insurance, Protection and Risk," *Canadian Journal of Economics* 22, 202–204.

Carmichael, L. (1983). "The Agent-agents Problem: Payment by Relative Output," *Journal of Labor Economics* 1, 60–65.

Chang, Y.-M., and I. Ehrlich. (1985). "Insurance, Protection From Risk and Risk-Leaving," *Canadian Journal of Economics* 18, 574–587.

Dionne, G., and P. Lasserre. (1988). "Dealing with Moral Hazard and Adverse Selection Simultaneously," Working Paper, Université de Montréal.

Ehrlich, I., and G. Becker. (1972). "Market Insurance, Self- Insurance and Self-Protection," *Journal of Political Economy* 623–648.

Grossman, S., and O. Hart. (1983). "An Analysis of the Principal-Agent Problem," *Econometrica* 1, 7–45.

Harris, M., and A. Raviv. "Some Results on Incentive Contracts," *American Economic Review* 1, 20–31.

Helpman, E. and J. J. Laffont. (1975). "On Moral Hazard in General Equilibrium," *Journal of Economic Theory*, 10, 8–23.

Holmström, B. (1979). "Moral Hazard and Observability," *The Bell Journal of Economics* 10, 74–92.

Holmström, B. (1982). "Moral Hazard and Teams," *The Rand Journal of*

Economics 13, 324–340.

Hosios, A., and M. Peters. (1989). "Repeated Insurance Contracts with Adverse Selection and Limited Commitment," *Quarterly Journal of Economics* 2, 229–254.

Huberman, G., D. Mayers and C. Smith. (1983). "Optimal Insurance Policy Indemnity Schedules," *Bell Journal of Economics* 8, 415–426.

Jewitt, I. (1988). "Justifying the First-Order Approach to Principal-Agent Problems," *Econometrica* 5, 1177–1190.

Kotowitz, Y. (1987). "Moral Hazard." In the New *Palgrave: a Dictionary of Economics*: the Macuillan Press Limited, London 549–551.

Lambert, R. (1983). "Long-term Contracts and Moral Hazard," *Bell Journal of Economics* 8, 441–452.

MacDonald, G. M. (1984). "New Directions in the Economic Theory of Agency," *Canadian Journal of Economics* 3, 415–440.

Mookerjee, D., and I. Png. (1989). "Optimal Auditing, Insurance and Redistribution," *Quarterly Journal of Economics* 2, 399–416.

Pauly, M. (1968). "The Economics of Moral Hazard: Comment," *American Economic Review* 58, 531–537.

Pauly, M. (1974). "Overinsurance and Public Provision of Insurance: The Roles of Moral Hazard and Adverse Selection," *Quarterly Journal of Economics* 88, 44–62.

Polinsky, A. M. (1983). *An Introduction to Law and Economics.* Boston: Little, Brown.

Polinsky, A. M., and S. Shavell. (1979). "The Optimal Tradeoff between the Probability and Magnitude of Fines," *American Economic Review* 69, 880.

Radner, R. (1981). "Monitoring Cooperative Agreements in a Repeated Principal-Agent Relationship," *Econometrica* 49, 1127–1148.

Radner, R., and J. Stiglitz. (1984). "A Non-concavity in the Value of Information." In *Bayesian Models in Economic Theory*, edited by M. Boyer and R. E. Kihlstrom. North-Holland Rogerson, W. P. (1985) "Repeated Moral Hazard," *Econometrica* 53, 69–76.

Rogerson, W. P. (1985). "The First-Order Approach to Principal-Agent Problems," *Econometrica* 6, 1357–1367.

Rubinstein, A., and Yarri, M. E. (1983). "Repeated Insurance Contracts and Moral Hazard," *Journal of Economic Theory* 30, 74–97.

Sappington, D. (1983). "Limited Liability Contracts between Principal and Agent," *Journal of Economic Theory* 29, 1–21.

Schlesinger, H., and E. Venezian. (1986). "Insurance Markets with Loss-Prevention Activity: Profits, Market Structure, and Consumer Welfare," *Rand Journal of Economics* 17, 227–238.

Shavell, S. (1979a). "Risk-Sharing and Incentives in the Principal and Agent Relationship," *The Bell Journal of Economics* 10, 55–73.

Shavell, S. (1979b). "On Moral Hazard and Insurance," *Quarterly Journal of Economics* 11, 541–562.

Singh, N. (1985). "Monitoring and Hierarchies: The Marginal Value of Information in a Principal-Agent Model," *Journal of Political Economy* 93(3), 599–610.

Spence, M., and R. Zeckhauser. (1971). "Insurance, Information and Individual Action," *American Economic Review* 61, 380–387.

Stiglitz, J. (1983). "Risk, Incentives and Insurance: The Pure Theory of Moral Hazard," *The Geneva Papers on Risk and Insurance* 8(26), 4–33.

Winter, R. (1990). "On Moral Hazard and Insurance Contracts," mimeo. University of Toronto.

ADVERSE SELECTION IN INSURANCE MARKETS: A SELECTIVE SURVEY*

Georges Dionne

Université de Montréal

Neil Doherty

University of Pennsylvania

Abstract

In this survey we present some of the more significant results in the literature on adverse selection in insurance markets. Section 1 discusses the monopoly model introduced by Stiglitz (1977) for the case of single-period contracts and extended by many authors to the multi-period case. The introduction of multi-period contracts raises many issues that are discussed in detail: time horizon, discounting, commitment of the parties, contract renegotiation, and accident underreporting. Section 2 covers the literature on competitive contracts. The analysis becomes more complicated since insurance companies must take into account competitive pressures when they set incentives contracts. As pointed out by Rothschild and Stiglitz (1976), there is not necessarily a Cournot-Nash equilibrium in presence of adverse selection. However, market equilibrium can be sustained when principals anticipate competitive reactions to their behavior or when they adopt strategies that differ from the pure Nash strategy. Multi-period contracting is discussed. We show that different predictions on the evolution of insurer profits over time can be obtained from different assumptions concerning the sharing of information between insurers about individual's choice of contracts and accidents experience. The roles of commitment and renegotiation between the parties to the contract are important. We then

* CRSH (Canada) and FCAR (Québec) provided financial support to this study. Comments by K. J. Crocker, I. Cromb, B. Dahlby, C. Fluet, T. Nilssen, D. A. Malueg and P. Viala were very useful. We wish to thank J. Lafontaine and A. Mathieu for their valuable assistance in the preparation of the manuscript.

97

discuss how risk categorization can be used to improve resource allocation under adverse selection. Finally, the last section introduces models that simultaneously consider moral hazard and adverse selection. A short conclusion summarizes the main results in recent literature and discusses some avenues of future research.

Key words: Adverse selection, insurance markets, monopoly, competitive contracts, self-selection mechanisms, single-period contracts, multi-period contracts, commitment, contract renegotiation, accident underreporting, risk categorization

Without asymmetric information and under the standard assumptions of insurance models that we shall use in this article (same attitude toward risk and same risk aversion for all individuals in all classes of risk, one source of risk, risk neutrality on the supply side, no transaction cost in the supply of insurance, and no moral hazard), a Pareto optimal solution is characterized by full insurance coverage for all individuals in each class of risk. Each insured sets his optimal consumption level according to his wealth. No other financial institution is required to obtain this level of welfare and both risk categorization and self-selection mechanisms are redundant. Moreover, there is no need for multi-period insurance contracts since they are not superior to a sequence of one-period contracts. Finally, the two standard theorems of welfare economics hold and market prices of insurance are equal to the corresponding social opportunity costs.

In insurance markets, adverse selection results from asymmetric information between the insured (agent) and the insurer (principal). The insureds are heterogeneous with respect to their expected loss and have more information than the insurance company, which is unable to differentiate between risk types. Naturally, the high-risk individual has no incentive to reveal his true risk, which is costly to observe by the insurer. As pointed out by Arrow, a pooling of risks is often observed in insurance markets. "In fact, however, there is a tendency to equalize rather than to differentiate premiums. . . .This constitutes, in effect, a redistribution of income from those with a low propensity of illness to those with a high propensity. . . ." (Arrow, 1963; p. 964).

Akerlof (1970) showed that if all insurers have imperfect information on individual risks, an insurance market may not exist, or if it exists, it may not be efficient. He proposed an explanation of why, for example, people over 65 have great difficulty buying medical insurance: "the result is that the average medical condition of insurance applicants deteriorates as the price level rises — with the result that no insurance sales may take place at any price" (1970; p. 492). The seminal contributions of Akerlof and Arrow have generated a proliferation of models on adverse selection. In this survey we shall, however, confine attention to a limited subset. Many authors have proposed mechanisms to reduce the inefficiency associated with adverse selection: the "self-selection mechanism" in one period contracts, which induces policyholders to reveal hidden information by selection from a menu of contracts (Rothschild and Stiglitz, 1976; Stiglitz, 1977; Wilson, 1977; Miyazaki, 1977; Spence, 1978; Hellwig, 1986), the "categorization of risks" (Hoy, 1982; Crocker and Snow, 1985, 1986), and multi-period contracts (Dionne, 1983, Dionne and Lasserre, 1985, 1987; Kunreuther and Pauly, 1985; Cooper and Hayes, 1987; Hosios and Peters, 1989; Nilssen, 1990; Dionne and Doherty (1991)). All of them address private market mechanisms. In the first case, insurers offer a menu of policies with different prices and quantity levels so that different risk types choose different insurance policies. Pareto improvements for resource allocation with respect to the single contract solution with an average premium to all clients can be obtained. In the second case, insurers use imperfect information to categorize risks and, under certain conditions, it is also possible to obtain Pareto improvements for resource allocation. In the third case, insurers use the information related to the past experience of the insured as a sorting device (i.e., to motivate high-risk individuals to reveal their true risk ex ante).

In this survey, we present some of the more significant results in the literature on adverse selection in insurance markets. Section 1 discusses the monopoly model introduced by Stiglitz (1977) for the case of single-period contracts and extended by many authors to the multi-period case. The introduction of multi-period contracts raises many issues that are discussed in detail: time horizon, discounting, commitment of the parties, contract renegotiation, and accident underreporting. Section 2 covers the literature on competitive contracts. The analysis becomes more complicated since insurance companies must take into account competitive pressures when they set incentives contracts. As pointed out by Rothschild and Stiglitz (1976) there is not necessarily a Cournot-Nash equilibrium in the presence of adverse selection. However, market equilibrium can be sustained when principals anticipate competitive reactions to their behavior or when they adopt strategies that differ from the pure Nash strategy. Multi-period contracting is discussed. We show that different predictions on the evolution of insurer profits over time can be obtained from different assumptions concerning the sharing of information between insurers about individual's choice of contracts and accident experiences. The roles of commitment and renegotiation between the parties to the contract are important. We then discuss how risk categorization can be used to improve resource allocation under adverse selection. As shown recently by Bond and Crocker (1991), risk categorization has two potential effects: 1) it may improve efficiency and 2) it may mitigate nonexistence of equilibrium problems. Finally, the last section introduces models that simultaneously consider moral hazard and adverse selection. A short conclusion summarizes the main results and discusses some avenues of future research.

Before proceeding let us comment briefly on some standard assumptions. We assume that all individuals maximize expected utility. The utility functions of the individuals in each risk group are identical, strictly concave, and satisfy the von Neumann-Morgenstern axioms. Utility is time independent, time additive, and event-independent. In many models there is no discounting. Individuals start each period with a given wealth, W, which is nonrandom. To avoid problems of bankruptcy, the value of the risky asset is lower than W. All risk in the individual's portfolio is assumed to be insurable. Income received in a given period is consumed in that period; effectively there is no saving and no banking. Insurers are risk neutral and maximize the value of their cash flows or profits. Insurers write exclusive insurance contracts and there are no transaction costs in the supply of insurance. Finally, the insureds are assumed to be unable to influence either the probabilities of accident or the damages due to accidents; this rules out any problem of moral hazard.

As indicated above, the design of optimal contracts when moral hazard and adverse selection are present simultaneously is discussed in the last section of the paper. Recently, the two information problems have been integrated by some authors into a single model (Laffont and Tirole, 1986; Guesnerie, Picard, Rey, 1988) where all the parties to the contract are risk neutral. However, such contributions cannot be applied directly to insurance contracts if at least one party to the contract is risk averse.

To simplify the presentation, we explicitly assume that insurers are risk neutral. An equivalent assumption is that shareholders are well diversified in the sense that much of their total risk is diversified in their personal portfolios. The presence of transaction costs would not affect the qualitative conclusions concerning the effects of adverse selection on resource allocation in insurance markets. However, proportional transaction costs (or proportional loadings) are sufficient to explain partial insurance coverage and their explicit introduction in the analysis would modify some conclusions in the reference models. For example, each individual in each class of risk would buy less than full insurance in the presence of full information, and the introduction of adverse selection will decrease further the optimal coverage for the low risk individuals.

The presence of many sources of noninsurable risks, or of many risky assets in individual portfolios, is also an empirical fact that is not considered in the models. As long as these risks are independent, the conclusions should not be affected significantly. However, the optimal portfolio and insurance decisions in the presence of many correlated risks and asymmetrical information in one or in many markets is still an open question in the literature.

In reality, we observe that banks coexist with insurers who offer multi-period insurance contracts. The presence of savings and banking may change the conclusions obtained for multi-period contracts under asymmetrical information. Particularly, it may modify accident-reporting strategies and commitment to the contracts. However, with few exceptions (Allen (1985), moral hazard; Dionne and Lasserre (1987), adverse selection; Fudenberg, Holmstrom and Migrom (1986), moral hazard) research on principal-agent relationships has not envisaged the simultaneous presence of several alternative types of institutions.

The assumption of exclusive insurance contracting in discussed in section 2 and some aspects of the discounting issues are discussed in section 1. There remain the assumptions on the utility function. Although the theory of decision making under uncertainty has been challenged since its formal introduction by von Neumann and Morgenstern (Machina, 1987), it has produced very useful analytical tools for the study of optimal contracts such as optimal insurance coverage and the associated comparative statics, as well as the design of optimal contracts under moral hazard or the characterization of optimal insurance policies under adverse selection. In fact, very few contributions use nonlinear models in insurance literature (see however Karni, 1991) and none of these has addressed adverse selection. In this survey we then limit the discussion to the linear expected utility model. We also assume that utility functions are not function of the states of the world and that all individuals in all classes of risks have the same level of risk aversion. These assumptions are not necessary to get the desired results, but they permit the discussion to focus on differences in risk types.

1. Monopoly

1.1. Public information

There are two possible states of the world ($x \in \{n, a\}$): state (n), "no accident" having the probability ($1 - p_i$) and state (a), "accident" having the probability $0 < p_i < 1$. Consumers differ only by their probability of accident. For simplicity, there are two types of risk in the economy ($i \in \{H, L\}$ for high and low risk) with $p_H > p_L$. Each consumer owns a risky asset with monetary value $D(x)$; $D(a) = 0$ in state (a) and $D(n) = D$ in state (n). Therefore, the expected damage for a consumer of type i ($E_iD(x)$) is p_iD.

Under public information and without transaction cost, a risk-neutral private monopoly[1] would offer insurance coverage (net of premium) (β_i) for an insurance premium (α_i), such that a consumer will be indifferent between purchasing the policy and having no insurance (Stiglitz, 1977). In other words, the private monopolist maximizes his total profit over α_i, β_i, and λ_i:

Problem 1: $\underset{\alpha_i, \beta_i, \lambda_i}{Max} \ \Sigma q_i((1 - p_i)\alpha_i - p_i\beta_i)$ (1)

under the individual rationality (or participating) constraints

$$V(C_i|p_i) - V(C^0|p_i) \geq 0 \quad i = H, L \tag{2}$$

where

$V(C_i|p_i)$ is the expected utility under the contract $C_i = \{\alpha_i, \beta_i\}$:

$$V(C_i|p_i) = p_iU(W - D + \beta_i) + (1 - p_i)U(W - \alpha_i);$$

$U(\cdot)$ is a twice differentiable, strictly increasing and strictly concave function of final wealth ($U'(\cdot) > 0$, $U''(\cdot) < 0$);

W is nonrandom initial wealth;

C^0 denotes self-insurance; $C^0 = \{0, 0\}$ implies that $V(C^0|p_i) \equiv p_iU(W - D) + (1 - p_i)U(W)$; $V(C^0|p_i)$ is the reservation utility. Below this level, individuals will self-insure.

q_i is the number of policies sold to consumers of type i;

λ_i is a Lagrangian multiplier for constraint (2).

It is well known that full insurance, $\beta_i^* = D - \alpha_i^*$ (for $i = L, H$), is the solution to the above problem and that (2) is binding for both classes of risk, which means that

$$V(C_i^*|p_i) = V(C^0|p_i) \quad i = H, L$$

or $\alpha_i^* = p_iD + z_i^*,$

where z_i^* is the maximum unit-profit (or the maximum risk premium) on each policy. In other words z_i^* solves $U(W - p_iD - z_i^*) = p_iU(W - D) + (1 - p_i)U(W)$.

The private monopoly extracts all the consumer surplus. However, there is no efficiency cost since each individual buys full insurance as under perfect competition.[2] This is the classical result that Pareto-efficient risk sharing between a risk-averse agent and a risk-neutral principal shifts all the risk to the principal. To sum up we can write:

> *Proposition 1*: In the presence of public information about insureds' underlying risk, an optimal contract between a private monopolist and any individual of type i is characterized by
> a) full insurance coverage, $\beta_i^* = D - \alpha_i^*$;
> b) no consumer surplus, $V(C_i^*|p_i) = V(C^0|p_i)$.

Both solutions are shown at C_H^* and C_L^* in Figure 1 where C^0 is the "initial endowment" or self-insurance situation and where the vertical axis is wealth in the accident or loss state.

Any point to the northwest of C^0 and below or on the 45° degree line represents the wealth of the insured with any contract where $\alpha_i \geq 0$ and $\beta_i \geq 0$. Since the monopoly solution implies no-consumer surplus, it must lie on each risk type indifference curve passing through C^0. These in-

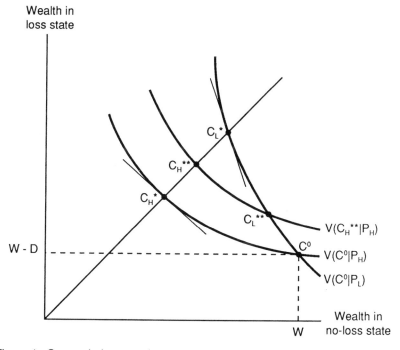

Figure 1. One-period monopoly contract.

difference curves are strictly convex since $U(\cdot)$ is strictly concave by assumption.[3]

1.2. Private information and single-period contracts

Under private information, the insurer does not observe the individual's risk type,[4] and must introduce mechanisms to ensure that agents will reveal this characteristic. Stiglitz (1977) extended the Rothschild-Stiglitz (1976) model to the monopoly case. In both contributions, price-quantity contracts[5] permit the separation of types by introducing incentives for individuals to reveal their type. Low-risk individuals reveal their identity by purchasing a policy that offers limited coverage at a low unit price. Thus they trade off insurance protection to signal their identity. Formally, risk revelation is obtained by adding two self-selection constraints to Problem 1:

$$V(C_i|p_i) - V(C_j|p_i) \geq 0 \quad i = H, L$$
$$j = H, L$$
$$i \neq j \tag{3}$$

Equation (3) guarantees that individual i prefers C_i to C_j. Let us use λ_{HL} and λ_{LH} for the corresponding Lagrangian multipliers where λ_{HL} is for the self-selection constraint of the H type risk. λ_{HL} and λ_{LH} cannot both the positive.[6] From Figure 1 it is easy to observe that, if the high risk individuals are indifferent between both contracts ($\lambda_{HL} > 0$), the low risk individuals will strictly prefer their own contracts ($\lambda_{LH} = 0$). Moreover, λ_{LH} cannot be positive when λ_{HL} is zero since this leads to a violation of (2). Therefore, a feasible solution can be obtained only when $\lambda_{HL} > 0$ and $\lambda_{LH} = 0$.

Figure 1 shows the solution to the maximization of (1) subject to (2) and (3) where low risk individuals choose a positive quantity of insurance[7] $\beta_L^{**} > 0$ and high risk individuals buy full insurance coverage ($\beta_H^{**} = \beta_H^*$). Separation of risks and profit maximization imply that $V(C_H^{**}|p_H) = V(C_L^{**}|p_H)$. As discussed above, it is clear that (3) and (2) cannot both be binding for the high risk individuals when it is possible for the low risks to buy insurance. In fact, Figure 1 indicates that C_H^{**} is strictly preferred to C_H^* which means that high risk individuals get some consumer surplus when the monopolist sells insurance to the low risk individuals. In other words, the rationality constraint (2) is not binding for the H individuals ($\lambda_H = 0$).

Another property of the solution is that good-risk individuals do not receive any consumer surplus ($\lambda_L > 0$). However, as discussed, they strictly prefer their contract to the contract offered to the bad-risk individuals. In other words

$$V(C_L^{**}|p_L) = V(C^0|p_L) \quad \text{and} \quad V(C_L^{**}|p_L) > V(C_H^{**}|p_L),$$

which means that the self-selection constraint is not binding for the low-risk individuals while the rationaliry constraint is.

In conclusion, one-period contracts with a self-selection mechanism increase the monopoly profits under private information compared with a single contract without any revelation mechanism, but they do not necessarily correspond to the best-risk allocation arrangement under asymmetrical information. In particular, good-risk individuals may not be able to buy any insurance coverage or, if they can, they are restricted to partial insurance. As we shall see in the next section, multi-period contracts can be used to relax the binding constraints and to improve resource allocation under asymmetrical information. In summary

Proposition 2: In the presence of private information, an optimal one-period contract menu between a private monopoly and individuals of types H and L has the following characteristics:

a) $\beta_H^{**} = D - \alpha_H^{**}; \beta_L^{**} < D - \alpha_L^{**}$
b) $V(C_H^{**}|p_H) > V(C^0|p_H); V(C_L^{**}|p_L) = V(C^0|p_L)$
c) $V(C_H^{**}|p_H) = V(C_L^{**}|p_H); V(C_L^{**}|p_L) > V(C_H^{**}|p_L)$

Proof: See Stiglitz (1977).

Stiglitz (1977) also considered a continuum of agent types and showed that some of the previous results can be obtained under additional conditions. However, in general, the presence of a continuum of agent types affects the results. For example, Riley (1979) showed that a Nash equilibrium never exists in the continuum case. (See also Riley, 1985).

1.3. Multi-period insurance contracts

Multi-period contracts are often observed in different markets. For example, in many countries, drivers buy automobile insurance with the same insurer for many years and insurers use bonus-malus systems (or experience rating) to relate insurance premiums to the individual's past experience. (Lemaire, 1985; Henriet and Rochet, 1984; Hey, 1985; Dionne and Vanasse, 1988). Long-term contracting also is observed in labor markets, workers' compensation insurance, service contracts, unemployment insurance, and many other markets. The introduction of multi-period contracts in the analysis gives rise to many issues such as the time horizon, discounting, commitment of the parties, myopic behavior, accident underreporting, and renegotiation. These issues are discussed in the following paragraphs.

Multi-period contracts are set, not only to adjust ex-post insurance premiums or insurance coverage to past experience, but also as a sorting device. They can be a complement or a substitute to standard self-selection mechanisms. However, in presence of full commitment, ex-ante risk announcement or risk revelation remains necessary to obtain optimal contracts under adverse selection.

In Cooper and Hayes (1987), multi-period contracts are presented as a complement to one period self-selection constraints. Since imperfect information reduces the monopolist's profits, the latter has an incentive to relax the remaining binding constraints by introducing contracts based on anticipated experience over time. By using price quantity contracts and full commitment in long-term contracts, Cooper and Hayes introduce a second instrument to induce self-selection and increase monopoly profits: experience rating increases the cost to high-risks from masquerading as low-risks by exposing them to second-period contingent coverages and premia.

Cooper and Hayes' model opens with a direct extension of the standard one-period contract presented above to a two-period world with full commitment on the terms of the contract. There is no discounting and all agents are able to anticipate the values of the relevant futures variables. To increase profits, the monopolist offers contracts in which premiums and coverages in the second period are a function of the accident history in the first period. Accidents are public information in their model. The two period contract C_i^2 is defined by:

$$C_i^2 = \{\alpha_i, \beta_i, \alpha_{ia}, \beta_{ia}, \alpha_{in}, \beta_{in}\}$$

where a and n mean "accident" and "no accident" in the first period and where α_{il} and $\beta_{il}(l = a, n)$ are "contingent" choice variables. Conditional on accident experience, the formal problem consists of maximizing two-period expected profits by choosing C_L^2 and C_H^2 under the following constraints:

$$V(C_i^2|p_i) \geq 2V(C^0|p_i) \tag{4.1}$$

$$\begin{aligned} V(C_i^2|p_i) \geq V(C_j^2|p_i) \quad &i = H, L \\ &j = H, L \\ &i \neq j \end{aligned} \tag{4.2}$$

where

$$V(C_i^2|p_k) \equiv p_k U(W - D + \beta_i) + (1 - p_k) U(W - \alpha_i)$$
$$+ p_k[p_k U(W - D + \beta_{ia}) + (1 - p_k) U(W - \alpha_{ia})]$$
$$+ (1 - p_k)[p_k U(W - D + \beta_{in}) + (1 - p_k)U(W - \alpha_{in})]$$
$$k = i, j \quad j = H, L \quad i = H, L \quad i \neq j$$

The above constraints show that agents are committed to the contract for the two periods. The model does not allow the parties to renegotiate the contract at the end of the first period. Moreover, the principal is committed to a loss-related adjustment of the insurance contract in the second period negotiated at the beginning of the first period; the insured is committed, for the second period, to buy the coverage and to pay the premium chosen at the beginning of the first period. It is also interesting to observe from (4) that the decisions concerning insurance coverage in each period depend on the anticipated variations in the premiums over time. In other words, (4) establishes that variations in both premia and coverages in the second period are a function of experience in the first period. Using the above model, Cooper and Hayes proved the following result:

Proposition 3: In the presence of private information, the monopoly increases his profits by offering an optimal two-period contract having the following characteristics:

1) High-risk individuals obtain full insurance coverage in each period and are not experience rated.

$$\hat{\alpha}_H = \hat{\alpha}_{Hn} = \hat{\alpha}_{Ha}, \hat{\beta}_H = \hat{\beta}_{Ha} = \hat{\beta}_{Hn}$$

where
$$\hat{\beta}_H = D - \hat{\alpha}_H$$

2) Low-risk individuals obtain partial insurance with experience rating.

$$\hat{\alpha}_{Ln} < \hat{\alpha}_L < \hat{\alpha}_{La}, \hat{\beta}_{La} < \hat{\beta}_L < \hat{\beta}_{Ln}$$

3) Low-risk individuals do not obtain any consumer surplus, and high-risk individuals are indifferent between the two contracts.

$$V(\hat{C}_L^2|p_L) = 2V(C^0|p_L),$$
$$V(\hat{C}_H^2|p_H) = V(\hat{C}_L^2|p_H)$$

Proof: See Cooper and Hayes (1987).

The authors also discussed an extension of their two-period model to the case in which the length of the contract may be extended to many periods. They showed that the same qualitative results as those in Proposition 3 hold with many periods.

Dionne (1983) and Dionne and Lasserre (1985, 1987) also investigated multi-period contracts in the presence of adverse selection.[8] Their models differ from that of Cooper and Hayes in many respects. The main differences concern the revelation mechanism, the sorting device, commitment assumptions, and the consideration of statistical information. Moreover, accidents are private information in their models. Unlike Cooper and Hayes, Dionne (1983) did not introduce self-selection constraints to obtain risk revelation. Instead risk revelation results from a Stackelberg game in which the insurer offers a contract in which the individual has to select an initial premium by making a risk announcement in the first period. Any agent who claims to be a low risk pays a corresponding low premium as long as his average loss is less than the expected loss given his declaration (plus a statistical margin of error to which we shall return). If that condition is not met, he is offered a penalty premium. Over time, the insurer records the agent's claims and offers to reinstate the policy at the low premium whenever the claims frequency becomes reasonable again.[9]

Following Dionne (1983) and Dionne and Lasserre (1985), the no-claims discount strategy consists of offering two full insurance premiums[10] $(F^1 = \{\alpha_L, \alpha_H\})$ in the first period and for $t = 1, 2, \cdots$

$$F^{t+1} \begin{cases} = \alpha_d \text{ if } \sum_{s=1}^{N(t)} \theta^s / N(t) < E_d D(x) + \delta_d^{N(t)} \\ \\ = \alpha_k \text{ otherwise} \end{cases}$$

where

α_d	is the full information premium corresponding to the declaration (d), $d\varepsilon\{L, H\}$
θ^s	is the amount of loss in contract period s, $\theta^s \in \{0, D\}$
α_k	is a penalty premium. α_k is such that $U(S - \alpha_k) < V(C_0 | p_H)$
$E_d D(x)$	is the expected loss corresponding to the announcement (d)
$\delta_d^{N(t)}$	is the statistical margin of error
$N(t)$	is the total number of periods with insurance; $N(t) \leq t$.

Therefore, from the construction of the model, $\sum_{s=1}^{N(t)} \theta^s / N(t)$ is the average loss claimed by the insured in the first $N(t)$ periods. If this number is strictly less then the declared expected loss plus some margin of error, the insurer offers α_d. Otherwise he offers α_k. The statistical margin of error is used to not penalize too often those who tell the truth. But it has to be small enough to detect those who try to increase their utility in announcing a risk class inferior to their true risk. From the Law of the Iterated Logarithm, one can show that

$$\delta_d^{N(t)} = \sqrt{2\gamma\sigma_d^2 \log\log N(t)/N(t)}, \quad \gamma > 1$$

where σ_d^2 is the variance of the individual's loss corresponding to the declaration (d), and $\delta_d^{N(t)}$ converges to zero over time (with arbitrary large values for $N(t) = 1, 2$).

Graphically, we can represent $E_d D(x) + \delta_d^{N(t)}$ in the following way: We see in Figure 2 that as $N(t) \to \infty$, $E_d D(x) + \delta_d^{N(t)} \to E_d D(x)$. Over time, only a finite number of points representing $(\Sigma\theta^s/N(t))$ will have a value outside the shaded zone.

Proposition 4 below shows that the public information allocation of risks is obtainable using the no-claims discount strategy as $T \to \infty$ and as long as the agents do not discount the future.[11]

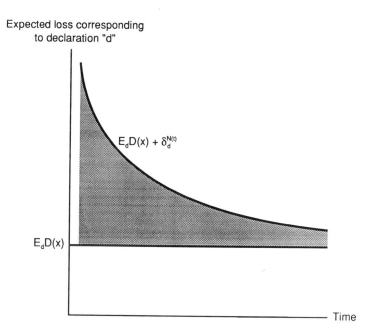

Figure 2. Graphical representation of $E_d D(x) + \delta_d^{N(t)}$.

Proposition 4: Let α_i be such that:

$$\alpha_i - E_i D(x) \geq 0 \text{ and } U(W - \alpha_i) \geq V(C^0 | p_i).$$

Then, when $T \to \infty$, there exists a pair of optimal strategies for the individual of type i and the private monopoly having the following properties:
1) the strategy of the monopoly is a no-claims discount strategy; the strategy of insured i is to tell the truth about his type in period 1 and to buy insurance in each period;
2) the optimal corresponding payoffs are $\alpha_i^* - E_i D(x) = z_i^*$ and $U(W - \alpha_i^*) = V(C^0 | p_i)$, $i = H, L$;
3) both strategies are enforceable.

Proof: See Dionne and Lasserre (1985).

It is also possible to obtain a solution close to the public information allocation of risks in finite horizon insurance contracts. Dionne and Lasserre (1987) showed how a trigger strategy with revisions[12] may establish the existence of an ε-equilibrium. This concept of ε-equilibrium is due to Radner (1981) and was also developed in a moral hazard context. Extending the definition to the adverse selection problem, Dionne and Lasserre (1987) defined an ε-equilibrium as a triplet of strategies (principal, low-risk individual, high-risk individual) such that, under these strategies, the expected utility of any one agent is at least equal to his expected utility under public information less epsilon. In fact, the expected utility of the high-risk individual is that of the full information equilibrium.

As for the case of an infinite number of periods,[13] Dionne and Lasserre (1987) showed that it is in the interest of the monopolist (he obtains higher profits) to seek risk revelations on the part of the insured rather than simply to use the statistical instrument to discriminate between low-risk and high-risk agents. In other words, their second main result shows that it is optimal to use statistical tools not only to adjust, ex-post, insurance premiums according to past experience, but also, to provide an incentive for the insured to announce, ex-ante, the true class of risk he represents. Finally, they obtained that a multi-period contract with announcement dominates a repetition of one-period self-selection mechanisms (Stiglitz, 1977) when the number of periods is sufficiently large and there is no discounting.

Another characteristic of the Dionne and Lasserre (1987) model is that low-risk agents do not have complete insurance coverage when the number of periods is finite; they chose not to insure if they are unlucky enough to be considered as high-risk individuals. However, they always choose to be insured in the fist period and most of them will obtain full insurance in each period. Finally, it must be pointed out that the introduction of a continuum of agent types does not create any difficulty in the sense that full separation of risks is obtained without any additional condition.

In Dionne (1983) and Dionne and Lasserre (1985) there is no incentive for accident underreporting at equilibrium since there is no benefit associated with underreporting. When the true classes of risk are announced, insureds cannot obtain any premium reduction by underreporting accidents. When the number of periods is finite, matters are less simple since each period does matter. In some circumstances, the insured has to evaluate the tradeoff between increased premiums in the future and no coverage in the present. This is true even when the contract involves commitment and no renegotiation as in Dionne and Lasserre (1987). For example, the unlucky good risk may prefer to receive no insurance coverage during a particular period in order to pass over a trigger date and have the opportunity to pay the full information premium as long as his average loss is less than the reasonable average loss corresponding to his class of risk.

The benefits of underreporting can be shown to be nil in a two-period model with full commitment and no statistical instrument and when the contract cannot be renegotiated over time (see the Appendix for a formalization of the following discussion). To see this, let us go back to the two-period model presented earlier (Cooper and Hayes, 1987) and assume that accidents are now private information. When there is ex ante full commitment by the two parties to the contract one can write a contract where the net benefit to any type of agent from underreporting is zero. High-risk individuals have full insurance and no experience rating at equilibrium and low-risk individuals have the same level of expected utility whatever the accident reporting at the end of the second period. However, private information about accidents reduces insurer's profits when we compare it with the situation where accidents are public information.

In all the preceding discussions it was assumed that the insurer can precommit to the contract over time. It was shown that an optimal contract under full commitment can be interpreted as a single transaction in which the incentive constraints are modified to improve insurance possibilities for the low-risk individuals and to increase profits. Since there is full commitment and no renegotiation, accident histories are uninformative on the risk type. This form of commitment is optimal in Dionne (1983) and Dionne and Lasserre (1985) since, as in the Arrow-Debreu world, neither party to the contract can gain from renegotiation. However, in a finite horizon world, the role of renegotiation becomes important since self-selection in the first period implies that future contracts might be inefficient given the public information available after the initial period. When the good risks have completely revealed their type, it becomes advantageous to both parties — the insurer and the low-risk individuals — to renegotiate a full insurance contract for the second period. Although the possibilities of renegotiation improve welfare in the second period (ex post), they violate the ex-ante self-selection constraints and reduce ex-ante welfare. In other words, renegotiation limits the commitment possibilities and reduces ex-ante parties' welfare. For example, if the high-risk individuals anticipate renegotiations in the second period, they will not reveal their type in the first period (Dionne and Doherty, 1991).

Formally, we can interpret the possibility of renegotiation as adding a new constraint to the set of feasible contracts: unless parties can pre-commit not to renegotiate, then contracts must be incentive compatible and renegotiation-proof (Dewatripont, 1989; Bolton, 1990). To reduce the possibilities for renegotiation in the second period, the insurer who is unable to commit not to renegotiate after new information is revealed, must set the contract so that the insured type will not be perfectly known after the first period. This implies that the prospect of renegotiation reduces the speed of information revelation over time. In other words, the prospect of renegotiation can never improve the long-term contract possibilities. In many circumstances, a sequence of one-period contracts will give the same outcome as a renegotiated-proof long-term contract; in other circumstances a renegotiation-proof long-term contract dominates (when intertemporal transfers are allowed, for example) (Hart and Tirole, 1988; Laffont and Tirole, 1987, 1990; Dionne and Doherty 1991).

Recently, Hosios and Peters (1989) presented a formal model that rules out any renegotiation by assuming that only one-period contracts are enforceable.[14] They also discussed the possibility of renegotiation in the second period when this renegotiation is beneficial to both parties. Although they cannot show formally the nature of the equilibrium under this alternative, they obtained interesting qualitative results. For example, when the equilibrium contract corresponds to incomplete risk revelation in the first period, the seller offers, in the second period, a choice of contract that depends on the experience of the first period. Therefore accident underreporting is possible with commitment and renegotiation. This result is similar to that obtained in their formal model where they ruled out any form of commitment for contracts that last for more than one period. Only one-period contracts are enforceable. They showed the following results:

Proposition 5: In the absence of any form of commitment from both parties to the contract:

1) Without discounting, separating equilibria do not exist; only pooling and semiseparating equilibria are possible.[15]
2) Accident underreporting can now affect the seller's posterior beliefs about risk types and insurance buyers may fail to report accidents in order to avoid premium increases.

Proof: See Hosios and Peters (1989).

The first result implies that the insurer does not have full information on the risk types at the end of the first period; therefore, accident reports become informative on the risk type (contrary to the Cooper and Hayes model). However, the authors did not discuss the optimality of such two-period contracts. It is not clear that a sequence of one-period contracts with separating equilibrium does not dominate their sequence of contracts.

2. Competitive contracts

The introduction of competition raises many new issues. The two main issues that will be discussed here are 1) the choice of an adequate equilibrium concept and 2) the nature of information between competitive insurers. It will be shown that many well-known and standard results are sustained under the strong assumptions that all the insurers share the same information about an individual's choice of contracts and accident experience. To discuss these and other issues clearly, let us first present the standard public information case.

2.1. Public information about an individual's characteristics

Under competition, firms are now constrained to earn zero expected profits. When information on individual risk characteristics is public, each firms knows the risk type of each individual. The optimal individual contract is the solution to:

Problem 2:

$$\underset{\alpha_i, \beta_i, \lambda_i}{\text{Max}} \; p_i \, U(W - D + \beta_i) + (1 - p_i) \, U(W - \alpha_i) + \lambda_i[(1 - p_i)\alpha_i - p_i\beta_i]$$

$$i = L, \quad H$$

where $(1 - p_i)\alpha_i = p_i\beta_i$ is the zero-profit constraint.

As for the monopoly case under public information, the solution to Problem 2 yields full insurance coverage for each type of risk. The optimal solutions, $\bar{C}_H$ and $\bar{C}_L$ in Figure 3 correspond to levels of con-

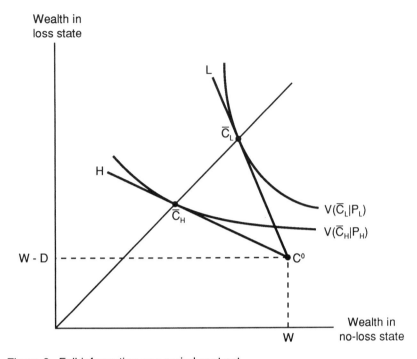

Figure 3. Full information one-period contract.

sumer welfare greater than in the no-insurance case (C^0). However, as already pointed out, the monopoly solution under private information also yields full insurance coverage and does not introduce any distortion in risk allocation. The difference between the monopoly and competitive cases is that, in the former, consumer surplus is extracted by the insurer, while in the latter it is retained by both types of policyholder.

Under competition, the zero-profit constraint passes through C^0 and the absolute value of its slope is equal to $(1 - p_i)/p_i$. Each point $\bar{C}_i$ represents the expected wealth of an individual of type i. The full information solutions are obtained when the slopes of indifference curves are just equal to the ratio of the probability of not having an accident to that of having an accident.

2.2. Private information and single-period contracts

It is clear that, under asymmetrical information, traditional full information competitive contracts are not adequate to allocate risk optimally. Consequently, many authors have investigated the role of sorting devices in a competitive environment. The first contributions on the subject in competitive markets are by Spence (1973), Pauly (1974), Rothschild and Stiglitz (1976), and Wilson (1977). The literature on competition in markets with adverse selection is now very large and it is not our intention here to review all significant contributions. Our selection of models was made with criteria that will be identified and explained when it will become appropriate.[16]

A first division that we can make is between models of signaling (informed agents move first) and of screening (uninformed agents move first) (Stiglitz and Weiss, 1984). Spence (1973) and Cho and Kreps (1987) models are of the first type and are mainly applied to labor contracts in which the workers (informed agents) move first by choosing an education level (signal). Then employers bid for the services of the workers and the latter choose the more appropriate or preferred bids. Cho and Kreps (1987) present conditions under which this three-stage game generates a Riley (1979a) single-period separating equilibrium.[17] Without restrictions (or conditions as those proposed by Cho and Kreps (1987)) on out-of-equilibrium beliefs, many equilibria arise simultaneously, which limit considerably the explanatory power of the traditional signaling models.[18]

Although it may be possible to find interpretations of the signaling models in insurance markets, it is generally believed that the screening interpretation is more natural. Rothschild and Stiglitz (1976) and Wilson (1977) introduced to the literature an insurance model with a screening behavior. In their model only a two-stage game is considered. First, the uninformed insurer offers some contracts to the informed agents who then choose among the contracts in the second stage.

Let us start with the Rothschild and Stiglitz (1976) example in which the insurers set premiums with constant marginal costs (as in the Bertrand model). Each insurer knows the proportions of good risks and bad risks in the market but has no information on an insured's type. Moreover, each insured cannot, by assumption, buy insurance from many insurers. Otherwise, the individual insurers would not be able to observe the individual's total amount of insurance coverage and would not be able to discriminate easily.[19]

It is clear that the nature of the equilibrium is a function of how individual firms anticipate the behavior of rivals. Rothschild and Stiglitz (1976) assumed that each insurer follows a pure Cournot-Nash strategy, in which each insurer takes the actions of its competitors as given. This results in an equilibrium having the following properties: a) no contract in the equilibrium set makes negative expected profits; b) there is no contract outside the equilibrium set that can make a positive profit when included in the original set. They obtained two significant results:

Proposition 6: When insurers follow a pure Cournot-Nash strategy in a two-stage screening game:
a) A pooling equilibrium is not possible; the only possible equilibria are separating equilibria.
b) A separating equilibrium may not exist.

A pooling equilibrium is an equilibrium in which both types of risk buy the same contract. Assume that the publicly observable proportions of good-risk and bad-risk individuals are respectively δ and $(1 - \delta)$, and the average price of insurance is $\bar{p}$. This corresponds to the line $C^\circ F$ in Figure 4a. To see why the Cournot-Nash definition of equilibrium is not compatible with a pooling equilibrium, assume that (C_1) in the figure is a pooling equilibrium contract for a given insurer. By definition, it corresponds to zero expected profits; otherwise another insurer in the market will offer another pooling contract. Because of the relative slopes of the risk type indifference curves, there always exists a contract (C_2) that will be preferred to contract (C_1) by the low-risk individuals. The existence of contract (C_2) contradicts the above definition of a Cournot-Nash equilibrium. Consequently, if there exists an equilibrium, it has to be a separating one in which different risk-type consumers receive different insurance contracts. As for the monopoly case, the formal solution is obtained by adding one self-selection constraint to Problem 2 and by verifying that, at equilibrium, the high-risk individuals receive full insurance and the low-risk types receive less than full insurance.[20] (See Wilson (1977) for a formal analysis.) Again the self-selection constraint is binding for the high-risk individuals only, and the profit constraint is binding at zero expected profits.

Graphically, $\mathring{C}_L$ and $\mathring{C}_H$ in Figure 4b correspond to a separating equilibrium. In equilibrium, high-risk individuals buy full insurance ($\mathring{C}_H = \bar{C}_H$), while low-risk individuals get only partial insurance ($\mathring{C}_L$).[21] Each firm earns zero expected profit on each contract. This equilibrium has the advantage for the low-risk agents that their equilibrium premium corresponds to their actuarial risk and does not contain any subsidy to the high-risk individuals. However, a cost is borne by low-risk insureds in that their equilibrium contract delivers only partial insurance compared with full insurance in the full information case. Only high-risk individuals receive the first best risk allocation. Finally, the separating equilibrium may not be Pareto optimal in the sense that it is possible to improve the welfare of individuals in each class of risk. We will come back to this issue.

The second important result from Rothschild and Stiglitz is that there

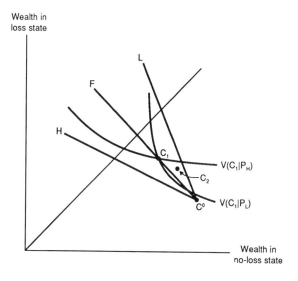

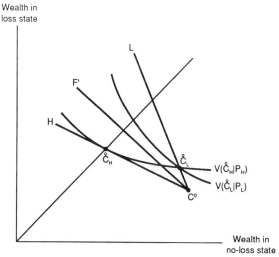

Figure 4. The Rothschild-Stiglitz model.

are conditions under which a separating equilibrium does not exist. In general, there is no equilibrium if the costs of pooling are low to the low-risk individuals (few high-risk individuals or low $(1 - \delta)$), which is not the case in Figure 4b since the line C^0F' corresponds to a value of δ lower than the critical level δ^{RS} permitting separating equilibria) or if the costs of separating are high (structure of preference). In the former case, given the separating contracts, the cost of sorting (partial insurance) exceeds the benefits (no subsidy) when profitable pooling opportunities exist. But, as already shown, a pooling contract cannot be an equilibrium. This negative result has prompted further theoretical investigations since many insurance markets do function even in the presence of adverse selection.

One such extension is to consider a mixed strategy in which an insurer's strategy is a probability distribution over a pair of contracts. Rosenthal and Weiss (1984) showed that a separating Nash equilibrium always exists when the insurers adopt this strategy.[22] However, it is not clear that a mixed strategy has any particular economic interpretation in insurance markets as in many other markets. Another extension is to introduce a three-stage game in which the insurer may reject in the third stage, the insured's contract choice made in the second stage. Hellwig (1986, 1987) showed that a pooling contract may correspond to a sequential equilibrium of the three-stage game or it can never be upset by a separating contract whenever pooling is Pareto preferred. Moreover, contrary to the Rothschild-Stiglitz two-stage model, the three-stage game always has a sequential equilibrium in pure strategies. The most plausible sequential equilibrium is pooling rather than sorting, while in a three-stage game in signaling models (Cho and Kreps, 1987) it is the pooling rather than the separating equilibria that lack robustness. As pointed out by Hellwig (1987), the conclusions are very sensitive to the details of game specification.

Another type of extension that permits the existence of equilibria is to allow firms to consider other firms' behavior or reactions in their strategies and then to abandon the pure Nash strategy in the two-stage game. For example, Wilson (1977) proposed an anticipatory equilibrium concept where firms drop policies so that those remaining (after other firms anticipated reactions) at least break even. The resulting equilibrium (pooling or separation) always exists. By definition, a Wilson equilibrium exists if no insurer can offer a policy such that 1) this new policy yields nonnegative profits and 2) remains profitable after other insurers have withdrawn all nonprofitable policies in reaction to the offer.

A Wilson equilibrium is a Nash equilibrium when a separating equilibrium exists; otherwise it is a pooling equilibrium.[23] Wilson also considered subsidization between policies, but Miyazaki (1977) and Spence (1977) developed the idea more fully. They showed how to improve welfare of both classes of risk (or of all n classes of risk; Spence (1977)) with low-risk class subsidizing the high-risk class. In fact, Spence has shown that, in a model in which firms react (in the sense of Wilson) by dropping loss-

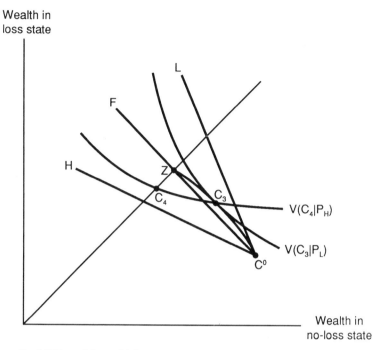

Figure 5. A Wilson-Miyazaki-Spence equilibrium with cross subsidization.

making policies, there is a unique equilibrium. In all the above models, each of the contracts in the menu available is defined to permit the low-risk policyholders to signal their true risk. The resulting equilibrium is a break-even portfolio of separating contracts, and exists regardless of the value of δ. More formally we have

Proposition 7: A Wilson-Miyazaki-Spence (WMS) equilibrium exists regardless of the value of δ. When $\delta \leq \delta^{RS}$, the WMS equilibrium corresponds to the Rothschild-Stiglitz equilibrium.

One such equilibrium (C_3, C_4) is presented in Figure 5 for the case of two risk classes with cross-subsidization from the low to the high-risk group. The line $(C^0 \, C_3 \, Z)$ is the zero-profit locus defined such that contract pairs yield a zero profit to the insurer.

The above equilibrium is second-best efficient in the sense of Harris and Townsend (1981). An allocation is second best efficient if it is Pareto optimal within the set of allocations that are feasible under the feasible constraints (self-selection constraints and the zero-profit constraints on the portfolio).[24] In fact Crocker and Snow (1985) proved the following proposition:

> **Proposition 8:** A Wilson-Miyazaki-Spence equilibrium is second-best efficient for all values of δ.

Proof: See Crocker and Snow (1985).

It can be shown that a Rothschild-Stiglitz equilibrium is second-best efficient if, and only if, δ is lower than some critical value $\hat{\delta}$, which is itself lower than the critical value δ^{RS}, permitting the existence of a Nash equilibrium. Then, as mentioned, a Nash equilibrium is not necessarily efficient. The same conclusion applies to the Riley equilibrium since it sustains the Rothschild-Stiglitz solution whatever the value of δ. Finally, as we will see in section 2.4, another possibility to deal with equilibrium issues is to use risk categorization (Bond and Crocker, 1990).

2.3. Multi-period contracts

Let us begin with Cooper and Hayes's (1987) analysis of two-period contracts with full commitment on the supply side. Cooper and Hayes used the Nash equilibrium concept in a two-stage, two-period game that implies that the equilibrium must be a separating equilibrium.[25] In fact, they considered two different behaviors about commitment. First, both insurers and insureds commit themselves to the two-period contracts (without renegotiation) and, second, the insurers commit to a two-period contract but the contract is not binding on insureds. We will refer the respective assumptions as contracts with full commitment and with semi-commitment. When competitive firms can bind agents to the two periods, it is easy to show that, in the separating solution, the contracts offered are qualitatively identical to that of the monopoly solution with commitment: high-risk agents receive full insurance at an actuarial price in each period while low-risk agents face price and quantity adjustments in the second period.

When the authors relax the strong commitment assumption in favor of semi-commitment, and consider that insureds can costlessly switch to other firms in the second period, they show that the presence of second-period competition limits, but does not destroy, the use of experience rating as a sorting device. The difference between the results with full commitment and semi-commitment is explained by the fact that the punishment possibilities for period one accidents are reduced by

.

the presence of other firms that offer single-period contracts in the second period.

The semi-commitment result was obtained by assuming that, in the second period, entrant firms offer single-period contracts without any knowledge of insureds' accident histories or their choice of contract in the first period. The new firms' optimal behavior is to offer a Rothschild-Stiglitz separating contract to those who switch.[26] By taking this decision as given, the design of the optimal two-period contract by competitive firms with semi-commitment has to take into account at least one supplementary binding constraint that reduces social welfare when we compare it to full commitment. In other words, the presence of competition, combined with agents' inability to enforce multi-period contracts, reduces the usefulness of long-term contracts as a sorting device and, consequently, the potential gains of long-term relationships. This conclusion is similar to that obtained in the monopoly case in which the principal cannot commit on nonrenegotiation.

These results can be summarized by the following proposition, which was derived from the maximization problem (A2) presented in the Appendix:

Proposition 9: Let us assume that a Nash equilibrium exists. Then the optimal two-period contracts are characterized by the following properties:
a) With full commitment

$$\alpha_{Ln} < \alpha_L < \alpha_{La}, \beta_{La} < \beta_L < \beta_{Ln}$$

b) With semi-commitment

$$\alpha_{Ln} < \alpha_L, \beta_L < \beta_{Ln}$$

c) In both cases

$$\alpha_{Hn} = \alpha_H = \alpha_{Ha}, \beta_{Ha} = \beta_H = \beta_{Hn}$$

An important result arising from semi-commitment concerns the evolution of profits over time. The insurers are constrained to earn zero expected profits for the two periods. For high-risk individuals, expected profits are zero in each period. At equilibrium, firms make positive expected profits on low-risk individuals' contracts during the first period and from the second-period contract corresponding to the loss state in the first period. Negative profits are earned on second-period contracts for low risks who suffered no first-period loss. In aggregate, expected two period profits for low risks are zero. This arrangement provides an appropriate bonus for accident free experience and ensures that low risks who suffer an accident remain with the firm.[27]

This temporal profit pattern for the good risks was labeled *highballing* by D'Arcy and Doherty (1990) and was shown to stand in contrast with the lowballing predicted by Kunreuther and Pauly (1985).[28] Nilssen (1990) also obtained a lowballing prediction. Despite the clear differences between the last two contributions, the results are quite similar. Insurers make negative expected profits in the first period and make positive profits on the policies they renew. The similarity in this lowballing prediction is mainly due to the fact that both articles assume that long-term contracts are not written while, as we saw, Cooper and Hayes permitted long-term contracting. The three contributions assume that insurers have private information on their own policyholders but Kunreuther and Pauly also assume that insurers have private information on current contracts, which does not allow them to use the price-quantity contracting. They argue that insurers are unable to write exclusive contracts; instead they propose that insurers offer only pure price contracts (Pauly, 1974), which implies that they necessarily obtain a pooling equilibrium. Over time, the contracting insurer obtains a Bayesian update of its policyholders' loss distribution not available to rivals so that policyholders do not sort themselves into distinct risk classes. In contrast to Kunreuther and Pauly, Nilssen (1990) use the basic framework of the Rothschild-Stiglitz model. This last difference explains the types of equilibrium obtained while their similar assumptions on commitment and observation of individual's accident history explain their similar conclusions on lock-in in which each firm earns a positive expected profit on its old customers since it controls information on past experience.[29] Finally, contrary to the monopoly case, absence of commitment in the Nilssen model does not rule out separation.

Table 1 compares the competing models. The table presents also some extensions of the Hosios-Peters model to competition. As for Kunreuther and Pauly, and Nilssen, Hosios and Peters assume no commitment on the supply side and consider that rivals observe all contract choices. According to Nilssen, accidents are private information between the insured and the insurer and are thus not observed by the rival firms. Accident reporting is public information according to Hosios and Peters, but accidents are not. This last distinction permits explicit consideration of accident underreporting, an important empirical phenomenon in the automobile insurance industry. Finally, Dionne and Doherty (1991) introduce renegotiation in a model with commitment. They first show that fully separating strategies (Cooper and Hayes (1987)), when renegotiated, degenerate to replications of single-period payoffs. They then present an alternative equilibrium that may involve partial pooling in the first period followed by separation. They show that the equilibrium is a full separating equilibrium when the discount factor is low and tends to a pooling for large discount factors.

Table 1. Comparison of Competitive Models

Characteristics	Kunreuther and Pauly single period equilibria	Cooper and Hayes nonbinding model	Nilssen	Hosios and Peters with competition	Dionne and Doherty
Price-quantity contracts	no	yes	yes	yes	yes
Commitment to more than one period					
insurer	no	yes	no	no	yes
insured	no	no	no	no	no
Insurers observe					
total contract choice	no	yes	yes	yes	yes
accidents	no (claims only)	yes	yes	no (claims only)	yes
Rivals observe					
contract choices	no	yes in the current period no for entrants	yes	yes	yes
loss experience	no	no	no	?	no
Type of equilibrium					
first period	pooling	separating	pooling or separating	pooling or separating	pooling or separating
second period	pooling	separating	separating	pooling or separating	separating

Table 1. Continued

Characteristics	Kunreuther and Pauly single period equilibria	Cooper and Hayes nonbinding model	Nilssen	Hosios and Peters with competition	Dionne and Doherty
Accident underreporting	?	no	no	yes when pooling in the second period	no
Consumer lock-in	yes	no	yes when pooling in the first period	?	no
Temporal profit pattern	lowballing	highballing	lowballing	?	highballing when pooling in the first period

The issue of consumer lock-in has motivated D'Arcy and Doherty (1990) to undertake an empirical investigation of the significance of adverse selection and of the testable predictions that permit discrimination between the competing models. Their results first show evidence of adverse selection in the U.S. automobile insurance markets, a result also found by Dahlby (1983, 1991) in the Canadian automobile insurance market. They also show empirical evidence of lowballing, which is consistent with the Nilssen and Kunreuther and Pauly models. Dionne and Doherty (1991) extended D'Arcy and Doherty's (1990) empirical analysis. Most of their results also favor the lowballing predictions.

2.4. Risk categorization

Adverse selection can explain the use of risk categorization in insurance markets based on variables that procure information at a low cost (Hoy, 1982). For example, in automobile insurance, age and sex variables are significant in explaining probabilities of accidents (Dionne and Vanasse, 1988). Particularly, young male drivers (less than 25) are much more risky to insure than the average driver. Since it is almost costless to observe age and sex, an insurer may find it profitable to offer policies with higher premiums to young males. However, such categorization is now prohibited in some states and countries.

As mentioned above, Dahlby (1983) provided some empirical evidence that adverse selection is present in the Canadian automobile insurance market. He also suggested that his empirical results are in accordance with the Wilson-Miyazaki-Spence model that allows for cross-subsidization between individuals in each segment defined by a categorization variable such as sex or age: low-coverage policies (low risks) subsidizing high-coverage policies (high risks) in each segment.[30] This important statistical result raises the following question. Does statistical categorization enhance efficiency in the presence of adverse selection? In other words, can welfare be improved by using the public information on agents' characteristics (such as age and sex) in offering insurance contracts in presence of adverse selection?

Crocker and Snow (1985, 1986) showed that, if the observable characteristics are correlated with hidden knowledge, costless imperfect categorization always enhances efficiency where efficiency is defined as in Harris and Townsend (1981). However, when categorization entails some positive cost, the results are ambiguous.[31]

Another important contribution in Crocker and Snow (1986) concerns the existence of a balanced-budget tax-subsidy policy that provides private incentives to use costless categorization. With appropriate taxes, no agent loses as a result of categorization. The results are shown for the Wilson-Miyazaki-Spence equilibrium concept but can also sustain an efficient allocation in a Nash equilibrium with a tax systen (Crocker and Snow, 1985). Finally, their conclusions can be applied to the Wilson anticipatory equilibrium or to the Riley reactive equilibrium, both with a tax system. It then becomes clear that prohibiting discrimination on equity considerations imposes efficiency costs in insurance markets (such as automobile insurance) where categorization based on age and sex variables is costless.

3. Moral Hazard and Adverse Selection

Although in many situations principals face adverse selection and moral hazard problems simultaneously when they design contracts, these two types of asymmetrical information have been given separate treatment so far in the economic literature on risk-sharing agreements. Recently, both information problems have been integrated into a single model in which all the parties of the contract are risk neutral (Laffont and Tirole, 1986; Picard, 1987; Caillaud, Guesnerie, Rey, and Tirole, 1988; Guesnerie, Picard, and Rey, 1988). Although these models involve uncertainty, they are unable to explain arrangements in which at least one party is risk averse. In particular they do not apply to insurance. More recently, some authors have attempted to integrate both information problems into a single model in which the agent is risk averse.[32]

As already discussed by Dionne and Lasserre (1988) such an integration of both information problems is warranted on empirical grounds. Applied studies are still few in this area, but they will find it difficult to avoid considering both kinds of information asymmetry. In the insurance literature, for example, one significant contribution is that by Dahlby (1983), who studied the relationship between statistical discrimination and adverse selection. On the basis of differences in accident frequencies between groups or insurance types, he concluded that adverse selection was present in the market studied. However it is not clear in his study that adverse selection is the only source of resource misallocation since moral hazard might also explain part of the frequency differences (see Dahlby (1991), Arnott (1991), and Dionne and Vanasse (1988) for a similar discussion).

3.1. Monopoly and multi-period contracts

Dionne and Lasserre (1988) showed how it is possible to achieve a first-best allocation of risks when moral hazard and adverse selection problems are present simultaneously. While they draw heavily on the contributions of Rubinstein and Yaari (1983), Dionne (1983) and Dionne and Lasserre (1985), the integration of the two types of information problems is not a straightforward exercise. Since an agent who has made a false announcement may now choose an action that is statistically compatible with his announcement, false announcements may go undetected. They proposed a contract under which the agent cannot profit from this additional degree of freedom. Under a combination of moral hazard and adverse selection, several types of customers can adopt different care levels so that they have identical expected losses. When this happens, it is impossible to distinguish those who produce an efficient level of care from the others on the basis of average losses. However, deviant behaviors can be detected by monitoring deviations from the mean.

Thus the insurer's strategy can be written with more than one simple aggregate (as in Dionne and Lasserre (1985) and Rubinstein and Yaari (1983)). In Dionne and Lasserre (1988) the principal has to monitor two aggregates, the average loss experienced by a given agent and its squared deviation from the mean. However, it was sufficient to get the desired result since, in their model, the information problem has only two dimensions. More generally, the insurer would have to monitor one moment of the distribution for each hidden dimension.

Combining moral hazard with adverse selection problems in models that use past experience might involve some synergetic effects. In the model presented in Dionne and Lasserre (1988), the same information required to eliminate either the moral hazard problem alone (Rubinstein and Yarri), or adverse selection alone (Dionne and Lasserre), is used to remove both problems simultaneously. A related subject concerns the efficient use of past information and the allocation of instruments toward the solution of each particular information problem. For a long time, self-selection mechanisms have been proposed in response to adverse selection while nonlinear pricing was advocated against moral hazard. In one-period contracts both procedures used separately involve inefficiency (partial insurance), which can be reduced by the introduction of time in the contracts. Dionne and Lasserre showed that self-selection may help solve moral hazard problems as well as adverse selection problems. We will now discuss how the use of two instruments may improve resource allocation and welfare when both problems are present simultaneously in single-period competitive contracts.

3.2. Competitive contracts and risk categorization

One of the arguments often used to justify the prohibition of risk categorization is that it is based on fixed or exogenous characteristics such as age, race, and sex. However, as pointed out by Bond and Crocker (1991), insurers also use other characteristics that are chosen by individuals. They extended Crocker and Snow's (1986) previous analysis of risk categorization in the presence of adverse selection and examined the equilibrium and efficiency implications of risk categorization based on the consumption of goods that are statistically related to an individual's risks, which they termed *correlative products*.

Formally, their model introduces endogenous categorization in an environment characterized by both moral hazard and adverse selection. They show that, while there is a natural tension between the sorting of risk classes engendered by adverse selection and the correction of externalities induced by moral hazard, the use of risk classification improves efficiency in resource allocation. They also discover that the sorting of risks based on correlative consumption may give a first-best allocation as a Nash equilibria when adverse selection is not too severe and when the insurer can observe individual consumption of the hazardous good. This is particularly interesting as an alternative view of how firms, *in practice*, may overcome the nonexistence of Nash equilibrium problems.

They then considered the case in which the insurer cannot observe both the individual's consumption and the individual's characteristics. However, the planner can observe aggregate production of the good. They showed that taxation of the consumption good has now two roles (it reduces moral hazard and relaxes self-selection constraints) that permit Pareto improvements.

Cromb (1990) analyzed the simultaneous presence of moral hazard and adverse selection in competitive insurance markets[33] and obtained that the addition of moral hazard to the standard Rothschild-Stiglitz (1976) model with adverse selection has qualitative effects on the nature and existence of equilibrium. Under certain circumstances the addition of moral hazard may eliminate the adverse selection problem but, more generally, it constitutes a new source of nonexistence of a Nash equilibrium. This result contrasts with the conclusion obtained by Bond and Crocker (1991) who showed that risk categorization makes Nash equilibrium more likely.

Conclusion

In this paper we have reviewed recent developments in the theory of adverse selection in insurance markets. Our objective was to highlight significant results in the literature. We started with the monopoly case. Since the article by Stiglitz (1977), many authors have investigated sorting devices other than self-selection in one-period contracts to improve resource allocation under adverse selection. One motivation was that low-risk individuals may not have any insurance coverage at the equilibrium of the single-period contract. Another motivation was that long-term relationships are observed in many insurance markets.

A first important result is that, in the presence of full commitment between the parties, multi-period contracts are optimal not only to adjust ex-post insurance premia, but also to seek risk revelation on the part of the insured. Multi-period contracts can be a complement (Cooper and Hayes, 1987) or a substitute (Dionne, 1983; Dionne and Lasserre, 1985) to the standard self-selection mechanims used in single-period contracts. However, the role of renegotiation has become important in recent literature. Under certain circumstances, when the good risks have declared their type in the first period, it becomes advantageous to both parties (the insurer and the good-risk individuals) to renegotiate full insurance contracts in the second period. However, although the possibilities of renegotiation improve welfare in the second period, when anticipated they violate the ex-ante self-selection constraints and reduce ex-ante benefits associated with risk revelation. The prospect of renegotiation reduces the speed of information revelation, and pooling or semi-pooling contracts may become optimal (Hosios and Peters, 1989; Dionne and Doherty, 1991).

The introduction of competition raised many issues. The two main issues that were discussed are 1) the choice of an adequate equilibrium concept and 2) the nature of information between insurers. In the case of a single-period contract, it was shown by Hellwig (1988) that when the sharing of information about customers is treated endogenously in a two-stage game, the resulted equilibrium is more akin to the Wilson reactive equilibrium than to the competitive Nash equilibrium. The predictions about the nature of contracts and the temporal profit patterns in multi-period contracting also depend upon the assumptions made on the nature of information between the insurers. Table 1 compares the competing models. It also compares assumptions made on both commitment between the parties to the contract and information about total contract choice and accident observation.

There was much literature in the 1970s on the nature of equilibrium concepts in the presence of adverse selection. The different contributions were motivated by the negative result obtained by Rothschild and Stiglitz that a Nash equilibrium may not exist in a two-stage game. More recently, three-stage games have been investigated in models with asymmetric information. Contrary to the Rothschild and Stiglitz result, it was shown in a model with a screening behavior that the game has always a sequential equilibrium in pure strategies (Hellwig, 1987). Efficiency of different equilibria was also studied. Crocker and Snow (1985) showed, for example, that a Wilson-Miyazaki-Spence equilibrium is second-best efficient in the sense of Harris and Townsend (1981) and that the Rothschild and Stiglitz equilibrium is not necessarily efficient when it exists. The same conclusion applies to the Riley equilibrium.

Adverse selection can explain the use of risk categorization in insurance markets. Crocker and Snow (1986) demonstrated that costless imperfect categorization always enhances efficiency. More recently, Bond and Crocker (1991) extended the contribution to consider moral hazard and showed that taxation permits Pareto improvements when the planner can observe aggregate production of the consumption goods that are statistically correlated with insurable hazards. But, more importantly, they showed that risk categorization may overcome the nonexistence of Nash equilibrium problems.

Many extensions of the above literature can be considered. In this conclusion we shall restrict ourselves to two of them. The first one concerns the integration of moral hazard and adverse selection into a single model. As mentioned in the last section, such extension is warranted on empirical grounds. In many cases, empirical studies are not able to dispense with considering both kinds of information asymmetries simultaneously. The same conclusion applies to private and public interventions that may improve resource allocation in practice. It is also warranted on theoretical grounds since very few contributions have proposed integrations of both problems in which at least one party to the contract is risk averse.

The second extension is to propose empirical tests to separate issues on commitment in different lines of insurance. Particularly, it would be interesting to have answers to the following questions: 1) Is competition in insurance markets strong enough to rule out pooling and semi-pooling contracts in the absence of commitment? 2) Is the role of experience rating limited to adjust over time premiums that were originally set in a pooling strategy? 3) Is the presence of moral hazard important enough in different markets to rule out the significance of theoretical predictions that do not consider both problems simultaneously?

Notes

1. For an analysis of several reasons why a monopoly behavior in insurance markets should be considered, see Dahlby (1987). For examples of markets with a monopoly insurer see D'Arcy and Doherty (1990) and Dionne and Vanasse (1988). The result of this section also applies to a cartelized market.

2. As in the perfect discrimination case, the monopolist charges a price of insurance to each consumer equal to marginal cost. All potential consumer surplus is connected into monopoly profits so there is no dead weight loss.

3. Since individuals of different types have the same degree of risk aversion, at each point in the figure, the absolute value of the slope of the high-risk indifference curve is lower than that of the low-risk individual. For example at point C^0, $U'(W)(1 - p_H)/U'(W - D)p_H < U'(W)(1 - p_L)/U'(W - D)p_L$. At equilibrium points C_H^* and C_L^*, the respective slopes (in absolute values) are $(1 - p_H)/p_H$ and $(1 - p_L)/p_L$. This is true since under full insurance, the insured of type i has $W - p_i D - z_i^*$ in each state.

4. For models where neither the insurer nor the insured know the individuals' probabilities of accident, see Palfrey and Spatt (1985), Malueg (1988), and Boyer, Dionne and Kihlstrom (1989).

5. We limit our discussion to private market mechanisms. On public provision of insurance and adverse selection, see Pauly (1974) and Dahlby (1981).

6. Technically the preference structure of the model implies that indifference curves of individuals with different risks cross only once. This single crossing property has been used often in the sorting literature (Cooper, 1984).

7. It is important to note that there is always a separating equilibrium in the monopoly case. However, the good risk individuals may not have any insurance coverage at the equilibrium. Property 4 in Stiglitz (1977) establishes that $C_L^{**} = 0$ when q_H/q_L exceeds a critical ratio of high to low risk individuals. The magnitude of the critical ratio is function of the difference in accident probabilities and of the size of the damage. Here, in order to have $C_L^{**} > 0$, we assume that q_H/q_L is below the critical ratio.

8. Townsend (1982) discussed multi-period borrowing-lending schemes. However, his mechanism implies a constant transfer in the last period that is not compatible with insurance in presence of private information.

9. This type of no-claims discount strategy was first proposed by Radner (1981) and Rubinstein and Yaari (1983) for the problem of moral hazard (see also Malueg (1986) where the good faith strategy is employed). However, since the two problems of information differ significantly, the models are not identical. First the information here does not concern the action of the agent (moral hazard) but the type of risk that he represents (adverse selection). Second, since the action of the insured does not affect the random events, the sequence of damage levels is not controlled by the insured. The damage function depends only on the risk type. Third, in the adverse selection model, the insured cannot change his declaration and therefore cannot depart from his initial risk announcement although he can always cancel his contract. Therefore, the stronger conditions used by Radner (1981a) (robust epsilon equilibrium) and Rubinstein and Yaari (1983) ("long proof") are not needed

to obtain the desired results in presence of adverse selection only. The Law of the Iterated logarithm is sufficient.

10. In fact their formal analysis is with a continuum of risk types.

11. In general, introducing discounting in repeated games reduces the incentive for telling the truth and introduces some inefficiency because players do not care for the future as much as they care for the current period. In other words, with discounting, players become less patient and cooperation becomes more difficult to obtain. See Sabourian (1989) and Abreu, Pearce and Stacchetti (1990) for detailed discussions on the discount factor issues in repeated contracts. See also footnote 15.

12. Radner's (1981) contribution does not allow for revisions after the initial trigger. However, revisions were always present in infinite horizon models [Rubinstein and Yaari (1983), Dionne (1983), Radner (1985), Dionne and Lasserre (1985)]. A trigger strategy without revision consists of offering a premium corresponding to a risk declaration as long as the average loss is less than the reasonable average loss corresponding to the declaration. If that condition is not met, a penalty premium is offered for the remaining number of periods. With revisions, the initial policy can be reinstate.

13. See also Gal and Landsberger (1988) on small-sample properties of experience rating insurance contracts in the presence of adverse selection. In their model, all insureds buy the same contract and resort to experience is made in the premium structure only. They show that the monopoly's expected profits are higher if based on contracts that take advantage of longer experience.

14. On limited commitment see also Freixas, Guesnerie, and Tirole (1985).

15. However, separating equilibria are possible with discounting since future considerations are less relevant. In a model with commitment and renegotiation, Dionne and Doherty (1991) obtain a similar result: when the discount factor is very low, a separating equilibrium is always optimal in a two-period framework. Intuitively, low discount factors reduce the efficiency of using intertemporal transfers or rents to increase the optimal insurance coverage of the low-risk individuals by pooling in the first period. See Laffont and Tirole (1990) for a general discussion on the effect of discounting on optimal solutions in procurement when there is no uncertainty.

16. See Cresta (1984) and Eisen (1989) for other analyses of problems of equilibria with asymmetric information.

17. A Riley or reactive equilibrium leads the Rothschild-Stiglitz separating equilibrium regardless of the number of individuals in each class of risk.

18. In fact, multiple equilibria are the rule in two-stage signaling models. However, when the stability of such equilibria is studied, the problem is to find at least one that is stable. For a more detailed analysis of signaling models see the survey by Kreps (1989). On the notion of sequential equilibrium and on the importance of consistency in beliefs see Kreps and Wilson (1982).

19. Jaynes (1978) and Hellwig (1988) analyzed the consequences of relaxing this assumption. More particularly they showed under what conditions an equilibrium exists when the sharing of information about customers is treated endogenously as part of the game among firms. They showed that it is possible to overcome Rothschild-Stiglitz's existence problem of an equilibrium if insurers compete on price-quantity contracts and exchange information so that insureds cannot buy more than one contract. Finally, Hellwig (1988) showed that the resulting equilibrium is more akin to the Wilson reactive equilibrium than to the competitive Nash equilibrium.

20. Partial coverage is generally interpreted as a monetary deductible. However, in many insurance markets the insurance coverage is excluded during a probationary period

that can be interpreted as a sorting device. Fluet (1991) analyzed the selection of an optimal time-deductible in presence of adverse selection.

21. On the relationship between the coverage obtained by a low-risk individual under monopoly compared to that under the pure Nash competitive equilibrium, see Dahlby (1987). It is shown, for example, that under constant absolute risk aversion, the coverage obtained by a low-risk individual under monopoly is greater than, equal to, or less than that obtained under competition as the monopolist's expected profit on a policy purchased by low-risk individuals is greater than, equal to, or less than its expected profit on the policy purchased by high-risk individuals.

22. See also Dasgupta and Maskin (1986). Mixed strategy and randomization are not equivalent. On randomization to improve market functioning in presence of adverse selection see Garella (1989) and Arnott and Stiglitz (1988).

23. As pointed out, the Riley (1979) reactive equilibrium is also a relevant alternative to the Nash equilibrium. See Grossman (1979) for an analysis of the Wilson type equilibrium with reactions of insureds rather than reactions of sellers.

24. See Crocker and Snow (1985, 1986) for more details.

25. In other words, they implicitly assumed that the conditions to obtain a Nash separating equilibrium in a single period contract are sufficient for their two-period model.

26. It is important to repeat here that the authors limited their focus on separating solutions.

27. In fact, the corresponding expected utility of the low-risk individual who did not have an accident in the first period (and stays) is strictly greater at equilibrium to that corresponding to the entrant one-period contract.

28. In our discussion on the Kunreuther and Pauly model we refer to their single-period equilibria in which firms can modify their prices from one period to the next and consumers are free to leave or stay.

29. Cromb (1990) considered the effects of different precommitment assumptions between the parties to the contract on the value of accident history. Under fully binding contracts, the terms of the contract depend only on the number of accidents over a certain time horizon while under other assumptions (partially binding and no binding) the timing of accidents becomes important.

30. However, Riley (1983) argued that the statistical results of Dahlby (1983) are also consistent with both the Wilson (1977) anticipatory equilibrium and the Riley reactive equilibrium (1979). Both models reject cross-subsidization.

31. On the social value of the acquisition of information by risk categorization in presence of imperfect information, see Doherty (1990), Rea (1991), Hoy (1989), and Crocker and Snow (1990).

32. On learning and moral hazard, see Malueg (1988). He showed that a simple good-faith strategy overcomes both the problem of differential learning and moral hazard when payoffs are evaluated by the limit of means.

33. See also Whinston for a model of social insurance.

34. Since (a.1) does not contain any H-type decision variables, introducing private information about accidents does not affect their optimal values.

References

Abreu, D., D. Pearce and E. Stacchetti. (1990). "Toward a Theory of Discounted Repeated Games with Imperfect Monitoring," *Econometrica 58*, 1041–1064.

Akerlof, G. A. (1970). "The Market for 'Lemons': Quality Uncertainty and the Market Mechanism," *Quarterly Journal of Economics* 84, 488–500.

Allen, F. (1985). "Repeated Principal-Agent Relationships with Lending and Borrowing," *Economics Letters 17*, 27–31.

Arnott, R. (1991). "Moral Hazard and Competitive Insurance Markets," in G. Dionne (Ed.), *Contributions to Insurance Economics*. Boston: Kluwer Academic Publishers.

Arnott, R., and J. E. Stiglitz. (1988). "Randomization with Asymmetric Information," *Rand Journal of Economics 19(3)*, 344–362.

Arrow, K. J. (1963). "Uncertainty and the Welfare Economics of Medical Care," *American Economic Review* 53, 941–969.

Bolton, B. (1990) "Renegotiation and the Dynamics of Contract Design," *European Economic Review* 34, 303–310.

Bond, E. W., and K. J. Crocker. (1991). "Smoking, Skydiving and Knitting: the Endogenous Categorization of Risks in Insurance Markets with Asymmetric Information," *Journal of Political Economy*. 99, 177–200.

Boyer, M., G. Dionne and R. Kihlstrom. (1989). "Insurance and the Value of Publicly Available Information" in *Studies in the Economics of Uncertainty: in Honor of J. Hadar*, T. B. Fomby and T. K. Seo. (eds). Springer Verlag, 137–155.

Caillaud, B., R. Guesnerie, P. Rey and J. Tirole. (1988). "Government Intervention in Production and Incentives Theory: A Review of Recent Contributions," *Rand Journal of Economics 19*, 1–26.

Cresta, J. P. (1984). "Théories des marchés d'assurance," Collection "Approfondissement de la connaissance économique," *Economica*, Paris.

Cho, I., and D. Kreps. (1987). "Signalling Games and Stable Equilibria," *Quarterly Journal of Economics* CII, 179–222.

Cooper, R. (1984). "On Allocative Distortions in Problems of Self-Selection," *Rand Journal of Economics 15*, (4) 568–577.

Cooper, R., and B. Hayes. (1987). "Multi–period Insurance Contracts," *International Journal of Industrial Organization 5*, 211–231.

Crocker, K. J., and A. Snow. (1985). "The Efficiency of Competitive Equilibria in Insurance Markets with Adverse Selection," *Journal of Public Economics 26*, 207–219.

Crocker, K. J., and A. Snow. (1986). "The Efficiency Effects of Categorical Discrimination in the Insurance Industry," *Journal of Political Economy 94*, 321–344.

Crocker, K. J., and A. Snow. (1990). "The Social Value of Private Information in Environments with Adverse Selection," working paper, Penn State University.

Cromb, I. J. (1990). "Competitive Insurance Markets Characterized by Asymmetric Information," Ph. D. thesis, Queen's University.

Dahlby, B. G. (1981). "Adverse Selection and Pareto Improvements through Compulsory Insurance," *Public Choice* 37, 547–558.

Dahlby, B. G. (1983). "Adverse Selection and Statistical Discrimination. An

Analysis of Canadian Automobile Insurance," *Journal of Public Economics* 20, 121–130.

Dahlby, B. G. (1987). "Monopoly Versus Competition in an Insurance Market with Adverse Selection," *Journal of Risk and Insurance* LIV, 325–331.

Dahlby, B. G. (1991). "Testing for Assymmetric Information in Canadian Automobile Insurance," *Contributions to Insurance Economics*, G. Dionne (Ed.) Boston: Kluwer Academic Publishers.

D'Arcy, S. P., and N. Doherty. (1990). "Adverse Selection, Private Information and Lowballing in Insurance Markets," *Journal of Business* 63, 145–164.

Dasgupta, P., and E. Maskin. (1986). "The Existence of Equilibrium in Discontinuous Economic Games, II: Applications," *Review of Economic Studies* 53(1), 27–41.

Dewatripont, M. (1989). "Renegotiation and Information Revelation over Time: The Case of Optimal Labour Contracts," *Quarterly Journal of Economics* 104(3), 589–619.

Dionne, G. (1983). "Adverse Selection and Repeated Insurance Contracts," *Geneva Papers on Risk and Insurance 8*, 316–333.

Dionne, G., and P. Lasserre. (1985). "Adverse Selection, Repeated Insurance Contracts and Announcement Strategy," *Review of Economic Studies 52*, 719–723.

Dionne, G., and P. Lasserre. (1987). "Adverse Selection and Finite-Horizon Insurance Contracts." *European Economic Review 31*, (4), 843–862.

Dionne, G., and P. Lasserre. (1988). "Dealing with Moral Hazard and Adverse Selection Simultaneously," working paper, Economics Department, Université de Montréal.

Dionne, G., and N. Doherty. (1991). "Adverse Selection, Commitment and Renegotiation with Application to Insurance Markets," Mimeo, University of Pennsylvania.

Dionne, G., and C. Vanasse. (1988). "Automobile Insurance Ratemaking in the Presence of Asymmetrical Information," working paper 603, CRT, Université de Montréal. *Journal of Applied Econometrics* (forthcoming).

Doherty, N. A. (1990). "Adverse Selection, Screening and the Value of Information in Insurance Markets," Mimeo, University of Pennsylvania.

Eisen, R. (1989). "Problems of Equilibria in Insurance Markets with Asymmetric Information," in *Risk, Information and Insurance*, H. Loubergé (Ed.) Norwell, MA: Kluwer Academic Publishers.

Fluet, C. (1991). "Probationary Periods and Time-Dependent Deductibles in Insurance Markets with Adverse Selection," in *Contributions to Insurance Economics*, G. Dionne (Ed.). Norwell, MA: Kluwer Academic Publishers.

Freixas, X., R. Guesnerie and J. Tirole. (1985). "Planning Under Incomplete Information and the Ratchet Effect," *Review of Economic Studies 52*, 173–191.

Fudenberg, D., B. Holmstrom and P. Milgrom. (1986). "Short-term Contracts and Long-term Agency Relationships," Mimeo, University of California, Berkeley.

Gal, S., and M. Landsberger. (1988). "On 'Small Sample' Properties of Experience Rating Insurance Contracts," *Quarterly Journal of Economics CIII*, 233–243.

Garella, P. (1989). "Adverse Selection and the Middleman," *Economica 56*, 395–399.

Grossman, H. I. (1979). "Adverse Selection, Dissembling, and Competitive Equilibrium," *Bell Journal of Economics 10*, 336–343.

Guesnerie, R., P., Picard, and P. Rey. (1988). "Adverse Selection and Moral Hazard with Risk Neutral Agents," *European Economic Review 33*, 807–823.

Harris, M., and R. Townsend. (1981). "Resource Allocation under Asymmetric Information," *Econometrica 49*, 33–64.

Hart, O. D., and J. Tirole. (1988). "Contract Renegotiation and Coasian Dynamics," *Review of Economic Studies 55*, 509–540.

Hellwig, M. F. (1986). "A Sequential Approach to Modelling Competition in Markets with Adverse Selection," Mimeo, University of Bonn.

Hellwig, M. F. (1987). "Some Recent Developments in the Theory of Competition in Markets with Adverse Selection," *European Economic Review 31*, 319–325.

Hellwig, M. F. (1988). "A Note on the Specification of Interfirm Communication in Insurance Markets with Adverse Selection," *Journal of Economic Theory 46*, 154–163.

Henriet, D., and J. C. Rochet. (1986). "La logique des systèmes bonus-malus en assurance automobile: une approche théorique," *Annales d'Économie et de Statistique*, 133–152.

Hey, J. (1985). "No Claim Bonus?" *The Geneva Papers on Risk and Insurance 10*, 209–228.

Hosios, A. J., and M. Peters. (1989). "Repeated Insurance Contracts with Adverse Selection and Limited Commitment," *Quarterly Journal of Economics CIV* (2), 229–253.

Hoy, M. (1982). "Categorizing Risks in the Insurance Industry," *Quarterly Journal of Economics 97*, 321–336.

Hoy, M. (1989). "The Value of Screening Mechanisms Under Alternative Insurance Possibilities," *Journal of Public Economics 39*, 177–206.

Jaynes, G. D. (1978). "Equilibria in Monopolistically Competitive Insurance Markets," *Journal of Economic Theory 19*, 394–422.

Karni, E. (1991). "Optimal Insurance: A Nonexpected Utility Analysis," in G. Dionne (Ed.), *Contributions to Insurance Economics*. Boston: Kluwer Academic Publishers.

Kreps, D. (1989). "Out-of-Equilibrium Beliefs and Out-of-Equilibrium Behaviour," in *The Economics of Information, Missing Markets and Games* (F. Hahn, ed.), Oxford: Clarendon Press, 7–45.

Kreps, D., and R. Wilson. (1982). "Sequential Equilibria," *Econometrica 50*, 863–894.

Kunreuther, H., and M. Pauly. (1985). "Market Equilibrium with Private Knowledge: An Insurance Example," *Journal of Public Economics 26*, 269–288.

Laffont, J. J., and J. Tirole. (1986). "Using Cost Observation to Regulate Firms," *Journal of Political Economy 94*, 614–641.

Laffont, J.-J., and J. Tirole. (1987). "Comparative Statics of the Optimal Dynamic Incentive Contracts," *European Economic Review 31*, 901–926.

Laffont, J.-J., and J. Tirole. (1990). "Adverse Selection and Renegotiation in Procurement," *Review of Economic Studies 57*, 597–625.

Lemaire, J. (1985). *Automoblle Insurance: Actuarial Models.* Boston: Kluwer-Nighoff Publishing.

Machina, M. J. (1987). "Choice Under Uncertainty: Problems Solved and Unsolved," *Journal of Economics Perspective 1*, 121–154.

Malueg, D. A. (1986). "Efficient Outcomes in a Repeated Agency Model Without Discounting," *Journal of Mathematical Economics 15*, 217–230.

Malueg, D. A. (1988). "Repeated Insurance Contracts with Differential Learning," *Review of Economic Studies LV*, 177–181.

Miyazaki, H. (1977). "The Rate Race and Internal Labour Markets," *Bell Journal of Economics 8*, 394–418.

Nilssen, T. (1990). "Consumer Lock-in with Asymmetric Information," working paper, Norvegian School of Economics and Business.

Palfrey, T. R., and C. S. Spatt. (1985). "Repeated Insurance Contracts and Learning," *Rand Journal of Economics 16(3)*, 356–367.

Pauly, M. V. (1974). "Overinsurance and the Public Provision of Insurance: The Roles of Moral Hazard and Adverse Selection," *Quarterly Journal of Economics 88*, 44–62.

Picard, P. (1987). "On the Design of Incentives Schemes Under Moral Hazard and Adverse Selection," *Journal of Public Economics 33*, 305–331.

Radner, R. (1981). "Monitoring Cooperative Agreements in a Repeated Principal-Agent Relationship," *Econometrica 49*, 1127–1148.

Radner, R. (1985). "Repeated Principal-Agent Games with Discounting," *Econometrica 53*, 1173–1198.

Rea, S. A. (1987). "The Market Response to the Elimination of Sex-Based Annuities," *Southern Economic Journal 54*, 55–63.

Rea, S. A. (1991). "Insurance Classifications and Social Welfare," in *Contributions to Insurance Economics*, C. Dionne (Ed.). Boston: Kluwer Academic Publishers.

Riley, J. G. (1979a). "Informational Equilibrium," *Econometrica 47*, 331–359.

Riley, J. G. (1979b). "Non-Cooperative Equilibrium and Markets Signalling," *American Economic Review* May, 303–307.

Riley, J. G. (1983). "Adverse Selection and Statistical Discrimination: Further Comments," *Journal of Public Economics 20*, 131–137.

Riley, J. G. (1985). "Competition with Hidden Knowledge," *Journal of Political Economy 93*, 958–976.

Rothschild, M., and J. Stiglitz. (1976). "Equilibrium in Competitive Insurance Markets: An Essay on the Economics of Imperfect Information," *Quarterly Journal of Economics 90*, 629–650.

Rubinstein, A., and M. Yaari. (1983). "Repeated Insurance Contract and Moral

Hazard," *Journal of Economic Theory 30*, 74–97.

Sabourian, H. (1989). "Repeated Games: A Survey," in the *Economics of Information, Missing Markets and Games* (F. Hahn, Ed.). Oxford: Clarendon Press, 62–105.

Spence, M. (1973). "Job Market Signalling," *Quarterly Journal of Economics 87*, 355–374.

Spence, M. (1978). "Product Differentiation and Performance in Insurance Markets," *Journal of Public Economics 10*, 427–447.

Stiglitz, J. (1977). "Monopoly, Nonlinear Pricing, and Imperfect Information: The Insurance Market," *Review of Economic Studies 44*, 407–430.

Stiglitz, J., and A. Weiss. (1984). "Sorting Out the Differences Between Screening and Signalling Models," working paper, Princeton University.

Townsend, R. (1982). "Optimal Multiperiod Contracts and the Gain from Enduring Relationships under Private Information," *Journal of Political Economy 90*, 1166–1185.

Whinston, M. (1983). "Moral Hazard, Adverse Selection and the Optimal Provision of Social Insurance," *Journal of Public Economics 22*, 49–71.

Wilson, C. (1977). "A Model of Insurance Markets with Incomplete Information," *Journal of Economic Theory 16*, 167–207.

Appendix

A1. Monopoly with Private Information about Accidents

Under private information about accidents, we must add one constraint to the two-period contract proposed by Cooper and Hayes to rule out underreporting. In this appendix we show that the following constraint is sufficient:

$$U(W - D + \beta_L) + p_L U(W - D + \beta_{La}) + (1 - p_L)U(W - \alpha_{La})$$
$$- U(W - D - \alpha_L) - p_L U(W - D + \beta_{LN}) - (1 - p_L)U(W - \alpha_{LN}) = 0.$$
$$(a.1)$$

The above constraint means that the low-risk individual is indifferent between accident reporting and accident underreporting when the event occurs in the first period. It reduces the gap between second-period levels of expected utility to

$$U(W - D + \beta_L) - U(W - D - \alpha_L) > 0$$

and, therefore, reduces the insurer's possibilities of profits, since the latter is now limited in his opportunities to relax the one-period binding constraints.

Maximizing the insurer two-period expected profits by choosing C_L^2 and C_H^2 under constraints (4.1), (4.2), and (a.1) yields as first-order conditions for the low-risk individual decision variables[34]:

$$\alpha_L: q_L = U'(W - \alpha_L)\left[\lambda_L - \frac{(1 - p_H)}{(1 - p_L)}\lambda_{HL}\right] - \frac{\lambda_{LL}}{(1 - p_L)}U'(W - D - \alpha_L)$$

$$\beta_L: q_L = U'(W - D + \beta_L)\left[\lambda_L - \frac{p_H}{p_L}\lambda_{HL}\right] + \frac{\lambda_{LL}}{p_L}U'(W - D + \beta_L)$$

$$\alpha_{La}: q_L = U'(W - \alpha_{La})\left[\lambda_L - \frac{(1 - p_H)}{(1 - p_L)}\frac{p_H}{p_L}\lambda_{HL}\right] + \frac{\lambda_{LL}}{(1 - p_L)}U'(W - \alpha_{La})$$

$$\beta_{La}: q_L = U'(W - D + \beta_{La})\left[\lambda_L - \frac{p_H p_H}{p_L p_L}\lambda_{HL}\right] + \frac{\lambda_{LL}}{p_L}U'(W - D + \beta_{La})$$

$$\alpha_{LN}: q_L = U'(W - \alpha_{LN})\left[\lambda_L - \frac{(1 - p_H)(1 - p_H)}{(1 - p_L)(1 - p_L)}\lambda_{HL}\right]$$

$$- \frac{\lambda_{LL}}{(1 - p_L)}U'(W - \alpha_{LN})$$

$$\beta_{LN}: q_L = U'(W - D + \beta_{LN})\left[\lambda_L - \frac{p_H(1 - p_H)}{p_L(1 - p_L)}\lambda_{HL}\right]$$

$$- \frac{\lambda_{LL}}{p_L}U'(W - D + \beta_{LN})$$

Under public information on accidents, $\lambda_{LL} \equiv 0$. Solving for α_L^{**} and β_L^{**} we have

$$U'(W - \alpha_L)\left[\lambda_L - \lambda_{HL}\frac{(1 - p_H)}{(1 - p_L)}\right] = U'(W - D + \beta_L)\left[\lambda_L - \frac{p_H}{p_L}\lambda_{HL}\right],$$

which implies that $U'(W - D + \beta_L) > U'(W - \alpha_L)$ and $\beta_L^{**} < D - \alpha_L^{**}$.

Similarly we can verify that $\alpha_{La}^{**} > \alpha_L^{**} > \alpha_{LN}^{**}$ and $\beta_{La}^{**} < \beta_L^{**} < \beta_{LN}^{**}$.

Under private information on accidents, (a.1) is binding and $\lambda_{LL} > 0$. This limits the monopoly's profits possibilities. One can verify that

$$\hat{\alpha}_L > \alpha_L^{**}, \hat{\beta}_L > \beta_L^{**}, \hat{\beta}_{La} > \beta_{La}^{**}, \hat{\alpha}_{La} < \alpha_{La}^{**}, \hat{\beta}_{La} < \beta_{LN}^{**}, \hat{\alpha}_{LN} > \alpha_{LN}^{**},$$

where $\hat{\alpha}$ and $\hat{\beta}$ are optimal values under private information on accident histories.

A.2. Two-period problem with competition

The proof here is limited to the low-risk contract.

a) Semi-commitment

Under competition and semi-commitment $C_L^2 = \{\alpha_L, \beta_L, \alpha_{La}, \beta_{La}, \alpha_{LN}, \beta_{LN}\}$ maximizes $V(C_L^2|p_L)$ subject to

$$2V(C_H^{**}|p_H) \geq V(C_L^2|p_H) \tag{a.2}$$

$$V(C_L^2|p_L) \geq 2V(C_H^{**}|p_L) \tag{a.3}$$

$$V(C_{La}|p_L) \geq V(C_L|p_L) \tag{a.4}$$

$$V(C_{LN}|p_L) \geq V(C_L|p_L) \tag{a.5}$$

$$(1 - p_L)\alpha_L - p_L\beta_L + p_L[(1 - p_L)\alpha_{LN} - p_L\beta_{LN}]$$
$$+ (1 - p_L)[(1 - p_L)\alpha_{La} - p_L\beta_{La}] = 0 \tag{a.6}$$

Constraints (a.2) and (a.3) are self-selection constraints where C_H^{**} corresponds to the single-period optimal contract of high-risk individuals and C_L^2 consider the option that high-risk agents can take the single-period contract (C_L) of the new firm (entrant) in the second period (see Cooper and Hayes for more details on C_L^2). Constraint (a.4) and (a.5) take into account the option that low-risk individuals can also switch to another firm in the second period whether they have an accident ($C_{La} = \{\alpha_{La}, \beta_{La}\}$) or not ($C_{LN} = \{\alpha_{LN}, \beta_{LN}\}$) in the first period, and (a.6) is the zero expected profit constraint. At the optimal solution constraints (a.2), (a.4), and (a.6) are binding.

b) Full commitment

Under competition and commitment by both parties, the contract is similar to that of the monopoly with commitment, which implies that constraints (a.4) and (a.5) do not have any usefulness or economic meaning and that constraint (a.2) does not contain any entrant component. At the optimal solution constraints (a.2)' and (a.6) are binding where (a.2)' is written for (a.2) without any entrant component and is similar to (4.2) in the text.

FINANCIAL PRICING OF PROPERTY AND LIABILITY INSURANCE

J. David Cummins

University of Pennsylvania

Abstract

Insurance companies are levered corporations that borrow money by issuing a specific type of debt instrument, the insurance policy. Insurance debt is more risky than conventional debt because neither the amount nor the timing of the debt repayments are known in advance. The debt analogy suggests financial modeling as a natural approach to the pricing of insurance. This paper reviews the theory of financial pricing of insurance and proposes some extensions. The review covers the insurance capital asset pricing model CAPM, discounted cash-flow models, and option-pricing models. The extensions include an option model of the insurance firm allowing for multiple asset and liability classes and an analysis of insurance company equity as a down-and-out option.

Key words: Insurance, insurance financial management, liability insurance, financial pricing models, contingent claims, option models, down-and-out option, risky debt

Since insurance companies are corporations and insurance policies can be interpreted as financial instruments or contingent claims, it seems natural to apply financial models to insurance pricing. Financial theory views the insurance firm as a levered corporation with debt and equity capital. The insurer raises debt capital by issuing insurance contracts.

Insurance contracts are roughly analogous to the bonds issued by non-financial corporations. Bonds tend to have fixed coupon payments and a fixed maturity date. Insurance policies are more risky than conventional bonds because both the payment time and amount are stochastic. In addition, the payout period for most policies does not have a fixed time limit. Thus, insurance pricing poses some difficult problems that are not present when dealing with conventional financial instruments.

Financial theory views the insurance underwriting and pricing decision as corporate capital budgeting. In capital budgeting, firms accept or reject projects based on decision criteria such as the net present value (NPV) or internal rate of return (IRR) rules (see Brealey and Myers (1988) or Copeland and Weston (1988)). These decision rules focus on the amount and timing of the anticipated cash flows from the candidate projects. The rate-of-return targets are based on market risk-return relationships such as the capital asset pricing model (CAPM) or arbitrage pricing theory (APT).

Financial pricing models for insurance are based on the premise that insurance prices are set in competitive markets. Thus, policy prices should reflect equilibrium relationships between risk and return or, minimally, avoid the creation of arbitrage opportunities. Adherence to these principles distinguishes financial models from most actuarial pricing models.

This paper reviews the principal financial models that have been proposed for pricing insurance contracts and proposes some new alternatives. The earliest models, based on the CAPM, provide important insights but are too simple to be used in realistic situations. More promising are discrete and continuous time discounted cash flow (DCF) models. Options models also provide important insights into insurance pricing. The most recent research focuses on perpetual options models that allow for default risk.

While the focus in this paper is on theoretical models, the reader should be aware that there is a growing empirical literature on the financial pricing of insurance (e.g., Cummins and Harrington (1985), D'Arcy and Garven (1989)). The intent here is to provide a concise analysis of the central theoretical contributions to the field rather than an exhaustive survey.

1. Insurance as Risky Debt

Insurance companies are levered corporations that raise debt capital by issuing a specific type of financial instrument — the insurance policy. Although some authors have argued that simple option pricing models can be used to price insurance debt, these models overlook important features of real-world insurance contracts. To develop realistic models it is usually necessary to start with the underlying stochastic processes and boundary conditions governing insurance debt rather than force-fitting the insurance contract into a conventional model. This section outlines the characteristics of insurance debt that should be reflected in financial pricing models.

The emphasis here is on long-tailed liability contracts. However, the same general characteristics apply to shorter-tailed property contracts. Life insurance (not discussed here) tends to have its own characteristics that distinguish it from property and liability insurance. The reader is cautioned against oversimplifying the insurance pricing problem.

Property-liability insurance tends to be characterized by an initial premium payment (i.e., a cash inflow to the insurer) followed by a stream of cash outflows representing loss payments. The premium inflow is analogous to the proceeds of a bond issue, and the loss payments are analogous to bond coupon and principal payments. During the period between the premium payment and the final satisfaction of all claims against the policy, the insurer invests the unexpended premium balance, receiving investment income. Also of significance are the federal tax flows that arise from operating as an insurance company.

Funds that flow into the company as policies are issued, are allocated between two liability accounts — the unearned premium reserve and the loss reserve. The unearned premium reserve reflects premiums that have been paid to the company for coverage not yet provided. If the policy is canceled before the coverage period has elapsed a refund is paid to the policy-holder on the basis of the unearned premium reserve. The unearned premium reserve amounts to a short-term loan (since most policy coverage periods are a year or less), with no unusual risk characteristics.

As the coverage period elapses, funds released from the unearned premium reserve are used to pay losses, expenses, and taxes or added to the loss reserve. The loss reserve represents the company's primary source of long-term debt. The reserve arises because loss payments lag loss occurrences, sometimes by considerable periods of time. The loss reserve for any given policy block represents the company's estimate of the losses it will eventually have to pay for that policy block less the payments that have already been made.[1] The loss reserve differs significantly from conventional long-term debt.

In a conventional bond, the borrower's obligation is to pay the bond coupons and to repay the principal of the bond on maturity.[2] The coupons and the bond principal are in nominal values (i.e., they do not depend upon inflation or other contingent events).[3] The payments occur at specified dates that are known in advance by both the borrower and the lender. In property and liability insurance, on the other hand, neither the amount nor the timing of the loss cash flows is known in advance. The aggregate losses paid for a given block of policies is the sum of n individual losses. A priori, both the number of losses (n) and the amount of each loss is a random variable. Loss amounts are random because the damage degree is random and because they are affected by inflation.[4] Since insurance inflation typically diverges from the general rate of inflation in the economy (Cummins and Nye (1981), Cummins and Weiss (1989)), the Fisher effect cannot be fully relied upon in discounting. The payout pattern (timing of claim payments) also can shift unpredictably.

Although the insurer's loss liability is nominally governed by the insurance contract, judicial decisions can radically alter the eligibility of losses for payment under both existing and future policies. Hazards that were unknown at the time the policies were issued (e.g., asbestos exposure) can lead to coverage of losses for which no premiums were collected. These risks are exacerbated in policies with longer coverage periods because there is more time for adverse events to occur. Thus, insurance debt is much more risky than conventional debt.

In addition to insurance policies, conventional short- and long-term debt are issued by some insurers. By law, this debt is junior to the company's obligations under its insurance policies. Since insurance regulation relies heavily on leverage ratios, the conventional debt is often issued by a holding company, which makes equity contributions to the insurer. Since the holding company and the insurer are separate legal entities, the conventional debt under this arrangement is not counted in the insurer's regulatory ratios.

Equity capital is the other major component of the capital structure of an insurance company. Companies maintain equity capital to achieve ruin probabilities sufficiently low to satisfy buyers and regulators. Ruin probabilities are never reduced to zero because buyers are not willing to pay for extremely low ruin probabilities. With complete information and buyer rationality, regulation would not be needed to ensure acceptable insolvency probabilities. One rationale for regulation is that consumers do not have adequate information or expertise to gauge insurer solvency levels.[5] Agents, brokers, and commercial monitoring firms (e.g., the A.M. Best Company) exist to provide private solvency monitoring.

In 1988, equity represented 25% of the capital structure of the property-liability insurance industry. In spite of this equity cushion, insurance insolvencies have been increasing during the past two decades. Eighty-five property-liability insurer insolvencies occurred from 1984 to 1988.

Assessments levied by state guaranty funds to pay the obligations of insolvent insurers totalled 2.5 billion from 1969 to 1988. Obviously, insurance debt carries default risk that must be taken into account in pricing.

The assets of insurers consist primarily of financial assets, with a heavy emphasis on stocks and bonds.[6] Insurers select assets with the objective of managing risk, including solvency risk and interest-rate risk. The latter element implies that insurers should be concerned about the net duration of their asset and liability portfolios (Staking(1990)). Other than financial assets, insurers have receivables, from agents and re-insurers, and a relatively small amount of real assets such as buildings and computer equipment.

The risks that should be taken into account in pricing insurance contracts are summarized in table 1. Insurance pricing models differ in the degree to which these risks are recognized. Actuarial models have focused on frequency and severity risk, payout pattern risk, and default risk (Cummins and Derrig (1988, 1989)), while the existing financial models focus on systematic risk, inflation risk, and interest-rate risk. At the present time, no model incorporates all types of pricing risk in a totally satisfactory manner.

One objective of this paper is to provide the motivation and background for the development of more realistic insurance pricing models. In the remainder of the paper, the central models are outlined and extensions are proposed. It is hoped that the paper will stimulate the development of new models reflecting the relevant types of risk in an operationally feasible framework.

2. A Simple CAPM for Insurance Pricing

The first financial models of the insurance firm were based on a very simple algebraic approach. Although these models are not very realistic, they do provide important insights into insurance pricing. The first model

Table 1.   Pricing Characteristics and Risks In Liability Insurance

Frequency and Severity Risk
Interest Rate (Duration) Risk
Inflation Risk
Payout Pattern Risk
Systematic (Market) Risk
Default Risk

of this type was developed by Ferrari (1969). His paper presents the basic algebraic model of the insurance firm but does not link the model to the concept of market equilibrium. An important advance in insurance financial pricing was the linkage of the algebraic model of the insurance firm with the capital asset pricing model (CAPM). The resulting model is often called the insurance CAPM.

The insurance CAPM was developed in Cooper (1974), Biger and Kahane (1978), Fairley (1979), and Hill (1979). The derivation begins with the following simple model of the insurance firm:

$$Y = I + \Pi_u = r_a A + r_u P \tag{1}$$

where

Y, I, and P = net income, investment income, and premiums, respectively,

A, L, and E = assets, liabilities, and equity,

Π_u = underwriting profit (premium income less expenses and losses),

r_a = rate of investment return on assets, and

r_u = rate of return on underwriting (as a proportion of premiums).

Writing (1) as return on equity and using the relationship $A = L + E$, one obtains:

$$r_e = r_a\left(\frac{L}{E} + 1\right) + r_u \frac{P}{E} = r_a(ks + 1) + r_u s \tag{2}$$

where

$s = P/E$ = the premiums-to-surplus ratio, and
$k = L/P$ = the liabilities-to-premiums ratio (funds generating factor).

Equation (2) indicates that the rate of return on equity for an insurer is generated by leveraging the rates of investment return and underwriting return. The leverage factor for investment income is $(ks + 1)$, a function of the premiums-to-surplus ratio and the funds-generating factor. The latter approximates the average time between the policy issue and claims payment dates. The underwriting return is leveraged by the premiums-to-surplus ratio.

By taking expectations in (2), one obtains the insurer's expected return on equity. This is essentially an accounting model. The model is given economic content by assuming that the equilibrium expected return on the insurer's equity is determined by the CAPM. The insurance CAPM is obtained by equating the CAPM return with the expected return given by (2) and solving for the expected underwriting profit (e.g., see Fairley (1979)). The result is

$$E(r_u) = -kr_f + \beta_u[E(r_m) - r_f] \tag{3}$$

where

$\beta_u = \text{Cov}(r_u, r_m)/\text{Var}(r_m) =$ the beta of underwriting profits.

The first term of (3), $-k\, r_f$, represents an interest credit for the use of policyholder funds. The second component of r_u is the insurer's reward for risk-bearing: the underwriting beta multiplied by the market-risk premium. The risk premium reflects only systematic risk (i.e., the risk of ruin is not priced and policies are treated as free of default risk).

Several limitations of the insurance CAPM have motivated researchers to seek more realistic models. One problem is the use of the funds generating factor (k) to represent the payout tail. Myers and Cohn (1987) argue that k represents a crude approximation of the discounted cash flow (DCF) approach and can lead to serious errors. A second problem is that the model ignores the problem of default risk. As a practical matter, errors in estimating underwriting betas can be significant (Cummins and Harrington (1985)). Most of the models discussed below are designed to deal with one or more of these problems.

3. Discrete Time Discounted Cash Flow (DCF) Models

The financial models that have been most widely used in practice in the United States are discrete time discounted cash flow models. These models are based on concepts of corporate capital budgeting. The two most prominent models, are the Myers-Cohn model and the National Council on Compensation Insurance (NCCI) model (Cummins (1990)). The following discussion focuses on the Myers-Cohn model.

The Myers-Cohn (MC) model is an application of Myers's adjusted present value (APV) method (see Brealey and Myers (1988, pp. 443–446)). The APV method discounts each expected cash flow from a project at its own risk-adjusted discount rate (RADR). Discounting each flow at its own RADR is consistent with the principle of value-additivity. The policy is priced as if the various flows could be unbundled and sold separately, avoiding the creation of arbitrage opportunities.

In insurance DCF analysis, it is important to adopt a perspective to avoid double counting. Flows can be measured from either the insurer's or the policyholder's perspective. Flows to one are the mirror image of flows from the other. The MC model adopts the policyholder perspective. The relevant cash flows are premiums, losses, expenses, and taxes. The flows from the company perspective are surplus commitment, underwriting profits (net of taxes), and investment income, also net of taxes.[7]

The policyholders pay the taxes arising out of the insurance transaction because the owners of the company have the alternative of investing directly in the capital markets. They will not place capital at risk in an insurer if by doing so they subject income on their capital to another layer of taxation.

The objective of the Myers-Cohn model is to determine the fair premium for insurance. The premium is defined as fair if the insurer is exactly indifferent between selling the policy and not selling it. The insurer will be indifferent if the market value of its equity is not changed by writing the policy. This principle is carried forward into the options models discussed later.

The cash flows can be illustrated by reference to a two-period model, with premiums paid at time 0 and losses paid at time 1. The cash flows for this case are shown in table 2. The generalization to multiple periods is straightforward. To simplify the discussion, expenses are ignored.

Premium flows occur at time 0 and loss flows at time 1. These flows are discounted at different rates (of course, the premium flow is not discounted at all in this simplified example because it occurs at time 0). Premium flows are virtually riskless and hence are discounted at the riskfree rate. Loss flows are discounted at an appropriate risk-adjusted discount rate (RADR). The underwriting profits tax is assumed to be paid at time 1. Since this is based on the difference between premiums

Table 2.   Cash Flows in Two-Period Myers-Cohn Model

Flow	Time 0	Time 1	Discount Rate
Premium	P	0	r_f
Loss	0	L	r_L
Underwriting Profits Tax	0	$\tau(P - L)$	r_f, r_L
Investment Balance	$P(1 + \delta)$	0	
Investment Blance Tax	0	$\tau r_f P(1 + \delta)$	r_f

Key: P = premiums, L = expected losses, r_f = risk-free rate, r_L = risk-adjusted discount rate for losses, τ = corporate income tax rate, and δ = surplus-to-premiums ratio.

and losses, the tax flow must be broken into two parts — the loss part and the premium part — each of which is discounted at the appropriate rate.

The other tax flow is the investment balance tax. Writing the policy creates an investment balance because the premium is paid in advance of the loss payment date and because the company commits surplus (equity capital) to the policy. The surplus and premium are invested and a tax must be paid on the investment income at time 1.[8] Myers has pointed out that the tax on both risk-free and risky investment income should be discounted at the risk-free rate. This result, known as the Myers Theorem, is discussed in Derrig (1985).

Discounting each flow and simplifying leads to the Myers-Cohn premium formula. The general formula for the multi-period case is the following:

$$P = \sum_{t=1}^{N} L \frac{c_t(1 + g)^t}{(1 + r_L)^t} + \frac{\tau S r_f}{1 - \tau} \sum_{t=1}^{N} \frac{(1 - \Sigma^{t-1}c_i)}{(1 + r_f)^t} \tag{4}$$

where

L, P, and S = expected losses, premiums, and surplus commitment,
g = loss inflation rate,
τ = the corporate income tax rate,
δ = the rate of surplus commitment (surplus-to-premiums ratio),
r_L = risk-adjusted discount rate for losses, and
c_t = the proportion of losses paid at time t, $\Sigma_t c_t = 1$.

The RADR for losses, r_L is equal to $r_f + \lambda$, where λ is the risk premium. Existing applications of the MC model use a RADR based on the CAPM:

$$r_L = r_f + \beta_L[E(r_m) - r_f] \tag{5}$$

where

β_L = $\text{Cov}[dL/L, r_m]/\text{Var}(r_m)$, and
dL/L = rate of growth of losses.

However, the MC model is not inherently a CAPM model, and any theoretically defensible RADR (such as one based on arbitrage pricing theory (APT)) could be used. A discount rate that is appropriate for an insurer with nonzero default probability is developed in Cummins (1988b).

An important feature of the MC model is the concept of the *surplus flow*. Myers and Cohn assume that surplus is committed to the policy when the policy is issued and gradually released as losses are paid. The surplus flow pattern has an important impact on the premium because it affects the investment balance tax.

An unanswered question in insurance financial modeling is the appropriate level of surplus commitment.[9] Usually, the surplus-to-premium ratio is based on the company's historical average or on the average for the insurance market as a whole. Neither approach is satisfactory, particularly in a multiple-line company. A solution to the surplus commitment and allocation problem would represent an important contribution to insurance financial theory.

The Myers-Cohn model is consistent with financial theory and relatively easy to apply in practice. The model is deceptively simple and avoids many subtle but important pitfalls in DCF modelling. It probably represents the state of the art in practical insurance financial models. Weaknesses include the difficulty of estimating the surplus-to-premiums ratio and the RADR as well as the omission of default risk. None of these problems is inherent in the MC model.

4. Options Pricing Models

Like options, insurance policies are derivative financial assets (contingent claims) with payments depending upon changes in the value of other assets. Payments under primary insurance policies are triggered by changes in the value of the insured assets, while reinsurance payments depend upon the experience of the covered primary insurance policies. Both types of insurance are candidates for pricing using the options approach.

Options models have an advantage over traditional actuarial models in their strict adherence to the rules of dominance and arbitrage. A security is dominant over another security if it has a higher return in some future states of the world and at least as high a return in all other states of the world. Rational options prices are based on the rule that options will be neither dominant nor dominated securities. This simple but powerful idea has far-reaching implications for the financial pricing of insurance.

4.1. Risk-Neutral Valuation Relationships

Two alternative approaches to options pricing have been applied to insurance: (1) Continuous-time, diffusion based options models, and (2) discrete-time models. Both types of models lead to risk-neutral valuation relationships (RNVRs). A risk-neutral valuation relationship is a formula for asset values in which all securities have the same rate of return (the risk-free rate) (Brennan (1979)). The equal return feature is just a fiction, of course — returns on most assets, including options, are not actually equal to the risk-free rate. Rather, a RNVR values assets as if returns were risk-free. Expectations are obtained using distributions for which the mean value is the risk-free rate but the other parameters are the same as those of the underlying asset. Discounting is then done using the risk-free rate.

To use a RNVR in a continuous time model, it is necessary to form a riskless hedge portfolio (e.g., the Black-Scholes option model is derived by forming a hedge portfolio containing the option and the underlying stock). By choosing the correct portfolio mix, risk is eliminated and the portfolio return must equal the risk-free rate. Since risk is eliminated, the option price will not depend upon investor risk preferences. In particular, the option price will be the same in an economy where investors are risk-neutral as in an economy where investors are risk-averse. Thus, the option price can be computed under conditions where the calculations are easiest, i.e., a risk-neutral economy.[10]

The key to the Black-Scholes derivation is the riskless hedge, which requires that assets be continuously tradable. This assumption applies only as an approximation for many assets, including insurance policies. The extent to which one loses accuracy by treating assets subject to discrete trading as if they were tradable continuously depends upon the asset under study. The continuous-time approach may produce reasonable values in insurance pricing. However, an alternative approach has been developed that does not require continuous trading. This approach is the discrete-time RNVR (Brennan (1979)).

Unlike the continuous-time RNVR approach, which places no restrictions on investor preferences, the discrete-time approach does require such restrictions. For example, Brennan shows that if asset returns are jointly lognormal, a RNVR exists if assets are priced as if there exists a single representative investor who exhibits constant relative risk aversion. Under these conditions, Brennan shows that prices can be calculated from risk-neutralized lognormal distributions.[11] The result is extended to multivariate lognormal distributions by Stapleton and Subramanyan (1984).

4.2. Basic Options Models in Insurance

Single period option models provide some important insights into insurance pricing and financial management. Smith (1977) proposes a

Black-Scholes put option model for insurance pricing. The proposed contract offers insurance against the decline in the value (V) of an asset below the insured value (X). The insurance premium is given by the formula:

$$P = -VN\left[\frac{-\ln(V/X) - (r_f + \sigma^2/2)\tau}{\sigma\sqrt{\tau}}\right] + Xe^{-r_f\tau}N\left[\frac{-\ln(V/X) - (r_f - \sigma^2/2)\tau}{\sigma\sqrt{\tau}}\right] \tag{6}$$

where τ, σ^2 = the time to expiration and risk parameter of the insured asset and $N[\cdot]$ = the standard normal distribution function. Smith suggests that this model might be applicable to mortgage insurance.

This approach can be extended to the pricing of reinsurance. Consider an excess of loss reinsurance agreement in which the insurer agrees to pay the property losses of a corporation in the event these losses exceed a fixed retention amount M. In this case, the insurance policy is a call option, paying $\text{Max}[0, Y - M]$ at maturity, where Y = losses. Under the appropriate conditions, both the Black-Scholes model and Brennan's discrete time lognormal RNVR models give the following formula for the reinsurance premium:

$$P_R = e^{-r_f\tau}\int_M^\infty (Y - M)\frac{1}{Y\sigma\sqrt{2\pi}}e^{-\frac{1}{2}\left(\frac{\ln Y - \mu}{\sigma}\right)^2}dY \tag{7}$$

where $\mu = r_f - \sigma^2/2$. Other contracts can be priced similarly. For example, if the contract has an upper limit (U), the price would be $C(Y, M, \tau) - C(Y, U, \tau)$, where $C(Y, S, \tau)$ is a call on asset Y with striking price S and time to expiration τ.

Equations (6) and (7) both require that the optioned variable be continuous. Thus, discrete jumps in the asset or loss values due to large claims are ruled out. Insurance applications of options models incorporating jumps have been provided by Merton (1978), Pennacchi (1987), and Cummins (1988a).

The role of the insurance company in pricing can be analyzed using the basic option model of the firm. This model rests on the put-call parity formula:

$$A = C(A, L, \tau) + [Le^{-r_f\tau} - P(A, L, \tau)] \tag{8}$$

where

A = the value of firm assets,
L = the value of firm liabilities,
$C(A, L, \tau)$ = a call option on asset A, with striking price L, and time to maturity τ,

$P(A, L, \tau)$ = a put option on asset A, with striking price L and time to
maturity τ.

The options are European options, implying that they can only be exercised at the maturity date. At that date (when $\tau = 0$), the value of the call
is $C(A, L, 0) = \text{Max}[0, A-L]$, while the value of the put is $P(A, L, 0) = \text{Max}[0, L-A]$.

The option model of the firm interprets the ownership interest as the
value of the call option because the owners have the right to receive the
residual value of the firm at the expiration date. If $A > L$ at that date, the
owners pay off the liabilities and receive the amount $A - L$. If $A < L$,
the owners default, turning the firm's assets over to the debt holders. The
put-call parity relationship shows how the value of the firm's assets is
divided between the stockholders (the call option) and the debt holders.
The debt value is the bracketed expression in (8), the riskless present
value of liabilities less the put value. The put expresses the value of the
owners' option to default at $\tau = 0$ if $A < L$ and is often called the
insolvency option.

Doherty and Garven (DG) (1986) apply the discrete time RNVR
option model of the firm to insurance pricing. Their model postulates an
insurer that begins with equity S and collects premiums P in return for the
promise to pay stochastic losses L at the expiration of the contract in one
period. Beginning assets $(P + S)$ are invested at stochastic interest rate
r_A. If the sum of investment income and underwriting $(P - L)$ income is
positive, the insurer must pay federal income tax on this amount at the
conclusion of the contract. The premium is obtained as the solution to the
following equation:

$$S = C[S+P + r_A(S+kP), L, \tau] - \tau C[\theta r_A(S+kP)+P, L, \tau] \qquad (9)$$

where k = the funds generating factor, and θ = proportion of assets in
taxable securities.

In this model, ending assets are $A = S + P + r_A(S + kP)$; and taxable
income is taxable investment income, $I = \theta r_A(S + kP)$, plus underwriting
income, $P - L$. At contract expiration, the owners receive $\text{Max}[A - L, 0] - \tau\text{Max}[I + P - L, 0]$. The premium is the amount such that the present value of the owners' net claim on the company is equal to the initial
surplus contribution. DG solve numerically for P under the assumption
that r_A and L are jointly normal and also jointly lognormal.

Although this model provides some important insights, there are
several problems: 1) The model uses a k factor to represent the payout
tail. This is inaccurate and leads to the strange implication that the
company collects P but potentially receives investment income on more

(less) than P if $k > (<)$ 1. Furthermore, the option expires in one period, even though investment income is potentially received for more or less than one period. 2) The presence of tax-exempt interest income is crudely modeled using a proportionality factor, θ. 3) The federal tax claim is assumed to expire worthless if taxable income is negative, whereas, in practice, insurers make extensive use of tax-loss carryovers. 4) The lognormal model presented in the article is awkward and probably incorrect because premiums seem to be used as the striking price rather than losses.

These and similar problems occurring elsewhere in the literature illustrate the hazards of attempting to force-fit an insurance problem into a financial model developed for other purposes. In fact, there are few insurance applications for which standard models can be used without modification.[12]

Single-period options models are appropriate for the calculation of premia for insurance guaranty funds and for stop-loss reinsurance.[13] In both cases, the option is on the entire firm and covers a single period. Cummins (1988a) uses the put-call parity relationship to obtain the premium for guaranty insurance as the value of the put, $P(A, L, \tau)$. Both continuous and jump models are developed, with stochastic assets and liabilities.

4.3. A Multi-Class Options Model

Because most insurers are multiple-line operations, it is of interest to extend the basic insurance options model to the case of multiple liabilities. Extensions to multiple-asset categories are straightforward and would follow the derivation given below. To conserve notation, the model is derived with two liability classes.

Assume that insurer assets and liabilities follow diffusion processes:

$$dA = \mu_A A dt + \sigma_A A dz_A$$
$$dL_1 = \mu_{L_1} L_1 dt + \sigma_{L_1} L_1 dz_{L_1}$$
$$dL_2 = \mu_{L_2} L_2 dt + \sigma_{L_2} L_2 dz_{L_2} \tag{10}$$

where

A, L_1, L_2	= market values of assets and liabilities (classes 1 and 2),
μ_A, σ_A	= drift and diffusion parameters for assets,
μ_{Li}, σ_{Li}	= drift and diffusion parameters for liability class i, $i = 1, 2$,
dz_A, dz_{L1}, dz_{L2}	= possibly dependent standard Brownian motion processes.

The Brownian motion processes are related as follows: $dz_A\, dz_{L1} = \rho_{A1}\, dt$, $dz_A\, dz_{L2} = \rho_{A2}\, dt$, $dz_{L1}\, dz_{L2} = \rho_{12}\, dt$, where ρ_{Ai}, $i = 1, 2$, = instantaneous correlation coefficients between the Brownian motion processes for assets and liability classes 1 and 2, respectively, and ρ_{12} = instantaneous correlation coefficient for liability classes 1 and 2.

Both assets and liabilities are assumed to be priced according to an intertemporal asset pricing model, such as the intertemporal capital asset pricing model (ICAPM). This implies the following return relationships:

$\mu_A = r_f + \pi_A$, for assets, and
$\mu_{Li} = r_{Li} + \pi_{Li}$, for liability class $i = 1, 2$.

where

r_{Li} = the inflation rate in liability class i, and
π_j = the market risk premium for asset liability $j = A, L_1, L_2$.

The Fisher hypothesis is assumed to hold so that $r_f = r + r_I$, where r = the real rate of interest and r_I = economy-wide rate of inflation. The economy-wide rate of inflation will not in general equal the inflation rates on the two classes of insurance liabilities. If assets (and liabilities) are priced according to the ICAPM, the risk premium would be

$$\pi_j = \rho_{jm}(\sigma_j/\sigma_m)[\mu_m - r_f]$$

where μ_m, σ_m = the drift and diffusion parameters of the Brownian motion process for the market portfolio, and ρ_{jm} = the correlation coefficient between the Brownian motion process for asset j and that for the market portfolio.[14]

The value of an option on the two-liability insurance company can be written as $P(A, L_1, L_2, \tau)$, where τ = time to expiration of the option. Differentiating P using Ito's lemma and invoking the ICAPM pricing relationships for assets and liabilities yields the following differential equation:

$$\begin{aligned}
Pr_f ={}& r_f P_A A + r_{L_1} P_{L_1} L_1 + r_{L_2} P_{L_2} L_2 - P_\tau \\
&+ \frac{1}{2}\sigma_A^2 P_{AA} A^2 + \frac{1}{2}\sigma_{L_1}^2 L_1^2 P_{L_1 L_1} + \frac{1}{2}\sigma_{L_2}^2 P_{L_2 L_2} L_2^2 \\
&+ P_{AL_1} AL_1 \sigma_{A1} + P_{AL_2} AL_2 \sigma_{A2} + P_{L_1 L_2} \sigma_{12} L_1 L_2
\end{aligned} \qquad (11)$$

Risk and the drift parameters (μ_j) have been eliminated by using the ICAPM and taking expectations. It would also be possible to do this by using a hedging argument, provided that appropriate hedging assets are available.

The next step is to use the homogeneity property of the options model to change variables so that the model is expressed in terms of the asset-to-liability ratio x, the option value-to-liability ratio $p = P/L$, and the liability proportions $w_1 = L_1/L$ and $w_2 = L_2/L$, where $x = A/L$ and $L = L_1 + L_2$. This requires the additional assumption that $L_1 + L_2$, the sum of two lognormal variables, can be treated as if it were lognormal. This is a common assumption in the literature (e.g., Doherty and Garven (1986)). The result is the following differential equation:

$$pr_n = xp_x r_n - p_\tau + \frac{1}{2} x^2 p_{xx} \sigma_n^2 \qquad (12)$$

where

$r_n = r_f - w_1 r_{L1} - w_2 r_{L2},$
$\sigma_n^2 = \sigma_A^2 + w_1^2 \sigma_{L1}^2 + w_2^2 \sigma_{L2}^2 - 2w_1 \sigma_{A1} - 2w_2 \sigma_{A2} + 2w_1 w_2 \sigma_{12},$
σ_j = the diffusion parameter for process j ($j = A$ = assets, $j = 1$ = liability class 1, and $j = 2$ = liability class 2), and
σ_{jk} = the covariance parameter for processes j and k.

Equation (12) is the standard Black-Scholes differential equation, where the optioned asset is the asset-to-liability ratio (x).

This model can be used to price various contingent claims on the insurer by solving the equation subject to the appropriate boundary conditions. For example, the call option $c(x, 1, \tau)$ = the value of owners' equity, is the solution to equation (12) with boundary condition $c(x, 1, 0) = \text{Max}(x-1, 0)$. The put option $g(x, 1, \tau)$ = the guaranty fund premium is the solution of (12) with boundary condition $g(x, 1, 0) = \text{Max}(1 - x, 0)$. The value of policy liabilities is obtained from the parity relationship as $b(x, 1, \tau) = 1 \exp(-r\tau) - g(x, 1, \tau)$. The striking price in each case is equal to 1 because of the normalization of asset and option values by L. The option values are given by the usual Black-Scholes call and put option formulas (see Jarrow and Rudd (1983)).[15]

4.4. Implications of the Multi-Class Model

A number of interesting implications about insurance markets can be gleaned from equation (12). The equation reveals that a portfolio effect exists for insurers that write multiple policies or multiple lines. The insolvency put on the portfolio is less than the weighted sum of insolvency puts if the lines were insured in mono-line companies.

To be more specific, assume the existence of two insurers, with assets

A_i, liabilities L_i, and risk parameters σ_i, $i = 1, 2$. The put values for the two insurers separately are $g_i(A_i, L_i, \tau)$, $i = 1, 2$. Now suppose that the two companies are merged, with no change in the asset or liability parameters. Assume that the correlation coefficient between the liability processes is ρ_{12}, and, to save notation, that there is no correlation between the asset and liability processes. Then, if $\sigma_1 = \sigma_2$, it can be shown that:

$$g_s(A_1+A_2, L_1+L_2, \tau) \leq g_1(A_1, L_1, \tau) + g_2(A_2, L_2, \tau) \qquad (13)$$

To prove relationship (13), use the homogeneity property to write:

$$(L_1 + L_2)g_s\left(\frac{A_1+A_2}{L_1+L_2}, \tau\right) \leq L_1 g_1\left(\frac{A_1}{L_1}\right) + L_2 g_2\left(\frac{A_2}{L_2}\right)$$

$$g_s(x_1 w_1 + x_2 w_2, \tau) \leq w_1 g_1(x_1) + w_2 g_2(x_2) \qquad (14)$$

where

$x_i = A_i/L_i$, $i = 1, 2$, and
$w_i = L_i/(L_1 + L_2)$, $i = 1, 2$.

The relationship is true owing to the convexity of European puts. Intuitively, the portfolio of puts (right-hand side) is worth at least as much as the put on the portfolio (left-hand side) because situations exist in which one of the individual puts finishes in the money but the portfolio does not. If $\sigma_1 \neq \sigma_2$, the relationship still is likely to hold as long as the difference between the two risk parameters is not too large.

Equation (14) implies that value is created by pooling different classes of risks in a portfolio. The portfolio will be safer than the individual portfolio segments taken separately as long as the liability processes are not perfectly correlated. Thus, multiple-line insurers have an advantage over mono-line insurers in that they can offer equally safe insurance with less capital.

A conjecture is that it may be optimal for an insurer to write business on a proportion of the liability-value-weighted "market" portfolio of all insured risks rather than to choose a portfolio consisting of a subset of these risks. Adjustments in the desired risk-taking posture of the company could be made by choosing a portfolio consisting of a weighted average of the market insurance portfolio and riskless debt. Investigation of the portfolio effect and this conjecture would be an interesting avenue for future research.

The model also can be used to gain some insights into the supply and demand for insurance (Cummins and Danzon (1991)). For example, assume that a company has an existing portfolio of policies L_1 that has one year until maturity. Its assets are A_1, and its existing portfolio will pay no additional premiums. The company has the opportunity to write a new block of policies, L_2. To write the new policies, it may have to issue new equity (E). The company is seeking a strategy for issuing new equity and pricing the new policy block.

Assuming that markets are efficient and that the policyholders know the characteristics of policies and potential insurers, pricing will be dependent upon the *liquidation rule*, i.e., the rule governing the disposition of the company's assets in the event of insolvency. Assume that the liquidation rule compensates policyholders in proportion to the nominal value of their claims against the company, so that policy class i obtains proportion $w_i = L_i/(L_1 + L_2)$ of assets. Then, the fair premium for the new policyholders is $L_2 [\exp(-r\tau) - g_s(x, \tau)]$, where $g_s(x, \tau) =$ the put option on the company after the new policies and new equity are issued and $x = (A_1 + A_2)/(L_1 + L_2)$.

Since the pricing rule of the new policyholders is satisfied for a wide range of x values, the amount of the equity issue is indeterminate unless additional structure is imposed on the problem. For example, equity owners could gain by issuing the new policies and obtaining little or no new equity. This would expropriate value from the existing (class 1) policyholders without affecting the new policyholders, who pay the fair value for their coverage.

In a competitive, efficient market, it is unlikely that the equity owners would gain by expropriation. Expropriating value from the old policyholders would adversely affect the firm's reputation and its future cash flows. For example, the new policyholders might not be willing to pay the fair value if it appears that the owners will adversely change the characteristics of the firm.

Assume that the firm's objective is for the value of equity after the equity/policy issue to be at least as large as the sum of its equity before the equity/policy issue and the amount of new capital raised, i.e.,

$$C_s(A_1+A_2, L_1+L_2, \tau) \geqslant C_1(A_1, L_1, \tau) + E$$

$$A_1 + A_2 - (L_1 + L_2)e^{-r\tau} + (L_1 + L_2)g_s(x, \tau)$$
$$\geqslant A_1 - L_1 e^{-r\tau} + L_1 g_1(x_1, \tau) + E \qquad (15)$$

$$A_2 - L_2[e^{-r\tau} - g_s(x, \tau)] + L_1[g_s(x, \tau) - g_1(x_1, \tau)] \geqslant E$$

Focusing on the third line in (15), it should be clear that the premium of the new policyholders is $(-1$ times) the first bracketed expression on the left-hand side of the inequality sign. The difference between A_2 and the premium must equal the new equity (E) since there is no other source of funds. Thus, the condition for writing the policies reduces to the following:

$$g_s(x, \tau; \sigma^2) - g_1(x_1, \tau; \sigma_1^2) \geqslant 0 \qquad (16)$$

where σ^2, σ_1^2 = the risk parameters of the firm after and before the policy issue.

In general, if the firm is safer after the new policies are issued, i.e., if $g_s(x, \tau, \sigma^2) < g_1(x_1, \tau, \sigma_1^2)$, the stockholders will lose money on the transaction.[16] They will gain if the firm is more risky following the policy issue, so that $g_s(x, \tau, \sigma^2) > g_1(x_1, \tau, \sigma_1^2)$. The first line of (15) is satisfied as an equality only if the value of the put (per dollar of liabilities) is the same before and after the policy issue.

Unless the new policies are unusually risky or highly correlated with the old policies, the risk parameter of the firm after the policies are issued will be less than it was before due to the diversification effect. Since $\partial g(x, \tau)/\partial \sigma > 0$ and $\partial g(x, \tau)/\partial x < 0$, this implies that the firm can operate at a lower leverage ratio without expropriating value from the old policyholders.

This model may help to explain market behavior observed during insurance price and availability crises. For example, assume that the risk of policy class 2 is sufficiently high that $\sigma^2 > \sigma_1^2$. Then, to avoid expropriation, the leverage ratio must increase, leading to higher costs for the new policies.

If there is an optimal leverage ratio (or range) and unexpected losses reduce the ratio to a suboptimal level, it may be difficult to restore the optimal ratio immediately. Expressions (15) and (16) imply that the firm cannot raise the ratio without incurring a capital loss unless it charges more than the expected value premium to the new policyholders. Writing more business at a suboptimal leverage ratio may affect the reputation of the firm and therefore dampen future cash flows. Thus, the firm may prefer to write business at higher-than-expected-value prices even if this means reducing its volume.

Some type of market imperfection or restriction on entry is necessary for firms to restore optimal leverage ratios by writing at higher-than-expected-value prices. For example, new entry may be difficult in lines such as liability insurance due to information asymmetries, regulation, and other market imperfections. A liability insurer gains significant information by observing its policyholders during the coverage and claims settlement periods. If this is private information that is not transmitted to subsequent insurers, it would provide an entry barrier.

4.5. The Insurer as a Down-and-Out Option

One of the implications of the simple options model of the firm is that the equity owners can gain at the expense of the debt holders by increasing the risk of the firm.[17] Nevertheless, in actual securities and insurance markets, stockholders usually do not exploit this feature of the call option. One way to explain this is through reputational arguments, as suggested above. Another approach is to examine penalties and restrictions that might be imposed on firms adopting expropriative strategies.

One type of restriction that is often used in bond markets is the safety covenant. For example, the bond agreement may specify that the firm will be reorganized if its value ever drops to a specified level. Although insurance contracts usually do not include safety covenants, regulation has a similar effect. Specifically, regulators will close down the insurer if the value of the firm's book liabilities ever exceeds the value of its book assets. The requirement is actually somewhat stricter than this, with the insurer being subject to regulatory restriction if the difference between assets and liabilities ever falls below some level $K > 0$.

The effect of the regulatory safety restriction is to terminate the equity-holders' claim on the firm if the difference between assets and liabilities ever reaches the boundary. The chance of reaching the boundary is an increasing function of risk. Consequently, the result of the regulatory safety restriction is to change equity owner incentives with regard to risk-taking.

The regulatory safety restriction can be modeled using a type of option known as the down-and-out option (see Merton (1973a) and Cox and Rubenstein (1985)). Let $W(A, L, \tau)$ equal the value of a down-and-out call option on an insurer with assets A and face value of liabilities L. The time-to-expiration of the option is τ. Prior to τ if the value of the assets ever reaches the knock-out boundary $K = bL\exp(-\eta\tau)$, the stocholders' interest in the firm is terminated and the assets revert to the debtholders, where b and η are constants.

To analyze the insurance case, assume that $\eta = 0$. Then the knock-out boundary is constant, and the value of the firm reverts to the debt holders *if* assets fall to bL. Also assume that the call option has an infinite life, i.e., $\tau = \infty$.[18] Since corporations have infinite lives, this is a reasonable abstraction of reality. The formula for the infinite down-and-out call is

$$W(A, L) = A - bL\left(\frac{A}{bL}\right)^{-2r_f/\sigma^2} \tag{17}$$

where $\sigma^2 =$ the dispersion parameter of the insurer. Because the value of an infinite-lived conventional call option equals the value of the assets (the value of an infinite-lived conventional put is zero), equation (17) implies that the value of the firm's debt is $D(A, L) = bL(A/bL)^{-\gamma}$, where $\gamma = 2r_f/\sigma^2$.

The effects of changes in risk on the equity and debt of the down-and-out firm are as follows:

$$\frac{\partial W}{\partial \sigma^2} = -\frac{\partial D}{\partial \sigma^2} = -bL\left(\frac{bL}{A}\right)^{2r_f/\sigma^2} \frac{2r_f}{\sigma^4} \ln\left(\frac{A}{bL}\right) \tag{18}$$

Expression (18) is < 0 if $bL < A$. Thus, increases in risk reduce the equity holders' share of the value of the firm and increase the debt holders' share. Equity holders have an incentive not to increase risk because this increases the chance that their share in the firm will be forfeited to the debt holders due to the knock-out feature. This provides a useful model of the value of the firm under solvency regulation.

Like the standard Black-Scholes model, the down-and-out option can be generalized to multiple asset and liability classes. For one asset class and two types of liabilities, the value of the down-and-out option is given by equation (17), with dispersion parameter σ_n^2 (defined following equation (12)).

If the liquidation rule allocates assets in proportion to nominal liabilities, the analysis of the firm's decision to accept new business is similar to the multivariate Black-Scholes analysis discussed previously. The firm will issue new business provided that the equity value of the firm after the policy (and stock) issue is greater than the value of the firm before the issue plus the amount of new capital raised. The condition is expressed as follows:

$$W(A_1+A_2, L_1+L_2) - W(A_1, L_1) \geqslant E$$

$$A_2 - bL_2\left(\frac{x}{b}\right)^{-2r/\sigma^2} - bL_1\left[\left(\frac{x}{b}\right)^{-2r_f/\sigma^2} - \left(\frac{x_1}{b}\right)^{-2r_f/\sigma_1^2}\right] \geq E \tag{19}$$

where

$x = (A_1 + A_2)/(L_1 + L_2)$,
$x_1 = A_1/L_1$,
σ^2 = dispersion parameter after the policy issue, and
σ_1^2 = dispersion parameter before the policy issue.

Assuming that new debt holders pay the expected value for their coverage, there is neither a gain nor a loss in equity if the term in brackets in (19) is equal to zero. The dispersion of the firm typically will be lower following the policy issue. Thus, the firm should be able to operate at a lower leverage ratio as a result of issuing new policies.

The down-and-out model provides an alternative options interpretation of the insurance firm which in some ways provides a better description of observed insurer behavior than the Black-Scholes model. Additional research is needed on the down-and-out model to further explore its implications for insurance pricing.

5. Continuous Time Discounted Cash Flow Models

5.1. Certainty Model

Continuous time models for insurance pricing have been developed by Kraus and Ross (KR) (1982) and Cummins (1988a). As an introduction, consider the Kraus-Ross continuous time model under conditions of certainty.

To simplify the discussion, assume that the current value of losses is determined by a draw from a random process at time 0. Loss payments occur at instantaneous rate θ, while loss inflation is at exponential rate ρ, and discounting is at rate r_f. The differential equation for the rate of change in outstanding losses at time t, in the absence of inflation, is: $dC_t/dt = -\theta C_t$. Solving this equation for C_t yields the amount of unpaid claims at any given time (the reserve): $C_t = C_0 e^{-\theta t}$. Thus, the assumption is that the claims runoff follows an exponential decay process with average time to payout $= 1/\theta$.

Considering inflation, the rate of claim outflow at any given time is: $L_t = \theta C_t e^{\pi t}$. The premium is the present value of losses, obtained as follows:

$$P = \int_0^\infty L_t e^{-r_f t} dt = \int_0^\infty \theta C_0 e^{(\pi - \theta - r_f)t} dt = \frac{\theta C_0}{r_f + \theta - \pi} \qquad (20)$$

In (20), π could be $>$, $=$, or $< i$, where $r_f = r + i$, $i =$ economy-wide inflation and $r =$ the real rate of interest. The model also can be used to estimate the market value of reserves, R_τ:

$$R_\tau = \int_\tau^\infty \theta L_0 e^{-(\theta + r_f - \pi)t} dt = \frac{\theta L_0}{\theta + r_f - \pi} e^{-(\theta + r_f - \pi)\tau} \qquad (21)$$

5.2. Uncertainty Models

Kraus and Ross also introduce a continuous time model under uncertainty. This model is based on arbitrage pricing theory (APT). The KR model allows for market-related uncertainty in both frequency and severity.

The following differential equation governs the claims process: $dC/dt = \alpha_t - \theta C_t$, where $\alpha_t =$ accident frequency. The frequency process affects the evolution of outstanding claims for a period of length T (the policy period). After that point, no new claims can be filed. During the entire period (0 to ∞) claims inflation takes place according to the price index q_t.

The parameters α_t and q_t are governed by the k economic factors of arbitrage pricing theory. These factors are modelled as diffusion processes:

$$dx_i = m_i x_i dt + \sigma_i x_i dz_i, \quad i = 1, 2, \cdots, k. \tag{22}$$

The parameters are log-linear functions of the factors, e.g.:

$$\log(q) = \sum_{i=1}^{k} q_i \log(x_i) + \log(q_0) \tag{23}$$

where q_0 = the price level of the average claim at policy inception.

Arbitrage pricing theory implies that the value of outstanding claims at any time t, $V(x, C, t)$, where x is the vector consisting of the x_i, is governed by the following differential equation:

$$E\left[\frac{dV}{V}\right] + \left[\frac{\theta q C}{V} - r_f\right] dt = \sum_{i=1}^{k} \lambda_i \sigma_i \left[\text{Cov}\left(\frac{dV}{V}, \frac{dx_i}{x_i}\right) \middle/ \text{Var}\left(\frac{dx_i}{x_i}\right) \right] dt \tag{24}$$

where

λ_i = the market price of risk for factor $i = (r_{mi} - r_f)/\sigma_i$, and
r_{mi} = the market return on a portfolio that is perfectly correlated with the ith risk factor.

The premium formula is obtained by applying the multivariate version of Ito's lemma (see Ingersoll (1987)) and then solving the resulting differential equation. The formula is:

$$P = \left(\frac{\theta a_0 q_0 L_0}{\rho + \theta}\right)\left(\frac{1 - e^{-\rho_a \tau}}{\rho_a}\right) \tag{25}$$

where

$\rho = r_f - \pi - \Sigma_i \lambda_i \sigma_i q_i,$
$\rho_a = r_f - \pi_a - \Sigma_i \lambda_i \sigma_i (q_i + \alpha_i),$
$\pi = \Sigma_i [.5\sigma^2 q_i(q_i - 1) + q_i m_i],$
$\pi_a = \Sigma_i [.5\sigma^2(\alpha_i + q_i)(\alpha_i + q_i - 1) + (\alpha_i + q_i)m_i].$

The premium given by (25) is similar to the premium for the certainty case except for the presence of the market risk loadings (λ_i terms). These loadings are the company's reward for bearing systematic risk. The α_i and q_i are the beta coefficients of the model.

For the company to receive a positive reward for risk bearing, the risk loading term must be negative, i.e., losses must be negatively correlated with some of the market factors such that the net loading is < 0. The model requires estimates of the market prices of risk for the k risk factors as well as the beta coefficients for insurance. This would be difficult given the available data. Like most other financial pricing models for insurance, this model gives the price for an insurance policy that is free of default risk.

A continuous time model that prices default risk has been developed by Cummins (1988a). Assets and liabilities are assumed to follow geometric Brownian motion:

$$dA = (a_A A - \theta L) \, dt + A\sigma_A dz_A$$
$$dL = (a_L L - \theta L) \, dt + L\sigma_L dz_L \tag{26}$$

where

a_A, a_L	= asset and liability drift parameters,
σ_A, σ_L	= asset and liability risk (diffusion) parameters,
A, L	= stock of assets and liabilities,
θ	= the claims runoff parameter, and
$dz_A(t), dz_L(t)$	= possibly correlated standard Brownian motion processes.

The model is more realistic than the standard options model since it does not have a fixed expiration date but rather allows the liabilities to run off over an infinite time horizon. In effect, it models liabilities as a perpetuity subject to exponential decay. Thus, it is a better model for long tail lines than the standard options model and avoids the use of the k (liabilities to premiums) factor.

Cummins uses the model to obtain the market value of default risk, $D(A, L)$. Using Ito's lemma to differentiate D and then using either a hedging argument or the ICAPM to eliminate the risk terms, one obtains the confluent hypergeometric differential equation. The solution is:

$$D(x) = \frac{\Gamma(2)}{\Gamma(2 + a)} \, b^a x^{-a} e^{-b/x} M(2, 2 + a, b/x) \tag{27}$$

where

$a\ = 2(r_f - r_L + \theta)/Q,$
$r_L =$ The liability inflation rate,
$b\ = 2\theta/Q,$
$Q\ = \sigma_A^2 + \sigma_L^2 - 2\sigma_A\sigma_L\rho_{AL},$ and
$M\ =$ Kummer's function (see Abramowitz and Stegun (1970)).

This perpetuity model has significant potential for pricing blocks of policies subject to default risk. It poses easier estimation problems than the Kraus-Ross model since one need only estimate the variance and covariance parameters of assets and liabilities rather than betas and factor risk premia.

Conclusions

This paper discusses the principal financial pricing models that have been developed for property-liability insurance and proposes some extensions. Insurance pricing models have been developed based on the capital asset pricing model, the intertemporal capital asset pricing model, arbitrage pricing theory, and options pricing theory. The models assume either that insurance policies are priced in accordance with principles of market equilibrium or minimally that arbitrage opportunities are avoided.

Additional research is needed to develop more realistic insurance pricing models. For example, most of the models assume that interest rates are nonstochastic even though insurers face significant interest-rate risk. Modeling multiple-line firms with multiperiod claim runoffs also poses challenging problems. With few exceptions, existing financial models do not price the risk of ruin. Estimation problems, especially for betas and market risk premia, are a major problem given the existing insurance data. Options models and perpetuity models such as Cummins' cohort model (Cummins (1988a)) may offer solutions to some of these problems, since they rely on relatively few parameters and can be modified to incorporate stochastic interest rates.

In addition to models now in existence, models based on consumption capital asset pricing theory (Breedon (1979)), martingale pricing (Duffie (1988)), and lattice modeling (Boyle (1988)) may provide promising avenues for future research. Modifications of the perfect information, perfect markets results for information asymmetries also will become increasingly important as the field continues to advance.

Notes

1. In economic terms, the true value of the reserve is its market value, reflecting the time value of money, a risk premium, and its value as a tax shield. However, state laws require that insurers state their policy obligations at nominal (nondiscounted) values.

2. Of course, there are many variations of this general pattern, such as the use of sinking funds, convertability, and call provisions.

3. Index bonds exist in some economies but are rarely used in the United States.

4. The damage degree is the "real" severity of loss, measured in physical units or constant dollars.

5. This rationale for regulation is debateable, but investigation of this issue is beyond the scope of this paper.

6. In 1988, 80% of the assets of property-liability insurers were invested in financial assets. About 75% of the financial assets were in bonds, and 13% were in stocks. See A. M. Best Company, *Best's Aggregates and Averages* (Oldwick, NJ, 1989).

7. It would be double counting to consider investment income as a flow from the policyholder perspective.

8. Of course, in practice, insurers invest in tax exempt as well as taxable securities. It would be useful to generalize the MC model to include both taxable and tax-exempt investment income.

9. In finance, this is known as the problem of optimal capital structure.

10. This argument was first developed by Cox and Ross (1976). The argument applies to most derivative securities, not just to the Black-Scholes model.

11. If asset prices are jointly normal, a RNVR exists if the representative investor's preferences exhibit constant absolute risk aversion.

12. Other options models, such as the *compound options model*, overcome some of the limitations of the single-period model. This model is discussed in Geske (1977) and (1979).

13. Property-liability insurance guaranty funds exist in all states to satisfy the financial obligations of insolvent insurers. The solvent insurers in the state are assessed after an insolvency to pay the claims of the insolvent insurer. Assessments are in proportion to company size. The options model can be used to calculate risk-based premiums, which have a number of advantages, as explained in Cummins (1988a).

14. Other models that could be used to define the risk premium include the inter-temporal CAPM with stochastic opportunity set (Merton (1971)) and the consumption CAPM (Breedon (1979)). The consumption CAPM seems especially promising since its risk premia are related to the rate of return on aggregate real consumption. This may lead to more accurate beta estimates for insurance liabilities than the traditional market portfolio of common stocks used in the conventional CAPM.

15. The options in terms of x can be rescaled in terms of dollars by multiplying by L. This is due to the homogeneity property.

16. The put value is directly related to risk, i.e., $\partial g/\partial \sigma$. The comparative statics of the Black-Scholes model are discussed in Jarrow and Rudd (1983).

17. The derivative of the call option on the firm with respect to the risk parameter is positive.

18. These assumptions are used to simplify the discussion. A closed form solution exists for finite-lived down-and-out options with $\eta > 0$. See Cox and Rubenstein (1985, p. 410).

References

Ang, James S., and Tsong-Yue Lai. (1987). "Insurance Premium Pricing and Ratemaking in Competitive Insurance and Capital Asset Markets," *Journal of Risk and Insurance* 54, 767–779.

Biger, Nihum, and Yehuda Kahane. (1978). "Risk Considerations In Insurance Ratemaking," *Journal of Risk and Insurance* 45, 121–132.

Boyle, Phelim. (1988). "A Lattice Framework for Option Pricing With Two State Variables," *Journal of Financial and Quantitative Analysis* 23, 1–12.

Brealey, Richard A., and Stewart C. Myers. (1988). *Principles of Corporate Finance*, 3rd ed. New York: McGraw-Hill Book Company.

Breedon, D. T. (1979). "An Intertemporal Asset Pricing Model with Stochastic Investment and Consumption Opportunities," *Journal of Financial Economics* 6, 273–296.

Brennan, M. J. (1979). "The Pricing of Contingent Claims In Discrete Time Models," *Journal of Finance* 24, 53–68.

Cooper, Robert W. (1974). *Investment Return and Property-Liability Insurance*

Ratemaking. Philadelphia: S.S. Huebner Foundation, University of Pennsylvania.

Copeland, Thomas E., and J. Fred Weston. (1988). *Financial Theory and Corporate Policy*, 3d. ed. Reading, MA: Addison-Wesley Publishing Company.

Cox, John D., and Stephen Ross. (1976). "The Valuation of Options for Alternative Stochastic Processes," *Journal of Finance* 31, 383–402.

Cox, John D., and Mark Rubinstein. (1985). *Options Markets.* Englewood Cliffs, N.J.: Prentice-Hall.

Cummins, J. David. (1990). "Multi-Period Discounted Cash Flow Rate making Models in Property-Liability Insurance," *Journal of Risk and Insurance* 57, 79–109.

Cummins, J. David and Patricia Denzon. (1991). "Price Shocks and Capital Flows in Liability Insurance," Working Paper, University of Pennsylvania.

Cummins, J. David, and Richard A. Derrig. (1988). *Classical Models of Insurance Solvency.* Kluwer Academic Publishers.

Cummins, J. David, and Richard A. Derrig. (1989). *Financial Models of Insurance Solvency.* Kluwer Academic Publishers.

Cummins, J. David, and Scott E. Harrington. (1985). "Property-Liability Insurance Rate Regulation: Estimation of Underwriting Betas Using Quarterly Profit Data," *Journal of Risk and Insurance* 52, 16–43.

Cummins, J. David, and Scott E. Haruington. (1987). *Fair Rate of Return In Property-Liability Insurance.* Kluwer Academic Publishers.

Cummins, J. David, and David J. Nye. (1981). "Inflation and Property-Liability Insurance," in John D. Long, ed., *Issues in Insurance*, V. II, 1–78. American Institute of Property Liability Underwriters, Malvern, PA

Cummins, J. David, and Mary A. Weiss. (1989). "The Auto Insurance Crisis and Solutions: Competing for Efficiency," *Contingencies* 1 (September-October): 46–51.

Cummins, J. David. (1988a). "Risk-Based Premiums for Insurance Guaranty Funds," *Journal of Finance* 43, 823–839.

Cummins, J. David. (1988b). "Capital Structure and Fair Profits In Property-Liability Insurance," working paper, University of Pennsylvania.

D'Arcy, Stephen, and Neil A. Doherty. (1988). *Financial Theory of Insurance Pricing.* Philadelphia: S.S. Huebner Foundation.

D'Arcy, Stephen, and James R. Garven. (1988). "Property-Liability Insurance Pricing Models: An Empirical Investigation," *Journal of Risk and Insurance* 57, 391–430.

Derrig, Richard A. (1985). "The Effect of Federal Income Taxes on Investment Income in Property-Liability Ratemaking," working paper, Massachusetts Rating Bureau, Boston, MA.

Doherty, Neil A., and James R. Garven. (1986). "Price Regulation in Property-Liability Insurance: A Contingent Claims Approach," *Journal of Finance* 41, 1031–1050.

Duffie, Darrell. (1988). *Security Markets: Stochastic Models.* New York: Academic Press.

Fairley, William. (1979). "Investment Income and Profit Margins In Property-Liability Insurance: Theory and Empirical Tests," *Bell Journal* 10, 192–210.

Ferrari, J. Robert. (1968). "A Note on the Basic Relationship of Underwriting, Investments, Leverage and Exposure to Total Return on Owners' Equity," *Proceedings of the Casualty Actuarial Society* 55, 295–302.

Geske, Robert. (1977). "The Valuation of Corporate Liabilities As Compound Options," *Journal of Financial and Quantitative Analysis* 541–552.

Geske, Robert. (1979). "The Valuation of Compound Options," *Journal of Financial Economics* 7, 63–81.

Hill, Raymond. (1979). "Profit Regulation in Property-Liability Insurance," *Bell Journal* 10, 172–191.

Ingersoll, Jonathan E., Jr. (1987). *Theory of Financial Decision Making*. Totowa, NJ: Rowman & Littlefield.

Jarrow, Robert, and Andrew Rudd. (1983). *Option Pricing*. Homewood, IL: Richard D. Irwin.

Karlin, Samuel, and Howard Taylor. (1981). *A Second Course in Stochastic Processes*. New York: Academic Press.

Kraus, Alan, and Stephen Ross. (1982). "The Determination of Fair Profits for the Property-Liability Insurance Firm," *Journal of Finance* 33, 1015–1028.

Merton, Robert C. (1973a). "Theory of Rational Option Pricing," *Bell Journal of Economics and Management Science* 4, 141–183.

Merton, Robert C. (1973b). "An Intertemporal Capital Asset Pricing Model," *Econometrica* 41, 867–880.

Merton, Robert C. (1977). "An Analytic Derivation of the Cost of Deposit Insurance and Loan Guarantees: An Application of Modern Option Pricing Theory," *Journal of Banking and Finance* 1 (June): 3–11.

Merton, Robert C. (1978). "On the Cost of Deposit Insurance When There Are Surveilance Costs," *Journal of Business* 51 (July): 439–452.

Myers, Stewart, and Richard Cohn. (1987). "Insurance Rate Regulation and the Capital Asset Pricing Model," in J. D. Cummins and S. E. Harrington, eds., *Fair Rate of Return In Property-Liability Insurance*. Norwell, MA: Kluwer Academic Publishers.

Pennacchi, George. (1987). "A Reexamination of the Over- (or Under-) Pricing of Deposit Insurance," *Journal of Money, Credit, and Banking* 19, 340–346.

Ross, Stephen A. (1976). "The Arbitrage Theory of Capital Asset pricing," *Journal of Economic Theory* 13, 341–360.

Ross, Stephen A. (1977). "Risk, Return, and Arbitrage," in I. Friend and J. Bicksler, eds., *Risk and Return in Finance*, V.I. Cambridge, MA: Ballinger Publishing Co.

Smith, Clifford W., Jr. (1979). "Applications of Option Pricing Analysis," in James L. Bicksler (ed.) *Handbook of Financial Economics*, North Holland Publishing Company, Amsterdam, 79–121.

Staking, Kim B. (1990). "Asset/Liability Management, the Duration Gap, and Insurer Stock Values," Ph.D. dissertation, Wharton School, University of Pennsylvania, Philadelphia.

Stapleton, R. C., and M. G. Subrahmanyam. (1984). "The Valuation of Multivariate Contingent Claims In Discrete Time Models," *Journal of Finance* 39, 207–208.

ECONOMETRIC MODELS OF ACCIDENT DISTRIBUTIONS*

Marcel Boyer

Université de Montréal

Georges Dionne

Université de Montréal

Charles Vanasse

Université de Montréal

Abstract

This paper deals with the econometrics of car accidents, that is, the estimation of the relative importance or significance of the factors explaining the number of accidents in a given period on an individual basis. The number of car accidents is a discrete variable and, therefore, represents a count process: the dependent variable takes only nonnegative integer values. Hence, the observed dependent variable is the number of accidents an individual i had in the period considered. The individual characteristics are considered exogenous or predetermined and may or may not be significant factors in explaining the number of accidents. We have estimated four categorical models (linear probability, probit, logit, and multinomial logit) and four count data models (Poisson and negative binomial models with and without individual characteristics in the regression component). It is difficult to compare the econometric results of the different models since some of these models are not nested. However, it is shown that the negative binomial model with a regression component produces a reasonable approximation of the true distribution of accidents. Different statistical tests reject the Poisson models (with and without a regression component) and the negative binomial model without individual characteristics. It is also observed that all estimated models provide the same qualitative

* We are grateful to the Régie de l'assurance automobile du Québec (R.A.A.Q.), FCAR (Québec), M.T.Q. (Québec) and S.S.H.R.C. (Canada) for their financial support and to M. Bisaillon, M. Bienvenu, P. Cossette, and M. Pellerin for their collaboration in different stages of this research. Comments by M. Beuthe, L. Bauwens, D. Bolduc, and C. Gouriéroux were particularly useful.

169

results (essentially the same significant variables), but differ when predictions of either the probabilities of accident or the expected number of accidents were made. For quantitative predictions, it is important to select the appropriate model. Moreover, it is shown that, in all models, the individual's past driving experience is a good predictor of risk. Finally, we apply the statistical results to a model of insurance rating in the presence of moral hazard.

Key words: econometric models, accident distributions, Poisson, negative binomial, linear probability, probit, logit, multinomial logit, moral hazard, insurance rating

This paper deals with the econometrics of car accidents, that is, the relative importance of factors explaining the number of accidents in a given period on an individual basis. The number of car accidents is a discrete variable and therefore represents a count process: the dependent variable takes only nonnegative integer values. We exploit a database consisting of the accident record and characteristics of individual drivers. Hence, the observed dependent variable is the number of accidents an individual *i* had in the period considered. The individual characteristics are considered exogenous and may or not be significant factors in explaining the number of accidents.

Count variables appear in the economic theory of individual behavior in two different but related sets of situations. In the first set, the individual is directly choosing a naturally discrete variable by selecting one among mutually exclusive possibilities. Examples of the first set of situations are the mutually exclusive choices of a particular brand in a discrete set of available goods, of a particular job among all the ex ante discrete available job opportunities, and of a mode of consumption like a transport mode among all the ex ante discrete available modes.

In the second set of situations giving rise to count variables, the individual really chooses a continuous variable, but this choice is private information to the agent and as such is unobservable by an outsider. However, the outsider can observe a proxy integer variable (a count variable) of the individual's choice. Examples of the second set of situations are the level of effort chosen by a worker or manager while an outside observer can only see if the firm succeeded or not in obtaining a contract, in entering a market, in avoiding bankruptcy, in avoiding a strike. Other examples are the probability of illness or health chosen by an insuree (through proper diet or exercise), while the outside observer or the insurer can only see, that is can only gather data on whether the individual was sick or not, on how many visits he made to a doctor, or on how many drug types he regularly consumes; the probability of divorce chosen by an individual (through a proper level of divorce preventing activities or behavior) while the outside observer can only observe whether the individual had a divorce or not; and so on.

Count data constitute a particularly important form of empirical observations not only in economics but also in all social sciences. Although their systematic use in econometrics is rather recent, they do have a long and successful history in biological research for which many of the statistical models were developed originally [Patil (1970)]. In economics, count data models have been or could be profitably used to explain the number of product varieties produced by a firm [Holland (1973), for the case of chemical products]; to explain the use of health services such as the number of visits to a doctor, to hospitals, the number or drugs consumed [Cameron, Trivedi, Milne, and Piggott (1988)]; the number of units bought of a good [Gilbert (1979)]; the number of patents applied for by firms [Haussman, Hall, and Griliches (1984)]; the number of airline incidents [Rose (1990)]; and many other cases relating to the number of strikes, the number of children in a family, the number of new firms created, the number of banks or other firms failures, and the number of layoffs spells. One can think of quite a few other examples; there are no doubt many other applications of count data models that could be made in applied econometrics and quantitative social sciences in general.

Although economic theory does provide many such examples of count data, it is in general silent regarding the proper statistical model to estimate the relevant parameters. For a survey of count data estimators, one can see Cameron and Trivedi (1986) and also Gouriéroux and Montfort (1989c). These authors suggest that the extensive statistics on stochastic discrete phenomena, which proved to be so helpful in biometrics where the theory itself often suggests using a particular statistical model, cannot oe applied too directly in econometrics (see, in particular, Cameron and Trivedi). There are good reasons for such a situation. In econometrics and sociometrics in general, the data-generating process involves rational agents interacting, competitively or cooperatively, over time under constraints of different types such as technological constraints, economic constraints, social constraints, physical constraints, and so on. These competitive and cooperative interactions give rise to a social or economic equilibrium, a particular set of allocations to and actions by each agent, at which the system is in some sense at rest, typically a dynamic rest (stationarity, ergodicity). Hence, interdependence and simultaneity are very important characteristics of economic outcomes and therefore important concepts in economic theory and applied econometrics; in other words, the future is never really determined until it has fallen into the past! In such a context, economic data-generating processes will rarely conform to standard statistical models and distributions: at best, it will be known that the true distribution — which will rarely exist in closed form — belongs to a certain family. Specification problems must continuously be addressed and robust estimators of parametric and nonparametric models must be developed.

The case of car accidents is, in many respects, typical of such problems [Greenwood and Yule (1920), Seal (1969), Johnson and Hey (1971), Ferreira (1974), and Lemaire (1985)]. Most accidents involve more than one individual, usually car drivers, but sometimes also pedestrians and cyclists. Each of those individuals must be assumed to behave rationally (the economic notion of rationality rests basically on the transitivity of constrained choices and not on their morality or social acceptability; moreover, it may be rational to express irrationality or bounded rationality) and make coherent choices over available possibilities in time and over time. Car accidents are the results of interactions between the individual drivers, pedestrians, and cyclists. Clearly, such a data-generating process is far from the natural, experimental, or biological inanimate processes that lead to most statistical models. Economic and social theories of data-generating processes are structural representations of individuals' information, constraints, and behavior interacting in a very complex way. These structural representations may or may not have simple reduced form counterparts whose parameters (identifiable, unidentifiable, or partly identifiable mixtures of structural parameters and constants) are to be estimated.

This paper deals almost exclusively with reduced form equations relating car accidents to individual characteristics seen as exogenous variables, but we will discuss in section 3 the use of our econometric results for the determination of an optimal pricing for car insurance, a very delicate calibrating exercise aimed at reducing (or increasing) the rate or number of car accidents to its socially optimal level. Before reaching those complex issues, we will present, in the first section, the database that will be used here. The particular features of the database will motivate many ulterior developments and choices of topics.

Section 2.1 will discuss the econometrics of count data models and more precisely the basic and traditional, although very restrictive, unique (requiring that the mean and the variance be equal) and constant (assuming homogeneous underlying individual car drivers) parameter Poisson distribution; and the similarly important negative binomial distribution, a specific and most interesting two-parameter form of the general Compound Poisson distribution (with a variance different from the mean by allowing the underlying individuals to differ according to their probability of accident, that is, to face different one-parameter Poisson distribution). These two distributions are benchmark models of count data and as such interesting ones, although they are unlikely candidates (even as reduced form) for representations of a data generating process as complex as that of car accidents.

Section 2.2 will discuss related models in which the dependent variable, the variable chosen by the individual agents, is continuous (in our case the individual's risk) and therefore not a count variable, but cannot be observed by an outside observer. This observer can only record a proxy variable which is a nonnegative categorical variable and therefore an apparent count variable. Four models will be discussed and estimated: the linear probability model, the probit and logit model, and the multinomial logit model. In each case, individual characteristics are introduced in the regression. Section 2.3 will let the moments of the Poisson and negative binomial distributions depend on individual characteristics; therefore, we will assume, as in section 2.2, that the underlying individuals are heterogeneous in driving skills and attitudes. We will make use of our data bank to define a space of characteristics in which each individual ($n = 19,013$) will be located. Section 2.4 will discuss advanced sampling and estimation issues such as endogenous sampling, simulation based inference and pseudo maximum likelihood estimators, three topics of great importance for count data econometrics. In section 2.5, we will compare the different estimated models by referring to estimated probability of accident of different fictitious individuals. Finally, in section 3, we will discuss the potential applications of our results to the determination of an optimal pricing formula for car insurance; of course, our econometric estimates of the link between individual characteristics and the probability of accident is only one element in such a determination. The conclusion summarizes the main results.

1. The Data

In Québec, the car insurance regime is a mixed system since 1978. Bodily injuries are insured, up to a maximum amount, by a provincial state-owned insurance company, the Régie de l'Assurance Automobile du Québec (RAAQ). Property damages are insured by a competitive system of private insurance companies. The public insurance scheme for bodily injuries is compulsory for all drivers. It is a centrally administered and no-fault system that covers every driver and pays indemnities for medical and rehabilitation costs (without a maximum) and for injuries, dismemberment, and pain and loss of enjoyment of life (with a maximum); there is also a maximum indemnity paid in the form of indexed annuities for disability (which represents full coverage for 85% of the population) and death (a pension-type indemnity when there are dependants; a small lump-sum payment otherwise). Although a driver has the option of purchasing additional insurance coverage from private companies (on which we have no data), the no-fault system suspends the right to sue for bodily injuries. Cars owners must also buy a minimum insurance from a private company covering responsibility for property damages to another party (on which we have no data). Everything else is optional.

There are two main types of pricing corresponding to the two main insurance plans: the public plan for bodily injury and the private plan for property damage and collision insurance. The pricing procedure in the former case is very simple. The main sources of financing are from drivers' permits and automobile registration fees (a tax on gasoline was used before March 1982; interest revenues are another source of funds). There is no classification of risks, and drivers pay the same premium whatever their personal characteristics (age, sex, marital status, territory), the car they use, their driving experience, and their accident record. Weight and type of vehicle driven are taken into consideration for vehicles other than pleasure vehicles. The private sector uses a traditional classification system for pricing property damage and collision insurance, based on personal characteristics, automoblie use, type of car, and past experience for the rating of both property damage insurance and collision insurance [see Boyer and Dionne (1987b), Gaudry (1991), Lefebvre and Fluet (1990), and Devlin (1991) for more details on the Quebec automobile insurance regime].

The sample upon which the study is based includes a similar set of data on 19,013 holders of a driving permit on August 1, 1983. The systematic sampling method was applied: first a driving permit was randomly selected on May 16, 1983, among the first 185 in the bank and afterwards each 185th was chosen (once eliminated, all the permits that were temporary, fictitious, expired before August 1, 1980, or belonging to nonresidents). This sample has many advantages. First, it was randomly gathered from among the entire population of Québec drivers and, therefore, is likely to be more representative than a sample of insured drivers from a given insurance company. Second, it contains five types of information on each driver: the personal characteristics appearing on the date of the sampling on the driver's license itself (age, sex, experience, place of residence, driving restrictions, class of license) and for the three year period from August 1, 1980, to July 31, 1983, the yearly number of accidents, the yearly number of demerit points, the yearly number of license suspensions for criminal offenses, and the number of days the permit was valid during each one-year period. It must be noted, however, that for reasons of confidentiality, the name and address of the individual drivers are not known to us, although a correspondence table is kept at the RAAQ for the purpose of updating the files.

It must be noted also that the data bank also has important and serious limits. The most important is certainly the absence of data measuring directly the individual exposure to risk and for the purpose of using the econometric estimates for determining a fair and efficient pricing formula for automobile insurance, the absence of data on private insurance premia (for property damage and for injuries in excess of the public maximum coverage). Boyer, Dionne and Vanasse (1990) present statistical tables that summarize the information contained in the sample.

2. The Econometrics of Categorical and Count Data Models

2.1. Count data models without individual characteristics

It is reasonable to suppose that for a given individual, the probability of being involved in a car accident satisfies the following conditions: the probability of accident is proportional to the length of the period considered, the instantaneous probability of accident is constant throughout the period, the probability of having more than one accident in a period is small and accidents are independent.

The Poisson distribution does satisfy the above characteristics and has therefore been used as a first choice to represent the distribution of accidents. The probability that an individual will be involved in k accidents over t years or periods is then:

$$P(k|t, \lambda) = \frac{e^{-\lambda t}(\lambda t)^k}{k!} \tag{1}$$

where λ is both the mean and variance of the distribution. However, using a Poisson distribution to represent the observed distribution of accidents for a group of individuals supposes implicitly that all individuals have the same probability of being involved in one or more accidents. This last feature is very restrictive. If, on the other hand, we assume that λ varies between individuals and that for a given individual the distribution of accidents follows a Poisson distribution, then it will be

Table 1. Estimates of the Univariate Poisson and Negative Binomial Distributions

Number of Accidents k	Observed Number of Individuals with k Accidents in 1982–1983 n_k	Predicted Number of Individuals with k Accidents in 1982–1983	
		Poisson ($\hat{\lambda} = 0.0701$)	Negative Binomial ($\hat{a} = 0.6960$; $\hat{\tau} = 9.9359$)
0	17,784	17,726.60	17,785.28
1	1,139	1,241.86	1,132.05
2	79	43.50	88.79
3	9	1.02	7.10
4	2	0.02	0.61
5+	0	0	0
	19,013	$\chi^2 = 133.06$ $\chi^2_{2,95} = 5.99$	$\chi^2 = 2.21$ $\chi^2_{1,95} = 7.82$
		LL $= -4,950.28$	LL $= -4,916.78$

mathematically convenient to suppose that λ is distributed as $f(\lambda)$. From the distribution of λ, the *average* probability of being involved in k accidents over t years becomes the negative binomial distribution if we assume that λ follows a Gamma density function with mean a/τ and variance a/τ^2:

$$P(k|t, a, m) = \frac{\Gamma(k + a)}{k!\Gamma(a)} \left(\frac{a}{a + mt}\right)^a \left(\frac{mt}{a + mt}\right)^k \qquad (2)$$

where the mean is $m = a/\tau$, the variance is $(a/\tau)(1 + 1/\tau)$ and $\Gamma(a)$ is the Gamma function [see Ferreira (1974) and Lemaire (1985) for more details]. If the distribution of accidents is better represented by the Poisson distribution (1), it would suggest that individuals are homogeneous insofar as their respective probabilities of accident are concerned. This would imply among other things that differential insurance pricing would have no supporting empirical evidence. We estimated the two distributions (1) and (2) for the 12-month period from August 1982 to July 1983 by the maximum likelihood method. Results are reported in table 1, where k is the number of accidents, n_k is the number of individuals with k accidents and LL is the log-likelihood. For the Poisson distribution, we obtain an estimated $\hat{\lambda}$ of 0.0701; observed and predicted values for n_k give a χ^2 statistic of 133.06 thereby rejecting the hypothesis that the distribution of accidents follows a Poisson distribution. As for the negative binomial distribution, the maximum likelihood estimates are $\hat{a} = 0.6960$ and $\hat{\tau} = 9.9359$ and therefore $\hat{m} = 0.0701$; observed and predicted values for n_k give a χ^2 statistic of 2.21. We cannot therefore reject the hypothesis that drivers are indeed heterogeneous insofar as their respective probabilities of accident are concerned. These results provide the necessary empirical justification for proceeding with the econometric estimation of the probability of accident by controlling for the individual characteristics to isolate properly the specific effects of different individual characteristics. It is interesting to note that based on the parameter estimates of the negative binomial distribution, equation 2 gives the probability of having 0 accident ($k = 0$) in 1982–1983 ($t = 1$) as 0.935 and, therefore, $P(k \geq 1 | t = 1, a, m) = 0.065$. This value corresponds to the mean of the estimated individual probabilities of accident to be obtained below from the probit and logit models.

2.2. Categorical models: linear probability, probit, logit, and multinomial logit models

The standard econometric models used to estimate probabilities of accident from the characteristics of individuals and with variables indirectly representing the individual's choice of safety activities are categorical models where the dependent variable, the number of accidents, is a binary variable (0 for no accident and 1 for a positive number of accidents) or a multinary (rarely more than three categories) variable. We will consider here the main models: the standard linear probability model estimated with the ordinary least squares estimator and the nonlinear probit, logit, and multinomial logit models; the first three are binary models and the fourth is a trinary model. In each case, a first group of variables, described in table 2, includes age, sex, number of years since the first license was obtained, place of residence, driving restrictions, class of the driver's license, and period of validity of the license; we will represent those by the vector v_i. Each variable, except for the last one, is represented by a set of dichotomous variables, as is customary the case in the insurance business. For example, the age variable is represented by eight dichotomous variables with the age group 16–19 as the reference group. A second group consists of proxy variables for the unobservable choices of self-protection activities by the individual; we will represent those by the vector w_i. It corresponds to the individual's past driving experience. Three such variables appear in our sample: the cumulative

Table 2.   List of Variables Used*

AGE: A16 = 1 if on 1/8/82 the driver was less than 16 (sampling date 16/5/83);
   A1619 if between 16 and 19 (omitted category); etc.

SEX: SEXM = 1 if male.

EXPERIENCE: (number of years with a driving license); EXP0 = 1 if license
   obtained in 82–83, EXPM1 = 1 if on 1/8/82 license less than one year old;
   EXP1 = 1 if license between one and two years old (omitted category); etc.

PLACE OF RESIDENCE: REG6 = 1 if driver lives in Montreal area (omitted
   category); REG3 = 1 if in Quebec city; REG5 = 1 if in Eastern Townships;
   REG9 = 1 if in Outaouais region; etc.

DRIVING RESTRICTIONS: RTSA, driver must wear glasses; RTSB can drive
   during daylingt only; RTSJ, must drive an automatic transmission car; RTSU,
   license valid for six months only; RTSY, cannot drive a taxi or an ambulance;
   RTS0, has no restrictions; etc. (no omitted category since categories are not
   mutually exclusive).

CLASS OF DRIVING LICENSE: CL1112, may drive a bus (includes CL13, 41,
   42, 61); CL21, may drive a vehicle (CL22) or a set of vehicles whose weight
   exceeds 11 000 kg (trucks and trailers); CL31, taxi; CL42, a set of vehicles
   whose weight is less than 11 000 kg; CL54, motorcycles; CL55, small
   motorcycles; CL56, velomotor (no omitted category since categories are not
   mutually exclusive).

VALIDITY: VALA, number of days the individual's license was valid in 80–81;
   VALB, in 81–82, VALC, in 82–83.

DEMERIT POINTS: number of demerit points cumulated by the individual from
   1/8/80 to 31/7/82 for infractions such as not stopping at a stop sign (2 points) or
   at a red light (3); illegal passing (2), crossing a continuous line (2), racing (6),
   not stopping for a school bus with blinking lights on (9), speed over limit by 1
   to 14 km/h (1), by 15 to 29 km/h (2), by 30 to 44 km/h (3), by more than
   45 km/h (4).

LICENSE SUSPENSIONS: number of license suspensions in 81–82 for criminal
   offenses such as negligence causing death or injury, hit and run, dangerous
   driving, impaired (alcohol) driving.

PAST INVOLVEMENTS IN ACCIDENTS: number of accidents the driver was
   involved in (at fault or not) between 1/8/80 and 31/7/82.

---

* For a detailed description of the variables, see Boyer, Dionne and Vanasse (1990).

number of demerit points D over the two previous years, the number of
license suspensions S for criminal offenses in the previous year (we have
no data on this for 1980–1981) and, finally, the number of accidents Z the
individual was involved in during the two previous years.

   The first model is the linear probability model:

$$k_i = X_i \beta + u_i \qquad (3)$$

where $X_i = (1, v_i, w_i)$ and $E(u_i) = 0$. The dependent variable k_i is dichotomous: $k_i = 1$ if the i th individual had one or more accidents during 1982–1983, and $k_i = 0$ otherwise. $E(k_i|X_i) = X_i\beta$ can be interpreted as the probability that $k_i = 1$ since

$$E(k_i|X_i) = p(1|X_i)1 + (1 - p(1|X_i))0 = p(1|X_i). \qquad (4)$$

Table 3 presents the results of the application of ordinary least squares to this model. The first column (model 1) corresponds to only one proxy for

Table 3. Least Squares Estimates

Variable	Model 1		Model 2	
D	—		.011	$(12.37)^{**}$
S	—		.057	$(2.77)^{**}$
Z	.048	$(12.48)^{**}$	.040	$(10.05)^{**}$
INTERCEPT	.049	$(2.33)^{**}$	.046	$(2.19)^{**}$
A16	−.039	(-1.11)	−.036	(-1.05)
A2024	−.004	(-0.42)	−.007	(-0.65)
A2534	−.033	$(-3.08)^{**}$	−.030	$(-2.82)^{**}$
A3544	−.044	$(-3.91)^{**}$	−.038	$(-3.40)^{**}$
A4554	−.046	$(-3.88)^{**}$	−.037	$(-3.14)^{**}$
A5564	−.058	$(-4.74)^{**}$	−.047	$(-3.88)^{**}$
A65+	−.058	$(-4.21)^{**}$	−.044	$(-3.22)^{**}$
SEXM	.044	$(10.74)^{**}$	.034	$(8.23)^{**}$
EXP0	−.015	(-0.75)	−.008	(-0.39)
EXPM1	−.001	(-0.07)	.3E-3	(0.02)
EXP2	−.018	(-1.19)	−.016	(-1.06)
EXP35	−.028	$(-1.78)^{*}$	−.028	$(-1.75)^{*}$
EXP610	−.030	$(-1.77)^{*}$	−.031	$(-1.84)^{*}$
EXP11	−.025	(-1.44)	−.026	(-1.49)
REG1	.008	(0.81)	.010	(1.03)
REG2	−.3E-3	(-0.03)	.004	(0.43)
REG3	.004	(0.69)	.007	(1.30)
REG4	.011	(1.44)	.011	(1.56)
REG5	.5E-3	(0.05)	.001	(0.12)
REG7	.008	(1.26)	.009	(1.32)
REG8	−.6E-4	(-0.01)	.3E-4	(0.01)
REG9	.028	$(3.08)^{**}$	.031	$(3.45)^{**}$
REG10	.017	(1.49)	.015	(1.32)
REG11	.016	(1.18)	.017	(1.30)

Table 3.   Continued

Variable	Model 1		Model 2	
RTSA	−.035	(−2.75)**	−.033	(−2.66)**
RTSB	.014	(0.49)	.015	(0.55)
RTSCG	−.021	(−1.32)	−.020	(−1.24)
RTSD	.1E-3	(0.01)	.5E-3	(0.03)
RTSH	.018	(1.36)	.017	(1.36)
RTSJ	.096	(1.69)*	.095	(1.68)*
RTSK	−.060	(−0.97)	−.061	(−0.98)
RTSM	−.027	(−1.46)	−.026	(−1.44)
RTSO	.014	(0.48)	.017	(0.61)
RTSQ	−.071	(−0.97)	−.066	(−0.90)
RTSU	.058	(2.14)**	.060	(2.23)**
RTSY	−.077	(−2.66)**	−.075	(−2.59)**
RTSØ	−.026	(−2.02)**	−.026	(−2.03)**
CL1112	.034	(2.08)**	.035	(2.10)**
CL13	−.035	(−0.67)	−.031	(−0.59)
CL21	.015	(1.78)*	.016	(1.89)*
CL22	.135	(4.06)**	.127	(3.85)**
CL31	.097	(4.55)**	.082	(3.88)**
CL42	.005	(0.73)	.006	(0.88)
CL54	.007	(0.74)	.007	(0.68)
CL55	−.067	(−1.57)	−.080	(−1.89)*
CL56	−.001	(−0.01)	.004	(0.04)
VALA	.8E-4	(1.43)	.4E-4	(0.78)
VALB	−.1E-3	(−2.36)**	−.7E-4	(−1.59)
VALC	.2E-3	(5.24)**	.2E-3	(4.82)**
$\bar{R}^2$		0.0325		0.0407
F		13.78		16.52
nb of variables		51		53
nb of observations		19013		19013

* significant at 90%   ** significant at 95%

F statistic (to test that $\beta_D = \beta_S = 0$) = 82.06 > $F_{(2,\infty)}^{99}$ = 4.60.

care activities, namely the Z variable; the second column (model 2) corresponds to all three proxies D, S, Z. Values in parentheses are t-statistics.

It is interesting to note that the age variables are significant. In comparison with the reference group (i.e., the 16–19-year-old drivers), we see that drivers over 25 will have a lower probability of accident by 3.3 to

5.8 percentage points in the first model, and by 3.0 to 4.7 percentage points in the second model. Sex is also significant, male drivers having a probability of accident 4.4 and 3.4 points higher respectively.

As was mentioned above, these variables can also be proxies for driver skill and, more important, risk exposure. Our results are similar to those obtained by Dahlby (1983) and somewhat justify their use by insurers when they are costless to observe [Crocker and Snow (1986)]. Clearly, individual measures of risk exposure and driver skill would be more appropriate here. However, variables VALA, VALB, and VALC measure the number of days during which the permit is valid. Those variables indirectly take into account the fact that a new driver may not have a full year of driving experience and also the fact that individuals with a license suspension do not drive during that time. We observe that the effect of VALC is positive and significant. The place of residence variable is not significant except for one region, meaning that when individual information is available, this variable, used as proxy of risk by insurers, is irrelevant. Finally, driving licenses for classes 11 and 12 (bus drivers), 21 and 22 (truck and trailer truck drivers), 31 (taxi drivers) and 55 (small motorcycles) are significant, with classes 11 and 12, 21 and 22, and 31 raising the individual probabilities of accident and class 55 reducing them.

Our results also indicate that the above variables explain only in part the differences in probabilities between drivers. Indeed, the three 'behavioral' variables D (demerit points), S (license suspensions for criminal offense), and Z (past accident involvements) are significant [the correlation coefficients between D, S and Z are $r_{DS} = 0.07901$, $r_{DZ} = 0.22110$ and $r_{SZ} = 0.09431$]. In the first model, a single accident during 1980–1981 or 1981–1982 raises the probability of being involved in an accident in 1982–1983 by 4.8 percentage points. Considering that the average probability of being involved in at least one accident is 6.5%, the increase is quite important. In the second model, each additional demerit point increases the probability of accident by 1.1 percentage point; an additional license suspension increases the probability of accident by 5.7 percentage points; and an additional involvement in an accident during 1980–1981 or 1981–1982 increases the probability of accident in 1982–1983 by 4.0 percentage points. Although the regressions are generally very significant ($F = 13.8$ and 16.5), the adjusted R^2 are only 0.03 and 0.04. This result was expected since the data is at the individual level and therefore very disaggregated, and since the event "accident" is rather rare [Theil (1971), p. 181]. [A regression on the data aggregated over 353 postal codes gave an adjusted R^2 of 0.76, with the three variables D, S, Z also being quite significant.] We can choose between the two models by testing the $\beta_D = \beta_S = 0$ hypothesis in model 2. We obtained an F-statistic of 82.06 well above the $F^{99}_{(2,\infty)} = 4.60$ bound and model 2 therefore appears significantly more adequate.

We made a thorough investigation of multicollinearity.[1] We ran auxiliary regressions of D, S, and Z on all the other explanatory variables. We obtained low R^2's (0.13, 0.09 and 0.05 respectively). However, those regressions are not appropriate if there exist other relations between the explanatory variables. We therefore used the approach proposed by Belsley, Kuh, and Welsch (1980) [referred to as BKW]. This method, based on the analysis of the characteristic roots and vectors of the matrix $X'X$ (scaled to unit length but not centered), can reveal the presence and perhaps the nature of multicollinearity. We found three near linear dependencies associated with condition indexes greater than 30 (the heuristic rule proposed by BKW says that condition indexes of 30 to 100 are associated with moderate to strong relations). The examination of the variance-decomposition proportions indicated competing dependencies involving the constant, the age variables, the number-of-years-with-a-driving-license variables, and the validity variables. Auxiliary regressions were performed as suggested by BKW (pp. 150–160) for the validity variables on all the other explanatory variables; we obtained R^2's of 0.87, 0.55 and 0.07 respectively for VALA, VALB, and VALC, which indicate that the relations are not very tight. These results indicate that the multicollinearity problem is not harmful in our case.

However, the linear regression model is far from being totally adequate when the dependent variable is dichotomous. First, there is a serious risk of heteroscedasticity problem and secondly, $X_i\beta$ could possibly be outside the range $[0, 1]$ for certain X_i; this is troublesome if we interpret $E(k|X_i)$ as a probability. Although these problems are likely to be less serious given the large number of observations and variables, we obtained $X_i\beta < 0$ for 602 individuals (3.2% of our sample). More adequate nonlinear models such as the probit and the logit models should be estimated.

Let us consider again the linear model $k_i = X_i\beta$ with the dependent variable being the individual's risk. This variable is not observed as such. What is observed is not the individual's risk but rather whether the individual had an accident or not. We may pose that the occurrence of an accident depends on the risk of accident itself and random elements which can be represented as u_i: hence, an individual has an accident if $X_i\beta + u_i > 0$ and no accident if $X_i\beta + u_i < 0$. Therefore, even if $X_i\beta$ does represent the risk of accident for driver i, we observe only that this driver had at least one accident ($k_i^* = 1$, i.e., $u_i > -X_i\beta$) or had no accident ($k_i^* = 0$, i.e., $u_i < -X_i\beta$). Therefore, the likelihood function will be given by

$$LF = \left[\prod_{k_i^*=0} F(-X_i\beta)\right]\left[\prod_{k_i^*=1} (1 - F(-X_i\beta))\right] \tag{5}$$

where $F(\ )$ is the cumulative distribution function of u_i. If u_i is normally distributed, an assumption that could be justified by the fact that the number of factors that influence the probability of accident other than those factors included in X_i is indeed very large, then

$$F(-X_i\beta) = \int_{-\infty}^{\frac{-X_i\beta}{\sigma}} (2\pi)^{-1/2}\exp\left(-\frac{s^2}{2}\right) ds \tag{6}$$

and the maximization of LF with respect to β (setting $\sigma = 1$, because LF is homogeneous of degree 0 in β and σ) gives the probit estimator. Probit estimates for model 1 and model 2 are presented in table 4 under the columns Original Coefficient. As a whole, the regressions are very signi-

Table 4. Probit Estimates

Variable	MODEL 1 Original Coefficient	(t)	MODEL 2 Original Coefficient	(t)	Transformed Coefficient
D	—	—	0.055	(9.62)**	0–1 :0.006 1–5 :0.028 5–31:0.434
S	—	—	0.290	(2.23)**	0–1 :0.039 1–2 :0.057 2–3 :0.077
Z	0.257	(10.12)**	0.211	(8.11)**	0–1 :0.025 1–2 :0.034 2–6 :0.239
INTERCEPT	−2.128	(−10.21)**	−2.295	(−10.30)**	NC
A16	−0.323	(−0.95)	−0.304	(−0.89)	−0.25
A2024	−0.014	(−0.18)	−0.028	(−0.35)	−0.003
A2534	−0.224	(−2.60)**	−0.207	(−2.40)**	−0.020
A3544	−0.330	(−3.53)**	−0.292	(−3.11)**	−0.027
A4554	−0.350	(−3.58)**	−0.288	(−2.93)**	−0.026
A5564	−0.482	(−4.62)**	−0.409	(−3.91)**	−0.033
A65	−0.468	(−3.93)**	−0.372	(−3.11)**	−0.030

Table 4.   Continued

	MODEL 1		MODEL 2		
Variable	Original Coefficient	(t)	Original Coefficient	(t)	Transformed Coefficient
SEXM	0.432	(11.69)**	0.370	(9.80)**	0.037
EXP0	0.054	(0.27)	0.227	(1.08)	0.029
EXPM1	0.050	(0.32)	0.116	(0.72)	0.014
EXP2	−0.157	(−1.22)	−0.145	(−1.10)	−0.014
EXP35	−0.241	(−1.81)*	−0.245	(−1.79)*	−0.022
EXP610	−0.239	(−1.66)*	−0.251	(−1.70)*	−0.024
EXP11	−0.187	(−1.27)	−0.194	(−1.29)	−0.021
REG1	0.090	(1.10)	0.107	(1.30)	0.012
REG2	0.004	(0.06)	0.035	(0.46)	0.004
REG3	0.046	(0.98)	0.073	(1.55)	0.008
REG4	0.097	(1.61)	0.106	(1.75)*	0.012
REG5	0.021	(0.25)	0.025	(0.30)	0.003
REG7	0.072	(1.31)	0.073	(1.32)	0.008
REG8	0.008	(0.16)	0.008	(0.18)	0.001
REG9	0.216	(3.07)**	0.245	(3.46)**	0.031
REG10	0.142	(1.61)	0.128	(1.43)	0.015
REG11	0.144	(1.34)	0.158	(1.46)	0.019
RTSA	−0.266	(−2.52)**	−0.254	(−2.40)**	−0.025
RTSB	0.138	(0.54)	0.155	(0.60)	0.019
RTSCG	−0.158	(−1.05)	−0.146	(−0.97)	−0.014
RTSD	0.040	(0.33)	0.034	(0.28)	0.004
RTSH	0.112	(1.00)	0.118	(1.04)	0.014
RTSJ	0.745	(1.77)*	0.736	(1.73)*	0.134
RTSK	−0.533	(−0.99)	−0.535	(−0.99)	−0.037
RTSM	−0.272	(−1.56)	−0.273	(−1.55)	−0.023
RTSO	0.104	(0.47)	0.145	(0.67)	0.017
RTSQ	−0.650	(−0.97)	−0.591	(−0.88)	−0.039
RTSU	0.343	(1.75)*	0.366	(1.86)*	0.520
RTSY	−0.997	(−2.34)**	−0.977	(−2.31)**	−0.480
RTSØ	−0.189	(−1.75)*	−0.186	(−1.71)*	−0.210
CL11,12	0.145	(1.30)	0.158	(1.41)	0.019
CL13	−0.298	(−0.59)	−0.256	(−0.51)	−0.022
CL21	0.121	(1.79)*	0.127	(1.88)*	0.014
CL22	0.581	(2.95)**	0.560	(2.81)**	0.091
CL31	0.438	(3.40)**	0.359	(2.74)**	0.050
CL42	0.039	(0.68)	0.045	(0.77)	0.005

Table 4. Continued

Variable	MODEL 1			MODEL 2		
	Original Coefficient	(t)	Original Coefficient	(t)	Transformed Coefficient
CL54	0.038	(0.49)	. 0.041	(0.52)	0.004
CL55	−0.476	(−1.32)	−0.579	(−1.55)	−0.038
CL56	−0.120	(−0.20)	−0.104	(−0.17)	−0.010
VALA	0.001	(1.49)	0.001	(0.97)	NC
VALB	−0.001	(−1.75)*	−0.000	(−0.42)	NC
VALC	0.002	(5.87)**	0.002	(5.70)**	NC
nb of observations	19013				19013
nb of variables	51				53
Likelihood ratio	620.99				716.64
Mean est'd prob. of accident	0.065				0.065
Est'd prob. of accident (avg. ind.)	0.053				0.052
(Standard error)	(0.002)				(0.002)

(* = significant at 90%; ** = significant at 95%; NC = not calculated)

Log likelihood ratio test for the restrictions $\beta_D = \beta_S = 0$: −2 (LL$_1$ − LL$_2$) = 95.40 > $\chi^2_{2,99}$ = 9.21.

ficant. Moreover, the sets of significant variables are basically the same as those obtained with OLS. Since the probit estimator is nonlinear in the parameters, we observe that the average individual, defined by the vector of average values of the explanatory variables, has an estimated probability of accident of 0.053 in model 1 and 0.052 in model 2. These are significantly smaller than the mean of the estimated probabilities of accident, which is 0.065 in both models, over the whole sample of 19,013 observations, which is explained by the nonlinearity of the model. This mean of estimated probabilities differ also from the mean (0.071) of the previously estimated negative binomial distribution. The last difference is due to the use of a cardinal count variable having values 0, 1, 2, 3, etc., to measure the number of accidents in the negative binomial model while the dependent variable in the probit model is an ordinal categorical 0–1 variable ($k = 1$ for one or more accidents).

We performed a log-likelihood ratio test of the $\beta_D = \beta_S = 0$ hypothesis in model 2 to discriminate between the two models; we obtained $-2(LL_1 - LL_2) = 95.40$ well above the $\chi^2_{2,99} = 9.21$ bound, again favoring significantly model 2 over model 1. This result corroborates the result of a similar test in table 3 and, from now on, we will therefore concentrate on model 2 with variables D, S, and Z.

Table 4 also presents transformed coefficient estimates that can be directly interpreted as the variation in the probability of accident due to the presence of a given variable. Consider a variable w_h and its sample mean W_h. The transformed estimate of the coefficient for w_h is the difference between the probability of accident estimated for ($w_h = 0$, $w_j = W_j$ for $j \neq h$) and its value estimated for ($w_h = v_h$, $w_j = W_j$ for $j \neq h$), where v_h equals 1 for a dichotomous variable and may take different step values for other variables. As an example of the former, consider the results of model 2: the otherwise average male driver ($SEXM = 1$) has a probability of accident 3.7 percentage points higher than the otherwise average female driver ($SEXM = 0$). As examples of the latter, consider again the results of model 2: the otherwise average driver with five demerit points in the previous two-year period ($D = 5$) has a probability of accident that is 3.4 (0.6 + 2.8) percentage points higher than that of the otherwise average driver with no demerit points and, similarly, the otherwise average driver with two previous accidents ($Z = 2$) has a probability of accident that is 3.4 points larger than that of the otherwise average driver with only one previous accident ($Z = 1$) and 5.9 (2.5 + 3.4) points larger than that of the otherwise average driver with no previous accidents ($Z = 0$).

It is interesting to note also that age is significant, drivers over 25 years of age having probabilities of accident 2.0 to 3.3 percentage points lower than that of the 16–19-year-old drivers. Experience, or more precisely the number of years with a driving license, is not very significant; the same is true for the region of residence with one exception. It appears that restriction A (must wear glasses or correcting lenses) reduces significantly the probability of accident, possibly because some (many) drivers who do not have such a restriction should in fact have it! On the other hand, drivers who can only drive automatic transmission equipped cars and drivers who have a temporary 6-month license are risky drivers. Finally, truck and trailer truck drivers and taxi drivers are significantly more risky drivers (they may also have more risk exposure).

We saw above that male drivers are more risky and that young drivers (less than 25) are also more risky. What about young female drivers? We looked at interaction effects between age and sex, a debated issue in the car insurance context. We obtained probit estimates for the age–sex interaction terms as follows. We constructed categorical variables $F19$ (females 19 years of age or younger on August 1, 1980; the omitted

Table 5. Probit Estimates with Age–Sex Interaction Variables

VARIABLE	PROBIT ESTIMATE (t-statistics)	
M19	0.478	(4.24)**
M2024	0.443	(3.65)**
M2534	0.218	(1.75)*
M3544	0.166	(1.28)
M4554	0.165	(1.23)
M5564	0.086	(0.62)
M65	0.021	(0.14)
F2024	0.033	(0.26)
F2534	−0.058	(−0.46)
F3544	−0.224	(−1.63)
F4554	−0.209	(−1.42)
F5564	−0.569	(−2.91)**
F65	−0.004	(−0.02)
D	0.056	(9.62)**
S	0.291	(2.23)**
Z	0.211	(8.11)**
INTERCEPT	−2.382	(−10.04)**

** significant at 95%; * significant at 90%

category), $M19$ (males 19 years of age or younger), $F2024$, $M2024$, $F2534$, $M2534$, etc. The results are summarized in table 5.

These results suggest the following comments: although the age coefficients for females have the expected negative sign, only the coefficient of $F5564$ is significant; as for males, we note that the probability of accident decreases with age but only the coefficients of the younger groups are significant; moreover, the reduction in the probability of accident happens sooner for males than for females but becomes more important at age 55–64 for females than for males; finally and most importantly, the coefficients of variables D, S, and Z were unaffected (all the other coefficients not reported here were also unaffected).

The results of table 4 show that the number of demerit points D and the number of license suspensions for criminal offences S cumulated over time are very significant to explain the individual probabilities of accident. These two variables are linear aggregates in the sense that they give the same weight to the number of demerit points corresponding to the different infractions or offenses. In a recent study [Boyer, Dionne and Vanasse (1988)], we investigated two questions related to the above results and form of aggregation. First, if we disaggregate those variables and use different variables for different infractions and offenses, which would have a larger effect on the individual probabilities of accident? Second, are the relative number of points for each infraction and obtained from the actual regulation of road safety in Québec adequate? In other words, do they represent the marginal effect of those infractions on the individual probabilities of accident? Our results, available upon request, indicate that the offenses for driving under the influence of alcohol are more significant than the other offenses and that among the driving infractions, the not stopping at a stop sign and not stopping at a red light infractions are not enough penalized (in the sense of carrying too few points) relatively to the excess speed infractions even if both are significant in explaining the individual probabilities of accident. Moreover, our results show that the effect of each infraction is nonlinear, which means that the adequate number of points for each infraction should be an increasing function of the number of infractions.

As for the linear probability model, it is desirable to check for the presence of multicollinearity in the probit model. Even if the methodology used previously for the analysis of multicollinearity in the linear model is not necessarily appropriate for nonlinear models such as the probit, we nevertheless undertook some analysis. The extension of the methodology to the probit model is far from being straightforward. The estimates of the probit model are the solution of

$$\frac{\partial LLF}{\partial \beta} = \sum_{i=1}^{n} \frac{k_i - F(X_i\beta)}{F(X_i\beta)[1 - F(X_i\beta)]} f(X_i\beta)X_i' = 0, \qquad (7)$$

where LLF is the log-likelihood function. The estimated variance-covariance matrix of the parameters is

$$[E(-\partial^2 L/\partial\beta\partial\beta')]^{-1} = (X'\Lambda X)^{-1}. \qquad (8)$$

where Λ is a diagonal matrix whose element (i, i) is

$$\frac{f^2(X_i\beta)}{F(X_i\beta)[1 - F(X_i\beta)]} . \qquad (9)$$

As pointed out by BKW, multicollinearity can lead to convergence problems (we have none) if the optimization algorithm uses the inverse of the Hessian matrix and can lead also to poor estimates of the variances of the parameters. We applied the same methodology to the matrix $X'\Lambda X$ (instead of $X'X$) and found the same kind of relations involving the same groups of variables as in the linear case. We then reestimated the probit model without the number-of-years-with-a-driving-license variables and the validity variables. We also applied the BKW method to the matrix of explanatory variables and the Hessian matrix of the reduced model and we found no evidence of multicollinearity. We obtained results very similar to those of the complete model except for the constant and the age variables. These results lead us to the conclusion that multicollinearity is not harmful in our case and that low multicollinearity is preferable to a misspecification of the model due to the omission of important variables.[2] Another fact is that the predictions will not necessarily be imprecise because of multicollinearity as long as the values of the independent variables for which a prediction is desired obey the same near exact restrictions as the X matrix. For all these reasons, we think that it is legitimate to use the full specification model.

The probit model was obtained above by supposing that $F(-X_i\beta)$ in (5) is the cumulative normal distribution. One may wish to verify whether the estimated coefficients of the explanatory variables are sensitive to that asumption. A standard alternative is to suppose that $F(-X_i\beta)$ is the logistic function:

$$F(-X_i\beta) = \frac{\exp(-X_i\beta)}{1 + \exp(-X_i\beta)} = \frac{1}{1 + \exp(+X_i\beta)}, \qquad (10)$$

which substituted in (5) leads to the logit estimator. The logit estimates [not presented here but available in Boyer, Dionne, and Vanasse (1990)] are very similar to those of the probit. First, the significant variables are the same and, second, the adjusted logit coefficients are quite close to their probit counterpart especially so for the more significant variables; the only noticeable difference is for the age and sex variables for which the logit estimates are about 20% larger (in absolute value). Indeed, with 19,013 observations, one could have expected even larger differences [Maddala (1983), pp. 23–24]. We can therefore be reasonably confident in either the probit or the logit estimates but since the probit model appears slightly better, we will use only the probit estimates in the comparison of models in section 2.5 below.

An important drawback of both the probit and logit models is that the dependent variable is restricted to 0 (if no accident) and 1 (if *one or more* accidents). Clearly, it may be interesting to consider more than two categories in the case of car accidents to better represent the tail of the distribution. Given that only 11 individuals in our sample had more than two accidents in 1982–1983, we will consider a multinomial model with three categories: no accidents, one accident, two and more accidents containing respectively 17,784, 1,139, and 90 individuals. Considering the relative computational complexity and cost of multinomial probit and logit models, we proceeded to the estimation of the multinomial logit model only. However, we should emphasize that the consideration of one more category (2+) implied the estimation of 53 additional parameters.

The transformed coefficients appearing in table 6 give, as in table 4, the impact of a variable on the probability of accident for the otherwise average individual. They were obtained as in table 4 except that we now have two probabilities: the probability of having exactly one accident Prob1 and the probability of having two and more accidents Prob2+. Consider, for example, the $SEXM$ variable: the otherwise average male driver ($SEXM = 1$, $w_h = W'_h$, $\forall h \neq SEXM$) has a probability of having one accident, which is 3.3 percentage points higher than the otherwise average female driver ($SEXM = 0$, $w_h = W_h$, $\forall h \neq SEXM$) and a probability of having 2+ accidents, which is 0.2 percentage points higher; considering that the average probabilities are respectively 4.74% and 0.19%, the relative variations are quite large in this case. Similarly, the otherwise average individual who had two license suspensions for criminal offense in 1981–1982 ($S = 2$) has a probability of having one accident in 1982–1983, which is 4.78 percentage points higher that the otherwise average driver who had only one such suspension ($S = 1$) and a probability of having two accidents or more in 1982–1983, which is 0.33 percentage points higher; again, these relative increases are quite large.

The above probit and multinomial logit models are categorical models and therefore may indeed miss the basic cardinal aspect of car accidents. In a sense, having two accidents is not simply being in a category of those with two or more accidents and not in the category of those with one accident, but it means that one had twice as many accidents as those in the one-accident category. It is also quite different from purely ordinal categorization, such as riding a bus or a train, given that one does not use a private car. In other words, car accidents represent a count process where numbers 0, 1, 2, 3, etc., are not simply categories but truly cardinal numbers that can be added and compared. Moreover, count data models will naturally discriminate between those with, say, 3 and 4 accidents by using all the information contained in the data. Hence, it seems desirable to look at count data models with individual characteristics, which we will do next.

2.3. Count data models with individual characteristics in the regression component

The constant individual probability of accident models of section 2.1. are clearly quite restrictive. The favorable χ^2 test of the negative binomial

Table 6. Multinomial Logit Estimates

Variable	Alternative 1 (1 accident)			Alternative 2 (2 accidents or more)		
	Original Coefficient	(t)	Transformed Coefficient	Original Coefficient	(t)	Transformed Coefficient
D	0.0959	(8.67)**		0.1337	(5.35)**	
0–1			0.0042			0.0002
1–5			0.0208			0.0013
5–31			0.3777			0.0518
S	0.5355	(2.09)**		0.7073	(1.38)	
0–1			0.0307			0.0018
1–2			0.0478			0.0033
2–3			0.0702			0.0059
Z	0.3830	(7.64)**		0.4780	(3.75)**	
0–1			0.0194			0.0010
1–2			0.0270			0.0015
2–6			0.2197			0.0170
INTERCEPT	−4.6116	(−9.02)**	NC	−7.1174	(−5.01)**	NC
A16-	−0.4123	(−0.54)	−0.0155	−5.8179	(−0.25)	−0.0019
A2024	0.0440	(0.27)	0.0021	−0.8866	(−1.85)*	−0.0013
A2534	−0.2931	(−1.63)	−0.0124	−1.7629	(−3.06)**	−0.0025
A3544	−0.4756	(−2.43)**	−0.0190	−1.9913	(−2.99)**	−0.0024
A4554	−0.4482	(−2.18)**	−0.0175	−2.3876	(−3.22)**	−0.0024
A5564	−0.7113	(−3.21)**	−0.0251	−2.4728	(−3.04)**	−0.0022
A65+	−0.6944	(−2.68)**	−0.0240	−2.3354	(−2.52)**	−0.0019
SEXM	0.7790	(9.30)**	0.0335	1.2107	(3.24)**	0.0021

Table 6. Continued

	Alternative 1 (1 accident)			Alternative 2 (2 accidents or more)		
Variable	Original Coefficient	(t)	Transformed Coefficient	Original Coefficient	(t)	Transformed Coefficient
EXP0	0.5150	(1.11)	0.0290	0.6040	(0.48)	0.0014
EXPM1	0.2392	(0.70)	0.0120	0.0382	(0.03)	0.0001
EXP2	−0.4384	(−1.63)	−0.0167	0.9395	(0.98)	0.0028
EXP35	−0.5978	(−2.15)**	−0.0223	0.7716	(0.77)	0.0021
EXP610	−0.6286	(−2.09)**	−0.0246	0.9485	(0.88)	0.0025
EXP11	−0.4826	(−1.57)	−0.0220	0.8309	(0.73)	0.0016
REG1	0.1747	(0.99)	0.0084	0.4144	(0.75)	0.0009
REG2	0.0678	(0.42)	0.0031	0.1289	(0.23)	0.0003
REG3	0.1456	(1.46)	0.0069	0.0759	(0.21)	0.0001
REG4	0.2302	(1.83)*	0.0114	−0.1531	(−0.31)	−0.0003
REG5	0.0255	(0.14)	0.0012	−0.2407	(−0.38)	−0.0004
REG7	0.1195	(1.01)	0.0056	0.4175	(1.16)	0.0009
REG8	0.0212	(0.22)	0.0010	−0.2610	(−0.72)	−0.0005
REG9	0.4696	(3.22)**	0.0256	0.9776	(2.32)**	0.0028
REG10	0.2334	(1.27)	0.0117	0.0992	(0.16)	0.0002
REG11	0.3246	(1.46)	0.0170	−0.3065	(−0.30)	−0.0005
RTSA	−0.5839	(−2.61)**	−0.0239	0.7302	(0.99)	0.0017
RTSB	0.3707	(0.68)	0.0199	−4.7744	(−0.22)	−0.0019
RTSGC	−0.3743	(−1.15)	−0.0144	0.3971	(0.34)	0.0009
RTSD	−0.1300	(−0.47)	−0.0064	2.5122	(3.64)**	0.0196
RTSH	0.2431	(1.03)	0.0121	0.3783	(0.43)	0.0008
RTSJ	1.3778	(1.76)*	0.1173	−2.3203	(−0.04)	−0.0017
RTSK	−0.9577	(−0.95)	−0.0287	−1.1703	(−0.03)	−0.0013
RTSM	−0.4174	(−1.12)	−0.0159	−7.1072	(−0.31)	−0.0021

RTSO	0.3185	(0.70)	0.0166	−0.1548	(−0.13)	−0.0003
RTSQ	−1.0159	(−0.79)	−0.0297	−1.2722	(−0.02)	−0.0013
RTSU	0.7210	(1.84)*	0.0450	1.0183	(0.87)	0.0030
RTSY	−2.0699	(−2.04)**	−0.0415	−5.0153	(−0.22)	−0.0019
RTSØ	−0.4383	(−1.91)*	−0.0214	1.0706	(1.37)	0.0018
CL1112	0.1200	(0.52)	0.0055	1.3103	(2.82)**	0.0049
CL13	−0.3465	(−0.33)	−0.0134	−4.1667	(−0.19)	−0.0019
CL21	0.2783	(1.98)**	0.0135	0.4812	(1.11)	0.0010
CL22	0.9972	(2.71)**	0.0708	1.1778	(1.34)	0.0037
CL31	0.6212	(2.52)**	0.0370	0.8989	(1.56)	0.0025
CL42	0.1125	(0.93)	0.0050	−0.1714	(−0.47)	−0.0003
CL54	0.0855	(0.53)	0.0038	−0.1999	(−0.43)	−0.0004
CL55	−1.6369	(−1.57)	−0.0379	−0.1010	(−0.08)	−0.0001
CL56	0.0262	(0.02)	0.0013	−3.9273	(−0.19)	−0.0018
VALA	0.9389E-3	(0.81)	NC	−0.2512E-4	(−0.01)	NC
VALB	0.6760E-4	(0.07)	NC	−0.2900E-3	(−0.11)	NC
VALC	4.7879E-3	(5.63)**	NC	0.8391E-3	(0.46)	NC

LL at zero	=	−4876.4237
LL at convergence	=	−4488.4113
Log likelihood ratio	=	776.0248
Number of observations	=	19,013
Number of alternatives	=	3
Number of parameters	=	106

* significant at 90%
** significant at 95%

model in table 1 suggests that individual car drivers are likely to have different probabilities of accident. Hence, it would be worthwhile to find out which individual characteristics are responsible for such heterogeneity. Moreover, allowing heterogeneity in individual probabilities of accident may make the basic Poisson model more attractive. In this subsection, we look at both the Poisson and the negative binomial models with heterogeneous car drivers. In both cases, we will assume that an individual's probability of accident depends on his personal characteristics: in the Poisson model, we assume that the distribution of accident an individual is involved in remains a one-parameter distribution (hence, mean and variance are equal), while in the negative binomial case, we allow for overdispersion (a variance larger than the mean) in the distribution by assuming that the individual characteristics leave some differences between the individual probabilities unexplained and that this unexplained portion follows a Gamma distribution. In a sense, the set of characteristics which the data allow us to define may not be rich enough to stick to the Poisson distribution with heterogeneous drivers.

Let K_i be the number of accidents in which an individual i is involved in a given period. Let us suppose that the assumptions underlying the one-parameter Poisson model are satisfied and, moreover, that the function linking the parameter λ_i to the individual's characteristics is

$$\lambda_i = \exp(X_i\beta)$$

where β is a $m \times 1$ vector of weights to be estimated. Then, the probability that the individual i will be involved in k accidents is

$$p(K_i = k|X_i) = \frac{e^{-\exp(X_i\beta)}\exp(X_i\beta)^k}{k!}.$$

The mean and variance of K_i are both $\lambda_i = \exp(X_i\beta)$; note that the form $\exp(\cdot)$ simply makes sure that λ_i is nonnegative. The likelihood function of the data (K_i, X_i) is given by

$$L(K;\beta) = \prod_{i=1}^{n} \frac{e^{-\exp(X_i\beta)}\exp(X_i\beta)^{K_i}}{K_i!} \tag{11}$$

The estimates of β are given in table 7, together with transformed coefficents which can be interpreted as in table 6.

The Poisson model with individual characteristics is restrictive in many ways. As we mentioned in section 2.1, the Poisson model rests on an assumption of independence of successive accidents. Hence, the probability that an individual will be involved in a car accident in period t is independent of whether or not he was involved in an accident in $t - 1$ or

Table 7. Maximum Likelihood Estimates of the Poisson Model with Individual Characteristics

Variable	Original Coefficient	(t)	Transformed Coefficients Prob1	Prob2+
D	0.0832	(10.23)**		
0–1			0.0039	0.0002
1–5			0.0186	0.0013
5–31			0.2702	0.1368
S	0.4624	(2.49)**		
0–1			0.0271	0.0020
1–2			0.0396	0.0048
2–3			0.0547	0.0114
Z	0.3370	(8.96)**		
0–1			0.0178	0.0011
1–2			0.0237	0.0022
2–6			0.1704	0.0516
INTERCEPT	−4.3318	(−10.20)**	NC	NC
A16−	−0.6992	(−0.96)	−0.0247	−0.0010
A2024	−0.0959	(−0.69)	−0.0044	−0.0002
A2534	−0.4738	(−3.06)**	−0.0208	−0.0010
A3544	−0.6427	(−3.76)**	−0.0262	−0.0012
A4554	−0.6696	(−3.71)**	−0.0261	−0.0012
A5564	−0.8841	(−4.51)**	−0.0314	−0.0013
A65+	−0.8542	(−3.71)**	−0.0296	−0.0012
SEXM	0.7810	(10.13)**	0.0356	0.0020
EXP0	0.5620	(1.43)	0.0341	0.0027
EXPM1	0.2531	(0.85)	0.0134	0.0008
EXP2	−0.1892	(−0.81)	−0.0084	−0.0004
EXP35	−0.3806	(−1.56)	−0.0161	−0.0008
EXP610	−0.3450	(−1.31)	−0.0152	−0.0008
EXP11	−0.2613	(−0.96)	−0.0125	−0.0007
REG1	0.1716	(1.12)	0.0088	0.0005
REG2	0.0828	(0.59)	0.0041	0.0002
REG3	0.1033	(1.17)	0.0051	0.0003
REG4	0.1439	(1.28)	0.0073	0.0004
REG5	−0.0294	(−0.19)	−0.0014	−0.0001
REG7	0.1409	(1.40)	0.0071	0.0004
REG8	−0.0238	(−0.28)	−0.0011	−0.0001
REG9	0.4677	(3.78)**	0.0271	0.0020

Table 7.   Continued

Variable	Original Coefficient	(t)	Transformed Coefficients Prob1	Prob2+
REG10	0.1750	(1.09)	0.0090	0.0005
REG11	0.2147	(1.07)	0.0113	0.0007
RTSA	−0.3324	(−1.72)*	−0.0150	−0.0008
RTSB	0.2342	(0.45)	0.0124	0.0008
RTSGC	−0.1850	(−0.64)	−0.0082	−0.0004
RTSD	0.2941	(1.28)	0.0159	0.0010
RTSH	0.2218	(1.07)	0.0116	0.0007
RTSJ	1.4493	(2.04)**	0.1299	0.0206
RTSK	−0.9161	(−0.98)	−0.0296	−0.0011
RTSM	−0.5860	(−1.65)*	−0.0219	−0.0009
RTSO	0.2402	(0.63)	0.0128	0.0008
RTSQ	−1.2459	(−1.06)	−0.0354	−0.0012
RTSU	0.4873	(1.50)	0.0289	0.0022
RTSY	−1.9646	(−1.95)*	−0.0434	−0.0013
RTSØ	−0.1831	(−0.92)	−0.0090	−0.0005
CL1112	0.4293	(2.56)**	0.0248	0.0018
CL13	−0.4499	(−0.45)	−0.0177	−0.0008
CL21	0.2745	(2.29)**	0.0141	0.0008
CL22	0.8311	(2.98)**	0.0575	0.0055
CL31	0.5504	(2.98)**	0.0336	0.0026
CL42	0.0681	(0.66)	0.0032	0.0002
CL54	0.0230	(0.17)	0.0011	0.0001
CL55	−0.6993	(−1.18)	−0.0247	−0.0010
CL56	−0.2090	(−0.21)	−0.0091	−0.0004
VALA	0.3382	(0.90)	NC	NC
VALB	0.0660	(0.22)	NC	NC
VALC	1.2803	(5.27)**	NC	NC
Average individual			0.0504	0.0014
LL		−4563.86		
Number of observations		19,013		
Number of parameters		53		

* = significant at 90%;   ** = significant at 95%

more generally $t' < t$. There are good reasons to believe that in the context of car accidents, this will not be the case. An accident may make someone more nervous on the road at least for some subsequent periods and increase or decrease the probability of accident; an accident may have occurred because the individual is in a state of intensive stress, which will last more than one basic period. Those are only two of the reasons one can think of why car accidents may occur in spells, that is, possibly linked to some form of dynamic dependency. In fact, our results indicate that past involvements in accidents raise the probability of accident significantly in a given period. This result may be due to missing individual characteristics that would be significant in explaining the probability of accident for an individual; but they may indicate the existence of spells of accidents, that is, a more fundamental breakdown in one of the basic assumptions of the model, the assumption that events are independent over time. We did not pursue the problem here [see, however, Heckman, and Borjas (1980)].

Another possibly restrictive assumption of the Poisson model is that for a given individual, the mean and variance of the distribution be equal. The problem here is of a different nature from the previous one: it is basically an estimation problem since it may produce an underestimate of the variance (towards the mean) and hence too large student-t values, that is too many and too strongly significant individual characteristics. Moreover, the Poisson model may attach two small probabilities to the possibility that the number of accidents is two or more. There are fortunately relatively simple remedies for this second problem. The idea is, of course, to break the strong link between mean and variance. We noted in a previous subsection that one could generate a two-parameter distribution of accidents by allowing the individual λ_i to follow a gamma distribution. And it turned out that allowing for a larger variance improved the results very significantly. In the present case, although the λ_i are different across individuals, it remains that the mean and variance of each individual Poisson distribution are both equal to $\lambda_i = \exp(X_i\beta)$. Of course, allowing the λ_i to differ across individuals through the different vector X_i of characteristics may or may not be sufficient to explain adequately the overdispersion uncovered in the preceding subsection.

One way to introduce additional flexibility in the model is to suppose that the vector of characteristics X_i is not sufficient to capture the whole difference between individuals and to assume that the additional unobserved characteristics can be modeled as a random addition μ_i to $X_i\beta$, that is, $\lambda_i = \exp(X_i\beta + \mu_i)$ with probability density function $h(\mu_i)$. Of course, μ_i may also represent pure randomness and not missing characteristics, that is not a specification error. Then, the marginal probability that the i-th individual will be involved in k accidents becomes:

$$\int \frac{e^{-(X_i\beta+\mu_i)}\exp(X_i\beta + \mu_i)^k}{k!} \, h(\mu_i)d\mu_i, \tag{12}$$

which is the general form of the Compound Poisson distribution: different specifications of $h(\mu_i)$ lead to different particular cases.

The particular form we will consider here is the negative binomial distribution obtained by writing $\lambda_i = \exp(X_i\beta + \mu_i) = \exp(X_i\beta)\varepsilon_i$ and assuming that $\varepsilon_i = \exp(\mu_i)$ follows a gamma density with a mean of 1 (the mean of μ_i is assumed equal to 0) and a variance $\frac{1}{a}$. Since $\lambda_i = \exp(X_i\beta)\varepsilon_i$, it will have a mean of $\exp(X_i\beta)$ and a variance of $\frac{1}{a}\exp(X_i\beta)^2$.

Integrating the expression for the distribution of accidents above, we find

$$P(K_i = k|X_i) = \frac{\Gamma(k + a)}{k!\Gamma(a)} \left(\frac{\exp(X_i\beta)}{a}\right)^k \left(1 + \frac{\exp(X_i\beta)}{a}\right)^{-(k+a)}, \tag{13}$$

which is the expression for the negative binomial distribution with parameters a and $\exp(X_i\beta)$: its mean is $E(K_i) = \exp(X_i\beta)$ and its variance $V(K_i) = \exp(X_i\beta)[1 + \exp(X_i\beta)/a]$. Hence, the variance is a strictly convex increasing function of the mean: the variance/mean ratio is a linear function of the mean. As mentioned by Cameron and Trivedi (1986), this is just one parameterization of the negative binomial distribution. We can rewrite $P[K_i = k]$ above more generally and directly as a two-parameter (v_i, ϕ_i) distribution

$$P[K_i = k] = \frac{\Gamma(k + v_i)}{\Gamma(k + 1)\Gamma(v_i)} \left(\frac{v_i}{v_i + \phi_i}\right)^{v_i} \left(\frac{\phi_i}{v_i + \phi_i}\right)^k; \quad \phi_i > 0, v_i > 0 \tag{14}$$

with $E[K_i] = \phi_i$ and $VAR(K_i) = \phi_i + \frac{1}{v_i}$, where both v_i and ϕ_i are functions of the individual characteristics X_i. Since we wish to stick to the interpretation $E(\lambda_i) = \exp(X_i\beta)$, we can set $\phi_i = \exp(X_i\beta)$. But we have some freedom in setting the relation between v_i and X_i. For instance, we could assume that

$$v_i = \frac{1}{r} [\exp(X_i\beta)]^q; \quad r > 0.$$

The above formulation for $P[K_i = k|X_i]$ corresponds to the special case $r = \frac{1}{a}$ and $q = 0$. Cameron and Trivedi do in fact consider two cases: $q = 0$

and $q = 1$. We consider only the case $q = 0$ here and hence the heterogeneity of the individual car drivers, composed of a fixed part $\exp(X_i\beta)$ and a random part μ_i or ε_i, allows for overdispersion in the data but a restricted form of overdispersion, namely that the variance of the distribution of accidents for individual i is a second-degree polynomial of the mean of the distribution: $V = E + gE^2$ where $g = \dfrac{1}{a}$ is the variance of ε_i, the random (or missing) term of the individual vector of characteristics. As $g \to 0$ (that is $a \to \infty$), we obtain the Poisson distribution as expected since then $VAR(\varepsilon_i) = 0$. The choice of parameterization of the negative binomial distribution is by no means a simple matter. We feel that assuming q = 0 above is a very reasonable assumption to make in the case of car accidents.

Coming back to the estimation of the parameters of $P[K_i = k|X_i]$, we should first note that this model or this particular parameterization of the negative binomial model is equivalent to that of Gouriéroux, Montfort, and Trognon (1984b), to that of Haussman, Hall, and Griliches (1984) and to the Negbin II model of Cameron and Trivedi (1986). The maximum likelihood estimates are given in table 8 together with transformed coefficients that can be interpreted as in tables 6 and 7.

Table 8. Maximum Likelihood Estimates of the Negative Binomial Model with Individual Characteristics

Variable	Original Coefficient	(t)	Transformed Coefficients Prob1	Prob2+
D	0.0863	(9.66)**		
0–1			0.0038	0.0003
1–5			0.0183	0.0019
5–31			0.2219	0.1671
S	0.4800	(2.19)**		
0–1			0.0266	0.0029
1–2			0.0380	0.0070
2–3			0.0501	0.0160
Z	0.3488	(8.40)**		
0–1			0.0175	0.0016
1–2			0.0230	0.0032
2–6			0.1486	0.0684
INTERCEPT	−4.3138	(−8.43)**	NC	NC
A16–	−0.7091	(−0.92)	−0.0241	−0.0015
A2024	−0.1048	(−0.70)	−0.0046	−0.0003

Table 8.   Continued

Variable	Original Coefficient	(t)	Transformed Coefficients Prob1	Prob2+
A2534	−0.4874	(−2.89)**	−0.0203	−0.0016
A3544	−0.6581	(−3.47)**	−0.0256	−0.0018
A4554	−0.6801	(−3.43)**	−0.0253	−0.0017
A5564	−0.8949	(−4.25)**	−0.0304	−0.0019
A65+	−0.8522	(−3.66)**	−0.0284	−0.0017
SEXM	0.7768	(9.66)**	0.0337	0.0027
EXP0	0.5493	(1.20)	0.0311	0.0034
EXPM1	0.2573	(0.71)	0.0129	0.0012
EXP2	−0.1854	(−0.65)	−0.0079	−0.0006
EXP35	−0.3850	(−1.32)	−0.0155	−0.0011
EXP610	−0.3423	(−1.10)	−0.0144	−0.0011
EXP11	−0.2565	(−0.80)	−0.0117	−0.0009
REG1	0.1791	(1.13)	0.0087	0.0007
REG2	0.0796	(0.56)	0.0037	0.0003
REG3	0.1059	(1.14)	0.0050	0.0004
REG4	0.1451	(1.20)	0.0069	0.0006
REG5	−0.0251	(−0.15)	−0.0011	−0.0001
REG7	0.1408	(1.36)	0.0067	0.0006
REG8	−0.0236	(−0.26)	−0.0011	−0.0001
REG9	0.4631	(3.50)**	0.0252	0.0027
REG10	0.1836	(1.09)	0.0090	0.0008
REG11	0.2188	(1.02)	0.0109	0.0010
RTSA	−0.3450	(−1.59)	−0.0148	−0.0012
RTSB	0.2412	(0.45)	0.0121	0.0012
RTSGC	−0.1871	(−0.56)	−0.0079	−0.0006
RTSD	0.2795	(1.22)	0.0142	0.0014
RTSH	0.2189	(0.85)	0.0108	0.0010
RTSJ	1.4465	(1.49)	0.1154	0.0262
RTSK	−0.9376	(−0.74)	−0.0290	−0.0017
RTSM	−0.5990	(−1.47)	−0.0214	−0.0014
RTSO	0.2458	(0.63)	0.0124	0.0012
RTSQ	−1.2141	(−0.84)	−0.0338	−0.0018
RTSU	0.5083	(1.44)	0.0285	0.0031
RTSY	−1.9666	(−1.84)*	−0.0421	−0.0019
RTSØ	−0.1936	(−0.87)	−0.0091	−0.0007
CL1112	0.4270	(2.54)**	0.0231	0.0025
CL13	−0.4715	(−0.42)	−0.0176	−0.0011

Table 8. Continued

Variable	Original Coefficient	(t)	Transformed Coefficients Prob1	Prob2+
CL21	0.2570	(1.99)*	0.0124	0.0011
CL22	0.8430	(2.64)**	0.0542	0.0075
CL31	0.5449	(2.64)**	0.0310	0.0035
CL42	0.0587	(0.53)	0.0026	0.0002
CL54	0.0333	(0.24)	0.0015	0.0001
CL55	−0.7309	(−1.11)	−0.0246	−0.0015
CL56	−0.2455	(−0.18)	−0.0101	−0.0007
VALA	0.3624	(0.76)	NC	NC
VALB	0.0131	(0.04)	NC	NC
VALC	1.3066	(4.78)**	NC	NC
a	0.4609	(3.18)**		
Average individual			0.0492	0.0020
LL		−4556.43		
Number of observations		19,013		
Number of parameters		54		

* =significant at 90%; ** = significant at 95%

The Poisson and negative binomial estimates are rather close and the transformed coefficients are similarly quite comparable. Moreover, the same variables are significant. Since the Poisson is a particular case of the negative binomial model — it corresponds to the restriction $\left(\frac{1}{a}\right) = 0$ on the negative binomial model — we can perform a log-likelihood ratio test of this restriction to decide if considering individual characteristics is sufficient to explain the overdispersion in the data or if we gain in adding a gamma-distributed random element to $X_i\beta$. We obtain $-2(LL(\text{Poisson}) - LL(\text{negative binomial})) = -2(-4563.86 + 4556.43) = 14.86$ which is larger than $\chi^2_{1,.99} = 6.63$ indicating that the negative binomial model does perform significantly better. Finally, the log-likelihood ratio test indicates that the standard negative binomial model estimated without individual characteristics is rejected when compared with the negative binomial model estimated with individual characteristics $[-2(-4,916.78 + 4,556.43) = 720.7$ while the critical value at a 5% significance level is 63.83].

2.4. Related sampling and estimation issues

Maximum likelihood estimators (MLE) are not always efficient or easily tractable and their properties are quite sensitive to the distributional assumptions and to the sampling process. Most importantly, MLE of the Poisson or negative binomial regression models will not be efficient if the true distribution is not the specified one (this also holds for other regression models). Gouriéroux, Monfort, and Trognon (1984a, GMT hereafter) show that, if the pseudo distribution is a member of the linear exponential family (LEF), pseudo maximum likelihood methods will be consistent, provided that the mean of the distribution is well-specified. Since Poisson and negative binomial distributions are members of the LEF, pseudo maximum likelihood methods can be used to estimate these regression models. The pseudo maximum likelihood functions will be

$$- \sum_{i=1}^{n} \exp(X_i \beta) + \sum_{i=1}^{n} K_i X_i \beta \quad \text{for the Poisson family, and} \quad (15a)$$

$$\sum_{i=1}^{n} \left\{ K_i X_i \beta - \left(\frac{1}{a} + K_i \right) ln(1 + a\exp(X_i \beta)) \right\} \quad \begin{array}{l} \text{for the negative} \\ \text{binomial family,} \end{array} \quad (15b)$$

where a is an estimator of the dispersion parameter of the negative binomial distribution. These estimators are shown to be strongly consistent and asymptotically normal. GMT (1984b) give the appropriate expression of the asymptotic covariance matrix of the estimated parameters.

GMT (1984a) also present quasi generalized pseudo maximum likelihood methods, which need stronger assumptions than pseudo maximum likelihood methods. They show that if the pseudo distribution is a member of the LEF, quasi generalized pseudo maximum likelihood estimators (QGPMLE) of the negative binomial regression model (not Poisson model) will be more efficient than the PMLE, provided that the mean and the variance are well specified. For the QGPMLE of the negative binomial regression model, the objective function is

$$\sum_{i=1}^{n} \left\{ K_i X_i \beta - \left(\frac{1}{\hat{\eta}^2} + K_i \right) ln(1 + \hat{\eta}^2 \exp(X_i \beta)) \right\} \quad (15c)$$

where $\quad \hat{\eta}^2 = \dfrac{\sum_{i=1}^{n} [(K_i - \exp(X_i \hat{\beta}))^2 - \exp(X_i \hat{\beta})] \exp(2X_i \hat{\beta})}{\sum_{i=1}^{n} \exp(4X_i \hat{\beta})}$

and $\hat{\beta}$ comes from PMLE. There is no way to be sure that the specified distribution is the true one, but, if estimators based on weaker assumptions are close to MLE, one can reasonably assume that the model is not misspecified. QGPMLE of the negative binomial regression model are presented in table 9. As one can see, coefficients are very close to those of the MLE of the negative binomial regression model based on strong distributional assumptions.

Gouriéroux and Monfort (1989b) also propose some simulation based methods for models with heterogeneity by replacing mathematical expec-

Table 9. Quasi-Generalized Pseudo Maximum Likelihood Estimates

Variable	Coefficient	(t)
D	0.0839	(10.64)**
S	0.4647	(2.32)**
Z	0.3400	(9.35)**
INTERCEPT	−4.3260	(−8.82)**
A16−	−0.7017	(−0.93)
A2024	−0.0981	(−0.70)
A2534	−0.4777	(−2.99)**
A3544	−0.6470	(−3.58)**
A4554	−0.6728	(−3.56)**
A5564	−0.8873	(−4.39)**
A65+	−0.8550	(−3.80)**
SEXM	0.7799	(9.96)**
EXP0	0.5580	(1.28)
EXPM1	0.2536	(0.73)
EXP2	−0.1896	(−0.71)
EXP35	−0.3823	(−1.38)
EXP610	−0.3442	(−1.17)
EXP11	−0.2601	(−0.86)
REG1	0.1727	(1.14)
REG2	0.0819	(0.60)
REG3	0.1036	(1.16)
REG4	0.1438	(1.25)
REG5	−0.0289	(−0.18)
REG7	0.1406	(1.43)
REG8	−0.0242	(−0.28)
REG9	0.4665	(3.73)**
REG10	0.1762	(1.10)
REG11	0.2152	(1.05)

Table 9. Continued

Variable	Coefficent	(t)
RTSA	−0.3346	(−1.62)
RTSB	0.2356	(0.45)
RTSGC	−0.1852	(−0.58)
RTSD	0.2912	(1.32)
RTSH	0.2214	(0.90)
RTSJ	1.4474	(1.60)
RTSK	−0.9169	(−0.78)
RTSM	−0.5881	(−1.48)
RTSO	0.2405	(0.64)
RTSQ	−1.2402	(−0.92)
RTSU	0.4922	(1.53)
RTSY	−1.9652	(−1.86)*
RTSØ	−0.1848	(−0.87)
CL1112	0.4284	(2.79)**
CL13	−0.4517	(−0.41)
CL21	0.2699	(2.22)**
CL22	0.8332	(2.87)**
CL31	0.5480	(2.95)**
CL42	0.0653	(0.63)
CL54	0.0254	(0.19)
CL55	−0.7042	(−1.15)
CL56	−0.2110	(−0.17)
VALA	0.3441	(0.76)
VALB	0.0537	(0.17)
VALC	1.2855	(4.98)**

Objective function: −4492.99
Nb of parameters: 53
Nb of observations: 19 013

tations in the objective functions by empirical means from simulated values of the error term. The sampling method is also important for the choice of the estimation method to be used with count data. The sample is said to be exogenous, as in our case, when decision makers (individuals) are sampled and their choices (accidents) observed. In that case of exogenous sampling, maximum likelihood and pseudo maximum likelihood methods are appropriate. The sample is said to be endogenous when choices are sampled and decision makers observed. For example, if one had sampled 50% of individuals with no accident and 50% of individuals with accidents, the resulting sample would overrepresent the population of drivers with accidents since 6.5% of the entire population had at least one accident. In that case of endogenous sampling, one should use some other estimation methods. Statistical methods have been developed to deal with that kind of problem [see Manski-McFadden (1981) for a survey]. Manski-Lerman (1977) propose a weighted maximum likelihood method called Weight Exogenous Sampling Maximum Likelihood (WESML) method. Gouriéroux and Monfort (1989a) showed that the Exogenous Sampling Berkson (ESB) method keeps interesting properties when the observations are endogenously stratified and they proposed the Modified Exogenous Sampling Berkson (MESB) method, which is shown to be asymptotically more efficient than the ESB method and the WESML method.

2.5. Comparison of estimated individual probabilities of accident by the different models

It is difficult to compare the econometric results of the different models insofar as these models are not directly comparable on a statistical basis. For instance, the categorical models of subsection 2.2 provide the probability of being in one category or another, that is to be in the category of those with no accident or in the category of those with at least one accident (for the linear probability model, the probit model and the logit model; for the multinomial logit, the latter category is divided into two categories), while the Poisson and negative bionomial models, both the homogeneous and heterogeneous drivers forms, give the probability of having 0, 1, 2, 3, etc., accidents. Since the Poisson model is a limited case of the negative binomial model and since the homogeneous drivers Poisson and negative binomial models are special cases of the corresponding heterogeneous drivers models, rigorous hypothesis tests can be performed to discriminate between the models. They were already discussed in the previous section. However, the reader may observe that all models provide the same qualitative results in the sense that the significant variables are essentially the same in the different models. Therefore, any of these models can be estimated when the objective is limited to the identification of significant explanatory variables.

In this section, the econometric results are compared on the basis of the predicted expected number of accidents for given individuals, that is for different X vectors. Table 10, 11, and 12 present the results. We observe that the predictions differ with the distributional assumptions.

Table 10.   The Otherwise Average Individual's Expected Number of Accidents
E(ACC) as a Function of Cumulated Demerit Points D

Demerit Points D *During 1980–1981 and 1981–1982*	*E(ACC) in 1982–1983 (for* S = Z = 0)		
	POISSON	*NEGBIN*	*MLOGIT*
0	0.047	0.046	0.044
5	0.071	0.071	0.071
10	0.107	0.110	0.111
15	0.162	0.169	0.171
20	0.246	0.260	0.256

Table 11.   The Otherwise Average Individual's Expected Number of Accidents
E(ACC) as a Function of License Suspensions S

Number of Suspensions S *During 1981–1982*	*E(ACC) in 1982–1983 (for* D = Z = 0)		
	POISSON	*NEGBIN*	*MLOGIT*
0	0.047	0.046	0.044
1(VALB = 281)[1]	0.073	0.075	0.074
2(VALB = 197)[1]	0.115	0.120	0.120

[1] The driver cannot drive during a suspension.

Consequently, in order to obtain consistent quantitative predictions, it is
important to select the appropriate model particularly when the true
distribution is not symmetric as for the Poisson and the negative binomial
family.[3] See Boyer, Dionne, Vanasse (1990) for other tables.

3. The Determination of an Optimal Pricing Formula for Automobile Insurance

In the presence of moral hazard between the principal (insurer) and the
agent (insured), the traditional one-period insurance contracts that do not
take into account this asymmetrical information problem are not optimal.
Many authors have investigated optimal insurance pricing in single-period
models when moral hazard is present [see, for example, Holmstrom
(1989) and Shavell (1979) and recent surveys by Arnott (1991) and
Winter (1991)].

More recently, Radner (1981, 1985), Rubinstein and Yaari (1983),

Table 12.   The Otherwise Average Individual's Expected Number of Accidents E(ACC) as a Function of Past Involvements in Accidents Z

Number of Accidents Z During 1980–1981 and 1981–1982	E(ACC) in 1982–1983					
	For D = S = 0			For D = 5 and S = 1 (VALB = 281)		
	Poisson	Negbin	Mlogit	Poisson	Negbin	Mlogit
0	0.0466	0.0462	0.0443	0.1110	0.1148	0.1157
1	0.0652	0.0655	0.0641	0.1554	0.1627	0.1629
2	0.0914	0.0929	0.0921	0.2177	0.2306	0.2251
3	0.1280	0.1317	0.1308	0.3050	0.3269	0.3035
4	0.1793	0.1866	0.1828	0.4272	0.4634	0.3971
5	0.2512	0.2645	0.2503	0.5984	0.6568	0.5019

Boyer and Dionne (1985, 1987a) have shown that multiperiod contracts are Pareto superior to a repetition of single-period contracts when the number of periods is large and the discount factor is close to one. One interesting characteristic of these contracts for automobile insurance concerns the use, by the principal, of statistical information obtained over time from the agent to relate insurance premiums to the individual's past experience. Since the insurer does not observe the individual's driving behavior, he may then use his past experience to enforce more care activities in each period.

The statistical results in the previous sections of this paper clearly show that the individual's past driving experience is a good predictor of risk. In this section, we will show how the Rubinstein-Yaari model for the pricing of insurance in the presence of moral hazard can be applied to the negative binomial model with a regression component.

Considering the Rubinstein-Yaari model, we can reformulate their contract in order to introduce all the information contained in the regression component.[4] The Rubinstein-Yaari no-claims-discount contract is expressed in terms of the observed past average claim and the expected claim obtained from a proper behavior regarding self-protection. In each period, the insurer sets the level of the insurance premium, $P(t)$, as a function of past experience and the insured must decide whether to purchase insurance or not and must choose the level of care activities. The insurer observes the insured's number of accidents when the latter buy insurance. Rubinstein and Yaari propose the following no-claims discounts strategy for the leader (insurer) in a Stackelberg game:

$$P(1) = P_i^*$$

$$P(t) = \begin{cases} P_i^* & \text{if } \dfrac{1}{N(t)}\displaystyle\sum_{s=1}^{t-1} L^s < \exp(X_i^*\beta) + a_i^{N(t)} \\[2mm] PP_i & \text{otherwise} \end{cases}$$

where $P(t)$ is the premium for period $t > 1$; P^* is the full information premium; L^s is the observed number of claims in period s; $N(t)$ is the number of periods during which the agent was insured; $a_i^{N(t)}$ is a statistical margin of error, on which we shall return; PP is a penalty premium; X_i^* is the vector of characteristics of a type i individual evaluated at the socially efficient level of self-protection activities generating different values of D_i^*, S_i^*, and Z_i^*.

The role of the penalty premium is important. It does not correspond to a simple adjustment to past experience of the previous period premium. Rubinstein and Yaari showed that, in order to have an optimal solution, PP_i has to be set such that the individual would prefer to self-insure than to buy insurance in a one-period contract. Then, in order to obtain the commitment of the insured to this type of contract, the insurer must use a statistical margin of error that guarantees to those who behave properly that they will not be penalized often.

The above contract can be interpreted as follows: considering that $\exp(X_i^*\beta)$ is the socially-optimal expected number of accidents corresponding to a type i individual, this individual is offered, at period t, a full insurance contract at the P_i^* premium if the average number of past accidents over the $(t - 1)$ previous periods is less than the socially-optimal expected number of accidents plus a statistical margin of error.

To illustrate how such a contract can be designed from our results, we shall consider a driver who corresponds to the average of individual vectors of characteristics $(\bar{X}_i)$. We shall simulate histories of accidents randomly by a negative binomial distribution with parameters (1.4663, 27.6306) implying that $\exp(\bar{X}_i\beta) = 0.0531$ with a corresponding variance equal to 0.0550. Let us assume that the socially-optimal expected number of accidents is also equal to 0.0531. Assuming that the individual takes insurance in each period, the corresponding statistical margin of error, a_i^t, is then equal to

$$\sqrt{\dfrac{2\gamma(0.0550)\ \log\log t}{t}}$$

where γ is a policy parameter and a_i^t is obtained from the law of the iterated logarithm [see Radner (1981) for more details]. In each $t \geq 3$ period, the individual will be charged the P_i^* premium if the past observed frequency of accidents $(1/t) \sum_{s=1}^{t-1} L^s$ is less than $exp(\bar{X}_i\beta) + \alpha_i^t$ where α_i^t is defined as above, He will be charged a penalty premium, otherwise. With an appropriately chosen PP_i (penalty premium), the individual is induced to select the proper level of care. However, even with the proper or optimal level of care, the insured may be unlucky and have to pay PP_i often. However, α_i^t prevents the insurer from penalizing too often those who choose the appropriate level of prevention.

The simulation permitted the verification of the above assertion. We simulated 1,000 cases of a 50-period contract and of a 100-period contract and 100 cases of a 1,000-period contract. The results for $\gamma = 1.05$ are summarized in table 13.

Table 13. Average Number (#) and Percentage (%) of Periods for which the Average Individual Will Be Wrongly Penalized

Contract		Periods with PP_i (#)	(%)
50-period	(1,000 cases)	4.17	8.34
100-period	(1,000 cases)	7.03	7.03
1,000-period	(100 cases)	27.80	2.78

Although Rubinstein and Yaari's results were derived from an infinite horizon model without discounting, it appears reasonable to design such a contract spanning a 50-year horizon or a 100-semester horizon. In Québec, for example, automobile insurance for bodily injuries is offered by a public monopoly and drivers must buy insurance in order to drive. Then their average length of contracts is about 50 years or 100 semesters. In both cases, they would be penalized less than 8% of the total number of periods if they behave properly. However, an individual who does not produce the optimal level of care and generates an accident frequency of 0.07 instead of 0.053, for example, will be penalized for more than 15% of the periods.

Conclusion

In this study, we reviewed and estimated eight econometric models of accident distributions. The estimation of the appropriate statistical model is important to implement insurance contracts that reduce the inefficiencies associated to asymmetrical information. We used a set of data on 19,013 car drivers for which we had five types of information: the personal characteristics, the number of accidents, the number of demerit points, the number of license suspensions for criminal offenses, and the number of days the driving permit was valid during each period. We have estimated four categorical models (linear probability, probit, logit, and multinomial logit) and four count data models (Poisson and negative binomial models with and without individual characteristics in the regression component).

It is difficult to compare the econometric results of the different models since some of these models are not nested. However, it was shown that the negative binomial model with a regression component produces a reasonable approximation of the true distribution of accidents. Different statistical tests rejected the Poisson models (with and without a regression component) and the negative binomial model without individual characteristics. It was also observed that all estimated models provide the same qualitative resluts (essentially the same significant variables), but differ when predictions of either the probabilities of accident or the expected number of accidents were made. For quantitative predictions, it is important to select the appropriate model. Finally, it was shown that, in all models, the individual's past driving experience is a good predictor of risk.

In section 3, we used the statistical results obtained from the negative binomial model with a regression component to show how the Rubinstein-Yaari model of insurance tarification in the presence of moral hazard could be applied. Other types of tarification models could also be investigated.

Notes

1. Our analysis of multicollinearity is limited to its effects on the estimation results for the β parameters and does not take into account its potential effects on other conclusions we may obtain from the model (prevision and tarification).

2. Details are available from the authors.

3. Those econometric results may also be used for risk classification. For different approaches to risk classification, see Dahlby (1983), Lemaire (1985), and Beuthe and Van Namen (1975).

4. For a reformulation of the Rubenstein-Yaari contract in terms of probabilities of accident estimated with a probit model, see Boyer and Dionne (1989).

References

Arnott, R. (1991). "Moral Hazard and Competitive Insurance Markets," in G. Dionne (ed.): *Contributions to Insurance Economics*, Norwell, MA: Kluwer Academic Publishers.

Belsley, David A. E. Kuh, and R. E. Welsch. (1980). *Regression Diagnostics, Identifying Influential Data and Sources of Multicollinearity*. New York: Wiley.

Beuthe, M., and Ph. Van Namen. (1975). "La sélection des assurés et la détermination des primes d'assurances par l'analyse discriminante," *Mitteilungen der Vereinigung Schweizerischer Versicherungsmathematiker* 2, 137–155.

Boyer, M., and G. Dionne. (1985). "Sécurité routière: responsabilité pour négligence et tarification," *Canadian Journal of Economics/Revue canadienne d'économique* 18, November, 814–830.

Boyer, M., and G. Dionne. (1987a). "The Economics of Road Safety," *Transportation Research B* 21(5), 413–431.

Boyer, M., and G. Dionne. (1987b). "Description and Analysis of the Québec Automobile Insurance Plan," *Canadian Public Policy/Analyse de politiques* XIII(2), 181–195.

Boyer, M., and G. Dionne. (1989). "An Empirical Analysis of Moral Hazard and Experience Rating," *Review of Economics and Statistics* LXXI(1), 128–134.

Boyer, M., G. Dionne, and C. Vanasse. (1988). "Infractions au code de la sécurité routière, infractions au code criminel et accidents automobiles," R.A.A.Q. report and Discussion Paper no. 583, Centre de recherche sur les transports, Université de Montréal, 85 pages. *Actualité Économique* (forthcoming).

Boyer, M., G. Dionne and C. Vanasse. (1990). "Econometric Models of Accident Distributions," Working Paper 9001, Département de sciences économiques, Université de Montréal.

Cameron, A. C., and P. K. Trivedi. (1986). "Econometric Models Based on Count Data: Comparisons and Applications of Some Estimations and Tests," *Journal of Applied Econometrics* 1, 29–53.

Cameron, A. C., P. K. Trivedi, F. Milne and J. Piggott. (1988). "A Microeconometric Model of the Demand for Health Care and Health Insurance in Australia," *Review of Economic Studies* 55, 85–106.

Crocker, K. J., and A. Snow. (1986). "The Efficiency Effects of Categorical Discrimination in the Insurance Industry," *Journal of Political Economy* 94, 321–344.

Dahlby, B. A. (1983). "Adverse Selection and Statistical Discrimination," *Journal of Public Economics* 20, 121–131.

Devlin, R. A. (1991). "Liability versus No-fault Automobile Insurance Regimes: An Analysis of the Experience of Quebec," in G. Dionne (ed.), *Contributions to Insurance Economics*. Norwell, MA: Kluwer Academic Publishers.

Ferreira, J. (1974). "The Long-Term Effects of Merit-Rating Plans on Individual Motorists," *Operations Research* 22, September-October, 954–978.

Gaudry, M. (1991). "Measuring the Effects of the 1978 Quebec Automobile Insurance Act with the DRAG Model," in G. Dionne (ed.), *Contributions to Insurance Economics*. Norwell, MA: Kluwer Academic Publishers.

Gilbert, C. L. (1979). "Econometric Models for Discrete Economic Processes." Discussion Paper, University of Oxford.

Gouriéroux, C., and A. Montfort. (1989a). "Econometrics Based on Endogenous

Samples." INSEE, Discussion paper 89.3.

Gouriéroux, C., and A. Montfort. (1989b). "Simulation Based Inference in Models with Heterogeneity." INSEE, Discussion Paper 89.5.

Gouriéroux, C., and A. Montfort. (1989c). "Econometrics of Count Data: The A.L.D.P. Model," paper presented at the European Society Econometric Meeting, Munich, September, 50 pages.

Gouriéroux, C., A. Montfort and A. Trognon. (1984a). "Pseudo Maximum Likelihood Methods: Theory," *Econometrica* 52, 681–700.

Gouriéroux, C., A. Montfort and A. Trognon. (1984b). "Pseudo Maximum Likelihood Methods: Applications to Poisson Models," *Econometrica* 52, 701–720.

Greenwood, M., and G. U. Yule. (1920). "An Inquiry into the Nature of Frequency Distribution of Multiple Happenings," *Journal of the Royal Statistical Society* A(83), 255–279.

Hausman, J., B. H. Hall and Z. Griliches. (1984). "Econometric Models for Count Data with an Application to the Patents-R & D Relationship," *Econometrica* 52, 909–938.

Heckman, J., and G. Borjas. (1980). "Does Unemployment Cause Future Unemployment? Definitions, Questions and Answers from a Continuous Time Model for Heterogeneity and State Dependence," *Econometrica* 47, 247–283.

Holland, P. W. (1973). "Poisson Regression," Discussion Paper, Princeton University.

Holmstrom, B. (1979). "Moral Hazard and Observability," *Bell Journal of Economics* 10, Spring, 74–91.

Johnson, P. D., and G. B. Hey. (1971). "Statistical Studies in Motor Insurance," *The Journal of the Institute of Actuaries* 97, 199–232.

Lefebvre, P., and C. Fluet. (1990). "L'évolution du prix réel de l'assurance automobile au Québec depuis la réforme de 1978," *Canadian Public Policy*, XVI, 375–386.

Lemaire, J. (1985). *Automobile Insurance: Actuarial Models*. Boston: Kluwer-Nihoff.

Maddala, G. S. (1983). *Limited-Dependent and Qualitative Variables in Econometrics*. New York: Cambridge University Press.

Manski, C. F., and S. R. Lerman. (1977). "The Estimation of Choice Probabilities from Choice Based Samples," *Econometrica* 45, 1977–1988.

Manski, C. F., and D. McFadden. (1981). "Alternative Estimators and Sample Designs for Discrete Choice Analysis," in *Structural Analysis of Discrete Data with Econometric Applications*, C. F. Manski and D. McFadden (eds.), M.I.T. Press.

Patil, G. P. (1970). *Random Counts in Models and Structures: Volume 1*. The Pennsylvania State University Press.

Radner, R. (1981). "Monitoring Cooperative Agreements in a Repeated Principal-Agent Relationship," *Econometrica* 49, September, 1127–1148.

Radner, R. (1985). "Repeated Principal-Agent Games with Discounting," *Econometrica* 53, September, 1173–1199.

Rose, N. (1990). "Profitability and Product Quality: Economic Determinants of Airline Safety Performance," Journal of Political Economy, 98, October, 944–969.

Rubinstein, A., and M. E. Yaari. (1983). "Repeated Insurance Contracts and Moral Hazard," *Journal of Economic Theory* 30, June, 79–97.

Seal, H. L. (1969). *Stochastic Theory of a Risk Business*. New York: Wiley.

Shavell, S. (1979). "Risk Sharing and Incentives in the Principal and Agent Relationship," *Bell Journal of Economics* 10, Spring, 55–74.

Theil, H. (1971). *Principles of Econometrics*. New York: Wiley.

Winter, R. (1991). "Moral Hazard in Insurance Contracts," in G. Dionne (ed.), *Contributions to Insurance Economics*. Norwell, MA: Kluwer Academic Publishers.

PART II ESSAYS

A) THEORETICAL MODELS

OPTIMAL INSURANCE: A NONEXPECTED UTILITY ANALYSIS

Edi Karni*

The Johns Hopkins University

Abstract

This paper reviews some of the recent developments in the theory of decision making under risk and applies them to selected problems in the theory of optimal insurance, namely, the choice of optimal insurance coverage and the comparative statics analysis of the optimal insurance coverage with respect to the consumer's risk aversion. The analysis highlights the methodology of local expected utility analysis.

Key words: Nonexpected utility, expected utility with rank-dependent probabilities, weighted utility, optimal insurance

Like the analysis of other arrangements designed to improve the allocation of risk bearing among economic agents, the economic analysis of insurance was conducted within the framework of expected utility theory. Mounting experimental evidence indicating systematic violations of the expected utility hypothesis inspired the development in recent years of alternative

* Useful comments by Mark Machina, Zvi Safra, and two anonymous referees are gratefully acknowledged. Part of the work reported here was done during the author's participation in BoWo 89; financial support by the Deutsche Forschungsgemeinschaft, Gottfried-Wilhelm-Leibniz-Forderpreis, is acknowledged with thanks.

decision theories that depart from expected utility theory and the examination of the validity of results obtained within the framework of the expected utility model in the new decision models.[1] In the present paper we survey some of these theories and examine some of their implications for the theory of optimal insurance.

The idea that in choosing among risky prospects decision makers behave as if they seek to maximize the expectation of a utility function (i.e., the expectation of a real valued function defined on the set of outcomes), goes back to Bernoulli (1738). However, only with the publication of von Neumann and Morgenstern's (1944) *Theory of Games and Economic Behavior* did the theory acquired an axiomatic foundation. The subsequent work of Marschak (1950), Samuelson (1952), Malinvaud (1950), and Herstein and Milnor (1953) clarified the behavioral meaning of the underlying axioms. The behavioral interpretation of the axioms seemed so normatively compelling that the resulting theory came to be regarded as a model of rational behavior.

According to the von Neumann-Morgenstern expected utility theory, decision makers are characterized by a preference relation, $\geq$, over a set, L, of risky prospects. Formally, let X be an arbitrary set of outcomes; then L is the set of all probability measures on X. Thus, L is a convex subset of a linear space. For any $f, g \in L, f \geq g$ has the interpretation f preferred (weakly) over g, $f > g$ means that f is strictly preferred to g, and $f \sim g$ means that f and g are equally preferred. The essence of expected utility theory is a set of restrictions on the preference relation $\geq$ that allows its numerical represenation as the mathematical expectation of a real–valued function u on X, in the sense that for all f and g in $L, f \geq g$ if and only if the mathematical expectation of u under f is larger or equal to that under g. u is referred to as a utility function.

In the von Neumann-Morgenstern theory the preference relations are complete (i.e., for all $f, g \in L$, either $f \geq g$ or $g \geq f$) and transitive (i.e., for all $f, g, h \in L, f \geq g$ and $g \geq h$ implies that $f \geq h$), and satisfy an Archimedean axiom, namely, for all $f, g, h \in L, f > g$ and $g > h$, then there exist numbers α and β between zero and one such that $\alpha f + (1 - \alpha)h > g > \beta f + (1 - \beta)h$. In addition, the preference relation satisfies the independence axiom, namely, for all f, g, and h in L and $0 \leq \alpha \leq 1$, if $f \geq g$ then $\alpha f + (1 - \alpha)h \geq \alpha g + (1 - \alpha)h$. The normative appeal of the independence axiom is easily understood if we interpret the mixture operation $\alpha f + (1 - \alpha)h$ as a representation of a two-stage compound lottery, i.e., a lottery in which the prizes in the first stage are themselves lottery tickets. For example, the first stage in the compound lottery $\alpha f + (1 - \alpha)h$ entails an α percent chance of winning the lottery ticket f and a

$(1 - \alpha)$ percent chance of winning the lottery ticket h. In the second stage either f or h is played out to determine the prize in X that is awarded to the decision maker. Comparing the risky prospects $\alpha f + (1 - \alpha)h$ and $\alpha g + (1 - \alpha)h$ the decision maker is supposed to reason that if the event that has a probability $(1 - \alpha)$ is realized in the first stage, then he wins h independently of which risky prospect he chose. However, if the event that has a probability α is realized in the first stage, then he gets to participate in f if he chose the first prospect, and in g if he chose the second. Since the decision maker prefers f over g, he is better off with the risky prospect $\alpha f + (1 - \alpha)h$ than with $\alpha g + (1 - \alpha)h$. Implicit in this reasoning is the assumption that if f is preferred over g in isolation, it is also preferred given that h could have been realized but was not.

The von Neumann-Morgenstern expected utility theorem asserts that $\geq$ satisfies the aforementioned axioms if and only if there exists a real-valued, affine, functional, V, on L representing $\geq$. Formally, there exists $V: L \to \mathbf{R}$ such that for all $f, g \in L$, $f \geq g$ if and only if $V(f) \geq V(g)$, and, for all $\alpha \in (0, 1)$, $V(\alpha f + (1 - \alpha)g) = \alpha V(f) + (1 - \alpha)V(g)$. For simple probability distributions this representation takes the form of the expectaton of a real-valued utility function, u, on X that is defined for each $x \in X$ by $u(x) = V(\delta_x)$, where δ_x is the element of L that assigns the unit probability mass to $x \in X$.[2] V is unique up to positive monotonic transformations and u, the von Neumann-Morgenstern utility function, is unique up to positive affine transformations. It is important to note that it is the independence axiom that is by and large responsible for the affinity of V.

In addition to representation theorems expected utility theory consists of a body of results describing the interaction between the decision maker's attitudes toward risk and the feasible set of risky prospects that he must choose from. The study of optimal insurance contracts is but one instance of this type of analysis.

1. Nonexpected Utility Theory

Nonexpected utility models of decision making under risk depart from one or more of the axioms of expected utility theory and, in some cases, restrict the set of risky prospects. In this survey we confine ourselves to nonexpected utility theories in which the preference relations are complete, transitive, and continuous in an appropriate sense, and the space of risky prospects has sufficient structure so that the preference relation is representable by a real-valued but not necessarily linear functional V. In other words we consider models that depart from the independence axiom of expected utility theory.[3]

1.1. Decision Theories with the Betweenness Property

A preference functional V on L is said to satisfy betweenness if for all f, g in L and $\alpha \in [0, 1]$ $V(f) \geqslant V(g)$ implies $V(f) \geqslant V(\alpha f + (1 - \alpha)g) \geqslant V(g)$. In other words, the preference ranking of a probability mixture of any two risky prospects is in between the two risky prospects. The indifference sets in L induced by a preference functional with the betweenness property are convex. In other words, the preference relation represented by V is both quasiconcave and quasiconvex. Expected utility theory is a specific case of this broader class of models. Under appropriate restrictions these models are consistent with the famous Allais paradox and other experimental observations contradicting the independence axiom.

Decision models with the betweenness property were developed by Chew and MacCrimmon (1979), Chew (1983), Fishburn (1983), Dekel (1986), and Nakamura (1984).[4] An interesting example of a decision model with the betweenness property is weighted utility theory. In weighted utility theory the independence axiom is weakened as follows: For all f, g in L, $f \sim g$ implies that for all $\alpha \in (0, 1)$ there exists $\beta \in (0, 1)$ such that for all h in L $\alpha f + (1 - \alpha)h \sim \beta g + (1 - \beta)h$. Unlike the independence axiom, this condition does not require that $\alpha = \beta$. As a result the representation functional is not linear on L. Instead $\geq$ is represented by an extended real-valued functional V such that for all f and $g \in L$ and $\alpha \in (0, 1)$,

$$V(\alpha f + (1 - \alpha)g) = \frac{\alpha W(f) V(f) + (1 - \alpha) W(g) V(g)}{\alpha W(f) + (1 - \alpha) W(g)},$$

where W is a nonnegative real-valued linear function on L. Note that if W is a constant function, then V is the expected utility functional. If $p = (p_1, p_2, \cdots, p_n)$ is a simple probability distribution on X (i.e., $p_i \geqslant 0$, $\Sigma_{i=1}^n p_i = 1$,) and p_i denotes the probability of the outcome $x_i \in X$, then

$$V(p) = \frac{\Sigma_{i=1}^n v(x_i) w(x_i) p_i}{\Sigma_{i=1}^n w(x_i) p_i},$$

where $w(x_i) = W(\delta_{x_i})$ and $v(x_i) = V(\delta_{x_i})$.

One interpretation of weighted utility theory is as follows: Let X be an arbitrary interval in the real line, **R**. For $i = 1, 2, \cdots, n$, define the transformed probabilities $p_i^* = w(x_i) p_i / \Sigma_{i=1}^n w(x_i) p_i$, and regard $V(p)$ as the expectation of v with respect to $p^* = (p_1^*, p_2^*, \cdots, p_n^*)$. In this interpretation the evaluation of risky prospects requires that monetary values be transformed into utilities as in expected utility theory and, in addition, the probabilities be transformed so that the probability of a outcome x depends on its size. In general, the utility and the transformed probability of each outcome depends only on that outcome.

1.2. Expected Utility with Rank Dependent Probabilities

The idea that the evaluation of risky prospects requires the transformation of the probabilities of the different outcomes is also inherent in the next class of nonexpected utility theories, which we refer to as expected utility with rank dependent probabilities. In these theories, risky prospects are represented by cumulative distribution functions on J, an arbitrary interval in the real line. We denote by D_J the set of all risky prospects. To grasp the nature of the representation functional consider first the case in which $F \in D_J$ is a simple cumulative distribution, i.e., $F(\cdot) = \Sigma_{i=1}^n p_i \delta_{x_i}(\cdot)$, $x_1 < x_2, \cdots, < x_n$, and p_i is the probability of x_i. Then,

$$V(F) = \sum_{i=1}^n u(x_i) \left[g\left(\sum_{j=i}^n p_i \right) - g\left(\sum_{j=i+1}^n p_i \right) \right],$$

where u is a monotonic increasing, continuous, real-valued function on J and $g: [0, 1] \to [0, 1]$ is continuous, strictly increasing, and onto. The utility function u is unique up to positive affine transformations and the probability transformation function g is unique. Note that if g is the identity function (i.e., if, for all $p \in [0, 1]$, $g(p) = p$), then V is reduced to the expected utility functional. In general, $[g(\Sigma_{j=i}^n pi) - g(\Sigma_{j=i+1}^n p_i)]$ may be regarded as a transformation of the probability p_i. Unlike in weighted utility theory where the probability transformation depends on the size of the outcome to which it is assigned, the probability transformation in this case depends on the relative rank of the outcome in the set of the relevant outcomes. If F is not a simple cumulative distribution function then

$$V(F) = - \int_J u(x) \, dg(1 - F(x)).$$

Models of expected utility with rank dependent probabilities were axiomatized independently by Quiggin (1982) for the case in which $g(1/2) = 1/2$ and Yaari (1987) for the case in which $u(x) = x$. Building upon the work of Quiggin and Yaari, respectively, Chew (1985) and Segal

(1989) axiomatized the general expected utility with rank dependent probability functionals. By an appropriate choice of the probability transformation function, g, these models can be made to be consistent with experimental evidence violating the independence axiom. (See Quiggin (1982), Segal (1987), and Karni and Safra (1987), (1990).)

1.3. Local Expected Utility Analysis

The widespread acceptance of expected utility theory is due largely to its clear implications for the analysis of institutional arrangements designed to improve the allocation of risk bearing. Fortunately, as shown by Machina (1982), many of these implications are robust to the weakening or the abandonment altogether of the independence axiom. More specifically, if the preference functionals are smooth, in the sense of having a local linear approximation along certain paths, then locally in the set of risky prospects, decision makers behave as if they were expected utility maximizers. Certain global comparative statics results analogous to those obtained under expected utility theory may then be obtained by integration along the relevant paths.

The analytical tool required for the extension of expected utility analysis is the local utility function. To illustrate this idea we follow Machina (1982), and identify the the set of risky prospects with the set, D_J, of all cumulative distribution functions on a bounded interval J in **R**, and suppose that D_J is normed by the L^1 norm. Suppose that preferences on D_J are representable by real-valued functional V that is smooth in the sense of being Frechet differentiable.[5] This implies that for each F in D_J there exists an absolutely continuous real-valued function, $U(\cdot; F)$, on J such that for all F and G in D_J,

$$V(F) - V(G) = \int_J U(x; F)(d(F(x) - dG(x)) + o(\| F - G \|).$$

A decision maker whose preferences are represented by V ranks differential shifts from the risky prospect F as if he is an expected utility maximizer with a von Neumann-Morgenstern utility function $U(\cdot; F)$. This function is the local utility function at F. Thus, if V is Frechet differentiable, expected utility analysis obtains locally. Global implications may be obtained via the Fundamental Theorem of Calculus. More specifically, the comparison of two risky prospects that are far apart requires finding a differentiable path in D_J connecting the two distributions and then integrating the differential of the preference functional (i.e., the derivative of V) along the path. Generally speaking, results in expected utility analysis that depend on the properties of the von Neumann-Morgenstern utility function but not on the linearity of the functional are preserved provided the same properties are imposed on all the local utility functions.

The local utility function is unique up to affine positive transformations such that the multiplicative constant is the same for every indifference class of the underlying preference relation. In other words, let V be a smooth preference functional representing a preference relation $\geq$ on D_J, and let $\{U(\cdot\,; F)|F \in D_J\}$ be the set of local utility functions corresponding to V. If V^* is another functional representation of $\geq$ with a corresponding local utility functions $\{U^*(\cdot\,; F)|F \in D_J\}$ then for each $F \in D_J$, $U^*(\cdot\,; F) = a(F) + b(V(F))U(\cdot\,;F)$, where $b(\cdot)$ is a continuous positive function on $\mathbf{R}$ and $a(\cdot)$ is a real-valued function on D_J.[6] Machina (1982) shows that if for every $x \in J$ the local utility functions display increasing absolute risk aversion at x as a result of a shift towards stochastically dominating distributions, then the corresponding preference functional may be consistent with experimental evidence (e.g., the Allais paradox, the common ratio effect, and the utility evaluation effect) that contradict the independence axiom. In expected utility theory, because all the local utility functions are identical, the possibility that the attitudes toward risk alter in the aforementioned manner does not exist.

Examples: (a) The local utility function at F corresponding to the weighted utility functional is defined for all $x \in X$ by

$$U(x; F) = \frac{w(x)[v(x) - V(F)]}{\displaystyle\int_X w(z)\,dF(z)}.$$

(b) The local utility function at F corresponding to expected utility with rank dependent probabilities functional is given by

$$U(x; F) = \int_{J^x} g'(1 - F(z))\,du(z),$$

where $J^x = (-\infty, x) \cap J$.

Frechet differentiability is quite restrictive, and may not be applicable in many cases. For instance, Chew, Karni, and Safra (1987) show that, in general, expected utility with rank-dependent probabilities functionals are not Frechet differentiable. [Intuitively speaking, the reason is the rank dependent nature of the representation functional. In particular, consider a simple, nondegenerate, probability distribution with support in $\mathbf{R}$ and let the highest ranking outcome, say x_n, be gradually reduced. As long as there is no crossing of ranks, the value of the functional declines at the rate $g(p_n)$ (see section 2.2). However, as soon as x_n becomes smaller than x_{n-1}, the second highest outcome, further decline in x_n reduces the value of the functional at the rate $g(p_n + p_{n-1}) - g(p_{n-1})$. Hence, the preference functional is not differentiable at the distribution where $x_{n-1} = x_n$. An insightful geometric description of this argument is provided in Wakker (1989).] Fortunately, however, the essential aspect of local expected utility analysis is not the concept of differentiability that is being imposed, rather it is the feasibility of approximating the preference functional on the relevant set of paths in the space of distributions by an expected utility functional. In many problems this does not require that the preference functional be Frechet differentiable. Thus, for instance, Chew, Karni, and Safra (1987) obtained comparative statics results in optimal portfolio theory under the weaker assumption that the preference functional is Gateaux differentiable but not necessarily Frechet differentiable. More generally, comparative statics analysis requires the study of properties of the preference functional along some path in the relevant space of distributions. Hence, the applicability of local expected utility analysis depends on the existence of linear approximation of the preference functional along the relevant path. Formally, a path in D_J is a function $H_{(\cdot)}: [0, 1] \to D_J$. A preference functional is smooth with respect to a path $H_{(\cdot)}$ at $F \in D_J$ if $H_0 \equiv F$ and there exists $u: J \times D_J \to \mathbf{R}$ such that

$$V(H_\alpha) - V(H_0) = \int_J u(\cdot\, ; H_0)\, d(H_\alpha - H_0) + o(\alpha).$$

If D_J is a metric space with a metric d then, as noted by Chew, Epstein, and Zilcha (1988), Frechet differentiability with respect to d amounts to V being smooth with respect to all paths such that $d(H_\alpha, H_0) = O(\alpha)$, where $O(\cdot)$ is zero at zero and is a function of the same order as its argument. Gateaux differentiability, the infinite dimensional analogue of the directional derivative in finite dimensional spaces, requires that V be smooth with respect to all the linear paths, i.e., all the paths such that $H_\alpha = (1 - \alpha)F + \alpha G$, $F, G \in D_J$, $\alpha \in [0, 1]$.

The possibility that even path smoothness may be unnecessarily restrictive in some cases is raised by a recent result due to Chew, Epstein, and Zilcha (1988) concerning the correspondence between certain theorems in expected utility theory and the analogous theorems under nonexpected utility theory.

1.4. The Theory of Risk Aversion

The study of the role of insurance in the allocation of risk bearing requires a formal measure of the intensity of decision makers' aversion to bearing risks. One such measure is based on the intuitive notion that a more risk averse decision maker is always ready to pay more than a less risk averse decision maker to avoid any given risk. Pratt (1964) formalized this notion as follows: Let $\mathscr{X}$ denote the set of random variables in **R**. Given a von Neumann-Morgenstern utility function u, and for every $Z \in \mathscr{X}$ such that the expectation $E\{u(Z)\}$ exists, define the certainty equivalent of Z according to u, $C^u(Z)$, by the equation $E\{u(Z)\} = u(C(Z))$. The existence and uniqueness of $C^u(Z)$ follows from the fact that u is continuous and strictly monotonic increasing. The risk premium, Π^u, corresponding to u is defined for every $Z \in \mathscr{X}$ such that $E\{u(Z)\}$ exists by $\Pi^u(Z) = E\{Z\} - C^u(Z)$. The risk premium is interpreted as the largest sum of money a decision maker with a utility function u is willing to forego for the right to exchange the risk Z for its expectation.

A utility function u is said to display risk aversion (strict risk aversion) if $\Pi^u(Z) \geq (>) 0$ for all $Z \in \mathscr{X}$. An immediate consequence of Jensen's inequality is that a utility function displays risk aversion (strict risk aversion) if and only if it is concave (strictly concave). A utility function u is said to display more risk aversion than another utility function v if $\Pi^u(Z) \geq \Pi^v(Z)$ for all $Z \in \mathscr{X}$.

Pratt (1964) showed that the latter definition is equivalent to the following condition: $u = T \circ v$, where T is monotonic increasing an concave. If u and v are twice differentiable then the definition is equivalent to the condition: $-u''(x)/u'(x) \geq -v''(x)/v'(x)$ for all x. The measure of risk aversion by $-u''(x)/u'(x)$ was discovered independently Arrow (1965) and Pratt (1964) and is known as the Arrow-Pratt measure of absolute risk aversion.

Intuitively speaking, if one decision maker is strictly more risk averse than another, then given any nonrandom initial wealth, every risk that is acceptable to the less risk averse decision maker should be acceptable to the more risk averse one but not vice versa (see Yaari (1969)). One way of formalizing this idea is as follows: Let Z and Y be random variables in $\mathscr{X}$ and denote their cumulative distribution functions by F_Z and F_Y, respectively. Z is said to be a simple mean utility preserving spread of Y from the viewpoint of u if $E\{u(Z)\} = E\{u(Y)\}$ and there exist $x^* \in \mathbf{R}$ such that $F_Z(x) \geq F_Y(x)$ for all $x \leq x^*$ and $F_Z(x) < F_Y(x)$ for all $x > x^*$. Z is said to be a simple mean preserving spread of Y if $E\{u(Z)\} = E\{u(Y)\}$

in the above definition is replaced by $E\{Z\} = E\{Y\}$. (See Rothschild and Stiglitz (1970) for more detailed discussion.) A utility function u is said to display risk aversion if and only if $E\{u(Z)\} \leq E\{u(Y)\}$ whenever Z is a simple mean preserving spead of Y, and to be more risk averse than another utility function v if all simple mean utility preserving spreads from the viewpoint of v are mean utility nonincreasing spreads from the viewpoint of u. Diamond and Stiglitz (1974) showed that this definition is equivalent to the definition of Pratt (1964).

To extend the theory of risk aversion to nonexpected utility functionals we begin by extending the definitions of mean utility preserving spreads and the notion of greater risk aversion. Let F and G be two cumulative distribution functions on a bounded interval J in **R**. Given the preference functional V, F is said to be a simple compensated spread from the viewpoint of V if $V(F) = V(G)$ and there exist x^* such that $F(x) \geq G(x)$ for all $x \leq x^*$ and $F(x) < G(x)$ for all $x > x^*$. A preference functional V is said to display risk aversion if $V(F) \leq V(G)$ whenever F is a simple mean preserving spread of G. A preference functional V displays greater risk aversion than another preference functional V^* if, for every F and G such that F is a simple compensated spread of G from the viewpoint of V^*, $V(F) \leq V(G)$. Note that, unlike in expected utility theory, the fact that the preference functional displays risk aversion in the aforementioned sense is not equivalent to the condition that for every F, $V(F) \leq V(\mu_F)$, where μ_F denotes the mean of F.

Let V and V^* be Frechet differentiable functionals on the set, D_J, of cumulative distribution functions on J with local utility functions $\{U(\cdot; F)|F \in D_J\}$ and $\{U^*(.; F)|F \in D_J\}$, respectively. Machina (1982) showed that V is more risk averse than V^* if and only if each of the following conditions holds: (a) For any $F, G \in D_J$ and $p \in (0, 1)$, define the conditional certainty equivalents c and c^*, by $V((1 - \alpha)F + \alpha G) = V((1 - \alpha)F + \alpha\delta_c)$ and $V^*((1 - \alpha)F + \alpha G) = V((1 - \alpha)F + \alpha\delta_c^*)$, respectively, then $c \leq c^*$. (b) For every $F \in D_J$ there exists a continuous, monotonic increasing, and concave transformation, T_F, such that $U(\cdot; F) = T_F \circ U^* (\cdot; F)$. If the local utility functions are twice differentiable then the above condions are equivalent to $-U_{11}(x; F)/U_1(x; F) \geq -U_{11}^*(x; F)/U_1^*(x; F)$ for all $x \in J$ and $F \in D_J$.[7]

These conditions are analogous to the definitions of the relation "more risk averse" in expected utility theory. The main difference is in condition (a) where the new concept of conditional certainty equivalent is introduced. This reflects the need to compare the certainty equivalents of a distribution function G according to the local utility functions, $U(\cdot; F)$ and $U^*(\cdot; F)$, of another distribution function F. In expected utility theory this problem does not arise as all the local utility functions are identical. The significance of this condition will become clear when we apply the definition to the analysis of insurance contracts in section 2.3.

Finally, Chew, Karni, and Safra (1987) show that if V and V^* are expected utility with rank dependent probabilities functionals with utility and probability transformation functions (v, g) and (v^*, g^*), respectively, then V is more risk averse than V^* if and only if v is a concave transformation of v^* and g is a convex transformation of g^*. Similarly, an expected utility with rank dependent probabilities functional V with a utility function v and a probability transformation function g displays risk aversion if v is concave and g is convex.

2. Optimal Insurance Policies

2.1. A Brief Review

Consider a risk averse decision maker with initial wealth w. Let X be a random variable representing possible losses of wealth in case of an accident, and denote by F its cumulative distribution function. Clearly, the support of F is $[0, w]$. Denote by I: $\mathbf{R} \to \mathbf{R}$ the indemnity function representing the insurance coverage, and by P the insurance premium. Then, the terminal wealth of the decision maker, Y, is the random variable defined by $Y(X) = w - P - X + I(X)$. We shall assume that insurance policies are priced according to the formula,

$$P = \zeta \int I(x) \, dF(x),$$

where $\zeta \geq 1$ is a proportional loading factor, and x denotes the realizations of X. Assume further that decision makers evaluate alternative policies according to the expected utility of the terminal wealth (i.e., a decision maker with von Neumann-Morgenstern utility function u behaves as if he seeks to maximize the following):

$$\int_0^w u(Y(x)) \, dF(x), \tag{1}$$

subject to

$$P = \zeta \int I(x) \, dF(x), \tag{2}$$

and

$$I(x) \geq 0 \quad \text{for all } x \in [0, w]. \tag{3}$$

The constraint (3), which is critical for the following result, requires that indemnity payments be nonnegative. In other words, it rules out insurance contracts that specify a payments from the insuree to the insurer in some states of nature while receiving payments in others.

The optimal insurance policy for the above problem is characterized by the following theorem which is due to Borch (1960) and Arrow (1971).

Theorem 1: If the decision maker is risk averse, then the optimal insurance policy, $I^*(X)$, for the insurance problem (1)–(3) specified above is characterized as follows: For every given P there exists an m such that

$$I^*(x) = \begin{cases} x - m & \text{if } x - m \geq 0, \\ 0 & \text{if } x - m < 0. \end{cases}$$

That is, for every given level of insurance premium, the optimal insurance policy is characterized by a complete coverage over a deductible minimum, m. The deductible minimum itself depends on the insurance premium. Under an optimal insurance policy the residual risk borne by the insured is the risk represented by losses smaller then the deductible minimum. Thus, it is reasonable to expect that, ceteris paribus, a more risk averse decision maker prefers a policy with smaller deductible minimum and a higher premium. This intuition is borne out by the analysis (see Karni (1983)). Formally,

Proposition 1: Let u and v be twice differentiable von Neumann-Morgenstern utility functions. For each $Z \in \mathcal{Z}$ denote by $m^u(Z)$ and $m^v(Z)$ the optimal deductible minimum of u and v, respectively. Then the following two conditions are equivalent:

(i) $m^u(Z) \leq m^v(Z)$ for all $Z \in \mathcal{Z}$

(ii) $-u''(w)/u'(w) \geq -v''(w)/v'(w)$ for all w.

2.2. Optimal insurance without the independence axiom

In expected utility theory strict risk aversion is equivalent to strict quasiconcavity of the expected utility functional over the set $\{I(X)|P = \zeta \int_0^w I(x)\,dF(x)\}$ for each given P. This implies that the demand for insurance is continuous and that the the first-order conditions for optimality of the indemnity function, $I(X)$, are both necessary and sufficient. The crucial property of the expected utility functional that is responsible for this result is betweenness. Hence, the same observations apply to weighted utility theory and, more generally, to all nonexpected utility theories with the betweenness property. Interestingly, the same conclusion holds in expected utility with rank dependent probability theory (see Chew, Karni, and Safra (1987)). The equivalence between risk aversion and quasiconcavity of the preference functional does not extend to general smooth preference relations. In particular, as shown in Dekel (1989), unless the preference functional is quasiconcave on the set, D_J, of probability distributions, risk aversion is not sufficient to guarantee that the preference functional be quasiconcave over the space of random variables.[8] Thus, while the characterization of the optimal indemnity function in Theorem 1 extends to Frechet differentiable preference functionals, it does not constitute sufficient condition for global maximum.

Consider the following restatement of the optimal insurance problem (1)–(3). Let $F_{w-P-X+I}(\cdot)$ denote the cumulative distribution function of the random variable $Y(X) = w - P - X + I(X)$. Then the optimal insurance problem is given by

$$\operatorname*{Max}_{I(\cdot)} \; V(F_{w-P-X+I}(\cdot)) \tag{4}$$

subject to

$$P = \zeta \int_0^w I(x) \, dF(x), \tag{5}$$

and

$$I(\cdot) \geq 0. \tag{6}$$

If V displays risk aversion, then the characterization of the optimal insurance policy is as follows:

Theorem 2: Let V be Frechet differentiable preference functional on D_J and suppose that the local utility functions corresponding to V are twice differentiable. If V displays risk aversion, then the optimal insurance policy, $I^*(X)$, for the insurance problem specified in (4)–(6) is characterized as follows: For every given P there exists a deductible minimum, m, such that

$$I^*(x) = \begin{cases} x - m & \text{if } x - m \geq 0 \\ 0 & \text{if } x - m < 0. \end{cases}$$

Proof: The necessary conditions for optimality of I^* are: For all $x \in [0, w]$

$$\frac{\partial}{\partial I(x)} \left\{ V(F_{w-P-X+I}(\cdot))|_{I=I^*} + \lambda \left[P - \zeta \int_0^w I(x) \, dF(x) \right] + \mu I(x) \right\} = 0, \tag{7}$$

$$P - \zeta \int_0^w I(x) \, dF(x) = 0, \tag{8}$$

$$\mu I(x) = 0, \quad \mu \geq 0. \tag{9}$$

By Frechet differentiability of V equation (7) may be written as follows: For all $x \in [0, w]$,

$$\frac{\partial}{\partial I(x)} \left\{ \int_{I'(w)-P}^{w-P+I'(0)} U(z; F^*) \, dF_{w-P-X+I}(z) \right.$$

$$\left. + \lambda \left[P - \zeta \int_0^w I(x) \, dF(x) \right] + \mu I(x) \right\} = 0, \qquad (7')$$

where $F^*(\cdot) \equiv F_{w-P-X+I}(\cdot)$. But, for all $x \in [0, w]$, $F_{w-P-X+I}(w - P - x + I(x)) = 1 - F(x)$. Hence, (7′) may be written as:

$$\frac{\partial}{\partial I(x)} \left\{ \int_0^w U(w - P - x + I(x); F^*) \, dF(x) \right.$$

$$\left. + \lambda \left[P - \zeta \int_0^w I(x) \, dF(x) \right] + \mu I(x) \right\} = 0. \qquad (7'')$$

However, (7″) in conjunction with (8) and (9) are the necessary conditions of the simple optimal control problem encountered in expected utility analysis, namely,

$$\underset{I}{\text{Max}} \int_0^w U(w - P - x + I(x); F^*) \, dF(x)$$

subject to

$$P - \zeta \int_0^w I(x) \, dF(x) = 0$$

$$I(\cdot) \geq 0.$$

But, by Machina (1982), risk aversion of V is equivalent to concavity of $U(\cdot; F^*)$. Hence, the optimality conditions are necessary and sufficient and the conclusion of the theorem follows from Theorem 1.

Corollary: If V is quasiconcave, then (7)–(9) are necessary and sufficient conditions for I^* to be a global maximum.

The corollary is an immediate consequence of the following lemma.

Lemma: Let V be Frechet differentiable preference functional on D_J. If V is quasiconcave and displays risk aversion then, for any positive P, V is quasiconcave in $I(\cdot)$ on the set

$$S(P) = \left\{ F_{w-P-x+I}(\cdot) \,|\, P = \zeta \int_0^w I(x) \, dF(x) \right\}.$$

Proof: Let $I, I' \in S(P)$ such that $V(F_{w-P-x+I}) = V(F_{w-P-x+I'}) = t$. Denote by I^α the indemnity function defined for all $x \in [0, w]$ by $\alpha I(x) + (1 - \alpha) I'(x)$. By Dekel (1989) $\alpha F_{w-P-x+I} + (1 - \alpha) F_{w-P-x+I'}$, is a mean preserving spread of

$F_{w-P-x+I^a}$. Since V is risk averse this implies $V(F_{w-P-x+I^a}) \geq V(\alpha F_{w-P-x+I} + (1 - \alpha)F_{w-P-x+I'})$. The quasiconcavity of V on D_J implies $V(\alpha F_{w-P-x+I} + (1 - \alpha)F_{w-P-x+I'}) \geq V(F_{w-P-x+I}) = t$. Thus, $V(F_{w-P-x+I^a}) > t$.

Notice that quasiconcavity of V is not a necessary condition for V to be quasiconcave in I on S, (see Dekel (1989)).

Remarks: Theorem 2 and its proof illustrate the methodology of local expected utility analysis. Note, however, the requirement of Frechet differentiability is much too strong for the conclusion. As a matter of fact, theorem 2 is a specific example of the a result due to Zilcha and Chew (1990). Zilcha and Chew studied the relationships between the sets of efficient random variables (i.e., given convex and closed sets of feasible random variables to chose from efficient random variables are optimal for some risk-averse decision maker) under expected and non-expected utility theories. They show that the efficient set under expected utility theory remains invariant when the set of admissible preferences includes all complete preference relations that satisfy first- and second-order stochastic dominance. Interesting analysis of the efficient sets under weaker definitions of risk aversion with application to optimal insurance is provided in Safra and Zilcha (1988).

Since preference functionals satisfying the betweenness property are quasiconcave in the space of distribution functions, it follows that, for such functionals, the corollary is applicable, and I^* is a global maximum.

2.3. Comparative statics: The effect of risk aversion

The qualitative effect of risk aversion on the deductible minimum as characterized in Proposition 1 extends to nonexpected utility analysis with some modifications. Using theorm 2 we measure the level of insurance coverage by the deductible minimum. Then, following Machina (1982) we define the conditional insurance demand as the value of the deductible minimum, m, that induces the most preferred distribution in the set $\{(1 - p)\hat{F} + pF_{Y(m, X)}|m \in [0, w]\}$, where $Y(m, X)$ is the random variable representing the terminal wealth of a decision maker with initial wealth w, facing the risk X who takes out an optimal insurance policy with a minimum deductible m. Thus, the conditional insurance demand may be thought of as the demand for insurance against the risk X when with probability $(1 - p)$ the disribution of wealth is given by $\hat{F}$ regardless of the level of insurance. Unlike in expected utility theory where the conditional insurance demand is independent of p and $\hat{F}$, in nonexpected utility analysis the conditional demand for insurance depends on both p and $\hat{F}$. We shall show that, *ceteris paribus,* higher risk aversion (or, equivalently, smaller conditional certainty equivalent) is equivalent to higher conditional demand for insurance.

Proposition 2: Let V and V^* be Frechet differentiable, risk averse, quasi-concave, preference functionals, and suppose that the respective local utility functions $\{U(\cdot; F)|F \in D_J\}$ and $\{U^*(\cdot; F)|F \in D_J\}$, are twice differentiable with respect to their first argument. For a given w, let $Y(m, X)$ be a random variable defined by $Y(m) = w - P(m) - x$, for $x \in [0, m]$, and $Y(m) = w - P(m) - m$ if $x \in [m, w]$. Then, V displays greater risk aversion than V^* if and only if for every $\hat{F} \in D_J$, and $p \in (0, 1]$, $m' \leqslant m^*$, where m' and m^* represent that most preferred distributions on the set $\{(1 - p)\hat{F} + pF_{Y(m, X)}|m \in [0, w]\}$ for V and V^*, respectively.

Proof: Given w, ζ, and F, the optimal insurance policy specified in theorem 2, implies

$$P(m) = \zeta \int_m^w (x - m)\, dF(x).$$

Differentiating P with respect to m we get,

$$\frac{dP}{dm} = -\zeta \int_m^w dF(x) < 0.$$

Upon taking out an optimal insurance policy, I^*, with a deductible minimum m, the risk facing a decision maker is given by:

$$F_{w-P-X+\Gamma}(w - P - z) = \begin{cases} 0 & m < z \leqslant w \\ 1 - F(m) & m = z \\ 1 - F(z) & m \geqslant z \geqslant 0. \end{cases}$$

The problem facing the decision maker is to maximize $V(F_{w-P-X+\Gamma})$ with respect to m. Denote $F_{w-P(m')-X+\Gamma}$ by F_V. Since V is quasiconcave in I the necessary and sufficient condition for optimality is:

$$0 = \frac{\partial}{\partial m} V(F_{w-P(m)-X+\Gamma})\big|_{m=m'}$$

$$= \frac{\partial}{\partial m} \int_0^w U(w - P(m) - z; F_V)\, dF_{w-P(m)-X+\Gamma}(w - P(m) - z)\big|_{m=m'}$$

$$= \frac{\partial}{\partial m} \left\{ (1 - F(m))\, U(w - P - m; F_V) \right.$$

$$+ \int_m^0 U(w - P - z; F_V)\, d(1 - F(z)) \Big\} \Big|_{m=m'}$$

$$= -F'(m')\, U(w - P(m') - m'; F_V)$$

$$- (1 - F(m'))\, U'(w - P(m') - m'; F_V)\left[1 + \frac{dP}{dm}(m')\right]$$

$$- \frac{dP}{dm}(m') \int_m^0 U'(w - P(m') - z; F_V)\, d(1 - F(z))$$

$$+ U(w - P(m') - m'; F_V)\, F'(m')$$

$$= -(1 - F(m'))\, U'(w - P(m') - m'; F_V)\left[1 + \frac{dP}{dm}(m')\right]$$

$$- \frac{dP}{dm}(m')\left[\int_{m'}^0 U'(w - P(m') - z; F_V)\, d(1 - F(z))\right].$$

Let $\underline{w} = w - P(m') - m'$, and define

$$y(m', V) = \frac{\partial}{\partial m}\, V(F_{w-P(m)-X+I})/U'(\underline{w}; F_V)\big|_{m=m'}$$

and

$$y(m', V^*) = \frac{\partial}{\partial m}\, V^*(F_{w-P(m)-X+I})/U^{*\prime}(\underline{w}; F_V)\big|_{m=m'}.$$

Since V, and V^* are quasiconcave in I, they are quasiconcave in m. Hence, $y(m', V) = 0$ is a necessary and sufficient condition for the optimality of m' for V. Similarly, $y(m^*, V^*) = 0$ is a necessary and sufficient condition for the optimality of m^* for V^*. Since V is more risk averse then V^* we get,

$$y(m', V^*) - y(m', V) = \frac{dP(m')}{dm}\left[\int_{m'}^0 \left\{ -\frac{U^{*\prime}(w - P(m') - z; F_V)}{U^{*\prime}(\underline{w}; F_V)}\right.\right.$$

$$\left.\left. + \frac{T'_{F_V}(U^*(w - P(m') - z; F_V))\, U^{*\prime}(w - P(m') - z; F_V)}{T'_{F_V}(U^*(\underline{w}; F_V))\, U^{*\prime}(\underline{w}; F_V)}\right\}\, d(1 - F(z))\right].$$

Since $U^*(w - P - z; F_V) > U^*(\underline{w}, F_V)$ for $z < m$, $T''_{F_V}(\cdot) \leq 0$ implies

$$\frac{T'_{F_V}(U^*(w - P(m') - z; F_V))}{T'_{F_V}(U^*(\underline{w}; F_V))} \begin{cases} \leq 1 & \text{if } 0 \leq z < m \\ = 1 & \text{otherwise.} \end{cases}$$

This and the fact that $\dfrac{dP}{dm} < 0$ imply that $y(m', V^*) \geq y(m', V) = 0$, where the equality follows from the optimality of m' for V. By quasiconcavity of the objective function in m this implies that $m^* \geq m'$.

To prove the "only if" part suppose that for some $\hat{F} \in D_J$, $T_{\hat{F}}$ is not concave. By continuity this implies that $T_{\hat{F}}$ is convex on some open interval in **R**. Then by Pratt (1964) there exist $x_1 < x_2$ in this interval and $\alpha \in (0, 1)$ such that

$$\frac{U'(x_2; \hat{F})}{U'(x_1; \hat{F})} > \alpha > \frac{U^{*\prime}(x_2; \hat{F})}{U^{*\prime}(x_1; \hat{F})}$$

Thus, there exists small positive ε such that

$$\frac{U(x_2 + \varepsilon; \hat{F}) - U(x_2; \hat{F})}{U(x_1; \hat{F}) - U(x_1 - \alpha\varepsilon; \hat{F})} > 1 > \frac{U^*(x_2; \hat{F}) - U^*(x_2 - \varepsilon; \hat{F})}{U^*(x_1 + \alpha\varepsilon; \hat{F}) - U^*(x_1; \hat{F})}.$$

This implies that for some positive probability p, $V(G) > V(H)$, and $V^*(H) < V^*(F)$, where F, H, and G are defined as follows:[9]

$$F = (1 - p)\hat{F} + p(\tfrac{1}{2}\delta_{x_1+\alpha\varepsilon} + \tfrac{1}{2}\delta_{x_2-\varepsilon}),$$
$$H = (1 - p)\hat{F} + p(\tfrac{1}{2}\delta_{x_1} + \tfrac{1}{2}\delta_{x_2}),$$
$$G = (1 - p)\hat{F} + p(\tfrac{1}{2}\delta_{x_1-\alpha\varepsilon} + \tfrac{1}{2}\delta_{x_2+\varepsilon}).$$

Let

$$m_f \equiv x_2 - x_1 - (1 + \alpha)\varepsilon < m_h \equiv x_2 - x_1 < m_g \equiv x_2 - x_1 + (1 + \alpha)\varepsilon.$$

Suppose that the initial wealth of the two decision makers being compared is $w = x_2$ and that they face the risk of losing $x = x_2 - x_1$ with probability 1/2. Let $\zeta = 2/(1 + \alpha)$ and $P = \varepsilon$. Then $I = (1 + \alpha)\varepsilon$, and the minimum deductible corresponding to this policy is $m = x_2 - x_1 - (1 + \alpha)\varepsilon$. Let $Y(m_f)$ be a random variable that takes the values $\{x_2 - P, x_2 - P + m_f\}$ with equal probabilities. Then, it is easy to verify that F, may be expressed as:

$$F = (1 - p)\hat{F} + pF_{Y(m_f)}$$

Similarly, defining $Y(m_h)$ and $Y(m_g)$ as the random variables that takes the values $\{x_2 - P, x_2 - P + m_h\}$ and $\{x_2 - P, x_2 - P + m_g\}$ with equal probabilities, respectively, we get,

$$H = (1 - p)\hat{F} + pF_{Y(m_h)}$$
$$G = (1 - p)\hat{F} + pF_{Y(m_g)}$$

Since V and V^* are risk averse and quasiconcave, $V(G) > V(H)$ implies that the optimal minimum deductible, m', corresponding to V is larger than m_h, and $V^*(H) < V^*(F)$ implies that the optimal minimum deductible, m^*, corresponding to V^* is smaller than m_h. Thus, $m^* < m'$, a contradiction.

Remarks: (a) The proof of proposition 2 is based on the analysis of the behavior of the preference functional along paths in the set $\{F_{w-P(m)-X-I(m)}(\cdot) | 0 \leq m < w\}$. The essential requirement is that the preference functionals be smooth in the sense of having linear approximation along these paths. Frechet differentiability is a sufficient condition for path smoothness. Whether or not it is also necessary is an open question. (b) The analysis of insurance presented in theorem 2 and proposition 2 may be extended to insurance problems such as personal injury or life insurance, involving state-dependent preferences. For an extension of the theory of risk aversion with state-dependent preferences to Frechet differentiable preference functional see Karni (1987).

3. Concluding Remarks

In this paper we surveyed some recent developments in the theory of decision making under risk, and explored few implications of these developments for the theory of optimal insurance contracts. Our aim was to highlight the similarities and the differences between expected utility and nonexpected utility analysis of optimal insurance contracts. In so doing we also exposed some of the techniques that are used in nonexpected utility analysis.

The comparative statics analysis in section 2.3 involved interpersonal comparison of risk aversion. In expected utility theory the same analysis applies to a given decision maker at different levels of wealth. In nonexpected utility analysis, since a shift in the level of the decision marker's initial wealth involves a change in the distribution, the comparative statics effects of such a change are complicated by the fact that the local utility function itself varies with the exogenous shift. For a detailed discussion of this problem the reader is referred to Machina (1989).

Finally, the present paper is not intended to provide a comprehensive nonexpected utility analysis of optimal insurance. The study of insurance contracts within the framework of nonexpected utility theory has the potential of producing testable implications of these theories.

Notes

1. For excellent surveys of the evidence see MacCrimmon and Larsson (1979), Machina (1982), and Fishburn (1988). For a more comprehensive survey of the theoretical developments see Karni and Schmeidler (1991).

2. Additional restrictions that would permit the extension of the expected utility representation to more general probability measures are given in Fishburn (1970). Note that if L is endowed with the topology of weak convergence, and if $\geq$ is continuous in the sense that for all $f \in L$, the sets $\{g \in L \mid g \geq f\}$ and $\{g \in L \mid f \geq g\}$ are closed in this topology, then V is weakly continuous and there exists a real bounded continuous function u on X such that, for all $f \in L$, $V(f) = \int u\,df$.

3. For a theory that departs from the completeness axiom, see Bewley (1986, 1987). Theories that depart from the transitivity axiom include Fishburn (1982), Loomes and Sagden (1982), Bell (1982).

4. A detailed survey of these models appears in Chew (1989).

5. A real-valued functional T defined on a domain D of a normed space X is Frechet differentiable at $x \in D$ if for each $h \in X$ there exists $\partial T(x, h) \in \mathbf{R}$ that is linear and continuous with respect to h, and $T(x + h) - T(x) = \partial T(x, h) + o(\| h \|)$, where $o(\cdot)$ denotes a function that is zero at zero and of a higher order than its argument. If T is Frechet differentiable at x for all x in D, then T is Frechet differentiable.

6. For further details see Machina (1988).

7. This result extends to Gateaux differentiable preference functionals provided that the local utility function approximate the preference functional. Karni and Safra (1988) give an example in which a preference functional that is not Frechet differentiable displays strong risk aversion (i.e., aversion to mean preserving spreads) and yet some local utility functions are convex.

8. In the terminology of Tobin (1957) a risk averse expected utility maximizer is necessarily a diversifier. This implication does not carry over to smooth preference functionals.

9. To see this note that for $p = 0$. $F = H = G = \hat{F}$. Differentiating with respect to p we get, $\dfrac{\partial V}{\partial p}(G)\Big|_{p=0} - \dfrac{\partial V}{\partial p}(H)\Big|_{p=0} = \frac{1}{2}\{U(x_1 - \alpha\varepsilon; \hat{F}) + U(x_2 + \varepsilon; \hat{F}) - U(x_1; \hat{F}) - U(x_2; \hat{F})\} > 0$. Thus, for some positive p, we have $V(G) > V(H)$. A similar argument establishes the inequality $V^*(F) > V^*(H)$.

References

Allais, M. (1953). "Le Comportement de L'Homme Rationnel Devant le Risque: Critique des Postulats et Axiomes de L'Ecole Americaine," *Econometrica* 21, 503–46.

Arrow, K. J. (1965). *Aspects of the Theory of Risk Bearing*. Helsinki: Yrjo Jahnsson Saatio.

Arrow, K. J. (1971). *Essays in the Theory of Risk Bearing*. Chicago: Markham.

Bell, D. (1982). "Regret in Decision Making Under Uncertainty," *Operations Research* 30, 961–981.

Bernoulli, D. (1738). "Specimen Theoriae Novae de Mensura Sortis," Commentarii Academiae Scientiarum Imperialis Petropolitanae V, 175–192. English translation: "Exposition of a New Theory on the Measurement of Risk," *Econometrica* 22(1954), 23–36.

Bewley, T. F. (1986). "Knightian Decision Theory: Part I," Cowles Foundation Discussion Paper No. 807.

Bewley, T. F. (1987). "Knightian Decision Theory: Part II," Cowles Foundation Discussion Paper No. 835.

Borch, K. (1960). "The Safety Loading of Reinsurance Premiums," *Skand. Aktuarietidskrift* 162–184.

Chew, S. H. (1983). "A Generalization of the Quasilinear Mean With Applications to the Measurement of Income Inequality and Decision Theory Resolving the Allais Paradox," *Econometrica* 51, 1065–1092.

Chew, S. H. (1985). "An Axiomatization of Rank Dependent Quasilinear Mean Generalizing the Gini Mean and the Quasilinear Mean," Johns Hopkins University Working Paper No. 156.

Chew, S. H. (1989). "Axiomatic Utility Theories with Betweenness Property," *Annals of Operations Research* 19, 273–298.

Chew, S. H., and K. R. MacCrimmon. (1979). "Alpha-Nu Choice Theory: A Generalization of Expected Utility Theory," University of British Columbia Faculty of Commerce and Business Administration Working Paper No. 686.

Chew, S. H., Karni, E., and Z. Safra. (1987). "Risk Aversion in the Theory of Expected Utility with Rank Dependent Probabilities," *Journal of Economic Theory* 42, 370–381.

Chew, S. H., L. G. Epstein, and I. Zilcha. (1988). "A Correspondence Theorem Between Expected Utility and Smooth Utility," *Journal of Economic Theory* 46, 186–193.

Dekel, E. (1986). "An Axiomatic Characterization of Preferences Under Uncertainty: Weakening the Independence Axiom," *Journal of Economic Theory* 40, 304–318.

Dekel, E. (1989). "Asset Demands without the Independence Axiom," *Econometrica* 57, 163–169.

Diamond, P. A., and J. E. Stiglitz. (1974). "Increases in Risk and in Risk Aversion," *Journal of Economic Theory* 8, 337–360.

Fishburn, P. C. (1970). *Utility Theory for Decision Making.* New York: John Wiley & Sons.

Fishburn, P. C. (1982). "Nontransitive Measurable Utility," *Journal of Mathematical Psychology* 26, 31–67.

Fishburn, P. C. (1983). "Transitive Measurable Utility," *Journal of Economic Theory* 31, 293–317.

Fishburn, P. C. (1988). *Nonlinear Preference and Utility Theory.* Baltimore: The Johns Hopkins University Press.

Herstein, I. N., and Milnor, J. (1953). "An Axiomatic Approach to Measurable Utility," *Econometrica* 21, 291–297.

Karni, E. (1983). "Risk Aversion in the Theory of Health Insurance." *In Social Policy Evaluation*, Helpman, Razin, and Sadka, eds. New York: Academic Press.

Karni, E. (1987). "Generalized Expected Utility Analysis of Risk Aversion with State-Dependent Preferences," *International Economic Review* 28, 229–241.

Karni, E., and Z. Safra. (1987). "'Preference Reversal' and the Observability of Preferences by Experimental Methods," *Econometrica* 55, 675–685.

Karni, E., and Z. Safra. (1988). "Some Observations On The Nature Of Risk Aversion," unpublished manuscript.

Karni, E., and Z. Safra. (1990). "Rank-Dependent Probabilities," *Economic Journal* Vol 100 487–495.

Karni, E., and D. Schmeidler. (1991). "Utility Theory with Uncertainty," Handbook of Mathematical Economics, Vol. 4, W. Hildenbrand and H. Sonnenschein, eds. Amsterdam: North-Holland.

Loomes, G., and R. Sugden. (1982). "Regret Theory: An Alternative Theory of

Rational Choice Under Uncertainty," *Economic Journal* 92, 805–824.

Machina, M. J. (1982). "'Expected Utility' Analysis without the Independence Axiom," *Econometrica* 50, 277–323.

Machina, M. J. (1988). "Cardinal Properties of 'Local Utility Functions'." In B. R. Munier (ed.) *Risk, Decision and Rationality*. Dordrecht, Holland: D. Reidel Publishing Co., 339–344.

Machina, M. J. (1989). "Comparative Statics and Non-expected Utility Preferences," *Journal of Ecomonic Theory* 47, 393–405.

MacCrimmon, K. R., and S. Larsson. (1979). "Utility Theory: Axioms versus 'Paradoxes'." In *Expected Utility Hypotheses and the Allais Paradox*, M. Allais and O. Hagen (eds.). Dordrechet, Holland: D. Reidel Publishing Co.

Malinvaud, E. (1952). "Note on von Neumann-Morgenstern's Strong Independence Axiom," *Econometrica* 20, 679.

Marschak, J. (1950). "Rational Behavior, Uncertain Prospects, and measurable Utility," *Econometrica* 18, 111–141. ("Errata," *Econometrica* 18, 312.)

Nakamura, Y. (1984). "Nonlinear Utility Analysis." Ph.D. dissertation, University of California, Davis.

Pratt, J. W. (1964). "Risk Aversion in the Small and in the Large," *Econometrica* 32, 122–136.

Quiggin, J. (1982). "A Theory of Anticipated Utility," *Journal of Economic Behavior and Organization* 3, 323–43.

Rothschild, M., and J. Stiglitz. (1970). "Increasing Risk I: A Definition," *Journal of Economic Theory* 2, 225–243.

Safra, Z., and I. Zilcha. (1988). "Efficient Sets with and without the Expected Utility Hypothesis," *Journal of Mathematical Economics* 17, 369–384.

Samuelson, P. A. (1952). "Probability, Utility, and the Independence Axiom," *Econometrica* 20, 670–687.

Segal, U. (1987). "The Ellsber Paradox and Risk Aversion: An Anticipated Utility Approach," *International Economic Review* 28, 175–202.

Segal, U. (1989). "Anticipated Utility: A Measure Representation Approach," *Annals of Operations Research*.

Tobin, J. (1957). "Liquidity Preference as Behavior Toward Risk," *Review of Economic Studies* 25, 65–86.

von Neumann, J., and O. Morgenstern. (1944). *Theory of Games and Economic Behavior*. Princeton: Princton University Press.

Wakker, P. (1989). "Transforming Probabilities without Violating Stochastic Dominance." In *Mathematical Psychology in Progress*, Roskam, E. E. (ed.). Berlin: Springer.

Yaari, M. E. (1969). "Some Remarks on the Measures of Risk Aversion and on Their Uses," *Journal of Economic Theory* 1, 315–329.

Yaari, M. E. (1987a). "The Dual Theory of Choice Under Risk," *Econometrica* 55, 95–116.

Zilcha, I. and S. H. Chew (1990). "Insurance of the Efficient Sets When the Expected Utility Hypothesis is Relaxed" *Journal of Economics Behavior and Organization* 13, 125–131.

BACKGROUND RISK, PRUDENCE, AND THE DEMAND FOR INSURANCE

Louis Eeckhoudt

Facultés Universitaires Catholiques de Mons (Belgium)
et de Lille (France)

Miles Kimball

University of Michigan

Abstract

This paper addresses the question of whether uninsurable background risk will lead people to buy more insurance against other risks that are insurable. The conditions of decreasing absolute risk aversion and decreasing absolute prudence on the utility function and either statistical independence or a general condition indicating a positive relationship between the background risk and the other risk are shown to be enough to guarantee that background risk will increase the optimal amount of insurance against the other risk. In particular, background risk raises the optimal coinsurance rate and reduces the optimal level of the deductible (for any given coinsurance rate).

Key words: absolute risk aversion, absolute prudence, background risk

With few exceptions [D. Mayers and C. Smith (1983), N. Doherty and H. Schlesinger (1983a,b), Turnbull (1983) and E. Briys, Y. Kahane, and Y. Kroll (1988)], papers on insurance demand consider that the

The authors sincerely thank E. Briys, C. Gollier, H. Loubergé, and H. Schlesinger for stimulating comments and suggestions on previous versions of the paper. M. Kimball gratefully acknowledges financial support from the National Science Foundation, grant #SES-8912252. L. Eeckhoudt has benefited from the support of EDHEC (Lille–France).

239

decision maker's opportunity set contains only *one* source of uncertainty against which coverage is sought. Although this literature has produced many insightful results, the single-risk assumption imposes severe limitations upon the relevance of the models. Hence, the introduction of multiple sources of uncertainty in the analysis of the demand for insurance beginning in 1983 has represented significant progress.

This paper extends some of the results obtained by the authors mentioned above. These extensions are made possible by using the notion of prudence recently proposed by M. Kimball (1990a,b,c) and the assumption that prudence decreases as wealth increases. Since the notion of prudence is still unfamiliar to many readers, section 1 surveys some basic results about prudence. We then show in section 2 the relevance of prudence for analyzing the optimal level of insurance coverage (as reflected in the co-insurance rate and the deductible) when the decision maker faces two independent sources of uncertainty. Sections 3 and 4 analyze the case of a positive dependence between the background risk and the insurable risk.

1. The Concept of Prudence and its Relationship with Risk-Aversion[1]

Consider an agent who owns safe assets of value x and a lottery $\tilde{y}$; then the risk premium, π, is given by:[2]

$$U(x - \pi(\tilde{y}, x)) = E[U(x + \tilde{y})]. \qquad (1)$$

Assuming that U is twice differentiable, one can use a second-order Taylor approximation as in Pratt (1964) to show that π is approximately equal to $(-U''/U') \cdot \sigma^2/2$ where $-(U''/U') = A$ is the degree of absolute risk aversion. Absolute risk aversion A indicates how much a decision maker dislikes the uncertainty and how much he or she is willing to pay to get rid of it.

Although the notion of absolute risk aversion is very rich, it is not suitable for answering questions that depend on the effect of risk on marginal utility rather than total utility. Kimball (1990a) defines the precautionary premium, ψ, as the quantity satisfying

$$U'(x - \psi(\tilde{y}, x)) = E[U'(x + \tilde{y})] \qquad (2)$$

where U' is marginal utility.

It is easy to show that ψ is approximately equal to $(-U'''/U'') \cdot \sigma^2/2$ where $(-U'''/U'') = \eta$ is the degree of absolute prudence as defined by Kimball (1990a).

Kimball (1990a,b,c and 1987) offers an economic interpretation of absolute prudence, η. He writes that "the term 'prudence' is meant to suggest the propensity to prepare and forearm oneself in the face of uncertainty, in contrast to 'risk aversion' which is how much one dislikes uncertainty and would turn away from uncertainty if one could."

For instance, in a model of saving under uncertainty, prudence represents the intensity of the precautionary saving motive. The concept of prudence is also useful for analyzing the demand for insurance in the presence of background risk, since insurance, like precautionary saving, is a way of increasing the resources one will have in the event of bad outcomes. However precautionary saving adds to the resources available in all future states, while insurance increases the resources one will have after bad events and reduces the available resources under good circumstances. This difference between precautionary saving and insurance explains one difference between the conditions needed to guarantee that uncertainty will lead to precautionary saving and the conditions needed to guarantee that background risk will increase the demand for insurance on other risks.

To wit, absolute prudence need only be positive to guarantee that uncertainty will lead to increased saving, but absolute prudence needs to be both positive and declining in wealth in order to guarantee that background risk will increase the demand for insurance on other risks.

We consider the conditions of positive and decreasing absolute prudence quite reasonable. Just as absolute risk aversion A is usually taken to be both positive and declining in wealth, it is attractive to assume that absolute prudence η (or equivalently the precautionary premium ψ) is positive and declining in wealth. Assuming that η and ψ are positive amounts to assuming that U''' is positive, which is actually one of the implications of decreasing absolute risk aversion. In fact, as will be shown, decreasing absolute risk aversion implies that absolute prudence η is greater than absolute risk aversion A and that the precautionary premium ψ is greater than the risk premium π.

The assumption that η (or ψ) is decreasing in wealth is more daring. There are a number of arguments in favor of such an assumption developed in Kimball (1990b). For example, he argues that given decreasing absolute risk aversion, decreasing absolute prudence can be guaranteed by a mild restriction on the rate of increase of the wealth elasticity of risk tolerance.[3] The idea that the strength of the precautionary saving motive measured by absolute prudence should be decreasing in wealth also seems quite plausible in and of itself. Kimball (1990b) offers the following thought experiment to bring out the intuition for decreasing absolute prudence: "Consider a college professor who has $10,000 in the bank and a Rockfeller who has a net worth of $10,000,000, who have the same preferences except for their differences in initial wealth. If each is forced to face a coin toss at the beginning of the next year, with $5,000 to be gained or lost depending on the outcome, which one will do more extra saving to be ready for the possibility of losing? If one's answer is that the college professor will do more extra saving, it argues for decreasing absolute prudence."

Furthermore, Kimball (1990c) shows that, given monotonicity and concavity of the utility function, decreasing absolute risk aversion and decreasing absolute prudence are jointly necessary and sufficient for the attractive property of *standard risk aversion*. A utility function is said to have standard risk aversion if any risk that makes a small reduction in wealth more painful also makes any statistically independent undesirable risk more painful.[4] One would expect the notion of standard risk aversion, which deals with the effect of one risk on the desirability of another to be relevant to the analysis of the decision of how much insurance to buy against one risk while facing other uninsurable risks. We show that this is indeed the case.

Before proceeding, we must redeem our promise to show that absolute prudence η is greater than absolute risk aversion A and that the precautionary premium ψ is greater than the risk premium π.

To show that $\psi > \pi$, differentiate (1) with respect to x, to obtain

$$\left(1 - \frac{\partial \pi}{\partial x}\right) \cdot U'(x - \pi(\tilde{y}, x)) = E[U'(x + \tilde{y})]$$
$$= U'(x - \psi(\tilde{y}, x)). \qquad (3)$$

If π is declining in x $(\partial \pi / \partial x < 0)$ it follows that

$$U'(x - \pi(\tilde{y}, x)) < U'(x - \psi(\tilde{y}, x)).$$

Given risk aversion and therefore $U'' < 0$, it is clear that ψ must be greater than π.

In fact, it is easy to show by such arguments that

$$\pi \gtreqless \psi \quad \text{as} \quad \frac{\partial \pi}{\partial x} \lesseqgtr 0.$$

Since A and η are closely related to η and ψ, it is not surprising that

$$A \gtreqless \eta \quad \text{as} \quad \frac{\partial A}{\partial x} \lesseqgtr 0.$$

This can be shown formally by differentiation of the logarithm of absolute risk aversion with respect to x:

$$\frac{1}{A}\frac{dA}{dx} = \frac{d}{dx}\ln\left(\frac{-U''(x)}{U'(x)}\right) = \frac{U'''(x)}{U''(x)} - \frac{U''(x)}{U'(x)} = A - \eta$$

2. Prudence and the Optimal Insurance Coverage in the Presence of Independent Background Risks

We are now ready to examine the impact of background risk on the optimal coverage of insurable risks.

As indicated in the introduction, this type of question has already been addressed to some extent in the literature. For instance, in their 1983 paper, D. Mayers and C. Smith consider many sources of (possibly correlated) uncertainties and analyze the optimal risk position in each type of uncertainty. However to arrive at explicit solutions, they need to restrict themselves to a mean-variance model.[5] In two almost simultaneous papers, N. Doherty and H. Schlesinger (1983a,b) discuss the effect of background risk on insurance decisions for an arbitrary risk averse utility function. However, they only address the question of whether full insurance is optimal in the presence of background risk and not the general question of the effect of background risk on the optimal (possibly incomplete) level of coverage.

In this paper, we use the notion of prudence, in addition to that of risk aversion, to examine the effect of background risk on the optimal level of insurance for a more general class of joint distributions of the two sources of uncertainty. We begin in this section with the case of independent risks using the following notation:

w = the level of safe initial wealth.
$\tilde{z}$ = the insurable risk
μ = the expected value of $\tilde{z}$
$F(z)$ = the distribution function for the random variable $\tilde{z}$
a = the coinsurance rate
λ = the (proportional) loading factor

Given these definitions, the insurance premium is $(1 + \lambda)\mu a$, and the optimization problem in the absence of background risk is

$$\underset{\alpha}{\text{Max }} E[U(w - (1 - \alpha)\tilde{z} - \alpha(1 + \lambda)\mu)] \qquad (4)$$

The optimal coinsurance rate α^* is 1 if $\lambda = 0$ but strictly less than 1 if $\lambda > 0$.

We want to analyze what happens to the optimal insurance rate α^* if the initial wealth w is replaced by $w + \tilde{y}$ where $\tilde{y}$ is statistically independent background risk with zero mean and cumulative distribution $G(y)$. The optimization problem in the presence of the background risk $\tilde{y}$ is

$$\underset{\alpha}{\text{Max}} \, E[U(w + \tilde{y} - (1 - \alpha)\tilde{z} - \alpha(1 + \lambda)\mu)]$$

or

$$\underset{\alpha}{\text{Max}} \int \left[\int U(w + y - (1 - \alpha)z - \alpha(1 + \lambda)\mu) \, dG(y) \right] dF(z) \qquad (5)$$

Its solution will be denoted α^{**}.

Following Kihlstrom, Romer, and Williams (1981), let us define a utility function $\hat{U}(w)$ obtained by integrating out the background risk $\tilde{y}$:

$$\hat{U}(w) = \int U(w + y) \, dG(y),$$

Then, (5) can be rewritten

$$\underset{\alpha}{\text{Max}} \, E[\hat{U}(w - (1 - \alpha)\tilde{z} - \alpha(1 + \lambda)\mu)], \qquad (6)$$

yielding of course the same α^{**} as in (5).

$\hat{U}$ inherits many of the properties of U. For instance it will be monotonically increasing and risk averse as U is. In addition, Kimball (1987) establishes another important fact about $\hat{U}$: it is more concave and therefore more risk averse than U.

We give here a different proof of this fact.

First observe that
$$\hat{U}(w) = E[U(w + \tilde{y})]$$
$$= U(w - \pi(\tilde{y}, w)).$$

Since $E(\tilde{y}) = 0$, $\pi(\tilde{y}, w) > 0$.

Differentiating with respect to w yields:

$$\hat{U}'(w) = \left(1 - \frac{\partial \pi}{\partial w}\right) \cdot U'(w - \pi(\tilde{y}, w))$$
$$= U'(w - \psi(\tilde{y}, w)) \qquad \text{from (3)}$$

so that

$$\hat{U}''(w) = \left(1 - \frac{\partial \psi}{\partial w}\right) \cdot U''(w - \psi(\tilde{y}, w))$$

Collecting the results, one obtains:

$$-\frac{\hat{U}''(w)}{\hat{U}'(w)} = \left(1 - \frac{\partial\psi}{\partial w}\right) \cdot \left[-\frac{U''(w - \psi(\tilde{y}, w))}{U'(w - \psi(\tilde{y}, w))}\right]$$

$$\geq -\frac{U''(w - \psi(\tilde{y}, w))}{U'(w - \psi(\tilde{y}, w))}$$

$$\geq -\frac{U''(w)}{U'(w)} \tag{7}$$

The first inequality follows from $\partial\psi/\partial w \leqq 0$. The second inequality follows from $\psi > 0$ and decreasing absolute risk aversion.[6]

Equation (7) proves our assertion that $\hat{U}$ is more risk averse than U. This fact can now be coupled with well-known results in the insurance economics literature to establish the following propositions.

Proposition 1: if $\lambda = 0$, $\alpha^* = \alpha^{**} = 1$.

Proof: Apply to the increasing and concave utility $\hat{U}$ the kind of reasoning that is used to prove that $\alpha^* = 1$ under U when $\lambda = 0$ (see Mossin (1968)).

Proposition 2: if $\lambda > 0$, the presence of independent background risk implies that $\alpha^* < \alpha^{**} < 1$.

Proof: $\alpha^{**} < 1$ follows by applying to $\hat{U}$ the standard result that the optimal coverage is incomplete when the loading factor is positive. Similarly, $\alpha^* < \alpha^{**}$ follows directly from the fact that $\hat{U}$ is more risk averse than U and from the standard result that increased risk aversion leads to an increase in the optimal coinsurance rate (Dionne-Eeckhoudt, 1985).

Finally, the results obtained for α carry over to the optimal level of a deductible. If D^* is the optimal level of the deductible in the absence of background risk, and D^{**} stands for the optimal level of D when the decision maker also faces independent background risk, then

Proposition 3: for $\lambda = 0$, $D^* = D^{**} = 0$ while for $\lambda > 0$, $0 < D^{**} < D^*$.

Again the result is the consequence of two facts:
(1) $\hat{U}$ is more concave than U.
(2) *Ceteris paribus*, a more risk averse individual always selects a lower deductible (see Schlesinger (1981)).

For the case of independent risks, these propositions confirm those of Doherty and Schlesinger (1983a,b) and extend them, both by allowing comparisons between α^* and α^{**} and by establishing results for any pair of statistically independent risks.

3. Positive Dependence Between Risks and the Optimal Coinsurance Rate

So far we have assumed that the background risk is independent of the risk to be insured. This may not always be the case. For example, in case of fire, a more severe damage to the building and machinery usually induces a longer interruption of business that would adversely affect many activities in the firm and hence worsen the distribution of $\tilde{y}$.

Under independence, background risk tends to increase the demand for insurance. Intuition suggests that a positive relationship between the background risk and the insurable one should reinforce this tendency. To verify this intuition formally, we must take care in the way we define a positive relationship. It is clear that more than just a positive correlation is needed since higher moments of the joint distribution are likely to matter. Therefore we make the stronger assumption that the distribution of background risk conditional upon a given level of insurable loss deteriorates in the sense of third-order stochastic dominance as the amount of insurable loss increases. More formally, if $\tilde{y}(z)$ represents the distribution of background risk conditional upon the level of loss z, we assume that if $z_2 > z_1$ then $\tilde{y}(z_1)$ weakly dominates $\tilde{y}(z_2)$ according to third-order stochastic dominance.

The aspect of third-order stochastic dominance that is important here is that if $\tilde{y}(z_1)$ weakly dominates $\tilde{y}(z_2)$, then

$$\pi(\tilde{y}(z_2), x) \geq \pi(\tilde{y}(z_1), x)$$

for any final wealth x and any monotonically increasing utility function with positive and decreasing absolute risk aversion.[7] By the same mathematical principle,

$$\psi(\tilde{y}(z_2), x) \geq \psi(\tilde{y}(z_1), x)$$

for any x and any risk-averse utility function with positive and decreasing absolute prudence.[8]

To allow for full use of the fact that third-order stochastic dominance includes first-order stochastic dominance as a special case, we weaken the previous assumption that $E(\tilde{y}) = 0$. In its place we assume only that the background risk is undesirable when $\tilde{z}$ is equal to the value which makes one indifferent *ex post* to the coinsurance rate chosen, or more formally, when $\tilde{z}$ is equal to the expected value of the insurable loss increased by the loading factor:

$$\pi(\tilde{y}([1 + \lambda]\mu), w - (1 + \lambda)\mu) \geq 0.$$

When we allow for the possibility that the background risk $\tilde{y}$ is not independent of the insurable risk $\tilde{z}$, the problem of choosing the optimal coinsurance rate can be written:

$$\text{Max}_{\alpha} \int \left\{ \int U(w + y - (1 - \alpha)z - \alpha(1 + \lambda)\mu)\, dF(y|z) \right\} dG(z),$$

where $G(z)$ represents the distribution of $\tilde{z}$ while $F(y|z)$ stands for the conditional distribution of $\tilde{y}$ given z (or, in our notation, the distribution of the variable $\tilde{y}(z)$).

The first-order condition is

$$\int (z - (1 + \lambda)\mu) \cdot \left\{ \int U'[w + y - (1 - \alpha^{**})z \right.$$

$$\left. - \alpha^{**}(1 + \lambda)\mu]\, dF(y|z) \right\} dG(z) = 0. \tag{8}$$

Using the definition of the precautionary premium, (8) becomes

$$\int (z - (1 + \lambda)\mu) \cdot U'(w - (1 - \alpha^{**})z - \alpha^{**}(1 + \lambda)\mu$$

$$- \psi(\tilde{y}(z), w - (1 - \alpha^{**})z - \alpha^{**}(1 + \lambda)\mu))\, dG(z) = 0$$

In the absence of the background risk $\tilde{y}$, the first-order condition is

$$\int (z - (1 + \lambda)\mu) \cdot U'(w - (1 - \alpha^{*})z - \alpha^{*}(1 + \lambda)\mu)\, dG(z) = 0. \tag{9}$$

To demonstrate that α^{**} is greater than α^{*} we need only to show that

$$\int (z - (1 + \lambda)\mu) \cdot U'(w - (1 - \alpha^{*})z - \alpha^{*}(1 + \lambda)\mu$$

$$- \psi(\tilde{y}(z), w - (1 - \alpha^{*})z - \alpha^{*}(1 + \lambda)\mu))\, dG(z) > 0, \tag{10}$$

or equivalently, that

$$\int (z - (1 + \lambda)\mu) \cdot U'(w - (1 - \alpha^{*})z - \alpha^{*}(1 + \lambda)\mu \tag{11}$$

$$\frac{- \psi(\tilde{y}(z), w - (1 - \alpha^{*})z - \alpha^{*}(1 + \lambda)\mu))}{U'(w - (1 + \lambda)\mu - \psi(\tilde{y}((1 + \lambda)\mu), w - (1 + \lambda)\mu))}\, dG(z)$$

$$> \frac{\int (z - (1 + \lambda)\mu) \cdot U'(w - (1 - \alpha^{*})z - \alpha^{*}(1 + \lambda)\mu)\, dG(z)}{U'[w - (1 + \lambda)\mu]} = 0.$$

The following Lemma is helpful in proving (11):

Lemma: If $U(x)$ is a monotonically increasing utility function with positive and decreasing absolute risk aversion and $h(x)$ is a function for which $h'(x) \lesseqgtr 0$ and $h(x_0) > 0$,

then
$$\frac{U'(x - h(x))}{U'(x_0 - h(x_0))} < \frac{U'(x)}{U'(x_0)} \quad \text{when } x > x_0 \tag{12}$$

and

$$\frac{U'(x - h(x))}{U'(x_0 - h(x_0))} > \frac{U'(x)}{U'(x_0)} \quad \text{for } x < x_0 \tag{13}$$

Proof of (12) and (13):
Since $h'(x) \leq 0$, when $x > x_0$, $h(x) \leq h(x_0)$, and $x - h(x) \geq x - h(x_0)$. Therefore,

$$\frac{U'(x - h(x))}{U'(x_0 - h(x_0))} \lesssim \frac{U'(x - h(x_0))}{U'(x_0 - h(x_0))} < \frac{U'(x)}{U'(x_0)}. \tag{14}$$

The first inequality follows from the decreasing marginal utility implied by risk aversion. The second inequality is a consequence of decreasing absolute risk aversion and the assumption that $h(x_0) > 0$; Pratt (1964) shows that the proportional decline in marginal utility between one point (x_0) and a higher one (x) increases with the level of risk aversion (Theorem 1, p. 128).[9]

Similarly, when $x < x_0$, $x - h(x) \leq x - h(x_0)$ and

$$\frac{U'(x - h(x))}{U'(x_0 - h(x_0))} \geq \frac{U'(x - h(x_0))}{U'(x_0 - h(x_0))} > \frac{U'(x)}{U'(x_0)} \tag{15}$$

(The proportional increase in marginal utility between one point (x_0) and a lower one (x) increases with risk aversion.)

To prove (11) with this lemma, let

$$x = w - (1 - \alpha^*)z - \alpha^*(1 + \lambda)\mu,$$

$$h(x) = \psi(\tilde{y}(z), x) = \psi\left(\tilde{y}\left(\frac{w - \alpha^*(1 + \lambda)\mu - x}{1 - \alpha^*}\right), x\right) \tag{16}$$

$$x_0 = w - (1 + \lambda)\mu,$$

and

$$h(x_0) = \psi(\tilde{y}((1 + \lambda)\mu), (1 + \lambda)\mu) > \pi(\tilde{y}((1 + \lambda)\mu), (1 + \lambda)\mu) \geq 0.$$

Clearly $h(x)$ as defined by (16) is decreasing in x through both the first and second arguments of ψ — through the first argument because the distribution of $\tilde{y}$ improves as x increases with the decrease in the loss z

and through the second argument because of decreasing absolute prudence. Thus the conditions of the lemma are satisfied.

The conclusions of Lemmas 12 and 13, together with the fact that $x \geq(\leq) x_0$ as $z - (1 + \lambda)\mu \leq(\geq) 0$ establish the desired result (11). The proof follows from the fact that the background risk increases conditional expected marginal utility more the greater is the insurable loss, both because of decreasing absolute prudence and because of the positive dependence between the insurable risk and the background risk.

4. Positively Dependent Risks and the Optimal Level of the Deductible

We can show that the negative effect of independent background risk on the optimal deductible (holding the coinsurance rate fixed) also extends to the case of a positive relationship between the insurable risk and the background risk.

The one new piece of notation needed is

$$\varphi(D) = \int_D^{z_{max}} (z - D)\, dG(z).$$

We will assume that the indemnification I is

$$I = 0 \quad \text{for} \quad z \leq D$$

$$I = \alpha(z - D) \quad \text{for} \quad z > D.$$

If $\alpha = 1$, this is an insurance policy with only a deductible and no co-insurance. In any case α is not a choice variable in the problem we are currently considering.

We assume again that the conditional distribution of the background risk is increasing in the outcome of the insurable risk in the sense of third-order stochastic dominance — or formally, that $\tilde{y}(z_1)$ dominates $\tilde{y}(z_2)$ if $z_1 < z_2$.

The last assumption we need is that if D^* is the optimal deductible in the absence of background risk and $\alpha(1 + \lambda)\varphi(D^*)$ is the price of insurance with that deductible, then

$$\pi(\tilde{y}(D^*), w - D^* - \alpha(1 + \lambda)\varphi(D^*)) \geq 0, \tag{17}$$

or in words, that the background risk is undesirable when the outcome of the insurable risk is exactly equal to the deductible chosen in the absence of the background risk. These assumptions, together with the standard assumptions we have made about the form of the utility function imply that $D^{**} \leqq D^*$ where D^{**} is the optimal deductible in the presence of background risk.[10]

D^{**}, the optimal deductible in the presence of background risk, is the solution to

$$\underset{D}{\text{Max }} v(D)$$

where

$$v(D) = \int_0^D \left\{ \int_{-\infty}^{+\infty} U(w + y - \alpha(1 + \lambda)\varphi(D) - z)\, dF(y|z) \right\} dG(z)$$

$$+ \int_D^{z\max} \left\{ \int_{-\infty}^{+\infty} U(w + y - \alpha(1 + \lambda)\varphi(D) \right.$$

$$\left. - D - (1 - \alpha)(z - D))\, dF(y|z) \right\} dG(z). \tag{18}$$

Using Leibniz's rule and the fact that $\varphi'(D) = G(D) - 1$ (also due to Leibniz's rule) we can calculate:

$$v'(D) = \alpha(1 + \lambda)(1 - G(D)) \cdot$$

$$\int_0^D \left\{ \int_{-\infty}^{\infty} U'(w + y - \alpha(1 + \lambda)\varphi(D) - z)\, dF(y|z) \right\} dG(z)$$

$$+ \alpha[(1 + \lambda)(1 - G(D)) - 1] \cdot$$

$$\int_D^{z\max} \left\{ \int_{-\infty}^{\infty} U'(w + y - \alpha(1 + \lambda)\varphi(D) \right.$$

$$\left. - \alpha D - (1 - \alpha)z)\, dF(y|z) \right\} dG(z) \tag{19}$$

We can eliminate the inner integrals in (4.3) by using precautionary premia:

$$v'(D) = \alpha(1 + \lambda)(1 - G(D)) \cdot$$

$$\int_0^D U'(w - \alpha(1 + \lambda)\varphi(D) - z - \psi(\tilde{y}(z), \cdot))\, dG(z)$$

$$+ \alpha[(1 + \lambda)(1 - G(D)) - 1] \cdot$$

$$\int_D^{z\max} U'(w - \alpha(1 + \lambda)\varphi(D) - \alpha D$$

$$- (1 - \alpha)z - \psi(\tilde{y}(z), \cdot\cdot))\, dG(z) \tag{20}$$

where $\cdot$ stands here for $w - a(1 + \lambda)\varphi(D) - z$
and $\cdot\cdot$ stands for $w - a(1 + \lambda)\varphi(D) - aD - (1 - a)z$.

The first-order condition for the optimal deductible in the presence of background risk is $v'(D^{**}) = 0$. We can show by contrast that $v'(D^*) < 0$, as long as there is an interior solution for D^*.

Assuming that $v''(D)$ is negative at least where $v'(D) = 0$,[11] $v'(D)$ can only cross zero going downward, as in figure 1. As a result D^* must be to the right of D^{**}, if we can show that $v'(D^*)$ is negative.

To show that $v'(D^*) < 0$ when $0 < D^* < z_{\max}$, consider the first-order condition for an interior value of D^*. By replacing the background risk $\tilde{y}$ with zero in (20) one finds the first-order condition for D^*:

$$a(1 + \lambda)(1 - G(D^*)) \int_0^{D^*} U'[w - a(1 + \lambda)\varphi(D^*) - z]\, dG(z)$$

$$+ a[(1 + \lambda)(1 - G(D^*)) - 1] \int_{D^*}^{z_{\max}} U'[w - a(1 + \lambda)\varphi(D^*)$$

$$- aD^* - (1 - a)z]\, dG(z) = 0 \qquad (21)$$

As long as $D^* > 0$, the first term is positive; for (21) to be satisfied, the factor $[(1 + \lambda)(1 - G(D^*)) - 1]$ must be negative. Setting $D = D^*$ in (20),
and applying the lemma of section 3 with

$$x = \begin{cases} w - a(1 + \lambda)\varphi(D^*) - z & \text{for } z \leq D^* \\ w - a(1 + \lambda)\varphi(D^*) - aD^* - (1 - a)z & \text{for } z \geq D^* \end{cases}$$

$$h(x) = \psi(\tilde{y}(z(x)), x)$$

and

$$x_0 = w - a(1 + \lambda)\varphi(D^*) - D^*$$

reveals after careful examination that $v'(D^*) < 0$. Again, the key to the proof is that the background risk increases conditional expected marginal utility more in situations with larger insurable losses.

We must still deal with the possibility that D^* has a corner solution. Of course $D^{**} \leq D^*$ when $D^* = z_{\max}$. The weak inequality is necessary because if the load is prohibitive for the purchase of any insurance in the absence of background risk it may also be prohibitive even in its presence. Similarly, as long as the coinsurance rate a is positive, $D^* = 0$ only when the loading factor $\lambda = 0$, in which case it follows that $D^{**} = D^* = 0$.

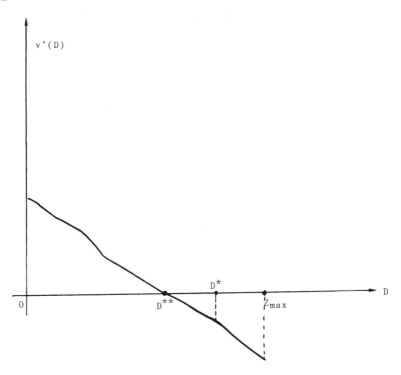

Figure 1.

Conclusion

The consideration of multiple sources of risks in the insurance economics literature has been one of the major areas of progress in the field since Mossin's important initial contribution (1968).

In this paper we have used the notion of prudence and plausible assumptions about its behavior to obtain a more complete understanding of the impact of background uninsurable risk on the optimal coverage of an insurable one. Though prudence was originally conceived as a tool for analyzing precautionary saving, it turns out to be a powerful tool of analysis for this new line of research in insurance economics as well.

Notes

1. This section contains no new theoretical developments beyond those in Kimball (1990a–c). However, the presentation of the material is largely new.

2. Calling π a risk premium is strictly correct only when $E(\tilde{y}) = 0$. When the lottery has a nonzero mean, π is equal to minus a certainty equivalent.

3. The restriction on the rate of increase of the wealth elasticity of risk tolerance is that *its* elasticity must be less than one plus the coefficient of relative risk aversion.

4. Standard risk aversion implies the weaker property of proper risk aversion introduced by Pratt and Zeckhauser (1987), which is exhibited by a utility function if any pair of statistically independent undesirable risks are jointly undesirable. Kimball (1990c) argues that standard risk aversion is the more natural concept.

5. An extension of that model, using a very similar criterion (the "reward to variability ratio") has been recently proposed by Briys, Kahane, and Kroll (1988).

6. C. Gollier suggested this shortened version of the proof of (7).

7. In fact, this will be true for any utility function satisfying $U'(\cdot) > 0$, $U''(\cdot) < 0$, and $U'''(\cdot) > 0$ — guaranteed by monotonicity and positive and decreasing absolute risk aversion.

8. This will be true for any utility function satisfying $U''(\cdot) < 0$, $U'''(\cdot) > 0$ and $U''''(\cdot) < 0$ — guaranteed by risk aversion and positive and decreasing absolute prudence.

9. Because of decreasing absolute risk aversion, the function $T(x) = U(x - h(x_0))$ is more risk averse than $U(x)$.

10. For simplicity we will also assume that the distribution of the insurable risk has no mass points. This assumption is not very restrictive since a distribution with mass points can be approximated arbitrarily closely by distributions without mass points.

11. An earlier version of the paper demonstrated that $v''(D)$ is indeed negative when $v'(D) = 0$.

References

Briys, E. Y. Kahane, and Y. Kroll. (1988). "Voluntary insurance coverage, compulsory insurance and risky-riskless portfolio opportunities," *Journal of Risk and Insurance* 4, 713–722.

Dionne, G. and L. Eeckhoudt. (1985). "Self-insurance, self-protection and increased risk aversion," *Economics Letters* 17, 39–42.

Doherty N. and H. Schlesinger. (1983a). "Optimal insurance in incomplete markets," *Journal of Political Economy* 91, 1045–1054.

Doherty, N. and H. Schlesinger. (1983b). "The Optimal deductible for an insurance policy when initial wealth is random," *Journal of Business* 56, 555–565.

Kihlstrom, R., D. Romer, and S. Williams. (1981). "Risk aversion with random initial wealth," *Econometrica* 49, 911–920.

Kimball, M. (1987). *Essays on Intertemporal Household Choice*, unpublished Ph.D. dissertation, Harvad University.

Kimball, M. (1989). "Precautionary saving due to income risk: Theory and Evidence," Economics Department, University of Michigan.

Kimball, M. (1990a). "Precautionary saving in the small and in the large," *Econometrica* 58, 53–73.

Kimball, M. (1990b). "Precautionary saving and the marginal propensity to consume," Economics Department, University of Michigan.

Kimball, M. (1990c). "Standard risk aversion," Economics Department, University of Michigan.

Mayers, D., and C. Smith. (1983). "The interdependence of individual portfolio decisions and the demand for insurance," *Journal of Political Economy* 91, 304–311.

Mossin, J. (1968). "Aspects of rational insurance purchasing," *Journal of Political Economy* 76, 553–568.

Pratt, J. (1964). "Risk aversion in the small and in the large," *Econometrica* 32, 217–229

Pratt, J., and R. Zeckhauser. (1987). "Proper risk aversion," *Econometrica* 55, 143–154.

Schlesinger, H. (1981). The optimal level of deductibility in insurance contracts," *Journal of Risk and Insurance* 48, 465–481.

Turnbull, S. (1983). "Additional aspects of rational insurance purchasing," *Journal of Business* 56, 217–229.

OPTIMUM INSURANCE WITH DEVIANT BELIEFS

John M. Marshall*

University of California, Santa Barbara

Abstract

Optimum insurance between a risk-neutral or risk-averse insurer and a risk-averse client has been widely studied under conditions of agreement about the distribution of probabilities of loss. The condition of agreement is relaxed here, and the client is assumed to be more optimistic than the insurer. When optimism is defined broadly, the optimum contracts can have almost any form and in general will not even resemble insurance contracts. However, the optimum contracts are insurance contracts under a condition that restricts the type of disagreement. Under the same condition, the optimum contract for a more optimistic client has a higher deductible than the optimum contract for a less optimistic one.

Key words: insurance, optimism, deductible, disagreement

Optimum insurance with deviant beliefs

A central problem of insurance theory is optimum insurance for a risk-averse client by a risk-averse or risk-neutral insurer. Karl Borch (1960, 1962) studies this problem in its pure form as a model of reinsurance.

*I thank the Huebner Foundation for Insurance Education for supporting this research. My views are not necessarily those of the Foundation. I also thank Georges Dionne and Christian Gollier for their comments.

In more recent treatments of the problem, the objective is to derive, using minimum further hypotheses, the real phenomena of deductibles, coinsurance, and maximums on coverage. Substantial contributions are made by K. J. Arrow (1971, 1974) and Artur Raviv (1979). They assume only that there are transactions costs attendant upon the insurance. Such solutions have the appeal of elegance and a predictive power beyond that of models dependent upon additional assumptions.

Raviv's version is noteworthy for explaining deductibles and co-insurance succinctly and clarifying the role of the minimal assumptions in the explanation. Raviv also extends the model to explain the existence of maximums, using additional assumptions about regulatory constraints. The added assumptions are realistic and usefully extend the fundamental theory. However, they are not a part of the fundamental theory, which would explain regulatory structure endogenously or omit it.[1]

In this paper I start from the fundamental version of the Raviv model. In the first section I interpret his results diagrammatically and heuristically, and I consider the effects of deviant beliefs upon the model. Even when one party is more optimistic than the other, the effects upon deductibles and the insurance premium are not determinate. To reduce this variety and to derive some consequences, limitations upon the form of belief deviance are needed. Following the section on heuristics, I generalize the formal model of Raviv to admit deviant beliefs of a specific type. I show that Raviv's main findings continue to hold in spite of such belief deviance. My derivations are simpler and more direct than those of Raviv and may thereby aid further developments in the theory. In the paper's final section I show that the type of belief-deviance considered has determinate effects upon the optimum levels of the deductible and the premium.

Belief-deviance in practice

Disagreement about probability occurs because agents possess different information. Aumann (1976) shows that disagreement must vanish when information is completely shared. Such sharing is not expected, however. Even supposing that agents desire to share information completely, costs of communication interfere. Agents continue to communicate until the marginal gains from further communication fall below the marginal costs. When net gains from further sharing have fallen to zero, some differences in information and probability beliefs will remain. This is true in practice and would remain true even in an optimally governed economy. Thus belief deviance is a natural, expected result of the cost of sharing information.

Belief deviance can also exist when all risks have in an objective sense the same, average distribution. In this case some consumers may stubbornly believe that they are luckier or unluckier than average.

Belief deviance is enlarged by the incentives associated with generating information. A number of authors have described how production of information may proceed too far and in the wrong directions.[2] This occurs because information is highly valuable to agents who hold it privately, even though the public finds the same information to be of lower, zero, or even negative value. Agents possess such information in secrecy and exploit the private gains from it. Thus the production of private information contributes to differences in probability beliefs.

Belief-deviant clients are relevant in selective underwriting. Here the client and underwriter recognize that the risk is less than that supposed in the rating formula. The problem is to tailor the contract to the client's needs, subject to the constraint that the contract is priced on the basis of average risk, not the risk of the client. A similar situation arises when insurance rates are regulated. An insurance firm sees that rates are too high on some class of business. In seeking to attract clients from this class, the firm must design contracts that suit the clients given the regulated rate structure. All of these situations call for an optimum insurance policy with deviant probability beliefs.

Representation of Preferences

Preferences of the insurer and the client are represented as expected utility. This must be justified because of experimental findings showing that expected utility is not a *universally applicable* representation of preferences.[3] Experimental work does not address the question of whether expected utility may be suitable for the *specific application* to optimum insurance.[4] Expected utility is appropriate in this case for several compelling reasons.

Necessity is the first reason that expected utility is used for the study of optimum insurance. Theories allowing more general preferences are being developed, but they are not yet applicable to optimum insurance. Even the question of what optimum means under general preferences is difficult to answer.[5] The second reason for using expected utility is its normative force. Because expected utility is implied by reasonable axioms, it is frequently argued that expected utility should be used when

prescribing, even though the behavior of consumers cannot be rational-
ized by it. This argument has distinguished support,[6] although many
writers including Marshall (1989) have suggested modifications. Finally,
expected utility is appropriate in the present case because it has been
used previously to study optimum insurance and in that application has
been highly predictive of the form of actual insurance policies.

There is a final question to answer here: Why do the very numerous
and impressive studies denying expected utility not show that it is inapplicable to optimum insurance? The reason is that the conceptual
experiments in optimum insurance theory are much simpler than actual
experiments with subjects. Typical experiments offer their subjects a
range of choices involving differing probability distributions, differing
semantic framing,[7] or differing degrees of ambiguity.[8] Optimum insurance
involves unvarying probabilities, constant framing, and a steady lack
of ambiguity. The experimental studies show that expected utility fails
when particular dimensions of the choices change, but in the problem of
optimum insurance these dimensions are unvarying.

1. Heuristics and Diagrams

A heuristic explanation of Raviv's results is desirable because the results
are important and because the heuristics will help explain the contributions of the present paper. The problem is to find an optimum pattern
of transfer of a continuum of state-contingent commodities (i.e., payments of money contingent upon losses) and one certainty commodity
(i.e., unconditional payments of money). The insurer can transfer any
commodity to the client, but *the client can transfer only the certainty
commodity*. This assumption is not absolutely required, as Gollier (1987)
has shown under some additional conditions. For present purposes the
assumption is useful and is justified by the idea that prohibitive transaction
costs prevent the client from transferring state-contingent commodities.

To define the commodities, the loss of the client is denoted by t, which
is also the state, where t is a member of the real interval $[0, T]$. There is
one state-contingent commodity for each value of t. The probability
density function of t is $f(t)$.

The losses t are on the horizontal axis in figure 1. Points of this axis
represent the continuum of goods, one for each loss t. On the vertical axis
is the shadow price of the contingent goods (i.e., prices for insurance in
the individual losses), expressed in terms of the certainty good. The
insurer and client are initially in a no-trade (autarky) situation. The

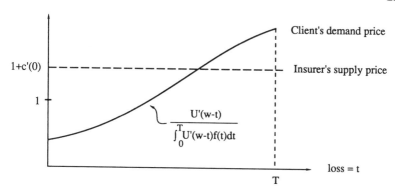

Figure 1. Autarky (no-insurance) shadow prices.

client's shadow-price of contingent goods, after adjustment for probability density, is an increasing function of the loss t, as shown in figure 1.

Specifically, the client has wealth of w-t in state t, where w (endowed wealth), is a constant. Utility is a risk-averse $U()$. The shadow-price of good t, adjusted for probability density is

$$\frac{U'(w-t)f(t)}{\int_0^T U'(w-t)f(t)\,dt} \cdot \frac{1}{f(t)} = \frac{U'(w-t)}{\int_0^T U'(w-t)f(t)\,dt} \tag{1.1}$$

By risk-aversion, the adjusted shadow-price rises with t. It is less than unity at $t = 0$, as illustrated, since

$$U'(w) < \int_0^T U'(w-t)f(t)\,dt. \tag{1.2}$$

The insurer's adjusted supply price in the initial, autarky situation at t is:

$$\frac{V'(w_0)f(t)}{\int_0^T V'(w_0)f(t)\,dt} \cdot \frac{1}{f(t)} \cdot (1 + c'(0)) = 1 + c'(0), \tag{1.3}$$

where w_0 is the wealth of the insurer. On the left, the first term is the shadow-price of consumption to the insurer. The middle term adjusts for the probability density at t. The right-hand term accounts for the transaction costs. This reduces to simply the probability loading (the 1) plus the marginal transaction cost loading, $c'(0)$.

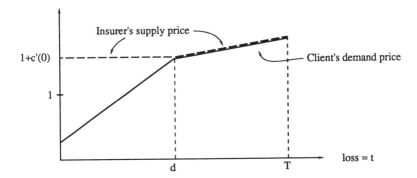

Figure 2. Shadow prices with optimum insurance

The insurer bears no risk and consequently has a supply price of contingent goods *per unit of probability* that is the same for all t, as shown in figure 1. Because the client has a rising demand price, there are potential gains for both parties from transfers, that is, from trade in insurance.

Leaving autarky and supposing that optimum transfers of contingent and certainty goods are made, the shadow-prices become related as shown in figure 2. The main features of optimum insurance are illustrated there and in figure 3.

1.1 Deductible

There is a critical value d, the deductible. For a contingent good t, where $t < d$, the good is not transferred from insurer to client because the client's demand price is below the insurer's supply price. Given the shadow-prices, transfers of contingent goods from client to insurer would be interesting in these states, but they are prevented by transaction costs.

1.2. Coinsurance

To the right of the deductible, the client's and insurer's shadow prices coincide in the optimum. A theoretically interesting case is that either the insurer is risk-averse or the marginal cost of transactions is rising. In either case the optimum scarcity price rises with t. Increments of loss are

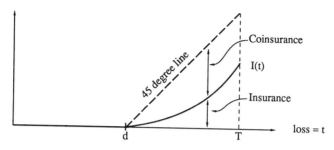

Figure 3. Optimum insurance, $I(t)$.

shared between insurer and client, as illustrated by the coinsurance in figure 3. Specifically, as the loss increases, each party has an increasing burden, as illustrated by the increasing shadow-prices. Because each increment of loss is shared, coinsurance is never negative.

If the insurer is risk-neutral and marginal transaction cost is constant (i.e., $c''() = 0$), the price line is flat, and all incremental losses above the deductible are absorbed by the insurer. Coinsurance is zero, but still not negative.

This is the intuitive explanation of Raviv's results. In section 2, a formal proof is given that encompasses these results. The important achievement of the theory is to explain deductibles and coinsurance.

1.3. Deviant Beliefs

The client's beliefs deviate from those of the insurer when she (the client) holds a probability density function $g(t)$ different from $f(t)$. The no-trade supply prices of the insurer remain as they were in figure 1, for $f(t)$ is still the adjustment factor. The effect of deviance is a distortion of the client's autarky shadow prices. With sufficiently deviant $g(t)$, this distortion can take almost any form.

Deviant probabilities could explain, for instance, the existence of binding maximums on insurance contracts. It suffices for the client to regard large losses as being much less likely than the insurer thinks. This argument is tidy and reasonable. It is not entirely convincing because a similar argument could explain *any* form of contract, no matter how bizarre. Thus in figure 1 it is possible to imagine the client's autarky shadow-price as a serpentine that crosses and recrosses the insurer's shadow-price line. The optimum insurance policy would be quite strange. It would have successive areas of coverage and no coverage, with co-insurance possibly negative where client shadow price is very high in autarky relative to that of the insurer.

More precisely, the client's shadow-price, after adjustment for $f(t)$, is

$$\frac{U'(w-t)f(t)}{\int_0^T U'(w-t)g(t)dt} \cdot \frac{g(t)}{f(t)} \qquad (1.4)$$

Relative to the previous case, this shadow-price is different in two ways. There is a proportional displacement either upward or downward, due to the change of probability density function in the denominator of the left-hand term. In addition, the factor $\dfrac{g(t)}{f(t)}$ distorts the curve, raising the client's shadow-price in areas the client considers to be more probable than does the insurer, and lowering it elsewhere.

Nothing useful can be said about a completely general deviation in beliefs. Some limitation is needed. A possible improvement would be to consider deviations that are ranked, relative to $f(t)$ as more optimistic. The ranking of Blackwell (1951) and of Rothschild and Stiglitz (1970) is the natural one. I will show that this ranking is not sufficient to give determinate predictions on the change in optimum insurance.

1.4. Blackwell-Rothschild-Stiglitz optimism

Optimism is defined through the distribution functions $G(t)$ and $F(t)$ corresponding to $f(t)$ and $g(t)$. The client is more optimistic if for all s

$$\int_0^s G(t)\,dt > \int_0^s F(t)\,dt \qquad (1.5)$$

This condition implies and is implied by the condition that for every risk-averse utility function $U()$, loss density of $g(t)$ is preferable to loss density $f(t)$. The condition is satisfied when $g(t)$ can be produced from $f(t)$ by moving probability mass from areas of large loss to areas of smaller loss. Note that this does not require equal means for f and g although it can accommodate them.

Under the assumption that $g(t)$ is more optimistic than $f(t)$, the shift of the client's autarky shadow-price can be visualized. Since $g(t)$ involves shifts of probability mass to areas of lower t, the denominator in (1.4) is less than in (1.1). Thus the general shift of shadow-prices is upward.

However, there is nothing to prevent the serpentine shape described in the general case. Therefore general optimism does not have any specific empirical content. The example given below shows specifically that an optimistic shift in probabilities can lead to optimum insurance that has a lower deductible.

1.4.1. Example: An optimistic shift that lowers the deductible. This example demonstrates that optimism of the Blackwell-Rothschild-Stiglitz type is consistent with *lower* optimum deductibles, as well as with the expected case of higher optimum deductibles.

The example uses a discrete space of losses $t = 1,2,11$. The insurer is risk-neutral, and he attributes probabilities $f(1) = .5$, $f(2) = .1$, and $f(11) = .4$ to the losses. Transactions costs are $c(I) = .1I$.

Since the insurer is risk-neutral, its autarky shadow-prices depend only upon probability and transaction cost, not upon scarcity. They must be $p(1) = .55$, $p(2) = .11$, and $p(11) = .44$. The adjusted prices, corresponding to values in figure 1, are $q(1) = q(2) = q(11) = 1.1$. Because of risk neutrality, these will also be the shadow-prices in the optimum.

The client's utility function is $U() = \ln()$, and her initial wealth is 11. At first she agrees about the density of probability $f()$. Then the optimum insurance policy is defined to be the solution to

$$\text{Maximize } .5\ln(10 - m + I(1)) + .1\ln(9 - m + I(2)) + .4\ln(-m + I(11)) \tag{1.6}$$

$$\text{subject to} \qquad m - .55I(1) - .11I(2) - .44I(11) = 0 \tag{1.7}$$

$$\text{and } m, I() \geq 0 \tag{1.8}$$

Here m represents the certainty payment from client to insurer, that is, the premium. This is a standard problem in nonlinear programming. Kuhn-Tucker techniques apply. The solution is $I(1) = 0$, $I(2) = 0$, $I(11) = 8.915314$, $m = 3.922738$, and Lagrange multiplier representing the marginal utility of numeraire is $.1820885$.

The deductible in this problem is between 2 and 11.[9] The task now is to show probabilities $g()$ that are more optimistic than $f()$ by the Blackwell-Rothschild-Stiglitz measure and lead to positive payments when the loss is 2. A density function satisfying the requirement is $g(1) = .5$, $g(2) = .4$, and $g(3) = .1$. Now the problem defining optimum insurance is

$$\text{Maximize } .5\ln(10 - m + I(1)) + .4\ln(9 - m + I(2)) + .1\ln(-m + I(11)) \tag{1.9}$$

subject to $m - .55I(1) - .11I(2) - .44I(11) = 0$ (1.10)

and $m, I() \geq 0$ (1.11)

The solution is $I(1) = 0$, $I(2) = 14.86364$, $I(11) = 5.147727$, $m = 3.9$, and Lagrange multiplier representing the marginal utility of numeraire is .1821494. The deductible is marked by the onset of insurance, which now lies between losses 1 and 2.

This optimum has properties that are unexpected in an insurance contract. The payment at a loss of 2 exceeds the loss itself and also the payment at a loss of 11. This could be interpreted as super coinsurance — a coinsurance that rises faster than the loss — but that interpretation is strained. It is better to recognize that the optimum contract needed here does not resemble insurance. The optimum is better interpreted as a gamble in which the client is betting on state 2 and the insurer is betting on state 11. Not only does belief deviance in the example cause a paradoxical shift of the optimum deductible, it makes insurance contracts inapplicable for optimum risk sharing.

The derivations of this section show that a very general definition of optimism cannot imply that optimists should have lower deductibles. In the specific example, optimism is inconsistent with insurance of any sort.

2. A Context for Deviant Beliefs

The discussion in the previous section shows that no specific results will be obtained in completely general cases. Further limitations on optimistic beliefs are needed to produce a theory in which the optimum contract resembles insurance. In this section, I describe optimum contracts under a limited form of belief deviance. These contracts have all of the usual characteristics of insurance contracts. In section 3, I place some further restrictions, under which a client who is more optimistic will have a higher optimum deductible.

The needed limitations have meaning when the Raviv (1979) theory is extended slightly to include a mass of probability at t equal to zero. The insurer attaches probability β to this no-loss outcome, and the client attaches a higher probability $\alpha > \beta$. However, the client and insurer agree upon the probability of loss $f(t)$, conditional upon loss $t > 0$, where $f(t) > 0$ for $0 < t \leq T$. Thus the client's probability density at loss t is $(1 - \alpha)f(t)$ and that of the insurer is the larger $(1 - \beta)f(t)$.

Other than that, the theoretical set-up follows Raviv. There is a fixed transactions cost of a units of the certainty good. It is incurred for any insurance contract. In addition, the payment $I(t)$ from insurer to client in state t costs $c(I(t))$-a in that state, where cost $c()$ satisfies $c' > 0$ and $c'' > 0$. This technology is convex in the usual sense of showing increasing marginal costs.[10]

The analysis uses conditions derived from a problem of economic efficiency. The problem may be written

$$\text{Maximize} \quad \alpha U[w - m] + (1 - \alpha)\int_0^T U[w - m - t + I(t)]f(t)dt \quad (2.1)$$

$$\text{subject to} \quad \beta V[w_0 + m] + (1 - \beta)\int_0^T V[w_0 + m - I(t) - c(I(t))]f(t)dt = k \quad (2.2)$$

$$\text{and } m, I(t) \geqslant 0 \quad (2.3)$$

Thus, an efficient insurance contract will maximize the client's expected utility holding the insurer's utility at a fixed level. The idea of solving this with control theory is due to Raviv. His solution involves a two-part structure that is quite lengthy and raises obstacles to the derivations connecting disagreement to optimum deductibles. Thus my starting point will be to prove Raviv's results for the extended case using a shorter proof.

Although control theory is used, there is no passage of time considered here. The time variable is loss t. The control variable is $I(t)$, the payment from insurer to client in case of loss t. One state variable is the premium paid by the client, $m(t)$, which never varies. The other state variable, $n(t)$, represents cumulative utility of the insurer from loss 0 through loss t, so that $n(T)$ is the insurer's total expected utility. The problem is

$$\text{Maximize} \quad \alpha U[w - m(0)] + (1 - \alpha)\int_0^T U[w - m(t) - t + I(t)]f(t)dt \quad (2.4)$$

$$\text{subject to} \quad \dot{n} = (1 - \beta)V[w_0 + m(t) - I(t) - c(I(t))]f(t) \quad (2.5)$$

$$\dot{m}(t) = 0 \quad (2.6)$$

$$I(t) = 0 \quad (2.7)$$

$$\beta V[\omega_0 + m(0)] - n(0) \geqslant 0 \quad (2.8)$$

$$n(T) \geqslant k \quad (2.9)$$

This system is unusual because of the unvarying state variable $m(t)$, for which neither starting nor terminal value is given. The problem is, however, completely within the formal framework of control theory in

Kamien and Schwartz (1972). That is important here because it shows that the conditions derived below are sufficient as well as necessary for optimum insurance. If one is concerned only with necessary conditions, it is possible to go directly from the problem at equation 2.1 to the condition at equation 2.17. Gollier (1987) demonstrates that variational calculus can also be used in solving problems of this type.

To maximize the Hamiltonian of this system, write its Lagrangian

$$L = U[w - m(t) - t + I(t)](1 - \alpha) f(t) + \lambda(t) V[w_0 + m(t) - I(t) - c(I(t))](1 - \beta) f(t) + \mu(t) \cdot 0 + \omega(t) I(t) \qquad (2.10)$$

where $\lambda(t)$ and $\mu(t)$ are the dual variables associated with equations 2.5 and 2.6, and $\omega(t)$ is the shadow price of the nonnegativity constraint on $I(t)$.

Some preliminary observations will simplify matters. From the Lagrangian, the differential equation governing λ is

$$\dot{\lambda} = -\frac{\partial L}{\partial n} = 0 \qquad (2.11)$$

Hereafter I will write λ for $\lambda(t)$. Note also that the condition for $n(0)$ is

$$r \frac{\partial}{\partial n(0)} [\beta V(w_0 + m(0)) - n(0)] + \lambda(0) = 0 \qquad (2.12)$$

where r is the Lagrange multiplier associated with the constraint of equation 2.9. Thus from equation (2.12) $r = \lambda(0) = \lambda$.

The differential equation governing μ is

$$\dot{\mu} = -\frac{\partial L}{\partial m} = U'[w - m(t) - t + I(t)](1 - \alpha) f(t) - \lambda V'[w_0 + m - I(t) - c(I(t))](1 - \beta) f(t) \qquad (2.13)$$

The initial and terminal values are found from the necessary condition

$$\frac{\partial}{\partial m(0)} [\alpha U[w - m(0)]]$$

$$+ r \frac{\partial}{\partial m(0)} [\beta V[w_0 + m(0)] - n(0)] + \mu(0) = 0, \qquad (2.14)$$

which reduces to

$$-\alpha U'[w - m(0)] + \lambda \beta V'[w_0 + m(0)] + \mu(0) = 0. \qquad (2.15)$$

Since there is no terminal condition on $m(T)$, the corresponding shadow price, $\mu(T)$, equals zero. Combining with (2.13) implies

$$\mu(t) = -\int_t^T \left\{ U'[w - m - t + I(t)](1 - \alpha) - \lambda V'[w_0 + m - I(t) \right.$$

$$\left. - c(I)](1 - \beta) \right\} f(t)dt \tag{2.16}$$

where m and I replace $m(t)$ and $I(t)$ for brevity. Evaluate this equation at $t = 0$ and combine with (2.15) to yield

$$\alpha U'[w - m] + (1 - \alpha) \int_0^T U'[w - m - t + I(t)] f(t)dt$$

$$-\lambda \left\{ \beta V'[w_0 + m] + (1 - \beta) \int_0^T V'[w_0 + m - I(t) - c(I)] f(t)dt \right\} = 0 \tag{2.17}$$

This is the first major condition needed to prove the results in section 3.

The other major condition is derived from the fact that the optimum control $I(t)$ must maximize the Hamiltonian. Because the Hamiltonian is a concave function of I and a check of the constraints reveals no violation of the constraint qualification, the conditions are collectively sufficient as well as individually necessary. The optimization condition is $\dfrac{\partial L}{\partial I} = 0$, or

$$U'[W - m - t + I(t)](1 - \alpha)$$

$$-\lambda V'[w_0 + m - I(t) - c(I)](1 + c'(I))(1 - \beta) = -\omega(t)/f(t) \tag{2.18}$$

for $t > 0$, where $\omega(t) \geq 0$ and $\omega(t) \cdot I(t) = 0$. It could happen that for all t, $\omega(t) > 0$, $I(t) = 0$, and there is no insurance. That would be the case if the insurer is too risk averse or the fixed cost of transactions, a, is too high. Such cases are uninteresting and trivial. Therefore consider the case that $\omega(t)$ is sometimes zero.

In that case the optimum deductible d is defined by the condition that

$$U'[w - m - d](1 - \alpha) -\lambda V'[w_0 + m - a](1 + c'(0))(1 - \beta) = 0 \tag{2.19}$$

For $t > d$, zero insurance would imply a negative value of $\omega(t)$, which is not allowed in an optimum. Thus, $I(t) > 0$ for all $t > d$. The optimum indemnity $I(t)$ is that which solves equation 2.18 with $\omega(t) = 0$. For $t < d$,

$$U'[w - m - d](1 - \alpha) -\lambda V'[w_0 + m - a](1 + c'(0))(1 - \beta) < 0 \tag{2.20}$$

Any positive insurance payment would reduce the value in (2.20) further by lowering the first, positive term, and raising or leaving unchanged the second term, which is negative. Thus from (2.18) we must have $\omega(t) > 0$

in this range. Consequently, $t < d$ implies $I(t) = 0$. Now Raviv's main results can be stated:

Theorem: (Raviv) Optimum insurance has a deductible, d, such that

$0 < d \leqslant T$, $I(t) = 0$ for $0 < t \leqslant d$, and $I(t) > 0$ for $d < t \leqslant T$.

Proof: The relation of d and $I(t)$ was proved above in discussion of equations (2.18) and (2.19). The relation continues to be true when $d = T$. It remains to show that $d > 0$. If $d = 0$ we have from (2.19)

$$U'[w - m](1 - \alpha) f(t) - \lambda V'[w_0 + m - a](1 + c'(0))(1 - \beta)f(t) = 0 \tag{2.21}$$

Since $\alpha > \beta$, this implies that

$$\alpha U'[w - m - d]f(t) - \lambda \beta V'[w_0 + m] > 0 \tag{2.22}$$

and $\omega(t) = 0$ for all t. Then because of $c'(\ ) > 0$ and (2.18), we have

$$(1 - \alpha)U'[w - m - t + I(t)] f(t) - \lambda(1 - \beta)V'$$
$$[w_0 + m - I(t) - c(I)]f(t) > 0 \tag{2.22}$$

Integrating this expression over t and adding (2.21) to it supplies a direct contradiction to the necessary condition of (2.17). Q.E.D.

Now an important lemma from Raviv (1979) can be restated for the case of disagreement:

Lemma: (Raviv) Optimum insurance satisfies

$$I'(t) = \cfrac{R_u(A)}{R_u(A) + \left(\dfrac{1 - \alpha}{1 - \beta}\right) R_v(B)(1 + c') + \dfrac{c''}{1 + c'}} \tag{2.24}$$

where $A = w - m - t + I(t)$, $B = w_0 + m - I(t) - c(I(t))$, $R_u(A) = \dfrac{-U''(A)}{U'(A)}$, and $R_u(B) = \dfrac{-V''(B)}{V'(B)}$.

Proof: The lemma follows from implicit differentiation of equation 2.18 with $\omega(t) = 0$, and using equation 2.17 to substitute for λ. **Q.E.D.** Several more results follow immediately from the lemma:

Proposition 1: (Nonnegative coinsurance) If $R_u(\ ) > 0$ and $c'' \geqslant 0$, then $I'(t) \leqslant 1$ and $I(t) \leqslant \max [0, t - d]$.

Proposition 2: (No binding maximum) If $R_u(\ ) > 0$ and $c'' \geqslant 0$, then $I'(t) > 0$ and $I(t) > 0$ for all t, $T \geqslant t > d$.

Proposition 3: (Full insurance) If $R_v(\ ) \equiv 0$ and $c'' \equiv 0$, then $I'(t) \equiv 1$ and $I(t) = \max [0, t - d]$.

The individual meanings of these results have already been discussed. Their collective meaning is also significant. They show that within the restraints considered here, optimum contracts in the case of disagreement have all of the expected properties of insurance contracts. That finding justifies examining the behavior of deductibles under the restraints.

3. Deductibles That Increase with Optimism

Now the main result of this paper can be demonstrated. Some limitations are needed: The insurer is risk neutral, and without further loss of generality, he has utility $V[x] = x$. Transactions costs are linear, that is, $c(I(t)) - a = c \cdot I(t)$, where c is a constant. The probability of no-loss must be great enough. Specifically, $\beta > \dfrac{c}{1 + c}$, a relatively mild restriction.

The restrictions lead to some simplification in the necessary conditions. They will be reduced to a pair of conditions connecting d, m, and α. The conditions are denoted $J^i(d, m, \alpha)$ and are the basis for proving the desired result. Under the assumptions, the constraint on utility of the insurer becomes a constraint on expected wealth. Without loss of generality that level will be set to w_0. Then (2.21) becomes

$$J^2(d, m, \alpha) = m - (1 - \beta)(1 + c)\int_0^T (t - d) f(t)dt = 0 \qquad (3.1)$$

Equation 2.17, which defines the deductible, becomes

$$(1 - \alpha)U'[w - m - d] - \lambda(1 + c)(1 - \beta) = 0 \qquad (3.2)$$

and equation 2.14, which defines λ, is now

$$\alpha U'[w - m] + \int_0^T U'[w - m - t - I(t)](1 - \alpha) f(t) dt - \lambda = 0 \qquad (3.3)$$

Combine these two equations by solving (3.2) for λ and substituting. The outcome will be called

$$J^1(d, m, \alpha) = \alpha U'[w - m] + \int_0^T U'[w - m - t - I(t)](1 - \alpha) f(t) dt$$

$$- \frac{1 - \alpha}{(1 + c)(1 - \beta)} U'[w - m - d] = 0 \qquad (3.4)$$

The signs of the partial derivatives of the J^i are needed. In writing them it is convenient to use $F(t)$ to denote the distribution function associated with the probability density function $f(t)$. Observe also that from the propositions proved in the general case, we have $I(t) = \max(0, t - d)$. It follows that

$$J_d^1 = -(1 - \alpha)\left[1 - F(d) - \frac{1 - \alpha}{(1 + c)(1 - \beta)}\right]U''[w - m - d] \quad (3.5)$$

$$J_m^1 = -\alpha U''[w - m] - (1 - \alpha)\int_0^d U''[w - m - t]f(t)dt$$

$$-(1 - \alpha)\left[1 - F(d) - \frac{1 - \alpha}{(1 + c)(1 - \beta)}\right]U''(w - m - d) \quad (3.6)$$

and

$$J_\alpha^1 = U'[w - m] + \frac{1}{(1 + c)(1 - \beta)}U'[w - m - d]$$

$$-\int_0^T U'[w - m - t + I(t)]f(t)\,dt \quad (3.7)$$

Lemma: If $\beta > \dfrac{1}{1 + c}$, then $\dfrac{1}{(1 + c)(1 - \beta)} > 1$, $1 - F(d) - \dfrac{1 - \alpha}{(1 + c)(1 - \beta)} < 0$, $J_d^1 < 0$, and $J_\alpha^1 > 0$.

Proof: The first conclusion follows directly from the hypothesis and immediately implies the second conclusion. That implies the third conclusion by inspection. The final conclusion depends upon the first and upon the fact that, for the risk-averse client, $U'[w - m - d] \geq U'[w - m - t + I(t)]$. **Q.E.D.**

Now consider the partial derivatives of $J^2 (d, m, \alpha)$.

$$J_d^2 = (1 - \beta)(1 + c)[1 - F(d)] \quad (3.8)$$

$$J_m^2 = 1 \quad (3.9)$$

$$J_\alpha^2 = 0 \quad (3.10)$$

The signs of these terms are not in doubt.

Now the theorem can be proved.

Theorem: Given the assumptions of this section and, in particular, that $\beta > \dfrac{c}{1 + c}$, the solutions $d(\alpha)$ and $m(\alpha)$ to the equations $J^1(d, m, \alpha) = 0$ and $J^2(d, m, \alpha) = 0$, satisfy $d'(\alpha) > 0$ and $m'(\alpha) < 0$.

Proof: The relation of $d'(\alpha)$ and $m'(\alpha)$ is given by

$$\begin{bmatrix} J_d^1 & J_m^1 \\ J_d^2 & J_m^2 \end{bmatrix} \cdot \begin{bmatrix} d'(\alpha) \\ m'(\alpha) \end{bmatrix} = \begin{bmatrix} -J_\alpha^1 \\ 0 \end{bmatrix} \tag{3.11}$$

If the matrix can be inverted, this becomes

$$\begin{bmatrix} d'(\alpha) \\ m'(\alpha) \end{bmatrix} = \frac{1}{\Delta} \begin{bmatrix} J_m^2 & -J_m^1 \\ -J_d^2 & J_d^1 \end{bmatrix} \cdot \begin{bmatrix} -J_\alpha^1 \\ 0 \end{bmatrix} \tag{3.12}$$

where $\Delta = J_d^1 J_m^2 - J_m^1 J_d^2$ is the determinant. One needs $\Delta \neq 0$ to assure that the matrix inversion is legitimate. But

$$\Delta = -(1 - \beta)(1 + c)(1 - F(d)) \left\{ -\alpha U''[w - m] \right.$$

$$- (1 - \alpha) \int_0^d U''[w - m - t] f(t)\, dt \bigg\}$$

$$- (1 - \alpha) \left[1 - F(d) - \frac{1}{(1 + c)(1 - \beta)} \right]$$

$$\cdot [1 - (1 - \beta)(1 + c)(1 - F(d))]\, U''[w - m - d] \tag{3.13}$$

This is composed of two additive parts. The first part contains the term in brackets which is, by inspection, positive. Consequently the first additive component is negative. In the second additive term, the first term in large parenthesis is negative by lemma 2, and the second term in large parenthesis is positive by application of the same lemma. Thus the second additive is also negative and therefore Δ is definitely negative.

Now $d'(\alpha) = -\dfrac{1}{\Delta} J_\alpha^1$. From lemma 2, J_α^1 is positive. Thus $d'(\alpha) > 0$. Similarly, $m'(\alpha) = \dfrac{1}{\Delta} J_d^2 J_\alpha^1 < 0$ by the lemma and by the earlier observation that $J_d^2 > 0$. **Q.E.D.**

The theorem shows that the optimum deductible rises and the premium declines as the insured becomes more optimistic. This is the desired result, but it should be considered in light of the restrictions used, since general optimism has no definite implications for optimum deductibles. The present result is achieved by assuming that insurer and client agree upon conditional probability. This limitation makes the result possible and confers a second advantage: it assures that the optimum contract for the optimistic client resembles insurance.

4. Concluding Observations

The attractive proposition that client optimism will lead to a higher optimum deductible is in general incorrect and can be proved only under strong assumptions. At first sight the need for strong assumptions is discouraging, but on further reflection it supplies new insights into the nature of insurance. Optimum contingent contracts are not necessarily insurance contracts. When beliefs are divergent, optimum contracts could resemble shares, bonds, options, or lottery tickets, or they could fail to resemble any known contract. They will be insurance contracts in the restricted case examined in sections 2 and 3 above. Given that type of belief deviance, insurance is the optimum contract and higher deductibles are optimum for more optimistic clients.

It is interesting to consider whether the restriction used here might be further relaxed without giving up the results. Are there other types of belief deviance that admit insurance contracts as the optimum? Does greater optimism necessarily lead to higher deductibles in such contracts? To approach these questions would be a considerable project. It would require, to begin, a careful discussion of how a contract of insurance differs from any other contingent contract, a question that the present paper has treated informally. Even with a more formal approach to this question, it is uncertain whether any relaxation of requirements can be made. Pending further discoveries in this area, the provisional finding is that deductibles rise with the client's optimism when optimum risk-sharing is achieved through contracts of insurance.

Notes

1. A related effort by Huberman, Mayers, and Smith (1983) introduces a different structure of transactions costs, some constraints related to principal-agent problems, and a risk-loving client. Their theory explains maximums convincingly as a product of risk-loving, but it relies heavily upon the constraints to rationalize deductibles and coinsurance of a realistic form. The theory if presented somewhat informally. For all of these reasons, it is not as hospitable to extension as the Raviv model.

2. See for instance, Hirshleifer (1971), Marshall (1974), and Boyer, Dionne, and Kihlstrom (1989).

3. See Mark Machina (1987) for an introduction and selected references. The literature is too extensive for exhaustive citation here.

4. Borch wrote in this context, "it is almost trivial that the Bernoulli hypothesis must hold for a company in the insurance business" (1962, sec. 2.2). Today many would disagree.

5. See Marshall (1989) for discussion and references.

6. For instance, Luce (1988) opens with "subjective expected utility is widely acknowl-

edged to be normatively compelling but not fully descriptive of behavior" (page 305). Fishburn (1988) cites past and present opinion that "expected utility theory is the only adequate normative theory for preference under risk," (page 280), although Fishburn himself is skeptical of this idea.

7. For instance, people gamble more freely in situations described to them as avoiding loss than in those described as opportunities for gain. Paul Slovic (1969) was among the first to find this effect.

8. For instance, see Kunreuther and Hogarth (1989).

9. Using proposition 3 of section 2, the deductible is in fact $2.084686 = 11.0 - 8.915314$.

10. Huberman, Mayers and Smith (1983) argue that transactions costs in state t should consist of a fixed cost and a region of decreasing costs. They assert correctly that this structure is realistic. However, their argument in favor of an optimum deductible is complicated and informal. The Arrow-Raviv assumption of convexity supplies a direct reason for the widely observed deductible. Because the latter result is formally demonstrated, it is a preferable basis for extending the theory.

References

Arrow, Kenneth J. (1971). *Essays in the Theory of Risk Bearing.* Chicago: Elsevier Publishing Company.

Arrow, Kenneth J. (1974). "Optimal Insurance and Generalized Deductibles," *Scandinavian Actuarial Journal*, 1–42.

Aumann, Robert J. (1976). "Agreeing to Disagree," *Annals of Statistics* 4, 1236–1239.

Blackwell, David. (1951). "Comparison of Experiments," *Proceedings of the Second Berkeley Symposium on Mathematical Statistics*, University of California Press, 93–102.

Borch, Karl. (1960). "The Safety Loading of Reinsurance Premiums," *Skandinavisk Actuarietidskrift*, 163–184.

Borch, Karl. (1962). "Equilibrium in a Reinsurance Market," *Econometrica 7*, 424–444.

Boyer, Marcel, Georges Dionne, and Richard Kihlstrom. (1989). "Insurance and the Value of Publicly Available Information," *Studies in the Economics of Uncertainty*. New York: Springer Verlag, 137–156.

Fishburn, Peter C. (1988) "Expected Utility: An Anniversary and a New Era," *Journal of Risk and Uncertainty* 1(3), 267–284.

Gollier, Christian. (1987). "The Design of Optimal Insurance Contracts without the Nonnegativity Constraint on Claims," *Journal of Risk and Insurance* 54(2), 314–324.

Hestenes, M. R. (1966). *Calculus of Variations and Optimal Control Theory.* New York: Wiley.

Hirshleifer, J. (1971). "The Private and Social Value of Information and the Reward to Inventive Activity," *American Economic Review*, 61 (September) 561–573.

Huberman, Gur, David Mayers and Clifford W. Smith, Jr. (1983). "Optimum Insurance Policy Indemnity Schedules," *Bell Journal of Economics* 14, Autumn 415–426.

Kamien, M. I. and Nancy L. Schwartz. (1971). "Sufficient Conditions in Optimal Control Theory," *Journal of Economic Theory* (June), 207–214.

Kunreuther, Howard and Robin M. Hogarth. (1989). "Risk, Ambiguity, and Insurance," *Journal of Risk and Uncertainty* 2(1), 5–36.

Luce, Duncan. (1988). "Rank-Dependent, Subjective Expected-Utility Representations," *Journal of Risk and Uncertainty* 1(3), 305–332.

Machina, Mark. (1987). "Choice under Uncertainty: Problems Solved and Unsolved," *Journal of Economic Perspectives* 1(1), 121–154.

Marshall, John M. (1974). "Private Incentives and Public Information," *American Economic Review* 64, (June), 373–390.

Marshall, John M. (1989). "Welfare Analysis under Uncertainty," *Journal of Risk and Uncertainty* 2, 385–404.

Raviv, Artur. (1979). "The Design of an Optimal Insurance Policy," *American Economic Review* 69(1), March, 84–96.

Rothschild, Michael and Joseph E. Stiglitz. (1970). "Increasing Risk I: A Definition," *Journal of Economic Theory* 2, 225–243.

Rothschild, Michael and Joseph E. Stiglitz. (1974). 'Equilibrium in Competitive Insurance Markets: An Essay on the Economics of Imperfect Information," *Quarterly Journal of Economics* 90, 629–649.

Slovic, Paul. (1969). "Manipulating the Attractiveness of a Gamble Without Changing its Expected Value," *Journal of Experimental Psychology* 79, (January) 139–145.

INCREASES IN RISK AND THE DEMAND FOR INSURANCE*

Yves Alarie

Université de Montréal

Georges Dionne

Université de Montréal

Louis Eeckhoudt

Facultés Universitaires Catholiques de Mons (Belgium)
et de Lille (France)

Abstract

Many people anticipate that a risk-averse agent faced with an exogenous mean preserving increase in risk will take a less risky position or will demand more insurance. This widespread belief does not always turn out to be true in the insurance market and, more generally, in many other economic examples. This negative result has prompted many theoretical investigations to obtain intuitively acceptable results. Some authors have searched for conditions on the utility function, others have presented subclasses of mean preserving increases in risk, while a third group has considered the two kinds of restrictions jointly. It is interesting to notice that none of these contributors have applied their analysis to the insurance problem, although Meyer and Ormiston (1989) have interpreted the nature of insurance contracts as simple risk-reducing transformations. The object of this article is to fill this gap in literature. By examining the study of the coinsurance coverage, we show that one of its specifications, namely the linearity of the payoff in the decision variable and in the random element, does not preclude the applicability of well-known theorems to the demand for insurance.

* We thank C. Gollier, H. Schlesinger, A. Twizeyemariya, and P. Viala for their comments on a previous version, and A. Mathieu, C. Laflamme, and J. Lafontaine for their contributions in the preparation of the manuscript. C.R.S.H. (Canada) and F.C.A.R. (Soutien équipe, Québec) provided financial support.

Key words: Mean preserving increases in risk, linear payoffs, demand for insurance, coinsurance, relatively strong increases in risk, strong increases in risk

Many people anticipate that a risk-averse agent faced with an exogenous mean preserving increase in risk will demand more insurance to maintain an adequate level of protection.

This widespread belief does not always turn out to be true as already implicitly shown in a very general context by Rothschild and Stiglitz (1970, 1971) when they first presented the notion of a mean preserving increase in risk (MPIR) or of a mean preserving spread. For instance, when they applied their model to the simplest portfolio problem, they were unable to obtain the a priori intuitive result that an MPIR in the return of the risky asset will reduce its holdings by all risk-averse individuals. To generate clearcut comparative statics results they needed to put additional restrictions either on the shape of the utility function or on that of the original density. They arrived at the same conclusion for many other applications such as savings under uncertainty, the behavior of the competitive firm under uncertainty, and the firm production problem. This observation has prompted further investigations. Indeed, some authors have searched for conditions on the utility function — besides monotonicity and risk aversion — that would yield the desired result [Drèze and Modigliani (1972), Diamond and Stiglitz (1974), Dionne and Eeckhoudt (1987), Dionne, Eeckhoudt and Briys (1989)]. Another branch of the literature has tried to stay close to the assumption of risk aversion while presenting subclasses of MPIR that would produce the kind of comparative statics results that one expects [Meyer and Ormiston (1983, 1985), Black and Bulkley (1989), Eeckhoudt and Hansen (1980, 1983, 1984)]. Notice also that, in some papers, the two kinds of restrictions are jointly considered [Sandmo (1970, 1971), Meyer and Ormiston (1989)].

One may notice that none of the authors mentioned so far have applied their analysis to the insurance problem, although Meyer (1989) and Meyer and Ormiston (1989) have interpreted the nature of insurance contracts as simple risk-reducing transformations.

The object of this article is to fill this gap in literature. By examining the study of the optimal coinsurance coverage, we find that one of its specifications, namely the linearity of the payoff in the decision variable and in the random element does not preclude the applicability of well-known theorems to the demand for insurance. We begin the paper with a review of the main contributions in the field. We then introduce the characteristics of the demand for coinsurance and, in section 3, we present our main result. A short conclusion proposes potential extensions.

1. Mean Preserving Increases in Risk: A Review

The first distinction to be made in the field of MPIR concerns the difference between global and marginal increases in risk. For a global increase in risk, the economic environment moves from initial certainty to an uncertain situation. This class of problems has been extensively analyzed by Kraus (1979) and Katz (1981) for one-dimensional utilities and by Drèze and Modigliani (1972) for general utility functions in a two-period context. An important finding, in the one-dimensional environment on which we shall concentrate the discussion, is to present conditions under which all risk averse agents react in a way that is in agreement with intuition. Kraus and Katz derived their results for global increases in risk by considering the following problem:

$$\text{Max}_{\alpha} \; E[U(Z(\alpha, x))] \tag{1.1}$$

where x is a random variable that is degenerate in the initial situation $(x \equiv x_0)$;

U is an increasing and concave utility function of Z;
Z is a payoff function; and
α is a decision variable.

In all reviewed contributions, Z is assumed strictly concave in α. It is assumed that x is an advantageous outcome by taking Z_x to be strictly positive. This arbitrary definition is not at all restrictive. However, we shall keep it in this review to simplify the discussion.

Let us define α^* as the optimal level of the control variable in the initial (here, nonrisky) situation.[1] The assumption that $Z_{\alpha\alpha}$ is always negative ensures that the second-order condition for a maximum is satisfied. When the agent is shifted to uncertainty (for exogenous reasons) from x_0 to x with $E(x) = x_0$, α^{**} will denote his new optimal position which is obtained by solving (1.1). In order to give a sign to $(\alpha^{**}\text{-}\alpha^*)$, Kraus and Katz simply needed to focus on the shape of Z and did not have to restrict U beyond the standard assumptions that $U' > 0$ and $U'' < 0$.

When marginal increases in risk are considered, two risky situations are compared and equation 1.1 becomes the starting point. This can be written:

$$\operatorname*{Max}_{a} \int_{x_2}^{x_3} U(Z(a, x))\, dF(x) \qquad (1.1')$$

where $F(x)$ is the original cumulative distribution function with support in the bounded interval $[x_2, x_3]$. $F(x)$ is assumed here to be continuous, but the following analysis could easily be accommodated for discrete random variables.

In the context of marginal changes in risk, the definition of an MPIR, namely a mean preserving spread, was formulated by Rothschild and Stiglitz (1970). They presented three equivalent definitions of an MPIR. One of them, called the integral condition, is written

(a) $$\int_{x_1}^{x_4} [G(x) - F(x)]\, dx = 0$$

$$(1.2)$$

(b) $$\int_{x_1}^{y} [G(x) - F(x)]\, dx \geqslant 0 \quad \text{for all } y\varepsilon[x_1, x_4]$$

where $G(x)$ is the cumulative distribution function after the exogenous increase in risk; $[x_1, x_4]$ is a bounded interval that contains the support of $G(x)$ with $x_1 \leqslant x_2 \leqslant x_3 \leqslant x_4$.

Specifically, condition (b) indicates that G has more weight in the tails than F, while condition (a) guarantees the equality of the means. One of the major results of Rothschild and Stiglitz (1970) is that a mean preserving spread reduces expected utility under risk aversion, but does not always reduce the optimal level of the risky activity (a^*). This "negative" result has prompted much further research. We concentrate here on the articles whose main focus was the restrictions on the changes from F to G.

In fact, Rothschild and Stiglitz themselves already took a step in that direction by showing that in the comparison between bets satisfying conditions (a) and (b), intuitive comparative statics results emerge in the sense that MPIR reduce both expected utility and the level of the risky activity. Notice, however, that bets represent a very specific case since only two outcomes for x are allowed both in the initial and final situations.[2]

This restriction was nicely removed by Meyer and Ormiston (1983, 1985) in two companion papers where they defined a "strong increase in risk." The basic idea behind the definition is the following: while Rothschild and Stiglitz redistribute probability mass located at a set of points to the right and to the left without restrictions, Meyer and Ormiston require that the shifts to the right and to the left have to be outside (or at the extreme points) of the initial interval of the distribution $F(x)$ [see Meyer and Ormiston (1985), p. 429 for more details]. Formally, a strong increase in risk is obtained by adding the following condition (c) to (a) and (b) in (1.2):

(c) $G(x) - F(x)$ is nonincreasing on (x_2, x_3)
           where support $F(x)$ in contained in $[x_2, x_3]$ (1.3)
           and support $G(x)$ is contained in $[x_1, x_4]$.

This additional condition means that the weight taken from $F(x)$ is never redistributed inside (x_2, x_3) but transferred either to x_2 and x_3 themselves or outside these limits. While the strong increase in risk is obviously a special case of Rothschild and Stiglitz's definition (because of the additional condition c) it results in a generalization of 1) the notion of a global increase in risk, 2) the case of bets, and 3) the concept of a squeeze [Eeckhoudt and Hansen (1980, 1983)].

Despite its advantages, the restriction imposed by Meyer and Ormiston remains rather strong and it is legitimate to try to improve it. This goal was reached by Black and Bulkley (1989) who presented the notion of a "relatively strong increase in risk" to compare risky situations. In their approach, they relax the need to transfer weight from inside the original density to points that are outside or just at its end points. More precisely, they use the idea that an increase in risk should raise the likelihood of the extreme values of the initial density and this is the reason why they consider the behavior of the likelihood ratio function $f(x)/g(x)$ where $f(x)$ and $g(x)$ are the probability density functions associated to F and G. Formally, the definition of a relatively strong increase in risk reads as follows:[3]

(a) $$\int_{x_1}^{x_4} [G(x) - F(x)]\, dx = 0;$$

(b)   For all points in $[x_5, x_6]$, $f(x) \geq g(x)$
           and for all points outside this interval
           $f(x) \leq g(x)$ with $x_1 \leq x_2 \leq x_5 \leq x_6 \leq x_3 \leq x_4$,
           where $[x_1, x_4]$ is defined here as the support of $G(x)$ and
           $[x_2, x_3]$ as the support of $F(x)$;

(c) $\dfrac{f(x)}{g(x)}$ is nondecreasing in the interval $[x_2, x_5)$;   (1.4)

(d) $\dfrac{f(x)}{g(x)}$ is nonincreasing in the interval $(x_6, x_3]$.

Condition (b) means that the weight taken from inside the support of $F(x)$, that is $[x_2, x_3]$, can be sent either outside $[x_5, x_6]$ or, even at its extremities, inside $[x_1, x_4]$. Conditions (c) and (d) specify how the weights sent to the extremities of $F(x)$ have to be allocated. This discussion reveals that the relatively strong increase in risk includes, as a special case, a strong increase in risk. To give an example different from those presented by Black and Bulkley, consider figure 1 in which two triangular densities are compared.

Obviously between x_2 and x_5, $\dfrac{f(x)}{g(x)}$ is increasing and the reverse occurs between x_6 and x_3. Notice that this example satisfies Black and Bulkley's definition without being a strong increase in risk.

After having presented the definition of both a strong increase and a relatively strong increase in risk, we now turn to a general presentation of the results obtained by using them. They can be synthesized in the following theorem:

Theorem 1: If α^* and α^{**} maximize $E[U(Z(\alpha, x))]$ under $F(x)$ and $G(x)$ respectively, sufficient conditions for $\alpha^{**} < \alpha^*$ for all risk-averse decision makers are such that

i) $G(x)$ represents either a strong or a relatively strong increase in risk;
ii) $Z_x \geqslant 0$, $Z_{\alpha x} \geqslant 0$, $Z_{\alpha x x} \leqslant 0$, $Z_{\alpha \alpha} < 0$.

Proof: See the corresponding articles.

Before introducing the insurance model, let us discuss briefly another type of risk increase often used for comparative statics analyses. First proposed by Sandmo (1970, 1971) as a "stretching" of a density around a constant mean , this notion of increasing risk was recently extended by Meyer (1989) and Meyer and Ormiston (1989) who showed that an initial random variable x can be transformed by using a single value function $t(x)$. The transformation $t(x)$ is defined as deterministic to distinguish it from other transformations presented above. Under particular conditions (a nondecreasing, continuous and differentiable function), the transformation $t(x)$ represents an MPIR of the random variable x if the function $k(x) \equiv t(x) - x$ is such that

(a)
$$\int_{x_2}^{x_3} k(x)\, dF(x) = 0$$

$$\tag{1.5}$$

(b)
$$\int_{x_2}^{y} k(x)\, dF(x) \leqslant 0 \quad \text{for all} \quad y\varepsilon[x_2, x_3]$$

As usual, condition (a) preserves the mean of the random variable, while condition (b) is equivalent to the second integral condition intro-

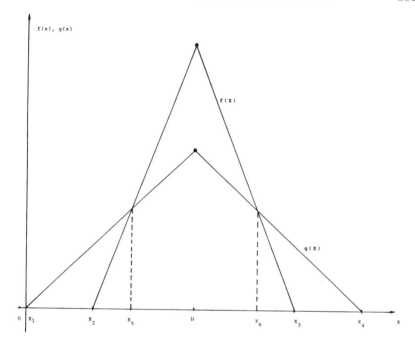

Figure 1. An example of a relatively strong increase in risk.

duced by Rothschild and Stiglitz. To obtain intuitive comparative statics results, the transformation $t(x)$ must be restricted to the case of a simple transformation and conditions on U must be introduced. For instance, linear transformations such as the stretching of Sandmo (1970) or the squeeze of Eeckhoudt and Hansen (1980) are examples of simple deterministic transformations. In fact, Meyer and Ormiston (1989) have proved the following theorem:

Theorem 2: If α^* and α^{**} maximize $EU(Z(\alpha, x))$ under x and $t(x) \equiv x + k(x)$ respectively, sufficient conditions to obtain $\alpha^{**} < \alpha^*$ for all risk averse decision makers are

a) $U(\cdot)$ corresponds to a decreasing (absolute) risk averse function;
b) $Z_x \geqslant 0$, $Z_{xx} \leqslant 0$, $Z_{\alpha x} \geqslant 0$, and $Z_{\alpha xx} \leqslant 0$;
c) $t'(x) \geqslant 0$ and $t(x)$ is a simple increase in risk.

Proof: See Meyer and Ormiston (1989).

It is interesting to observe that theorem 2 contains conditions related to both the utility function and the transformation of the random variable. This suggests that even simple deterministic transformations of random variables represent quite general increases in risk. We are now ready to analyze the demand for insurance.

2. The Coinsurance Model

In this paper, we refer to the classical insurance problem (Mossin, 1968; Briys, Dionne, Eeckhoudt, 1989) in which the individual is endowed with a wealth, W_0, and a risk of damage defined by a random variable x with support contained in the interval $[0, L]$, where L stands for the value of the physical asset submitted to the risk.

To protect himself against this damage, the individual has the opportunity to buy a coinsurance contract paying an indemnity $\alpha x (0 \leq \alpha \leq 1)$ for a fixed premium $P = \lambda \alpha \mu$, where λ is equal to unity plus the loading factor and $\mu \equiv E(x)$.

Given these specifications, the individual's optimization problem is

$$\text{Max}_{\alpha} \; E[U(W_0 - (1 - \alpha)x - \lambda \mu \alpha)] \tag{2.1}$$

with first-order condition

$$E[U'(Z)(x - \lambda \mu)] = 0 \tag{2.2}$$

where Z stands for the value of final wealth. Strict concavity of U guarantees that the second-order condition for a maximum is satisfied. Notice also that the value of λ will always be such that the optimal α that solves (2.2) is an interior solution for all transformations of the distribution function.

At this stage, it is worth pointing out the differences between the present problem and those presented in the preceding section. A major distinction concerns the sign of $Z_{\alpha\alpha}$. In the two models that are the closest to our own problem [Meyer and Ormiston (1985), and Black and Bulkley (1989)], $Z_{\alpha\alpha}$ needs to be strictly negative in order to derive theorem 1 (see especially p. 431 in Meyer and Ormiston and the definition of b* in Black and Bulkley, p. 126). Of course, in our problem $Z_{\alpha\alpha}$ is equal to zero. However, as we shall see this difference will not preclude the applicability of both Black and Bulkley's and Meyer and Ormiston's conditions to obtain comparative statics results.[4]

Other differences are given in table 1. The second difference, which results from the fact that x is a damage, is unimportant since it only alters the type of proof. Condition (3) in the insurance problem will be useful in the proof of our main result while it seems unimportant in theorem 1.

Table 1. Comparison between conditions of Theorem 1 and characteristics of the insurance problem

Conditions of Theorem 1	Characteristics of the insurance problem
1 $Z_{aa} > 0$	$Z_{aa} = 0$
2 $Z_x \geq 0$	$Z_x < 0$
3 ----	$Z_{xx} = 0$
4 $Z_{ax} \geq 0$	$Z_{ax} = 1$
5 $Z_{axx} \leq 0$	$Z_{axx} = 0$

The last two conditions illustrate other specific aspects of the insurance problem.

3. Increases in Risk and the Demand for Insurance

Proposition: If a^* and a^{**} maximize $E[U(Z(x, a))]$ under $F(x)$ and $G(x)$ respectively, sufficient conditions to obtain a greater insurance coverage $(a^{**} > a^*)$ for all risk-averse decision makers are such that
  i) $G(x)$ represents a relatively strong increase in risk;
  ii) $Z(x, a)$ is linear in a and x.

Proof: The proof starts from the first order condition corresponding to the initial density $f(x)$

$$E[U'(Z) \cdot (x - \lambda\mu)] = 0. \tag{3.2}$$

Under the new density $g(x)$, one has to show that the above expression evaluated at a^* is positive. Consequently, we want to show that

$$\int_0^L U'(Z)(x - \lambda\mu)s(x)\,dx > 0 \tag{3.3}$$

where $s(x) \equiv g(x) - f(x)$ is positive (negative) whenever the likelihood ratio $\dfrac{f(x)}{g(x)}$ is less (greater) than 1.

To establish (3.3), one has to consider three cases: (i) $x_5 \leq \lambda\mu \leq x_6$; (ii) $x_5 \geq \lambda\mu$; (iii) $\lambda\mu \geq x_6$. We shall restrict ourselves to cases (i) and (iii) since the proof can be repeated with appropriate modifications for the other case.

For case (i), we can rewrite (3.3) as[5]

$$\int_0^{x_5} U'(Z)(x - \lambda\mu)s(x)\,dx + \int_{x_5}^{\lambda\mu} U'(Z)(x - \lambda\mu)s(x)\,dx$$

$$+ \int_{\lambda\mu}^{x_6} U'(Z)(x - \lambda\mu)s(x)\,dx + \int_{x_6}^{L} U'(Z) \cdot (x - \lambda\mu)s(x)\,dx > 0$$

$$(3.4)$$

where Z stands for $Z(\alpha, x)$. From the definition of a relatively strong increase in risk, the integrands in (3.4) alternate in sign starting with a negative, as can be seen from figure 2 where $\lambda\mu$ happens to lie in the interval $[x_5, x_6]$.

Because $U'(Z)$ is *increasing* in x when $\alpha^* < 1$, the left-hand side of (3.4) is greater than

$$U'(Z_5)\left[\int_0^{\lambda\mu} (x - \lambda\mu)s(x)\,dx\right] + U'(Z_6)\left[\int_{\lambda\mu}^{L} (x - \lambda\mu)s(x)\,dx\right] \qquad (3.5)$$

where $Z_i = W_0 - x_i + \alpha^* x_i - \lambda\mu\alpha^*$, $i = 5,6$.

The sum of the two expressions in brackets is clearly equal to zero. Indeed

$$\int_0^{L} (x - \lambda\mu)s(x)\,dx = \int_0^{L} x s(x)\,dx - \lambda\mu \int_0^{L} s(x)\,dx \qquad (3.6)$$

and the two terms on the right-hand side of (3.6) are zero because of the definition of a mean preserving increase in risk.[6]

To complete the proof, since $U'(Z_5) < U'(Z_6)$, we now show that the first bracket in (3.5) is negative. Integrating by parts, one obtains

$$\int_0^{\lambda\mu} (x - \lambda\mu)s(x)\,dx = (x - \lambda\mu)S(x)\Big|_0^{\lambda\mu} - \int_0^{\lambda\mu} S(x)\,dx$$

$$= -\int_0^{\lambda\mu} S(x)\,dx, \qquad (3.7)$$

which is negative by the definition of a relatively weak increase in risk.

Q.E.D.

Figure 2 gives an example with the following two triangular densities:

$$g(x) = 1/25x \qquad\qquad 0 \leqslant x \leqslant 5 = \mu$$
$$\quad\;\; = -1/25x + 2/5 \quad \mu = 5 \leqslant x \leqslant 10 = L$$

$$f(x) = 1/9x - 2/9 \qquad x_2 = 2 \leqslant x \leqslant 5 = \mu$$
$$\quad\;\; = -1/9x + 8/9 \qquad \mu = 5 \leqslant x \leqslant 8 = x_3$$

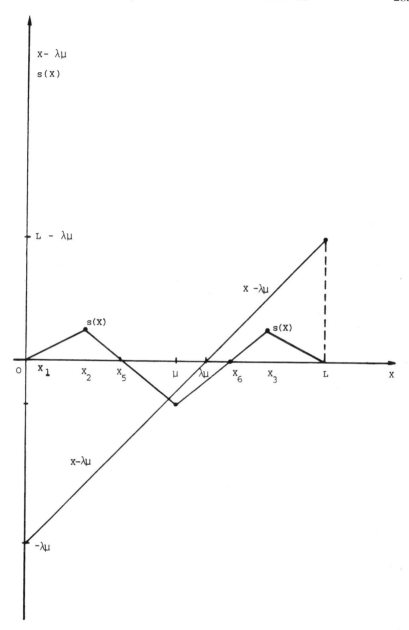

Figure 2. Representation of the $s(X)$ and $(X-\lambda\mu)$ functions when densities are triangular and the payoff is linear.

Since $s(x) \equiv g(x) - f(x)$, $s(x)$ is negative in the interval $[x_5, x_6]$ and positive otherwise, which is in accordance with condition (b) in the definition of a relatively strong increase in risk (1.4).

Remark: It is interesting to notice that when $\lambda\mu$ lies in the interval $[x_5, x_6]$ neither condition (c) nor condition (d) in (1.4) are necessary to prove the desired result. In the Appendix we show explicitly how condition (d) is useful for the case $x_6 \leqslant \lambda\mu$ and the reader can verify that condition (c) has a symmetric role for the case $x_5 \geqslant \lambda\mu$. Finally, since the Meyer and Ormiston's definition of increasing risk implies that $x_5 = x_2$ and $x_6 = x_3$, $\lambda\mu$ lies, by definition, in the interval $[x_2, x_3]$.

After having made the proof for marginal changes in risk, a few words about a global increase in risk are in order. If $F(x)$ were a degenerate distribution with probability 1 at x_0 inside $[0, L]$, it is clear that a risk-averse individual would never buy nonactuarial insurance so that a corner solution ($\alpha^* = 0$) prevails. The transition from certainty to uncertainty (with distribution $G(x)$) will necessarily create a positive insurance demand for a risk-averse agent if λ is not prohibitive ($\lambda < \bar{\lambda}$). Hence, theorem 3 also applies for a global increase in risk despite the fact that $Z_{\alpha\alpha}$ equals zero.

Finally, we can apply directly the definition of deterministic transformations of random variables to the coinsurance problem and obtain the result that a risk-averse individual with decreasing absolute risk aversion will increase α from α^* to α^{**} if a simple increase in risk is applied to the initial random variable. This result can easily be verified since the characteristics of the payoff function in the coinsurance problem (given in table 1) satisfy the conditions of theorem 2. (Let us remember that condition 2 in table 1 is unimportant to get the desired results.)

Conclusion

In the same manner as restrictions on the shift from F to G are substitutes to restrictions on U to obtain intuitively comparative statics results, this paper has shown that restricting the class of the payoff functions to a linear one did not preclude the applicability of well-know theorems to the demand for insurance.

This general conclusion, applied here to the coinsurance problem, can of course be extended to other problems with a linear payoff such as the simple portfolio problem or the competitive firm under uncertainty with constant marginal costs [see Dionne and Eeckhoudt (1990)]. Another potential extension concerns other forms of insurance contracts. An example is the choice of the optimal deductible that involves kinked linear payoffs.

Notes

1. When the initial situation is nonrisky, (1.1) amounts to: $\underset{a}{\text{Max}}\ U(Z(a, x_0))$ where x_0 is the degenerate value of x.

2. For example, in the insurance problem that will be analyzed in detail in the next section, two sufficient restrictions to obtain the result that a risk averse individual will demand a greater insurance coverage when the distribution of losses becomes riskier (mean preserving spread) is either because U is quadratic or because the random variable can take only two values: no loss with probability $(1 - p)$ and a positive loss with probability p.

3. As pointed out by Black and Bulkley (1989), (a) and (b) in (1.4) are sufficient for $G(x)$ to represent a mean preserving spread in the Rothschild and Stiglitz sense. Moreover, as we shall see in section 3, conditions (c) and (d) are not always required to obtain the desired results of comparative statics analysis.

4. See Dionne and Eeckhoudt (1990) for a more general discussion.

5. The proof of case (iii) is presented in the Appendix.

6. Let us notice that the assumption Z_{xx} plays its role here. Indeed, $Z_{xx} = 0$ implies that the expression on the left-hand side of (3.6) can easily be evaluated.

References

Black, J. M., and G. Bulkley. (1989). "A Ratio Criterion for Signing the Effects of an Increase in Uncertainty," *International Economic Review* 30, 119–130.

Briys, E., Dionne, G. and L. Eeckhoudt. (1989). "More on Insurance as a Giffen Good," *Journal of Risk and Uncertainty* 2, 415–420.

Diamond, P. A., and J. E. Stiglitz. (1974). "Increase in Risk and in Risk Aversion," *Journal of Economic Theory* 8, 333–361.

Dionne, G., and L. Eeckhoudt. (1987). "Proportional Risk Aversion, Taxation and Labour Supply Under Uncertainty," *Journal of Economics* 47, 353–366.

Dionne, G., and L. Eeckhoudt. (1990). "Increases in Risk and Linear Payoffs," Working paper, Economics Department and C.R.T., Université de Montréal.

Dionne, G., L. Eeckhoudt and E. Briys. (1989). "Proportional Risk Aversion and Saving Decisions Under Uncertainty," in Henri Loubergé (ed.), *Risk, Information and Insurance*. Boston: Kluwer Academic Publishers.

Drèze, J., and F. Modigliani. (1972). "Consumption Decisions Under Uncertainty," *Journal of Economic Theory* 5, 308–335.

Eeckhoudt, L., and P. Hansen. (1980). "Minimum and Maximum Prices,

Uncertainty and the Theory of the Competitive Firm," *American Economic Review* 70, 1064–1068.

Eeckhoudt, L., and P. Hansen. (1983). "Micro-economic Applications of Marginal Changes in Risk," *European Economic Review* 22, 167–176.

Eeckhoudt, L., and P. Hansen. (1984). "Mean-Preserving Changes in Risk with Tail-Dominance," Working paper #8413, Economics Department, Université de Montréal.

Katz, E. (1981). "A Note on a Comparative Statics Theorem for Choice under Risk," *Journal of Economic Theory* 25, 318–319.

Kraus, M. (1979a). "A Comparative Statics Theorem for Choice under Risk," *Journal of Economic Theory* 21, 510–517.

Meyer, J. (1989). "Stochastic Dominance and Transformations of Random Variables." In Thomas B. Fomby and Tae Kun Seo (eds.), *Studies in the Economics of Uncertainty: In Honor of Josef Hadar*. New York: Springer Verlag.

Meyer, J., and M. B. Ormiston. (1983). "The Comparative Statics of Cumulative Distribution Function Changes for the Class of Risk Averse Agents," *Journal of Economic Theory* 31, 153–169.

Meyer, J., and M. B. Ormiston. (1985). "Strong Increases in Risk and their Comparative Statics," *International Economics Review* 26, 425–437.

Meyer, J., and M. B. Ormiston. (1989). "Deterministic Transformations of Random Variables and the Comparative Statics of Risk," *Journal of Risk and Uncertainty* 2, 179–188.

Mossin, J. (1968). "Aspects of Rational Insurance Purchasing," *Journal of Political Economy* 76, 553–568.

Rothschild, M., and J. Stiglitz. (1970). "Increasing Risk I: A Definition," *Journal of Economic Theory* 2, 225–243.

Rothschild, M., and J. Stiglitz. (1971). "Increasing Risk II: Its Economic Consequences," *Journal of Economic Theory* 3, 66–84.

Sandmo, A. (1970). "The Effects of Uncertainty on Saving Decisions," *Review of Economic Studies* 37, 353–360.

Sandmo, A. (1971). "On the Theory of the Competitive Firm under Price Uncertainty," *American Economic Review* 61, 65–73.

Appendix

Proof for the case in which $\lambda\mu \geq x_6$

We have to show that

$$\int_0^L U'(Z)(x - \lambda\mu)\,s(x)\,dx > 0. \tag{A.1}$$

Let us first consider the case in which

$$\int_{x_6}^{L} (x - \lambda\mu) s(x) \, dx > 0.$$

Equation (3.6) in the text implies

$$\int_{0}^{x_6} (x - \lambda\mu) s(x) \, dx < 0$$

and the proof in the text gives the desired result without any additional condition. This is true since (A.1) is greater than the following positive expression:

$$U'(Z_5) \left[\int_{0}^{x_6} (x - \lambda\mu) s(x) \, dx \right] + U'(Z_{\lambda\mu}) \left[\int_{x_6}^{L} (x - \lambda\mu) s(x) \, dx \right].$$

When

$$\int_{x_6}^{L} (x - \lambda\mu) s(x) \, dx < 0 \qquad (A.2)$$

we have to introduce condition (d) in (1.4) to get the desired result.

To see this, let us first notice that (A.2) implies

$$\int_{0}^{x_6} (x - \lambda\mu) s(x) \, dx > 0$$

and, consequently,

$$\int_{0}^{x_6} U'(Z)(x - \lambda\mu) s(x) \, dx > 0$$

Therefore, by definition,

$$\int_{0}^{L} U'(Z)(x - \lambda\mu) s(x) \, dx > \int_{x_6}^{L} U'(Z)(x - \lambda\mu) s(x) \, dx. \qquad (A.3)$$

To complete the proof we now show that the right-hand side of (A.3) is positive. This expression can be rewritten as

$$\int_{x_6}^{x_3} U'(Z)(x - \lambda\mu) s(x) \, dx + \int_{x_3}^{L} U'(Z)(x - \lambda\mu) s(x) \, dx. \qquad (A.4)$$

The second term in (A.4) is nonnegative. The first integral is equal to

$$\int_{x_6}^{x_3} U'(Z)(x - \lambda\mu)(r(x) - 1) f(x) \, dx$$

where $r(x) \equiv \dfrac{g(x)}{f(x)}$. Condition (d) in (1.4) implies that

$$\int_{x_6}^{x_3} U'(Z)(x - \lambda\mu)(r(x) - 1)f(x)\,dx >$$

$$(r(\lambda\mu) - 1) \int_{x_6}^{x_3} U'(Z)(x - \lambda\mu)f(x)\,dx.$$

Finally, since by (3.2)

$$\int_{x_2}^{x_3} U'(Z)(x - \lambda\mu)f(x)\,dx = 0$$

it follows that

$$\int_{x_6}^{x_3} U'(Z)(x - \lambda\mu)f(x)\,dx > 0,$$

which completes the proof, since $r(\lambda\mu) > 1$ by definition of a relatively strong increase in risk.

Q.E.D.

CROP INSURANCE IN INCOMPLETE MARKETS

Bharat Ramaswami

University of Minnesota

Terry L. Roe

University of Minnesota

Abstract

When there are multiple risks threatening the loss of an asset, insurance schemes contingent on one risk alone are incomplete. Such is the case with crop insurance schemes when price variability is uninsured. This paper considers the effect of price risk on crop insurance decisions when price risk is due to supply-and-demand shocks. If demand shocks satisfy the principle of increasing uncertainty, increasing demand uncertainty reduces optimal crop insurance whenever risk aversion is constant or decreasing. In fact, the insurance is so limited for decreasing risk-averse individuals that they strictly prefer those states of the world in which no indemnity is forthcoming to those in which they receive indemnities. Special cases arise when either output risk or demand uncertainty is the sole cause of price risk. In the first case, the optimal insurance is complete even though price variability affects the demand for crop insurance through the correlation between price and output. In the second case, the principle of increasing uncertainty is trivially satisfied and price risk affects optimal insurance levels even though it is independent of output risk.

* We thank Theodore Graham-Tomasi, Harris Schlesinger, and Jan Werner for valuable discussions and criticisms. We are also indebted to an anonymous referee and Georges Dionne for comments that have improved the paper. The first author gratefully acknowledges the support of a Doctoral Dissertation Fellowship from the Graduate School of the University of Minnesota.

Key words: multiple risks, risk markets, price risk, crop insurance, insurance compensation incomplete markets.

In recent years, researchers have directed their attention to the analysis of insurance schemes in economies that do not possess a full set of risk markets. Since complete market economies exist only as allegorical entities, the study of incompleteness enriches the theory of insurance.

This paper examines crop insurance decisions in economies with incomplete risk markets. While economic activity in agriculture is subject to a variety of risks, crop insurance is a claim contingent only on states of output. If the markets for other agricultural risks are absent, insurance decisions have to be taken against the background of uninsurable risks. In this paper, we take price risk to be the principal example of the "other agricultural risks" for which markets may be absent. The objective is to investigate the effect of price risk on crop insurance decisions.

To motivate the key issues, consider the following example. Suppose that the output of a farmer is either one hundred bushels (of say, corn) with probability 0.6, or sixty bushels with probability 0.4. The insurance compensation is the physical loss of 40 bushels valued at the "price election."[1] The problem is to choose the price election (and hence the amount of insurance) at the beginning of the planting season when price and output are unknown. Now compare the choice of price election in two situations that differ only with respect to the extent of price uncertainty. In the first case, the output price is known with certainty to be $2.00 per bushel. In the second case, the output price could be $3.00 per bushel or $1.00 per bushel, with equal probability. So the expected output price is $2.00 per bushel. In which instance, will the farmer buy more insurance? Or could it be that the choice of the price-election is unaffected by price risk?

These questions cannot be resolved in models of agricultural insurance where only output risk is present (Ahsan, Ali, and Kurian (1982), Nelson and Loehman (1987)). It is, however, well known that if price and output are negatively correlated, the resulting natural hedge will reduce the demand for crop insurance. In the above example, though, price and output are independently distributed random variables. Assuming a constant absolute risk aversion coefficient of 0.003, part A of the appendix calculates the optimal insurance to be $80.00 when price is known to be $2.00 but is only $70.40 in the second case when prices are uncertain. Price risk seems to matter even when it is independent of output risk.

So what exactly is the relationship between price risk and crop insurance decisions? To answer the question the next section presents a model in which price variability is caused by output fluctuations and demand shocks. Since crop insurance is contingent only on output risk, demand shocks constitute a source of incompleteness in the insurance scheme. Section 2 examines the effect of incompleteness on the optimal amount of insurance. Two special cases, considered in section 3, arise when either demand uncertainty or output risk is the sole cause of price risk. In the first case, price risk is independent of output risk and for an important class of utility functions, it is shown that price risk affects crop insurance decisions in the manner of the above numerical example. If, on the other hand, price risk is completely induced by output shocks then the optimal insurance is complete even though price variability affects the demand for crop insurance through the correlation between price and output. This is because incompleteness is the consequence of an independent source of risk additional to output risk. In section 4, the change in optimality conditions (as compared to complete insurance schemes) is examined from the point of view of potential moral hazard. The last section discusses the implications of the results and its applicability to other insurance schemes.

1. A Model of Incomplete Insurance

1.1. Output and Price Distributions

The insurance decision of a risk-averse farmer is considered in a simple stylized world in which price and output risk are the only sources of uncertainty. Suppose that output has a subjective probability distribution of the following form:

$$q = \begin{cases} Q_1 \text{ with probability } (1 - \gamma) \\ Q_2 \text{ with probability } \gamma \end{cases} \tag{1}$$

where q is output. Without loss of generality we can assume $Q_1 > Q_2$.

In competitive markets, price variability can be attributed to shifts in either the demand curve or the supply curve or to a combination of the two.[2] Even if supply-and-demand shocks are independent, the subjective probability distributions of output and price need not be independent for an individual farmer. Crop hazards such as drought, floods, and hailstorms affect many farmers in a particular geographical area and so their outputs are likely to be positively correlated. A price-taking farmer may

therefore view the probability distribution of price as conditional on
output.

Let θ be a random demand shock independent of the output realization and suppose that it is a two-point distribution taking the value θ_1
with probability λ and the value θ_2 with probability $(1 - \lambda)$. Due to these
demand shocks the price conditional on an output realization is itself
random. More specifically,

$$P|Q_i = \begin{cases} P(Q_i, \theta_1) \text{ with probability } \lambda \\ P(Q_i, \theta_2) \text{ with probability } (1 - \lambda) \end{cases} \quad \text{for } i = 1, 2 \quad (2)$$

where $P(Q_i, \theta_j)$ is the output price conditioned on the output realization
Q_i and demand realization θ_j. Without loss of generality, we can assume
θ_1 is the favorable demand shock, i.e., $P(Q_i, \theta_1) > P(Q_i, \theta_2)$ for $i = 1, 2$.

The value of output is a random variable w distributed as

$$w = \begin{cases} W_1 \equiv W(Q_1, \theta_1) = P(Q_1, \theta_1)Q_1 \text{ with probability } (1 - \gamma)\lambda \\ W_2 \equiv W(Q_1, \theta_2) = P(Q_1, \theta_2)Q_1 \text{ with probability } (1 - \gamma)(1 - \lambda) \\ W_3 \equiv W(Q_2, \theta_1) = P(Q_2, \theta_1)Q_2 \text{ with probability } \gamma\lambda \\ W_4 \equiv W(Q_2, \theta_2) = P(Q_2, \theta_2)Q_2 \text{ with probability } \gamma(1 - \lambda) \end{cases} \quad (3)$$

Since θ_1 corresponds to the higher price, crop revenue can be order in
one of two ways. Either $W_1 > W_2 > W_3 > W_4$ or $W_1 > W_3 > W_2 > W_4$.

1.2. Insurance

As the state of the world is the two-tuple (q, θ) a complete insurance
contract would be contingent on q and θ. Since crop insurance contracts
are contigent on output alone, the demand shock θ is the source of
incompleteness. Let I be the indemnity, which is payable only if the event
Q_2 occurs. We suppose the insurance firm is risk neutral and offers
actuarially fair insurance.[3] So the premium is γI.

Denoting r as the revenue with insurance, we have

$$r = \begin{cases} R_1 \equiv R(Q_1, \theta_1) = P(Q_1, \theta_1)Q_1 - \gamma I \text{ with probability } (1 - \gamma)\lambda \\ R_2 \equiv R(Q_1, \theta_2) = P(Q_1, \theta_2)Q_1 - \gamma I \text{ with probability } (1 - \gamma)(1 - \lambda) \\ R_3 \equiv R(Q_2, \theta_1) = P(Q_2, \theta_1)Q_2 + (1 - \gamma)I \text{ with probability } \gamma\lambda \\ R_4 \equiv R(Q_2, \theta_2) = P(Q_2, \theta_2)Q_2 + (1 - \gamma)I \text{ with probability } \\ \gamma(1 - \lambda), \end{cases} \quad (4)$$

since θ_1 is associated with a higher price compared to θ_2, $R_1 > R_2$ and
$R_3 > R_4$. A complete ordering of incomes is not possible without further
information about I.

1.3. Conditions for Interior Solution

From the set of actuarially fair contracts the optimal insurance is found by maximizing the expectation of an increasing and strictly concave von Neumann-Morgenstern utility function.

$$\underset{I}{\text{Max }} \eta(I) = (1 - \gamma)\lambda U(R_1) + (1 - \gamma)(1 - \lambda)U(R_2)$$
$$+ \gamma\lambda U(R_3) + \gamma(1 - \lambda)U(R_4)$$

The optimal level of insurance is positive if $\eta'(I)$ evaluated at $I = 0$ is also positive.[4] Now

$$\eta'(I) = \gamma(1 - \gamma)\{\lambda U'(R_3) + (1 - \lambda)U'(R_4)$$
$$- \lambda U'(R_1) - (1 - \lambda)U'(R_2)\} \tag{5}$$

and since $R_k|_{I=0} = W_k$

$$\eta'(I)|_{I=0} = \gamma(1 - \gamma)\{\gamma(U'(W_3) - U'(W_1))$$
$$+ (1 - \lambda)(U'(W_4) - U'(W_2))\} \tag{6}$$

A sufficient condition for I to be positive is for W_1 to be greater than W_3 and for W_2 to be greater than W_4. This can be described more compactly by the following notation.

Let $\delta w(\theta) \equiv W(Q_1, \theta) - W(Q_2, \theta)$. δw is the revenue loss (for a given state of demand θ) when the output Q_2 is realized. Then optimal insurance is positive if $\delta w(\theta_1) > 0$ and $\delta w(\theta_2) > 0$

The above condition simply says that, in the absence of insurance, the farmer's revenue is higher when output is higher irrespective of what demand state is realized. If the price-output correlations are sufficiently negative the condition may not be satisfied and the optimal insurance may be zero or even negative.[5]

1.4. The Principle of Increasing Uncertainty

An essential assumption of the analysis is that the random demand shocks are such that $\delta w(\theta_1) > \delta w(\theta_2)$, i.e., the revenue loss is higher in the favorable demand state θ_1.[6] The assumption is equivalent to the *principle of increasing uncertainty*, which may be stated as follows: if increases in output lead to higher expected revenue, then increases in output also lead to greater riskiness of revenue. Thus, if $W(Q_1, \theta)$ has a higher mean revenue than $W(Q_2, \theta)$, then $W(Q_1, \theta)$ is also riskier than $W(Q_2, \theta)$. The equivalence of the assumption $\delta w(\theta_1) > \delta w(\theta_2)$ with the principle of increasing uncertainty is demonstrated in part B of the appendix. The principle of increasing uncertainty was first stated by Leland (1972) who used it to demonstrate the impact of demand uncertainty on firms' output decisions.[7]

2. The Effect of Demand Uncertainty

Proposition 1: Let I^* be the optimal amount of insurance. If the demand shocks satisfy the principle of increasing uncertainty, $R_1(I^*) > R_3(I^*) > R_4(I^*) > R_2(I^*)$ or equivalently $\delta w(\theta_1) > I^* > \delta w(\theta_2)$.

Proof: From (4) note that $R_3 > R_4$ for all I. So what needs to be shown is $R_1(I^*) > R_3(I^*)$ and $R_4(I^*) > R_2(I^*)$.

The optimal insurance satisfies

$$\eta'(I^*) = \gamma(1 - \gamma)\{\lambda U'(R_3^*) + (1 - \lambda)U'(R_4^*) - \lambda U'(R_1^*) - (1 - \lambda)U'(R_2^*)\} = 0 \tag{7}$$

where R_j^* denotes $R_j(I^*)$ for $j = 1, \cdots 4$.

Let $\eta_1(I) \equiv U'(R_3) - U'(R_1)$ and $\eta_2(I) \equiv U'(R_2) - U'(R_4)$.

Substituting and rearranging terms, (7) becomes

$$\lambda\eta_1'(I^*) - (1 - \lambda)\eta_2(I^*) = 0 \tag{8}$$

Clearly $\eta_1(I^*)$ and $\eta_2(I^*)$ must both be of the same sign. Suppose they are both negative.

$$\eta_1 < 0 \Rightarrow R_3^* > R_1^* \Rightarrow W(Q_2, \theta_1) + (1 - \gamma)I^* > W(Q_1, \theta_1) - \gamma I^*,$$
$$\text{and so } I^* > \delta W(\theta_1). \tag{9}$$

$$\eta_2 < 0 \Rightarrow R_2^* > R_4^* \Rightarrow W(Q_1, \theta_2) - \gamma I^* > W(Q_2, \theta_2) + (1 - \gamma I^*),$$
$$\text{and so } I^* < \delta W(\theta_2). \tag{10}$$

Combining the two inequalities, $\delta w(\theta_2) > I^* > \delta w(\theta_1)$. But this contradicts the assumption that θ_1 and θ_2 are such that $\delta w(\theta_1) > \delta w(\theta_2)$. Similarly, η_1 and η_2 cannot both be zero. Hence η_1 and η_2 are positive. This means $R_3^* < R_1^*$ and $R_2^* < R_4^*$. Since $R_3^* < R_4^*$, we obtain the ordering $R_1^* > R_3^* > R_4^* > R_2^*$. Notice also that the inequalities in (9) and (10) are reversed, and so we obtain upper and lower bounds on the amount of optimal insurance, i.e., $\delta w(\theta_1) > I^* > \delta w(\theta_2)$.

The complete ordering of the R_j's is a direct consequence of the first-order condition and the principle of increasing uncertainty. Recall, that in the absence of insurance, we know that either $W_1 > W_2 > W_3 >$

W_4 or $W_1 > W_3 > W_2 > W_4$. In either case the worst income state is W_4 when both price and output are low. With insurance, however, the ordering changes in a significant way. Now the worst income state is R_2, when price is low but output is high. In this state, premium payments have to be made, even though the farmer suffers losses due to low prices. For the farmer, the incomplete nature of insurance creates a difficult trade-off between output and price risks. While output risks are clearly reduced, the farmer is worse off in the low price-high output state R_2. Further the fact that R_2 *decreases with greater pruchase of insurance,* *suggests that I^** cannot be too high. The argument is made more precise in the following propositions.

Proposition 2: If the principle of increasing uncertainty is satisfied and if risk aversion is nonincreasing, the optimal insurance is strictly less than expected value of crop loss.

Proof: The proof consists in showing $\eta'(I)$ to be negative for all values of I greater than or equal to the expected value of crop loss.[8]

Let $\bar{p}|Q_1$ denote the expected price when output is Q_1 and let $\bar{p}|Q_2$ denote the expected price when output is Q_2. Then the expected value of crop loss is $E[\delta w(\theta)] = (\bar{p}|Q_1)Q_1 - (\bar{p}|Q_2)Q_2$.

Let $r_G(\theta)$ denote the random income in the high crop output "good" states and $r_B(\theta)$ the random income in the low crop output "bad" states, i.e.,

$$r_G(\theta) = (p|Q_1)Q_1 - \gamma I$$

$$= \begin{cases} R_1 = P(Q_1, \theta_1)Q_1 - \gamma I \text{ with probability } \lambda \\ R_2 = P(Q_1, \theta_2)Q_1 - \gamma I \text{ with probability } (1 - \lambda) \end{cases} \quad (11)$$

and

$$r_B(\theta) = (p|Q_2)Q_2 + (1 - \gamma I)$$

$$= \begin{cases} R_3 = P(Q_2, \theta_1)Q_2 + (1 - \gamma)I \text{ with probability } \lambda \\ R_4 = P(Q_2, \theta_2)Q_2 + (1 - \gamma)I \text{ with probability } (1 - \lambda) \end{cases} \quad (12)$$

Then from (5), (11) and (12), $\eta'(I)$ can be written more compactly as

$$\eta'(I) = \gamma(1 - \gamma)\{E^\theta U'(r_G(\theta)) - E^\theta U'(r_B(\theta))\} \quad (13)$$

where the superscript on the expectations operator denotes that the expectations are with respect to the distribution of demand shock θ. The sign of $\eta'(I)$ therefore, depends on the difference in expected marginal utilities between the low and high crop states. Now, $r_G(Q_1, \theta)$ —

$r_B(Q_2, \theta) = \delta w(\theta) - I$. So $E^\theta U'(r_G(\theta)) = E^\theta U'(r_B(\theta) + \delta w(\theta) - I)$. Let $v(\theta) = \delta w(\theta) - E[\delta w(\theta)]$. Clearly $E^\theta v(\theta) = 0$ and since $\delta W(\theta_1) > \delta W(\theta_2)$, $v(\theta_1) > 0$ and $v(\theta_2) < 0$.

Substituting, $\quad EU'(r_G) = EU'(r_B + v + E[\delta w(\theta)] - I)$.

If $I \geq E[\delta w(\theta)]$, $E^\theta U'(r_G) \geq E^\theta U'(r_B + v) > E^\theta U'(r_{BL})$ where the second inequality follows from the convexity of marginal utility ($U''' > 0$)[9] and from the observation that $r_B + v$ is a mean preserving spread of r_G. Therefore, the optimal insurance is less than the expected value of crop loss.

The result for the certainty case is the following:

Proposition 3: If the price conditional on an output realization is certain and equal to its conditional expectation, then the optimal insurance is equal to the expected value of crop loss.

Proof: If demand uncertainty vanishes such that $P(Q_1, \theta_1) = P(Q_1, \theta_2) = \bar{p}|Q_1$ and $P(Q_2, \theta_1) = P(Q_2, \theta_2) = \bar{p}|Q_2$, then $R_1 = R_2$ and $R_3 = R_4$. First-order condition (7) reduces to $U'(R_1) = U'(R_3)$. Therefore, $I^* = (\bar{p}|Q_1)Q_1 - (\bar{p}|Q_2)Q_2$.

If we refer to $(\bar{p}|Q_1)Q_1 - (\bar{p}|Q_2)Q_2$ as the certainty level of insurance, then proposition 2 proves that optimal level of insurance under demand uncertainty is less than the certainty level of insurance. The next proposition is concerned with the marginal impact of demand uncertainty, i.e., the effect of making the conditional price distribution slightly more risky.

Proposition 4: If the principle of increasing uncertainty is satisfied and if risk aversion is constant or decreasing, an increase in demand uncertainty reduces optimal insurance.

The proof is in part C of the appendix.

3. Two Special Cases

In the earlier section, price variability was the consequence of supply and demand shocks, i.e., $p = p(q, \theta)$. Two special cases of this formulation are when $p = p(q)$ and $p = p(\theta)$. In the first case, all the price variability is due to output fluctuations. In the second case, all price variability is due to demand uncertainty, which leads to price risk being independent of output risk.

3.1. Price Risk Due to Output Variability

Output q has a two outcome distribution given by (1). If there is no demand risk, price is also a two-outcome distribution with

$$p = \begin{cases} P(Q_1) \text{ with probability } (1 - \gamma) \\ P(Q_2) \text{ with probability } \gamma \end{cases} \tag{14}$$

Then it is not difficult to see that $I^* = P(Q_1)Q_1 - P(Q_2)Q_2$, i.e., the optimal amount of insurance is simply the value of the crop loss.[10]

Clearly, price variability affects the optimal value of insurance. More specifically, the optimal insurance depends on the correlation between price and output. But the optimal insurance is not incomplete. There is only one source of risk in the model. Price variability is completely induced by supply variability for which insurance is available. So the insurance scheme is complete. The incompleteness in crop insurance is not a consequence of price variability per se but rather it is due to the presence of a source of uninsurable risk (demand uncertainty) different from output risk.

3.2. Price Risk Due to Demand Uncertainty

Let $P(\theta_1) \equiv P_1$ and $P(\theta_2) \equiv P_2$. Then

$$p = \begin{cases} P_2 \text{ with probability } \lambda \\ P_2 \text{ with probability } (1 - \lambda) \end{cases} \tag{15}$$

where without loss of generality, we assume $P_1 > P_2$.

If price and output are independent, it is not necessary to assume the principle of increasing uncertainty as it is trivially true.[11] So by proposition 2, the optimal insurance is less than the expected revenue loss for all constant and decreasing risk aversion utility functions. This explains the comparisions of optimal insurance levels in the example in the introduction.

4. Incentive Implications

The effect of demand uncertainty on the optimal crop insurance can also be seen in another way. In the absence of demand shocks, it is optimal to equalize the farmer's income across the two output states of nature. The individual is consequently indifferent between them. What can we infer when insurance is incomplete, i.e., is $E^\theta U(r_G) \gtreqless E^\theta U(r_B)$?

Proposition 5: If the demand shocks satisfy the principle of increasing uncertainty, then

(i) $E^\theta U(r_G(\theta)) > E^\theta U(r_B(\theta))$ for decreasing absolute risk aversion utility functions

(ii) $E^\theta U(r_G(\theta)) = E^\theta U(r_B(\theta))$ for constant absolute risk aversion utility functions

(iii) $E^\theta U(r_G(\theta)) < E^\theta U(r_B(\theta))$ for increasing absolute risk aversion utility functions

Proof: Define the inverse of the marginal utility function by $z : z \equiv (U')^{-1}$. Also define ϕ as the composite function of U and $z : \phi = U \circ z$. Denoting by α a value of marginal utility of income the following relation holds $\phi(\alpha) = U(z(\alpha))$.

Lemma: $\phi''(\alpha)$ is greater than, equal to, or less than zero depending on whether the utility function exhibits decreasing, constant, or increasing absolute risk aversion.

Proof of lemma: See Imai, Geanakoplos, and Ito (1981).

From the first-order condition $E^\theta U'(r_G) = E^\theta U'(r_B)$. From proposition 1, we also know $U'(R_2^*) > U'(R_4^*) > U'(R_3^*) > U'(R_1^*)$. At the optimum, therefore, $U'(r_G)$ is a mean preserving spread of $U'(r_B)$. But if absolute risk aversion is decreasing, ϕ is a strictly convex function of marginal utility (from lemma). Therefore, by Jensen's inequality, $E^\theta \phi(U'(r_G)) = E^\theta U(r_G) > E^\theta U(r_B) = E^\theta \phi(U'(r_B))$. The proof is similar for other cases.

When individuals are decreasing risk-averse, incompleteness limits the amount of insurance so much that the individual prefers ex ante the high output state. If we allow for moral hazard so that the individual's actions affect the probabilities of high and low output, then the incentive problem is least serious for decreasing risk-averse individuals simply because their insurance coverage is already curtailed by price risk.[12]

5. Concluding Remarks

This paper has explored some properties of incomplete crop insurance schemes. It is well known that actuarially fair complete insurance results in equalization of marginal utilities and hence net incomes across different states of nature. Incomplete insurance schemes, by contrast, cannot stabilize incomes completely. This is reflected in the first-order condition that requires the expected marginal utilities to be equal across the high and low output states. Since the marginal costs of insurance are evaluated at different utility levels corresponding to the different price states, the demand for insurance is, in many circumstances, sensitive to price risk. The farmer buying crop insurance risks greater exposure to the uninsured price variability, so the demand for crop insurance emerges from a tradeoff between output and price risks.

The implication is that introducing the market for price risks would increase the demand for crop insurance. In a study of crop insurance in the United States, Gardner and Kramer (1986) state that a "general reason for coordinating price support programs and output insurance programs is that either one by itself may have only small risk reducing effects in the absence of the other. This situation arises when price fluctuations are caused by random output variations that are correlated across farms since in this situation, low yields tend to be compensated by higher prices." As we have seen, the above argument could be made even if price and output shocks are independently distributed. Further, the analysis can be extended to show that introducing futures markets increases the optimum level of crop insurance (see Ramaswami and Roe, (1989)).

In the analysis it was convenient to assume actuarially fair insurance. If the premium includes a loading fee or a subsidy the results need to be qualified. The key result is proposition 1, which states that if insurance is actuarially fair, the optimal insurance is bounded below by the revenue loss in the low-price state and bounded above by the revenue loss in the high-price state. However, if the premium is higher than actuarial cost, the optimal insurance may be less than the lower bound and if the premium is below the actuarial cost, the optimal insurance may be greater than the upper bound. So whether proposition 1 is violated depends on the extent of mark-up or subsidy on the actuarial cost.[13]

The results of this paper apply to all situations where the insurable and the uninsurable risks interact multiplicatively.[14] Earlier Doherty and Schlesinger (1983) have studied the properties of optimal insurance when the multiple risks are additive. An implication of their analysis is that uninsurable risks are inconsequential for the demand for insurance if the multiple risks are independent. This, as we have seen, is not true in the multiplicative case. The multiplicative specification of risks arises quite naturally in contexts where the assets that are insured against physical loss are also subject to uninsured fluctuations in unit value. Of course, real-world insurance schemes may also occur in settings that satisfy neither the additive nor the multiplicative specification.[15] For this reason, it would be worthwhile in future investigations to consider more general structures capable of accomodating a variety of cases.

Appendix

Part A

From (7) and (12) the optimal insurance satisfies $E^{\theta}U'(r_G) = E^{\theta}U'(r_B)$. In the example price risk is independent of output risk. For the constant risk aversion case the first-order condition reduces to $Ee^{-Ar_G} = Ee^{-Ar_B}$ where the expectations are with respect to price and A is the risk aversion coefficient. Substituting for $r_B = pQ_2 + (1 - \gamma)I$ and $r_G = pQ_1 - \gamma I$, we obtain

$$e^{A\gamma I} E(e^{-ApQ_1}) = e^{-A(1-\gamma)I} E(e^{-ApQ_2})$$

Solving for I,

$$I^* = -1/A[\ln(Ee^{-ApQ_1}/Ee^{-ApQ_2})]$$

Using a value of $A = .003$, $I^* = \$80.00$ when $P_1 = P_2 = \$2.00$, and $I^* = \$70.40$ when $P_1 = \$3.00$ and $P_2 = \$1.00$ with equal probability.

Part B

We wish to show that the assumption $\delta w(\theta_1) > \delta w(\theta_2)$ is equivalent to the principle of increasing uncertainty. According to the principle, if $W(Q_1, \theta)$ has a higher mean revenue than $W(Q_2, \theta)$, then $W(Q_1, \theta)$ is also riskier than $W(Q_2, \theta)$.

Suppose $EW(Q_1, \theta) > EW(Q_2, \theta)$. Then we need to show that if $\delta w(\theta_1) > \delta w(\theta_2)$ then $W(Q_1, \theta)$ is riskier than $W(Q_2, \theta)$ after adjusting for the difference in means, i.e.,

(a) $W(Q_1, \theta_1) > W(Q_2, \theta_1) + EW(Q_1, \theta) - EW(Q_2, \theta)$ and

(b) $W(Q_1, \theta_2) < W(Q_2, \theta_2) + EW(Q_1, \theta) - EW(Q_2, \theta)$.

Consider the right-hand side of (a):

$W(Q_2, \theta_1) + EW(Q_1, \theta) - EW(Q_2, \theta)$
$\quad = W(Q_2, \theta_1) + \lambda(W(Q_1, \theta_1) - W(Q_2, \theta_1)) + (1 - \lambda)(W(Q_1, \theta_2)$
$\quad\quad - W(Q_2, \theta_2))$
$\quad = (1 - \lambda)(\delta w(\theta_2) - \delta w(\theta_1)) + W(Q_1, \theta_1)$
$\quad < W(Q_1, \theta_1)$.

Consider the right-hand side of (b):

$$W(Q_2, \theta_2) + EW(Q_1, \theta) - EW(Q_2, \theta)$$
$$= W(Q_2, \theta_2) + \lambda(W(Q_1, \theta_1) - W(Q_2, \theta_1)) + (1 - \lambda)(W(Q_1, \theta_2)$$
$$- W(Q_2, \theta_2))$$
$$= \lambda(\delta w(\theta_1) - \delta w(\theta_2)) + W(Q_1, \theta_2)$$
$$> W(Q_1, \theta_2).$$

Since each of the above steps can be reversed, the reverse implication is also true.

Part C

Proof of Proposition 4. The initial conditional price distribution can be represented as

$$p \,|\, Q_i = \begin{cases} P(Q_i, \theta_1) - k_1 \text{ with probability } \lambda \\ P(Q_i, \theta_2) + k_2 \text{ with probability } (1 - \lambda) \end{cases} \quad i = 1, 2$$

where $k_1 = k_2 = 0$ (initially). Now an increase (decrease) in the riskiness (in the Rothschild-Stiglitz 1970 sense) of the $p \,|\, Q_i$ distribution is represented by a decrease (increase) in k_2, $\bar{p} \,|\, Q_i$ held constant. Since $\bar{p} \,|\, Q_i = \lambda[P(Q_i, \theta_1) - k_1] + (1 - \lambda)[P(Q_i, \theta_2) + k_2]$, $dk_1/dk_2 = (1 - \lambda)/\lambda$. As $\eta''(I) < 0$, $\partial I^*/\partial k_2$ is of the same sign as $\partial\eta'(I)/\partial k_2$ evaluated at I^*.

$$\partial\eta'(I)/\partial k_2 \big|_{I^*} = \gamma(1 - \gamma)\{\lambda(U''(R_3^*)Q_2 - U''(R_1^*)Q_1)dk_1/dk_2$$
$$- (1 - \lambda)(U''(R_2^*)Q_1 - U''(R_4^*)Q_2)\}$$

Substituting for dk_1/dk_2

$$\partial\eta'(I)/\partial p_2 \big|_{I=I^*} = \gamma(1 - \gamma)(1 - \lambda)\{U''(R_1^*)Q_1 - U''(R_3^*)(Q_1 - (Q_1 - Q_2))$$
$$+ U''(R_4^*)(Q_1 - (Q_1 - Q_2)) - U''(R_2^*)Q_1\}.$$
$$= \gamma(1 - \gamma)(1 - \lambda)\{(U''(R_1^*) - U''(R_3^*))Q_1\}$$
$$+ (U''(R_4^*) - U''(R_2^*))Q_1 + (U''(R_3^*)$$
$$- U''(R_4^*))(Q_1 - Q_2)\},$$

which is strictly positive because $R_1^* > R_3^* > R_4^* > R_2^*$ and $U''' > 0$.

Notes

1. The price-election is the price at which the insurance company compensates the farmer for a unit loss of the commodity. In this United States the current crop insurance

practice is to offer a farmer buying insurance a choice between three price elections. For a description of the crop insurance program, see the report by the U.S. General Accounting Office (1984).

2. See Newbery and Stiglitz (1981), ch. 4, for a discussion about the causes of price variability in agricultural commodity markets.

3. Considering that the government is often the principal insurer in agriculture, this is not an unreasonable assumption. The consequences of departing from this assumption are indicated later. In the United States the administrative expenses of the Federal Crop Insurance Corporation are excluded from premium calculations and premiums are priced below actuarial cost. The subsidy depends on the level of deductible but is not greater than 30% of the actuarial cost.

4. As noted later, strict concavity of the utility function guarantees the strict convacity of η in I.

5. It is not essential for the analysis that the optimal insurance be positive.

6. Another way of saying this is that θ induces the same ordering over revenue losses as over prices.

7. Sandmo (1971) analysed the impact of price uncertainty on a competitive firm's output decisions. Leland extended the analysis to consider the impact of demand uncertainty on a monopolist firm. As generalized by Coes (1977), the principal result is that if stochastic demand shocks satisfy the *principle of increasing uncertainty*, increases in demand uncertainty reduce the optimal output of a decreasing risk-averse firm.

8. This is enough since η is strictly concave in I. From (8), $\eta''(I) = \lambda\eta_1'(I) - (1 - \lambda)\eta_2'(I)$ where $\eta_1'(I) = (1 - \gamma)U''(R_3) + \gamma U''(R_1) < 0$ and $\eta_2'(I) = -(1 - \gamma)U''(R_4) - \gamma U''(R_2) < 0$.

9. All constant and decreasing absolute risk aversion utility functions have a strictly positive third derivative. It can also be shown that the optimum insurance is equal to the expected value of crop loss when marginal utility is linear and greater than the expected value of crop loss when marginal utility is concave. Therefore, convexity of marginal utility is a necessary and sufficient condition for demand uncertainty to reduce optimal insurance.

10. This is the result of proposition 3 in which the prices are assumed to be certain at their expected values.

11. $\delta W(\theta_1) = P_1(Q_1 - Q_2) > P_2(Q_1 - Q_2) = \delta W(\theta_2)$.

12. Imai, Geanakoplos, and Ito report a result opposite to ours. They consider unemployment insurance schemes where severance payments are made to laid-off workers. But "since severance payments usually do not depend on outcomes at alternative opportunities after layoff they are considered at best incomplete insurance for layoff" (Ito (1986)). The issue that is investigated is whether the laid-off worker could be better off, in an ex-ante sense, than the retained worker. This is indeed the case for individuals with decreasing risk-averse utility functions. Individuals with constant risk-aversion utility functions are indifferent between the two states while increasing risk-averse individuals prefer to be retained. So, the incentive problem is most serious for decreasing risk-averse individuals. The difference between their model and ours lies in the asumption about the uninsured variable. The uncertainty in the rehiring wage, in the Imai model, affects only the marginal benefit of insurance (the expected marginal utility if the worker is laid off) and not the marginal cost (the marginal utility of the *sure* wage net of premium payments). See Ito and Machina (1983), and Ito for further variants of the problem.

13. Suppose C is the actuarial cost of insurance. Then, by continuity arguments, there exists insurance prices $C_1 > C > C_2$ such that proposition 1 is true for all premiums that lie in the interval $[C_1, C_2]$.

14. Some examples of incomplete insurance for multiplicative risks are
(a) when a firm faces price and output uncertainty but can obtain insurance only against price risks,
(b) when an exporter can obtain insurance against exchange rate risks but not against fluctuations in world market price, and
(c) when a work of art can be insured against loss of theft but not against changes in its market value. This example is due to Turnbull (1983).
15. The unemployment insurance scheme considered by Imai, Geanakoplos, and Ito is an example.

References

Ahsan, S. M., A. A. G. Ali, and N. Kurian. (1982). "Towards a Theory of Agricultural Insurance," *American Journal of Agricultural Economics* 64, 520–529.

Coes, D. V. (1977). "Firm Output and Changes in Uncertainty," *American Economic Review* 67, 249–251.

Doherty, N., and H. Schlesinger. (1983). "Optimal Insurance in Incomplete Markets," *Journal of Political Economy* 91, 1045–1054.

Gardner, B., and R. Kramer. (1986). "Experience with Crop Insurance Programs in the United States" in *Crop Insurance for Agricultural Development*, P. Hazell, C. Pomareda and A. Valdes, eds. Baltimore: the Johns Hopkins University Press.

Imai, H., J. Geanakoplos, and T. Ito. (1981). "Incomplete Insurance and Absolute Risk Aversion," *Economics Letters* 8, 107–112.

Ito, T. (1986). "Implicit Contracts and Risk Aversion," in *Equilibrium Analysis, Essays in Honor of Kenneth J. Arrow*, Volume II, W. P. Heller, R. M. Starr and D. P. Starrett, eds. Cambridge University Press.

Ito, T., and M. Machina. (1983). "The Incentive Implications of Incomplete Insurance: The Multiplicative Case," *Economics Letters* 13, 319–323.

Leland, H. E. (1972). "Theory of the Firm Facing Uncertain Demand," *American Economic Review* 62, 278–291.

Nelson, C., and E. T. Loehman. (1987). "Further Toward a Theory of Agricultural Insurance," *American Journal of Agricultural Economics* 69, 523–531.

Newberry, D. M. G., and J. E. Stiglitz. (1981). *The Theory of Commodity Price Stabilization*, New York: Oxford University Press.

Ramaswami, B. and T. Roe. (1989). "Incompleteness in Insurance: An Analysis of the Multiplicative Case," Bulletin No. 89–7, Economic Development Center, University of Minnesota.

Rothschild, M., and J. Stiglitz. (1970). "Increasing Risk I: A Definition," *Journal of Economic Theory* 2, 225–243.

Sandmo, A. (1971). "On the Theory of the Competitive Firm under Price Uncertainty," *American Economic Review* 61, 65–73.

Turnbull, S. M. (1983). "Additional Aspects of Rational Insurance Purchasing," *Journal of Business* 56, 217–229.

U.S. General Accounting Office. (1984). "More Attention Needed in Key Areas of the Expanded Crop Insurance Program," Report to the Secretary of Agriculture, GAO/RCED-84-65, March 14, Washington, D.C.

HOW DOES AMBIGUITY AFFECT INSURANCE DECISIONS?

Howard Kunreuther
The Wharton School, University of Pennsylvania

Robin M. Hogarth
Graduate School of Business, University of Chicago

Abstract

There is increasing empirical evidence that one reason the insurance industry has been reluctant to cover a number of risks is the ambiguity or uncertainty associated with either the probability of specific events occurring or the magnitude of their potential consequences or both.

This paper briefly reviews the literature on ambiguity as it relates to decision making under uncertainty and indicates why it creates theoretical challenges. Empirical evidence is then presented on the importance of ambiguity on the insurance premium setting process based on recently completed national surveys of both actuaries and undewriters. At a prescriptive level the paper explores whether new institutional arrangements are required to replace traditional insurance mechanisms for providing protection that is currently unavailable.

Key words: ambiguity, loss estimates, risk assessment

There is increasing empirical evidence that one reason the insurance industry has been reluctant to cover a number of risks is the ambiguity

Our appreciation to Larry Berger, Georges Dionne, and Neil Doherty for helpful comments on an earlier draft of this paper. This research was partially supported by NSF grant No. SES88-09299, a contract from the Office of Naval Research, and a grant from the Russell Sage Foundation.

307

associated with either the probability of specific events occurring or the magnitude of the potential consequences or both.

Regarding ambiguity on the probability dimension, political risk provides an example in which few companies offer protection against potential losses of industrial firms investing in developing countries with unstable political systems. Insurers have indicated that their principal reason for not providing coverage has been the difficulty in estimating the probabilities associated with losses of different magnitudes (Kunreuther and Kleindorfer, 1983).

Providing protection to manufacturers of the pertussis vaccine against possible brain damage caused by the use of the vaccine illustrates a case where there is considerable ambiguity on the loss dimension (Hinman and Kaplan, 1984). In this case the probability of such serious side effects from the vaccine are well known but the size of court awards from product liability suits against the manufacturer have made the costs of insurance prohibitive to them. In fact, manufacturers decided not to produce the vaccine because of concern with the potential costs of such liability (Huber, 1983).

For risks where there is considerable ambiguity on both the probability and outcome dimensions the insurance industry has been unwilling to extend coverage very widely. For example, environmental pollution coverage has been considered uninsurable by practically all major insurance firms (Carter, 1990). Not only is the probability of a claim against the insurer uncertain, but should a suit be filed against the insured party there is no guarantee that the costs to the insurer will be bounded by the stated limits of coverage (Abraham, 1988; Katzman, 1983).

In the case of earthquake coverage the insurance industry is willing to provide coverage against damage to residential homes and to commercial structures but at premiums that greatly exceed expected loss. One reason for this behavior is that it enables the insurance industry to build up reserves for a large quake. However, for residential insurance where losses are not expected to be high, the premium-to-loss ratio over the first 60 years that such insurance was offered in California (1916–76) averaged 30 to 1 (Atkisson and Petak, 1981). Firms are reluctant to lower their rates and are anxious to develop some type of government involvement to avoid the potentially large losses they feel they would face (National Committee of Property Insurance, 1989).

This paper investigates the impact of ambiguity on insurance premiums based on recently completed surveys of both actuaries and underwriters. The data strongly suggest that ambiguity related to both probabilities and losses plays a key role in insurers' decisions on what premiums to charge and what coverage to offer. At a descriptive level this behavior raises questions as to what models of choice each of these groups utilize in making their premium recommendations. At a prescriptive level a relevant question is whether new institutional arrangements are required to replace traditional insurance market mechanisms for providing protection that is currently unavailable.

1. Ambiguity and Insurers Price-Setting Decisions

The premium setting decisions of actuaries and underwriters need to be viewed in the context of an insurance firm's decision on offering coverage in a market setting. To motivate this analysis consider a situation in which the insurer is considering selling contingent claims for one time period against a risk where there is a nonambiguous probability p that a specific loss L will occur. Assume for ease of exposition that only one loss can occur for any given policy during this time period. If the firm sells m different policies against this risk, then let p_j represent the nonambiguous probability estimate that j losses will occur $j = 0 \cdots m$.

Let us suppose that the insurer determines what premium to set based on an expected profit maximization criterion. For the case where the probability is nonambiguous and the loss is specified as L, let r_1 be the premium for which the insurer is indifferent between offering coverage or maintaining the status quo. If A represents the insurer's assets prior to providing coverage, then r_1 is determined by

$$A = A - \sum_{j=0}^{m} jp_jL + mr_1 \tag{1}$$

In other words $r_1 = \sum_{j=0}^{m} (jp_j) L/m$. Since the insurer is risk neutral, he sets r_1 equal to the expected loss from a single risk whether the risks of the m policies are independent of each other or correlated in any way.

Now consider the cases in which either the probability is ambiguous and/or the loss is uncertain. We define an ambiguous probability to be one in which the experts disagree on the chances of j out of m losses so that some type of aggregation procedure is needed. Specifically, consider the case in which k different expert opinions are combined, with p_{ij} representing the probability estimate by expert i that j losses will occur. By according each expert's estimate a weight w_i, with $\sum_{i=1}^{k} w_i = 1$, then a linear weighting rule yields an estimate $p \cdot_j = \sum_{i=1}^{k} w_i p_{ij}$. Suppose the weights are chosen so that $p \cdot_j = p_j$ for all values of $j = 0 \cdots m$. An ambiguous loss is defined here to be one in which the claim against the insurer can vary between some lower bound $L_{\min}$ and an upper bound (normally the policy limit) $L_{\max}$ with a mean value given by L.

Under these definitions it can be easily seen from equation 1 that a risk-neutral insurer will charge a premium r_1 whether or not the probability or loss is ambiguous. Risk neutrality implies that the variance does not matter in premium determination and, hence, uncertainty on estimates of probabilities and losses should have no effect on insurers' pricing decisions.

The assumption that insurers are risk neutral with respect to potential losses has been challenged by David Mayers and Clifford Smith (Mayers and Smith, 1983) in a paper on the corporate demand for insurance and more recently in their study of the demand for reinsurance by property/liability insurance companies (Mayers and Smith, 1990). Neil Doherty has made a similar point in a study of insurance contracts written between a corporate insurer and a corporate buyer (Doherty, 1989).

The variance associated with potential losses may be an important feature for an insurer to consider for several reasons. For one thing, the provisions of the corporate tax code implies a convex tax function for low levels of taxable income and a linear function for taxable income above $100,000. Hence, an insurer's tax liability will be lower if the variance of pretax income is reduced. As the variance of a loss increases then the chances of insurer insolvency also increases. If there are transaction costs associated with bankruptcy, then the expected cost associated with any risk portfolio will be lower as one is more certain of the magnitude of the outcomes.

If insurers prefer to be in a situation with a lower variance, then this implies that they will charge a higher premium the more volatility there is in the probability distribution of losses. This situation is equivalent to being risk averse. At a more general level, Bruce Greenwald and Joseph Stiglitz examine firm behavior when there is asymmetries of information between outside investors who provide capital and inside managers who control its use (Greenwald and Stiglitz, 1990). They show that if professional managers in firms are rewarded with a share of profits but suffer a large penalty in case the firm suffers bankruptcy, then the firm will behave as if it maximized expected utility u where u is characterized by decreasing absolute risk aversion.

A simple example adapted from Kunreuther (Kunreuther, 1989)

contrasts the impact of nonambiguous and ambiguous probabilities on expected utility for a risk-neutral and risk-averse firm when $L = 100$ and only two policies are sold by the insurer. Two experts, whose estimates are equally credible (so $w_1 = w_2 = .5$) are utilized by the insurer. Expert 1 estimates the probability of L on any single policy to be .1 and the other expert estimates this same probability to be .3. This situation can be contrasted with the case where both experts agree that the probability of L on any single policy is .2. Suppose an insurer with assets A arbitrarily sets $U(A) = 0$ and utility $U(A - 100) = -1$. If two losses were experienced and the insurer were risk neutral then $U(A - 200) = -2$. A risk averse insurer would set $U(A - 200) < -2$, say $U(A - 200) = -3$.

Figure 1 provides four simple decison trees to illustrate the impact of ambiguity in the probability for independent and perfectly correlated risks. For a risk-neutral insurer the expected utility is the same in all four cases since this is equivalent to maximizing expected profits. A risk-averse insurer will want to charge a higher premium when losses are correlated and when probabilities are ambiguous.[1]

Ambiguity is thus an important component in determining the market price for coverage if the insurer is risk averse. The variance in either the probability or the actual loss has a negative impact on the insurer's expected utility and thus necessitates a higher premium for the firm to want to market coverage.

2. How Actuaries and Underwriters Determine Premiums

The above discussion implicitly assumed that the insurer was making pricing decisions that satisfied its shareholders who would otherwise invest in other companies. No attention was given to the actual decision makers in the firm — the actuaries and the underwriters. Both of these groups play critical roles in the premium-setting process and may create additional reasons premiums will be higher as the variance associated with a given risk increases.

How actuaries and underwriters actually behave will be determined in part by how they are evaluated and remunerated. Agency theory arguments have been used to determine optimal compensation packages for corporate decision makers and the nature of such compensation reflects a tradeoff between risk sharing and efficiency considerations. (Lambert and Larcker, 1985; Mayers, and Smith, 1989) For example, payment by salary may be efficient from a risk-bearing viewpoint if shareholders have a comparative advantage over managers in bearing

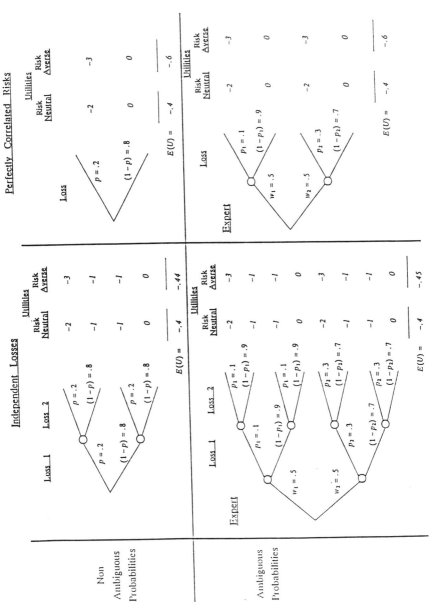

Figure 1. Decision trees and expected utilities for two risks under different probability and loss conditions.

risk. However, a fixed salary does not align rewards to managers and shareholders and the subsequent agency problem ensues. Optimal contracts often require that managers bear some risk and, hence, require an appropriate risk premium. This risk premium is with the firm (i.e., owner). These considerations imply that if risk to the insurer can be reduced, there is a gain that can be divided between the various corporate shareholders.

We will assume that actuaries and underwriters in different insurance companies are paid the same salary regardless of the risks they insure against. In this situation the only way for these employees to reduce the chances of insolvency of the firm on high-variance risks is to suggest charging a higher premium than if the probability distribution of losses were more stable.

In practice actuaries and underwriters utilize heuristics, which explicitly address these concerns in recommending premiums for coverage against specific risks. Actuaries first determine a premium based on expected value under the assumption that the probability and loss is known. They then increase this value to refect the amount of perceived ambiguity in either the probability or loss.[2]

For example, one formula utilized for determining a premium r is

$$r = (1 + \lambda)\mu$$

where μ = expected value (i.e., $p \times L$) and λ ($\lambda > 0$) is a factor reflecting ambiguity. The value of λ varies depending upon the situation but is considered by actuaries as a global security loading independent of any adjustment to cover administrative costs. (Lemaire, 1986)

Other models of behavior explicitly focus on the impact of constraints on individual behavior under uncertainty. Forty years ago A. D. Roy (1952) developed a model of choice in which firms were guided in their actions by keeping the probability of a large loss (which might cause bankruptcy) to be as low as possible. In other words, firms were first concerned with their safety and then with profit maximization. Hence the term *safety-first* behavior was used to describe their actions.

James Stone (1973a,b) developed a model of underwriting behavior that incorporated some of the ideas of safety-first behavior. Let X be a random variable representing the total loss from the insurer's current portfolio of risks. If the underwriter is considering insuring an additional risk in which the firm expects to sell m policies, each of which can create a loss L, then the underwriter will recommend a premium r so that

$$\sum_{j=j^*}^{m} \{\text{Probability } [(X + jL) > (A + mr)]\} < p^* \qquad (2)$$

where j^* is the minimum number of losses where $X + j^*L > A + mr$, and p^* is a preassigned probability that reflects safety first considerations. The expression in brackets represents events where the total loss is greater than the assets of the firm, thus leading to insolvency. As the variance associated with the loss distribution increases, there is a greater chance of insolvency and hence a need to raise the premium r to satisfy the safety-first constraint given by (2). Stone provides illustrative examples as to how variance in losses leads the underwriter to set higher premiums than would have been predicted if he were behaving as if he maximized expected profit for the firm.

3. Empirical Evidence on Insurers Decision Processes

To determine the impact of ambiguity on insurer behavior one can construct a matrix such as table 1. It specifies the four different premiums based on whether probability and/or loss are ambiguous or precise.

To better understand the premium-setting behavior of insurers when the risks are ambiguous or nonambiguous, questionnaires were developed with different scenarios. One mail survey was conducted with professional actuaries and another with underwriters, each one tailored to the types of decisions that these groups make. In the case of the actuaries, the survey compared the pure premiums for situations where the loss was known and the probabilities were either precise (r_1) or ambiguous (r_2). Losses were either independent of each other or perfectly correlated. [See Hogarth and Kunreuther, 1989a, 1992, for more details.] For the underwriters another set of scenarios were constructed that examined all four cells in table 1 for a single risk in different contexts [see Kunreuther et al. 1991 for more details].

3.1. Actuary Survey

In the case of the professional actuaries, data were obtained from a mail survey of members of the Casualty Actuarial Society residing in North America. Of this population, 489 of 1,165 persons (i.e., 42%) provided usable responses, all anonymously.

Scenarios were designed around five different situations: (1) Defective product: The owner of a small business with net assets of $110,000 seeks to insure against a $100,000 loss that could result from claims against a defective product; (2) Brown River: A small businessman faces a potential loss of $100,000 from the possible flooding of the Brown River;

Table 1.   Different Levels of Knowledge for Loss and Probabilities

		Probabilities	
		Precise	Ambiguous
Loss	Precise	r_1	r_2
	Uncertain	r_3	r_4

(3) Palcam; a firm wants to set the price of a warranty for a possible defect in a new personal computer called Palcam-X that would cost $400 to repair; (4) Computeez: A manufacturing company wants to determine the price of a warranty to cover the $100 cost of repairing a component of a personal computer; (5) Health: A major health insurance company wants to determine what additional premium to charge for complications arising from a certain surgical procedure.

All these scenarios specified precise loss estimates but defined the probabilities to be either precise or ambiguous. Hence, actuaries were only asked to indicate the premiums r_1, or r_2 from table 1. In the scenarios with precise probabilities, the actuaries were given a specific probability level (ranging from .001 to .90) and were told that they could feel confident about the estimate either because they had sufficient data from past experience (e.g., the defective product scenario) or the experts agreed on the chances of a loss (e.g., Computeez). For the case of an ambiguous probability, the actuaries were given the same probability estimate as in the nonambiguous case but were told that they experienced considerable uncertainty concerning the estimate (e.g., defective product scenario) or there was considerable disagreement among the experts (e.g., Computeez). With the exception of the Brown River scenario, no range of probability estimates were given when the experts disagreed.[3]

The ratio of coverage per dollar premium (denoted by C) provides an indication of the impact that ambiguity has on the prices charged by insurers.[4] Table 2 contrasts the median values of C when actuaries were asked to specify the minimum pure premium they would charge when probabilities were either nonambiguous (precise) [NA (p)] or ambiguous [$A(p)$] for the defective product and Computeez scenarios specified above.[5] The figures are revealing. The first row in each scenario, labeled $1/p$, specifies the value of C if an actuarially fair premium were charged for a risk that has a probability p of occurring. Values of C less than $1/p$ implies that the insurer is charging a premium in excess of expected loss. The next two rows present the median values of C for the nonambiguous and ambiguous probabilities respectively. In all cases the value of C is decreasing when the probability of a loss changes from precise to ambiguous. The differences are particularly striking when the probabilities are relatively low (i.e., $p = .01$ and $p = .001$).

The Computeez scenario is of particular interest as the actuaries were asked to specify premiums when losses were independent or perfectly correlated. If actuaries are setting premiums so as to maximize expected profits of the firm, then the premiums should be unaffected by either ambiguous probabilities or correlated losses. If, on the other hand, the actuaries are risk averse, then expected utility theory implies that premiums should be higher for ambiguous probabilities than for nonambiguous probabilities if losses are independent. For perfectly correlated risks, the premiums should remain the same whether the actuary is risk neutral or risk averse.

The values of C presented in table 2 indicate that the actuaries specified considerably higher premiums for perfectly correlated risks than independent risks when 100,000 units are insured. For ambiguous probabilities they reacted by increasing the premium (i.e., reducing C)

Table 2. Actuaries Estimates of Coverage per Dollar Premium (C) for Different Scenarios (Median Values) For Nonambiguous Probabilities [NA(p)] and Ambiguous Probabilities [A(p)]

	Defective Product Scenarios*			
	p = 0.01	p = 0.35	p = 0.65	p = 0.90
1/p	100	2.86	1.54	1.11
NA(p)	65	2.34	1.43	1.11
A(p)	20	2.00	1.25	1.05

Loss = $100,000

	Computeez Scenarios**					
	Independent Risks			Perfectly Correlated		
	p = 0.001	p = 0.01	p = 0.10	p = 0.001	p = 0.01	p = 0.10
1/p	1000	100	10	1000	100	10
NA(p)	909	95	10	1000	82	8.3
A(p)	200	50	8.3	100	9	4.0

100,000 units Insured

Loss = $100

* The number of actuaries responding to these scenarios ranged from 9 to 15

** The number of actuaries responding to these scenarios ranged from 14 to 22 particularly for the perfectly correlated case. Thus when $p = .01$, the actuarially fair value is $C = 100$. When losses are perfectly correlated and the actuary faces an ambiguous probability, the median value is $C = 9$. The probability would have to be $p = .111$ for this median premium to be actuarially fair.

These data suggest that actuaries are extremely risk averse when they face a potentially large loss and are uncertain about the chances of it occurring. They may feel that they will be held responsible should such an event occur. By charging a premium somewhat in excess of expected loss they can provide some type of justification for their actions to others, in this case the underwriters (Tetlock 1985).

A focus group with four actuaries from a large insurance firm in the Philadelphia area provided considerable insight into the basis for the questionnaire responses. There was general agreement in the group that ambiguity on probabilities greatly increases the perceived risk, particularly if there is a large exposure (as in the perfect correlation Computeez case). One actuary in response to this scenario, indicated that if the risks were perfectly correlated and the probability was ambiguous he would either refuse to provide coverage or demand a premium that was 'near 100 cents to the dollar.'

3.2. Underwriter Survey

The questionnaire on the underwriter premium-setting process was constructed so that data for all four cases in table 1 could be collected. After conducting informal group discussions and personal interviews with underwriters in the Philadelphia area, we mailed packets of questionnaires to the chief property and casualty underwriters in 190 insurance companies throughout the United States, asking each to distribute them to underwriters who reported to them in their firms. We received 222 completed questionnaires from 47 insurance companies.[6]

Each underwriter was asked to respond to four different neutral scenarios reflecting the conditions on probability and loss depicted in table 1.[7] For example, to determine r_1 in table 1 the underwriter was told that he faced a given risk where, if a loss occurred, it would equal L dollars and that all the experts agree that the annual probability of the loss was p. Ambiguous probabilities were defined as "wide disagreement and a high degree of uncertainty among the experts." The precise loss was specified at $L = \$1$ million or $L = \$10$ million. Precise values of the probability were set at $p = .01$ or $p = .005$. For the case of an uncertain loss, estimates ranged from negligible to either $2 million or to $20 million depending on whether the best estimate was $1 million or $10 million.

To determine whether specific risk contexts influenced the premium-setting process, each underwriter was given either a set of four scenarios related to insuring a commercial building against earthquake damage of $L million or providing coverage against pollution damage of $L million from the leakage of an underground storage tank.[8]

Figure 2 provides a summary of the values of C for three sets of scenarios where $p = .01$ and $L = $ 1 million. The actuarially fair value is $C = 100. As with the actuaries, the underwriters charge higher premiums when either p is ambiguous and/or L is uncertain. Even for the case where precise estimates of p and L are given the values of C are relatively low ranging from 63 in the neutral scenario to 51 in the earthquake scenario. For the case where both p and L are ambiguous then the C ratio is very low for all three types of scenarios. Although the data depicted in figure 2 did not reveal a large difference between the three types of scenarios, it was generally true that a potential hazardous waste loss induced underwriters to charge a higher premium than for the other two scenarios. Hence, C was the lowest for this situation. In general, ambiguity of probability had more of an impact in raising premiums than uncertainty of the loss.

4. Implications for Market Behavior

The empirical data on actuary and underwriter behavior suggest that ambiguity on probability and/or uncertainty of losses will lead to higher premiums than if the risk was precisely specified. In certain cases, such as political risk and environmental pollution there is a reluctance by most insurers to offer *any* coverage on the market. For other risks such as earthquake, private insurers are looking for ways to bring the federal government in as partners.

The principal reason why actuaries and underwriters want to charge higher premiums when there is ambiguity is because all potential policyholders are affected in the same way by the uncertainty regarding probability or losses. If there is a lack of understanding of the mechanism causing a loss, then this uncertainty will affect all of the risks. Similarly if one is uncertain as to what type of liability ruling will be invoked should a claim be made on one policy, then this uncertainty will affect all policies.

Risk assessment techniques can shed light on the perceived probability, and clearer specification of liability rules can reduce the uncer-

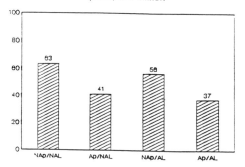

Mean Coverage/$, Neutral Scenario
p=.01, L=1 million

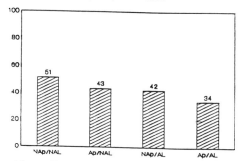

Mean Coverage/$, Earthquake Scenario
p=.01, L=1 million

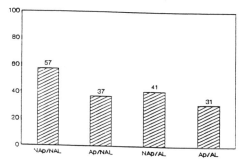

Mean Coverage/$, Haz. Waste Scenario
p=.01, L=1 million

Figure 2. Mean coverage under three scenarios.

tainty of losses. However, there is little indication that there will be rapid movement in these directions in the next few years. Hence, one may want to turn to alternative institutional arrangements rather than standard insurance contracts as a way of resurrecting the market.

4.1. Mutual Insurance

Mutual insurance arrangements should be an attractive way of providing protection to individuals or industrial firms facing an ambiguous risk. Each member of the mutual company contributes a sum of money entitling them to insurance protection and at the end of the year dividends are paid out if there is a surplus. The parameters associated with the risk do not have to be precisely estimated and claims experience over the years can help specify the loss distribution. Neil Doherty and Georges Dionne (1989) have shown that mutual-like insurance is preferable to standard coverage when losses are correlated.

Risk retention groups have now emerged as a type of mutual arrangement whereby industrial firms contribute their own capital to a pool of companies as a way of obtaining insurance protection. Risk assessments are needed to delineate differences between firms and to determine how contributions to the group should vary. At the same time there needs to be appropriate monitoring and control procedures at regular intervals to assure that the firms are meeting prescribed standards and to avoid moral hazard problems.

Although in theory the concept of risk retention groups appears to be a viable institution, few have formed over the past few years. One difficulty associated with creating these groups is that many potential members feel that they are better than average and will contribute more in capital contributions than they will receive in return. Hence the importance of risk assessment procedures and enforcement of standards to allay these concerns. Another reason is the feeling on the part of firms who already are part of a pool that they would prefer not to have competitors join the group since those insured feel they have a comparative advantage over uninsured rivals. The insurer who forms this pool needs to clarify at the outset that their intention is to expand it to many companies and that there are large advantages to the size and stability of the pool through diversifying.

4.2. Government Reinsurance

One way to reduce the concern by insurers with uncertainty on the loss side is to have some partial government involvement for handling unusually large unanticipated losses if the reinsurance industry is unwilling to do so. For example, if there is a severe earthquake that damages a large number of homes, it may be necessary for the government to cover a portion of the catastrophic losses.

There is precedence for this type of arrangement for risks in which there is considerable uncertainty regarding losses. The Price Anderson Act of 1975 formed two insurance pools that provided $60 million of liability coverage to protect nuclear power plant operators. The federal government provided up to $500 million of additional indemnity due to the limited experience with nuclear power at the time and to encourage the construction of nuclear power plants. Today the government has phased out the program and each nuclear power plant's liability has been increased so that should an accident occur the total amount of financial protection would exceed $7.2 billion (American Nuclear Insurers, 1989).

The National Flood Insurance Program was passed in 1968 because private companies refused to market coverage for water damage partly due to the uncertainty associated with potentially catastrophic losses. One of its principal features was a government reinsurance program. The insurance industry has proposed a similar arrangement for earthquake protection (National Committee of Property Insurance 1989). Current rates would be lowered from their present level on all structures in exchange for government reinsurance protection in case of a catastrophic quake that exceeded a certain level of damage.

Conclusions

A principal conclusion emerging from surveys of actuaries and under-writers is that they will add an ambiguity premium in pricing a given risk whenever there is uncertainty regarding either the probability or losses. At a descriptive level both decision makers are utilizing heuristics that may lead to different predictions from standard economic theory. In particular when presented with a single risk or a perfectly correlated set of risks, standard models of choice predict that the premiums will be the same whether the probability is precise or ambiguous. In fact, they are not.

These findings raise a number of questions regarding the decision-making process in an insurance firm. For example, it is important to understand more fully the types of constraints affecting underwriters and actuaries in their determination of premiums and how the two groups interact with each other in both formal and informal ways. What specific quantitative and qualitative factors are important to actuaries and underwriters when confronted with uncertain risks? What role does availability of reinsurance, surplus, and capacity of the firm play in determining recommended premiums and whether coverage should be offered by the insurer? How important is the portfolio of other insured risks in the actuary and underwriter's process?

By understanding more fully the answers to these questions, one can determine whether certain prescriptive measures are likely to affect the decision-making process in insurance firms. What is the value to insurers of additional data designed to reduce the ambiguity associated with the risk? What efforts should be undertaken by the insurer to increase the amount of its reinsurance given the nature of its portfolio of risks? Finally what are the potential roles of new institutional forms such as mutuals and public-private sector programs in resurrecting markets for coverage? It is clear that ambiguity matters to insurers and for this reason alone we need both to understand it better and to develop more creative approaches for dealing with it.

Notes

1. This example could be extended to the case in which losses are ambiguous. In comparing situations where the expected loss is the same, a risk-averse insurer would always charge a higher premium if there were variation in L than if L were constant.

2. This procedure is similar to the model proposed by Hillel Einhorn and Robin Hogarth (1985) on how people assess ambiguous probabilities. Their theory is based on the principle that people first anchor on an initial estimate of the probability and adjust this anchor by imagining other values that the probability can take.

3. In the Brown River scenario the nonambiguous case was presented as a flood with probability .01. In the ambiguous scenario actuaries were told that hydrologists were "sufficiently uncertain about this annual probability that it could range anywhere from zero to 1 in 50 depending on climatic conditions."

4. We are indebted to David Hildebrand for suggesting the use of this measure.

5. For the defective product scenario each actuary responded to both the ambiguous and nonambiguous version. For the Computeez scenario, each actuary responded to either a nonambiguous or ambiguous version. The versions were the first and last questions of several the actuaries were asked to answer. Each question appeared on a different page of the questionnaire and the order of the ambiguous and nonambiguous versions were randomized across subjects.

6. Our thanks to Norman Baglini and his colleagues at the American Institute for Property and Liability Underwriters for critiquing our questionnaire. Dong Ping Yin was most helpful in analyzing the data.

7. The scenarios were labeled *neutral* in that there was no context associated with the particular risk.

8. A Latin Square design was constructed for determining what values of p and L each underwriter was given for the different sets of four scenarios.

References

Abraham, Kenneth. (1988). "Environmental Liability and the Limits of Insurance, *Columbia Law Review* 88, 942–988.

American Nuclear Insurers. (1989). "Nuclear Liability Insurance: Protection for the Public," Report #2, March (mimeo).

Atkisson, Arthur, and Petak, William. (1981). "Earthquake Insurance: A Public Policy Analysis." Report prepared for the Federal Insurance Administration, Federal Emergency Management Agency, Washington, D.C. 20472.

Berger, Larry and Kunreuther, Howard (1991). "Safety First and Ambiguity," Wharton Risk and Decision Processes Center Working Paper.

Carter, Robert. (1990). *Liability for Accidental Pollution: Obstacles to the Supply of Insurance*. London: The Chartered Insurance Institute.

Doherty, Neil. (1989). "The Design of Insurance Contracts when Liability Rules are Unstable." Unpublished Paper, Wharton School, University of Pennsylvania.

Doherty, Neil, and Dionne, Georges. (1989). "Risk Pooling, Contract Structure and Organizational Form of Insurance Firms." Working Paper, Wharton School, University of Pennsylvania.

Einhorn, Hillel J., and Hogarth, Robin M. (1985). "Ambiguity and Uncertainty in Probabilistic Inference," *Psychological Reveiw* 92, 433–461.

Greenwald, Bruce, and Stiglitz, Joseph. (1990). "Asymmetric Information and the New Theory' of the Firm: Financial Constraints and Risk Behavior," *American Economic Review: Papers and Proceedings* 80, 160–165.

Hinman, Alan, and Kaplan, J. (1984). "Pertussis and Pertussis Vaccine," *Journal of American Medical Association* 251, 3109–3113, June 15.

Hogarth, Robin, and Kunreuther, Howard. (1989a). "Risk, Ambiguity and Insurance," *Journal of Risk and Uncertainty* 2, 5–36.

Hogarth, Robin, and Kunreuther, Howard. (1992). "Pricing Insurance and Warranties: Ambiguity and Correlated Risks," *The Geneva Papers on Risk and Insurance Theory*.

Huber, Peter. (1983). *Liability: The Legal Revolution and Its Consequences*. New York: Basic Books.

Katzman, Martin. (1983). *Chemical Catastrophes*, Homewood, IL: Richard D. Irwin.

Kunreuther, Howard C., and Kleindorfer, Paul R. (1983). "Insuring Against Country Risks: Descriptive and Prescriptive Aspects." In R. Herring (ed.), *Managing International Risk*. Cambridge, UK: Cambridge University Press.

Kunreuther, Howard. (1989). "The Role of Actuaries and Underwriters in Insuring Ambiguous Risks," *Risk Analysis* 9, 319–328.

Kunreuther, Howard, Meszaros, Jacqueline, Hogarth, Robin and Spranca, Mark (1991). "Ambiguity and Underwriter Decision Processes," Wharton Risk and Decision Processes Center Working Paper.

Lambert, Richard, and Larcker, David. (1985). "Executive Compensation,

Corporate Decision-making and Shareholder Wealth: A Review of the Evidence," *Midland Corporate Finance Journal* 2, 6–22.

Lemaire, Jean. (1986). *Théorie Mathématique des Assurances*. Belgium: Presses Universitaires de Bruxelles.

Mayers, David, and Smith, Clifford. (1983). "On the Corporate Demand for Insurance," *Journal of Business* 55, 281–296.

Mayers, David, and Smith, Clifford. (1990). "On the Corporate Demand for Insurance: Evidence from the Reinsurance Market," *Journal of Business* 63, 19–40.

Mayers, David, and Smith, Clifford. (1989). "Executive Compensation in the Life Insurance Industry." Working Paper, University of Rochester.

National Committee of Property Insurance. (1989). "Catastrophic Earthquakes: The Need to Insure Against Economic Disaster," Mimeo, Boston, MA: The Earthquake Project.

Roy, A. D. (1952). "Safety-First and the Holding of Assets," *Econometrica*, 20, 431–49.

Stone, John (1973a). "A Theory of Capacity and the Insurance of Catastrophic Risks," *Journal of Risk and Insurance* (Part I), 40, 231–243.

Stone, John (1973b). "A Theory of Capacity and the Insurance of Catastrophic Risks," *Journal of Risk and Insurance* (Part II), 40, 339–355.

Tetlock, Phillip. (1985). "Accountability: The Neglected Social Context of Judgements and Choice," *Research in Organizational Behavior*, vol 7. Greenwich, Conn: JAI Press.

MORAL HAZARD
AND COMPETITIVE
INSURANCE MARKETS

Richard J. Arnott*

Boston College

Abstract

Most work on the theory of moral hazard in the context of insurance investigates the properties of the schedule relating the net insurance payout to the accident damage in a partial equilibrium context. This paper reviews some results from a long-term research project undertaken by Joseph Stiglitz and the author, which in contrast focuses on moral hazard in general equilibrium. Topics addressed include the properties of indifference curves, the form of competitive insurance contracts, the existence of competitive equilibrium, and the descriptive and welfare properties of equilibrium.

The central finding is that the presence of moral hazard radically alters the nature of competitive equilibrium:

a) At one extreme, equilibrium may not exist; at the other, there may be an infinity of equilibria.

*This essay reviews some of the results obtained from a long-term research project on moral hazard with Joseph Stiglitz. Financial support for our research from the National Science Foundation, the Olin Foundation, the Hoover Institution, and the Social Sciences and Humanities Research Council of Canada is gratefully acknowledged. Part of this paper was written when I was visiting the Faculty of Commerce at U.B.C. in the summer of 1989. I would like to thank the faculty there for their hospitality. We have received many useful comments on our work; those of Martin Hellwig have been particularly insightful. I would also like to thank Georges Dionne for helpful comments on an earlier version of this paper.

b) When equilibrium exists, some insurance markets may be inactive even though there is demand for insurance.

c) In active insurance markets, equilibrium may be characterized by positive profits, rationing of insurance, and/or random premia and payouts.

d) Neither the first nor the second welfare theorem holds.

e) Market prices do not reflect social opportunity costs. As a result, the potential scope for efficiency-improving government intervention is considerable.

Key words: Moral hazard, insurance, competition, equilibrium, existence, uniqueness, welfare economics, principal-agent, first-order approach, adverse selection

In the standard (Arrow-Debreu) treatment of risk and insurance in competitive equilibrium, the states of nature, which occur with exogenous probabilities, are observable. Insurance entails lump-sum transfers across realized states and therefore has no adverse incentive or (equivalently) substitution effects.

Moral hazard arises when neither the states of nature nor individuals' actions are observable to an insurer.[1] What is observable is whether a particular accident has occurred. In these circumstances, there is no mechanism by which the insurer can induce an insured individual to reveal either the state of nature or his precaution truthfully. Thus, the insured–against events are accidents of varying degrees of severity, conditional on neither the state of nature nor the insured's actions. The provision of insurance against these events will generally affect the individual's incentives to take precautions,[2] i.e., has adverse incentive or substitution effects. There is therefore a tradeoff between risk-bearing and incentives. This is the moral hazard problem.

Moral hazard is pervasive in the economy. It occurs whenever risk is present, individuals are risk-averse, and "effort" is costly to monitor. And it arises not only in insurance markets, but in all other contexts in which insurance is provided — by governments, through social institutions, or in principal-agent contracts.

During the past decade, Joseph Stiglitz and I have been engaged in a long-term, collaborative research project on moral hazard. This essay will review some of our findings, as well as some related results in the literature. The treatment will be illustrative, selective, and nontechnical. The central message is that *the presence of moral hazard radically alters the nature of competitive equilibrium*:

a) At one extreme, equilibrium may not exist; at the other, there may be an infinity of equilibria.

b) When equilibrium exists, some insurance markets may be inactive even though there is demand for insurance.

c) In active insurance markets, equilibrium may be characterized by positive profits, rationing of insurance, and/or random premia and payouts.

d) Neither the first nor the second welfare theorem holds.

e) Market prices do not reflect social opportunity costs. As a result, the potential scope for efficiency-improving government intervention is considerable.

Moral hazard arises because of a particular form of informational asymmetry — the insured's actions are unobservable by the insurer. *Adverse selection* is a conceptually distinct insurance-related phenomenon caused by another form of informational asymmetry — the insurer is unable to identify individuals' risk types. In real-world insurance contexts, both phenomena are ubiquitous and occur simultaneously. In this essay, to simplify the analysis, adverse selection is assumed away. Only limited progress has been made by theorists in analyzing moral hazard and adverse selection together, which has considerably hindered empirical investigation of the economics of insurance. In the course of the essay, reference will be made to features of real-world insurance provisions that can be explained by moral hazard. The reader should keep in mind, however, that, because of the neglect of adverse selection, such explanations are partial and tentative.

Though some examples will be given, the essay will proceed at an abstract level. To put flesh on the bones, the reader may find it useful to think in terms of a somewhat hackneyed example — housing fire insurance. There are many activities a tenant or homeowner may undertake to reduce the probability of fire, or to lessen the expected damage conditional on a fire occurring — not dumping cigarette ashes in wastepaper baskets, not smoking in bed, not leaving the stove unattended while cooking, dousing the ashes in the fireplace before retiring, replacing frayed electrical cords immediately, keeping a functioning fire extinguisher in every room, spending extra on fire-resistant materials in home construction and household furnishings, ensuring easy exits from each room in the house, holding family fire drills, etc. All these activities entail economic decisions that are affected by the provision of insurance.

1. The Basic Model[3]

Throughout most of the paper, the simplest model in which moral hazard is present will be employed. Each individual in the economy engages in a single activity that has two possible outcomes: either a fixed-damage accident occurs or else it does not (an alternative interpretation is that an accident always occurs but is either high damage or low damage). The output of the economy is a single consumption good, which is the only good in the economy. An individual's level of output depends on whether or not an accident occurs to him. The probability that he has an accident is a function of his accident-prevention effort — a catch-all for the myriad preventive activities or expenditures an individual can undertake.

Individuals are risk-averse and so want to insure against the accident. The insured's effort is unobservable by the insurer. As a result, the provision of insurance is characterized by moral hazard, and insurance is provided against the accident without reference to the insured's effort.

Let y_0 and y_1 denote consumption in the no-accident and accident events, respectively. In the absence of insurance

$$y_0 = w \qquad y_1 = w - d,$$

where w is the no-accident output and d is the damage due to the accident, so that $w - d$ is output in the event of accident. An insurance policy provides a (net of premium) payout or benefit of α if an accident occurs, and otherwise charges a premium β. Thus, with insurance

$$y_0 = w - \beta \qquad y_1 = w - d + \alpha \qquad (1.1)$$

The probability that an accident occurs to an individual, p, is a function of his level of effort, e. At some points in the paper, it is assumed that the individual has a choice of only a finite number of effort levels, each corresponding to a different accident-prevention technique. It is additionally assumed that there is no effort level for which the accident is certain to occur; nor is it possible for the insured to deliberately cause an accident. At other points in the paper, the individual has a choice over a continuum of effort levels. Where $p(e)$ is the probability of accident with effort e, with $e = 0$ corresponding to no effort, it is assumed that $p(0) = \bar{p} < 1$, $p'(e) < 0$, and $p''(e) > 0$; more effort reduces the probability of accident, and successive units of effort reduce the probability of accident by successively lower amounts. Different individuals' accident probabilities are statistically independent.

In the discrete effort levels case, the individual's expected utility is

$$EU^j = (1 - p^j)u_0^j(y_0) + p^j u_1^j(y_1), \qquad (1.2a)$$

where j indexes the effort level, u_0^j is the utility function if an accident does not occur, and u_1^j the utility function when one does. The expected utility function is said to be *separable* if expected utility can be written as

$$EU^j = (1 - p^j)u_0(y_0) + p^j u_1(y_1) - e^j. \tag{1.2b}$$

In many contexts, effort is ordinal; thus, the above definition assumes a particular cardinalization of effort — that effort is measured by the disutility it causes. If "effort" entails expenditure on some accident-prevention good, the expected utility function is said to be *monetized* and has the form

$$EU^j = (1 - p^j)u_0(y_0 - e^j) + p^j u_1(y_1 - e^j). \tag{1.2c}$$

The utility function when an accident occurs may differ from that when one does not, either because the accident causes pain or because it affects tastes (Dionne [1982]). The accident is said to be *utility-decreasing* if $u_1(y) < u_0(y)$ for all y, and *marginal-utility-decreasing* if $u_1'(y) < u_0'(y)$ for all y where $'$ denotes a derivative. When $u_1(y) = u_0(y)$ for all y, the expected utility function is *event-independent*. The appropriate choice of functional form of the expected utility function depends on context.

The terminology for the discrete effort levels case applies equally well to the continuum of effort levels case. The expected utility function is

$$EU = (1 - p(e))U_0(y_0, e) + p(e)U_1(y_1, e). \tag{1.3}$$

If it is separable $U_i(y, e) = u_i(y) - e$; if it is event-independent $U_0(y, e) = U_1(y, e)$ for all y, e; and if it is separable and event-independent $U_i(y, e) = u(y) - e$.

In some contexts, the model is appropriately interpreted as static, in others as describing a stationary state.[4]

Some discussion may help to clarify the terminology. An accident is utility-decreasing if, holding consumption constant, utility is lower when the accident occurs. Most common accidents are utility-decreasing because they are aggravating, unpleasant, or painful. However, a worker disabled by a back problem that will cause him no pain if he does not work, may be happier living on a full disability pension than having to work. Whether an accident is marginal-utility-increasing or marginal-utility-decreasing is more difficult to judge. One would expect, for instance, that an accident that caused severe brain damage would be marginal-utility-decreasing. However, even this extreme example is moot since an individual might purchase extensive coverage against such an accident to relieve his friends and family from the worry that he be well cared for. The expected utility from "financial accidents" is likely to be close to event-independent.

2. The Individual's Effort Decision

Intuition suggests that as more insurance is provided, an insured individual will take less care. Such will normally, but not always, be the case.

The individual's effort choice problem is

$$\max_{e} EU = (1 - p(e))U_0(w - \beta, e) + p(e)U_1(w - d + \alpha, e). \quad (2.1)$$

The first-order condition, with positive effort, is

$$\{-p'(U_0 - U_1)\} + \left[(1 - p)\frac{\partial U_0}{\partial e} + p\frac{\partial U_1}{\partial e}\right] = 0. \quad (2.2)$$

The term in curly brackets is the marginal benefit of effort — the reduction in the probability of an accident from an extra unit of effort $(-p')$ times the gain in utility from a unit reduction in the probability of accident $(U_0 - U_1)$. And the term in square brackets is the expected marginal cost of effort — the probability-weighted marginal disutility of effort for the two events. The second-order condition is

$$A \equiv -p''(U_0 - U_1) - 2p'\left[\frac{\partial U_0}{\partial e} - \frac{\partial U_1}{\partial e}\right] + \left[(1 - p)\frac{\partial^2 U_0}{\partial e^2} + p\frac{\partial^2 U_1}{\partial e^2}\right] < 0 \quad (2.3)$$

There is no guarantee that A is negative. As a consequence, effort may be discontinuous in the parameters of the insurance contract, and may *increase* discontinuously in response to an increase in the amount of insurance provided.

Even when the second-order condition is always satisfied, effort can rise when the amount of insurance increases. To see this, consider increasing the insurance payout, holding the premium fixed

$$\left.\frac{\partial e}{\partial \alpha}\right|_\beta = -\left[p'\frac{\partial U_1}{\partial y_1} + p\frac{\partial^2 U_1}{\partial e\partial y_1}\right] \div A \quad \text{for } e > 0; \quad (2.4)$$

this expression is positive if $\frac{\partial^2 U_1}{\partial e\partial y_1}$ is sufficiently positive — if an increase in y_1 substantially decreases the disutility of effort. An example is the tenancy contract between landlord and tenant in a poor country; if the landlord assists his tenants who have suffered from crop failure, he can prevent their becoming undernourished, which will improve their productivity for the next harvest season.

With separable utility, however, increases in insurance can never cause increases in effort. Furthermore, beyond a level of insurance characterized by $\lim_{e \downarrow 0} p'(e)(-u_0 + u_1) - 1 = 0$, effort is zero — this equation characterizes the *zero effort locus* (ZEL), which in the separability case divides the set of (α, β) for which effort is positive from the set for which effort is zero.

The results of this section are summarized in

Proposition 1: Normally, and always with separable utility, increases in insurance do not cause effort to increase. However, with nonseparable utility, effort can increase either continuously or discontinuously with increases in insurance.

3. The Peculiar Shape of Indifference Curves

From analysis of the individual's effort decision, one can derive a correspondence relating effort to the parameters of the insurance contract, $e = e(\alpha, \beta)$. Substitution of this correspondence into (2.1) gives expected utility as a function of only exogenous parameters and the parameters of the insurance contract, i.e., $V(\alpha, \beta) \equiv EU(e(\alpha, \beta), \alpha, \beta)$. It will prove very useful to conduct the analysis in $\alpha - \beta$ space (see figure 1).

The procedure in this section will be to analyze the shape of indifference curves in $\alpha - \beta$ space first for fixed effort, then for two effort levels, and finally for a continuum of effort levels.

3.1. A Single Effort Level

From (1.2a)

$$\frac{d\beta}{d\alpha}\bigg|_{V_0^j} = \left[\frac{\partial EU^j/\partial \alpha}{\partial EU^j/\partial \beta} \right] = \frac{(u_1^j)' \, p^j}{(u_0^j)'(1 - p^j)} \equiv s^j > 0, \qquad (3.1)$$

while

$$\frac{d^2\beta}{d\alpha^2}\bigg|_{V_b} = -s^j(A_1^j + s^j A_0^j) < 0, \qquad (3.2)$$

where $A_i^j \equiv -\dfrac{(u_i^j)''}{(u_i^j)'}$ is the coefficient of absolute risk aversion with event i. Indifference curves are positively sloped since, from the individual's point of view, the payout is a good and the premium a bad; and they have negative curvature because of risk aversion — as more insurance is provided, the individual is willing to pay a smaller increase in premium for each increase in payout.

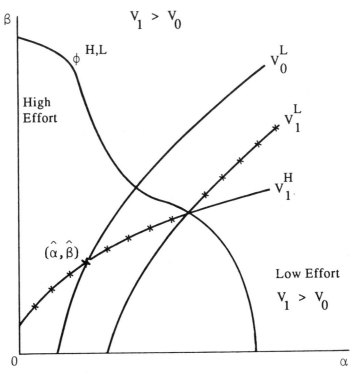

Figure 1. Two activities, separable utility: derivation of indifference curves.

3.2. Two Effort Levels, Separable Utility

Suppose there are two effort levels, low (L) and high (H); with a lower effort level the probability of accident is higher. If the utility function is separable, then the low-effort indifference curve through any point is steeper than the high-effort indifference curve; with lower effort, the probability of accident is higher and therefore the individual is willing to pay a larger increase in premium for a given increase in payout.

As noted in the previous section, with separable utility and a continuum of effort levels, effort decreases as the amount of insurance increases. The analogous result for the two-effort-level case is that the individual expends high effort with low levels of insurance, and vice versa. The boundary separating the high- and low-effort regions is called the *switching locus*.

The pieces are now assembled to construct an effort-variable indifference curve. Turn to figure 1. The switching locus is denoted by $\phi^{H,L}$. V_1^H is the indifference curve yielding utility U_1 when the individual chooses high effort, and V_1^L the corresponding indifference curve when the individual expends low effort. Below $\phi^{H,L}$, the individual chooses high effort and so the high-effort indifference curves are relevant; above $\phi^{H,L}$, the low-effort indifference curves are relevant. Thus, V_1, the indifference curve corresponding to utility level U_1 with effort endogenous, coincides with V_1^H below the switching locus, and V_1^L above. It is apparent from the figure that indifference curves for the two-effort-level case with effort endogenous have a scalloped shape and are never convex.

3.3. Continuum of Effort Levels, Separable Utility

The shape of an indifference curve when there is a continuum of effort levels is determined by two forces. Risk aversion by itself causes indifference curves to be convex (negative curvature). However, as more insurance is provided, effort falls, which increases the slope of an indifference curve; this effect concavifies indifference curves. Which effect dominates depends on the relative power of the two forces. Elementary manipulation gives

$$\frac{d^2\beta}{d\alpha^2}\bigg|_{\bar{V}} = \{-s(A_1 + sA_0)\} + \frac{u_1'}{u_0'(1-p)^2}\frac{dp}{d\alpha}\bigg|_{\bar{v}} \qquad (3.3)$$

where s is defined analogously to s^j in (3.1). The expression in curly brackets gives the risk aversion effect, which convexifies the indifference curve; the second term is the effort disincentive effect, which concavifies the indifference curve. The former is larger, the higher the degree of risk aversion; the latter is larger, the more sensitive is the probability of accident to the amount of insurance provided.

The important result is that when the effort disincentive effect dominates the risk aversion effect, indifference curves are nonconvex. It will be demonstrated that the nonconvexity of indifference curves (in benefit-premium space) caused by moral hazard has significant implications for the existence and nature of equilibrium.

The results are summarized in

Proposition 2: With effort fixed, indifference curves are convex in benefit-premium space; with a finite number of discrete effort levels, indifference curves have a scalloped shape and are never convex; with a continuum of effort levels, indifference curves may or may not be convex, depending on the relative strengths of the risk aversion and effort disincentive effect.

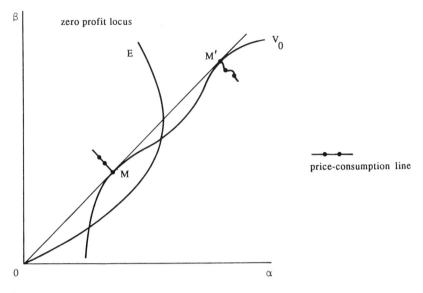

Figure 2. Nonconvexity of indifference curves may cause discontinuities in the price-consumption line.

3.4. Price- and Income-Consumption Lines May Be Discontinuous

Price- and income-consumption lines are defined in the normal way. The price of insurance, q, is defined as the premium paid per unit of benefit, i.e., $q \equiv \dfrac{\beta}{\alpha}$. Thus, the price-consumption line is the locus of points of maximal utility along the price lines $\beta = q\alpha$. An income-consumption line is defined for a specific price, and a q-income-consumption line is defined as the locus of points of maximal utility along price lines with slope q.

The nonconvexity of indifference curves can cause price- and income-consumption lines to be discontinuous. This is illustrated in figure 2, which shows a situation where the price-consumption line is discontinuous across the zero profit locus, $(1 - p)\beta - p\alpha = 0$ (the properties of this locus are discussed in the next section), which will prove significant later on.

Arnott and Stiglitz [1988a] derive the conditions that determine whether price- and income-consumption lines jump inward or outward at a point of discontinuity. In the case of the price-consumption line, what matters is whether, in terms of figure 2, utility increases faster below M or below M' as the price of insurance is reduced. This result indicates that the existence and properties of discontinuities in price- and income-consumption lines depend on global rather than local properties of the utility and probability-of-accident functions. Thus:

> **Proposition 3:** Nonconvexity of indifference curves can generate discontinuities in price- and income-consumption loci. The existence and properties of these discontinuities depend on global properties of the utility and probability-of-accident functions.

4. The Feasibility Set Is Never Convex

The *feasibility set* is the set of contracts for which nonnegative profits are made, i.e., the (α, β) for which $(1 - p(e(\alpha, \beta)))\beta - p(e(\alpha, \beta))\,\alpha \geq 0$, and the *zero profit locus* (ZPL) is the locus of contracts on which zero profits are made.

4.1. Separable Utility

With effort fixed at $\tilde{e}$, the zero profit locus is a ray from the origin with slope $\tilde{q} = \dfrac{\tilde{p}}{1 - \tilde{p}}$. The method of constructing the zero profit locus with two effort levels is analogous to that employed in constructing the indifference curves for this case, and is demonstrated in figure 3. For (α, β) below the switching locus, the high-effort budget constraint is relevant, while for (α, β) above $\phi^{H,L}$, the low-effort budget constraint is relevant. The effort-endogenous feasibility set is evidently nonconvex.

With a continuum of effort levels, the slope of the zero profit locus is given by

$$
\left. \frac{d\beta}{d\alpha} \right|_{ZPL} = \begin{cases} \dfrac{p + (\beta + \alpha) \dfrac{\partial p}{\partial \alpha}}{(1 - p) - (\beta + \alpha) \dfrac{\partial p}{\partial \beta}} & \text{for } e > 0 \\[4mm] \dfrac{\bar{p}}{1 - \bar{p}} & \text{for } e = 0 \end{cases} \tag{4.1}
$$

Two properties of the feasibility set are of particular interest. First, from (4.1), at any point on the zero profit locus where it is positively sloped,

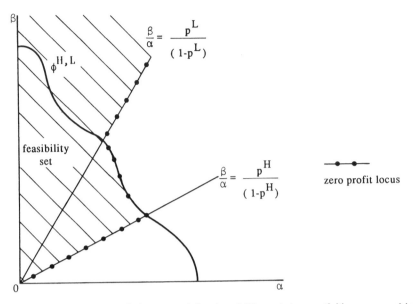

Figure 3. The zero-profit locus and the feasibility set, two activities, separable utility.

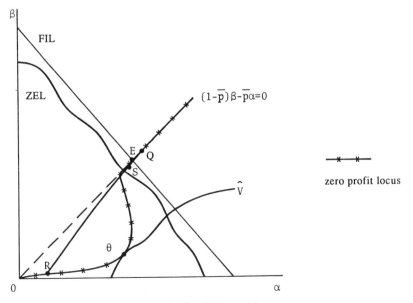

Figure 4. With separable utility, the feasibility set is nonconvex.

and where effort is positive, the locus is steeper than the ray joining the point to the origin $\left(\text{which has slope } q \equiv \dfrac{\beta}{\alpha} = \dfrac{p}{1-p}\right)$. Second, the zero profit locus is nonconvex. This is most-easily demonstrated geometrically. Turn to figure 4. Draw in the zero effort line (ZEL) which was characterized in section 2 by $\lim_{e \downarrow 0} p'(e)(-u_0 + u_1) - 1 = 0$. Next, note that the slope of the zero profit locus at the origin is $\dfrac{p(e(0,0))}{1 - p(e(0,0))} < \dfrac{\bar{p}}{1 - \bar{p}}$. Now take a point Q on the ZPL above the ZEL, and another point R on the ZPL near the origin. Since it is impossible for the line joining the two points to lie inside the feasibility set, the set is nonconvex. Other properties of the zero profit locus for the separability case worthy of note are that i) it is continuous, ii) its curvature is a priori indeterminate, iii) it can have a negatively sloped segment, but never a zero slope, iv) its slope can be discontinuous at the zero effort line.

4.2. Nonseparable Utility

Because effort need not be continuous in the parameters of the insurance contract when utility is nonseparable, the feasibility set need not be connected and segments on the boundary of the feasibility set can have positive profits.

The results established thus far in this section are summarized in the following:

Proposition 4: With separable utility, the feasibility set is connected but non-convex and the zero profit locus is continuous. With nonseparable utility, the feasibility set need not be connected and can contain positive profit segments on its boundary.

4.3. Additional Geometrical Results

The stage is almost set for an examination of the existence and nature of competitive equilibrium. But a few additional results are needed.

Define the *full insurance line* (FIL) to be the locus of (α, β) for which the marginal utility of consumption is the same in the accident and no-accident events. In the case of separable utility, the FIL line is given by

$$u_0'(w - \beta) = u_1'(w - d + \alpha). \tag{4.2}$$

Note that when the utility function is also event-independent, the full insurance line is given by $w - \beta = w - d + \alpha$ or $d = \alpha + \beta$ — consumption is equalized in the two events.

Recall that with separable utility, the zero effort line is given by

$$\lim_{e \downarrow 0} p'(e)(-u_0 + u_1) - 1 = 0. \tag{4.3}$$

The relative positions of the ZEL and FIL lines for separable, event-independent utility will be of interest in the analysis that follows. If $\lim_{e \downarrow 0} p'(e) = -\infty$, then $(-u_0 + u_1) = 0$ along the ZEL, which with event-independent utility implies $u_0' = u_1'$. Thus, when $\lim_{e \downarrow 0} p'(e) = -\infty$, the FIL and ZEL coincide and are given by $d = \alpha + \beta$. If, alternatively, $\lim_{e \downarrow 0} p'(e)$ is finite, then $(-u_0 + u_1) < 0$, which with event-independent utility implies that $w - \beta > w - d + \alpha$ or $d > \alpha + \beta$. In this case, therefore, the ZEL lies strictly inside the FIL (the case drawn in figure 4).

5. The Existence and Properties of Competitive Equilibrium

A full analysis of the existence and properties of competitive equilibrium with moral hazard is very involved for reasons that shall be explained. Even Arnott and Stiglitz [1989a] provide only a partial analysis for the special case of separable, event-independent utility. As a result, this section will only touch on points of special interest.

The way Arnott and Stiglitz proceed is to define competitive equilibrium as a Nash equilibrium in admissible contracts, with free entry and exit, and then to examine the nature of equilibrium under alternative definitions of admissible contracts.

5.1. When Insurance Purchases Are Observable, Equilibrium Will Entail Rationing of Insurance Purchases, and Possibly Random Insurance

The instinctive reaction of an economist trained in the Arrow-Debreu tradition is to say "Why is the definition of admissible contracts an issue? In standard competitive economies, any Pareto optimum can be decentralized by a price system, along with lump-sum transfers. Won't this result extend to economies with moral hazard?" Because of moral hazard, at any price of insurance, insured individuals will typically take less than the socially optimal amount of care. Since insured individuals will typically be more careful if less insurance at a given price is provided, a Pareto improvement can normally be made by rationing the quantity of insurance individuals can purchase.[5] Furthermore, if feasible, competitive insurers will provide contracts that entail rationing.

This argument is now formalized, employing the geometric apparatus developed in the previous sections. Separability is assumed. Turn to figure 4. The contract that provides individuals with maximum utility conditional on moral hazard and on insurers making nonnegative profits occurs at $\theta \equiv (\alpha^*, \beta^*)$, the point of maximum utility along the zero profit locus, which is the point of tangency of the ZPL and $\hat{V}$. We term θ the constrained optimum — the optimum conditional on the unobservability of effort. It was noted earlier that at any point on the zero profit locus where the locus is positively sloped and where effort is positive, the slope of the ZPL exceeds that of the ray from the origin to the point. Since θ satisfies these conditions, this result implies that $\left.\dfrac{d\beta}{d\alpha}\right|_{\hat{V} \atop \theta} > q^*$, which in turn implies that the contract (α^*, β^*) entails rationing at the price q^*.

An insurance company can ration an individual's total insurance purchases only if it can control his insurance purchases from other firms. The simplest way for the firm to do this is to insist that it be the individual's exclusive insurance agent. Such a provision is enforceable only when the individual's total insurance purchases are observable. Suppose they are. Then (α^*, β^*) is the equilibrium contract. It upsets any other contract that makes nonnegative profits, but cannot itself be so upset.

Proposition 5: When insurance purchases are observable, and utility is separable, competitive equilibrium will entail firms offering exclusive contracts that forbid its clients from purchasing insurance from other firms. The equilibrium exclusive contract is characterized by the point of maximum utility on the zero profit locus, and entails quantity rationing at the equilibrium price.

Proposition 5, which was first stated by Pauly [1974], should be qualified. Its proof implicitly considers only deterministic contracts. In fact, (α^*, β^*) may be upset by an exclusive contract that randomizes premia and payouts. Randomization may be Pareto-improving because of the nonconvexities generated by moral hazard. The conditions under which random exclusive contracts dominate deterministic exclusive contracts are given in Arnott and Stiglitz [1988b]. In the rest of the paper, only deterministic contracts will be considered.

It is worth noting that when utility is nonseparable, the exclusive contract equilibrium is at the point of maximum utility in the feasibility set, which may be characterized by positive profits. The reason for this is that effort may be discontinuous in the parameters of the insurance contract. If a firm offers a more attractive contract than the equilibrium contract, the individual reduces his effort discontinuously, which renders the entering contract unprofitable.

5.2. When Only Price Contracts Are Admissible, Competitive Equilibrium May Entail Positive Profits or Inactivity

The analysis of competitive equilibrium with moral hazard becomes subtle when individuals' total insurance purchases are unobservable. What contracts should be deemed admissible? Should negative insurance contracts in which an individual pays when an accident occurs be allowed? Should the definition of equilibrium allow for firms to offer policies that, though not purchased in equilibrium, serve to deter entry? Before addressing these questions, it will prove instructive to examine the characteristics of equilibrium when firms are restricted to offering price contracts in which individuals may purchase as much insurance as they wish at the quoted price.

It is straightforward to establish that when firms are restricted to offering only price contracts, equilibrium always exists and is unique, and individuals' equilibrium insurance purchases are characterized by the lowest point on the price-consumption line consistent with nonnegative profits.

Pauly [1974] investigated the active, zero profit price equilibrium. Since equilibrium purchases are positive, equilibrium is at a point of tangency of a price line and an indifference curve:

$$q = \frac{\beta}{\alpha} = \frac{p\, \dfrac{\partial U_1}{\partial y_1}}{(1 - p)\, \dfrac{\partial U_0}{\partial y_0}}, \tag{5.1}$$

and since zero profits are made,

$$\frac{\beta}{\alpha} = \frac{p}{1 - p}. \tag{5.2}$$

Comparison of (5.1) and (5.2) establishes that in an active zero profit price equilibrium, full insurance is provided. Thus, an active zero profit price equilibrium lies at the point of intersection of the zero profit locus and the full insurance line, marked as E in figures 2 and 4.

The price equilibrium need not, however, be of this type because of discontinuities in the price-consumption line caused by nonconvexity of the indifference curves. Figure 2 illustrates a situation where the price-consumption line jumps across, and never intersects, the zero profit locus. In this case, M is the equilibrium point since it is the lowest point on the price-consumption line consistent with nonnegative profits. But at M, positive profits are made! The reason that positive profits can occur in equilibrium is that at points of discontinuity in the price-consumption line, effort is discontinuous in the price of insurance. If the price of insurance is lowered slightly below q^M, the individual reduces his effort discontinuously, which renders the insurance unprofitable.

The price equilibrium may also be at the origin. At high prices of insurance, the individual would prefer to make no purchases. As the price of insurance is lowered, a point is reached where the individual purchases a large amount of insurance and discontinuously decreases effort, which renders the insurance unprofitable. Thus, no insurance is sold in equilibrium, in which case the market is said to be inactive.

Proposition 6: When only price insurance contracts are allowed, equilibrium occurs at the lowest point on the price-consumption line consistent with non-negative profits. The price equilibrium may be one of three types: a) a zero profit price equilibrium which provides full insurance, b) a positive profit price equilibrium, and c) a zero insurance or inactive price equilibrium.

5.3. Possible Nonexistence of a Quantity Equilibrium

In the previous section, firms were restricted to offering price contracts. But with unobservable insurance purchases, there is no good reason to exclude (nonexclusive) quantity contracts in which firms specify a contract (α, β) or equivalently a quantity α and a price $q \equiv \frac{\beta}{\alpha}$ of insurance. In fact, firms may find it preferable to offer quantity contracts rather than price contracts, since doing so may give them at least partial, indirect control over their clients' total purchases of insurance.

When all firms offer quantity contracts, the characteristics of equilibrium depend on how many firms are in the market and what contract each offers which together constitute the market structure. For example, equilibrium may be different if each firm supplies half of each individual's aggregate insurance purchases than if each firm provides one-quarter.

No attempt shall be made here to provide a thorough analysis of non-exclusive quantity equilibria. Only the possible nonexistence of a quantity equilibrium is demonstrated.

Assume that equilibrium exists with one firm in the market offering a single policy, constrained by potential entry. To simplify the argument, the utility function is assumed to be separable. If the contract the incumbent firm offers makes a profit, an entering firm can make a profit by offering a small, supplementary policy at a slightly lower price; hence, the equilirium contract must lie on the zero profit locus. If the contract the incumbent firm offers rations the quantity of insurance that can be purchased at the quoted price, an entering firm can make a profit by offering a small, positive supplementary policy at a slightly higher price; while if the incumbent firm's contract provides more insurance than individuals would like at the quoted price, an entering firm can offer a small, negative supplementary policy at the same price and make a profit. Thus, the equilibrium contract must lie on the price-consumption line. Putting these results together implies that equilibrium must lie at the point of intersection of the price-consumption line and the zero profit locus. But it has been shown that there may be no such intersection, in which case there is no equilibrium with one firm in the market.

5.4. Expanding the Set of Admissible Contracts — the Possibility of an Infinity of Equilibria

Where individuals' total insurance purchases are unobservable, two cases have been considered thus far, that where all firms offer price contracts, and that where all firms offer a single quantity policy. In both cases, the set of admissible contracts is unjustifiably restricted. When the set of admissible contracts is expanded to allow firms to offer multiple quantity policies in their contracts, to combine price and quantity contracts in their contracts, and to offer policies which are not purchased in equilibrium, there may be an infinity of equilibria.

This is demonstrated in figure 5. Suppose there is a single firm in the market which offers a contract containing a quantity policy (α', β') and a price policy with price q''. (α', β') is the lowest point on the q''-income-consumption line inside the feasibility set. If the contract can be upset, it must entail the insured individual purchasing an amount of insurance, say $(\bar{\alpha}, \bar{\beta})$, from the entering firm. Hence, without loss of generality, attention may be restricted to entering quantity contracts. No entering quantity contract with price greater than q'' with be bought, since the

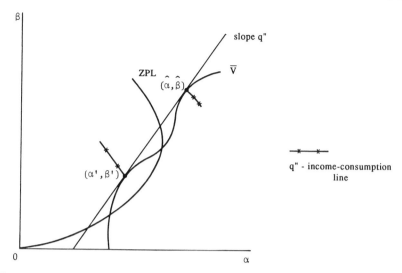

Figure 5. A possible infinity of equilibria with expansion of the admissible contract set.

incumbent firm's contract allows the individual to purchase as much insurance as he wishes at the price q''. The most profitable entering contract per unit of insurance is a small, supplementary positive contract at a price only slightly lower than q''. If such a contract is offered, the individual will purchase (α', β') plus the supplementary contract plus some insurance at the price q'', providing him with aggregate purchases characterized by a point slightly below $(\hat{\alpha}, \hat{\beta})$ on the q''-income-consumption line. If $\dfrac{p(e(\hat{\alpha}, \hat{\beta}))}{1 - p(e(\hat{\alpha}, \hat{\beta}))} > q''$, the entering contract will make a loss. Since the argument relied on no local arguments, if $\{(\alpha', \beta'), q''\}$ is an equilibrium contract, then there is an infinity of analogous equilibrium contracts, each corresponding to a different utility level.

Note that, though the price policy in the equilibrium contract may not be purchased in equilibrium, it serves to deter entry. Such a policy is termed a latent policy.

5.5. Comments

The last three subsections have shown that, when insurance firms cannot observe individuals' insurance purchases, the nature of equilibrium is sensitive to what contracts are deemed admissible. What contract forms real-world competitive insurance companies choose depends, inter alia, on their knowledge of the market, the costs of administration, and consumer acceptance and understanding. Thus, what contract forms are reasonably deemed admissible is moot.

In this section, it has been assumed that firms either have no knowledge of their clients' purchases from other firms or complete knowledge. Hellwig [1983] has analysed intermediate cases where inter-firm communication is endogenous. He argues that equilibrium will entail some firms exchanging information on insurance sales to each client, but never all firms. Another approach to the treatment of intermediate cases is to assume that firms can obtain information about their clients' purchases, but at a cost.

What light does the analysis of this section cast on actual insurance contracts? All standard insurance contracts, except life and air flight insurance, contain exclusivity provisions.[6] This is consistent with the analysis, since moral hazard is likely to be unimportant for life and air flight insurance, but important for all other standard forms of insurance. Other features, such as the absence of random insurance, negative insurance, and latent policies, and the unavailability of insurance against small-damage, high-probability accidents, are probably due to transactions costs, broadly interpreted. In the applied literature on imperfect information, one comes across statements that the absence of insurance against certain contingencies can be ascribed to moral hazard and adverse selection. Without transactions costs, such assertions appear to have little theoretical foundation.

The analysis has been static. The extension to a dynamic environment is an active topic of current research.

6. Nonmarket Insurance

The analysis was applied to an insurance *market*, but can readily be adapted to treat other forms of insurance.

6.1. Principal-agent problems

Almost all principal-agent relationships are characterized by moral hazard. A classic example is the choice of contract between landlord and laborer (e.g., Stiglitz [1974]). Should the landlord rent the land to the laborer, pay the laborer a wage, or share output with the laborer under a sharecropping contract? The output from the land depends on the weather and the laborer's effort, neither of which can be perfectly observed by the landlord — hence moral hazard. If the landlord rents the land, the laborer has a strong incentive to work hard but faces considerable risk since he is the residual claimant. If, however, the landlord pays the laborer a wage, the laborer has little incentive to work hard, since he can blame low output on bad weather. Thus, share-cropping may provide the optimal balance between risk-bearing and incentives. To formalize this, suppose there are two output levels, with the probability of the higher output level increasing in the laborer's effort. Let θ^H and θ^L denote the high and low values of the laborer's marginal product (VMP), y^H and y^L the corresponding laborer consumption levels, and e effort. Then with the transformation of variables $\theta^H \leftrightarrow w$, $\theta^H - \theta^L \leftrightarrow d$, $y^H \leftrightarrow w - \beta$, and $y^L \leftrightarrow w - d + \alpha$, the model is identical to the one analysed in the essay. Analogous to the analysis of exclusive contracts, one obtains the result that, where the landlord can ensure that the laborer will not obtain insurance against output variability from a third party, sharecropping will typically occur.

6.2. Social insurance

Almost all forms of social insurance are affected by moral hazard. One example will be given here — the optimal replacement rate (the ratio of unemployment benefits to employment income) in unemployment insurance.

The replacement rate affects a variety of margins — the worker's choice of hours of work a week, his occupational choice which entails trading off income against job satisfaction, and his decisions to quit and to accept a job offer. The focus here will be on yet another margin, search effort. The two events are to find a job and to not find a job. A higher replacement rate provides the unemployed worker with more insurance against the uncertainty of his success in search, but weakens his search incentives. The model is completely analogous to that presented in the paper, and the analogous result is obtained that if exclusivity can be enforced, typically only partial replacement will be provided. There are a couple of interesting wrinkles to this example. First, if being unemployed is more pleasant than working, the accident is utility-increasing. Second, assistance to the unemployed worker from family and friends undermines the benefits from exclusivity and may actually be socially harmful. The last point is elaborated in Arnott and Stiglitz [1991].

7. The Welfare Economics of Moral Hazard — One Accident, One Consumer Good

Can the government improve efficiency by intervention when moral hazard is present? In answering this question, it is important to specify what information the government has at its disposal. It shall be assumed here that the government has the same information as private insurers.

In this section, attention shall be restricted to the case treated thus far in the paper, where there is a single type of accident and a single consumer good.

It was demonstrated in section 5 that when individuals' total insurance purchases are observable, equilibrium is characterized by exclusive contracts and is efficient, contingent on the presence of moral hazard.

When insurance purchases are unobservable, the appropriate treatment of the welfare economics is problematical since those constraints that affect the forms of admissible contract may also affect the cost and scope of government intervention.

This problem does not arise, however, when indifference curves are convex. In this case, in the absence of government intervention, equilibrium always exists and lies at the point of intersection of the zero profit locus and the full insurance line. Now consider the effect of the government taxing insurance firms on their total payouts and distributing the proceeds to households as a lump sum. This forces firms to offer insurance at less than actuarially fair odds, which stimulates effort. It can be shown that by setting the tax rate at the right level, the government can force the economy to the constrained social optimum.[7] Thus, when insurance purchases are unobservable and indifference curves are convex, the constrained optimum can be achieved by the taxation of insurance payouts. When indifference curves are nonconvex, the taxation of insurance is normally desirable even though the constrained optimum may not be achievable. The taxation of insurance induces firms to offer insurance at less than fair odds. As a consequence, individuals will typically purchase less insurance and expend more effort. This argument is formalized in Arnott and Stiglitz [1989b]. The beneficial effects of government intervention in this context stem from the government's monopoly on coercive taxation.

8. The Welfare Economics of Moral Hazard in a Multi-Market Setting

This section reviews material contained in Arnott and Stiglitz [1986], [1989c], and [1990]. It has been shown that when insurance purchases are observable, and there is a single good and a single type of accident, competitive equilibrium is efficient conditional on moral hazard being present. In this section, it is shown that competitive equilibrium is inefficient, even with observability if there is more than one good or if individuals purchase insurance against different accidents from different agents.

The general explanation for this generic inefficiency result is that the provision of insurance in the presence of moral hazard causes the insured individual to receive less than the full social benefit of his care. As a result, not only will the individual typically expend less than the socially optimal amount of care, but also there will be an insurance-induced externality that will cause market prices to deviate from the corresponding social opportunity costs.

Consider first an economy with an accident-prevention good, say fire extinguishers, a consumer good, a single type of accident — fire — and accident-prevention effort. The presence of moral hazard typically causes individuals to purchase too little of the accident-prevention good and to expend too little accident-prevention effort, relative to the first-best situation where effort and fire extinguisher purchases are observable. The subsidization of fire extinguishers typically encourages their purchase and reduces the probability of accident. This reduces the efficiency loss relative to the first best and is therefore welfare-improving. Arnott and Stiglitz [1986] develop this point. By this line of reasoning, industrial safety should be subsidized, and alcohol should be taxed to discourage drunk driving.

This line of reasoning also establishes that in a competitive equilibrium in a multi-market economy with moral hazard, market prices do not coincide with shadow prices. As a result, neither the first (any competitive equilibrium is Pareto optimal) nor the second (any Pareto optimum can be decentralized as a competitive equilibrium with lump-sum transfers) theorems of welfare economics holds. This in turn implies that the *potential* scope for government intervention with moral hazard is substantial.[8] To establish the actual desirability of government intervention in a specific context, however, it needs to be established that the benefits of government intervention exceed the costs.

Next consider an economy with a single consumer good but two types of statistically independent accidents, say house fire and occupational disability. Assume that the technology of insurance provision is such that insurance companies specialize in the types of insurance they provide; in the current context, that one group of firms provides house fire insurance and another occupational disability. There are two different sources of market failure. First, relative to the market equilibrium, a Pareto improvement can be made by transferring a dollar from one type of insurance company to the other. Taking a dollar away from home fire insurers forces them to offer insurance at less than actuarially fair odds, which will typically stimulate their clients' care in preventing fires. Giving the dollar to occupational safety insurers will typically reduce job safety. However, the net result may be an improvement in efficiency. Second, even though the accident probabilities are statistically independent, the effort expended to prevent one accident generally affects the effort expended to prevent the other, through the expected utility function. Thus, there is an uninternalized externality — the insurance contract offered by house fire insurers affects the profitability of occupational disability insurers.[9] If the assumption that the technology of insurance provision is such that insurance companies specialize in the types of insurance they provide is relaxed, then the above results can be re-interpreted to state that all an individuals' insurance needs (and at all points in time) should be, and in competitive equilibrium will be, provided by a single insurance company — an extended exclusivity result.

In the discussion of unemployment insurance in the last section, it was noted that assistance to the unemployed from family and friends may be socially harmful because it undermines the beneficial effects of exclusivity. Because unemployment insurance is rationed, family and friends have an incentive to make pacts of mutual assistance — for the employed to help the unemployed. In making such pacts, they neglect that when everyone does so, the moral hazard associated with job search will increase throughout the economy, which will cause the government to increase taxes or decrease the replacement rate. This is an example of a general phenomenon that may be of considerable importance — when moral hazard is present, dysfunctional nonmarket insurance institutions may arise, which undermine the effectiveness of market and government insurance provision.

Thus far in the discussion of the welfare economics of moral hazard, the traditional dichotomy of market versus government has been maintained: When the market fails, the government should intervene to improve the market's performance as long as the benefits of doing so exceed the costs. In recent years, however, largely in response to work on mechanism design, the focus of welfare economics has been changing. The traditional dichotomy neglects that the market is not the only institutional mechanism for delivering goods and services in general, or insurance in particular. Social custom (e.g., the reciprocation of support), the firm (e.g., the insurance provided in long-term labor contracts), nonprofit organizations, and government are all important sources of insurance. Thus, the central question of welfare economics is more appropriately posed as "What is the best institutional mechanism for the provision of a particular good or service?" than as "What government intervention is warranted to correct market failure?" Future research on the welfare economics of insurance should adopt this new perspective.

9. A Continuum of Outcomes[10]

To simplify the analysis, it was assumed that there are only two possible outcomes — either a fixed-damage accident occurs or it does not. This was a convenient simplifying assumption for the purpose of investigating the positive and normative properties of competitive equilibrium at a general level. Practically, however, accident damage is typically continuously variable, in which case the question naturally arises as to how the insurance payout should vary with the level of accident damage.[11]

This problem has been extensively analyzed. It has typically been treated as a principal-agent problem, but as we have seen principal-agent and insurance problems are isomorphic. The principal-agent problem asks: How with moral hazard should an agent's wage, s, be related to his output, y, subject to his receiving expected utility of $\bar{U}$? Now, accident damage equals maximum output minus actual output, $d = \bar{y} - y$, and the wage equals output plus net payout, $w = \bar{y} - d + \alpha(d)$. Thus, if one solves $s = s(y)$ in the principal-agent formulation, one can straightforwardly translate this into $\alpha = \alpha(d)$ in the insurance formulation. In conformity with the literature, the problem will be analyzed in the principal-agent context.

Assume that the agent's utility function is separable and event-independent. Then expected utility is

$$EU = \int_{\underline{y}}^{\bar{y}} (u(s(y)) - e)f(y, e)dy, \qquad (9.1)$$

where $\bar{y}$ and $\underline{y}$ are maximum and minimum output, respectively, which are assumed to be independent of e, and $f(y, e)$ is the probability density function of output with effort e.

The problem facing the risk-neutral principal is to choose the wage schedule so as to maximize profit, subject to the agent receiving at least his reservation utility level $\bar{U}$, and the agent's choosing effort so as to maximize his expected utility, taking the wage schedule as given. The second constraint is an incentive compatibility constraint, and is written as

$$e = \underset{e'}{\text{argmax}} \; EU \left(\langle s(y) \rangle, e' \right). \tag{9.2}$$

The first constraint is

$$EU(\langle s(y) \rangle, e) - \bar{U} \geqslant 0. \tag{9.3}$$

And expected profits are

$$\pi = \int_{\underline{y}}^{\bar{y}} (y - s(y)) f(y, e) dy. \tag{9.4}$$

Thus, the principal's problem is to

$$\underset{\langle s(y) \rangle, \, e}{\max} \; (9.4) \quad \text{such that,} \quad \begin{array}{l} \text{i) } (9.3) \\ \text{ii) } (9.2) \end{array} \tag{9.5}$$

Since one is solving for an optimal function, one would like to use optimal control theory. Unfortunately, (9.2) as written is not a differentiable constraint.

One approach to solving the problem, called the first-order approach, is to replace (9.2) with the first-order condition of the individual's effort choice problem,

$$\int_{\underline{y}}^{\bar{y}} u(s(y)) f_e(y, e) dy - 1 = 0, \tag{9.6}$$

where subscript e denotes a partial derivative. The problem will now be "solved" using the first-order approach. Then conditions will be investigated under which the first-order approach is "valid." The approach may be said to be strongly valid if it identifies only the globally optimal solution, weakly valid if it identifies the globally optimum solution but identifies other solutions as well, and invalid if it fails to identify the globally optimal solution.

The principal's maximization problem written in Lagrangean form is

$$\mathcal{L} = \int_{\underline{y}}^{\bar{y}} (y - s(y)) f(y, e) dy + \lambda \left(\int_{\underline{y}}^{\bar{y}} (u(s(y)) - e) f(y, e) dy - \bar{U} \right)$$
$$+ \mu \left(\int_{\underline{y}}^{\bar{y}} u(s(y)) f_e(y, e) dy - 1 \right). \tag{9.7}$$

λ is the Lagrange multiplier on (9.3); it should be positive since $\lambda = -\dfrac{\partial \mathcal{L}}{\partial \overline{U}}$ and expected profits should go up as the agent's reservation utility level falls. μ is the Lagrange mutliplier on (9.6); it should be positive since $\mu = -\dfrac{\partial \mathcal{L}}{\partial \S}$, where $\S$ is the marginal disutility of effort, and expected profits should rise with a fall in the agent's marginal disutility of effort.

This appears to be a straightforward optimal control problem with control parameter e, control variable $s(y)$, and two isoperimetric constraints. The Euler condition with respect to s is

$$(-1 + \lambda u')f + \mu u' f_e = 0, \tag{9.8}$$

or, in the form familiar in the literature, as

$$\frac{1}{u'(s(y))} = \lambda + \mu \frac{f_e(y, e)}{f(y, e)}, \tag{9.9}$$

where u' is the marginal utility of consumption. Two features of this equation are worthy of note. First, if moral hazard is absent, $u'(s(x)) = \dfrac{1}{\lambda}$ for all x; as expected, in the absence of moral hazard, full insurance is provided. Second, since $\dfrac{1}{u'(s(y))} \infty \dfrac{f_e(y, e)}{f(y, e)}$ and $s(y) \infty \dfrac{1}{u'(s(y))}$, then $s(y) \propto \dfrac{f_e(y, e)}{f(y, e)}$. Now, $\dfrac{f_e(y, e)}{f(y, e)}$ is the proportional change in the probability of output y as effort rises. Ordinarily, one expects an increase in effort to increase the probability of high output and by proportionally more the higher the output, and to decrease the probability of low output. Thus, the wage will normally be increasing in output, which is what intuition suggests should occur when moral hazard is present.

Unfortunately, the first-order approach is not in general valid. It may be invalid, weakly valid, or strongly valid.

There are essentially two different problems with the first-order approach. The first relates to the possible nonequivalence of (9.2) and (9.6). The first-order condition for effort identifies local extrema. There may be multiple local extrema, and the global maximum may not be a local extremum. The second problem relates to properties of the overall maximization problem.

With regards to the first problem: It will prove convenient for subsequent analysis to integrate the first-order condition of the individual's effort choice problem by parts, yielding

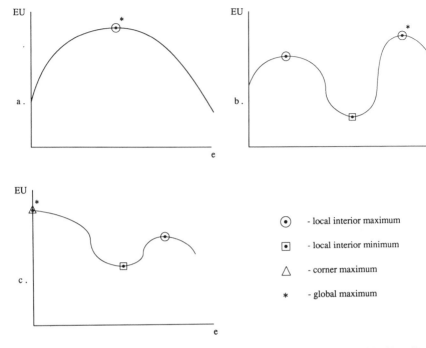

Figures 6a–6c. Problems with the first-order approach: the individual's effort choice problem.

$$(u(s(y))F_e(y, e))\big|_{\underline{y}}^{\overline{y}} - \int_{\underline{y}}^{\overline{y}} u'(s(y))s'(y)F_e(y, e)dy - 1 = 0.$$

Since the first term on the left-hand side is zero,[12]

$$-\int_{\underline{y}}^{\overline{y}} u'(s(y))s'(y)F_e(y, e)dy - 1 = 0. \tag{9.6'}$$

The corresponding second-order condition is

$$-\int_{\underline{y}}^{\overline{y}} u'(s(y))s'(y)F_{ee}(y, e)dy < 0. \tag{9.10}$$

This is not necessarily satisfied since $s'(y)$ need not be positive for all y, and $F_{ee}(y, e)$ need not be negative for all y and e. Thus, there may be multiple local extrema.[13] Furthermore, as in the two-outcome case, the optimal effort level may be zero — a corner maximum that does not satisfy the first-order condition. Figures 6a–6c show three possible graphs of expected utility as a function of effort. In Figure 6a, the first-order condition picks out only one local extremum, which is the global maximum; this is the well-behaved case. In Figure 6b, the first-order condition identifies two local interior maxima and one local interior minimum, with one of the local interior maxima being the global maximum. And in Figure 6c, the first-order condition identifies a local interior maximum and a local interior minimum, while the global maximum is at a corner.

The second problem stems from the fact that (9.5) is not necessarily a concave programming problem. Suppose that the individual's effort choice problem has been correctly solved. To simplify the exposition, let us switch from the problem with a continuum of output levels to the problem with a discrete number, for which wage s_i is associated with output level y_i, $i, = 1$ __, I. Suppose that the problem has been completely solved, and that the optimum entails $\{s_i^*\}$. Then allow s_1 and s_2 to vary, holding all the other s_i at their optimal levels, and plot the indifference curves corresponding to $\bar{U}$, as well as isoprofit contours, in s_2-s_1 space, as done in figures 7a–7c.

Now, the indifference curves are continuous in s_2-s_1 space, though not necessarily convex for the reasons identified in section 3. The isoprofit contours may, however, be discontinuous, since a small change in one of the contract parameters may cause a discontinuous change in the individual's choice of effort (corresponding to a jump from one local maximum to another in the individual's effort choice problem) and correspondingly in the profit level. Also, even when continuous, the isoprofit contours need not be concave. In figure 7a, the first-order conditions identify a unique extremum which is the global optimum (in s_2-s_1 space; the problem need not be as well-behaved in s_1 __ s_2-s_1 space). In figure 7b, the first-order conditions identify two local interior maxima, of which one is the global maximum, as well as one local interior minimum. In figure 7c, the first-order conditions identify a unique local interior maximum, but miss the global maximum which is at a point of discontinuity of an isoprofit contour (and correspondingly of effort).

Since the solution employing the first-order approach is much easier than using alternative solution procedures (one of which is given in Grossman and Hart [1983]), a lot of effort has gone into attempts to obtain an economically persuasive set of conditions under which the first-order approach is valid (most notably, Mirrlees [1975], Rogerson [1985], and Jewitt [1988]).

The set of conditions specified by Rogerson can be easily motivated. Observe that if one rules out corner solutions to the individual's effort choice problem *and* if (9.10) is satisfied for all y, e then the first-order

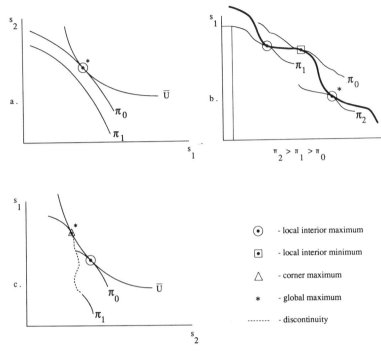

Figures 7a–7c. Problems with the first-order approach: the contract choice problem.

approach is weakly valid. Equation 9.6 is then equivalent to 9.2, and e is continuous in $s(y)$. Equation 9.10 is satisfied for all y, e if $F_{ee}(y, e) > 0$ for all y, e *and* $s'(y) > 0$ for all y. From the discussion of (9.9), it follows that with $\lambda > 0$ and $\mu > 0$ (which Rogerson proves) $s'(y) > 0$ for all y if $\dfrac{f_e(y, e)}{f(y, e)}$ is increasing in y for all y and e. Thus, ruling out corner solutions to the individual's effort choice problem, a pair of sufficient conditions for the first-order approach to be valid are

i) $F_{ee}(y, e) > 0$ for all y, e

ii) $\dfrac{f_e(y, e)}{f(y, e)}$ is increasing in y for all y, e.

Rogerson refers to condition *i* as the convexity of the distribution function (CDFC) condition, and condition *ii* as the monotone likelihood ratio condition (MLRC). We argued earlier that the MLRC is intuitively reasonable. While $F_e(y, e) < 0$ (higher effort reduces the probability that output will be below any given level) is economically sensible, $F_{ee}(y, e) > 0$ has no intuitive economic justification and is indeed (as Jewitt demonstrates) not satisfied for many reasonable probability-of-accident functions $F(y, e)$. Noting these points, Jewitt [1988] derives an alternative set of conditions, which entails strengthening condition ii and weakening condition i.

10. Moral Hazard cum Adverse Selection

It was noted in the introduction that empirical work in insurance economics must take account of the simultaneous presence of adverse selection and moral hazard. In view of its importance for empirical work, it is therefore remarkable that there is virtually no theoretical work that treats adverse selection and moral hazard simultaneously.[14]

Theorists have been deterred by the inherent complexity and messiness of the problem. With even only two events and two groups, one encounters a tedious cataloguing of cases (Cromb [1987]). And the complexity of the general case can be appreciated by considering the optimal income tax problem (Mirrlees [1971]). There the government designs a schedule relating after-tax income to before-tax income when individuals differ according to unobservable ability and make an unobservable labor-leisure choice. The problem entails hidden action and hidden type, but no uncertainty. An insurance problem with both adverse selection and moral hazard, meanwhile, contains hidden action, hidden type, and unobservable (realization of) uncertainty. Thus, the general insurance problem is at least as complex as the optimal income tax problem with unobservable uncertainty. The optimal income tax problem is difficult enough. Providing a complete analysis of the problem extended to treat unobservable uncertainty is positively daunting. One can only hope that there will be a conceptual breakthrough, or that some brave and talented soul will take on the task.

11. Concluding Comments

This essay has, I believe, made a persuasive case that the nonconvexities and externalities to which moral hazard gives rise fundamentally alter the qualitative properties of competitive equilibrium.

Moral hazard is pervasive. Whether its presence in the economy should cause us to rethink the way in which most economic analysis — which ignores moral hazard — is done, depends on its quantitative importance. There are no estimates of this, since the necessary empirical work requires as its theoretical foundation a general, dynamic model that treats moral hazard and adverse selection simultaneously. In my opinion, the development of such a model should be the highest priority item on the research agenda in the theory of insurance economics.

Notes

1. This is the extreme form of moral hazard. When the states of nature and/or individuals' actions are partially observable (i.e., with noise) moral hazard problems remain but are diluted. See Holmstrom [1979].

2. The provision of insurance therefore affects the probabilities of the events. For this reason, one may define moral hazard to occur whenever the provision of insurance affects the probabilities of the insured-against events.

3. The material in sections 1–4 is based on Arnott and Stiglitz [1988a], which builds on the classics in the literature: Arrow [1970], Helpman and Laffont [1975], Marshall [1976], Pauly [1974], Shavell [1979], and Spence and Zeckhauser [1971].

4. In this interpretation, however, the possibility of experience-rating — basing the insurance offered on the accident experience of the insured individual — is ignored.

5. This intuition is imprecise since it neglects that rationing at a given price of insurance exposes the individual to more risk.

6. How effective these provisions are depends on context.

7. This statement is subject to a technical qualification. See Arnott and Stiglitz (1989b).

8. These results contrast with those of Prescott and Townsend [1984] who prove that multimarket competitive equilibrium with moral hazard *is* Pareto optimal. The differences between the Arnott and Stiglitz conclusions and those of Prescott and Townsend derive from differences in assumptions.

Arnott and Stiglitz assume that insurance companies cannot observe their clients' consumption bundles, and cannot therefore write insurance contracts contingent on their clients' consumption choices. The government, meanwhile, can observe and therefore tax market transactions, but only anonymously; for example, they can tax the sale of a pack of a cigarettes, but cannot vary the tax rate depending on who purchases or will smoke the cigarettes. The government has an advantage over the collectivity of insurance companies in its monopoly on taxation.

In contrast, Prescott and Townsend assume that insurance companies can observe their clients' consumption bundles, and therefore write insurance contracts contingent on their clients' consumption choices. Under these assumptions, the government has no advantage over the collectivity of insurance firms. The Prescott and Townsend assumptions strike me as unrealistic.

9. This is a technological and not a pecuniary externality since it operates through the individual's effort decision and not through prices.

10. The reader may wish to skim or skip this section since the subject matter is intrinsically rather difficult technically.

11. This question is investigated at length in another essay in this book, 1991 Winter [1991].

One idealized payout schedule specifies a deductible (if $d \le \bar{d}$, the insurance company pays out nothing) and a coinsurance rate (for every dollar of damage above $\bar{d}$, the insured receives c (≤ 1) dollars).

12. Since the maximum and minimum output levels are independent of the level of effort, $F(\bar{y}, e) = 1$ and $F(\underline{y}, e) = 0$, independent of e.

13. Note that this is in contrast to the two-outcome case with separable and event-independent utility.

14. I know of seven papers — Stiglitz [1982], Whinston [1983], Prescott and Townsend [1985], Greenwald and Stiglitz [1986], Hoy [1987], Cromb [1987], and Gravelle [1989]. Stiglitz [1982] mentions how one result for the optimal income tax problem is modified when uncertainty is introduced (see below in the body of the paper for a discussion of the optimal income tax problem). Whinston [1983] extends the Diamond-Mirrlees model of optimal social insurance to two unidentifiable groups. Prescott and Townsend [1985] provide a general analysis, but under unrealistic informational assumptions (see fn. 8). Greenwald and Stiglitz [1986] provide a general analysis of the externalities to which moral hazard and adverse selection give rise. And, Hoy [1987], Cromb [1987], and Gravelle [1989] extend Arnott and Stiglitz [1988a] to two unidentifiable groups.

References

Arnott, R., and J. E. Stiglitz. (1986). "Moral Hazard, and Optimal Commodity Taxation," *Journal of Public Economics* 29, 1–24.

Arnott, R., and J. E. Stiglitz. (1988a). "The Basic Analytics of Moral Hazard," *Scandinavian Journal of Economics* 90, 383–413.

Arnott, R., and J. E. Stiglitz. (1988b). "Randomization with Asymmetric Information," *Rand Journal of Economics* 19, 344–362.

Arnott, R., and J. E. Stiglitz. (1989a). "Equilibrium in Competitive Insurance Markets with Moral Hazard," mimeo.

Arnott, R., and J. E. Stiglitz. (1989b). "Price Equilibrium, Efficiency, and Decentralizability in Competitive Insurance Markets," mimeo.

Arnott, R., and J. E. Stiglitz. (1989c). "The Welfare Economics of Moral Hazard," in H. Loubergé, ed., *Risk, Information, and Insurance: Essays in the Memory of Karl H.Borch*. Norwell, MA: Kluwer Academic Publishers.

Arnott, R., and J. E. Stiglitz. (1991). "Moral Hazard and Non-market Institutions: Dysfunctional Crowding Out or Peer Monitoring?" *American Economic Review* 81, 170–190.

Arrow, K. (1970). *Essays in the Theory of Risk-Bearing*. London: North-Holland.

Cromb, I. (1987). "Competitive Insurance Markets with Moral Hazard and Adverse Selection," mimeo. Queens' University.

Dionne, G. (1982). "Moral Hazard and State Dependent Utility Function," *Journal of Risk and Insurance* 49, 405–423.

Gravelle, H. E. S. (1989). "An Exposition of Some Basic Analytics of Observability in Insurance Contracts," mimeo. University of London.

Greenwald, B., and J. E. Stiglitz. (1986). "Externalities in Economies with Imperfect Information and Incomplete Markets," *Quarterly Journal of Economics* 100, 229–264.

Grossman, S., and O, Hart. (1983). "An Analysis of the Principal-Agent Problem," *Econometrica* 51, 7–45.

Hellwig, M. F. (1983). "Moral Hazard and Monopolistically Competitive Insurance Markets," University of Bonn, discussion paper 105.

Helpman, E., and J.-J. Laffont. (1975). "On Moral Hazard in General Equilibrium," *Journal of Economic Theory* 10, 8–23.

Holmström, B. (1978). "Moral Hazard and Observability," *Bell Journal of Economics* 10, 74–91.

Hoy, M. (1987). "The Value of Information and Screening Mechanisms under Alternative Insurance Possibilities," Department of Economics, University of Guelph, 4.

Jewitt, I. (1988). "Justifying the First-Order Approach to Principal-Agent Problems," *Econometrica* 56, 1177–1190.

Marshall, J. M. (1976). "Moral Hazard," *American Economic Review* 66, 880–890.

Mirrlees, J. A. (1971). "An Exploration in the Theory of Optimum Income Taxation," *Review of Economic Studies* 38, 175–208.

Mirrlees, J. A. (1975). "The Theory of Moral Hazard and Unobservable Behaviour," mimeo. Nuffield College, Oxford.

Pauly, M. (1974). "Overprovision and Public Provision of Insurance: The Roles of Adverse Selection and Moral Hazard," *Quarterly Journal of Economics* 88, 44–62.

Prescott, E., and R. Townsend. (1984). "Pareto Optima and Competitive Equilibrium with Adverse Selection and Moral Hazard," *Econometrica* 52, 21–46.

Rogerson, W. (1985). "The First-Order Approach to Principal-Agent Problems," *Econometrica* 53, 1357–1368.

Shavell, S. (1979). "On Moral Hazard and Insurance," *Quarterly Journal of Economics*, 93, 541–562.

Spence, M., and R. Zeckhauser. (1971). "Insurance, Information, and Individual Action," *American Economic Review* 61, 380–387.

Stiglitz, J. E. (1974). "Incentives and Risk Sharing in Sharecropping," *Review of Economic Studies* 41, 219–255.

Stiglitz, J. E. (1982). "Self-selection and Pareto Efficient Taxation," *Journal of Public Economics* 17, 213–240.

Whinston, M. D. (1983). "Moral Hazard, Adverse Selection, and the Optimal Provision of Social Insurance," *Journal of Public Economics* 22, 49–71.

Winter, R. (1991). "Moral Hazard in Insurance Contracts," in G. Dionne (Ed.) *Contributions to Insurance Economics*. Norwell, MA: Kluwer Academic Publishers.

PROBATIONARY PERIODS AND TIME-DEPENDENT DEDUCTIBLES IN INSURANCE MARKETS WITH ADVERSE SELECTION

Claude Fluet

Université du Québec à Montréal

Abstract

Insurance policies sometimes allow the extent of coverage to vary over the life of the policy according to the timing of the loss. In markets with adverse selection, contracts with time-dependent coverage are shown to provide a desirable screening mechanism whenever ex post information about the date of occurrence of a loss is available to insurers. In the situation considered, individuals face the risk of a given monetary loss over some given time horizon; the loss can occur only once and its date of occurrence is random. As in the standard analysis of separating equilibria under adverse selection, high-risk individuals purchase full coverage, while low risks are offered partial coverage; in contrast to the standard analysis, coverage can be made dependent on the date of occurrence of the loss. The paper shows under what conditions coverage for the low risks should be constant, increasing or decreasing over the life of the policy.

Key words: Insurance contracts, adverse selection, separating equilibrium, timing of losses, probationary periods, time-dependent deductibles

Many insurance policies, for instance dental or medical policies, include a probationary period by which coverage is excluded or reduced for events

I wish to thank Georges Dionne, Louis Eeckhoudt, Jacques Robert, and Pascale Viala for very helpful suggestions. Financial support from the Québec Fonds FCAR is gratefully acknowledged.

that occur during some specified period after the inception of the policy. A standard justification for such contracts is that they rule out insurance for individuals with preexisting conditions. A somewhat more general one would be that probationary periods allow insurers to sort out individuals with different risk characteristics. The purpose of the present paper is to give a formal expression to this idea.

Consider a competitive insurance market with asymmetric information about consumer's risk characteristics. For simplicity, there are only two risk types, each type being differentiated by the risk individuals face of suffering a given monetary loss within some given time-horizon. By assumption, the loss can occur only once. Insurers know the characteristics of each risk type, but are unable to tell beforehand to which type an individual belongs. In the situation usually examined in the literature, insurance contracts do not take into account the timing of the loss. That is, insurers determine their policies as if, *ex post*, they knew only whether or not the loss has occurred over the life of the policy, and not when it has occurred. In such a situation, contracts can be differentiated, as in Rothschild-Stiglitz [1976], only in terms of the premium paid to the insurer and the indemnity paid to the insured if a loss occurs. In a separating equilibrium, in which individuals reveal their type by selecting a preferred contract among the available policies, full coverage would be offered to high-risk individuals (those who face a greater probability of suffering the loss over the given time-horizon) and partial coverage to low-risk individuals. Partial coverage can be described here as implying a *deductible* with respect to the actual amount of the loss.

By construction, the insurance coverage in the equilibrium just described is independent of the date at which a loss occurs. Each risk type being characterized by a different probability of loss function over time, this suggests that more elaborate contracts could arise in equilibrium whenever *ex post* information about the timing of a loss, should a loss occur, is in fact available to the insurer. This requires of course that insurers be able to ascertain at reasonable cost the true date of occurrence of a loss (or, equivalently, that individuals, when making a claim, be unable to cheat on the true date of occurrence). Because information about the timing of a loss introduces the possibility of an additional instrument to sort out the high- and low-risk types, one would expect that the latter situation could be strictly preferred by low-risk agents; that is, the equilibrium that would obtain with such contracts would constitute a more efficient sorting mechanism.

Contracts with probationary periods are therefore examined. In their simplest form, these could allow full monetary coverage of a loss, but only after some agreed period has elapsed. Such contracts correspond to the pure time-deductible policies analysed in Eeckhoudt, et al. [1988], and would therefore be formally defined by a premium and a probationary period during which no claim can be recovered. In a less restrictive formulation, a probationary period contract is one that allows for a different amount of coverage according to whether or not the loss occurs within some specified period; in other words, such a contract involves a time-dependent deductible. A typical example of such policies would be the stepwise increasing coverage of some dental plans. Contracts with time-dependent deductibles obviously include as special cases the standard constant monetary deductible (when the deductible is independent of the timing of the loss) and the pure time-deductible (when the deductible is either zero or equal to the loss).

Under appropriate conditions, it is possible to characterize the probationary period contracts in a separating equilibrium. As in the standard situation, high-risk individuals purchase full insurance, while low-risks choose partial insurance. In the equilibrium contract purchased by the low risks the deductible may be either constant over the life of the policy (a pure monetary deductible contract), stepwise decreasing, or even stepwise increasing. The conditions leading to a specific form of contract are formulated in terms of the relative likelihood of being a high- or a low-risk type as a function of the date of occurrence of a loss, should a loss in fact occur. For instance, the equilibrium contract for low-risk individuals will include a positive probationary period with stepwise decreasing deductible if high-risk individuals are *relatively more likely* than the low risk to suffer an early rather than a later loss. The standard equilibrium with constant monetary deductible is obtained as a special case when the relative likelihood of being the high- or low-risk type in the event of a loss is constant over the life of the policy. It is also shown that a pure time-deductible policy, with zero coverage in one subperiod and full coverage in the other subperiod, cannot be optimal if the high-risk agents' hazard rate is always strictly greater than that of the low risk.

The fact that contracts with probationary periods may provide a more efficient sorting mechanism than simple monetary deductibles is not unlike the use of experience rating in multiperiod self-selection models (as for example in Dionne and Lasserre [1985] or Cooper and Hayes [1987]). It is worthwhile emphasizing, however, that experience rating as such is not feasible here, even though the situation explicitly involves a time dimension, because by assumption a loss can occur only once (experience is equivalent to observing the loss).[1] That a loss can be suffered only once should not be taken literally. What matters is that the occurrence of a loss, which in the model takes place at some specific (though random) date, corresponds to the revelation of a condition at that date (say a health condition), which implies a relatively well-defined string of expenses in the future. The amount of the loss appearing in the model can then be interpreted as the present value of these future expenses.

It should probably also be emphasized that a probationary period is different from a waiting period.[2] The latter is often seen in disability or unemployment insurance. In this case, it is the occurrence of a disability episode that constitutes the random-loss event. A waiting period begins with the disability episode and is basically a delay in benefits between the onset of the disability and eligibility for benefits. Since what is at stake is a loss of income proportional to the length of the disability episode, a waiting period is essentially equivalent to a monetary deductible. Waiting periods can of course also serve as screening devices.

1. Basic Framework

Let us abstract from any explicit consideration of a time dimension for the moment. Individuals have initial wealth W and face the risk of a loss D, so that their final wealth is W is no loss is suffered and $W - D$ if a loss takes place. They possess strictly increasing and strictly concave von Neumann-Morgenstern utility functions, $U(\cdot)$, defined in terms of final wealth. The probability of loss is π_L for low-risk and π_H for high-risk individuals, where $\pi_L < \pi_H$. These are exogenous so that no moral hazard problem arises. Except for their probability of loss (and its time characteristics later on), individuals are identical in every respect.

Standard insurance contracts are defined in terms of the premium P paid with certainty by the insured and of the indemnity that will be paid to him in the event of a loss. To emphasize that they may involve a deductible, contracts will be denoted by $\alpha = \{k, P\}$, where k is the monetary deductible, so that $D - k$ is the indemnity paid to the insured. In a competitive market, the equilibrium contracts under full information are $\bar{\alpha}_L = \{0, \pi_L D\}$ and $\bar{\alpha}_H = \{0, \pi_H D\}$; thus, individuals of each type purchase full coverage and pay the fair price for this coverage. The notation $\bar{\alpha}_i$ will describe these full coverage contracts with premium $\bar{P}_i \equiv \pi_i D$, for $i = H, L$. By contrast, under asymmetric information between insurer and insured, when an individual's probability of loss is not an observable characteristic, contracts must take into account the fact that individuals will misrepresent their risk class if they can benefit by this.

As shown by Rothschild-Stiglitz [1976], if the equilibrium concept is

Nash (as opposed, say, to Wilson's [1977] anticipatory equilibria), the competitive equilibrium in the asymmetric information situation must be a separating one where different risk-type agents reveal their type by purchasing contracts offering a different insurance coverage. Let $\hat{a}_L$ and $\hat{a}_H$ denote the contracts in a separating solution. These have the following characteristics: i) all contracts make zero expected profits; ii) high-risk individuals purchase full coverage, while low-risk individuals receive less than full insurance; hence, $\hat{a}_H = \bar{a}_H$ and $\hat{a}_L = \{\hat{k}_L, \pi_L(D - \hat{k}_L)\}$, where $\hat{k}_L > 0$; iii) high-risk individuals are indifferent between $\bar{a}_H$ and $\hat{a}_L$. In what follows, it is assumed that the proportion of high-risk agents in the market is sufficiently large (given the agents' preferences and the size of the loss) for a separating equilibrium to exist.

Let $V_i(a)$ denote the expected utility of type-i individuals from some arbitrary contract $a = \{k, P\}$:

$$V_i(a) \equiv \pi_i U(W - k - P) + (1 - \pi_i) U(W - P). \qquad (1)$$

It will be useful for later developments to note that the separating solution with contracts $\hat{a}_L$ and $\bar{a}_H$ is such that $\hat{a}_L$ solves the following problem:

$$\max_{a_L = \{k_L, P_L\}} V_L(a_L), \qquad (2)$$

subject to

$$V_H(\bar{a}_H) \geq V_H(a_L), \qquad (3)$$

$$P_L \geq \pi_L(D - k_L). \qquad (4)$$

The constraint (3) is the self-selection constraint for the high-risk group; (4) is the nonnegative profit contraint on contracts a_L. In the solution described above, (3) and (4) are binding.

Reintroducing explicitly the timing of losses, the market described until now can be reinterpreted as follows: insurance policies are purchased at date 0 for a period of coverage running up to date T, where T is the time horizon considered. Coverage is therefore bought against the risk of a loss D being suffered between date 0 and date T, the probability of such an event being π_L for low-risk individuals and π_H for high-risk individuals; only wealth at date T matters and there is no discounting. Under symmetric information, the timing of the loss is irrelevant since the solution is characterized by full insurance. When an individual's risk-type is private information, the separating solution analysed above is also an equilibrium if contracts are restricted to being differentiated only through their monetary deductible. Taking into account the time dimension of the problem makes it clear, however, that contracts could now also be differentiated by the fact that coverage is made dependent upon the timing of the loss.

The date of occurrence of a loss is represented by the random variable $\tilde{t}$ with cumulative distribution function $F_i(t)$ for type-i individuals (with $i = H, L$), where F_i is taken to be twice continuously differentiable and such that

$$F_i(0) = 0. \tag{5}$$

By definition, the overall probability of loss discussed earlier satisfies

$$\pi_i \equiv F_i(T). \tag{6}$$

An individual's risk type is therefore completely characterized by his probability of loss function $F_i(t)$. Insurers know the characteristics of each risk type (they know the distribution function F_i of each risk group), but they cannot observe directly to which type an individual belongs. Although an individual's risk type is private information, insurers are assumed to be able to ascertain the timing of a loss, once it was occurred. A consequence of the potential availability of such *ex post* information is that the relevant characteristics of a risk type do not reduce, as earlier, to the overall probability of loss $\pi_i \equiv F_i(T)$, but now comprise the entire path of $F_i(t)$ over the given time horizon.

With *ex post* information, coverage can be made dependent on the timing of the loss. In a contract with probationary period t and deductibles k_1 and k_2, the indemnity paid to the insured is $D - k_1$ if the loss occurs in the interval $(0, t]$ and $D - k_2$ if it occurs in the interval $(t, T]$. Such a contract will be denoted by $\beta = \{t, k_1, k_2, P\}$, where as earlier P is the premium paid. For a type-i individual, the expected utility of contract β is

$$V_i(\beta) = F_i(t) U(W - k_1 - P) + [\pi_i - F_i(t)] U(W - k_2 - P)$$
$$+ (1 - \pi_i) U(W - P), \tag{7}$$

A fair premium will be denoted by P^f. The fair premium on a contract with probationary period t and deductibles k_1 and k_2, if it were purchased by type-i individuals, is

$$P_i^f(t, k_1, k_2) = F_i(t)(D - k_1) + [\pi_i - F_i(t)](D - k_2)$$
$$= (D - k_2)\pi_i - (k_1 - k_2) F_i(t). \tag{8}$$

Let $\bar{\beta}_i$ refer to the fair premium, full coverage contract for a type-i individual. One way of characterizing such a contract is to write $t = k_1 = k_2 = 0$ and $P = \bar{P}_i \equiv \pi_i D$; it is clear that $\{0, k, 0, \bar{P}_i\}$, $\{T, 0, k, \bar{P}_i\}$ and

$\{t, 0, 0, \bar{P}_i\}$ also describe the same contract, for arbitrary t and k. A pure time-deductible contract has $t > 0$ and $k_i = D$, $k_j = 0$ for $i \neq j$; a pure monetary deductible can be represented by $k_1 = k_2$ and an arbitrary t, although other representations are also possible here. Consider now the contracts $\bar{\beta}_H$ and $\hat{\beta}_L = \{\hat{t}_L, \hat{k}_{L1}, \hat{k}_{L2}, \hat{P}_L\}$ such that $\bar{\beta}_L$ solves the problem

$$\max_{\beta_L = \{t_L, k_{L1}, k_{L2}, P_L\}} V_L(\beta_L), \tag{9}$$

subject to

$$V_H(\bar{\beta}_H) \geq V_H(\beta_L), \tag{10}$$

$$P_L \geq P_L^f(t_L, k_{L1}, k_{L2}). \tag{11}$$

Comparing with the previous optimisation problem, it should be obvious that the solution to problem (9) will necessarily satisfy $V_L(\hat{\beta}_L) \geq V_L(\hat{a}_L)$. In the next section, I analyse the properties of $\hat{\beta}_L$.

2. Separating Equilibria with Time-Dependent Deductibles

Two extreme situations are illustrated in figures 1a and 1b. In both cases, the equilibrium contract for low-risk individuals is a pure time-deductible policy amounting to full insurance. This results from the fact that in each case there exists some date $\hat{t}$, such that an agent's risk type is perfectly revealed by the occurrence of a loss in the intervals $(0, \hat{t}]$ or $(\hat{t}, T]$. For the situation represented in figure 1a, the best policy for low-risk agents is clearly the decreasing deductible contract $\hat{\beta}_L = \{\hat{t}, D, 0, \bar{P}_L\}$; since $F_L(\hat{t}) = 0$, this is equivalent to full insurance. Conversely, in the situation of figure 1b, the best contract involves an increasing deductible and is given by $\hat{\beta}_L = \{\hat{t}, 0, D, \bar{P}_L\}$; this is also equivalent to full insurance because $F_L(\hat{t}) = \pi_L$, so that type-L agents face no risk of a loss beyond $\hat{t}$. These extreme situations serve to illustrate that the form of the equilibrium contract depends on what information about an agent's risk type is generated by the date of occurrence of the loss. A somewhat less trivial but similar set of situations would be obtained if the probability of loss functions F_L and F_H were modified slightly so that the densities F_L' and F_H' were strictly positive everywhere: perfect revelation of one's risk type would not be possible now, but it is obvious that the form of the contract (whether the deductible is stepwise decreasing or increasing) would be essentially the same, although not necessarily of the pure time-deductible form and without the implication of full coverage.

$F_i(t)$

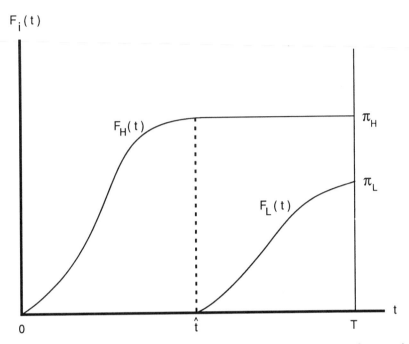

Figure 1a. First-best efficiency with a pure time deductible contract for type L. Coverage is stepwise increasing.

A second problem is illustrated in figures 1a and 1b which would still arise even if the distribution functions were modified slightly as indicated. This is the possibility that type-H agents may not be unambiguously the high-risk type, even when $\pi_H > \pi_L$. This is clearly the case in figure 1b, since there are values of t for which $F_L(t) > F_H(t)$; in fact, type-L agents are the high-risk type at the beginning of the time-horizon. In figure 1a, we have $F_H(t) > F_L(t)$ for all $t > 0$, but type-L agents are nevertheless the high-risk type in the second half of the time-horizon; that is, if an individual has not yet suffered a loss by date $\hat{t}$, he stands a greater chance of suffering one by the end of the life of the contract if he is a type-L agent. In what follows, the situations considered will be restricted to those where densities are everywhere strictly positive. Furthermore, a condition is introduced which ensures that type-H agents are unambiguously the high-risk type.

The latter condition is stated in terms of hazard rates. By definition, the hazard rate of type-i agents is

$F_i(t)$

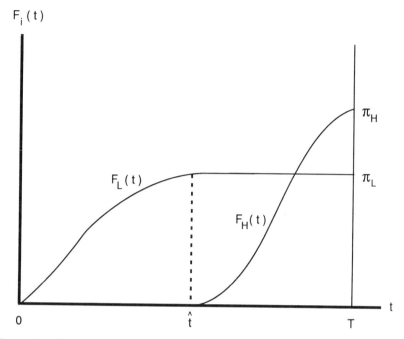

Figure 1b. First-best efficiency with a pure time-deductible contract for type L. Coverage is stepwise decreasing.

$$h_i(t) \equiv -d \log[1 - F_i(t)]/dt = F_i'(t)/[1 - F_i(t)]. \qquad (12)$$

To interpret this, note that for small ε the expression $h_i(t) \cdot \varepsilon$ is the conditional probability of suffering a loss in the interval $(t, t + \varepsilon)$, given that no loss has yet occurred by date t. Type-H agents are unambiguously the high-risk ones, in any subperiod, if they are characterized by a greater hazard rate. With strictly positive densities, this leads to the following characterization of the two risk types:

Assumption: For all t, $h_H(t) > h_L(t) > 0$.

To see the implications of this assumption, observe that the relation between the type-H and type-L hazard rates is equivalent to the statement that $\log[(1 - F_H)/(1 - F_L)]$ be everywhere strictly decreasing in t, that is,

$$[1 - F_H(t)]/[1 - F_L(t)] > [1 - F_H(\tau)]/[1 - F_L(\tau)], \quad \text{for all} \quad t < \tau. \qquad (13)$$

Setting $t = 0$ in (13) and recalling that $F_i(0) = 0$, the preceding inequality implies $F_H(\tau) > F_L(\tau)$ for all $\tau > 0$, which corresponds to a first degree stochastic dominance ordering. In particular, $\pi_H \equiv F_H(T) > F_L(T) \equiv \pi_L$.

Inequality (13) also implies that, at any point of time, type-H agents remain more likely to suffer a loss (over the rest of the time horizon), given that no claim has yet been recovered. For a type-i agent, this conditional probability is

$$Pr\{\tilde{t} \leqslant T | \tilde{t} > t\} = [\pi_i - F_i(t)]/[1 - F_i(t)]. \tag{14}$$

Setting $\tau = T$ in (13) and recalling that $\pi_i \equiv F_i(T)$, we have

$$[1 - F_H(t)]/[1 - F_L(t)] > (1 - \pi_H)/(1 - \pi_L), \quad \text{for all} \quad t < T, \tag{15}$$

or equivalently

$$- (1 - \pi_H)/[1 - F_H(t)] > - (1 - \pi_L)/[1 - F_L(t)],$$
$$1 - (1 - \pi_H)/[1 - F_H(t)] > 1 - (1 - \pi_L)/[1 - F_L(t)],$$

where the latter is easily seen to imply the desired relation between the conditional probabilities:

$$[\pi_H - F_H(t)]/[1 - F_H(t)] > [\pi_L - F_L(t)]/[1 - F_L(t)]. \tag{16}$$

The assumption on hazard-rates is basically only a definition of who constitutes the high-risk type. It is insufficient by itself to characterize the form taken by the equilibrium contracts. Clearout results are obtained, however, when the expression $[F_H(t)/F_L(t) - \pi_H/\pi_L]$ does not change sign with different values of t. In this expression, $F_H(t)/F_L(t)$ is the relative likelihood of being a high-risk type if a loss occurs by date t; similarly, π_H/π_L is the relative likelihood of being a type-H individual when a loss is known to have occured during the life of the policy (i.e., when a loss occurs by date T).

Proposition: The solution to the self-selection optimisation problem is a fair premium contract $\hat{\beta}_L = \{\hat{t}_L, \hat{k}_{L1}, \hat{k}_{L2}, P_L^f\}$ with $\hat{t}_L, \hat{k}_{L1}, \hat{k}_{L2} > 0$ and such that

$$\hat{k}_{L1} \gtreqless \hat{k}_{L2} \quad \text{if, for all } t \in [0, T), \; F_H(t)/F_L(t) \gtreqless \pi_H/\pi_L.$$

A proof of the proposition is given in the appendix. The proposition states that the deductible is positive in both subperiods; that is, full coverage in one subperiod (as in a pure time-deductible contract) cannot be an equilibrium. When the relative likelihood of being a high risk is constant,[3] the equilibrium is the pure monetary deductible contract as in the standard Rothschild-Stiglitz situation. When it is not constant, coverage is time dependent. In this case, since we are solving an optimisation problem, the equilibrium with time dependent deductibles strictly Pareto dominates the equilibrium that would obtain if only constant monetary deductibles were feasible. If $F_H/F_L > \pi_H/\pi_L$ everywhere, the deductible is stepwise decreasing. It is increasing if the opposite inequality holds; to call $\hat{t}$ a probationary period may then be somewhat inappropriate. Note that these conditions for a stepwise decreasing or increasing deductible were satisfied trivially in figures 1a and 1b: for all $t < T$, we had $F_H/\pi_H > F_L/\pi_L$ in figure 1a and $F_H/\pi_H < F_L/\pi_L$ in figure 1b.

An increasing deductible may seem surprising in view of the fact that by assumption a type-H individual is always more likely than a type-L to suffer a loss in the interval $(0, \hat{t}]$. What matters, however, is whether he is relatively more likely to suffer the loss in that interval than over the whole life of the contract.[4] As noted in the introduction, policies with stepwise increasing coverage are often found in medical or dental insurance. An illustration of a policy with decreasing coverage would be the supplementary automobile protection plans sold by car manufacturers. These generally involve optional three, four- or five-year coverage. Analytically, a four-year coverage may for instance be interpreted as a five-year policy with 100% deductible in the fifth year. To see why a consumer may end up purchasing the shorter plan, suppose that the probability for a car component to fail is related to the possibility of its having some hidden defect *and* to the a priori unknown "intensity" of use by the car owner (i.e., the individual's risk type, intensity of use being assumed exogenous for the sake of the argument). If the effect of use intensity is considered as building up over time, an early failure, as opposed to a later one, could be more indicative of an initially defective part than of a high-use owner. Conversely, a later loss would suggest that the part had no intrinsic defect and would be more indicative of a high-use intensity. In such a situation, low-use owners would choose the shorter plan.

Two examples are given in figure 2. The curve labeled a depicts a possible trajectory for $F_H(t)/F_L(t)$. Along curve a, F_H/F_L is everywhere greater than π_H/π_L: since type-H individuals are relatively more likely to suffer an early loss, the deductible is stepwise decreasing. Note that by definition F_H/F_L equals π_H/π_L at T. If the ratio F_H/F_L is represented by a curve such as b, an early loss, as opposed to a loss by date T, is relatively more likely for type-L individuals and the equilibrium deductible is accordingly stepwise increasing.

$F_H(t)/F_L(t)$

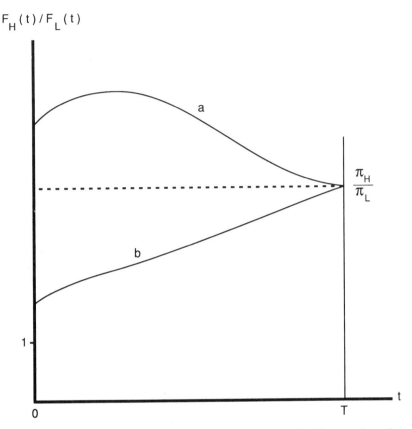

Figure 2. Possible trajectories of the relative likelihood F_H/F_L. With a path such as a, coverage for the low risks is stepwise increasing. With a path such as b, it is seepwise decreasing.

3. Concluding Remarks and Extensions

The results discussed here extend naturally to multiprobationary period contracts in which the deductible is allowed a predetermined number of steps over the life of the policy; more generally still, they extend to contracts of the form $\{\{k(t)\}, P\}$ defined in terms of continuous (possibly only stepwise continuous) time-dependent deductible functions. Solving the self-selection problem with the later form of contract, it can be shown that the deductible is decreasing over the life of the policy when the likelihood ratio $F'_H(t)/F'_L(t)$, defined in terms of densities, is decreasing (the deductible is increasing in the opposite situation). The assumption that hazard rates are always strictly positive ensures that the deductible can never decrease to zero over some interval. The condition on the likelihood ratio is more restrictive than the one analysed previously and which referred to the relative likelihood F_H/F_L. It is easily shown, however, that a decreasing likelihood ratio implies a decreasing relative likelihood. The interpretation of the conditions is otherwise the same as that given in the preceding section.[5]

A second extension would be to examine the contracts offered in the market when non Nash behavior is allowed. It is well known that, depending on the proportion of high risks in the market, a Rothschild-Stiglitz set of contracts may not be sustainable as a Nash equilibrium and that, even when it is, it may not be second best efficient. Second best efficiency is obtained, in particular, if each firm possesses Wilson foresight and if it competes by offering a menu of policies admitting cross-subsidization between risk types. The equilibrium outcome in such a situation is either identical to the Rothschild-Stiglitz set of separating contracts (if the proportion of high risks is "large," in which case these contracts are second best efficient) or is given by a break-even portfolio of separating contracts with cross-subsidization from the low to the high risk group.[6] These equilibrium contracts are such as to maximise the benefits to low-risk individuals, subject to the self-selection constraints imposed by the informational asymmetries and to the zero-profit constraint on the portfolio. Solving such a problem for the kind of situation examined in the present paper,[7] it is easily shown that high risks will purchase full insurance and that the low risks will be offered a partial coverage contract with the same characteristics as the policy analyzed in the previous section; that is, coverage increases or decreases over time depending on the path followed by the risk types' relative likelihood.

As a final remark, it may be useful to compare the contracts obtained here with the experience rating found in multiperiod insurance situations. In the latter case, a contract is a sequence of premiums and deductibles that depends on previous loss experience. As noted in the introduction, experience rating as such is not feasible in the situation examined in the present paper because a loss occurs only once; that is, further insurance is not warranted once the loss has been suffered. A similar form of contract is nevertheless conceivable. For instance, in the simple two-step deductible case, a contract with endogenous probationary period $\hat{t}$ could specify a premium payable at date 0 for coverage up to date $\hat{t}$, together with a premium payable at $\hat{t}$ for coverage beyond date $\hat{t}$ if a loss has not been suffered by that date; the contract would also specify the deductibles in the two subperiods. It can be shown, however, that such a contract cannot be an equilibrium; the reason is that only final wealth matters here and that such a contract would introduce additional risks by making the effective payment of one's premium conditional on the date of occurrence of the loss. In other words, it is always preferable to pay the whole premium unconditionally at the beginning of the time horizon.[8]

Appendix: Proof of the proposition

The Lagrangian of problem (9) is:

$$
\begin{aligned}
\mathscr{L} = & \{F_L(t_L)\,U(W - k_{L1} - P_L) + [\pi_L - F_L(t_L)]\,U(W - k_{L2} - P_L) \\
& + (1 - \pi_L)\,U(W - P_L)\} - \mu\{F_H(t_L)\,U(W - k_{L1} - P_L) \\
& + [\pi_H - F_H(t_L)]\,U(W - k_{L2} - P_L) + (1 - \pi_H)\,U(W - P_L)\} \\
& - \lambda\,[(D - k_{L2})\,\pi_L - (k_{L1} - k_{L2})\,F_L(t_L) - P_L],
\end{aligned}
$$

where γ and μ are respectively the multipliers associated with the nonnegative profit constraint and the type-H self-selection constraint.

The derivation uses the fact that any contract (and therefore also the solution) can be described with $t > 0$. Writing $U_A = U(W - k_{L1} - P_L)$, $U_B = U(W - k_{L2} - P_L)$, $U_C = U(W - P_L)$, and denoting $F_i(t)$ by F_i, the first-order conditions for an interior solution are:

$\mu\,\partial\mathscr{L}/\partial\mu = \lambda\,\partial\mathscr{L}/\partial\lambda = 0$, where $\lambda, \mu \geq 0$, together with

$$\partial\mathscr{L}/\partial k_1 = (\mu F_H - F_L)\cdot U_A' + \lambda F_L = 0, \qquad (A1)$$

$$\partial\mathscr{L}/\partial k_2 = [\mu(\pi_H - F_H) - (\pi_L - F_L)]\cdot U_B' + \lambda(\pi_L - F_L) = 0, (A2)$$

$$
\begin{aligned}
\partial\mathscr{L}/\partial P_L = & - [F_L U_A' + (\pi_L - F_L)\,U_B' + (1 - \pi_L)\,U_C'] \\
& + \mu[F_H U_A' + (\pi_H - F_H)\,U_B' \\
& + (1 - \pi_H)\,U_C'] + \lambda = 0,
\end{aligned}
\qquad (A3)
$$

$$\partial\mathscr{L}/\partial t = (\mu F_H' - F_L')\cdot(U_B - U_A) + \lambda F_L'(k_{L1} - k_{L2}) = 0. \quad (A4)$$

I first show that $\mu > 0$ and $\lambda > 0$. From (A1) to (A3), assuming $\lambda = 0$ and $U_A \neq U_B$ is shown to lead to $F_L = F_H$, which contradicts the assumption on hazard rates unless $t = 0$; but $t = 0$ or $U_A = U_B$ describe a standard constant deductible contract and we know that the profit constraint is binding in that case, which contradicts $\lambda = 0$. Assuming $\mu = 0$ implies a full coverage, fair premium contract for type L; because of the assumption on hazard rates, this requires $t = 0$ and $k_2 = 0$ (or some other equivalent combination) with the result that the type-H self-selection constraint would not be satisfied. Hence, $\mu, \lambda > 0$.

For $t > 0$, the conditions (A1) and (A2) lead to

$$U'_A/U'_B = \frac{F_L[(\pi_L - F_L) - \mu(\pi_H - F_H)]}{(\pi_L - F_L)(F_L - \mu F_H)}. \tag{A5}$$

From the same conditions, $F_L - \mu F_H > 0$ and $(\pi_L - F_L) - \mu(\pi_H - F_H) > 0$, so that both the numerator and denominator in (A5) are positive. Hence, (A5) implies

$$U'_A/U'_B \gtreqqless 1 \leftrightarrow k_1 \gtreqqless k_2 \leftrightarrow F_H/F_L \gtreqqless \pi_H/\pi_L.$$

I now show that $k_{L1}, k_{L2} > 0$. From the first-order conditions (A1), (A2) and (A3),

$$U'_B/U'_C = \frac{(\pi_L - F_L)[(1 - \pi_L) - \mu(1 - \pi_H)]}{(1 - \pi_L)[(\pi_L - F_L) - \mu(\pi_H - F_H)]}, \tag{A6}$$

where by the same conditions both the numerator and denominator are positive. It follows that

$$U'_B/U'_C > 1 \leftrightarrow k_2 > 0 \leftrightarrow (\pi_H - F_H)/(1 - \pi_H) > (\pi_L - F_L)/(1 - \pi_L).$$

The last inequality is equivalent to

$$\frac{(\pi_H - F_H)/(1 - F_H)}{(1 - \pi_H)/(1 - F_H)} > \frac{(\pi_L - F_L)/(1 - F_L)}{(1 - \pi_L)/(1 - F_L)},$$

which follows from the assumption on hazard rates (see the inequalities (15) and (16) in the text).

From the same first-order conditions,

$$U'_A/U'_C = \frac{F_L[(1 - \pi_L) - \mu(1 - \pi_H)]}{(1 - \pi_L)(F_L - \mu F_H)}. \tag{A7}$$

Hence,

$$U'_A/U'_C > 1 \leftrightarrow k_1 > 0 \leftrightarrow F_H/(1 - \pi_H) > F_L/(1 - \pi_L),$$

where the last inequality follows directly from $F_H > F_L$ and $\pi_H > \pi_L$, which are implied by the assumption on hazard rates.

Q.E.D.

Notes

1. Life insurance would be an extreme illustration of such a situation. Of course, experience (or "information") is also obtained over time through the fact that the loss has not yet occurred.

2. This distinction has been stressed by Mehr and Gustavson [1984].

3. This is satisfied for instance by the uniform distribution $F_i(t) = \phi_i t$, where ϕ_i is a constant and where $\phi_H > \phi_L$.

4. This could be formulated differently. From Bayes' formula (or see Milgrom [1981]), it can be shown that, for any prior probability distribution on the agents' risk types, we have:

$$\text{for }\ t < T,\ F_H(t)/F_L(t) \gtreqqless \pi_H/\pi_L \leftrightarrow Pr\{i = H | \tilde{t} \leq t\} \gtreqqless Pr\{i = H | \tilde{t} \leq T\}.$$

Thus, when for instance $F_H(t)/F_L(t) > \pi_H \pi_L$, a loss by date t, for $t < T$, is more indicative of a type-H individual (in terms of posterior probabilities) than a loss by date T.

5. With respect to figure 2, a curve such as a would not imply a monotonously decreasing deductible. It may be noted that with exponential distribution functions, that is functions of the form

$$F_i(t) = 1 - e^{-\gamma_i t},$$

where γ_i is the constant hazard rate (with $\gamma_H > \gamma_L$), the likelihood ratio

$$F_H'(t)/F_L'(t) = (\gamma_H/\gamma_L) e^{-(\gamma_H - \gamma_L)t}$$

is everywhere decreasing in t, so that coverage should be increasing over time. Exponential distribution functions are likely candidates in many applications.

6. See Wilson (1977), Miyazaki [1977], Spence [1978], and Crocker and Snow [1985, 1986]. By contrast, a Riley (1979) equilibrium would lead to the Rothschild-Stiglitz set of contracts and would not necessarily be second best efficient. An allocation is second best efficient if it is Pareto optimal within the set of allocations that are feasible under the information constraints (see Harris and Townsend [1981]).

7. Letting q denote the proportion of high risks in the market, the problem consists in finding contracts $\beta_i = \{t_i, k_{i1}, k_{i2}, P_i\}$, for $i = H, L$, so as to maximize $V_L(\beta_L)$, subject to $V_H(\beta_H) \geq V_H(\bar{\beta}_H)$, $V_H(\beta_H) \geq V_H(\beta_L)$, and $q[P_H - P_H^f(t_H, k_{H1}, k_{H2})] + (1 - q)[P_L - P_L^f(t_L, k_{L1}, k_{L2})] \geq 0$.

8. Multiperiod insurance contracts are typically analyzed under the assumption that individuals cannot save or borrow between time periods. In a sense, the opposite assumption is made here by supposing that only final wealth matters.

References

Cooper, R., and B. Hayes. (1987). "Multi-period Insurance Contracts," *International Journal of Industrial Organization* 5, 211–231.

Crocker, K. J., and A. Snow. (1985). "The Efficiency of Competitive Equilibria in Insurance Markets with Adverse Selection," *Journal of Public Economics* 26, 207–219.

Crocker, K. J., and A. Snow. (1986). "The Efficiency Effects of Categorical Discrimination in the Insurance Industry," *Journal of Political Economy* 94, 321–344.

Dionne, G., and P. Lasserre. (1985). "Adverse-Selection, Repeated Insurance Contracts and Announcement Strategy," *Review of Economic Studies* 52, 719–23.

Eeckhoudt, L., J. F. Outreville, M. Lauwers, and F. Calcoen. (1988). "The Impact of a Probationary Period on the Demand for Insurance," *Journal of Risk and Insurance* 55, 217–228.

Harris, M., and R. M. Townsend. (1981). "Resource Allocation Under Asymmetric Information," *Econometrica* 49, 33–64.

Mehr, R. I., and S. G. Gustavson. (1984). *Life Insurance: Theory and Practice.* Plano, Texas: Business Publications Inc.

Milgrom, P. R. (1981). "Good News and Bad News: Representation Theorems and Applications," *Bell Journal of Economics* 12, 380–391.

Miyazaki, H. (1977). "The Rat Race and Internal Labor Markets," *Bell Journal of Economics* 8, 394–418.

Riley, J. G. (1979). "Informational Equilibrium," *Econometrica* 47, 331–359.

Rothschild, M., and J. Stiglitz. (1976). "Equilibrium in Competitive Insurance Markets: An Essay on the Economics of Imperfect Information," *Quarterly Journal of Economics* 90, 629–650.

Spence, M. (1978). "Product Differentiation and Performance in Insurance Markets," *Journal of Public Economics* 10, 427–447.

Wilson, C. (1977). "A Model of Insurance Markets with Incomplete Information," *Journal of Economic Theory* 16, 167–207.

INSURANCE CLASSIFICATIONS AND SOCIAL WELFARE

Samuel A. Rea, Jr.

University of Toronto

Abstract

This paper investigates the welfare implications of rate classifications when classification is costly, and these results are compared with the market outcome. The private decision by an insurer whether to monitor the extent of an activity reflects social costs and benefits, but the gains may not exceed the costs. With respect to variables that separate low-risk from high-risk individuals, the gains from separation may be small, and the market may give overinvestment in information from society's point of view. When neither the insurer nor the insured know the expected loss, it may be efficient to determine the risk, despite the added variance in premiums.

Key words: Insurance classifications, discrimination

Automobile insurance rate classifications have been widely criticized as being arbitrary and discriminatory, suggesting that the classifications should either be made more precise or eliminated entirely.[1] The absence of variables that measure the driver's level of activity, such as mileage,

The research was supported by the Civil Liability Program, Yale Law School.

and the reliance on measures such as age, sex, and marital status are features that are frequently criticized. Economists usually defend the classifications by pointing out that there are efficiency gains from attempting some classification and that more precise classification is costly.[2] They argue that the survival of the rate classification system in the market is evidence that it is efficient. A similar controversy is raging over the use of gender as a basis for the pricing of life annuities and life insurance.

This paper investigates the welfare implications of rate classifications when classification is costly, and these results are compared with the market outcome. It is concluded that the private decision by an insurer whether to monitor variables such as mileage reflects the social costs and benefits but that the gains are unlikely to exceed the costs, given the estimated price elasticities. Therefore, one need not be concerned if there is a limited amount of monitoring of such variables by insurance companies. With respect to variables that separate low-risk from high-risk individuals, the gains from separation may be small, and the market may give overinvestment in information from society's point of view.[3] The models in this paper are based on the assumption that the amount of insurance can be effectively regulated, preventing low-risk customers from signaling their characteristics through the choice of the amount of insurance.[4]

1. Risky Activities and Insurance

Many activities create risk for an individual or for others. For example, a driver may injure himself, other drivers or pedestrians. Depending on the context, the legal system creates liability for all harm done to others (strict liability) or only for harm resulting from negligent conduct. Risk-averse individuals will want to insure against the risk of personal losses and against the liability for losses suffered by others. The insurance decision will interact with the decision to engage in the risky activity and the decision concerning the amount of care. In the absence of perfect information the insurance will lead to moral hazard and reduced levels of care, but for the purpose of this analysis of insurance classifications, it will be assumed that the level of care is efficient. The analysis will focus on the level of the risky activity, assuming that the third-party victim's care and activity levels are given.

The classification system will affect the price of insurance, which in turn will affect the demand for the risky activity and the amount of insurance that is purchased. If the price of insurance deviates from the cost of the insurance for an individual, the insurance and the activity level will not be optimal. The welfare implications of insurance classifications will depend on the cost of these distortions compared with the cost of administering the classification system.

The models presented below are based on the assumptions that the amount of insurance is fixed for those engaged in an activity and that consumers can choose whether to engage in that activity. For concreteness, liability insurance for drivers is used as the example. To avoid extraneous issues it is assumed that all losses fall on the nondriving party and that the driver is required to insure against his liability for these losses. The questions addressed are 1) to what extent is it efficient to charge different prices for these expected losses, 2) will the market outcome be efficient, and 3) what are the consequences of preventing the use of variables such as gender in rate determination?

2. Information Assumptions

Insurance markets are plagued by numerous types of imperfect information that affect their ability to achieve first-best efficiency. This paper investigates the impact on insurance markets of three type of imperfect information. First, the level of an insured's activity may be known by him but not by the insurer. Second, given the activity level, the insured's expected losses may be known by him but not by the insurer. Third, the expected loss per unit of activity for different groups may not be known by either the insurer or the insured. In all three cases the information can be acquired at a cost, but is it efficient to do so? Will the market insurance rates be the socially desired rates? What are the costs of eliminating existing classifications based on variables such as age and sex?

3. Activity Level Known Only by Individual

One of the characteristics of existing North American automobile insurance markets is that there is little monitoring of activity levels, such as mileage.[5] Instead, variables such as age and sex have been used.[6] It is possible that much of the difference in the accident experience between men and women reflects a greater amount of driving by men.[7] If mileage were measured, it would reduce some of the criticism of the use of sex or eliminate its predictive power. Efficiency gains would occur because drivers would pay for the marginal cost of their driving, but these gains

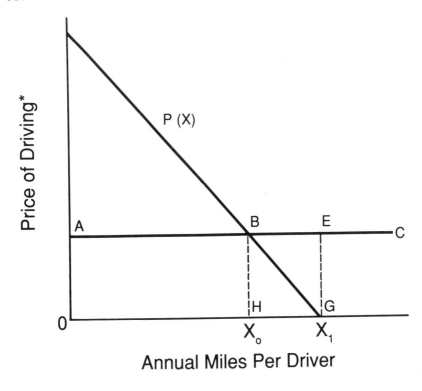

Figure 1. Demand for driving.

may be exceeded by the cost of monitoring. In this section I examine the
market incentives to invest in such information and compare these with
the efficient amount of investment in information. It is assumed that all
individuals are alike.

Consider the representative individual with a demand curve for driving
shown in figure 1. The vertical axis measures the price over and above the
marginal nonaccident cost of driving (fuel for example). The marginal
social cost of the activity (the expected accident cost per mile) is indicated
by the line C. In the absence of a marginal cost associated with insurance,
the insured will drive X_1 miles. This imposes an accident cost on society
equal to OAEG. The cost of the last $X_1 - X_0$ miles, BEGH, exceeds the
benefit from driving by an amount equal to the triangle BEG. Assume
that the cost of monitoring mileage is fixed per period and equal to

S. This cost includes outlays by the insurance company and the inconvenience for the customer. It will be efficient to monitor mileage when the cost of doing so (S) is less than the excess accident costs, in other words S is less than the area of the triangle BEG.

Assuming that it is efficient to monitor mileage, the efficient pricing scheme will be one that maximizes the net social benefit. This is accomplished by finding the amount of driving, X_0, which maximizes benefits from driving minus costs,

$$\left[\int_0^{X_0} P(X)dX \right] - S - CX_0 \tag{1}$$

where $P(X)$ is the inverse of the demand function. The net benefit is maximized where $P(X_0) = C$, as shown in figure 1. This output can be achieved with a two-part tariff in which the cost of driving is S per period and C per mile.

Insurance companies will have an incentive to introduce monitoring of mileage (and charge a two-part tariff) if it is socially efficient. This is shown as follows. Assume that insurance is initially offered in a competitive market at a price that just covers losses, CX_1, with no monitoring of mileage. This generates consumer surplus equal to

$$\text{Consumer surplus at } X_1 = \int_0^{X_1} P(X)dX - CX_1 \tag{2}$$

Consider an alternative fee schedule with an annual fee, F, and a charge per mile, M. The value to the consumer of this contract when he chooses to drive X_0 miles will be

$$\text{Consumer Surplus at } X_0 = \int_0^{X_1} P(X)dX - MX_0 - F \tag{3}$$

The profit of the firm is

$$\text{Profit at } X_0 = MX_0 + F - CX_0 - S \tag{4}$$

The value of the contract to the consumer is at a maximum, given the profit of the firm, if

$$P(X_0) = C \tag{5}$$

In other words, those that monitor mileage will charge a per-mile cost equal to marginal cost ($M = C$). As an alternative to the market price CX_1 a firm will offer a contract with an annual fee, F, and a charge per mile, C, if the firm can earn nonnegative profits

$$F \geq S \tag{6}$$

and customers prefer this new contract to the old contract:

$$\int_0^{X_0} P(X)dX - CX_0 - F \geq \int_0^{X_1} P(X)dX - CX_1 \tag{7}$$

Combining equations 6 and 7, one obtains:

$$C(X_1 - X_0) - \int_0^{X_1} P(X)dX \geq S \tag{8}$$

The monitoring will be undertaken if the costs are less than the reduction in annual losses minus the reduction in benefits from driving. In other words, the screening costs must be less than BEG in figure 1.

Since the decision to monitor mileage depends on the monitoring costs and the responsiveness of demand, it is useful to derive an expression that relates the costs to the elasticity of demand. Monitoring will be profitable if

$$(1/2)(X_1 - X_0)C \geq S \tag{9}$$

Letting $X_1 - X_0$ equal $-\dfrac{dX}{dP} C$ gives

$$(1/2)\left(-\frac{dX}{dP}\right) C^2 \geq S \tag{10}$$

This condition can be related to the elasticity of demand for driving with respect to the price of gasoline. If X_1 miles are driven per year and the price of gasoline is P_G, equation 10 becomes

$$(1/2)(e_G) (CX_1) \left(\frac{C}{P_G}\right) \geq S \tag{11}$$

where e_G is the absolute value of the elasticity of demand for vehicle usage with respect to the price of gasoline.[8]

Equation 11 indicates that the per mile cost of monitoring must be compared to an expression that contains the (gasoline) price elasticity of demand for vehicle usage, accident costs per period (CX_1), and the ratio of per-mile liability costs to gasoline costs. There has been considerable recent empirical research on the elasticity of demand for driving because of its importance for the demand for gasoline. The range of estimates is zero to $-.5$.[9] The relevant measure for this purpose would be the elasticity of accident cost with respect to the per-mile cost of driving. There is some evidence that the per-mile accident costs decline with the number of miles driven.[10] In the middle range of annual miles driven, accidents per driver go up only .43% for each percentage increase in miles driven. Therefore, the elasticity of accident costs with respect to the marginal cost of driving would be at most .43 times −.5, or −.22.

Assume that the elasticity of accident costs with respect to the marginal cost of driving is −.22, that the expected accident costs per year are $690, and that insurance costs are 55% of gasoline costs.[11] The monitoring will be worthwhile if the cost of monitoring is less than $42 (equation 11). The cost of monitoring should include the direct cost of measurement, the inconvenience to the customer, the cost of resolving disputes, and the cost of adding another set of price categories. This last cost reflects added billing costs of all types and costs of maintaining more detailed statistical records. Odometer reading would be done at least once each year and whenever a vehicle changed ownership. It would probably be difficult to organize at-home metering of odometers. If the motorist were required to visit a central location, the value of his time might add significantly to the cost.[12]

The relationship derived in equation 11 indicates that the failure of insurance companies to monitor activities of insured individuals may be perfectly rational and socially optimal when elasticities of demand are relatively low and costs are sufficiently high. Although this general conclusion is not surprising, it is surprising that the costs do not have to be very high (6% of annual premiums in the example above) to render monitoring inefficient, given low price elasticities. Consequently, it is not surprising that there is relatively little monitoring of mileage in the market.

4. Expected Losses Differ Between Individuals

Suppose that it is uneconomical to monitor variables such as mileage but that different individuals have different expected losses, in part based on their different mileage, but also because of other factors. Assume that there are two classes of drivers. The expected loss per period of driving is defined as C_H for high-risk drivers and C_L for low-risk drivers. C_A is the average expected loss. For graphical purposes it is convenient to assume (with no loss of generality) that the number of drivers equals N_A in each group, that each group has the same demand curve, and that all drivers are initially charged the same price, C_A. The demand curve in figure 2 is the demand for car ownership as a function of the fixed cost of

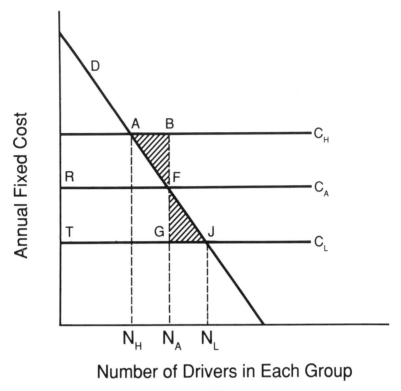

Figure 2. Demand for automobile ownership.

ownership, holding the cost per mile constant. Is it worthwhile to incur classification costs in order to assign different costs to the two groups?

If the two groups are each charged the group specific expected cost, instead of the overall average cost (C_A), the number of high-risk drivers will fall to N_H and the number of low-risk drivers will rise to N_L. It is assumed that there is no income effect and therefore that the marginal utility of income is constant along the demand curve. The reduction in losses of the high-risk drivers will exceed the loss of consumer surplus by the area ABF. The increase in consumer surplus of the low-risk drivers will exceed the increased losses by the area FGJ. These two amounts must be compared with the cost of screening, which is S per person. It will be shown below that it will only be necessary to screen the low-risk individuals. The classification costs will be worthwhile for society if

$$(N_L - N_A)(C_A - C_L) > S N_L \tag{12}$$

or

$$e_D[(C_A - C_L)^2/C_{LT}] > S \qquad (13)$$

where e_D is the absolute value of the price elasticity of demand for ownership, evaluated at the low-risk driver's total cost of ownership, C_{LT}. The left-hand side of equation 12 is the gain from classification. More generally, if C_T is the total fixed cost under uniform pricing, and n_i is the number of drivers in group i, the screening will be preferred if the total screening costs are less than

$$\sum_i .5e_D[(C_i - C_A)^2/C_T]n_i \qquad (14)$$

To evaluate the efficiency of screening, it is necessary to know the elasticity of demand for automobile ownership. The relevant price variable is the annual fixed cost of ownership. This elasticity may be very small. Gallini (1983, 324) estimated that the elasticity of fleet size with respect to fuel costs, holding mileage constant, was $-.05$ to $-.06$.[13] On the other hand, Devlin (1988) found an elasticity of $-.32$ for the fixed costs of ownership. It is not likely to be worthwhile to incur significant costs of classification if the elasticities are sufficiently low. For example, assume that $e_D = |-.3|$, $C_A = 700$, $C_H = 1000$, $C_L = 400$, and $C_{LT} = 3500$. It would not be worth separating the two groups if the screening cost exceeded \$7.71 per low-risk person.[14]

There are some variables that can be used to separate risk groups at a little or no cost. Sex, race, marital status, and age are examples of low-cost screening variables. If there is no classification cost, such classification can only yield net benefits (neglecting the social insurance provided by not charging high-risk people their full cost, discussed later). Given the low price elasticities, equation 14 suggests that the economic cost of banning the use of such variables might be small enough that society might be willing to bear this modest cost to avoid the use of variables that are felt to be inappropriate.

Will the market introduce the efficient amount of classification when there are two risk groups that can only be separated by incurring some cost? Assume that initially both groups are being charged the average expected loss and that the insurance company knows the expected loss for each group. An insurance company will have an incentive to introduce a new rate classification if it appears that it can make a profit, holding the prices of the competitors constant. The market dynamics will operate as follows: Customers will be told that they must pay more for insurance if they have a characteristic that is associated with high risk.

Those with high-risk characteristics will refuse the policy, preferring instead to take an alternative policy priced at C_A at another firm. Low-risk customers will be offered a policy that is slightly lower than C_A to lure those customers from other firms. As long as $C_A - C_L$ is large enough to cover the costs of verifying low-risk status,[15] the policy will survive in the market. Other firms will find that they have only high-risk customers and will be forced to charge them a higher price or to screen for low-risk customers.

High-risk customers will never have to pay the screening costs. If a firm were to charge a high-risk person a price higher than C_H, he would simply admit to another firm that he was a high-risk person and pay C_H. Therefore, all of the screening costs are borne by low-risk customers. Eventually, high-risk applicants would not apply for low-risk insurance policies, leaving the low-risk customers bearing the cost of their own screening.

The classification will thus survive in the market if

$$C_A - C_L \geqslant S. \tag{15}$$

In the case in which the two groups are of equal size, there will tend to be too much screening in the market. Excessive screening will occur when S is larger than the critical value in equation 12 but satisfies equation 15:[16]

$$C_A - C_L \geqslant S > \frac{(N_L - N_A)}{N_L}(C_A - C_L) \tag{16}$$

The reason for the excessive screening can be most easily seen in the extreme case in which $S = C_A - C_L$. The low-risk group is no better off after screening and has the same number of drivers. The high-risk group is worse off and some have chosen not to drive. Accident victims are indifferent because they are fully compensated. Since no group is better off, society would be better off if the screening had not taken place. There is a net loss to society because the benefit from the reduction in high-risk drivers (the triangle ABF) is less than the cost of screening (the rectangle RFGT).

The introduction of classification in the market was illustrated with two risk classifications, but the principle holds when there are more possible classifications and cross-classifications. For instance, assume that characteristic J was used to separate the pool into high-risk and low-risk groups. There might be another characteristic, K, that would allow each of those two groups to be separated on the basis of characteristic K. The first insurance company that decides to screen with characteristic K will do so as long as it can identify a group whose expected loss plus screening cost falls below the price they are being charged by other companies. These groups will be offered policies and the other groups will be left for the other companies. As before, the other companies will be forced either to cater to high-risk customers or to incur the screening costs. The net result may yield no net social gains unless there is sufficient elasticity of demand for the risky activity to outweigh the costs of screening.

5. Individual's Marginal Expected Loss Unknown

The equity implications of statistical discrimination have been examined by looking at the impact of imperfect discrimination on indices of inequality (Schmalensee (1984) and Hoy (1984)), but another perspective on the statistical discrimination issue can be gained by asking what pricing system would an individual choose if he did not know his risk category. Alternatively, one might ask whether it is worthwhile to incur costs in order to discover cost differences that are not yet known by anyone.

The current debate over AIDS testing raises similar issues. Is it worthwhile to acquire information on individual mortality risk? The answer to this question depends on three considerations. First, more accurate information will permit insurance pricing to more closely approximate the individual risk and may allow individuals to reflect the individual costs in their consumption or production behavior; second, the possibility of improved information adds a risk of higher insurance premiums; and third, the acquisition of information is costly.

The second consideration refers to the adverse effects of added risk. If new information allows individuals to be divided into risk categories, the individual faces two types of risk, the risk of being shown to be in a high-risk category and the risk of the loss. Consider a simple example with two categories of individuals facing the loss of their wealth, W, with probabilities, θ_L and θ_H. If the loss can be fully insured, the expected utility with known risk is:

$$U[(1 - \theta_i)W], i = L \text{ or } H.$$

If the fraction of low-risk individuals is r, the expected utility for someone who does not yet know his risk category is:

$$rU[(1 - \theta_L)W] + (1 - r)U[(1 - \theta_H)W].$$

If the risk is never known, the expected utility after purchasing insurance is:

$$U[(1 - r\theta_L - (1 - r)\theta_H)W],$$

which is higher if there is diminishing marginal utility of wealth. Therefore, the risk-averse individual will not want to know his risk category.[17] This conclusion is reinforced if there is a cost of acquiring the information. This same result can be applied to efforts of insurance companies to use experience rating in long-term insurance contracts (Boyer, Dionne and Kihlstrom, 1989). With public information and no behavioral response to the changing prices, constant insurance prices are preferred to experience rating.

There may be situations in which the information is known or can be known by either the insurance company or the insured. If the individual knows his risk category, he can overinsure (subject to restrictions on the amount of indemnity insurance) or underinsure. The cost of acquiring the information must be weighed against the private gain from such activity. From a social point of view the acquisition of this information is not desireable. Similarly, if the insurance company can acquire the information, it will have an incentive to do so. From a social point of view these expenditures are wasteful, as discussed above.

The conclusions change when the risk is a by-product of the consumption of a specific activity (or subset of activities). Assume that the insurance company can monitor the consumption of the risky activities. The revelation of individual risk category affects the cost of consuming the risky activity. *Ex ante*, before the probability of loss is known, the consumer may prefer a risky price to the average price because an individual who is risk averse with respect to changes in income is not necessarily risk averse with respect to changes in the price. Turnovsky, et al, (1980) have shown that a consumer would prefer price instability to the arithmetic mean of prices if

$$s(\eta - \rho) - e > o \qquad (17)$$

where s is the share of the good in the consumer's budget, η is the income elasticity of demand for the good, ρ is the coefficient of relative risk aversion, and e is the price elasticity of demand.

Although risk averse individuals may prefer to gamble to some extent on price changes, but there may be other costs and benefits associated with the introduction of screening. Screening costs reduce the advantages of investigating price change. On the other hand, the consumer will adjust his activities when the risks are known. For example, in the driving context, low-risk drivers will drive more and high-risk drivers will drive less, resulting in lower total accident costs. The resulting cost saving may make it worthwhile to refine the risk categories, despite the costs of doing so and the added risk (of classification) imposed on consumers.

This situation can be examined by assuming that the level of activity of an individual can be monitored, that individuals impose different marginal accident costs, and that neither the individual nor his insurance company knows his expected loss without incurring some costs. Assume that initially individuals are being charged according to the average marginal expected loss. In such circumstances would it be efficient to determine the marginal expected loss for each individual?

A simple model can illustrate the tradeoff between insurance against price change and accident cost reduction, assuming that screening is worthwhile.[18] The utility of an individual i is a function of his consumption of good X and good Y:

$$U^i[X(P_i), Y_i] \qquad (18)$$

The price of good Y is set equal to one and income, I^*, is exogenous. Consumption of the two goods is a function of the price of X, given the level of income and the price of Y. The budget constraint is:

$$I^* = P_i X(P_i) + Y_i(P_i) \qquad (19)$$

Assume that a fraction r of the population is low risk, indicated by L and a fraction $1 - r$ is high risk, indicated by H. The representative individual's expected utility

$$rU^L[X(P_L), I^* - P_L X(P_L)] + (1 - r)U^H[X(P_H), I^* - P_H X(P_H)] \qquad (20)$$

is maximized with respect to the prices, subject to a constraint that the insurance must break even:

$$rX(P_L)(C_L - P_L) + (1 - r)X(P_H)(C_H - P_H) = 0 \qquad (21)$$

If we assume that the liability rule is strict liability, the losses suffered by the victims need not appear in the calculation because they are fully compensated by the third-party insurance. The response of the individual to the price gives the following relationship:

$$U_1^i = U_2^i P_i \quad \text{for} \quad i = L, H \qquad (22)$$

The first-order conditions for the classification problem (maximization of equation 20 subject to equations 21 and 22) are

$$\frac{U_2^L}{U_2^H} = \frac{e_D^L[(C_L - P_L)/P_L] + 1}{e_D^H[(C_H - P_H)/P_H] + 1} \qquad (23)$$

plus equation 21, where e_D^i is the absolute value of the price elasticity of demand for X for individual i evaluated at P_i, $X(P_i)$. U_2^i is the marginal utility of income.

The solution depends on the effect of a change in the price of X on the marginal utility of income. If the marginal utility of income were constant, the solution would be marginal cost pricing.[19] It is possible that the marginal utility of income might rise as the price of X falls. If this were the case, the low-risk people would be charged less than their marginal cost and the high-risk people would be charged more than their marginal cost. In other words, the solution would be one in which the high-risk people subsidize the low-risk people. This surprising result indicates that equality of prices would not necessarily be chosen by individuals who did not yet know their risk classification.

If a two-part tariff could be used, the solution would be marginal cost pricing accompanied by lump sum transfers, which may or may not involve a subsidy to high-risk individuals. If screening is costly, the screening cost would be incorporated in the lump sum portion of the tariff. If screening is sufficiently costly, equality of prices would be chosen.

A decision to charge different prices makes some groups better off and others worse off. The Pareto criterion would not allow such a move to take place even if the net gains were positive, but one concept of justice which has some appeal is based on the hypothetical choice of individuals before they know which position in society they will occupy (Harsanyi, 1955; Rawls, 1971). The discussion above indicates that price discrimination might be chosen over equality of prices. For example, before one's sex is known one might choose to permit pricing based on sex. With a two-part tariff, the outcome could be marginal cost pricing and a lump sum transfer *to* the low-risk sex.

6. Extensions of the Model

6.1. Expected Losses Unknown

In practice insurance companies do not have information on the expected losses of all of the possible classification groups. The only good source for such information is actual claims experience. Consequently, firms will face the risk of incorrectly pricing new classifications. This will reduce the tendency of the industry to introduce new classifications.

If it were possible for a company to generate expected loss data (at a cost), the firm may not be able to capture the full return on its investment because other firms can free-ride on the investment in information. This is one reason why industry organizations gather actuarial data. If this were the only source of data on expected losses, new classifications would not be introduced because the industry, as opposed to the firm, would not assume that prices would remain constant following the new classification. Industry-wide databases are sufficiently imperfect that there are opportunities for investment in better analysis of the data. Unfortunately, the results of this analysis are revealed to competitors as soon as the price structure of the firm is made public. Other firms can avoid paying for the analysis if they can obtain the pricing information of the competitor.[20] The nonappropriability of investment in information on expected losses and the reliance on industry databases may reduce the incentive for firms to overclassify, as suggested in section 4.

6.2. Quantity of Insurance Variable — Asymmetric Information

The automobile liability insurance example was selected because it was reasonable to assume that the liability insurance can be made mandatory, as it is in many jurisdictions. When the quantity of insurance can vary, the impact of a ban on the use of variables such as gender in insurance pricing can lead to larger welfare losses because low-risk customers will have an incentive to choose high deductible policies that are unattractive to the high-risk customers.

The original papers on asymmetric information by Wilson (1977) and Rothschild and Stiglitz (1976) have been extended to incorporate gender classifications by Hoy (1982, 1984), Riley (1983), Dahlby (1983), and Crocker and Snow (1986). Dahlby (1983) estimates the reduction in collision insurance coverage that might result from mandatory unisex pricing. Riley (1983) presents a model of automobile insurance in which individuals differ in their probability of an accident, but there is a group of men with the highest risks. Each individual is assumed to know his or her own risk. Assuming that there cannot be a pooling equilibrium, there is a separating equilibrium for each sex. The presence of the high-risk group forces all men to choose larger deductibles than women of identical risk. A ban on gender-based insurance would force all women to choose higher deductibles because of the presence of the highest risk men. The lowest-risk women would drop out of the insurance market if the load factor were sufficiently high.

As Riley (1983) points out, the nature of the equilibrium depends on the way in which the risks of men and women differ. In the automobile insurance context it seems likely that the individual has more information about the probability of an accident than the insurance company.

This assumption is more controversial in the annuity and life insurance market because the insurance company can observe the results of medical examinations.[21]

6.3. Quantity of Insurance Variable — Use of Group Risk Prohibited

Assuming that each risk group is homogeneous, Rea (1987) shows that the elimination of gender-based pricing will lead to a pooling of risks and that the high-risk individuals will buy additional insurance at high-risk rates.[22] Welfare losses arise because low-risk groups buy less insurance as a result of the ban. A ban on the use of variables such as gender in insurance pricing will generally have much greater welfare costs if the amount of insurance per customer is not regulated.

7. Conclusions

The policy debate concerning classification variables in the insurance industry has been carried out without any economic analysis of the pattern of classification that is likely to occur in a competitive insurance industry. This paper has considered the welfare implications of classification of insurance risks, with particular emphasis on costly classification. It was shown that the industry will introduce the efficient amount of monitoring of the insured's activity. Given the low estimates of the elasticity of demand for driving, monitoring of mileage may not be efficient. Similarly, the efficiency gains from classifying individuals with known differences in expected losses are small, implying that the cost of eliminating sex discrimination in mandatory third party automobile insurance rates may be small. In the absence of regulation, competition in insurance markets could produce too much costly classification. A countervailing influence is the lack of appropriability of investment in actuarial data, and the tendency of firms to rely on industry-wide data sources. The efficiency cost of eliminating a rating variable may be very small when the quantity of insurance is fixed and demand is inelastic, but the cost could be considerably larger when the quantity of insurance purchased can be varied. Finally, risk-averse individuals will not want to know their risk group, unless that information would induce sufficiently large changes in the consumption of risky activities.

Notes

1. See for example Massachusetts (1978).

2. See for example Hoy (1982) and Benston (1982).

3. Stiglitz (1975) examines costly screening in the education context.

4. The literature in which insurance is variable is summarized later.

5. Some broad mileage categories are used, but there is no enforcement of the insured person's statement concerning his mileage.

6. Some jurisdictions have restricted private insurers' ability to price based on these variables.

7. Canadian data from a national survey indicate that among single individuals under age 20, men drive 71% more per year than women. Third-party liability rates for single men age 18 were 137% higher than for single women in Toronto (Rea and Trebilcock, 1982, 20). The mileage data are from the Canadian Health Survey, a microeconomic data tape available from Statistics Canada. The survey is described in Canada (1981). The data were collected in 1978 and 1979. The differences are underestimates because of truncation of the upper end of the mileage data. The averages are limited to those who reported some miles driven.

8. The analysis is similar if the monitoring must be done for each unit of consumption rather than each period. The two-part tariff will include the per unit cost of monitoring, S^*, in addition to the marginal accident cost. The monitoring will be undertaken if

$$[(C - S^*)/S^*] \, e_D \geqslant 2.$$

9. Meyer and Gomez-Ibanez (1981, 145) state that estimates of the elasticity of demand for gasoline cluster around $-.2$, allowing for a 1-to-5-year response. This measure incorporates shifts to more fuel-efficient cars, a substitution that is not relevant for the present discussion unless per-mile accident rates vary by vehicle size. Using quarterly data, Eckstein (1979, 91) estimated an elasticity of $-.104$ over one quarter and $-.312$ over one year, holding the auto stock and the average fuel efficiency of new cars constant. Gallini (1983, 323) estimated short-run elasticities of miles driven between $-.25$ and $-.34$ in Canada. Devlin (1988) found an elasticity of $-.5$ for Ontario and Quebec. Cross-national studies should give much higher elasticities because they reflect very long-run responses to price changes, such as residential location decisions. Using data from 25 countries Wheaton (1982, 447) estimated an elasticity of $-.50$. On the other hand Pindyck (1979, 230) found that the price of gasoline had an insignificant effect on miles driven.

10. *California Driver Fact Book*, revised July, 1976, derived from Table 14. Reprinted from Massachusetts Division of Insurance (1978, 11).

11. The accident and fuel costs (including oil) are from the Canadian Automobile Association, *Car Costs 1988–1989*, pp. 6–7. The accident costs are based on insurance costs. These include coverage other than liability, but any monitoring of liability coverage could also be used to price collision coverage.

12. The same considerations should influence the decision to meter usage of other services such as public utilities.

13. The cross-national studies referred to above include estimates of the elasticity with respect to the price of new automobiles. Pindyck (1979, 240) found that the elasticity of new registrations was $-.78$ but that this was nearly offset by reduced depreciation. Wheaton (1982, 447) found that taxes on new cars had a statistically insignificant (and positive) effect on ownership.

14. More generally, the elasticities of demand may vary with the risk group. For example, high-risk teenage drivers may have a more elastic demand for automobiles than low-risk older drivers.

15. Ideally, the firms would sample the customers, but this would not sufficiently deter lying unless there were a way to fine those who misrepresented their status. Ex post denial of benefits is permitted under the common law for material misrepresentation of risk, but this sanction is limited by statute in some jurisdictions.

16. Note that $(N_L - N_A)/N_L$ is always less than one.

17. Chapman (1987) argues that life annuities should be priced on a unisex basis because otherwise the high-risk group will increase current consumption and reduce planned future consumption (because consumption after death has no utility). However, death may not be unique in this respect. Ex ante, before one's risk category is known, it is in everyone's interest to pool any type of risk that affects the marginal utility of wealth and does not alter the relative price of a subset of consumption activities. There must be precommitment to maintaining insurance levels once the pattern of risk is revealed, otherwise those with lower risk will find the insurance overpriced and reduce the quantity of insurance purchased. Thaler (1982) discusses this point in the context of expenditures on safety.

18. See Boyer, Dionne, and Kihlstrom (1989) for an analogous situation in which production changes in response to insurance prices.

19. e_D^L does not have to equal e_D^H because equation 23 is not defined when $C_L = P_L$ and $C_H = P_H$.

20. This assumes that the customers of both firms do not differ in some unobservable way.

21. The greater longevity of annuitants compared to the general population may be due to a correlation between longevity and the decision to purchase an annuity, not better information on the part of the individual annuitant. For the insurance company the financial consequences are the same, but for economic modeling of the markets, the difference is important.

22. In the general case the Rea (1987) model is based on the assumption that the insurer can monitor the total amount of insurance purchased by the insured. In the case of life annuities, the focus of the article, the high-risk (long lived) customers are the only customers for upward-tilting annuities, and these annuities will be priced accordingly.

References

Benston, George. (1982). "The Economics of Gender Discrimination in Employee Fringe Benefits: *Manhart* Revisited," *University of Chicago Law Review* 49, 489–542.

Borenstein, Severin. (1989). "The Economics of Costly Risk Sorting in Competitive Insurance Markets," *International Review of Law and Economics* 9, 25–39.

Boyer, Marcel, Georges Dionne, and Richard Kihlstrom. (1989). "Insurance and the Value of Publicly Available Information." In *Studies in the Economics of Uncertainty In Honor of Josef Hadar*, edited by Thomas B. Fomby and Tae Kun Seo. New York: Springer-Verlag, 137–155.

Brilmayer, Lea, Richard W. Hekeler, Douglas Laycock, and Teresa A. Sullivan.

(1980). "Sex Discrimination in Employer-Sponsored Insurance Plans: A Legal and Demographic Analysis," *University of Chicago Law Review* 47, 505–560.

Canada, Statistics Canada. (1981). *The Health of Canadians: Report of the Canada Health Survey*, Catalogue 82-538E.

Chamberlin, J. R. (1985). "Assessing the Fairness of Insurance Classifications," *Research in Law and Economics* 7, 65–87.

Chapman, Bruce. (1987). "Pensions, Sex Discrimination, and the value of Life after Death," *International Review of Law and Economics* 7, 193–214.

Crocker, Keith J., and Snow, Arthur. (1986). "The Efficiency Effects of Categorical Discrimination in the Insurance Industry," *Journal of Political Economy* 94, 321–344.

Dahlby, B. G. (1983). "Adverse Selection and Statistical Discrimination: An Analysis of Canadian Automobile Insurance," *Journal of Public Economics* 20, 121–130.

Devlin, Rose Anne. (1988). "Liability Versus No-Fault Automobile Insurance Regimes: An Analysis of the Experience in Quebec," Unpublished Ph.D. dissertation, University of Toronto.

Eckstein, Otto. (1979). "Shock Inflation, Core Inflation, and Energy Disturbances in the DRI Model." In *Energy Prices, Inflation, and Economic Activity*, edited by Knut Anton Mork. Cambridge, MA: Ballinger, 63–98.

Gallini, Nancy T. (1983). "Demand for Gasoline in Canada," *Canadian Journal of Economics* 16, 299–324.

Harsanyi, John C. (1955). "Cardinal Welfare, Individualistic Ethics, and Interpersonal Comparisons of Utility," *Journal of Political Economy* 63, 309–321.

Hoy, Michael. (1982). "Categorizing Risks in the Insurance Industry," *Quarterly Journal of Economics* 97, 321–336.

Hoy, Michael. (1984). "The Impact of Imperfectly Categorizing Risks on Income Inequality and Social Welfare," *Canadian Journal of Economics* 17, 557–568.

Hoy, Michael. (1989). "The Value of Screening Mechanisms Under Alternative Insurance Possibilities," *Journal of Public Economics*, 39, 177–206.

Massachusetts Department of Insurance. (1978). *Automobile Insurance Risk Classifications: Equity and Accuracy*.

Meyer, John R., and José A. Gomez-Ibanez. (1981). *Autos, Transit and Cities*. Cambridge, Mass.: Harvard University Press.

Pindyck, Robert S. (1979). *The Structure of World Energy Demand*. Cambridge, Mass.: M.I.T. Press.

Rawls, John. (1971). *A Theory of Justice*. Cambridge, Mass.: Harvard University Press.

Rea, Samuel A., Jr. (1987). "The Market Response to the Elimination of Sex-Based Annuities," *Southern Economic Journal* 54, 55–63.

Rea, Samuel A., Jr., and Michael J. Trebilcock, (1982). *Rate Determination in the Automobile Insurance Industry in Ontario: The Use of Age, Sex and Marital Status as Rating Variables*. Toronto: Insurance Bureau of Canada.

Riley, John G. (1983). "Adverse Selection and Statistical Discrimination: Further Comments," *Journal of Public Economics* 20, 131–137.

Rothschild, Michael, and Joseph E Stiglitz. (1976). "Equilibrium in Competitive Insurance Markets: An Essay on the Economic of Imperfect Information," *Quarterly Journal of Economics* 90, 629–649.

Schmalensee, Richard. (1984). "Imperfect Information and the Equitability of Competitive Prices," *Quarterly Journal of Economics* 99, 441–460.

Stiglitz, Joseph E. (1975). "The Theory of 'Screening,' Education, and the Distribution of Income," *American Economic Review* 65, 283–300.

Thaler, Richard. (1982). "Precommitment and the Value of A Life." In *The Value of Life and Safety*, edited by M. W. Jones-Lee. Amsterdam: North-Holland, 171–183.

Turnovsky, Stephen J., Haim Shalit, and Andrew Schmitz. (1980). "Consumer's Surplus, Price Instability, and Consumer Welfare," *Econometrica* 48, 135–152.

Wheaton, William C. (1982). "The Long-run Structure of Transportation and Gasoline Demand," *Bell Journal of Economics* 13, 439–454.

Wilson, Charles. (1977). "A Model of Insurance Markets with Incomplete Information," *Journal of Economic Theory* 16, 167–207.

B) EMPIRICAL MODELS

SOCIAL INSURANCE IN MARKET CONTEXTS: IMPLICATIONS OF THE STRUCTURE OF WORKERS' COMPENSATION FOR JOB SAFETY AND WAGES*

Michael J. Moore
Duke University

W. Kip Viscusi
Duke University

Abstract

Social insurance programs whose costs are tied to particular behaviors represent more than simple income transfers between members of the economy. In the case of job safety insurance programs such as workers' compensation, in which the costs of the program are tied to the firm's safety records, the market incentives for safety that are created by the insurance program can be quite strong. At the same time, when those programs benefit injured workers, they simultaneously provide disincentives for safety and incentives for workers to extend periods of recovery and to file more claims.

We analyze these issues using a large data set on worker wages and characteristics, coupled with information on fatality risks and workers' compensation benefits. We find that workers' compensation insurance provides incentives for safety to firms that outweigh the

* An early version of this paper was presented at Northwestern University and at Duke University. Comments provided by seminar participants, and also the comments provided by Georges Dionne, John Ruser, Gary Zarkin, and two anonymous referees are gratefully acknowledged. Viscusi's research was supported by the endowment of the George G. Allen chair, and Moore's research was supported in part by the Business Associates Fund at the Fuqua School of Business, Duke University.

moral hazard effects. We further find that the insurance provided to workers on unsafe jobs reduces the net compensation paid to these workers. In particular, workers' compensation benefits create a negative compensating differential that offsets the positive compensating differential that must be paid for exposure to job risks. This negative wage differential leads to a reduction in the wage bill that compensates employers for the cost of workers' compensation premiums. Reductions in fatality risks, and the resultant reduction in the wage, supplement the direct wage-benefit effect.

Key words: compensating differentials, job safety, workers' compensation, social insurance

The principal purpose of social insurance programs is generally to address the economic needs of individuals who have either suffered a drop in income or who experience increased demands on their resources, such as higher medical bills. Workers' compensation addresses each of these classes of needs for workers who experience an on-the-job injury. Workers' compensation provides at least partial income replacement for the earnings lost due to the injury, and it also covers associated medical expenses.

The ramifications of this and other social insurance efforts extend beyond these two redistributive effects. Particularly in the case of workers' compensation, it is important to consider the broader implications of the program since it operates in a market context. Six effects can be distinguished. First, because employers fund workers' compensation benefits through premiums linked at least in part to their firm's safety record, there is a safety incentive. Higher benefit levels increase the marginal cost of accidents to the firm, providing an incentive to increase the investment in health and safety capital.

Second, this reduction in risk in turn will affect workers' wages. Since workers generally receive a compensating differential for the risks they face, a reduction in these risks through the safety incentives created by workers' compensation will partially offset the added safety costs. This reduction will not be complete. If there were a full or more than full offset, firms would have already undertaken the investment induced by workers' compensation.

Third, workers' compensation exerts a direct effect on the wages a firm must pay its workers. Providing social insurance for job injuries will increase the attractiveness of risky employment to workers. For workers in hazardous jobs, there will be a negative compensating differential in response to the social insurance just as there would be to any other positively valued aspect of the job. Social insurance through workers' compensation is not a deadweight loss to workers. Rather, it constitutes a valued component of the pay package. As a result, wages will decline in response to increases in benefits.

Fourth, workers' compensation will lead to a potential moral hazard problem for workers on the job. This ex ante moral hazard arises because workers' incentive to exercise care will be diminished, since insurance covers the financial and medical losses associated with the injury. To the extent that the losses represent irreplaceable effects on one's life and health, as with death or extensive permanent disability, there could be less of a moral hazard problem than if losses were purely financial. Dionne (1982) shows that, when the average coverage (wage replacement rate) is less than the optimal coverage, moral hazard will not present a problem for fatality insurance if the coverage does not cover direct utility losses or if incentives for safety are substantial.

The fifth effect concerns workers' incentives to return to work once injured. This ex post moral hazard problem arises because it is not economically feasible to monitor workers' employability perfectly and make payments contingent upon this status. Sixth, higher benefits will lead workers to file claims for accidents that may not have occurred or for off-the-job accidents.

This paper focuses on two general relationships that capture all of these effects — the effect of workers' compensation on fatality risk levels and the effect of workers' compensation on wages. The risk incentive effect includes the safety incentives for the firm net of any influence of moral hazard. The findings that we present, which indicate a beneficial effect of workers' compensation, run counter to the consensus in the literature, which is correctly summarized in the 1987 *Economic Report of the President* (p. 197): "A growing body of research has found that workers' compensation benefits have unfavorable effects on safety. Higher benefits appear to increase both the frequency of work injuries and the number of compensation claims filed." Our findings differ from the consensus primarily due to our focus on fatalities. As a consequence, moral hazard effects and reporting problems are minimal. Our findings will also differ in part because of our use of a new data series on occupational fatalities. These data are less susceptible to measurement error. Most important, they represent a severe accident category for which misrepresentation and moral hazard problems are less pronounced.

The second matter of interest concerns the wage effects of workers' compensation. We estimate both the direct wage offset due to the value workers place on social insurance, as well as the indirect wage benefit that arises through the fatality risk reduction induced by workers' compensation.

The analysis presented here provides an alternative perspective on the results in Moore and Viscusi (1989, 1990), which analyze the effects of experience rating on the firm's provision of safety. It focuses on the implications of the specific structure of workers' compensation across states, including benefit levels and benefit ceilings, and also on the role of the characteristics of workers and their jobs.

The organization of the paper is as follows. Sections 1 and 2 analyze the economic relationships involved and relate these economic effects to the specific components of the empirical analysis. Section 3 summarizes the variables used in the empirical analysis, which involve use of the University of Michigan Panel Study of Income Dynamics in combination with workers' compensation benefit information and death risk data. After discussing the estimation procedure in section 4, we present the estimates of the risk and wage equations in section 5. As indicated in sections 6 and 7, workers' compensation has dramatic effects, including substantial wage offsets and a reduction in the fatality rate, which could have been as much as 45% greater in the absence of the program. Workers' compensation clearly provides more than social insurance that simply transfers resources. It fundamentally affects the risk level and the compensation package.

1. A Conceptual Model of Worker and Firm Responses to Insurance Benefits

A complex array of influences operates among workers' compensation benefits, wages, and safety levels. Increases in accident insurance theoretically should induce two opposing effects. Increased benefits impose net additional financial costs on firms, leading them to devote more resources to providing safety. The extent of the safety incentive effect hinges on the extent to which additional accidents cause an increase in a firm's insurance premium through the experience-rating procedure. The incentive effect should be particularly strong for large firms, which either self-insure or are rated according to their own experience and thus pay most or all of the costs of the accident in terms of increased premiums.[1] Higher benefits also may produce an opposite influence on safety through moral hazard problems for covered workers. If the higher benefit levels on belance reduce injury risks, workers' compensation insurance could provide an effective means of regulating safety by acting as an injury tax.

To illustrate the direct effect of benefits on safety levels conceptually, consider a simple model in which firms choose the level of safety, $s \in$

(0, 1), to maximize profits. Safety enters the profit function through the safety cost function $c(s)$, where $c_s > 0$ and $c_{ss} > 0$, and through the expected value of output, sv. The safety level also affects profits through its effect on expected wages, sw, and expected benefits, $(1 - s)b$. In this simplified variant of the model we abstract from the dependence of w on s and b. The unit profit function is

$$\pi = sv - c(s) - sw - (1 - s)b,$$

where v is the unit of output. The first-order condition for a maximum with respect to s is

$$\pi_s = v - c_s - w + b = 0.$$

Note that, in order for the firm to make nonnegative profits, it must be true that $v > w$. The costs of safety improvements to the firm include the increased wage bill and the safety expenditures, while the benefits depend on the insurance level, b, and on the value of output, v. Totally differentiating the first-order condition yields

$$\frac{ds}{db} = \frac{1}{c_{ss}} > 0,$$

which is positive given the assumption $c_{ss} > 0$. The curvature of the safety-benefit relationship is theoretically ambiguous, since the second-order effect

$$\frac{d^2s}{db^2} = \frac{-1}{c_{ss}^2} c_{sss}$$

depends upon the sign of the third derivative of the safety cost function.

Extensions of this simple model that are explored in the empirical analysis include recognition of moral hazard and the feedback effects of benefits and risks on wages. If there are feedback effects of benefits and risks on wages the benefit-induced safety expenditures are partially financed by wage reductions on two margins — wages will fall in response to both lower risks and higher benefits. In the empirical analysis we estimate these "financing" effects. More importantly, we estimate the effect of benefits on fatality rates and find results that suggest that moral hazard does not play a dominant role in the determination of fatality risks. Workers' compensation benefits exert significant downward pressure on fatality risk levels. This effect decreases with benefit increases.

To analyze the effects of the two types of moral hazard, introduce the worker reaction function, which measures the extent of the worker's risk-taking $e = e(s, b)$, where $e_s > 0$, $e_b > 0$. The safety level now depends on firm expenditures on safety, s, benefit levels, b, and on the worker's reaction to s and b, $e(s, b)$, which firms will take into account in determining expenditures on safety.

Let $p^*(s, b) = p(s, e(s, b)) \in (0, 1)$ indicate the probability that a worker remains "uninjured," net of moral hazard effects. The assumptions concerning p are $p_s > 0$ and $p_e < 0$. Let $p_s^* = p_s + p_e e_s > 0$ denote the situation in which the moral hazard effect described in Viscusi (1979) is not dominant, while $p_s^* < 0$ indicates a serious moral hazard problem. Furthermore, $p_b^* = p_e e_b < 0$, so that the effect of benefit increases on the frequency and duration of claims decreases the probability that a worker works.

The dependence of wages on risks and benefits is captured by the wage function $w = w(s, b)$, where w_s, $w_b < 0$ reflect the desirability of both insurance and safety to workers. The profit function for the most general version of the model is

$$\pi = p^*(s, b)v - c(s) - p^*(s, b)w(s, b) - (1 - p^*(s, b))b.$$

The first-order condition is

$$\pi_s = -c_s + (b + v - w)p_s^* - p^*w_s = 0. \tag{1}$$

Equation 1 consists of three terms: the marginal cost of safety, $-c_s$, the marginal profitability of safety expenditures, $(b + v - w)p_s^*$, and worker expenditures on safety, p^*w_s. The last two terms in equation 1 are critical for interpreting the comparative static result to follow. The first of these, $(b + v - w)p_s^*$, represents the net change in profits that results from changes in accident rates. The remaining term, p^*w_s, equals the wage savings due to increased safety, since w_s is the implicit price of safety to the worker, and p^* is the quantity of safety. In other words, p^*w_s equals expenditures by the worker on safety.

Totally differentiating equation 1, the effect of an increase in benefits on the level of safety is

$$\frac{ds}{db} = H^{*-1}((w - v)p_{sb}^* - p_s^*(1 + \eta)) + H^{*-1}p_s^*w_b + H^{*-1}(w_s p_b^* + p^*w_{sb}),$$
$$\tag{2}$$

where η is the benefit elasticity of p_s^*, and H^* is the Hessian matrix for the problem.

It seems plausible that marginal changes in the safety level will induce a greater shirking reaction on the part of workers the higher the benefit level, so that $e_{sb} > 0$. Since $p_e < 0$, p_{sb}^* is < 0, and the first term in equation 2, $H^{*-1}(w - v)p_{sb}^*$ is positive, given $w < v$.

The second term depends on η, the elasticity of p_s^* with respect to benefits. If p_s^* and the elasticity are both positive, then $-H^{*-1}p_s^*(1 + \eta)$ is positive. If p_s^* is greater than zero, and η is negative, then $-H^{*-1}p_s^*(1 + \eta)$ is still positive if the elasticity is less than one in absolute value. If there is significant shirking due to the firm's provision of safety ($p_s^* < 0$), the term $-H^{*-1}p_s^*(1 + \eta)$ is negative, and benefit increases may decrease safety levels.

The third term in equation 2, $H^{*-1}p_s^*w_b$ is also positive if there is not a substantial moral hazard problem ($p_s^* > 0$). The final term, which represents the effect of a benefit increase on worker expenditures on safety, is negative. Thus, the total impact of benefit changes on risk levels is indeterminate when moral hazard is considered.

The importance of moral hazard is illustrated most clearly by analyzing the solution to the problem when there are no wage-risk or wage-benefit feedbacks (i.e., $w_s = w_b = w_{sb} = 0$). In this case, profits are

$$\pi = p^*(s, b)v - c(s) - p^*(s, b)w - (1 - p^*(s, b))b,$$

and the optimal level of s is given by the first-order condition

$$\pi_s = -c_s + p_s^*(v - w) + p_s^*b = 0,$$

or

$$-c_s + (b + v - w)p_s^* = 0.^2 \tag{3}$$

Equation 3 illustrates the interactive relationship between benefits and wages that exists on the firm side. If $p_s^* > 0$, so that moral hazard is not serious, a necessary condition for a positive level of safety is that the value of a healthy worker, output plus benefits, exceeds wages. Given some level of $b + v$, increases in w reduce the optimal level of s, as healthy workers become relatively more expensive. The effect of a benefit increase on safety in equation 3 is

$$\frac{ds}{db} = H^{*-1}((w - v - b)p_{sb}^* - p_s^*).$$

The sign of this term thus depends on both p_{sb}^* and p_s^*. Rearranging terms,

$$\frac{ds}{db} = H^{*-1}(w - v)p_{sb}^* - H^{*-1}p_s^*(1 + \eta).$$

As discussed above following equation 2, equation 4 is ambiguous in sign. As noted in the introduction, most empirical research has found a negative overall relationship.

Table 1.   Summary of Main Mechanisms of Influence

Explanatory Variable	*Nature of Effect on Risk Level*
Workers' compensation	Negative accident cost incentive effect, positive moral hazard effect.
(Workers' compensation)^2	Curvature of workers' compensation-risk relationship. Positive if marginal cost of safety is increasing.
	Nature of Effect on Wage Rate
Risk level	Positive compensating wage differential.
Workers' compensation	Negative compensating wage differential.
Workers' compensation-benefit	Captures workers who are above the benefit maximum.
Maximum binding interaction	Increased magnitudes of effects of benefits on wages.

2. Overview of the Economic Relationships

The empirical analysis focuses on two equations — a risk equation and a wage equation. Although neither of these equations is unprecedented in the literature, several of the key variables that we include are new. In addition, our focus on a new set of death risk data is also novel. Here we discuss the economic forces reflected in the main variables of interest. Table 1 provides a summary of these influences.

All of the variables of interest in the risk equation are related to workers' compensation. The funding mechanism for workers' compensation creates safety incentives for firms that should increase the safety level provided. Even for relatively small firms, which are not perfectly experience-rated, the insurance underwriting procedures create some link between workplace conditions and insurance premiums.[3]

A potentiallly offsetting influence is that of ex ante moral hazard, as more generous benefit levels will lead workers to decrease their level of care. This aspect of worker behavior is just as unambiguous theoretically as is the opposite safety incentive effect for employers. In addition, there are a number of studies indicating that more generous benefits lead to ex post moral hazard through more extended periods of recovery and possible over-reporting of injuries.[4] These abuses are likely to be more responsive to the benefit level than the fatality rate, which is the subject of this study. Although one cannot rule out the possibility of a dominant moral hazard effect on theoretical grounds, the high estimated value of life that workers receive through wage-risk tradeoffs suggests that it is highly implausible that workers would endanger their lives to a substantial degree because of more generous ex post compensation that will benefit their surviving heirs. Our working hypothesis is that higher benefits will lower fatality risk levels, so that the workers' compensation variable should have a negative sign in the risk equation.

The second variable of interest — the square of the workers' compensation variable — pertains to the nonlinearity of the effect of workers' compensation on risk. This relationship is highly complex once all feedback effects, such as moral hazard, are taken into account. However, in the simple model of the firm's safety decisions it was shown that the square of workers' compensation should have a positive effect on safety if the marginal cost curve for safety is rising at an increasing rate. Evidence regarding the marginal costs of compliance with OSHA standards for arsenic and cotton dust exposures presented in Viscusi (1983, 1985) indicates that the marginal cost curve for safety increases very steeply at low risk levels. To the extent that this pattern holds more generally, the negative risk incentive effect of workers' compensation should be dampened at higher benefit levels.

The final aspect of workers' compensation that will be considered is the structure of benefit payments. Under the institutional structure of the existing workers' compensation systems, increases in the benefit ceiling are costly to firms only if the benefit ceiling is binding. Figure 1 illustrates the effect of a benefit increase in three distinct cases. In the first case, the standard replacement rate for wages leads to benefits below the ceiling (CAP), as at wage W_1, and an increase in the benefit maximum to CAP' has no effect on workers' compensation costs, WC_1. If two-thirds of the wage is just equal to or slightly above the ceiling, as at wage W_2, an increase in the benefit cap from CAP to CAP' causes an increase in insurance costs from WC_2 to WC_2' that is less than CAP' − CAP. In the final case, a firm that pays a very high wage, W_3 or greater, pays the full cost of the increase in the benefit cap, $WC_3' - WC_3$. The predicted effect of workers' compensation on high-wage firms who pay the full cost of increases in WCOMP is therefore greater than that of low wage firms who receive less than a one-for-one effect of CAP increases in the intermediate wage range (W_2) and experience no effect if their workers are in the low wage range (W_1). More generally, in a world of uncertainty over wages and hours, an increase in the maximum will affect expected costs for all workers. The negative risk incentive effect of workers compen-

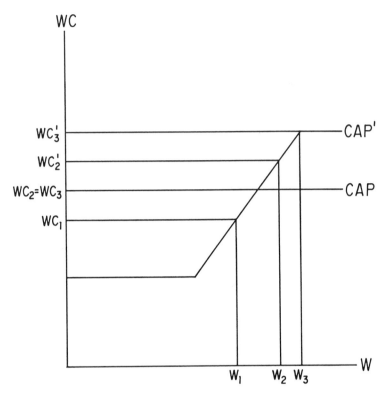

Figure 1. The effect of changes in the benefit ceiling (CAP) on the costs of workers' compensation (WC), given the wage level (W).

sation should be greater for workers at firms for which the cap is a binding constraint.

The variables included in the wage equation represent less complex influences. Wages should increase with the risk level, following Adam Smith's proposition that hazardous jobs will command compensating differentials. For economically similar reasons, higher levels of the benefit maximum should lead to a wage reduction. The extent of the reduction will depend upon whether the ceiling is binding. Ex post compensation for job risks should decrease the level of ex ante compensation required. The extent of the offset depends on the attractiveness of the insurance provided, which is determined by factors such as the degree of insurance loading.

3. The Sample and the Variables

Our primary data source in this study is the University of Michigan Panel Study of Income Dynamics (PSID). These survey data provide much of the information related to the worker and his job, which we augment using information on risk levels and workers' compensation. The PSID is a longitudinal survey that provides information on the characteristics of workers and their jobs for the years 1968–1984. We will focus on the 1982 survey year since it includes the state and industry information needed to establish a precise matching of the workers in our sample with the primary variables of interest — the job risk and workers' compensation variables, and also for comparability with our related research. The 1982 survey year also represents the midpoint of the time period covered by the risk data we will use. The PSID has been widely used in labor economics, including previous applications of the compensating differential model, such as Viscusi (1979) and Moore and Viscusi (1988, 1989, 1990a,b).

Our empirical analysis focuses on the national random sample of workers included in the PSID. We exclude the PSID subsample pertaining to low-income workers since this oversampling distorts the worker mix. The 1982 survey year pertains to labor market outcomes for 1981. The sample that we analyze, which is identical to the sample in More and Viscusi (1988), contains 1349 observations. The workers excluded from the sample were farmers and farm managers, workers who are not household heads, government employees (for whom no risk data are available), blacks, and cases with missing data. The variable definitions and sample characteristics appear in table 2.

The demographic variables are quite extensive, including information on the worker's sex (FEMALE dummy variable (d.v.)), family status (i.e., number of dependent children (KIDS), and marital status (MARRIED d.v.). The human capital variables included in the analysis pertain to health impairments (HEALTH d.v.), years of formal schooling (EDUCATION), and acquired training that is either general (EXPERIENCE and its square) or specific (JOB TENURE and its square). The extensive set of education and training variables precludes the inclusion of an age variable. Three regional dummy variables (NEAST, NCENT, and SOUTH d.v.'s) are included to reflect inter-regional differentials in wages and the cost of living. We include as an urban variable CITY, which increases with the size of the largest city in the worker's area.

The measure of pecuniary compensation is the worker's hourly wage

Table 2. Definitions of the Variables and Sample Characteristics

	Mean (Std. Dev.)	
FEMALE	0.15 (0.36)	Sex dummy variable (d.v.): 1 if worker is female, 0 otherwise.
KIDS	0.99 (1.15)	Number of dependent children
MARRIED	0.72 (0.45)	Marital status d.v.: 1 if worker has ever been married, 0 otherwise.
HEALTH	0.07 (0.26)	Health status d.v.: 1 if worker has a serious physical or nervous condition that limits the amount of work he can do, 0 otherwise.
EDUCATION	12.98 (2.50)	Number of grades completed.
EXPERIENCE	11.91 (10.56)	Years worked full time since age 18.
JOB TENURE	4.97 (6.21)	Years worked on current job.
NEAST	0.22 (0.41)	Region d.v.: 1 if worker lives in the Northeastern U.S.: 0 otherwise.
NCENT	0.31 (0.46)	Region d.v.: 1 if worker lives in the Northcentral U.S.: 0 otherwise.
SOUTH	0.27 (0.44)	Region d.v.: 1 if worker lives in the Southeastern U.S.: 0 otherwise
CITY	331.90 (378.92)	City size variables in 1,000's. (size of nearest city)
WAGE	7.01 (2.42)	Computed after-tax hourly wage, 1981.
UNION	0.28 (0.44)	Union status d.v.: 1 if worker's job is covered by a collective bargaining agreement, 0 otherwise.
BLUE	0.52 (0.50)	Collar color d.v.: 1 if worker is in a blue collar occupation, 0 otherwise.
RISK	7.92 (9.74)	NTOF risk variable. Number of fatal accidents per 100,000 workers in the worker's industry on a state-specific basis.
WCOMP	219.44 (67.59)	Weekly benefits for temporary total disability under state workers' compensation program.
REPRATE	0.89 (0.46)	Workers' compensation weekly after-tax wage replacement rate.

(WAGE) for 1981 and its natural logarithm (lnWAGE). These measures are superior to annual earnings variables frequently used in compensating differential studies. Since workers' compensation benefits are tax exempt, ideally one should place wages and workers' compensation on comparable after-tax terms. We have done this by putting the wage variables in after-tax dollars, based on the marginal tax rate reported by PSID members.

The job characteristic variables pertain to whether the worker is covered by a collective bargaining agreement (UNION d.v.) and whether the worker is in a blue-collar job (BLUE d.v.). The blue-collar variable reflects the influence of omitted job characteristics correlated with blue-collar occupations.

Two key variables of interest pertaining to job risks and workers' compensation benefits were constructed using information that was matched to workers in the PSID. Our death risk measure uses a new set of death risk data that became available in 1987. The National Institute for Occupational Safety and Health (NIOSH) has undertaken The National Traumatic Occupational Fatality (NTOF) project to obtain a more accurate assessment of fatality risks. As we indicate in Moore and Viscusi (1990a), this measure yields a higher risk level than does the Bureau of Labor Statistics (BLS) data. In addition to this difference, there is also evidence of substantial measurement error in the BLS data. Our results suggest that the NTOF data represent a superior risk measure.

The NTOF data also are better suited to analyzing workers' compensation since benefit structures vary by state, and the NTOF data are also available on a state-specific basis. Since most previously published risk data do not reflect state differences, use of such measures to analyze workers' compensation creates problems.[5] Use of the national data level BLS risk data introduces potentially major errors by ignoring interstate variation in industry levels.[6] Use of the NTOF Survey avoids these difficulties since these fatality rates were based on a census of occupational fatalities during the years 1980–1985 and are classified by both state and industry.

We will denote the NTOF risk measure by RISK, which is the average number of fatalities per 100,000 workers for the years 1980–1985. This variable is available by state and by industry. The mean fatality rate for the PSID sample is 7.8 deaths. This risk level is almost 50% higher than BLS death rates for this period.

The second key variable that must be constructed is the measure of workers' compensation benefits.[7] Most previous studies have generally used the benefits for the most frequent type of claim — temporary total disabilities — as a proxy for the ex ante level of all types of benefits, including those for temporary total, permanent total, and permanent partial disabilities, and for fatality benefits. In Viscusi and Moore (1987) we document the high correlations among the various benefit categories. This correlation makes separation of the effects of each benefit component difficult. Regardless, the relative uniformity of maxima across categories and the fact that compensating differentials are generated ex ante for insurance against any type of injury make this benefit category a reasonable measure for workers' compensation.

The basic workers' compensation insurance variable — WCOMP — equals weekly maximum insurance benefits for temporary total disability, as reported annually by the United States Chamber of Commerce (1982). The variable WCOMP is matched to workers only by state, but it is calculated on a worker-specific basis using benefit formulas that adjust for such factors as marital status and family size. The other insurance variable is REPRATE, which equals the weekly after-tax wage replacement rate:

$$\text{REPRATE} = \frac{\text{WCOMP}}{\text{WAGE} \times 40}$$

where WAGE is the hourly after-tax wage. The structure of workers' compensation benefits is captured by the binary variable D, which equals 1 if two-thirds of the workers' weekly wage exceeds the maximum and equals zero otherwise.

4. The Empirical Framework

The empirical model consists of a two-equation system, with the natural logs of the wage rate and of the risk level serving as the two dependent variables. In the risk equation, the subscript i denotes worker i (including the intercept), X_{ij} is explanatory variable j for worker i, and ε_{Ri} is the random error term.

The first equation pertains to determination of the risk level, and is of the form

$$\ln\text{RISK}_i = \sum_{j=0}^{J} a_j X_{ij} + \phi_1 D_i \text{WCOMP}_i + \phi_2 D_i \text{WCOMP}_i^2$$
$$+ \phi_3 (1 - D_i)\,\text{WCOMP}_i + \phi_4 (1 - D_i)\,\text{WCOMP}_1^2 + \varepsilon_{Ri}. \quad (5)$$

The wage equation to be estimated is

$$\ln\text{WAGE}_i = \sum_{k=0}^{K} \beta_k X_{ik} + \gamma_1 \text{RISK}_i + \delta_1 D_i \text{RISK}_i \times \text{REPRATE}_i$$

$$+ \delta_2(1 - D_i)\,\text{RISK}_i \times \text{REPRATE}_i + \varepsilon_{wi}. \qquad (6)$$

In our formulation wages, risks, and workers' compensation are inter-related in the following manner. The WAGE variable enters the RISK equation through the variable D only. The WAGE variable does not appear separately in the risk equation since, in the hedonic system, we can express the risk as a function of characteristics of the worker or the firm.[8] The RISK variable enters the wage equation directly to test for compensating differentials. Workers compensation affects both wages and risks directly, and also affects wages indirectly through the risk equation. The two-equation system is estimated using two-stage least squares, with WAGE, RISK, and D treated as endogenous.

The analysis in sections 1 and 2 indicates that if the safety incentive effect dominates the role of moral hazard, the expected coefficient signs are $\phi_1 < 0$, $\phi_2 > 0$, $\phi_3 < 0$, and $\phi_4 > 0$. Workers' compensation should reduce the risk level (ϕ_1, $\phi_3 < 0$) at a diminishing rate (ϕ_2, $\phi_4 > 0$). This reduction should be greater for higher wage workers. If moral hazard offsets the safety incentive effect the net effect of workers' compensation will be to raise fatality risk (ϕ_1, $\phi_3 > 0$), so that the results also serve as a test of the moral hazard dominance hypothesis. Furthermore, if the effects of WCOMP are pronounced when $D = 1$, we would also expect $|\phi_1| > |\phi_3|$ and $|\phi_2| > |\phi_4|$. However, the differential effects are more likely to appear in the wage equation, since the WAGE variable is worker-specific.

Equation 6 represents the lnWAGE equation. In equation 6 the RISK variable is expected to have a positive effect, using the familiar compensating differential rationale. This effect should not depend on the value of the variable D. In Viscusi and Moore (1987) we show that the theoretically appropriate benefit measure interacts benefits with the risk measure, because insurance benefits are only of value to the worker at positive risk levels. Equation 6 therefore interacts the NTOF fatality risk measure with the replacement rate measure. A wage offset from workers' compensation is expected, so that the predicted workers' compensation coefficients, δ_1 and δ_2, are negative. Thus the lnWAGE equation hypotheses are $\gamma_1 > 0$, δ_1, δ_2, < 0, and $|\delta_1| > |\delta_2|$.

In the empirical analysis of the compensating differential model, a number of issues arise with respect to the estimation of the model. Most importantly, the model itself consists of a regression of wages on job risks and benefit levels, all of which reflect the utility maximizing choices of workers. Since unobservable worker characteristics such as ability are correlated with all of these choice variables, ordinary least-squares estimates of compensating differential wage equations may not yield unbiased estimates of the wage-risk and wage-benefit tradeoffs. A similar problem arises when aggregate data are matched to workers in the sample and taken as a measure of the risk a particular worker faced in his job. The measurement error caused by this, in conjunction with the ability bias described above, exerts a downward influence on the estimated coefficients and tends to inflate the estimated standard errors.[9]

Our solution to this problem is similar to Biddle and Zarkin (1988). We use a standard wage equation that consists of the human capital variables (HEALTH, EDUCATION, JOB TENURE, JOB TENURE^2, EXPERIENCE, and EXPERIENCE^2), location variables (NEAST, NCENT, SOUTH, CITY), job-related variables (BLUE, UNION), and personal characteristics (KIDS, MARRIED, FEMALE, BLACK), and instrumented values of the endogenous right-hand side variables. Instrumental variables include all possible interactions of the exogenous variables, and the included variables. Unlike Biddle and Zarkin, we do not include interaction terms that appear significant in a variable selection process. The estimated coefficients on the key variables in each equation do not appear to be sensitive to the exclusion of these interactions. We therefore report the results from the simpler regressions only, as the coefficient estimates are easier to interpret.[10]

We use a similar procedure to estimate the risk regression. Individual and job characteristics, excluding the location measures, are included in the regression. The excluded higher order terms enable us to identify the coefficients of this regression.

5. Estimates of the RISK and WAGE Equation

5.1. RISK Equation

Table 3 presents estimates of the RISK and WAGE equations given by equations 5 and 6. The regressions restrict the WCOMP coefficients to be equal across values of the dummy variable, D.

Consider first the variables in the RISK regressions other than those related to workers' compensation. It is often argued in the wage-risk trade-off literature that wealth effects, ability, and worker characteristics lead workers to sort themselves into jobs with different risks. In terms of the explanatory variables in table 2, proxies for lifetime wealth such as

Table 3. Two-Stage Least-Squares Estimates of the Risk and Wage Equations[a] Coefficients (Standard Errors)

Independent Variable[a]	RISK	WAGE
KIDS	0.018	0.029[a]
	(0.023)	(0.008)
MARRIED	−0.011	0.064[a]
	(0.078)	(0.024)
HEALTH	−0.135	−0.081[a]
	(0.094)	(0.028)
EDUCATION	−0.036[a]	0.041[a]
	(0.012)	(0.004)
FEMALE	−0.271[a]	−0.206[a]
	(0.090)	(0.028)
UNION	0.056	0.150[a]
	(0.058)	(0.019)
JOB TENURE	−0.004	0.008[a]
	(0.005)	(0.003)
	----	$-0.73E{-}3$
		$(1.11E{-}3)$
EXPERIENCE	−0.004	0.019[a]
	(0.003)	(0.003)
	----	$-3.95E{-}4^{a}$
		$(0.78E{-}4)$
BLUE	0.194[a]	−0.065[a]
	(0.063)	(0.024)
WCOMP	$-5.78E{-}3^{a}$	$-1.25E{-}2^{a}$
	$(1.88E{-}3)$	$(0.31E{-}2)$
$WCOMP^{2}$	$8.57E{-}6^{a}$	----
	$(3.83E{-}6)$	
RISK	----	$1.42E{-}2^{a}$
		$(0.28E{-}2)$
INTERCEPT	2.852[a]	1.147[a]
	(0.296)	(0.069)
Summary Statistics		
R^{2}	0.082	0.476
x^{2}	92.2	85.58

[a] Statistically significant at the 0.05 confidence level, one-tailed t-test (critical value = 1.645).

EDUCATION and MARRIED, which are both positively related to wealth, should reduce RISK, since job safety is a normal good. This is empirically supported in the RISK regression, where the effect of EDUCATION is negative and highly significant. Marital status also has a negative effect, but it is not statistically significant. The variable KIDS, which measures the number of dependent children, has no discernible effect on RISK.

An extensive theoretical literature analyzes the relationship between risks and age, particularly as it relates to a worker's learning about risk. The theoretical propositions in these learning models are supported empirically in quit rate studies (Viscusi, 1979) and a reservation wage rate study (Viscusi, 1984). Risk equations have been estimated for other risk variables in Viscusi (1979), but the analysis of state-industry death risk variables in table 3 addresses a more refined risk measure.

In the table 3 results, EXPERIENCE has a negative effect on risks that is significant at the .10 confidence level. This could reflect the sorting of workers into safer jobs as they observe working conditions over time. There is not a similar JOB TENURE effect, which is probably due to the nature of the risk variable, which is only industry-specific. Increases in job tenure for a given level of experience will have no effect on one's industry risk level, though one's job-specific risk may change.

The FEMALE dummy variable is negative and highly significant in the RISK equation, indicating that women tend to work on safer jobs. On the other hand, HEALTH impairments are not strongly related to RISK. The impact of UNION status does not indicate a strong effect. The remaining coefficient, BLUE, is positive and significant, as expected.

The table 2 results indicate that workers' compensation on balance serves as a safety incentive mechanism. The WCOMP variable, which has the expected negative sign and strong statistical significance, is associated with a large impact on safety. Insurance costs exert strong downward pressure on fatal accident rates. The nonlinearity of the WCOMP effect is also very strong, as is evidenced by the positive coefficients for $WCOMP^2$. This result is consistent with the evidence that the marginal cost of providing safety rises at an increasing rate.[11]

5.2. WAGE Equation

Table 3 also presents estimates of equation 6. In table 3 the RISK and REPRATE efects are not allowed to vary across values of D. Alternative specifications are discussed below.

Workers with KIDS have higher wages and limitations caused by

HEALTH impairments decrease wages. The rate of return to education is about four percent, and JOB TENURE and EXPERIENCE increase wages, the latter at a decreasing rate. Workers who are FEMALE are paid significantly lower wages. The UNION coefficient of about 15% is consistent with most other studies.

In the equation reported in table 3, there is strong statistical evidence of a positive tradeoff between lnWAGE and RISK. The estimates of the coefficients γ and δ indicate that a 1/100,000 increase in the death risk will change wages by 1%, taking into account the effect of the risk change on expected benefits. The associated implicit value of life is $5.1 million in 1986 prices. This result is quite robust. As indicated in our sensitivity analyses the rate of trade-off net of the workers' compensation replacement rate is .2%.

The benefit structure variable D, which measures the effect of changes in the benefit ceiling conditional or whether a worker is above or below the ceiling, has an important effect on the wage equation coefficients δ_1 or δ_2. As expected, increases in the maximum are more highly valued by workers for whom the maximum is binding, so that $|\delta_1| > |\delta_2|$. The benefit structure variable did not lead to differences in the WCOMP coefficients in the RISK equation, probably due to differences in the level of aggregation of the variables RISK and D.

5.3. Other Issues Relating to the Estimation Procedure

The results in table 3 are quite strong in terms of their statistical significance, and the RISK and INSURANCE variables perform consistently with our a priori expectations. The estimation techniques are not typical, however, as previous research has relied almost exclusively on ordinary least squares (OLS) estimation of single equation models. To compare our results with the more standard OLS estimates, equations 5 and 6 were also estimated using OLS. The results indicated that in both the RISK and lnRISK regressions the coefficients on the insurance variables, WCOMP and $WCOMP^2$, are practically identical to the coefficients estimated using two-stage least squares in terms of their signs and significance levels.

6. Safety and Wage Effects

The empirical results indicate that there are statistically significant wage and risk effects of workers' compensation. The magnitude of these influences is also of considerable economic and policy interest. Consider first the effect on safety. Based on the estimates of equation 5, a decrease in benefits to zero would increase the average risk level by 3.53 deaths per 100,000 workers, which is an increase of 45%.

The RISK effects of workers' compensation also imply a wage adjustment, since risks and wages are positively related. Based upon the wage equation estimates in table 3, a one unit increase in the RISK level will increase the after-tax hourly wage by 2.2 cents, or about 45 dollars per year. If workers' compensation benefits were eliminated entirely and the risk level rose by 3.53, annual wages would rise by about $160.

The table 3 results also indicate that benefits exert downward pressure on fatality rates that diminishes as benefits rise. Setting the derivative of the benefit effect equal to zero and solving for WCOMP yields a value of $336. Of the states in our sample, Connecticut, Illinois, Iowa, Maine, and Wyoming had benefit ceilings in excess of this amount.

The effect of workers' compensation on wages consists of two components — a direct wage offset for the social insurance and a wage offset for the reduced risk level. The estimates in table 3 imply that the direct wage effect will be the larger of the two wage effects of workers' compensation.

Based on the coefficients in table 3, we can calculate the full wage effect of a benefit increase, i.e., the direct wage offset plus the wage decrease resulting from the diminished risk. For a worker with an hourly wage equal to $7, wages fall by about 8 cents per week per dollar of additional benefits. This effect consists primarily of the 1.25% reduction due to the direct effect of benefits on wages, but also includes a wage reduction of 0.03% a week due to the indirect effect of benefits on risks and risks on wages. In the absence of benefits, a linear extrapolation of these figures implies that wages would be $1,100 higher. The direct wage offset is consequently many times greater than the wage offset due to the reduced risk.

The total impact of workers' compensation on wages consist of two parts — the $1,100 wage offset from higher benefits and the $160 savings due to risk reduction. This difference in financial incentives for safety is evidenced in the greater safety impact of workers' compensation, compared with OSHA. The $160 per worker wage reduction is almost three times greater than the reported per worker expenditures on health and safety for the year 1981 of $57, expressed in 1986 prices, but these expenditure figures are highly speculative.[12] The $1,100 wage offset and the additional $160 offset from risk reduction also exceeds the $261 average cost of workers' compensation premiums per worker.[13]

7. Conclusion

Because workers' compensation is a social insurance program that operates within a market context, it has broad economic effects on the behavior of firms and prospective beneficiaries of the insurance. Workers' compensation is not a simple income transfer. Rather, it represents a targeted insurance effort that enhances the attractiveness of hazardous jobs by reducing the income loss associated with these positions. Since workers value this social insurance there is a substantial wage offset, which in turn diminishes the premium cost to firms.

The second class of effects stems from the safety incentives created by the funding arrangements. Since workers' compensation premiums dwarf the magnitude of penalties levied by OSHA, it is not surprising that workers' compensation has a greater safety incentive effect net of the influence of any moral hazard. Indeed, death risks could have been almost 50% greater in the absence of this program. There is also a small wage reduction that firms experience because of this decreased risk.

Perhaps the main lesson from this analysis of workers' compensation is that social insurance efforts have far reaching effects that should be taken into account in program design.[14] Society is not simply transferring money in these programs. It is also establishing powerful incentives for safety. Indeed, these incentives appear to be a driving force in promoting worker safety.

In addition, the frequent complaints by firms about the rising premium levels may be overstated. These premiums translate into benefits for which workers willingly accept substantial wage cuts. An attractive social insurance program that operates through the market will be at least partially self-financing.[15]

Notes

1. See Ruser (1985), and Moore and Viscusi (1989, 1990).
2. Note that $p_s^* > 0$ is a necessary condition for an interior solution to this problem.
3. For analyses of the role of experience rating, see Ruser (1985) and Moore and Viscusi (1989).
4. See Butler and Worral (1985) and Kniesner and Leeth (1987).
5. In those studies that have analyzed the impact of workers' compensation on injury rates, Butler (1983) uses time series data on risks and benefits within a single state (South Carolina) to circumvent this problem. Chelius (1982) uses unpublished data on two-digit (SIC) manufacturing industries for 36 states, and Ruser (1985) uses BLS injury data for 25 three-digit manufacturing industries across 41 states. Of the three studies, only Butler attempts to analyze the combined impact of benefits on both injury rates and wages.

6. In the NTOF data, the average risks within one-digit SIC industry classifications are typically 2–5 times the size of their standard errors, so that the interstate risk variation is more pronounced for some industries than for others.

7. Previous analyses have utilized a range of measures that include the weekly wage replacement rate [Chelius 1982, Viscusi and Moore 1987, and Arnould and Nichols 1983], weekly benefits (Ruser, 1985), annual payments by industry (Butler, 1983), and workers' compensation premium rates (Dorsey and Walzea 1983). Butler attempts to separately identify the effects of each type of benefit with some success and also constructs a benefit index using principal components analysis.

8. Moore and Viscusi (1989) analyze a RISK equation with firm characteristics.

9. See Brown (1980), Duncan and Holmlund (1983), and Moore (1990) for analyses of these problems.

10. The results of this estimation were reported in an earlier version of this paper.

11. Technically speaking, the estimation should take into account the fact that the dependent variable is grouped. One solution to this problem (the random effects model) requires longitudinal data, which we do not utilize in the study. An important finding in Ruser (1990) is that the results in our RISK equation are replicated using microdata on fatality risks.

12. Actual expenditures on employee safety and health in 1981 for all businesses, reported by McGraw-Hill (1983), were 5,120.4 million dollars. The total civilian labor force in 1981 included 106,940 workers, as reported by the Council of Economic Advisers (1987). Safety expenditure data are taken from The McGraw-Hill Survey of Investment in Employee Safety and Health (1986).

13. Total premiums paid for 1981 equal $22.9 billion dollars reported in Price (1984), for per worker premium costs of $214 in 1981 prices, and $261 in 1986 prices.

14. See Weiler (1986).

15. See Moore and Viscusi (1989).

References

Arnould, R. J., and L. M., Nichols. (1983). "Wage-Risk Premiums and Workers' Compensation: A Refinement of Estimates of Compensating Wage Differential," *Journal of Political Economy* 91(2), 332–340.

Biddle, J., and G. Zarkin. (1988). "Worker Preferences and Market Compensation for Job Risk," *Review of Economics and Statistics* 77, 660–667.

Butler, R. J. (1983). "Wage and Injury Rate Response to Shifting Levels of Workers' Compensation." In Worrall, John, D., ed., *Safety and the Workforce: Incentives and Disincentives in Workers' Compensation*, 61–86, Ithaca, NY: Industrial and Labor Relations Press.

Butler, R. J., and J. D. Worrall. (1985). "Work Injury Compensation and the Duration of Nonwork Spells," *Economic Journal* 95, 714–724.

Brown, C. (1980). "Equalizing Differences in the Labor Market," *Quarterly Journal of Economics* 94(1), 113–134.

Chelius, J. R. (1982). "The Influence of Workers' compensation on Safety Incentives," *Industrial and Labor Relations Review* 35(2), 235–242.

Council of Economic Advisers. (1987). *Economic Report of the President*, Washington, D.C.: U.S. Government Printing Office.

Dionne, G. (1982). "Moral Hazard and State-Dependent Utility Function," *J. of Risk and Insurance* 48(3), 422–435.

Dorsey, S., and N. Walzer. (1983). "Workers' Compensation, Job Hazards, and Wages," *Industrial and Labor Relations Review* 36(4), 642–654.

Duncan, G. J., and B. Holmlund. (1983). "Was Adam Smith Right After All? Another Test of the Theory of Compensating Wage Differentials," *Journal of Labor Economics* 1(4), 366–379.

Kniesner, T. J., and J. D. Leeth. (1987). "Separating the Reporting Effects from the Injury Rate Effects of Workers' Compensation. A Hedonic Simulation," Center for the Study of Business Regulation Working Paper No. 87–10, Duke University, Durham, North Carolina.

Moore, M. J., and W. K. Viscusi. (1988). "Doubling the Estimated Value of Life: The Implications of New Occupational Fatality Data," *Journal of Policy Analysis and Management* 7(3), 476–490.

Moore, M. J., and W. K. Viscusi. (1989). "Promoting Safety Through Workers' Compensation: The Efficacy and Net Wage Costs of Injury Insurance," *RAND Journal of Economics* 20(4), 499–515.

Moore, M. J., and W. K. Viscusi. (1990a). *Compensation Mechanisms for Job Risks: Wages, Workers' Compensation, and Product Liability*. Princeton, NJ: Princeton University Press.

Moore, M. J., and W. K. Viscusi. (1990b). *Have Increases in Workers' Compensation Benefits Paid for Themselves?* David Appel and Philip Borba eds. Dordrecht: Kluwer Academic Publishers.

Moore, M. J. (1990). "The Impact of Measurement Error and Ability Bias Estimates of Compensating Differentials." Working paper, Duke University, Durham, North Carolina.

Price, D. N., (1981) "Workers' Compensation Program Experience" *Social Security Bulletin*, 47(4), 8–12.

Ruser, J. W. (1985). "Workers' Compensation Insurance, Experience Rating, and Occupational Injuries," *RAND Jounal of Economics* 16(4), 487–503.

Ruser, J. (1990). "The Impact of Workers' Compensation Insurance on Occupational Injuries and Fatalities: Reporting Effects and True Safety Effects." BLS Working Paper.

U.S. Chamber of Commerce. (1982). *Analysis of Workers' Compensation Laws*, 1982 Ed. Washington, D.C.: U.S. Chamber of Commerce.

Viscusi, W. K. (1979). *Employment Hazards: An Investigation of Market Performance*. Cambridge, MA: Harvard University Press.

Viscusi, W. K. (1983). *Risk by Choice: Regulating Health and Safety in the Workplace*. Cambridge, MA: Harvard University Press.

Viscusi, W. K., and C. O'Connor. (1984). "Adaptive Responses to Chemical Labeling: Are Workers Bayesian Decision Makers?" *American Economic Review* 74(5), 942–956.

Viscusi, W. K. (1985). "Cotton Dust Regulation: An OSHA Success Story?" *Journal of Policy Analysis and Management* 4(3), 325–343.

Viscusi, W. K., and M. J. Moore. (1987). "Workers' Compensation: Wage Effects, Benefit Inadequacies, and the Value of Health Losses," *Review of Economics and Statistics* 69(2), 249–261.

Weiler, P. (1986). "Legal Policy for Workplace Injuries." American Law Institute Report, American Law Institute, Philadelphia, PA.

TESTING FOR ASYMMETRIC INFORMATION IN CANADIAN AUTOMOBILE INSURANCE

Bev Dahlby

University of Alberta

Abstract

An increase in an insurance policy's premium, holding the deductible constant, should increase the average claim frequency for the policy if the insurance market is subject to an adverse selection process. A model of adverse selection is developed to test this proposition using data on collision insurance in Canada over the period 1974–1986. The equations for the demand for collision insurance and for the average claim frequency for the policy are derived assuming that consumers have a constant absolute risk aversion utility function and that the underlying distribution function for the probability of loss is a member of the gamma distribution. The parameters of the models are estimated using a nonlinear estimation procedure, and a linear version of the model is also estimated. In general, the results are consistent with the presence of adverse selection in the market.

Key words: insurance, adverse selection, moral hazard, asymmetric information

As John Riley (1985) has observed, the principal-agent literature can be divided into those papers that focus on hidden actions (moral hazard) and

I would like to thank R. Arnott, D. Cummins, N. Dastoor, R. Devlin, G. Dionne, N. Doherty, D. Ryan, P. Townley, C. Vanasse, and two anonymous referees for their comments. The support of the Endowment Fund for the Future at the University of Alberta is gratefully acknowledged.

those that focus on hidden knowledge (adverse selection). Both problems arise because of asymmetric information. A voluminous theoretical literature has developed on these topics,[1] but there have been relatively few empirical studies of adverse selection and moral hazard in insurance markets. Doherty (1980) tested whether premium incentives in the fire insurance market in the U.K. influenced the decision to utilize a sprinkler system. Dahlby (1983) estimated a three-equation model of the market for collision insurance in Canada to determine whether low-risk in-dividuals had a greater propensity to drop their insurance coverage than high-risk individuals. Marquis and Phelps (1987) tested whether those who anticipate requiring more health services have a greater propensity to purchase health insurance. Waswansky (1988) found that the rate of return on annuities in the United States was lower than what would be expected based on average mortality rates, and this is consistent with the presence of adverse selection in the market for annuities. D'Arcy and Doherty (1990) tested the Cooper-Hayes and Kunreuther-Pauly models of self-selection with multiperiod contracts using data on automobile insurance in the United States. Boyer and Dionne (1989) used Quebec automobile insurance data to test whether a driver's record of claims was a good predictor of future claims.

This paper tests for asymmetric information in the market for collision insurance in Canada over the period 1974–1986. The model of asymmetric information that is tested in this paper is based on a simple adverse selection process, but it is argued that a moral hazard process could be observationally equivalent. This paper extends the research in Dahlby (1983) in two important ways. First, the model of adverse selection is derived from maximizing behaviour by consumers and an underlying distribution function for the probability of loss for the population. Second, the model is estimated over a longer period using less aggregate data.

Deriving a theoretically consistent model that is empirically tractable has been achieved, albeit at the cost of producing a model that is highly nonlinear and somewhat messy. However, the intuition underlying the model can be described very simply. An individual has an exogenously determined probability of suffering a loss and is faced with the choice of purchasing an insurance policy with a given deductible. The probability of a loss is assumed to vary across the population, and the insurance policy is only purchased by those individuals with the highest loss probabilities. The higher the premium, holding the deductible constant, the smaller the number of individuals who purchase the insurance policy and the higher the policy's average claim frequency because the purchasers of the policy

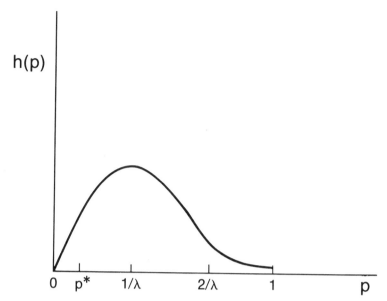

Figure 1.

are increasingly concentrated among the highest risks. A positive relationship between the premium and the average claim frequency is a key prediction of this adverse selection model.

1. A Model of Adverse Selection with Price Competition

The theory of adverse selection assumes that a) individuals have different probabilities of suffering a loss, b) each individual knows his own loss probability, and c) insurance companies do not know the individual's loss probability. It is assumed that the probability of loss, p, varies across the population with a continuous probability density function, $h(p)$, such as the one shown in figure 1. An individual, faced with the decision of whether to purchase an insurance policy with a given deductible or go without insurance coverage, will purchase the insurance policy if the gain from insurance is greater than the premium that is charged for the policy. The gain from insurance varies directly with the individual's loss probability, and therefore insurance is only purchased by those individuals with a loss probability greater than some critical loss probability level, p^*. The value of p^* will depend on the premium that is charged for the policy, the distribution of losses that the individual faces, the insurance policy's deductible, and the individual's attitude toward risk. The proportion of the population that purchases the insurance policy is given in figure 1 by the area under $h(p)$ to the right of p^*, and the average claim frequency will be based on the average probability of loss for this truncated distribution. Note that as the premium for a policy with a given deductible increases the average claim frequency for the policy will also increase because p^* will increase.

This adverse selection model can be written as follows:

$$Z = 1 - H(p^*) \tag{1a}$$

$$K = (1 - F(D))\,E(p|p \geqslant p^*) \tag{2a}$$

$$P = M(KC) \tag{3a}$$

where

Z is the proportion of individuals who purchase the insurance policy;
$H(p)$ is the distribution function for the probability of loss;[2]
p^* is the critical loss probability such that only individuals with a loss probability greater than p^* will buy insurance;
K is the average claim frequency for the policy;
$F(L)$ is the distribution function of the individual's loss, L;
D is the deductible for the policy;
E is the expectations operator;
P is the premium for the policy;
C is the average claim severity; and

$M(KC)$ is a function that relates the average loss cost to the premium. It is assumed that the magnitude of the loss and the probability of a loss are independently distributed. Therefore, in (2a) the average claim frequency, K, is the product of the average probability of a loss among those who purchase the insurance policy and the probability that the loss exceeds the deductible. The details of the model are described in the remainder of this section.

To derive an empirically tractable version of 1a, it is assumed that the probability density function for p follows the gamma distribution.[3] To make the use of the gamma distribution tractable, it is assumed that the shape parameter is equal to two. The resulting truncated probability density function is given below:

$$h(p) = \Psi^{-1}\lambda^2 p e^{-\lambda p}; \quad 0 \leqslant p \leqslant 1 \tag{4}$$

where $\Psi = 1 - (1 + \lambda)e^{-\lambda}$ and $\lambda > 1$. This probability density function is shown in figure 1. The mode occurs at $1/\lambda$, and there is an inflection point at $2/\lambda$. The average loss probability is the following:

$$E(p) = \Psi^{-1}[2\lambda^{-1} - e^{-\lambda}(\lambda + 2 + 2\lambda^{-1})] \tag{5}$$

Note that when λ increases, Ψ approaches 1, and the mean approaches $2/\lambda$ from below. The distribution function is the following:

$$H(p) = \Psi^{-1}(1 - (1 + \lambda p)e^{-\lambda p}) \tag{6}$$

Based on equations 1a and 6, the proportion of the population purchasing insurance can be approximated as the following if λ is large and hence Ψ is close to one:[4]

$$Z = (1 + \lambda p^*)e^{-\lambda p^*} \tag{1b}$$

To derive an empirically tractable version of (2a), it is assumed that the magnitude of the loss follows the exponential distribution:

$$F(L) = 1 - e^{-\phi L}; \quad L > 0 \tag{7a}$$

Note that the expected loss, $E(L)$, is ϕ^{-1}. The average claim made against the policy, C, is defined in (8), and it is also equal ϕ^{-1}.

$$C = \int_D^\infty (L - D)\phi e^{-\phi L}dL = \phi^{-1} \tag{8}$$

Therefore, the probability of making a claim, given that a loss has occurred is:

$$1 - F(D) = e^{-D/C} \tag{7b}$$

The average probability of a loss for those individuals who purchase insurance is the mean of the truncated distribution shown below:

$$E(p|p \geqslant p^*) = (1 - H(p^*))^{-1} \int_{p^*}^1 ph(p)\,dp \tag{9a}$$

Substituting (4) into (9a), the following is obtained:

$$\begin{aligned}
E(p|p \geqslant p^*) &= \Psi^{-1}\lambda^2(1 - H(p^*))^{-1} \int_{p^*}^1 p^2 e^{-\lambda p}\,dp \\
&= (\lambda\Psi(1 - H(p^*)))^{-1}[e^{-\lambda p^*}(1 + (\lambda p^* + 1)^2) \\
&\quad - e^{-\lambda}(1 + (\lambda + 1)^2)]
\end{aligned} \tag{9b}$$

Using (7b) and (9b), the average claim frequency can be approximated as the following if λ is large:[5]

$$K = e^{-(D/C)}\left[\frac{1 + (1 + \lambda p^*)^2}{\lambda(1 + \lambda p^*)}\right] \tag{2b}$$

To complete the specification of equations 1b and 2b, p^* must be derived. Suppose that each individual has the same constant absolute risk aversion utility function, and therefore the individual's utility in the absence of insurance is the following when a loss occurs:

$$U = -e^{-R(Y-L)}; \quad R > 0 \tag{10a}$$

where R is the coefficient of absolute risk aversion and Y is the individual's wealth in the absence of a loss. The individual's expected utility if he purchases the insurance policy is the following:

$$
\begin{aligned}
EU &= -p \int_0^D e^{-R(Y-P-L)}\phi e^{-\phi L}dL - p\int_D^\infty e^{-R(Y-P-D)}\phi e^{-\phi L}dL \\
&\quad - (1-p)e^{-R(Y-P)} \\
&= -e^{-R(Y-P)}\left\{1 + p\left(\frac{R}{\phi - R}\right)(1 - e^{(R-\phi)D})\right\}
\end{aligned} \tag{11a}
$$

If the individual does not purchase insurance, his expected utility can be determined from (11a) with $P = 0$ and $D \Rightarrow \infty$, and this is given below:

$$EU = -e^{-RY}\left(1 + \frac{pR}{\phi - R}\right); \quad \phi > R \tag{11b}$$

where the restriction, $\phi > R$, is required for expected utility in the absence of insurance to be convergent. It is assumed that this restriction holds in the rest of this paper. The gain from insurance, G, is defined as the maximum premium that the individual is prepared to pay for the insurance policy, and this can be determined from (11a) and (11b), and it is equal to the following:

$$G = R^{-1}\ln\left(\frac{\phi - (1-p)R}{\phi - R(1 - p(1 - e^{(R-\phi)D}))}\right) \tag{12a}$$

An individual will purchase the insurance policy if $G > P$. The critical loss probability level, p^*, occurs where $G = P$ and is given below:

$$p^* = \left(\frac{\phi - R}{R}\right)\frac{(1 - e^{RP})}{(e^{RP}(1 - e^{(R-\phi)D}) - 1)} \tag{13a}$$

Using a first-order Taylor expansion about the point $P = 0$ and replacing ϕ by C^{-1}, p^* can be approximated by the following:

$$p^* = (P/C)(1 - RC)e^{(1-RC)(D/C)}; \quad RC < 1 \tag{13b}$$

Note that p^* varies directly with P and D and inversely with C and R. Substituting (13b) into (1b) and (2b), the following equations can be obtained:

$$Z = (1 + \lambda(P/C)(1 - RC)e^{(1-RC)(D/C)})$$
$$\exp(- \lambda(P/C)(1 - RC)e^{(1-RC)(D/C)}) \qquad (1c)$$

$$K = e^{-(D/C)}\left[\frac{1 + (1 + \lambda(P/C)(1 - RC)e^{(1-RC)(D/C)})^2}{\lambda(1 + \lambda(P/C)(1 - RC)e^{(1-RC)(D/C)})}\right] \qquad (2c)$$

The specification of the third equation of the model, which determines the premium for the insurance policy is the following:

$$P = (\sigma_1 + KC)(1 + I)^{-\sigma_2}; \quad \sigma_i > 0 \qquad (3b)$$

where I is the interest rate. The coefficient σ_1 is included to capture the administration and other overhead costs of providing insurance which do not vary with the average loss cost per policy, KC. The interest variable has been included because the interest income on the policy reserves allows an insurance company to provide the policy at a lower premium.[6] The parameter, σ_2, can be interpreted as the average holding period for the premiums.

The equilibrium premium and claim frequency, $\hat{P}$ and $\hat{K}$, are shown in figure 2 by the intersection of the $K(P)$ curve that represents equation 2c and the $P(K)$ curve which represents equation 3b. The equilibrium shown in figure 2 is stable. Starting from some initial claim frequency, such as K_0, the market would converge to the equilibrium at E. A sufficient condition for the stability of the equilibrium at E is that the slope of the tangent to the $P(K)$ curve at E should be less than the slope of the $K(P)$ curve at E. This stability condition implies that the product of the elasticity of P with respect to K and the elasticity of K with respect to P is less than one, i.e.

$$\left(\frac{\partial P}{\partial K}\frac{K}{P}\right)\left(\frac{\partial K}{\partial P}\frac{P}{K}\right) < 1 \qquad (14)$$

The deductible for the insurance policy is treated as an exogenous variable. This makes the model similar to those developed by Pauly (1974), Kunreuther and Pauly (1985) and Abel (1986) in which firms are assumed to be engaged in price competition, not price and quantity competition as in the Rothschild and Stiglitz (1976) model. Recent research by D'Arcy and Doherty (1988) on automobile insurance pricing in the United States lends support to the price competition models. The main reason for treating the deductible as exogenous is that the deductibles for collision insurance in the Canadian insurance market, which is analyzed in section 2, were fixed in nominal terms for more than 10 years. The lack of adjustment in the deductibles, in spite of the double

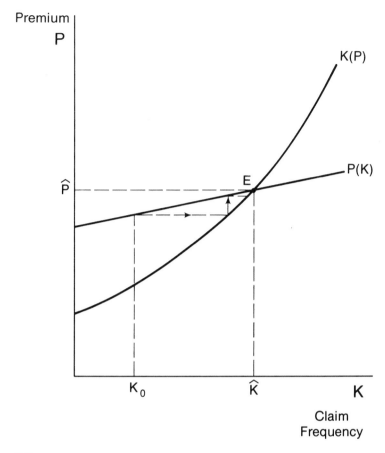

Figure 2.

digit inflation that occurred in some years over this period, suggests that
the firms treated the deductible as exogenous. This feature of the market
might arise because it is costly for a firm to gather the information
required to properly assess the expected loss cost of a policy with a new
deductible and to print new contracts, rate manuals, etc.[7]

This model of asymmetric information, based on a simple adverse
selection process, leads to the prediction that the claim frequency for
a policy will vary directly with its premium. This prediction would also
be generated by the following moral hazard model. Suppose that an
individual can reduce the probability of a loss by devoting time to loss

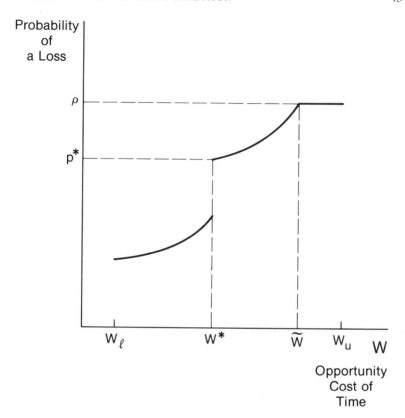

Figure 3.

prevention. The individual's opportunity cost of time, W, is private information, and it varies across individuals over the interval $[W_1, W_u]$. Those individuals with a higher opportunity cost of time devote less time to loss prevention and have higher loss probabilities. (If an insurance company cannot observe the individual's opportunity cost of time, it will not be able to tell the individual's loss probability.) Individuals can protect themselves against losses by purchasing an insurance policy with a deductible, or by devoting time to loss prevention. The insurance policy will only purchased by those individuals whose opportunity cost of time exceeds some critical value, W^*. The resulting distribution for the probability of a claim is shown in figure 3 where ρ is the probability of a loss if an individual does not devote any time to loss prevention. It is assumed in this diagram that individuals with an opportunity cost of time in the interval $[W^*, \widetilde{W}]$ will devote some time to the loss prevention activity because of the policy's deductible. (With full coverage, individuals who purchased insurance would not devote time to the loss prevention activity, and they would all have a loss probability of p.) The average probability of a loss for those who purchase insurance is the expected value for p computed over the truncated distribution $[p^*, p]$. An increase in the premium for the insurance policy, holding the deductible constant, increases W^* and hence p^* increases. This will increase the average claim frequency for the policy as long as some individuals who purchase insurance also devote some time to the loss prevention activity.

Thus a model which combined hidden action (the amount of time devoted to loss prevention) with hidden knowledge (the opportunity cost of time) would generate the same qualitative predictions as the adverse selection model. The main difference between the two types of models is that in the moral hazard model, Z and K depend on the underlying distribution of the opportunity cost of time. If this distribution does not vary over the observation period, then the models are equivalent. We do not have data on the distribution of opportunity cost of time across the population and over time. (The observed average real wage rate showed little variation over the sample period, and this may indicate that the distribution of the opportunity cost of time was relatively stable.) Therefore, it seems advisable to adopt Occam's razor and model the market as if it was based on an adverse selection process.[8]

2. Empirical Results

The data that are used to test the adverse selection model are described section 2.1. In section 2.2, the estimation of the parameters in equations 1c, 2c, and 3b is presented. Section 2.3 describes the results obtained by estimating a system of linear equations that can be considered an approximation to the adverse selection model.

2.1. The Data

The data on the Canadian automobile insurance market were taken from the Insurance Bureau of Canada's annual publication *Automobile Insurance Experience* (Green Book) for the policy years 1974 to 1986.[9] The data are based on the experience of private passenger automobiles (excluding farmers) in urban areas.[10] Cars insured in British Columbia, Saskatchewan, and Manitoba are excluded because these provinces have government-run automobile insurance schemes. Quebec is excluded in the policy years after 1976 because the Quebec government has introduced its own bodily injury automobile insurance.[11] The data are based on the experience of principal operators 25 years and older, with no occasional male operator under 25 and no occasional unmarried female operator under 25 without driver training. The 01 driver class is for pleasure driving only (no commuting) with a maximum distance of 16,000 kilometers, and the 02 driver class is for those commuting less than 16 kilometers (one way). The 01 and 02 driver classes represent about two-thirds of all cars insured.[12]

Each of these driver classes is further subdivided on the basis of the number of claim-free years of driving, and these categories are denoted by the third digit in the Insurance Bureau of Canada's driver class designation system. Thus the 015 and 025 driver classes include drivers with five or more years of claim-free driving. The other categories are three, two, one, and zero years of claim-free driving.[13] For the 01 driver class for the policy years 1984–1986, 91% of the cars insured were in the 015 class, 5.5% were in the 013 class, 1.0% were in the 012 class, 1.2% were in the 011 class, and 1.4% were in the 010 class. The average claim frequencies for the 01 driver class for these years for bodily injury and property damage (BIPD) coverage were 0.052 for the 015 class, 0.0898 for the 013 class, 0.0822 for the 012 class, 0.0872 for the 011 class, and 0.1038 for the 010 class.[14] The large difference between the claim frequencies of the 015 and the other driver classes indicates that the 01 class is not homogeneous with respect to the probability of incurring a loss, and this is, of course, a basic premise of the adverse selection model.[15]

This study focuses on the market for collision insurance that is voluntarily purchased by drivers, and therefore potentially subject to an adverse selection problem. The data relate primarily to policies with $100 and $250 deductibles. (After 1980, the data also include $200 and higher deductibles.[16]) Summary statistics for the variables used in the regressions are shown in table 1. There is considerable variation in the number of cars insured between the driver classes, with the largest numbers in the 015 and 025 categories and the fewest in the 010 and 020 categories. The average claim frequency, K, displays similar variation. Note that the average claim frequency was generally lower in the 01 class than in the 02 class, and this undoubtedly reflects the lower mileage (exposure) in the 01 driver class. The real premium, P, was obtained by dividing the

Table 1.   Statistics on The Variables Used in The Regression

Variable	Mean	The 01 Driver Class Standard Deviation	Minimum	Maximum
Q	163670	267770	8947	1048600
K	0.089835	0.018804	0.06000	0.14910
P	78.360	25.907	39.839	160.80
C	448.42	38.653	358.40	529.29

Variable	Mean	The 02 Driver Class Standard Deviation	Minimum	Maximum
Q	165420	240600	9029.0	802440
K	0.11346	0.026491	0.07020	0.18280
P	94.808	29.813	46.664	194.86
C	462.97	36.013	382.99	538.79

Q is the number of cars insured for collision insurance. K is the claim frequency. P is the average premium (1971$). C is the average loss and loss adjustment cost per claim (1971$). The data are for the 13 policy years, 1974 to 1986. For each year there are observations on the five driving record groups. There are 65 observations for each driver class.

total collision premiums collected in a given driver class by the number of cars insured for collision insurance in that class and deflating it by the Consumer Price Index (with 1971 equal to one). Note that the average premium for the 01 driver class was lower than that for the 02 driver class, and this reflects the lower average claim frequency for that driver class. Note also that the average real cost per claim, C, is similar for both driver classes.

2.2. Estimation of the Adverse Selection Model

The adverse selection model was estimated by pooling the five annual driving record observations for a given driver class for the policy years 1974–86. To estimate equation 1c, it was necessary to measure Z_{ij}, the proportion of the cars insured for collision insurance in driver class i, $i = 01$ or 02, with j years of claim-free driving, $j = 0, 1, 2, 3,$ or 5 (or more). Z_{ij} is equal to Q_{ij}/N_{ij}, where Q_{ij} is the number of cars insured for collision insurance in driver class–driver record group ij, and N_{ij} is the potential number of cars insurable for collision insurance in driver class–

driver record group ij. While Q_{ij} is observable, N_{ij} is not. However, the total number of cars potentially insurable in driver class i, N_i, can be approximated by the total number of cars insured for *BIPD* in driver class i because *BIPD* coverage is compulsory. If it is assumed that a constant fraction, v_{ij}, of the cars in driving class class i are insurable in driver class–driver record ij, then N_{ij} is equal to $v_{ij}N_i$, and (1a) can be written as:

$$Z_{ij} = \frac{Q_{ij}}{v_{ij}N_i} = 1 - H(p_{ij}^*) \qquad (1d)$$

or,

$$\widetilde{Z}_{ij} \equiv \frac{Q_{ij}}{N_i} = v_{ij}(1 - H(p_{ij}^*)) \qquad (1e)$$

The v_{ij}'s can be treated as additional parameters to be estimated. Using the adding-up condition, the estimated equation has the following form:

$$\widetilde{Z}_{ij} = (5 + \sum_{j=0}^{3} \psi_{ij})^{-1}(1 + \sum_{j=0}^{3} \psi_{ij}D_{ij})(1 - H(p_{ij}^*)) \qquad (1f)$$

where the D_{ij}'s are dummy variables (with five years claim-free the excluded group).[17]

Given that we are pooling the data from different accident record groups, the distribution of p_{ij} should be based on the gamma distribution for the entire driver class i. Instead, for reasons of empirical tractability, it has been assumed that each p_{ij} follows a different gamma distribution, and therefore in the estimated equations the λ parameter is allowed vary across driving record groups in the following fashion:

$$\lambda_i = \lambda_{i5} + \delta_{i0}D_{i0} + \delta_{i1}D_{i1} + \delta_{i2}D_{i2} + \delta_{i3}D_{i3} \qquad (15)$$
$$\delta_{i0} < \delta_{i1} < \delta_{i2} < \delta_{i3} < 0.$$

where λ_{i5} is the λ coefficient for the five year claim-free group in driver class i and the D_{ij}'s are dummy variables for driver classes i with j years of claim-free driving. In addition to the dummy variables for the number of claim-free years, a dummy variable for the years 1974 to 1976 was includedin the regression equations to capture any differences that the inclusion of Quebec in the data in those years might have had. The coefficient of this dummy was $DQUE_Z$ in the equation 1c and $DQUE_K$ in equation 2c.

Our model is an approximation to the "true" model, and it is assumed that the error terms in each equation are normally distributed with zero

Table 2.   Estimation of The Parameters of The Adverse Selection Model

	The 01 Driver Class		The 02 Driver Class	
	Estimated Coefficient	T-Ratio	Estimated Coefficient	T-Ratio
λ_{i5}	27.275	15.332	22.719	15.324
δ_{i0}	−11.117	5.9168	−10.531	6.8847
δ_{i1}	−9.1250	4.8455	−8.3216	5.3080
δ_{i2}	−7.8220	4.1716	−7.7745	5.1619
δ_{i3}	−7.4985	4.2865	−5.7185	3.8346
R_i	0.0021795	88.628	0.0021304	70.788
σ_{i1}	42.215	2.4874	24.289	2.3455
σ_{i2}	0.40811	0.20981	−2.0480	1.6489
$DQUE_Z$	−0.073128	2.5081	−0.063397	2.3443
$DQUE_k$	0.0098535	2.0905	0.014631	2.5633
ψ_{i0}	−0.92101	21.327	−0.90814	23.390
ψ_{i1}	−0.92912	23.196	−0.91332	24.694
ψ_{i2}	−0.92245	23.018	−0.90922	23.966
ψ_{i3}	−0.70116	16.757	−0.69000	17.640

R^2 Between Observed and Predicted				
$\tilde{Z}$	0.8514		0.8689	
K	0.6162		0.7061	
P	0.4251		0.5467	

mean. The model was estimated as a system of nonlinear equations using SHAZAM (see White 1987), and the estimated parameters and their t-ratios are shown in table 2. The estimates of λ_{i5} indicate that the overall probability of a loss (including those who do not purchase collision insurance) for those who have five or more years of claim-free driving is approximately 0.073 in the 01 group and 0.088 in the 02 group. The signs and relative magnitudes of the δ_{ij} coefficients follow the anticipated pattern. As one might expect, the estimates of the coefficient of absolute risk aversion, R_i, are very similar in the two sets of regressions. The estimate for the 01 group implies that relative risk aversion would be equal to one if wealth is equal to $459 (in 1971 dollars). Since relative risk aversion increases with wealth, this suggests that the estimates of R are rather high. The restriction that $RC < 1$ is not satisfied for 31 of the 65 observations for the 01 driver class, and for 26 of the 65 observations for the 02 driver class.[18] (The maximum values of RC were 1.1536 and 1.1478 for the 01 and 02 driver classes respectively.) The estimates of σ_{i1} are positive and statistically significant. The estimate of σ_{i2}, which can be interpreted as the average holding period for the insurance premium, is positive for the 01 driver class, and negative for the 02 driver class, but neither estimate is statistically significant. Finally, the estimated coefficients of the dummy variables for the years 1974–1976 indicate that the demand for collision insurance is lower and the claim frequency is higher in Quebec.

Table 3 shows the mean, minimum, and maximum values of the elasticities of Z with respect to P, K with respect to P, and P with respect to K based on all of the observations for the two samples. The sample mean elasticity of demand for collision insurance was -0.087 for the 01 group and -0.064 for the 02 group. The sample mean elasticity of the claim frequency with respect to the premium was 0.083 for the 01 group and 0.067 for the 02 group. As previously noted, this positive relationship between the claim frequency and the premium is a key prediction of the adverse selection model, but the model indicates that the relationship is relatively weak. The sample mean elasticity of the premium with respect to the claim frequency was 0.521 for the 01 group and 0.710 for the 02 group. The stability condition given by (14), which requires that the product of the two latter elasticities be less that one, was satisfied for all of the observations in the two samples.

2.3. Estimation of a Linear Model

A linear version of the adverse selection model, shown below, was also estimated:

$$\widetilde{Z}_{ij} = \alpha_1 + \alpha_2(P_{ij}/C_{ij}) + \alpha_3(D/C_{ij}) + \alpha_4\text{DQUE} + \sum \alpha_{ij}D_{ij} \quad (16)$$

$$K_{ij} = \beta_1 + \beta_2(P_{ij}/C_{ij}) + \beta_3(D/C_{ij}) + \beta_4\text{DQUE} + \sum \beta_{ij}D_{ij} \quad (17)$$

$$P_{ij} = \gamma_1 + \gamma_2(K_{ij}C_{ij}) + \gamma_3I \quad (18)$$

$$\alpha_2 < 0, \ \alpha_3 < 0, \ \beta_2 > 0, \ \beta_3 < 0, \ \gamma_2 > 0, \ \gamma_3 < 0$$

where DQUE is a dummy variable for the years 1974–1976 when the data include the Quebec experience, and the D_{ij}'s are dummy variables for the driver classes (the 015 driver class was the excluded category). Equations 16, 17, and 18 were estimated by combining the observations for the 01 and 02 driver classes for the period 1974–1986.[19] There

Table 3. Computed Elasticities

| | 01 Group | | | 02 Group | | |
	mean	minimum	maximum	mean	minimum	maximum
$\frac{\partial Z}{\partial P}\frac{P}{Z}$	-0.0866	-0.712	-0.248×10^{-3}	-0.0643	-0.447	-0.597×10^{-4}
$\frac{\partial K}{\partial P}\frac{P}{K}$	0.0830	0.250×10^{-3}	0.859	0.0666	0.594×10^{-4}	0.534
$\frac{\partial P}{\partial K}\frac{K}{P}$	0.521	0.284	0.808	0.710	0.445	1.06

The elasticities were calculated for the 65 observations for each group.

Table 4. Estimation of The Adverse Selection Model Using Three Stage Least Squares

	Dependent Variables		
	$\bar{Z}$	K	P
P/C	−0.13493	0.09730	—
	(0.26025)	(1.2191)	
D/C	−0.12632	−0.055211	—
	(0.79619)	(2.2231)	
KC	—	—	1.8642
			(12.856)
I	—	—	−150.05
			(2.0059)
Constant	0.64351	0.068236	16.269
	(11.897)	(8.3594)	(1.4282)
R-Square	0.8708	0.7438	0.5600

The absolute values of the asymptotic t ratios are shown in brackets. The observations for the 01 and the 02 driver classes are combined. The number of observations is 130. The Wald test for the null hypothesis $a_2 = a_3 = \beta_2 = \beta_3 = \gamma_2 = \gamma_3 = 0$ is 186.878 which is asymptotically distributed as a chi-square statistic with six degrees of freedom. The critical value for χ_6^2 at the five percent significance level is 12.592. The estimated coefficients of the dummy variables are contained in an appendix which is available from the author upon request.

were 10 observations for each year (corresponding to the 10 driving record–driver classes) and, therefore, a total of 130 observations.

Table 4 shows the results obtained by estimating the equations using three-stage least squares. (The estimated coefficients of the dummy variables are available from the author upon request.) All of the coefficients in table 4 have the anticipated sign, but only β_3, γ_2, and γ_3 are significant by the t test. The null hypothesis, $a_2 = a_3 = \beta_2 = \beta_3 = \gamma_2 = \gamma_3 = 0$, is rejected by the Wald test.

3. Conclusion

The evidence from our nonlinear and the linear estimation results are generally consistent with the existence of an adverse selection process in the market for collision insurance. Future refinements to the model should include the explicit modeling of the distribution of the probability of loss on the basis of driving record. Although the estimated model is based on a simple adverse selection process, the qualitative predictions of the model are consistent with a model which combined hidden action with hidden information.

Notes

1. See Pauly (1968), Akerlof (1970), Ehrlich and Becker (1972), Pauly (1974), Rothschild and Stiglitz (1976), Marshall (1976), Wilson (1977), Spence (1977), Riley (1979), Shavell (1979), Rubinstein and Yaari (1983), Dionne (1983), Kunreuther and Pauly (1985), Arnott and Stiglitz (1986), Cooper and Hayes (1987), and Dionne and Lasserre (1987).

2. The p should be considered the probability of one or more losses.

3. The gamma distribution has been used in actuarial studies of heterogeneity of risk classes. See Hossack, Pollard, and Zehnwirth (1983, pp. 96–101), Lemaire (1985, pp. 121–124), and Dionne and Vanasse (1988).

4. It is reasonable to assume that λ is large because we expect the average probability of a loss in collision insurance to be around 0.10.

5. If λ is large the second term in the square bracket in (9b) goes to zero and Ψ goes to one. The expression for $(1 - H(p^*))$ is approximated by (1b) and the expression for $1 - F(D)$ is given by (7b). Equation 2b follows directly.

6. To see why the nominal interest rate should be included in equation (3b), suppose $\sigma_2 = 1$. In the absence of inflation, the following equation would hold:

$$(1 + r)P = \sigma_1 + KC$$

If inflation occurs at the rate ρ, the left-hand side would be multiplied by $(1 + \rho)$. Let σ_1' and C' stand for the nominal values of σ_1 and C. On the right-hand side, r would be replaced by I, the nominal interest rate where $(1 + I) = (1 + \rho)(1 + r)$, P would be replaced by the nominal premium, P', but note that P would equal P'. If we deflate the nominal values P', σ_1', and C' by the CPI which equals $(1 + \rho)$, we obtain the following equation:

$$(1 + I)\frac{P'}{CPI} = \sigma_1 + \frac{KC'}{CPI}$$

Therefore, when we estimate the premium equation using the deflated nominal premium and the deflated nominal loss cost with σ_1 estimated as a parameter, the nominal interest rate, I, should be included in the equation.

7. In a letter to the author (dated December 14, 1988) R. L. Monte, Vice President, Insurance Operations, Insurance Bureau of Canada, notes that "there is no particularly overbearing need from the insurer's point of view to adjust deductibles annually by a little — in fact this would be an administrative nightmare. The existence of a nonzero deductible presumably creates an element of deterrence, but the exact size of such a deductible seems to be of lesser importance."

8. In an earlier version of this paper, this type of moral hazard model was derived and estimated. The model did not perform as well as the adverse selection model perhaps because of its greater complexity.

9. The policy year T runs from the July 1 in year T-1 to June 30 in year T.

10. The analysis was restricted to the data on automobile insurance experience in urban areas to ensure that the sample of observations in each driver class was relatively large.

11. See Boyer and Dionne (1987). The government insurance program in Quebec was introduced in 1978, but our figures for BIPD cars in 1977 and 1978 are based on the 1979 Green Book, which excludes Quebec.

12. For a description of all driver classes, see Dahlby and West (1986, table 1).

13. Drivers with four years of claim-free driving are presumably classified in the 013 and 023 classes.

14. Similar results are obtained for the 02 driver class. The analysis was restricted to the data on automobile insurance experience in urban areas in order to ensure that the sample of observations in each driving record–driver class was relatively large.

15. See Lemaire (1985) and Hossack, Pollard, and Zehnwirth (1983) on measurement of the heterogeneity of automobile insurance driver classes.

16. About 5% of cars insured for collision had smaller deductibles ($25 and $50) in 1974. However, by 1986, the proportion of cars insured with the $25 or $50 deductible had dropped to 0.6%. (This relative decline is understandable in view of the increase in the price level over this period). The proportion with the $100 deductible was 31.5%. The proportion with $200 or $250 deductibles was 64.3%. The proportion with other deductibles was 3.6%.

17. Therefore the v_{ij} is equal to $(1 + \psi_{ij})(5 + \sum_{j=0}^{3} \psi_{ij})^{-1}$. An adjustment was also made to this ratio to reflect the number of cars insured with $25 and $50 deductibles.

18. The frequent rejection of the $RC < 1$ condition may be caused by the fact that our measure of C includes loss adjustment expenses or our assumption that losses follow an exponential distribution.

19. The linear model was also estimated for the 01 and the 02 groups separately. The results which were qualitatively similar to those shown in table 4 and are available from the author upon request.

References

Abel, A. (1986). "Capital Accumulation with Adverse Selection and Uncertain Lifetimes," *Econometrica* 1079–1098.

Akerlof, G. (1970). "The Market for Lemons: Qualitative Uncertainty and the Market Mechanism," *Quarterly Journal of Economics* 84, 488–500.

Arnott, R., and J. Stiglitz. (1986). "Moral Hazard and Optimal Commodity Taxation," *Journal of Public Economics* 29, 1–24.

Boyer, M., and G. Dionne. (1987). "Description and Analysis of the Quebec Automobile Insurance Plan," *Canadian Public Policy* 13, 181–195.

Boyer, M., and G. Dionne. (1989). "An Empirical Analysis of Moral Hazard and Experience Rating," *Review of Economics and Statistics* 71, 128–134.

Cooper, R., and B. Hayes. (1987). "Multi-Period Insurance Contracts," *International Journal of Industrial Organization* 5, 211–231.

Dahlby, B. G. (1983). "Adverse Selection and Statistical Discrimination: An Analysis of Canadian Automobile Insurance," *Journal of Public Economics* 20, 121–130.

Dahlby, B. G., and D. S. West. (1986). "Price Dispersion in an Automobile Insurance Market," *Journal of Political Economy* 94, 418–438.

D'Arcy, S. P., and N. A. Doherty. (1990). "Adverse Selection, Private Information, and Low Balling in Insurance Markets," *Journal of Business* 63, 145–164.

Dionne, G. (1983). "Adverse Selection and Repeated Insurance Contracts," *Geneva Papers on Risk and Insurance* 8, 316–332.

Dionne, G., and P. Lasserre. (1987). "Dealing with Moral Hazard and Adverse Selection Simultaneously," discussion paper, University of Montreal.

Dionne, G., and C. Vanasse. (1988). "Automobile Insurance Ratemaking in the Presence of Asymmetrical Information," Centre de Recherche sur les Transports, discussion paper number 603, University of Montreal. Forthcoming *Journal of Applied Econometrics*.

Doherty, N. A. (1980). "Moral Hazard and Pricing in the U.K. Fire Insurance Market," *Journal of Risk and Insurance* 67, 240–257.

Ehrlich, I., and G. S. Becker. (1972). "Market Insurance, Self-Insurance, and Self-Protection," *Journal of Political Economy* 80, 623–648.

Hossack, I. B., J. H. Pollard and B. Zehnwirth. (1983). *Introductory Statistics With Applications in General Insurance*. Cambridge, U.K.: Cambridge University Press.

Insurance Bureau of Canada, *Automobile Insurance Experience* (Green Book), various years, Toronto.

Kunreuther, H., and M. Pauly. (1985). "Market Equilibrium with Private Information," *Journal of Public Economics* 26, 269–288.

Lemaire, J. (1985). *Automobile Insurance: Actuarial Models*. Hingham, MA: Kluwer-Nijhoff.

Marquis, M. S., and C. E. Phelps. (1987). "Price Elasticity and Adverse Selection in the Demand for Supplementary Health Insurance," *Economic Inquiry* 25, 299–313.

Marshall, J. M. (1976). "Moral Hazard," *American Economic Review* 66, 880–890.

Pauly, M. V. (1968). "The Economics of Moral Hazard," *American Economic Review* 58, 531–537.

Pauly, M. V. (1974). "Overinsurance and Public Provision of Insurance: The Roles of Moral Hazard and Adverse Selection," *Quarterly Journal of Economics* 88, 44–62.

Riley, J. G. (1979). "Informational Equilibrium," *Econometrica* 47, 331–359.

Riley, J. G. (1985). "Competition with Hidden Knowledge," *Journal of Political Economy* 93, 958–976.

Rothschild, M., and J. Stiglitz, (1976). "Equilibrium in Competitive Insurance Markets," *Quarterly Journal of Economics* 90, 629–649.

Rubinstein, A., and M. E. Yaari. (1983). "Repeated Insurance Contracts and Moral Hazard," *Journal of Economic Theory* 30, 74–97.

Shavell, S. (1979). "On Moral Hazard and Insurance," *Quarterly Journal of Economics* 93, 541–562.

Spence, M. (1977). "Product Differentiation and Performance in Insurance Markets," *Journal of Public Economics* 10, 427–447.

Wasawsky, M. (1988). "Private Annuity Markets in the United States: 1919–1984," *The Journal of Risk and Insurance* 55, 518–528.

White, K. J. (1987). "SHAZAM: A General Computer Program for Econometric Methods (Version 5)," *American Statistican* 41, 80.

Wilson, C. (1977). "A Model of Insurance Markets with Incomplete Information," *Journal of Economic Theory* 16, 167–207.

INCENTIVE EFFECTS OF NO-FAULT AUTOMOBILE INSURANCE: EVIDENCE FROM INSURANCE CLAIM DATA

J. David Cummins
University of Pennsylvania

Mary A. Weiss
Temple University

Abstract

This paper investigates the effects of no-fault on automobile property damage claim frequency in the United States. No fault restricts the right to sue for bodily injury liability (BIL), but most U.S. no fault laws make no change in the legal rules involving property damage claims. Thus, an analysis of property claims can reveal the indirect effects of no fault on incentives. The principal finding is that no fault induces drivers to shift property claims from property damage liability (PDL) coverage into collision (first-party property damage) coverage. With the elimination of some BIL claims under no fault, the expected recovery under tort is reduced so that first-party property claims become more attractive relative to PDL claims. Thus, no fault may facilitate experience rating since a higher proportion of claims come to the attention of the driver's insurer. The effect no fault on total claims is less conclusive. However, controlling for the size of the residual market, no fault appears to be positively associated with total property claims frequency.

Key words: automobile insurance, no fault, liability insurance, insurance claims frequency

No-fault automobile insurance was developed to remedy purported defects in the tort system as a method for compensating the victims of automobile accidents. Proponents of no fault argued that the tort system

445

was slow, inefficient, and inequitable (Conard (1964), Keeton and O'Connell (1965)). Auto accidents were said to be largely random so that the expensive process of assessing fault did not provide significant deterrent effects (Keeton and O'Connell (1965)). No fault eliminates the ability to sue for relatively small losses, reserving tort for more serious injuries. Compulsory first-party insurance is provided to compensate auto accident victims for their economic losses (medical costs and lost wages). The savings in general damages and claims settlement expenses resulting from the tort restriction are reallocated to help pay the costs of the first-party coverage.

No fault was endorsed by the U.S. Department of Transportation (DOT) (see DOT (1971)) and first implemented in Massachusetts in 1971. By 1976, sixteen states had adopted no fault. Eight additional states elected not to restrict tort liability but to require or make available first-party economic loss coverage as an add-on to auto liability policies.

No fault has achieved some of its goals. Several studies have found that the system delivers auto accident compensation more efficiently than tort (for example, Grabowski, Viscusi, and Evans (1989)). A study of closed claims found that no fault compensates a higher proportion of injured victims and that loss ratios are less variable than under tort (Rand Corp. (1985)). Yet, some no-fault states have experienced escalating auto insurance costs due partly to the prevalence of nominal-dollar thresholds that are not revised to keep up with inflation.[1]

The principal argument against no fault is that it increases moral hazard by reducing incentives to drive safely. Thus, no fault may result in higher injury and fatality rates. A substantial increase in injuries or fatalities would significantly weaken the case for no fault.

Studies of the moral hazard effects of no fault have been inconclusive. Landes (1982) found a positive relationship between no fault and fatal accident rates, but subsequent research has contradicted this finding (e.g., Kochanowski and Young (KY) (1985) and Zador and Lund (ZL) (1986)). These studies are flawed in their econometric methodology. The two major defects are 1) They do not take into account the potential endogeneity of no fault. The adoption of no fault may reflect interstate differences in accident rates. Failure to recognize this feedback effect could lead to inconsistent coefficient estimates. 2) The existing studies do not account adequately for differences in state characteristics other than no fault that may affect accident rates. This probably accounts for the findings by KY and ZL that no fault is inversely related to fatality rates.

The authors have shown elsewhere (Cummins and Weiss (1989)) that correcting these econometric problems makes a difference. In that study, no fault was not significantly related to injury accident rates and had a weak positive relationship with fatal accident rates.

The purpose of this study is to provide additional evidence on the incentive effects of no fault by analyzing the effects of no fault on insurance claim frequency rates.[2] Claims frequency is the result of a two-stage process in which an accident occurs followed by the filing of j claims, $j \geq 0$. Thus, studying claims frequency rates tests the combined impact of no fault on accident rates and on the propensity to file claims. Because one objective of no fault is to reduce the frequency of bodily injury liability claims, this study focuses on property damage claims, which are only incidentally affected by no fault. This provides a more reliable indication of the impact of no fault on accidents.

Studying claims frequency is useful for the following reasons 1) If the number of claims is not significantly affected by no fault, tests of claims frequency provide a test of the moral hazard effect of no fault on accident rates. 2) The impact of no fault on system costs is more directly related to claims frequency than to accident frequency. 3) Claims frequency data, which are collected by the insurance industry, are likely to be superior in accuracy and consistency to accident frequency data, which are collected from individual states by the DOT. 4) Apart from any impact on accidents, no fault may also affect the propensity to file certain types of claims or the allocation of claims by coverage. Thus, claim rates may provide an important source of information on driver behavior as it relates to economic incentives and asymmetrical information.

The study proceeds by presenting a theoretical model of the effects of no fault on care expenditures. The model is used to formulate hypotheses regarding the incentive effects of no fault. Hypotheses on claim filings are then developed based on a model of the claims generating process. The hypotheses are tested using claims frequency data and data on state economic, demographic, and environmental characteristics. The empirical analysis controls for the potential endogeneity of no fault by estimating a probit equation for the propensity of states to adopt no fault. The predicted adoption probabilities are used as an instrumental variable in the claim frequency equation.[3] Generalized least squares estimation is used to control for autocorrelation and heteroskedasticity.

1. Theoretical Analysis

The objective of the theoretical analysis is to develop hypotheses with regard to levels of care under no fault and tort. The theoretical models are specified in the following section. Subsequent sections develop hypotheses about levels of care.

1.1. The Model

The model considered in this paper is similar to the *bilateral* case discussed in the prior literature (e.g., Shavell (1987)), i.e., each accident is assumed to involve two drivers, both of whom suffer losses. The analysis is conducted from the perspective of driver 1; driver 2 represents the other driver.

Drivers are assumed to begin with equal initial wealth $W_1 = W_2 = W$, which is nonstochastic, and to select a level of expenditures on automobile safety (the level of care). The selected level of care (x) affects the accident probability λ. This parameter is a function of the care decisions of both drivers and can be written $\lambda_i(x_1, x_2)$, $i = 1, 2$, where the subscripts refer to drivers 1 and 2 and $\lambda_1(x_1, x_2) = \lambda_2(x_1, x_2)$. The characteristics of λ_1 and λ_2 are given below:[4]

$$\frac{\partial \lambda_i(x_1, x_2)}{\partial x_j} < 0, \quad \frac{\partial^2 \lambda_i(x_1, x_2)}{\partial x_j^2} > 0, \quad i, j = 1, 2; \quad \text{and} \lim_{\substack{x_1 \to \infty \\ x_2 \to \infty}} \lambda_i = \lambda_{i0} > 0$$

$$(1)$$

In most of the discussion, subscripts are suppressed; and both λ and x are understood to refer to driver 1.

When an accident occurs, both drivers sustain two types of losses: economic losses and pain and suffering (general damages). Economic losses (denoted ℓ) include medical bills and lost wages, while pain and suffering has value g.[5] Both ℓ and g are nonstochastic.

The assignment of negligence in the model is the probabilistic result of a two-stage process. The first stage is the occurrence of an accident, while the second involves assigning liability. The assignment of liability is summarized in table 1.

The functions p_1 and p_2 have the following characteristics:[7]

Table 1.   Assignment of Liability

Event	Probability
Driver 1 negligent	p_1
Driver 2 negligent	p_2
Neither negligent	$1 - p_1 - p_2$

Table 2.   Examples of Auto Accident Compensation Systems

System	System Parameters
No Insurance, No Liability Rule	$\delta_g = \delta_l = f_l = F^T = 0$
Pure No Fault	$\delta_g = \delta_l = F^T = 0; f_l = 1$
Pure Tort	$\delta_g = \delta_l = F^T = 1; f_l = 0$
No Fault With Threshold	$\delta_l = 0; \delta_g = f_l = 1; 0 < F^T < 1$
Tort With First-Party Economic Loss Coverage	$\delta_g = \delta_l = f_l = 1; F^T = 1$
No Fault With Subrogation	$\delta_g = \delta_l = f_l = 1; 0 < F^T < 1$

Note: F^T = probability that any given claim will exceed the no fault threshold; $\delta_g = \delta_l = 1$ if a negligence rule is present for general damages and economic losses, respectively, 0 otherwise; and $f_l = 1$ if first-party coverage available for economic loss, 0 otherwise.

$$\frac{\partial p_i(x_1, x_2)}{\partial x_i} < 0, \; \frac{\partial p_i(x_1, x_2)}{\partial x_j} > 0, \; \frac{\partial p_i}{\partial x_i} = -\frac{\partial p_i}{\partial x_j} \qquad (2)$$

In addition, $p_1 + p_2 \leq 1$.

Automobile accident compensation systems are modeled through system parameters, allowing for a wide range of alternative compensation systems and facilitating comparative statics analysis. The following parameters are used:

$\delta_g = 1$ if an injured party can sue for general damages, 0 otherwise.

$\delta_l = 1$ if an injured party can sue for economic losses, 0 otherwise. When an injured party can sue for economic losses that are covered by first-party insurance under no fault, the system is said to permit *subrogation*.

$f_l = 1$ if first-party coverage is available for economic losses, 0 otherwise.

F^T = probability that an accident qualifies for tort, $0 \leq F^T \leq 1$. Under a pure no fault system, $F^T = 0$; while under a tort system $F^T = 1$. Intermediate values of F^T represent various degrees of tort restriction under no fault;

Z = credibility factor used in pricing automobile insurance, $0 \leq Z \leq 1$.

If $Z = 1$ policies are fully *experience rated*; while $Z = 0$ corresponds to premium determination based on overall average losses for a class of drivers rather than the driving behavior of individual drivers purchasing insurance.[8]

Examples of compensation systems defined using the above parameters are presented in table 2. The systems in the table include those usually considered in public policy discussions plus a reference system with no insurance and no negligence rule where each driver is responsible only for his own losses.

Insurance premiums are assumed to be actuarially fair, i.e., no transactions costs or other administrative expenses are incurred in operating the insurance system. Full insurance against economic losses is purchased when it is available. First-party insurance against pain and suffering is not available in our model.[9]

Pareto optimal driving behavior would occur if each driver maximizes the following utility function (see Boyer and Dionne (1987) and Landes (1982)):

$$EU = \lambda_1 U_1(W - x_1 - \ell) + (1 + \lambda_1) U_1(W - x_1) + \lambda_2 U_2(W - x_2 - \ell)$$
$$+ (1 - \lambda_2) U_2(W - x_2) \tag{3}$$

where subscripts refer to drivers 1 and 2. Under Pareto optimality, each driver takes into account the impact of his care expenditures on the other driver's utility. In a market economy, drivers maximize their own expected utility, and liability rules are used to induce behavior consistent with equation (3). The model focuses on the impact of liability rules on driving behavior.

Drivers are assumed to maximize the following utility function:

$$EU = \lambda_L U(W - x - \pi - L) + (1 - \lambda_L) U(W - x - \pi) \tag{4}$$

where

EU = expected utility of driver 1,
λ_L = probability of the loss state, i.e., the state of the world in which an uncompensated accident loss occurs,
$U(\cdot)$ = driver 1's utility function,
L = the amount of loss not covered by insurance (including non-monetary losses),
π = the insurance premium, and
x = the selected level of care.

The variables appearing in equation (4) are defined as follows:

$$\lambda_L = \lambda[1 - p_2 F^T \delta_g] \tag{5a}$$

$$L = \ell(1 - f_\ell) + g \tag{5b}$$

$$\pi_1 = \ell \lambda f_\ell (1 - \delta_{\ell p2} F^T) + p_1 \lambda F^T (\delta_g g + \delta_\ell \ell) \tag{5c}$$

$$\pi = Z\pi_1 + (1 - Z)\pi_{AV} \tag{5d}$$

where ℓ, g = economic losses and pain and suffering, respectively,
π_{AV} = marketwide average premium, $\partial \pi_{AV}/\partial x \approx 0$,
π_1 = fully experience rated premium for driver 1, and
Z = degree of experience rating, $0 \leq Z \leq 1$.

The premium, the uncompensated loss, and the probability of the loss state all differ depending upon the accident compensation system. For example, in a no fault system with subrogation (table 2), the uncompensated loss in the loss state would be $L = g$, since no fault provides full first-party economic loss coverage. The loss (g) occurs if there is an accident *and* if the driver cannot collect in tort from driver 2. Thus, the probability of the loss state is $\lambda(1 - p_2 F^T)$. Under full experience rating $(Z = 1)$, the premium equals the expected value of first and third party claims: $\pi = \lambda(1 - p_2 F^T)\ell + \lambda p_1 F^T(\ell + g)$. Other systems are defined analogously.

1.2. Effects of System Design on Incentives

Consumers maximize utility by choosing the level of care (x). The general first-order condition based on equation (4) is the following:

$$\lambda'_L[U(W - x - \pi - L) - U(W - x - \pi)]$$
$$- Z\pi_{1x}[(1 - \lambda_L)\, U'(W - x - \pi) + \lambda_L U'(W - x - \pi - L)]$$
$$= [(1 - \lambda_L)\, U'(W - x - \pi) + \lambda_L U'(W - x - \pi - L)] \qquad (6)$$

where $\pi_{1x} = \partial\pi_1/\partial x < 0$.

Equation (6) can be written more compactly as:

$$-\lambda'_L \Delta U - (Z\pi_{1x} + 1)\, E[U'] = 0 \qquad (6a)$$

where $\Delta U = U(W - x - \pi) - U(W - x - \pi - L)$, and

$$E[U'] = \lambda_L U'(W - x - \pi) + (1 - \lambda_L)\, U'(W - x - \pi - L).$$

The first term in (6a) represents the marginal benefit of reductions in the loss state probabilty, while the second term represents the marginal cost of care expenditures. The marginal cost is mitigated by any premium reduction that takes place as a result of driver 1's increased care. The marginal cost of an additional unit of care is $1 + Z\pi_{1x}$, where $\pi_{1x} < 0$.

To analyze the effects of system parameters on accident rates, it is helpful to solve equation (6) for λ':

$$\lambda' = \frac{-1 - \lambda Z F^T[-\delta_\ell f_\ell/p'_2 + p'_1(\delta_g g + \delta_\ell \ell)] + \lambda p'_2 F^T \delta_g L\Omega}{(1 - p_2 F^T \delta_g)\, L\Omega + Z[\ell f_\ell(1 - \delta_\ell p_2 F^T) - p_1 F^T(\delta_g g + \delta_\ell \ell)]} \qquad (7)$$

where

$$\Omega = \frac{U(W - x - \pi) - U(W - x - \pi - L)}{L[\lambda_L U'(W - x - \pi - L) + (1 - \lambda_L)\, U'(W - x - \pi)]}$$

$$= \Delta U/(L E[U']) \qquad (8)$$

The quantity Ω equals 1 under risk neutrality.

Because $\lambda' < 0$, $\lambda'' > 0$, and the denominator is positive, the numerator of (7) must eventually become negative in order for an optimum to exist. If an optimum exists, any increase in either the numerator or the denominator of the right-hand side of (7) will lead to higher care expenditures.[10]

The interpretation of equation (7) is as follows: The first term in the numerator is the marginal cost of an additional unit of care expenditures. The second term (which is >0) reflects the marginal impact of care expenditures on the premium due to the reduction in the probability that driver 1 will be held negligent (the term involving p'_1) and the increased chance of successful subrogation against driver 2 (the term involving p'_2). This term vanishes if there is no experience rating ($Z = 0$), i.e., experience rating increases the numerator of (7) and hence is positively related to care expenditures (x). The final term in the numerator reflects the effect of care on the probability of a successful tort suit against driver 2 for general damages. This term also has a positive effect on x.

The terms in the denominator of (7) reflect the marginal benefits of an additional unit of care expenditures due to a reduction in the probability of having an accident. The first term reflects the expected value of an uncovered general damage loss, while the second term quantifies the impact on the premium of a marginal reduction in the accident probability.

The principal impact of no fault on incentives is captured by the parameter F^T, the probability that an accident qualifies for tort (exceeds the no fault threshold). In a pure tort system $F^T = 1$, while under pure no fault $F^T = 0$.

As an illustration of the potential effects of system design on care expenditures, consider equation (7) under the assumption of risk neutrality. In this case, the right-hand side of (7) equals $-1/(g + \ell)$ under pure no fault and $-1/[2(g + \ell)]$ under pure tort. Thus, the level of care is lower under no fault than under tort. Other compensation systems fall in between these two extremes. No fault is certain to lead to lower care levels as long as $-\lambda'/\lambda < -p'_1/p_1$, i.e., the elasticity of the accident rate with respect to care expenditures is less than the elasticity of the probability of being held negligent. If this inequality does not hold, no fault is likely but not certain to lead to lower care. This is because no fault increases the probability of being uncompensated for pain and suffering.

The ambiguity of the effect of no fault on care expenditures is exacerbated under risk aversion. Again, no fault increases the likelihood of uncompensated pain and suffering. If the responsiveness of liability assignment to care expenditures ($-p'_1/p_1$) is low and experience rating is minimal, no fault may have little or no effect on care expenditures. The importance of liability responsiveness was implicitly recognized by the developers of no fault. They maintained that findings of negligence are often designed to assist plaintiffs in reaching the deep pockets of insurers and may be only tenuously connected to driving behavior (Keeton and O'Connell (1965, p. 253)). This is equivalent to arguing that ($-p'_1/p_1$) is relatively small.

In principle, policymakers can fine-tune the liability system to approach more closely a target accident rate. Changing the amount of general damage awards or judicial responsiveness to care levels could have this effect. The resulting level of care could be higher or lower than the Pareto optimal level. If liability standards are set too high, excessive care levels could result and the system could destabilize.

It is possible that credibility factors are higher under no fault than under tort. This could occur because no fault transfers first-party claims from the health insurance system, which is not individually experience rated, into the automobile insurance system, which is merit rated. In addition, it increases the number of claims handled by automobile insurers, thus reducing sampling error and potentially increasing Z. An increase in Z could partially and perhaps fully offset a reduction in F^T as one moves from tort towards no fault.

On balance, the theory supports the hypothesis that no fault is likely to lead to lower levels of care than tort. However, this effect is likely to be mitigated if 1) The no-fault system has a low threshold so that few tort claims are eliminated; 2) the rationality of tort assignment is low, i.e, liability judgments imperfectly reflect care expenditures; and 3) the degree of experience rating is low in both systems or is significantly higher under no fault.

2. Empirical Tests

2.1. Determinants of Claims Frequency

The expected costs of automobile insurance can be expressed as follows:

$$G = \lambda\theta\mu_s/(\ell - e) \qquad (9)$$

where

λ = expected accident frequency,
θ = expected claims frequency per accident,
$\mu_s = \mu_s(p_1, p_2, l, g)$ = average accident severity, and
e = expense ratio.

Each of the components of expected aggregate costs (λ, θ, μ_s, and e) is a function of environmental variables, economic variables, the demographics of drivers and victims, and the characteristics of the legal and insurance systems. This study focuses on the claims frequency rate $\chi = \lambda\theta$

The tendency of any given driving environment to generate accidents depends upon a number of factors, such as the weather, highway construction, the number and quality of automobiles, and the amount each automobile is driven. Economic and demographic variables such as income, age, and education also affect the care levels. The legal system (civil and criminal penalties for adverse driving behavior) and law enforcement also play a role. Thus, λ can be expressed as follows:

$$\lambda = \lambda(y, d, w, s) \tag{10}$$

where $\lambda(\cdot)$ = an accident generating function, and

y, w, d, s = vectors of economic, environmental, demographic and legal variables, respectively.

Similarly, the tendency of accidents to generate claims also depends on both exogenous and endogenous variables. It is hypothesized that the decision to file a claim depends upon the probability of recovery, the expected amount of recovery, and the costs of filing the claim. Thus, $\theta = \theta(q, \mu_c, c)$, where q = the probability of recovery, μ_c = the expected amount of recovery, and c = the costs of filing the claim. The claim will be filed if $q\mu_c > c$.

The probability, amount, and costs of recovery are functions of economic variables such as income, automobile value, and price levels and by the structure of the legal system. The type of coverage under consideration also plays a role. For example, first-party claims are less costly to file than third-party claims; and the probability of collection is higher for first-party claims. The amounts of recovery depend upon the policy limits, the generosity of the legal system, and the types of expenses that are eligible for recovery.

One objective of no fault is to prevent less serious accidents from generating bodily injury liability claims by removing them from eligibility under the tort system. Thus, bodily injury claims frequency rates should be lower under no fault and claim recovery amounts should be higher. On the other hand, no fault has no direct impact on property claims arising from auto accidents. For this reason, property claims rates should provide a better indication of the impact of no fault on accident rates and of the indirect incentive effects of no fault.

Three types of automobile coverages are available for property claims: property damage liability (PDL), collision, and comprehensive. PDL is a third party coverage insuring the motorist against liability suits for damage to the property of others. This coverage is compulsory or quasicompulsory in all states. Collision and comprehensive are voluntary coverages reimbursing the insured for damage to his or her automobile. Collision covers damage due to auto accidents, while comprehensive covers other types of losses such as fire and theft. Since the focus of this study is on auto accidents, the PDL and collision coverages are examined.

The majority of insured drivers (about 70%) carry collision coverage. In an accident involving damage to two cars, the owners of the cars typically file collision claims with their own insurers, even if one of the drivers is at fault. The insurers then decide which driver is at fault, usually through an arbitration process, and allocate the costs accordingly. The insurer's recovery of costs from the negligent driver after paying a first party claim is known as subrogation.

As an alternative to the usual scenario, some accidents occur in which collision coverage is never invoked. This could occur if one or both drivers do not carry collision coverage, and it also could occur if the nonnegligent driver carries collision but chooses not to report the accident to his or her insurer. Instead, the driver files a property damage liability claim with the negligent driver's insurer. The reason a driver may bypass his or her own company is to avoid a premium increase. Drivers tend to believe, with some basis in fact, that filing a claim will increase their premium, even if the other driver is at fault. Systems for reporting accidents to state departments of motor vehicles are sufficiently imprecise that the driver may succeed in concealing the claim from his or her insurer.

No fault could affect claims frequency by changing the accident frequency, λ, or by changing the rate of claims filing, θ, in the following principal ways: 1) No fault could change λ due to weakened care incentives. 2) No fault could change λ for property claims by changing the characteristics of drivers who buy collision coverage. This change could be independent of the overall effect of no fault on accident rates. 3) No fault could affect the rate of claims filing for either property damage liability or collision coverage.

Although several nonmutually exclusive scenarios are possible, the most likely is that no fault alters the relative attractiveness of liability and collision coverages as sources of recovery for property claims. Under tort, many claims involve both bodily injury and property damage. If both types of loss are involved, the expected recovery is higher, the driver is more likely to interest a lawyer in handling the case, and the claim is more likely to be filed. No fault is designed to eliminate a significant number of small liability suits. To the extent that this is accomplished, motorists will find their expected recovery from tort to be significantly reduced. This may reduce the frequency of PDL claims.

For drivers who carry both PDL and collision coverage, adoption of no fault may decrease the likelihood that they will try to hide claims from their insurers by filing liability suits against the other driver involved in the accident. Again, if no fault reduces the expected recovery in tort by eliminating the bodily injury part of the claim, the balance may tip in favor of filing a collision claim, where recovery is certain, rather than a liability claim, where the probability of recovery is less than 1. Thus, even if no fault does not affect accident rates, it may induce drivers to substitute collision claims for liability claims.

No fault also could affect the composition of the driver pool carrying collision insurance. For example, if no fault increases the mandatory component of the insurance premium (i.e., the premium for liability and personal injury protection (PIP) coverages), it may induce drivers to drop their collision coverage. If the drivers dropping out are good risks, due to imprecise risk classification (asymmetrical information), collision claims frequency could increase even if the overall accident rate is unchanged. On the other hand, the dropouts may be drivers with relatively low incomes who can no longer afford to carry collision insurance. If this effect dominates and if the dropouts are primarily young and urban, collision frequency could decline. While much more detailed data would be needed to sort out these effects, this study provides significant new information regarding the effects of no fault on claims frequency rates.

2.2. Data, Methodology, and Hypotheses

2.2.1. Selection of Dependent Variables. As mentioned above, the rate of claim filing per accident for bodily injury coverages is critically

affected by the legal system. Table 3, discussed in more detail below, shows that the claims frequency rate for bodily injury liability in no fault states averages about 23% less than the rate in tort states. The bodily injury claims severity (average paid claim), on the other hand, is about 23% higher in no-fault states than in tort states. The claims frequency for personal injury protection (PIP), the no fault bodily injury coverage, is quite high in no fault states but nonexistent in tort states. These results confirm that bodily injury claims frequency rates are not informative with regard to the relative accident rates under no fault and tort.

PDL and collision claims frequency are analyzed in this study because no fault has no direct effect on these coverages. Only two states have no-fault laws that incorporate provisions dealing with property damage claims. With minor exceptions, Michigan has no fault for both bodily injury and property damage. The property damage liability claims rate in Michigan is much lower than the national average and the collision claims rate is much higher. We allow for this effect in the analysis by using a dummy variable for Michigan and by doing some runs in which Michigan is omitted. The other state with some no-fault property damage provisions is Massachusetts, which was eliminated from the study due to missing data.

2.2.2. The Sample.

Data on automobile insurance claims frequency and average paid claim costs (severity) by coverage are maintained by the National Association of Independent Insurers (NAII) in its FastTrack data base. The data are available quarterly from 1975 through the present. Data are reported to FastTrack by all companies that are members of the Insurance Services Office (ISO), the principal rating bureau in the United States, and the NAII, which represents companies that file rates independently. The FastTrack companies account for about 90 percent of the automobile insurance premium volume in the United States. The data are for the voluntary auto market, i.e., residual market experience is excluded.

The claims frequency statistics reported for the property damage coverages in FastTrack are paid claim frequencies. This is likely to result in minimal distortion because of the relatively short payout tail for property coverages. In contrast, arising (incurred) rather than paid claim frequencies are reported for bodily injury liability. The paid claim frequency rates used in this study are defined as follows:

$$F_t = \frac{N_t}{Y_t} \tag{11}$$

where

F_t = paid claim frequency in period t,
N_t = number of paid claims in period t, and
Y_t = number of earned car years in period t.

Earned car years is an accrual measure of the amount of auto insurance coverage provided during the period. Paid claim frequency for the collision, PDL, and collision and PDL combined are used in this study.[11]

The other variables used in the study were obtained from various business and governmental sources. The variable definitions and sources are presented in the Appendix.

Because most of the explanatory variables are available only on an annual basis, annualized FastTrack frequency rates were computed for use as dependent variables. The resulting pooled cross-section, time-series data base consists of twelve years of data (1975–1986) for fifty states. Since the generalized least squares procedure used in the study requires complete blocks, ten states were eliminated due to missing values. Comparison of the ordinary least squares (OLS) results for the fifty and forty-state samples suggest that the elimination of these states has no qualitative impact on the results.

2.2.3. Econometric Methodology. The following equations were estimated:

$$F^C = X_c\beta_c + \gamma_c D_N + \varepsilon_c \tag{12a}$$

$$F^P = X_p\beta_p + \gamma_p D_N + \varepsilon_p \tag{12b}$$

$$D_N = X_N\beta_N + \gamma_{NC}F^C_{t-1} + \gamma_{NP}F^P_{t-1} + \varepsilon_N \tag{12c}$$

where

F^C, F^P = collision and PDL paid claim frequency, respectively, $(NT \times 1)$ vectors, where N is the number of states and T the number of years,
D_N = 1 if a state has a no fault law, 0 otherwise, $(NT \times 1)$
X_i = $(NT \times k_i)$ matrix of explanatory variables for equation i, and
ε_i = $(NT \times 1)$ random error vector for equation i.

Except for qualitative variables, all variables are in natural logarithms.

No fault is an explanatory variable in the equations for collision and property damage frequency, while the lagged values of the frequency rates are hypothesized to affect the adoption of no fault. Lagged rather than current frequency rates are used in equation (12c) because policymakers know the history of frequency but not current values when designing the legal system (see Maddala (1984)).

Because the model is recursive rather than truly simultaneous, one might conjecture that consistent estimates of the parameters could be obtained by ordinary least squares. This is not the case if the residuals are autocorrelated. Preliminary testing revealed the presence of autocorrelated residuals in equations (12a) and (12b). The following specification of the residuals was adopted:

$$\varepsilon_{it} = \rho_i \varepsilon_{it-1} + \mu_{it} \tag{13}$$

where

$$E(\varepsilon_{it}\varepsilon_{jt}) = E(\mu_{it}\mu_{jt}) = 0, \ i \neq j,$$

$$E(\mu_{it}\mu_{it-1}) = 0, \ \text{and}$$

$$\mu_{it} \sim N(O, \sigma_{it}^2).$$

Thus, the residuals are hypothesized to be autocorrelated and heteroskedastic.

To obtain consistent estimates and improve efficiency, the following procedure was adopted.[12] The system was treated as simultaneous, with F_{t-1}^C and F_{t-1}^P endogenous. These variables were regressed on $[X, X_{-1}]$ and the fitted values from this reduced form were used as explanatory variables in the no fault equation.

The no fault equation (12c) is a qualitative variable model, where the dependent variable can be interpreted as the sentiment for no fault. However, what is observed is not the sentiment for no fault but a $(0, 1)$ variable indicating the presence or absence of a no fault law. This is the classic situation in which logit or probit analysis is appropriate. Probit analysis was used in this study.

The probit model yields the estimated coefficient vector $[\hat{\beta}_N, \hat{\gamma}_{NC}, \hat{\gamma}_{NP}]$. This vector is used to compute adoption probabilities:

$$\hat{\pi}_i = N[X_N\hat{\beta}_N + F_{-1}^C\hat{\gamma}_{NC} + F_{-1}^P\hat{\gamma}_{NP}] \tag{14}$$

where $\hat{\pi}_i$ = the estimated probability that state i has a no fault law. The probability vector is then used as an instrumental variable in equations (12a) and (12b) to estimate the effects of no fault.

In estimating equations (12a) and (12b), an iterated feasible Aitken instrumental variables (IGLSIV) procedure was used. This procedure is designed to correct for autocorrelated errors, where the autoregressive parameters ρ_i vary by state, and for heteroskedasticity across states. The procedure is iterated until convergence. Iterated Aitken estimates have been shown to approach maximum likelihood estimates as the number of iterations increases (Kmenta (1986)). The primary reason for using the IGLSIV procedure was to obtain more efficient parameter estimates. The instrumental variable for no fault is used to achieve consistency.

2.2.4. Additional Hypotheses, Independent Variables. Besides no fault, demographic, environmental, and economic variables could affect claims frequency. The influential economic variables include the proportion of new cars in the automobile fleet. The anticipated impact of this variable is ambiguous. With more new cars on the road, additional drivers may purchase collision insurance. If these are low risks, the collision frequency rate may decline. On the other hand, with more new vehicles, the anticipated recovery from making a collision claim is higher and is more likely to offset the driver's expectation of a premium increase as the result of making a claim. Thus, a higher proportion of new cars may lead to higher than normal collision claims frequency. Similar arguments apply to PDL.

The characteristics of the driving population also should affect frequency rates. Age is an important variable in automobile insurance underwriting, and a priori should be negatively related to claims frequency, perhaps as a proxy for driving experience and maturity. Several age variables were tested including the median age, median age of drivers, and the proportion of the population above age 17. The latter variable yielded the most useful results. Accident frequency is hypothesized to be directly related to alcohol consumption (e.g., Bruce (1984)). The variable used in this study is gallons of alcohol consumed per capita.

The physical characteristics of the driving environment have an important impact on accident rates. Adverse weather conditions also are anticipated to be directly related to accident and therefore to claims frequency. After testing several variables, the average snowfall in inches (by state) was selected for use in the study. Traffic densities also should affect frequency. Several traffic density variables were tested including vehicle miles driven per mile of roadway and the proportion of urban roads to total miles of roadway. These variables are highly correlated, but the ratio of urban miles of roadway to total miles of roadway yielded the most useful results. A possible explanation for this is that the miles of roadway variable is more reliable statistically than number of vehicle miles driven.

The proportion of drivers in the residual market was used to control for differences in the composition of the collision insurance pool. As this proportion increases, other things equal, the property claims frequency in the voluntary market should decline as more bad drivers are removed from the pool. On the other hand, if the size of the residual market is due to information asymmetries or if assignment to the residual market is arbitrary, this variable may have little effect on voluntary market frequency.

2.3. Empirical Results

A statistical profile of states by type of automobile accident compensation system is presented in table 3. No-fault states have higher real income,

Table 3.   Statistical Profile of States by Compensation System

VARIABLE	NO FAULT	ADD ON	TORT
REAL INCOME/CAPITA	$5,674	$5,359	$5,315
TRAFFIC DENSITY	0.617	0.473	0.458
URBAN ROADS	0.575	0.455	0.456
MILES PER CAR	12,619	14,341	14,007
POP % URBAN	0.744	0.630	0.561
POP % > 17 YR	0.716	0.715	0.710
SNOW (inches/year)	35.2	16.1	30.4
ALCOHOL (gallons/capita)	34.7	33.7	36.9
OPEN RATING	0.556	0.327	0.323
FATALITY RATE	0.0255	0.0266	0.0295
INJURY RATE	1.369	1.0677	1.2094
RESIDUAL MARKET %	0.0728	0.0510	0.0293
COLLISION FREQUENCY	0.0974	0.0773	0.0864
PDL FREQUENCY	0.0499	0.0485	0.0493
BIL FREQUENCY	0.0121	0.0166	0.0160
BIL AVG LOSS	9,200.63	4,354.64	4,295.89
COL/BIL CAR YEARS	0.694	0.695	0.710
Averages of data for all Years and States:			
NEW CAR %	0.083		
MEDIAN POP. AGE	30.2		

Note: Sample period is 1975–1986. Detailed definitions and data sources are given in the Appendix. Brief definitions: TRAFFIC DENSITY = total vehicle miles driven (millions)/ miles of roadway, URBAN ROADS = miles of urban roadway/miles of roadway, FREQUENCY = claims paid (arising for BIL)/earned car years, PDL = property damage liability, BIL = bodily injury liability, COL = collision, NEW CAR % = new auto sales/auto registrations, FATALITY RATE = fatal accidents/[vehicle miles (millions)], INJURY RATE = injury accidents/[vehicle miles driven (millions)].

higher traffic densities, and are more urbanized than tort or add-on states. No fault states are also more likely to have competitive rating laws. The percent of population over age 17 is slightly larger in no-fault states than in tort states and alcohol consumption is slightly lower. Average snowfall is higher in no-fault states.

Injury accident rates and all types of claims rates tend to be higher in no-fault states than in tort states. The fatal accident rate is lower in tort states, reflecting the fact that fatalities are lower in states where traffic congestion reduces average driving speed. The differences among states emphasize the need for controlling for state characteristics when estimating the impact of legal system variables on accident and claims frequencies.

The probit equation for the dichotomous no fault variable is presented in table 4. States with automobile insurance problems such as high accident and claims rates are expected to be more likely to adopt no fault. Several variables were tested to measure this effect. The fitted value (from the reduced form regression) of the lagged collision frequency rate is significant and positively related to no fault as anticipated.

States with open rating laws are significantly more likely to adopt no fault. Since open rating tends to be associated with higher premiums in auto insurance, this variable may be proxying the average auto insurance costs in the state. It also may reveal a tendency for the state to be willing to modify its legal system in an attempt to control insurance costs. The percentage of drivers in the state's residual market is also significantly related to the adoption of no fault.

The ratio of the number of lawyers in the state to the number of auto registrations is positively related to no fault. Lawyers are the primary interest opposing the adoption of no-fault laws. However, the presence of a relatively large number of lawyers in a state may be a demand effect relating to the number of potential bodily injury suits. The results presented in table 4 suggest that the demand effect is dominant.

The state's political environment is proxied by a dummy variable for the political party of the governor. As anticipated, states with Democratic governors are more likely to have a propensity for no fault.

The iterated generalized least squares instrumental variables results are presented in table 5. The table shows two equations for each of three dependent variables: collision frequency, PDL frequency, and total property claim frequency. The equations in the last three columns of table 5 include the percentage of drivers in the residual market (LRESPCT) as an explanatory variable, while those in the first three columns do not.

Table 4.   Probit Equation for No Fault

Variable	Coefficient
CONSTANT	5.8091
	(2.348)
LAWYERS/AUTO	0.6379
	(1.579)
RESIDUAL MARKET %	0.1123
	(2.530)
TRAVEL EXPENDITURES	0.0738
	(0.802)
OPEN RATING	0.5661
	(3.553)
DIRECT WRITER %	0.1464
	(0.415)
DEMOCRATIC GOVERNOR	0.548
	(2.955)
ROAD MAINTENANCE	−0.0206
	(−0.137)
COL CLAIM FREQ (t-1)	2.5538
(Predicted)	(2.296)
HOSPITAL COST	0.4172
(Per Day)	(1.461)
Percent Predicted	0.7938
Rank Correlation	0.5087

Note: TRAVEL EXPENDITURES = amounts spent in state on overnight trips, DIRECT WRITER % = pct. of auto premiums written by direct writers, DEMOCRATIC GOVERNOR = 1.0 if state has Democratic governor, 0 otherwise, ROAD MAINTENANCE = state expenditures on road maintenance per mile of roadway.

The results in the first three columns of table 5 reveal that no fault is directly related to collision claims frequency, inversely related to property damage liability claims frequency, and inversely related to total property claims frequency. At overall-sample mean values of the independent variables, these equations imply that no fault states have collision claims frequency rates 7.2% higher, property damage liability frequency rates 10.8% lower, and total property claims frequencies 3.8% lower than the corresponding rates in tort states. The results are consistent with the hypothesis that no fault discourages the filing of some PDL claims and encourages drivers to submit collision claims.

Table 5.   Claims Frequency Equations: Generalized Least Squares

Independent Variable	Dependent Variable: Collision	PDL	Total	Dependent Variable: Collision	PDL	Total
CONSTANT	-2.805	-3.897	-2.478	-2.880	-3.946	-2.768
	(-34.373)	(-41.175)	(-27.804)	(-32.265)	(-40.354)	(-30.117)
NO-FAULT	0.057	-0.114	-0.038	0.078	-0.105	0.045
	(2.877)	(-3.981)	(-2.344)	(3.594)	(-3.566)	(2.814)
ADD-ON	-0.085	-0.096	-0.155	-0.052	-0.085	0.004
	(-4.276)	(-5.233)	(-9.830)	(-2.261)	(-3.486)	(0.777)
SNOW	-0.001	0.012	0.026	-0.008	0.011	0.014
	(-0.109)	(2.477)	(6.417)	(-1.336)	(2.105)	(3.956)
URBAN ROADS	0.101	0.114	0.161	0.098	0.122	0.115
	(9.592)	(16.185)	(19.141)	(8.859)	(14.084)	(13.767)
ALCOHOL	0.137	0.100	0.134	0.149	0.112	0.174
	(7.463)	(5.207)	(7.005)	(7.926)	(5.687)	(9.874)
POP % > 17YRS	-1.936	-4.369	-2.665	-2.006	-4.356	-2.696
	(-13.954)	(-23.608)	(-16.632)	(-13.876)	(-23.878)	(-19.246)
NEW CAR %	0.240	0.269	0.245	0.250	0.273	0.293
	(10.518)	(11.058)	(10.040)	(11.005)	(11.237)	(12.757)
RESID MARKET %				-0.007	-0.007	-0.024
				(-1.658)	(-1.347)	(-6.326)
MICHIGAN	0.279			0.293		
	(4.495)			(4.458)		
R Squared	0.710	0.733	0.703	0.714	0.737	0.708

Note: NO-FAULT = probability of adopting no-fault, from probit equation (12c); ADDON = 1.0 if state has add-on law. 0 otherwise; SNOW = snowfall in inches per year; URBAN ROADS = miles of urban roadway/total miles of roadway; ALCOHOL = alcohol consumption in gallons per capita; POP % > 17YRS = percent of population over age 17; NEW CAR % = new car sales/auto registrations; MICHIGAN = 1.0 for Michigan, 0 otherwise; RESID MARKET % = percent of insured autos in the residual market. T-ratios are in parentheses.

The results presented in the last three columns of table 5 reinforce the conclusions. The coefficient of the no fault variable in the collision frequency equation is larger and more significant when the residual market variable is included, implying a 9% difference in claims rates between no fault and tort states. The no fault coefficient is smaller and somewhat less significant in the PDL equation, implying claims frequencies for this coverage about 10% lower in no fault states than in tort states. The major difference in the results when the residual market variable is included is that the no fault coefficient in the total property damage frequency equation is positive and significant, implying that total property claims frequency rates are about 4% higher in no-fault states.

The two major conclusions are the following: 1) No fault changes the incentive structure with regard to filing liability claims, resulting in a substitution of collision for property damage liability claims in no fault states. 2) After controlling for the proportion of drivers in the residual market, total property claims frequency is higher in no-fault states. If there are no additional quality differences in the collision insurance pools in no-fault and tort states, this implies that accident rates are higher under no fault, consistent with the hypothesis that no fault weakens the tort deterrent leading to lower care levels.

If the collision pool is either about the same or of lower quality in tort states than in no-fault states, there would be a strong presumption that no fault is associated with higher accident rates. However, if the collision pool is inferior in no-fault states, this might account for the higher property claim frequency under no fault. For the sample period as a whole, the proportion of drivers insured for collision is slightly lower under no fault than under tort (.694 vs. .713). The proportion insured under no fault was lower at the beginning of the period and higher at the end of the period. Thus, progressively more drivers purchased collision insurance in no-fault states, relative to tort states, over the sample period. This seems to argue against an income effect holding down collision purchases under no fault because no fault premiums relative to tort premiums were higher at the end of the sample period than at the beginning.

Thus, the steady increase in collision purchases under no fault may be attributable to more good risks being brought into the market due to progressively more accurate experience rating (lower information asymmetries) under no fault as compared with tort. Experience rating is expected to be more accurate under no fault because more first-party claims of all types are filed and because drivers are less likely to hide property damage incidents by filing liability rather than collision claims. If more good risks are accountable for the increased collision purchases under no fault, this would support the conclusion that accident rates are higher under no fault.

The coefficients of the other explanatory variables in table 4 are almost all consistent with expectations. The coefficients of the residual market variable generally support the hypothesis that larger residual markets improve the claims experience in the voluntary market. Snow has a positive and significant effect on claims rates in all but one of the six equations shown in the table. The traffic density proxy (URBAN ROADS) is significant and positive in all six equations, as are the alcohol consumption and new car variables. The proportion of the population over age 17 is significant and negative as expected.[13]

3. Conclusions

The conventional hypothesis in the law and economics literature is that no fault weakens driver incentives and leads to higher accident rates. This paper presents theoretical and empirical evidence that the incentive effects of no fault are far more complex than is usually recognized. To understand fully the effects of no fault, it is important to explore the complexities of the liability and insurance systems that govern auto accident compensation. This study goes beyond the usual analysis of accident rates to investigate the effects of no fault on claim frequency.

On balance, the theoretical analysis provides some support for the usual hypothesis that no fault weakens incentives. However, significant ambiguities are present. One reason for this is that no fault increases the probability that the driver will not be able to collect for his or her own general damages, thus partially countering the reduction in incentives due to the tort exemption. Ambiguities also arise because most real-world no-fault laws incorporate only moderate exemptions from tort liability and because of imperfections in experience rating. Thus, the theoretical case that no fault weakens incentives is not clearcut.

The empirical analysis investigates the effects of no fault on claims frequency rates. Property claims frequency rates are investigated because they provide a more direct indication of the effects of no fault on care levels and claim filing incentives than bodily injury claims, which are lower under no fault due to the tort exemption. The results support the hypotheses that no fault raises collision claims frequency rates and lowers property damage liability frequency rates. Part of the explanation for these effects is a substitution of collision claims for liability claims under no fault due to the reduced attractiveness of small liability suits.

After controlling for the proportion of drivers in the residual market, the total property claims rate is higher under no fault than under tort. If there are no other differences in the quality of the voluntary insurance pools under the two systems, this would imply that no fault is associated with higher accident rates. The proportion of drivers purchasing collision coverage was lower in no-fault states than in tort states at the beginning of the sample period but higher under no fault by the end of the period. If this effect resulted from good drivers joining the pool due to reduced information asymmetries, it would reinforce the conclusion that accidents are higher under no fault.

However, no-fault states also showed a gain in real income relative to tort states over the sample period. Consequently, the increase in the proportion buying collision insurance could be a combination of an income effect and an increase in the proportion of newer automobiles. The presence of these effects would argue against the hypothesis that accident rates are higher under no fault. Thus, the property damage liability/collision substitution effect may play a major role in determining claims frequency by coverage but the overall effects of no fault on accident rates may be small. This finding is consistent with evidence presented in Cummins and Weiss (1989) that fatality rates are slightly higher in no-fault states than in tort states but that injury accident rates are not significantly different.

The presence of substitution effects and driver strategies favoring liability suits over first-party claims have important implications for incentives and information asymmetries. If this effect is strongly present, it implies that a significant proportion of drivers may be able to hide important driving characteristics such as collision accidents from their insurers. Thus, insurers may be misclassifying drivers even after they have been insured with the company for some time. This may make the insurance system more prone to market failure than if information asymmetries primarily apply to newly underwritten drivers.

To the extent that no fault improves experience rating by bringing additional information into the first-party insurance system for use in classification, it may help to stabilize the insurance market. Thus, one adverse effect of the tort liability system is that it exacerbates information asymmetries. Investigation of this effect and other less obvious consequences of no fault have the potential to add significantly to our understanding of the automobile insurance market.

Table A1.   Definitions and sources of variables

VARIABLE	DEFINITION AND SOURCE
ADD-ON	Dummy variable equal to 1 if add-on rule exists and 0 otherwise (Rand Corp[5]).
ALCOHOL	Gallons of alcoholic beverages consumed per capita (Distilled Spirits Council of the U.S.[3]).
COL CLAIM FREQ	Number of Collision claims paid (NAII[4]).
DEMOCRATIC GOV	Dummy variable equal to 1 if state has Democratic governor, 0 otherwise.
DIRECT WRITER %	Percent of state bodily injury automobile insurance premium written by direct writers (BEDS[2]).
HOSPITAL COST	Average daily hospital charge (DOC[5]).
LAWYERS/AUTO	Number of lawyers divided by auto registrations (DOC[6] and FHWA[7]).
MICHIGAN	Dummy variable equal to 1 if state is Michigan, 0 otherwise.
NEW CAR %	Number of new car sales divided by auto registrations (DOC[6] and FHWA[7]).
NO FAULT	Dummy variable equal to 1 if no-fault law exists, 0 otherwise (Rand[5]).
OPEN RATING	Dummy variable equal to 1 if competitive (versus regulated) rating exists, and 0 otherwise (Rand[5]).
PDL CLAIM FREQ	Number of property damage liability claims paid (NAII[4]).
POP >17 YRS	Percent of population over age 17 (DOC[6]).
RESID MARKET %	Percent of autos in residual market (AIPSO[1]).
ROAD MAINTENANCE	State expenditures on road maintenance per mile of roadway (DOC[6]).
SNOW	Average snowfall in inches (DOC[6]).
TOTAL CLAIM FREQ	Total number of collision and PDL claims paid (NAII[4]).
URBAN ROADS	Urban roadway miles divided by total roadway mileage (FHWA[7]).

* The following abbreviations are used in the source descriptions:
AIPSO   Automobile Insurance Plan Services Office
BEDS   Best's Executive Data Service
NAII   National Association of Independent Insurers
DOC   U.S. Department of Commerce
FHWA   U.S. Federal Highway Administration

Sources:
1. Automobile Insurance Plan Services Office. *AIPSO Insurance Facts*. New York, various years.
2. A. M. Best Co. *Best's Executive Data Service*. Oldwick, NJ.
3. Distilled Spirits Council of the U.S., *Annual Statistical Review, Distilled Spirits Industry*, various years.
4. National Association of Independent Insurers. *Fast Track Monitoring System*, Des Plaines, IL, various years.
5. RAND Corporation [1985] *Auto Accident Compensation*, Santa Monica.
6. U.S. Department of Commerce. *Statistical Abstract of the U.S.* Washington, D.C.
7. U.S. Federal Highway Administration. *Highway Statistics*. Washington, D.C.
8. U.S. Travel Center. *Impact of Travel on State Economies*.

Notes

1. The threshold is the criterion that must be satisfied to qualify for a tort claim. In most states, the threshold is expressed in terms of dollars of economic loss. However, the types of losses that can be used to satisfy the threshold vary by state. Three states have verbal thresholds. It is a well-known actuarial result that policies with deductibles (mathematically the same as thresholds) have premium inflation in excess of claims inflation.

2. The Rand Corporation (1985) analyzes the closed claim data base discussed in All-Industry Research Advisory Committee (AIRAC) (1979). The AIRAC data base includes claim amounts and claim characteristics for a sample of insurers during a three-month period in 1977. This data base provides no direct evidence on overall system costs or accident frequencies.

3. Harrington and Fields (1986) also address this issue.

4. It is also assumed that $\partial^3 \lambda_i / \partial x_i^3 < 0$, $\partial \lambda_i / \partial x_j < 0$, $\partial^2 \lambda_i / \partial x_j^2 > 0$, and $\partial^3 \lambda_i / \partial x_j^3 < 0$.

5. Pain and suffering can be modeled either as a monetary loss or as an irreplaceable commodity. To simplify the discussion, the analysis is conducted on the assumption that pain and suffering can be treated as a replaceable commodity (denoted g). The effects of irreplaceability are considered in an Appendix available from the authors.

6. Actually, p_1 represents the probability that driver 1 is negligent and driver 2 is not negligent, p_2 is the probability that driver 2 is negligent and driver 1 is not negligent, and $1-p_1-p_2$ is the probability that neither one or both are negligent. There is no loss of generality in using the compound probabilities p_1 and p_2.

7. It is also assumed that $\partial^2 p_i / \partial x_i^2 > 0$ and $\partial^2 p_i / \partial x_j^2 < 0$. In the analysis to follow, it is often assumed that drivers are identical and, hence, that in equilibrium $p_1 = p_2$. This invokes the implicit assumption that $p_i < .5$, $i = 1, 2$.

8. Auto insurers employ merit rating plans that provide debits and credits for accident and conviction records. However, little is known about the accuracy of these plans. Even an ideal merit rating plan would involve Z factors less than 1 for most drivers because of sampling error.

9. This is consistent with real-world insurance markets.

10. The existence of an optimum is assumed in the following discussion.

11. The sum of collision and property damage liability claims frequency rates is referred to as total property claims frequency. This is not precisely correct because comprehensive claims also are property claims. The terminology is used primarily for convenience.

12. The method is a generalization of the approach proposed in Kmenta (1986, pp. 607–625 and 707–711).

13. This result is consistent with expectations, but this variable is probably also serving as a proxy for time-correlated effects such the introduction of safer automobiles, which could not be measured effectively using the available data. Thus, the magnitude of its coefficient should not be ascribed totally to the age/experience effect.

References

All-Industry Research Advisory Committee. (1979). *Automobile Injuries and Their Compensation in the United States*. 2 vols. Chicago: Alliance of American Insurers.

Boyer, Marcel, and Georges Dionne. (1987). "The Economics of Road Safety," *Transportation Research B 21* (5), 413–431.

Bruce, Christopher J. (1984). "The Deterrent Effects of Automobile Insurance and Tort Law: A Survey of the Empirical Literature," *Law and Policy* 6(1), 67–100.

Conard, Alfred F., et al. (1964). *Automobile Accident Costs and Payments.* Ann Arbor: University of Michigan Press.

Cummins J. D., and Mary A. Wiess. (1989). "An Economic Analysis of No Fault Automobile Insurance," Working paper. University of Pennsylvania.

Grabowski, Henry, W. Kip Viscusi, and W. Evans. (1989). "The Effects of Regulation on the Price and Availability of Automobile Insurance," *Journal of Risk and Insurance.*

Harrington, Scott E., and Joseph E. Fields. (1986). "Interest Group Pressure and Political Influence: The Case of No-Fault Automobile Insurance Legislation," Working paper, University of South Carolina.

Keeton, Robert E., and Jeffrey O'Connell. (1965). *Basic Protection For the Traffic Victim.* Boston: Little, Brown and Company.

Kmenta, Jan. (1986). *Elements of Econometrics.* 2d ed. New York: Macmillan Publishing Co.

Kochanowski, Paul S., and Madelyn V. Young. (1985). "Deterrent Aspects of No-Fault Automobile Insurance: Some Empirical Findings," *Journal of Risk and Insurance* 52, 268–288.

Landes, Elisabeth M. (1982). "Insurance, Liability, and Accidents: A Theoretical and Empirical Investigation of the Effect of No-Fault Accidents," *Journal of Law and Economics* 25, 49–65.

Maddala, G. S. (1983). *Limited-Dependent and Qualitative Variables In Econometrics.* New York: Cambridge University Press.

Rand Corporation. (1985). *Automobile Accident Compensation.* 4 vols. Santa Monica, CA.

Shavell, Steven. (1987). *Economic Analysis of Accident Law.* Cambridge, MA Harvard University Press.

U.S., Department of Transportation. (1971). *Motor Vehicle Crash Losses and their Compensation In the United States.* Washington, D.C.: U.S. Government Printing Office.

Zador, Paul, and Adrian Lund. (1986). "Re-Analysis of the Effects of No-Fault Auto Insurance on Fatal Crashes," *Journal of Risk and Insurance* 53, 226–241.

MEASURING THE EFFECTS OF THE NO-FAULT 1978 QUEBEC AUTOMOBILE INSURANCE ACT WITH THE DRAG MODEL

Marc Gaudry

Economics Department and Centre for Research on Transportation
Université de Montréal

Abstract

In this paper, we summarize the various effects on road safety of the new automobile insurance regime introduced in the Province of Quebec on March 1, 1978, as these effects are estimated by the DRAG model of the Demand for Road use, Accidents and their Gravity. To this end we provide a short overview of the DRAG model structure and methodology described at length in a number of technical reports available since 1984 and explain how changes brought about by the new law are taken into account in the model. We briefly present estimates of the effects, measured on police data, such as: an increase in accidents with material damages only of 7%, an increase in injuries of 24% and an increase in fatalities of 9%. We argue that these partial estimates are conservative when compared to the results of visual analyses of the same police data and the claim experience of automobile insurance companies. We conclude that, once proper account is taken of the reporting effects, compulsory insurance and flat premium rating features of the new law, very little of significance, if anything, can be attributed to the no-fault feature proper of the law.

Key words: DRAG accident model, Quebec automobile insurance act, road accidents, material damages, injuries, fatalities, no-fault, adverse selection, moral hazard

In this paper, we review the evidence concerning the various effects on road safety of the new automobile insurance régime introduced in the Province of Quebec on March 1, 1978, and discuss their significance with particular reference to the modified driver care levels associated with the

---

*The author wishes to thank Georges Dionne and a good-willed referee well versed in the French language text (Gaudry, 1984) for particularly useful comments.

471

compulsory insurance, flat premium rating, and no-fault features of the new law. We present a visual analysis of the main insurance company and police report data and summarize the results of a statistical analysis of police data made with our DRAG model (Gaudry, 1984): we both present an outline of the model and use it here to study the impact of the 1978 law, controlling simultaneously for other explanatory factors. To establish the significance of the statistical results as they pertain to the 1978 law, we also provide corroborating evidence on the modified average quality of the total stock of drivers resulting from the law.

1. Evidence

The new Quebec law came into force on March 1, 1978. Primary evidence of its effects on road safety consists of claims against insurance companies and of police reports on accidents of various categories and on the number of victims. Claims against insurance companies are recorded on the basis of the policy year, which starts on July 1 and ends on June 30 of the following year; police reports are available on a monthly basis.

1.1. Claims Against Insurance Companies

One can see in table 1 that, between 1977 and 1978, claim frequency per insured pleasure vehicle increased 20.1%, a number that almost certainly underestimates the true value because the policy year 1977 includes 4 months of data under the new régime. Under the specific heading of third-party liability that had been made compulsory by the new law, claims per insured vehicle increased 41.3% in Quebec during the same period, as compared to a 2.9% increase in frequency in the rest of Canada. Although some of the increase might have been caused by the fact that the 15% of vehicles not previously insured might have differed somewhat from the rest of the vehicles and included an unusual proportion of high-risk drivers, the huge increase in the average claim frequency constitutes prima facie evidence of an important increase in accidents.

1.2. Police Data on Accidents and Road Victims

An even stronger increase occurs in the official monthly data from police reports on accidents and road victims when the values for the twelve

Table 1. Claims Against Insurance Companies, Quebec 1973–1984

| Policy year | *Claims per 100 insured private automobiles (farmers included)* | | | | | | | | | | | |
	73	74	75	76	77	78	79	80	81	82	83	84
A. Overall claim frequency:	28.7	29.2	28.4	25.5	23.4	28.1	31.8	33.2	33.0	26.7	26.5	28.2
B. Third party liability:												
.Quebec	10.6	10.6	9.8	8.6	7.5	10.6	12.1	12.0	11.8	9.3	9.1	9.8
.rest of Canada	n.a.	8.5	7.8	7.1	6.9	7.1	6.9	6.7	6.7	6.0	5.4	5.6
difference	---	2.1	2.0	1.5	0.6	3.5	5.2	5.3	5.1	3.3	3.7	4.2

Source: Table 3.1, Table 3.2 and Table 3.B in Fluet and Lefebvre (1986).

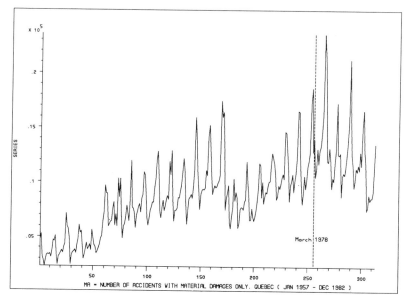

Figure 1. Number of accidents with material damages only, Quebec.

months before March 1, 1978, are compared to the values during the first
twelve months of the new régime: the total number of accidents increased
by 26.9%[1] and the number of victims by 29.7%. Moreover, all the
components of these two totals increased significantly. As shown in figure
1, accidents with material damages only reported to the police and
involving estimated damages greater than a certain criterion value
increased by 26.3% despite the fact that the reporting criterion was
increased from \$200 to \$250 in 1978; accidents with at least one injury
(no deaths) increased by 31.8% and fatal accidents increased by 7.0%.
In these accidents with bodily damages, the number of injuries shown
in figure 2 increased by 30.6% and the number of fatalities shown in
figure 3 increased by 6.4%. We now turn to the DRAG model used to
explain these data.

2. An Outline of the DRAG Comprehensive Road Safety Model

The DRAG model (Gaudry, 1984) is an econometric model designed to
explain the number of road accident victims. It appears to be the most

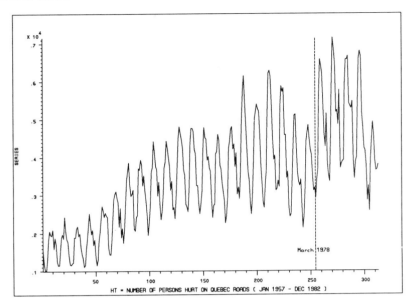

Figure 2. Number of persons hurt on Quebec roads.

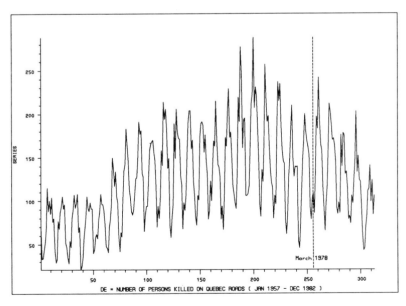

Figure 3. Number of persons killed on Quebec roads.

ambitious modeling effort of its kind ever made, or at least the most comprehensive in terms of structure, categories of factors taken into account and parameter estimation technique used. Some of its results are new, have policy implications, and have influenced the modeling efforts of other researchers. Basic model development was financed in 1983–1984 by the Quebec Automobile Insurance Board (Régie de l'assurance automobile du Québec (R. A. A. Q.)) where the model is currently under implementation.

2.1. Structure, Explanatory Factors and Estimation Technique

2.1.1. A Comprehensive Structure.   One approach to the problem of explaining the number of road victims is to relate it, or its components (*fatalities* and *injuries*), directly to the demand for road use and to a set of other factors, as in this structure:

Victims ← [DEMAND FOR ROAD USE, OTHER FACTORS]: *Risk.*

However, the approach taken in DRAG is not so direct: instead, an accounting identity is used that decomposes the number of victims into three elements, namely exposure, frequency and severity, which themselves become the objects to be explained. Thus, the number of victims is equal to the product of exposure (kilometers driven), accident frequency (accidents per kilometer), and the severity of accidents (victims per accident). This means that an explanation of the number of victims is effectively derived from the separate explanation of the three terms of the identity, as in:

$$
\text{VICTIMS} \leftarrow
\begin{bmatrix}
\text{Demand for road use} & \leftarrow \begin{bmatrix} \text{OTHER FACTORS} \\ (X_1) \end{bmatrix} \\
(DR) & \\
\text{Accident frequency} & \leftarrow \begin{bmatrix} \text{DR, OTHER FACTORS} \\ (X_2) \end{bmatrix} \\
(A) & \\
\text{Accident severity} & \leftarrow \begin{bmatrix} \text{DR, OTHER FACTORS} \\ (X_3) \end{bmatrix} \\
(G) &
\end{bmatrix}
\begin{array}{l}
: \textit{Exposure risk,} \\[1.0em]
: \textit{Frequency risk,} \\[1.0em]
: \textit{Severity risk.}
\end{array}
$$

Such a structure makes it possible to search for evidence of risk substitution among exposure, frequency, and severity risk dimensions. For instance, snow, a factor included in the three groups of explanatory variables X_1, X_2 and X_3, might lead to less driving (DR decreases) and, at the reduced exposure level, to more accidents (A increases) but less severe accidents (G decreases): the net impact on the number of road victims results from the relative strength of these potentially offsetting effects. The model acronym reflects these three dimensions: "*la* D*emande* R*outière, les* A*ccidents et leur* G*ravité*"; or "*D*emand for *R*oad use, *A*ccidents and their *G*ravity." The advantage of adding a demand level to the performance level sometimes studied alone by other authors is that one can obtain estimates of the 'total' impact of various factors that explain both road use and safety performance (i.e., that appear in X_1, X_2 and X_3) by tracing their influence on the number of accidents or victims through changes in road use in addition to their effects on performance for a given level of road use. For instance, snow certainly has a direct impact on accidents or their severity at any level of road use but it also has an indirect effect through its influence on the amount of driving. The same will be the case below for the new 1978 automobile insurance régime.

In fact, the DRAG model structure is comprehensive in another sense: each important dimension is broken up by subcategory. We distinguish between two measures of the demand for road use (the demand for gasoline and the demand for diesel fuel), three classes of accidents (with material damages only, with bodily injury and fatal),[2] and two measures of severity (morbidity and mortality rates, defined respectively as the number of injured persons and the number of persons killed per accident with corporal damages — with injuries or fatalities). Victims are persons injured and persons killed. Aggregates of these components, such as the number of accidents with corporal damages, the total number of accidents or the total number of victims, are also considered to facilitate comparison with authors who only considered aggregates.

Disaggregation of the risk dimensions into their subcategories means that patterns of substitution that are not too coarse can be detected: clearly, single-equation models (say on the number of fatalities) make it difficult to detect substitution because the substitute (say injuries) is not jointly considered.

2.1.2. A Comprehensive List of Explanatory Factors.

More than 40 explanatory factors are used simultaneously in the model. They belong to almost all categories of explanatory variables found in the literature on accidents, where very few are usually considered at the same time. This means that a very large number of models found in the literature are included as special cases and that one can obtain an idea of the relative importance of the various categories of factors. A partial list includes

PRICES		• prices of gasoline and diesel fuels
		• price of vehicle maintenance
VEHICLE	availability characteristics	• quantity of personal and utility vehicles
		• proportion of small cars
		• proportion of cars equiped with safety belt
NETWORK	legal	• speed limit reduction and compulsory belt use 1976
		• breathalyser law since December 1969
		• demerit point system since March 1973
		• higher penalties since April 1982
		• police patrol frequency and strikes
	modal mix	• urban transit strikes
		• intercity bus strikes
	infrastructure and	• proportion of highways in network
		• urban street maintenance strikes
	weather	• hot and cold
		• rain and snow
CONSUMER	characteristics	• driving licence availability
		• unemployment
		• automobile insurance régimes
	age and sex	• lower driving age (from 18 to 16)
		• pregnancy
	vigilance	• weekly hours worked
		• drug consumption
		• alcohol consumption
ACTIVITY	level or purpose	• employment
		• shopping
		• vacation

The considerable list of variables used in the original 1984 paper has a strong regulatory content: the impact of 10 laws is measured. It also contains factors never considered in earlier studies, such as the cost of maintaining vehicles, the introduction of compulsory insurance in 1961 and of the 1978 regime of so-called no-fault insurance discussed at length here, police surveillance, pregnancy, and trip purpose. Naturally, proper account is taken of the ADMINISTRATIVE measurement practices of the police who produce the accident reports.

This comprehensiveness is made possible by the use of monthly time series: all variables are defined by month. As our original series all start in 1956 and end in 1982 or later, more than three hundred data points are available. The monthly database is fully documented (Gaudry, Baldino and Liem, 1984) and makes it possible to ask questions about the role of any variable while holding the others constant (i.e., makes it possible to control for many factors).

2.1.3. A comprehensive estimation technique. There are two senses in which the technique used to obtain parameter estimates is comprehensive. First, we do not assume that the causal relationships are linear, or multiplicative, as is usually done: we allow the data to decide on the best-fitting form through the use of Box-Cox transformations. This means in particular that we do not make the popular assumption of proportionality between exposure and accidents, but test whether accidents are proportional to exposure. Second, we use special techniques to purge the unexplained part of each equation (the so-called residuals) from systematic information that could remain there, in order to obtain homoskedastic and white noise residuals, using a new algorithm (Liem, Dagenais and Gaudry, 1983) that has previously been successfully used with urban travel data (Dagenais, Gaudry and Liem, 1987).

In view of the high level of aggregation of the data, the white noise residuals are assumed to have a normal distribution (and tests of the appropriateness of that assumption are performed). Results for each dimension of risk considered are expressed in terms of the expected value of the dependent variable and in terms of the elasticity of this expected value.

2.2. An Idea of the Application and of the Results

An overview should mention a limited number of new results, drawn from Gaudry (1984).

2.2.1. Structure. The first interesting result associated with model structure is that most factors influence exposure very differently from the way in which they influence accident frequency or severity: this means that substitution occurs among the three dimensions of risk or that, if we had explained the number of victims directly — without the three-way decomposition into exposure, frequency and severity — we could have missed the relevance of particular factors because they often work through offsetting impacts on these components.

The second result is that there is also strong evidence of risk substitution among the categories of accidents or among severity rates: when conditions change, risk substitution exists both in the weak sense that categories of accidents or severity rates do not change in the same proportions, and in the stronger sense that they sometimes even change in opposite directions.

Risk substitution can imply paradoxical results as consumers trade up or down: for instance, increased police surveillance on average increases the total number of accidents and victims.[3] However, close examination of the results by subcategory shows that fatal accidents and the number of fatalities both decrease: other categories of accidents and victims increase and are responsible for the observed change in the totals. The reason for this may be that reduced speeds associated with police presence go with higher accident frequencies and injury rates, as consumers "trade down" at rates that imply more than one accident with material damage only (loss) per accident with bodily damage (gain) and more than one injury (loss) per fatality (gain).

2.2.2. Particular factors. Generally speaking, it is possible to identify particular factors for which there is strong evidence of behavioral adjustment or risk compensation. And the available evidence has strong policy implications, for instance:

- holding road use constant, the increased availability of seat belts increased all categories of accidents and the morbidity rate but reduced the mortality rate sufficiently to leave the number of fatalities essentially unchanged. However, increased gasoline sales imply indirect increases in road use (no doubt in speeds) and in all categories of victims. This suggests that freely wearing seat and shoulder belts leads to compensatory behavior or increased speeds;
- weather that is uncomfortable (warmer or colder than the average for September) increases the total number of accidents but involves a substitution between fatalities and injuries.[4] Rain and snow also increase the total number of accidents but have no significant effect on the number of injuries and fatalities because of very small or offsetting changes in the number of accidents with bodily damage or in their severity. All weather variables therefore reveal the presence of substitution between numbers of accidents and their severity.

By contrast, many results associated with more stringent laws and penalties, such as the 1973 demerit point system and the 1982 stiffening of penalties listed above, indicate that these factors reduce the number of accidents of all categories, and, despite mixed effects on the severity of remaining accidents, decrease the number of victims of all categories.

Two results associated with physiological states are very interesting. The first one is that there is a higher risk of accident and a lower severity of accidents associated with pregnancy, but marked differences between the first two months of pregnancy, when the severity of accidents increases, and the remaining months. As an explanatory hypothesis, we developed conjecture 7, which states that "an increased ratio of estrogen hormones to progesterone that is not compensated by a sufficient increase in androgen hormones reduces the ability to perform learned mechanical tasks." The second result is that higher aggregate consumption of alcohol is associated with reduced fatalities. This led to the development of the following "driver-mix" conjecture, which states that "if the individual risk curve is U-shaped (quadratic), the aggregate effect of an increase in alcohol consumption will depend on its distribution among drivers." More details are given in Gaudry (1984, 1989), including references to similar results on the role of alcohol in other countries.

2.2.3. Estimation technique. Generally speaking, one confidently rejects, for two-thirds of the equations of the model, both the linear and loglinear forms often used a priori and without testing in many studies. These results have in particular the following implication: one strongly rejects the view that accident frequency is proportional to exposure. This means that a model explaining accidents per kilometer is strongly inferior to a model that does not assume this proportionality: the effect found in the data is much less than proportional.

3. The 1978 Quebec Automobile Act

We now characterize the features of the 1978 Act that could explain the increase in accidents and road victims noted above, and discuss their representation for modeling purposes. This will point to features affecting two categories of factors: i) quantitative factors, such as the cost of maintaining a car, the number of licensed drivers per car and the number of cars per person; ii) qualitative factors, such as the quality of drivers (e.g., the proportion of high-risk drivers), and the quality of driving (the level of care), which are not measured as such but captured by a dummy.

3.1. Main Characteristics for Our Purposes

The Act split the previous accident insurance system. For BODILY DAMAGES, it established a basic public plan that

[78.1] was financed jointly from general revenues[5]
[78.2] and from a uniform premium system (for given classes of vehicles) independent from an individual's risk class and safety record. These two

characteristics reduced the average premium[6] for corporal damages, and the total premium (Lefebvre and Fluet, 1990). This should

A. be expected to increase EXPOSURE risk by all drivers and perhaps to have side effects on driver care to the extent that large decreases in insurance prices must, in a nonlinear world, imply changes in the marginal trade-offs involved in optimal care activity determination;

B. be expected to increase the total number of drivers through both the lower average premium and the important further relative price reduction for individuals belonging to the worst risk classes (as their demand for driving licenses is probably more elastic than the demand of those who face a relative price rise). This increase in the number of drivers would also naturally be expected to increase EXPOSURE risk and perhaps to have side effects on driver care through the modified average occupancy of cars resulting from the increased supply of drivers;

B*. be expected to increase the average riskiness because of the ADVERSE SELECTION brought about by the replacement, at a much lower average price, of the old multiple-class price structure by a class-independent uniform-price structure. The relative price increase for a few low-risk groups (such as women) and the relative price decrease for high-risk groups would create the significant adverse selection effect;

[78.3] introduced a centralized administrative mechanism that effectively made it almost impossible to own a car and not to be insured for bodily damages, effectively forcing the 15% of owners that were not insured to carry bodily damage insurance both for themselves and for others;[7]

[78.4] was not experience rated;

[78.5] removed the notion of fault for corporal damages (injuries or fatalities) for all drivers;

C. These three changes affected the motivation to drive carefully — almost certainly reduced it by reducing the benefits of care, thereby increasing *EX ANTE* MORAL HAZARD (see Cummins and Weiss, 1988). Moreover, [78.3] also affected risk composition;

[78.6] introduced a centralized compensation system that generally increased greatly the speed, frequency, and size of compensations (Fluet and Lefebvre, 1986). This

D. encouraged individuals to classify as accidents with injuries accidents previously declared as accidents with material damages only, because of the more favourable compensation system. This increased *EX POST* MORAL HAZARD.

For MATERIAL DAMAGES, it maintained the notion of fault[8] and

[78.7] introduced a centralized administrative mechanism that effectively made it almost impossible to own a car and not hold civil liability insurance, effectively forcing the 15% of drivers that were not insured to carry such insurance. This

E. raised the price of keeping a car for the 14–18% of pleasure vehicle owners not previously insured, thus reducing the number of cars, and EXPOSURE. As the average quality of the stock of cars changed when older cars were scrapped, driver care was almost certainly reduced;

F. changed the motivation to prudence of these newly insured owners — increased *EX ANTE* MORAL HAZARD.

[78.8] introduced mechanisms for the direct and fast payment of indemnities by the private insurers. This:

G. increased slightly the incentive to report to the police and to insurers minor accidents (with material damages only), because of faster compensation, thereby increasing *EX POST* MORAL HAZARD.

In summary form, A, B, and E are quantitative factors that are expected to influence principally EXPOSURE but may also have a qualitative REDUCED CARE effect. B* is a qualitative ADVERSE SELECTION effect. C and F are qualitative *EX ANTE* MORAL HAZARD effects. D and G are qualitative reporting problems of the *EX-POST* MORAL HAZARD type.

3.2. Representation of These Changes for Modeling Purposes

There are two ways of measuring the impact of these changes. Changes such as A on the average level of automobile insurance prices, B on the total number of licenced drivers, and E on the level of car ownership occur through three variables describing respectively the cost of maintaining a car, the number of licensed drivers per car, and the number of cars per person. DRAG results suggest that the effects on road safety caused by CHANGED LEVELS OF THESE THREE QUANTITATIVE FACTORS are not negligible but are difficult to be precise about. Moreover, the variations brought about by the new Act may have been qualitatively different from previous variations.

Such modifications in the qualitative significance of price, in the tenure of driving licences, or in the quality of the stock of cars, are captured by a qualitative dummy variable that also simultaneously measures the effect of other clearly QUALITATIVE changes B*, C, and F in the quality of drivers and driving, or the unexplained part of the increase in the number of accidents. DRAG results show that the net effect of the qualitative changes are very important and that the new Act clearly increased all categories of accidents and victims, but the exact value of the increase cannot always be ascertained exactly because some of the estimates may sometimes be tainted by the presence of declaration effects D and G.

3.3. Effects of Three Quantitative Factors

In table 2, one finds the elasticities of selected dependent variables of the model with respect to the three explanatory variables affected by the 1978 Act. These elasticities are defined as the ratio of the percentage change of the expected value of each explained variable with respect to the percentage change of the explanatory variable considered and are evaluated at the sample means.

Increases of the real price of maintaining a car, defined as the maintenance and insurance price (excluding any fuel and depreciation components), are associated with increased consumption of fuels, a result also found in Germany (Foos, 1986), and significant reductions in the number of accidents (and of their severity but, for these results, only the t-statistics are shown). This suggests that higher maintenance prices reduce engine tune-ups, causing higher fuel consumption, and reduce general maintenance, stimulating driver care and lower speed adjustments that reduce accidents and their severity. Lefebvre and Fluet have studied the evolution of the real price of insurance in Quebec and have estimated that the price of a dollar of compensation for material and bodily damages fell from $1.69 to $1.37 because of the Act (Lefebvre and Fluet, 1990, p. 48). If this 22% decrease is taken as the best educated guess of the price change, the Quebec part of the national index used in the model fell by 8.54% and the index itself by approximately 2.15% (the structural change being absorbed by the qualitative variable).

Increases of the number of licensed drivers per car reduce the number of all categories of accidents but, because of opposite effects on the severity of accidents with injuries and fatal accidents (again, only the t-statistics are shown), injuries decrease and fatalities increase: presumably, with fewer occupants per car, drivers increase speed (gasoline consumption increases slightly, but that may also be due to increased exposure). Visual analysis of figure 4 shows a sudden increase of about 6% immediately after the implementation of the Act, followed by continuing increases. This 6% increase is then a conservative "best educated guess" of the short-run effect of the new price structure, perhaps half of which is due to the increased supply of drivers.

Increases of the number of cars per person increase road use and, indirectly, accidents and victims. One notices on figure 5 the dramatic

Table 2. Elasticities of Quantitative Factors Modified by 1978 Insurance Act

	Independent variable used in reference model								
	Price of maintaining a car			Number of licensed drivers per car			Number of cars per person		
Dependent variable	Direct (t-st.)	Ind.	Total	Direct (t-st.)	Ind.	Total	Direct (t-st.)	Ind.	Total
ROAD USE									
::: Gasoline sales	0.205 (1.96)			0.073 (0.40)			0.269 (1.32)		
::: Diesel sales	0.273 (0.68)								
ACCIDENTS with									
(1) Property damage only	−0.629 (−3.03)	0.193	N	−0.371 (−1.78)	0.064	−.307		0.234	
(2) At least one injury, no deaths	−0.728 (−3.97)	0.107	N	−0.089 (−0.47)	0.035	−.054		0.130	
(3) At least one death	−1.01 (−3.90)	0.133	N	−0.604 (−1.95)	0.043	−.561		0.158	
(2) + (3) Bodily damage	−0.740 (−3.77)	0.108	N	−0.060 (0.64)	0.036	−.024		0.131	
(1) + (2) + (3) Total accidents	−0.653 (−3.91)	0.174	N	−0.303 (−2.22)	0.058	−.245		0.211	

Table 2.   Continued

	Independent variable used in reference model								
	Price of maintaining a car			Number of licenced drivers per car			Number of cars per person		
Dependent variable	Direct (t-st.)	Ind.	Total	Direct (t-st.)	Ind.	Total	Direct (t-st.)	Ind.	Total
SEVERITY									
• Morbidity	(−0.47)			(−1.87)					
• Mortality	(−0.82)			(1.05)					
VICTIMS									
(4) Injuries	−0.797	0.118	N	−0.313	0.041	−.272		0.149	
(5) Fatalities	−1.018	0.258	N	0.257	0.091	.348		0.333	
(4) + (5) Total victims	−0.840	0.123	N	−0.293	0.042	−.251		0.155	

Direct: holds road use constant.

Indirect: allows for variation in road use.

Total: direct + indirect, unless the sum is not relevant (indicated by N).

Reference model: found in Gaudry (1984).

t-statistics of underlying regression coefficients shown in parentheses are computed conditionally upon the estimated functional form of the regression equations and differ from the unconditional values presented in Gaudry (1984).

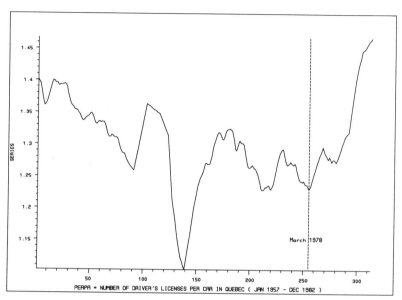

Figure 4. Number of driver's licenses per car in Quebec.

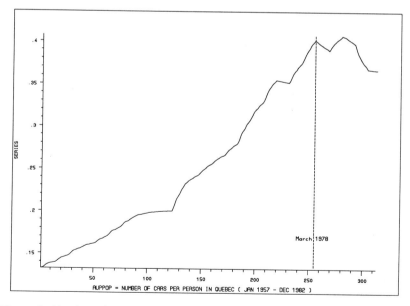

Figure 5. Number of cars per person in Quebec.

turn-around of car ownership in Quebec since the implementation of the
Act. The first significant drop in car ownership ever seen — about 3% —
is followed by a relatively slow recovery and a massive fall of ownership
levels. The influence of extraordinarily high real gasoline prices after
1979 (they increased by 60% between 1979 and 1982), the exodus of
households with higher than average car ownership levels and the re-
cession of 1982 may all have contributed to breaking the trend. The
3% drop during the first year of the Act is a best educated guess of the
impact of forcing owners to have insurance by requesting a proof of
insurance for material damages and tying the registration fee to the
payment of a premium for bodily damages: registering many (presumably
old) cars became too expensive.

3.4. Effects of Qualitative and Structural Changes

Table 3 shows the percentage variation of each dependent variable due
to the qualitative change brought by the Act. These variations are
computed at the mean value of the sample, i.e., for an average point
rather than at the specific moment of implementation of the legislation.[9]
We do not report in full the results concerning the qualitative impact of
the Act on the severity of accidents due to space limitations, but we show
the t-statistics.

   These direct elasticity results on the frequency of accidents by category
(8.5%, 26.3%, and 3.3%) can be compared with Devlin's (1991) more
recent results obtained with annual data comparing Quebec and Ontario:
in view of the very different nature of the data and estimation methods
used, they are surprisingly similar, as she obtains 5.33%, 26.74% and
9.62%. Unfortunately she did not estimate severity equations or equations explaining the number of injured and killed victims, so a complete
comparison of the qualitative effects of the 1978 Act is not feasible.

4. Significance of the Results

4.1. The Principal Effects of the 1978 Act

Table 4 summarizes the main effects of the 1978 Act, estimated both
visually and with the help of a combination of DRAG model results and
educated guesses. Estimates based on the model are lower than the visual
estimates: if model elasticities had been evaluated for the 12 months

Table 3. Qualitative Effect of 1978 and 1961 Insurance Acts

| | March 1978 Act | | | July 1961 Act | | | | | |
| | Reference Model | | | Reference Model | | | Model Variant | | |
Dependent variable	Direct (t-st.)	Ind.	Total	Direct (t-st.)	Ind.	Total	Direct (t-st.)	Ind.	Total
ROAD USE									
::: Gasoline sales	2.6 (0.76)			3.4 (1.35)			3.5 (1.44)		
::: Diesel sales	5.0 (0.42)			12.4 (1.56)			11.9 (1.44)		
ACCIDENTS with									
(1) Property damage only	8.5 (1.08)	2.5	11.0	24.9 (6.53)	3.6	28.5	26.5 (7.45)	3.9	30.4
(2) At least one injury, no deaths	26.3 (8.13)	1.4	27.7	13.1 (3.50)	2.0	15.1	15.2 (4.24)	2.2	17.4
(3) At least one death	3.3 (0.58)	1.7	5.0	-3.7 (-0.63)	2.6	-1.1	12.6 (1.86)	2.4	15.0
(2) + (3) Bodily damage	25.3 (7.18)	1.4	26.7	12.4 (3.14)	2.0	14.4	15.1 (3.81)	2.2	17.3
(1) + (2) + (3) Total accidents	12.1 (2.39)	2.3	14.4	22.2 (6.76)	3.3	25.5	24.0 (7.71)	3.5	27.5

% change due to

Table 3. Continued

| | March 1978 Act | | | July 1961 Act | | | | | |
| | Reference Model | | | Reference Model | | | Model Variant | | |
Dependent variable	Direct (t-st.)	Ind.	Total	Direct (t-st.)	Ind.	Total	Direct (t-st.)	Ind.	Total
SEVERITY									
• Morbidity	(−0.23)			(−3.53)					
• Mortality	(−2.73)			(3.72)					
VICTIMS									
(4) Injuries	24.8	1.5	26.3	5.9	2.1	8.0	10.1	2.3	12.4
(5) Fatalities	3.6	3.2	6.8	−9.1	4.4	−4.7	1.7	5.2	6.9
(4) + (5) Total victims	24.0	1.6	25.6	5.4	2.2	7.6	9.9	2.4	12.3

Direct: holds road use constant.
Indirect: allows for variation in road use.
Total: direct + indirect.
Reference model: found in Gaudry (1984).
Variant model: unpublished results with driver quality risk index.
t-statistics of underlying regression coefficients shown in parentheses are computed conditionally upon the estimated functional form of the regression equations and differ from the unconditional values presented in Gaudry (1984).

Table 4 Main Effects of 1978 Insurance Act

	% change					Visual
	Based on DRAG results and due to					
Dependent Variable	Price of maintaining a car	Licenced drivers per car	Cars per person	Qualitative structural change	Total	Total
ACCIDENTS with						
(1) Property damage only	1.34	−1.84	−0.70	11.00	9.81 7.43*	26.29
VICTIMS						
(4) Injuries	1.70	−1.63	−0.45	26.30	25.93 24.04*	30.58
(5) Fatalities	2.17	2.09	−1.00	6.80	10.06 9.12*	6.35

Values for the first three columns are obtained by multiplying respectively the direct, total and indirect elasticities of Table 2 by the best educated guesses described in the text. Starred values denote values obtained by evaluating the model elasticities on the same basis as that used for the visual estimates—the twelve months previous to the implementation of the Act.

previous to the implementation of the Act, and not for the whole sample period, they would be somewhat lower (as indicated by the starred values). This being said, it is clear that, although it is difficult to be precise about the impact of the Act on the level of the three quantitative factors considered, most of the impact of the Act occurs through its qualitative or structural change: in table 4, adding up the first three columns yields −1.19%, −0.37% and 3.26%, or values that would not offset the corresponding values of 11.0%, 26.3% and 6.8% unless the best educated guesses used to obtain the results for the three quantitative factors were dramatically modified. It is clear that we must discuss the significance of the qualitative-structural factor.

4.2. Increased Moral Hazard and Forced Adverse Selection

4.2.1. Reporting Effects or Moral Hazard After the Fact. In section 2, we pointed out the possible presence of a reporting effect and distinguished between characteristic (D), a motivation to report some accidents with material damages only as accidents with injuries, and characteristic

(G), a motivation to report accidents with material damages only more willingly to insurance companies. In the absence of further data, for instance on the number of hospital admissions related to road accidents, the possible tendency to exaggerate claims for injuries cannot be ascertained exactly; neither can we measure the net reporting effect on accidents with material damages only. However, it is certain that reported increases in such accidents and in injuries are not solely due to a possible reporting effect: this would imply that fatalities (that can be neither faked nor hidden) had increased[10] because of higher road use and qualitative change associated with the Act, but that all other measures of road safety had remained unchanged. Moreover, other considerations to be presented shortly also imply real increases in all measures of road accidents and victims.

4.2.2. Compulsory Insurance and Moral Hazard. The first consideration that points to a strong real component in all three main measures listed in table 4 is the effect of characteristic E of the Act, which effectively increased to about 100% the proportion of vehicles insured by insurance companies. This may seem unexpected because the obligation to carry a minimal amount of third-party liability insurance existed since July 1961; it appears that the added obligation to show proof of private insurance for material damages and to pay a premium for bodily damages simultaneously with the vehicle registration application made it more difficult than before to avoid insurance. The 1961 law, which was experience rated as it applied to private insurance, increased the proportion of insured vehicles approximately from 0.65 to 0.81, a variation that is comparable to that of the 1978 law. An idea of the effect of this forced insurance may be had by consulting table 3 where two estimates of the effects of the 1961 law are given.[11] Both models indicate increased fuel sales, increased accidents with material damages only and increased injuries; the effect on fatalities is uncertain, but on balance probably positive. It seems that forcing consumers to be insured reduces their care; in this respect, the 1978 law simply had more administrative teeth than the 1961 law, and certainly reduced driver care, but one cannot assign a precise part of the total increase to it, even on the basis of the 1961 results, because the remaining 15% of uninsured vehicles must have been different from the previous group that had been responsive to the requirements of the previous law.

4.2.3. No-fault and Moral Hazard. Essentially, being forced to be insured reduces the consumer's size and variability of loss in the event of an accident; the no-fault provision of the law also reduces the rewards of driver care but, in the absence of previous experience with this feature of the Act, there is no way to assess its importance, let alone compare it with the forced insurance and flat premium parts of the total effect. For other jurisdictions, we have not found modeling results on comparable complete no-fault systems for bodily damages; neither do Landes' (1982) results on the introduction of limited no-fault insurance in 16 American states provide any guidance: they were obtained with a very simple model and shown by Zador and Lund (1986) to be very sensitive to slight changes in specification. Cummins and Weiss (1988, 1991) also pertain to limited no-fault.

4.2.4. Flat Premium Rating and the Subsidization of Bad Risks. A third consideration pointing to a strong real component in the totals for (1) and (4) in table 4 is the indirect evidence of the impact of the uniform premium system for bodily damages. By forced subsidization of bad risks, this system created what amounts to a form of forced adverse selection. Of course, bad risks have higher accident rates in all accident categories — not only in the fatal category. Evidence of this additional adverse selection, with a significant effect on the risk composition of the stock of drivers, is extremely strong.

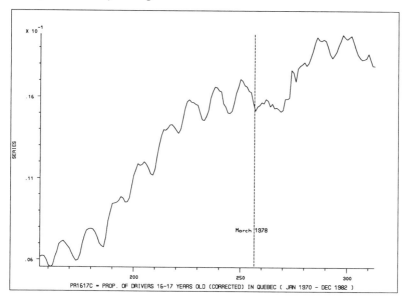

Figure 6. Proportion of drivers 16–17 years old in Quebec.

Consider figure 6 showing the proportion of drivers belonging to the 16–17 age group. The age pyramid was such that their share of the total stock of drivers was stabilizing around 1976 and 1977. The new Act shifted this plateau upwards by about 2–3 percentage points, a 15–20% increase of the share. In Gaudry (1984), we show that the relative participation rate of the 18–19 age group also increased rapidly for two years before getting back on trend.

Of course, the effect of the subsidization of relatively bad risks did not occur only in these obvious classes. One can see on figure 7 that the proportion of women in the stock of drivers, which had been increasing according to a linear trend, suddenly started increasing much more slowly along a new trend line — the slope suddenly changed, as one would expect from a structural price change taxing women to the benefit of men.

Our best educated guess of a 3% increase in the number of driver permits does not mean that all of this increase consisted in bad risks. The Act lowered the average price of insurance and changed relative prices, and perhaps also some absolute prices, to the disadvantage of "good risks", some subcategories of which might have shrunk. Adverse selection only means that the average quality of the stock of drivers fell.

5. Conclusion: Deterrence and Efficiency

With the help of the DRAG model, we conclude that the 1978 no-fault law in Quebec certainly increased real (not only reported) road accidents and victims but that the estimated increases, although plausible and conservative when compared to the results of intuitive visual analyses, are not all very significant in a statistical sense. Our results also suggest that the main effects of the law did not occur because of the subsidized and reduced average real price of insurance, the resulting increased number of drivers, or the decreased number of cars: they apparently occurred because of the qualitative and structural change of the new system. This structural change consisted mainly of i) forcing 14–18% of uninsured vehicles to carry insurance, ii) removing the notion of fault for bodily damages, and iii) charging a flat-premium insurance premium for bodily damages independently from the driver's safety record. It is not possible to unravel the influence of each of these three simultaneous components, but previous moral hazard experience with compulsory automobile insurance and the very strong evidence of forced adverse selection caused by the subsidization of high-risk drivers suggest that the contribution of no-fault, as such, to the reduction of driver care and deterrence, if it existed at all, was very small compared to the contributions of the two

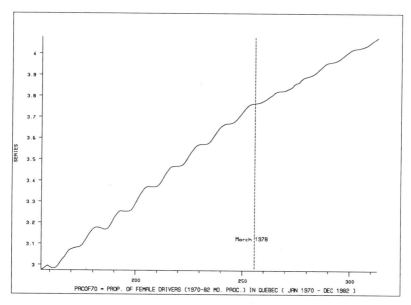

Figure 7. Proportion of female drivers in Quebec.

other elements. It is not surprising that the more recent work by Cummins and Weiss shows very weak relationships between low money or verbal no-fault thresholds and accident rates or insurance claims.

It is in principle possible to correct most of the inefficiencies caused by the law by setting up an adequate rating system that induces individuals to face the true social road safety cost of driving. Boyer and Dionne (1985, 1987) have shown that multiperiod no-fault insurance contracts based in part on the individual's past driving record can give individually rational self-protection activity levels that are socially efficient over time in the presence of both moral hazard and externalities; they are studying the empirical foundations of such a system and have already shown (Boyer and Dionne, 1989) that an individual's previous accident, demerit point, and infraction record are significantly related to the probability of accident. The detailed design of an experience-rated pricing system, particularly of one compatible with the absence of discrimination on the basis of age or sex, or the formulation of an equivalent combination of insurance premia and fines, is an empirical matter that will take time to evolve. It is also clear that the potential inclusion of information from police records into the pricing system is easy in the presence of a centralized rating agency or mechanism. Once proper account is taken of the various components of the 1978 Quebec law, and ways of improving its rating mechanism are considered, one would be hard put to build a case against it solely on the basis of its specific no-fault feature. The implied net welfare gains of the no-fault feature proper point to the existence of a political market opportunity in other jurisdictions as well.

Notes

1. As the proportion of insured vehicles increased by 19% from 84% to 100%, this number is compatible with the 20% increase in the frequency of claims per vehicle experienced by insurance companies.

2. Accidents with material damages only are in effect only those above a certain damage value ($250 in 1982) estimated by policemen in their reports. Only one injured person is sufficient to constitute an accident with bodily injury. Only one fatality is sufficient to constitute a fatal accident.

3. This result does not appear to hold for provincial (state) police patrols — for which more surveillance results in fewer injuries and fatalities — but for Montreal Urban Community police and for the overall average.

4. The implicit tradeoff associated with uncomfortable weather is 22 injuries per fatality.

5. A part of the existing tax revenues from fuel sales was earmarked to finance the public regime, but the tax rates on fuel were not increased.

6. As shown in Fluet and Lefebvre (1986), it is difficult to estimate the real price change as one has to take into account the new structure of the private sector as well as the respective roles of economies of scale, subsidies from general revenue and internal accounting rules within the new public administration.

7. We shall not be able to isolate directly this effect, but we will get a good idea of its importance by looking at the effect if the 1961 compulsory insurance law that also "convinced" 15% of drivers to carry insurance.

8. In practice, insurers used the notion of fault to determine compensations, but it is not clear that they used it coherently to set premia because they had no way of verifying the past experience of those who shopped around until Bill 133 gave them in January 1990 the possibility of constructing a central file in which each driver's dossier over the previous 10 years contained accident and fault information. Before January 1990, they certainly had a tendency to increase a client's premium after an accident irrespective of fault — hence the motivation for Bill 133.

9. The DRAG report uses a new analytical formula to compute these "elasticities" for dummy variables. The formula used is exact in the case of linear equations and approximate in the case of nonlinear equations.

10. On a calendar year basis, fatalities increased from 1556 to 1765 (13.43%) in Quebec as they fell from 3697 to 3664 (0.89%) in the rest of Canada between 1977 and 1978. (Reported in G. Ledoux, 1985).

11. Estimates obtained with the model variant are probably more accurate than those of the reference model because they are based on a more refined representation of the influence of the lowering of the minimum driving age a year later.

References

Boyer, M., and G. Dionne. (1989). "Moral Hazard and Experience Rating: an Empirical Analysis," *Review of Economics and Statistics* LXXI (1), 128–134.

Boyer, M., and G. Dionne. (1987). "The Economics of Road Safety," *Transportation Research B* 21(5), 413–431.

Boyer, M., and G. Dionne. (1985). "Sécurité routière: responsabilité pour négligence et tarification." *Canadian Journal of Economics/Revue Canadienne d'Economique* 18, 814–830.

Cummins, J. D., and M. A. Weiss. (1991). "Incentive Effects of No-Fault automobile Insurance: Evidence from Insurance Claim Data," in G. Dionne (ed.) *Contributions to Insurance Economics*. Norwell, MA: Kluwer Academic Publishers.

Cummins, J. D., and M. A. Weiss. (1988). "An Economic Analysis of No-Fault Insurance," Working paper No 88-4, Center for Research on Risk and Insurance, University of Pennsylvania.

Dagenais, M. G., M. Gaudry, and T. C. Liem. (1987). "Urban Travel Demand: the Impact of Box-Cox Transformations with Nonspherical Residual Errors," *Transportation Research B* 21(6), 443–477.

Devlin, R. A. (1991). "Liability versus No-Fault Automobile Insurance Regimes: An Analysis of the Experience of Quebec." in G. Dionne (ed.) *Contributions to Insurance Economics*. Norwell, MA: Kluwer Academic Publishers.

Fluet, C., and P. Lefebvre. (1986). "L'assurance automobile au Québec: bilan d'une réforme," Régie de l'Assurance Automobile du Québec, Février, 230 pages.

Foos, Gertraud. (1986). "Die Determinanten des Verkehrsnachfrage," *Karlsruher Beiträge zur Wirtschaftspolitik und Wirtschaftsforschung*, v. Loeper Verlag, Karlsruhe.

Gaudry, M. (1989). "Responsibility for Accidents: Relevant Results Selected from the DRAG Model," *Canadian Business Law Journal/Revue canadienne de droit de commerce* 16(1), 21–33.

Gaudry, M. (1984). "DRAG, un modèle de la Demande Routière, des Accidents et de leur Gravité, appliqué au Québec de 1956 à 1982." Publication #359, Centre de recherche sur les transports, Université de Montréal, octobre, 216 pages. Forthcoming in English in *Accident Analysis and Prevention*.

Gaudry, M., D. Baldino, and T. C. Liem. (1984). "FRQ, un Fichier Routier Québécois." Publication #360, Centre de recherche sur les transports, Université de Montréal, octobre, 225 pages.

Landes, E. (1982). "Insurance Liability and Accidents: A Theoretical and Empirical Investigation of the Effect of No-Fault Accidents," *Journal of Law and Economics* 25, 49–65.

Ledoux., G. (1985). "Bilan international des victimes de la circulation routière de 1970 à 1981: le Québec et le Canada." Rapport technique, Régie de l'Assurance Automobile du Québec, Avril.

Lefebvre, P., and C. Fluet. (1990). "L'évolution du prix total de l'assurance automobile au Québec depuis la réforme de 1978." *Canadian Public Policy*, XVI, 375–386.

Liem, T. C., M. G. Dagenais, and M. Gaudry. (1983). "L-1.1, A Program for Box-Cox Transformations in Regression Models with Heteroskedastic and Autoregressive Residuals," Publication #301, Centre de recherche sur les transports, Université de Montréal.

Zador, P., and A. Lund. (1986). "Re-analyses of the Effects of No-Fault Auto Insurance on Total Crashes," *Journal of Risk and Insurance* 53, 226–241.

LIABILITY VERSUS NO-FAULT AUTOMOBILE INSURANCE REGIMES: AN ANALYSIS OF THE EXPERIENCE IN QUEBEC*

Rose Anne Devlin

University of Ottawa.

Abstract

This paper examines the debate regarding the incentive effects of legal liability in the presence of liability insurance. Specifically, it examines the impact on road accidents of moving from a liability to a no-fault automobile insurance regime. A model is developed in which individuals choose driving care and kilometers driven within each type of insurance system. The theoretical results from the choice of care and kilometers suggest that the overall direction of change in each of these variables is an empirical matter. An investigation is conducted of the province of Quebec which switched to a pure no-fault system for all bodily-injury accidents in 1978. The empirical results indicate that there was an increase in total kilometers driven, and that driving care fell in the new insurance regime. These results suggest that there may indeed be a deterrence effect stemming from legal liability in the presence of liability insurance.

Key words: Automobile insurance, legal liability, no-fault, accident models, Quebec experience

A crucial conclusion found in the law and economics literature is that the tort system provides incentives for individuals to behave efficiently — the

* This paper is derived from my Ph.D. dissertation for the Department of Economics, University of Toronto. Samuel A. Rea, Jr., and Donald N. Dewees made invaluable contributions to this research. Useful comments were also provided by Georges Dionne and three anonymous referees. I retain sole responsibility for any remaining errors.

499

so-called deterrence effect. Opponents of this view argue that liability insurance eliminates these incentive effects and that emphasis should be placed on compensating victims regardless of fault. Both of these views stem from the notion that the primary purpose of accident law is to facilitate the maximization of net social benefits from participating in risky activities.[1]

The crux of the deterrence versus compensation debate is whether or not the tort system in the presence of insurance leads to efficient precautions against accidents. This paper provides evidence in this debate by examining empirically the experience of the province of Quebec. The situation in Quebec provides an almost ideal environment in which to analyze this problem, since it is the only jurisdiction in North America that has a purely no-fault system for bodily injury automobile accidents.[2] A number of studies have attempted to address this debate by analyzing the various U.S. states that have some form of no-fault automobile insurance, with contradictory conclusions (Landes, 1982; U.S., 1985; Kochanowski and Young, 1985; and Zador and Lund, 1986). However, each of these states permits tort action once damages exceeds some specified threshold.[3] Thus, U.S. evidence on the impact of no-fault on behavior will underestimate the impact of a true no-fault system.

In 1978 Quebec switched from a fault-based insurance system to a no-fault one for all bodily injuries resulting from automobile accidents. Gaudry (1987) is the only study that attempts to estimate the impact of no fault on the number and severity of accidents. Boyer and Dionne (1987, 1989) have examined the effects on moral hazard of nonexperience-rated premiums in Quebec. This paper presents a theoretical framework from which to analyze the new regime in Quebec; as well as some empirical results from the analysis.

Insurance theory suggests that if insurance companies can observe a driver's care and activity, then premiums can be geared precisely to that driver's behavior, eliminating moral hazard problems. Of course, the extent to which care cannot be measured determines the extent to which moral hazard problems prevail. In the real world, driving care cannot be measured and the risk class of individuals is unobservable; hence, various proxies are used that indicate how risky any particular driver might be. Commonly used proxies are age, sex, and driving record. Boyer and Dionne (1989) show, for instance, that all three of these proxies are significant predictors of drivers behavior. Others have shown, in more general terms, why some form of risk-rating should be practiced (Hoy, 1982; Rea, 1991).

The paper begins by presenting a model of an individual's choices of care and kilometers driven under full and asymmetric information assumptions. Next, the legal regime is added to the asymmetrical information model — which corresponds to the situation in pre- and post-no-fault Quebec. A brief description of the principal changes in Quebec is provided along with how these changes are shown by the model. The model shows that the overall impact of these changes on the probability of an accident is theoretically indeterminable. Consequently, an empirical investigation is done on the kilometers driven decision and the care decision — by way of various accident equations. These results indicate that the probability of an accident increased significantly with the new regime in Quebec.

1. The Model

The common approach to modeling an individual's choice of care and level of participation in an activity is to assume one of these variables is fixed — usually the level of activity (Shavell, 1987; Rea, 1987).[4] Care is then chosen to minimize expected accident costs for a given level of activity. Recognition has been given to the fact that the level of activity is affected by the type of legal rules that govern individuals' behavior.

The model below allows individuals to choose both the level of driving care x_i and kilometers driven K_i. However, the simultaneity of the care and kilometers driven decisions renders it difficult to determine how each of the choices will react to exogenous changes. The model concludes that the direction of individuals' responses to changing decision-making parameters (prices, legal environment) cannot be determined unequivocally.

Individuals are separated into high- and low-risk groups. The probability of an accident is dependent upon the individual's own care (x_i) and own kilometers driven (K_i) as well as the average level of driving care (x^m) and total kilometers driven (K^T).

The probability of an accident for any individual is conditional on average care and total kilometers driven as follows:

$$\pi_i(x_i, K_i \mid x^m, K^T) \tag{1}$$

Individuals are assumed to have an expectation of average care and total driving activity, the realization of which affects their probability of an accident. The anticipated values of these aggregates will affect the choices of x_i and K_i. In fact, it is assumed that (dropping the subscripts for the moment):

$$\frac{\partial \pi}{\partial x} < 0, \quad \frac{\partial^2 \pi}{\partial x^2} > 0, \quad \frac{\partial \pi}{\partial K} > 0, \quad \frac{\partial^2 \pi}{\partial K^2} < 0, \quad \frac{\partial \pi}{\partial x^m} < 0, \quad \frac{\partial \pi}{\partial K^T} > 0, \quad (2)$$

$$\frac{\partial^2 \pi}{\partial x \partial x^m} < 0, \quad \frac{\partial^2 \pi}{\partial x \partial K^T} > 0, \quad \frac{\partial^2 \pi}{\partial K \partial x^m} < 0, \quad \frac{\partial^2 \pi}{\partial K \partial K^T} > 0 \quad (3)$$

Note that (2) results from concavity assumptions and (3) results from restrictions on the probability function itself (homotheticity of the probability function is a sufficient condition). Intuitively, the restrictions in (3) imply that the safer a group of drivers is, the smaller the probability that any one will be in an accident, and thus the smaller the effect of an increment of care on the probability of an accident. This model implicitly assumes that there is a lag between what individuals perceive to be market riskiness and activity and what it actually is.

Assume that individuals choose to participate in the driving activity only if it is utility enhancing. Let Z_i^0 define the minimum expected utility level that an individual must achieve before purchasing a car. Then Z_i must be at least as great as Z_i^0 before individuals participate in the driving activity. Let U_i^j define the utility of a member of group i if the event j occurs — where $j = 1$ if an accident occurs and 0 otherwise. Z_i is defined as:

$$Z_i = \pi_i, K_i \mid x^m, K^T) * U_i^1(K_i, G_i^1) \\ + [1 - \pi_i(x_i, K_i \mid x^m, K^T)] * U_i^0(K_i, G_i^0) \quad (4)$$

In which:

π_i = probability of an accident per period for an individual in group i
i = individual's risk group where: 1 is high risk, 2 is low risk
x_i = care of individual
K_i = kilometers driven of individual
x^m = average care taken in market
K^T = total kilometers driven
G_i^1 = other goods purchased given an accident occurred
G_i^0 = other goods purchased if no accident occurred

Assume that individuals choose how many kilometers to drive, an accident either occurs or does not, and then the purchase of other goods is made. Individuals choose kilometers driven, care taken per kilometer driven, and other goods, to maximize their expected utility (4) subject to the relevant. budget constraint. However, the nature of the budget constraint will depend upon how premiums are set and the type of legal regime in operation.

1.1. Optimal Care with Full Information

If the insurance company can observe care, x, then full coverage will be provided with premiums responding to care chosen $P_{ins}(x)$. Thus the budget constraint under which Z is maximized is

$$P_{Ki}K + P_G G_i = Y_i - P_{ci}(x_i) \qquad (5a)$$

P_{Ki} = price per kilometer, which equals $P_g + a_i x_i$ where
  P_g = price of gasoline
  $a_i x_i$ = price of care times total units of care per kilometer
P_G = price of other goods (which is set equal to one)
Y_i = income of individual in group i
P_{ci} = fixed cost of purchasing an automobile, which equals
  $P_p + P_m + P_{ins}(x_i)$ − the user cost of purchasing an automobile, as well as maintaining and insuring the automobile (which depends upon care)[5] per year

Notice that (5a) is nonstochastic as a result of full-insurance (individuals are fully compensated in the event of an accident). The first-order conditions for the choice of care and kilometers driven are given in (6) and (7) and are shown to facilitate comparisons with later results.

$$\pi_x U^1 - \pi_x U^0 - \lambda[aK + P'_{ins}(x)] = 0 \qquad (6)$$

where λ is the Lagrangian multiplier or the marginal utility of income; π_x refers to the marginal effect of care on the probability of an accident (when subscripted with K it refers to the marginal effect of kilometers driven). Equation (6) is equivalent to $-P'_{ins}(x) = aK$ under full insurance with no nonpecuniary losses (i.e., when $U^1 = U^0$; see Rea 1982).[6] Thus, one obtains the standard result that care is chosen until its marginal benefit (the reduction in insurance premiums resulting from a unit increase in care: dP_{ins}/dx) equals its marginal cost (yielding x^*). The condition for choice of kilometers driven (K^*)[7] is:

$$\pi_K U^1 - \pi_K U^0 + \pi U_K^1 + (1 - \pi)U_K^0 - \lambda(P_g + ax) = 0 \qquad (7)$$

or, $P_g + ax = 1/\lambda(U_K^1)$ (whereby $U_K^1 = U_K^0$) with full insurance and no non-pecuniary losses.

The above results depend upon the full-information assumption.

1.2. Insurance with Asymmetrical Information

Insurance companies cannot observe care. This results in the well-known moral hazard problem (Shavell, 1987; Boyer and Dionne, 1989). Assume that drivers are classified into high- and low-risk groups based on certain characteristics. High-risk drivers pay a premium higher than low-risk drivers — thus $P_{c2} < P_{c1}$. In addition, less than full insurance is provided. Define the net accident costs of a driver as

$$A_i = TC_i - C_i, \tag{8}$$

in which TC are the total costs of the accident and C denotes compensation received. Then the relevant budget constraint facing any driver becomes

$$P_{Ki}K + P_G G_i^1 = Y_i - P_{ci} - A_i \text{ (with probability } \pi) \tag{5b}$$

$$P_{Ki}K + P_G G_i^0 = Y_i - P_{ci} \qquad \text{(with probability } (1 - \pi)) \tag{5c}$$

or, alternatively,

$$\begin{aligned}\pi[Y_i - P_{ci} - A_i - P_{Ki}K + P_G G_i^1] \\ + (1 - \pi)[Y_i - P_{ci} - P_{Ki}K + P_G G_i^0]\end{aligned} \tag{5d}$$

Note that now P_{ins} is independent of care ($P'_{ins}(x) = 0$).

Maximizing expected utility (Z_i) with respect to x, and K subject to (5d) using the Lagrangian method (dropping all subscripts) yields the following first-order conditions:

$$\pi_x U^1 - \pi_x U^0 - \lambda a K = 0 \tag{9}$$

$$\pi_K U^1 - \pi_K U^0 + U_K^1 \pi + U_K^0 (1 - \pi) - \lambda(P_g + ax) = 0 \tag{10}$$

Notice that under full insurance when $P'_{ins}(x) = 0$ care chosen $\hat{x}$ will be less than x^*. Thus, partial insurance is an optimal strategy when care is not observable. Moreover, condition (10) implies that fewer kilometers will be driven whenever there is less than full insurance coverage. Now there is an additional cost to drivers for each kilometer driven — namely the marginal effect upon the probability of an accident, π_K, weighed by the impact on total utility in the event of an accident (note that in this case $(U^1 - U^0) < 0$; whereas $(U^1 - U^0) = 0$ under full insurance)

1.3. Asymmetrical Information and Choice of Legal Rule

The above assumes that insurance premiums are fixed for each class of driver and that less than full compensation is provided. However, insurance coverage generally depends upon the type of legal regime in operation. In a liability system, third-party insurance is purchased and the amount any particular driver receives in compensation depends upon the degree of fault in an accident. A no-fault system, however, has drivers purchasing first-party insurance, and compensation is independent of fault. Net accidents costs, therefore, depend upon the type of legal/ insurance regime in operation, as follows:

$$A_i^L(\tilde{x}) = TC_i^L - C_i^L(\tilde{x}) \tag{8a}$$

Where the superscript $L = 1$ for liability and 2 for no-fault. Compensation is a function of care — the ex post determination of care (denoted by $\tilde{x}$) — with $C^{1'}(\tilde{x}) > 0$ and $C^{2'}(\tilde{x}) = 0$. Note that $\tilde{x}$ is related to true care x, such that $dC(\tilde{x})/dx > 0$. Replacing (8) with (8a) yields first-order conditions in which the choice of care is higher in the liability system than under no-fault.

In addition, the premiums charged in a liability system also depend upon the ex post determination of fault insofar as if the driver makes a claim against his insurance company, his premiums increase in the following period for some specified length of time (usually 6 years). Thus, a further component is added to net accident costs to reflect this increase:

$$A_i^L(\tilde{x}) = TC_i^L - C_i^L(\tilde{x}) + \theta_i^L(\tilde{x}) \sum_{j=1}^{n} \frac{1}{(1 + r)^j} \tag{8b}$$

Where θ is the additional charge if a claim is made, which depends upon the determination of care; n is the number of years for which the surcharge is levied; and r is the discount rate. Notice that $\theta^1 > 0$ and $\theta^2 = 0$. Substituting (8b) as the budget constraint in the expected utility maximization problem results in individuals taking more care and driving fewer kilometers in a liability system versus the no-fault system.

2. The Quebec Regime

There were a number of changes that occurred in 1978 when Quebec introduced its no-fault system for automobile accidents. This paper concentrates on the three principal changes that are relevant to drivers' choices of care and kilometers driven: the switch from variable premiums across individuals to a pooled premium for all drivers; the switch from experience-rated to nonexperience-rated premiums; and the switch from liability to no-fault administration and compensation.[8] In terms of the model, the first change results in P_c being independent of risk-group (i.e., $P'_{ins}(x) = 0$); the switch to nonexperience-rated premiums results in $\theta = 0$ in (8b); and switching to no-fault compensation implies that $C'(\tilde{x}) = 0$. The move to a pooled premium across risk groups implies that the residual income of individuals ($Y_i - P_{ci}$) changes for each risk group. The other two changes affect A_i (net accident costs).

The rest of the analysis assumes that care and kilometers driven are normal goods, and, thus,

$$\frac{dK}{d(Y - P_c)} > 0, \qquad \frac{dx}{d(Y - P_c)} > 0 \tag{11}$$

2.1. Pooling Premiums Across Individuals

The result of pooling premiums across individuals is that residual income, $Y - P_c$, increases for the high-risk group (since $P_c < P_{c1}$) and decreases for the low-risk group. Thus, from (11), the residual income effect will result in more high-risk kilometers driven and fewer low-risk kilometers driven. Care taken, however, will increase by the high-risk drivers and fall by the low-risk drivers *ceteris paribus*.

2.2. Switching to Nonexperience-Rated Premiums

Moving to a regime in which premiums are invariant over time regardless of accident history implies that the direction of change in net accident costs may also differ across risk groups. Under no-fault, $\theta = 0$ and hence for those drivers who would have been found to be at-fault in a liability system net accident costs are reduced. One expects there to be relatively more at-fault drivers in the high-risk group (which has a fatal accident propensity three times greater than the low-risk group) compared to the low-risk one (Devlin 1988). Consequently, proportionately more high-risk drivers will experience a fall in net accident costs (A_i). As A_i declines then residual income will increase and thus kilometers driven will increase and care will fall. Thus there will be relatively more high-risk kilometers driven and relatively less care taken.

2.3. No-Fault Administration

The switch to no-fault administration implies that compensation is no longer a function of observed care $\tilde{x}$ when the accidents occur. Hence, *all* individuals have the incentive to take less care.

2.4. The Overall Effect

The impact of the above on total kilometers driven is uncertain — however, there will be relatively more high-risk drivers on the road. The direction of change in total care is indeterminate since net income is affected differently for each risk group. Furthermore, as overall care falls, all individuals are induced to be more careful, from (3).

The purpose of the remainder of this paper is to present the empirical findings of the investigation in Quebec.

3. The Equations to Be Estimated[9]

The empirical analysis investigates how the care and activity decisions of individuals are affected by Quebec's new automobile insurance regime. The model suggests that the decision of how many kilometers to drive is a function of the price of kilometers, residual income (after a car is purchased), and the number of vehicles on the road.

The effect of the new regime on the care taken by drivers is discerned indirectly by examining what happened to the number of accidents before and after the changes. Separate accident equations are estimated for fatal (*F*), bodily-injury (*BI*), and property-damage-only (*PD*) accidents. The results from the fatal accidents are the most reliable insofar as the reported number of fatal accidents over the relevant time period is unlikely to be affected by the new insurance regime (there is no incentive to cheat when reporting a fatal accident). The reported number of *BI* and *PD* accidents are affected by the new regime since there is no longer any penalty to reporting a bodily-injury accident (in fact, the "victim" may be compensated). However, an estimate of the reporting bias of the new scheme can be obtained from estimates of the *BI* and *PD* accidents.

The equations were estimated as follows. First, a linear specification was postulated and then a series of Lagrange-Multiplier (LM) tests were done for each equation to ascertain if the equation was specified correctly.[10] Next, each equation was estimated separately by province (Ontario and Quebec) using the explanatory variables suggested from the above model (the time period used is approximately 1966–1984 — it differs between equations due to data constraints. The actual period used is noted in table 1). Tests were then done to detect any autoregressive errors, and in those equations in which first-order serial correlation was detected, the data were appropriately corrected (Johnston, 1960,

Table 1.   OLS Results of Equation (12): The Demand for Kilometers Driven[a]

Dependent Variable: Total annual kilometers driven (K)
Mean of Dependent Variable: $521*10^8$
Sample Period: Quebec, 1963–1984; Ontario, 1963–1984.

Variable	Estimate of Coefficient	t-statistic	Elasticity[b]
Constant	$.10447*10^{11}$	1.70	
NFQ	$.37945*10^9$	.27	
RPG	$-.52055*10^{10}$	5.90	$-.48$
NPDIR	$.23793*10^{13}$	2.72	.50
V	14430.00	8.65	.59

[a] Adjusted R-squared = .99, number of observations = 44, Bartlett's M = 2.78.
[b] The elasticity is evaluated at 1977 values.

259–260). Next, the Ontario and Quebec series were pooled for each equation, and the classical linear model assumption of homoscedastic variances across the two provinces was tested using the Bartlett test (Judge, 1980, 147). Finally, a series of F-tests were done on each pooled equation by adding an additional variable for each explanatory variable in the equation which was the product of the Quebec data times a dummy variable which was 1 for Quebec and 0 otherwise. These tests determine if the pooling restrictions that the coefficients are the same in Ontario and Quebec were valid. Most of these restrictions could not be rejected (the occasions when they were rejected are highlighted).

3.1. The Demand for Kilometers Driven

The equation estimated to capture the demand for kilometers driven was

$$K = d_0 + d_1\text{NFQ} + d_2\text{RPG} + d_3\text{NPDIR} + d_4\text{V} \qquad (12)$$

where

K   = total kilometers driven
NFQ   = Dummy variable for the new regime in Quebec, 1 = new regime, and 0 = old regime
RPG   = real price of gasoline per kilometer
NPDIR   = real personal disposable income per population sixteen and over
V   = total vehicles registered

This was estimated using OLS, and all coefficients were statistically the same across the provinces; these estimates are presented in table 1.

In addition to having a dummy variable denoting the switch in regime, (12) was estimated with an interactive dummy on total vehicles (VNF) in order to ascertain if there was a change in the number of kilometers driven per registered vehicle after no-fault. This interactive dummy variable VNF, however, did not contribute to explaining the number of kilometers driven.

The results of table 1 are used to estimate the impact of the change in residual income — income net of the fixed cost of motoring — on the number of kilometers driven.[11] This income effect is estimated to result in an increase of 58 deaths (a 3.72% increase in the fatal accident rate) per year in Quebec.[12]

3.2. Care Taken After No-Fault

The fatal accident equation, which was estimated to determine the direction of change in care after no-fault was

$$F = g_0 + g_1 NFQ + g_2 \frac{LMH}{DL} + g_3 \frac{MH}{DL} + g_4 LKM + g_5 KM + g_6 DA$$
$$+ g_7 SB + g_8 SP + g_9 CCDL + g_{10} D1 + g_{11} TIME \qquad (13)$$

In which

F	= number of fatal accidents
NFQ	= dummy variable denoting no-fault insurance in Quebec (new regime) (1 = new regime, 0 = otherwise)
LMH/DL	= lagged male drivers under 25 divided by total drivers
MH/DL	= male drivers under 25 divided by total drivers
LKM	= lagged total kilometers driven
KM	= total kilometers driven
DA	= dummy variable denoting the decrease in minimum drinking age from 21 to 18 in 1971 in both province (1 = 18 years, 0 = 21 years)
SB	= dummy variable denoting the enforcement of mandatory seat-belt legislation[13], 1976 Ontario, and 1982 Quebec (1 = enforcement, 0 = pre-enforcement)
SP	= dummy variable denoting the decrease in the maximum speed limit from 70mph to 60mph in 1976 in both provinces (1 = 60mph, 0 = 70mph)
CCDL	= number of criminal code traffic offenses per licenced driver[14]

Table 2. IV Estimates of Equation (13): The Fatal Accident Equation[a] (Using Transformed Data)

Dependent Variable: Number of fatal accidents (F)
Mean of Dependent Variable: 1387
Sample Period: Quebec, 1971–1984; Ontario, 1967–1984.
First-order Serial Correlation Coefficients: Quebec, −.8115, Ontario, −.6668

Variable	Estimate of Coefficient	t-statistic	Percentage Change in F
Constant	2106.8	3.66	
NFQ	133.46	2.63	9.62%
LMH/DL	−6887.2	1.02	
MH/DL	6932.9	1.02	
LKM	0.0209	0.03	
KM	1.6375	2.19	
DA	254.32	2.44	18.33%
SB	−93.110	1.39	−6.71%
SP	−182.43	1.93	−13.15%
CCDL	−0.0477	0.43	
D1	−858.73	3.59	
TIME	−51.830	4.59	

[a] Adjusted R-squared = .97, number of observations = 32, Bartlett's M = 1.37.

D1   = dummy variable which is "1" for Quebec observations, "0" otherwise (additional constant for Quebec)
TIME   = time trend

First of all, note that although theoretically one ought to be estimating fatal accidents per unit of driving activity (i.e., kilometers), this was not done since the kilometers driven data were considered unreliable. Hence, equation 13 was estimated using an instrumental variables technique to correct for the errors in variables problem associated with an unreliable measure of kilometers driven (lagged kilometers driven were also instrumented). First-order serial correlation was detected, and corrected. Table 2 presents the Instrumental Variables (IV) estimates of equation (13).[15]

The use of the IV technique allows for the fact that one would expect care and kilometers driven to be jointly determined, and the fact that kilometers driven are likely to be measured with error. In fact, given that the instruments are the independent variables in the kilometers driven equation this procedure is the same as a two-stage-least-squares estimation.

Table 3. Weighted IV Estimation of Bodily-Injury Accident Equation[a] (Transformed Data)

Dependent Variable: Number of bodily injury accidents (BI)
Mean of Dependent Variable: 36,676.
Sample Period: Quebec, 1971–1984; Ontario, 1967–1984.
First-order Serial Correlation Coefficients: Quebec, −.9653, Ontario, −.8692

Variable	Estimate of Coefficients	t-statistic	Percentage Change in BI
Constant	12425	1.25	
NFQ	9805.2	8.98	26.74%
LMH/DL	−397730.0	3.25	
MH/DL	257240.0	1.89	
LKM	9.8960	1.02	
KM	2.1349	.40	
DA	−792.270	0.48	
SB	−3167.10	2.89	−8.64%
SP	476.09	0.37	
CCDL	2.2395	1.03	
D1	29840.0	6.96	
TIME	−139.80	0.61	

[a] Adjusted R-squared = .997, number of observations = 32, Bartlett's M'' = 6.08.

In addition to estimating the pooled Ontario and Quebec data, equation 13 was estimated for Quebec only. This was done to ensure that the results from the pooled equation were not unduly influenced by the cross-coefficient restrictions stemming from pooling the data.[16] There were only 3 degrees of freedom in the Quebec only equation. However, the results were consistent with the results reported in table 3.[17]

Equation 13 uses kilometers driven as the measure of driving activity even though this variable is measured with error. Rather than kilometers driven, one could have used total vehicles or total passenger cars on the road as alternative measures of driving activity.[18]

A number of interesting observations can be made from these results, both with respect to the introduction of no fault, and regarding the efficacy of other regulations designed to influence accident causing behaviour. Note, for instance, that the results in table 2 indicate that the drop in the drinking age in 1971 from 21 to 18 resulted in an 18.33% increase in fatal accidents. This result is compatible with a recent study of drinking age legislation done in the United States (Saffer and Grossman,

1987). Lowering the speed limit from 70 miles per hour to 60 miles per hour lead to a spectacular 13% decrease in fatal accidents. This is interesting in light of other work that has found that the impact of speed on traffic accidents is not unequivocal (Friedland et al., 1987).

The most important observation from table 2 is that the no-fault dummy variable (NFQ) indicates that fatal accidents increased by 9.62% after no-fault was introduced. Thus, driving care fell significantly after no fault. This estimate of the increase in fatal accidents arising from the decrease in driving care in Quebec differs considerably from Gaudry's estimate of 4%.[19]

Equation 13 was also estimated using bodily-injury and property-damage-only accidents as the dependent variables.[20]

Notice from the results of the BI estimation (table 3) that there was a 26.74% increase in annual bodily-injury accidents (8,232) after no-fault was introduced. Fatal accidents, however, increased by 9.62%. The reporting of fatal accidents is believed to be highly reliable. If one

Table 4. Weighted IV Estimation of Property-Damage Accidents Equation[a] (Transformed Data)

Dependent Variable: Number of property-damage-only accidents (PD)
Mean of Dependent Variable: 140,546
Sample Period: Quebec, 1971–1984; Ontario, 1967–1984.
First-order Serial Correlation Coefficient: Quebec, −.7884, Ontario, −.6442

Variable	Estimate of Coefficient	t-statistic	Elasticity
Constant	−176760	4.16	
NFQ	20767.0	4.22	5.33%[b]
LMH/DL	1620500.0	3.25	
MH/DL	−405570.0	0.75	
LKM	−37.9730	1.04	
KM	26.4880	1.20	
DA	879.58	0.15	
SB	4606.9	1.09	
SP	−2969.8	0.62	
CCDL	−10.691	1.31	
D1	163980.0	9.45	
REALMIN	−21.383	2.01	0.5
TIME	1570.9	1.75	

[a] Adjusted R-squared = .995, number of observations = 32, Bartlett's M = 8.09.
[b] Denotes the change in the dependent variable as a result of a dummy variable.

assumes that this 9.62% is the appropriate indicator of the actual decline in care, the remaining 17.12% increase in BI accidents (7,639) is actually a *reporting* effect. (Recall that drivers are not penalized for reporting a BI accident under the no-fault insurance scheme. In fact, they most likely will benefit by receiving some form of compensation.)

Examining the PD accident equation estimates in table 4 one finds that the no-fault dummy indicates a 5.33% change in property-damage-only accidents after no-fault.[21] Assuming that the 9.62% increase in fatal accidents can be used as an indicator of the real increase in all accidents, the observed 5.33% increase in PD accidents is a consistent result. Applying the 9.62% increase in accidents to both bodily-injury and property-damage-only accidents, one finds that the large reporting effect left over for BI accidents (7,639) is consistent with the discrepancy between the 9.62% real increase in PD accidents and the 5.33% observed increase. If PD accidents actually increased by 9.62%, then there are 6,449 fewer accidents than expected — which is 84% of the reporting effect manifested in the BI equation results.

Thus, these accident results strongly suggest that there was a decrease in average care such that real accidents increased by at least 9.62% after no fault was introduced. In addition, there was a change in the mix of accidents from property damage only to bodily injury accidents. The efficiency implications of these results are detailed elsewhere (Devlin, 1988).

4. Some Conclusions Concerning the Deterrence Versus Compensation Debate

This paper examines how the liability system affects individuals' behavior in the presence of liability insurance. The magnitude of the increase in accidents resulting from the decline in average care by drivers is consistent with the hypothesis that the liability system does indeed affect drivers' behavior oven when liability insurance exists.

Recall that there are three main aspects to the switch to no-fault insurance in Quebec — premiums switched from being based on drivers' characteristics to being a flat-rate; premiums also switched from experienced to nonexperienced rated; and liability for bodily injury accidents was abolished. Each of these changes affects the care taken by drivers. Boyer and Dionne (1987) argue that the decrease in driving care in Quebec after no-fault is attributable mainly to uniform premium pricing. If premiums were to respond adequately to driving conduct, then the moral hazard effect that results in a decline in care would be eliminated. However, the fact that drivers are compensated for an accident regardless of fault is a necessary component of a no-fault insurance system. Thus, even if the flat-rate pricing structure of the insurance in Quebec were to change to a merit-rated structure, this would not eliminate the decrease in care attributable to the fact that drivers receive some compensation regardless of fault.

In conclusion, the presence of third-party (liability) insurance may dampen the incentives to take care emanating from the liability system, but it does not eliminate them. A no-fault system, with its attendant first-party insurance, severs the link between compensation for an accident and amount of driving care. Thus, irrespective of how the first-party insurance is priced, the fact that individuals are compensated regardless of care taken implies a moral hazard that may result in a decline in care taken. The empirical analysis of the Quebec experience is consistent with this conclusion. Note, however, that this paper does not deal with the potential benefits that arise as a result of the new regime in Quebec (see Fluet and Lefebvre, 1986). Before policy implications emerge from this analysis, all costs and benefits must be evaluated.

Appendix

Data Descriptions and Sources

Variable name	Description and source
BI:	The number of bodily-injury accidents reported: same sources as F.
CCDL:	The number of reported criminal code traffic offenses per driver in each of Ontario and Quebec. Statistics from Statistics Canada (85-206) and (85-001)
DL:	The number of driving license holders, from Statistics Canada (53-219).
F:	The number of fatal accidents reported per annum. In Quebec, from the Ministry of Transports, Quebec, reports up to 1978; then the Regié's annual reports from 1978 onwards. In Ontario, from the Ministry of Transportation and Communication (MTC) annual reports. Note that the definition of a fatality did not change in Quebec over the period in question; however, it did change in Ontario. In 1982 Ontario changed the definition of a fatal accident from one in which a fatality arose within one year of the accident,

Data Descriptions and Sources

Variable name	Description and source
	to one in which a fatality arose within 30 days of the accident. MTC officials estimated that this change resulted in a 5% decrease in reported fatal accidents after 1982. These figures were adjusted accordingly.
K: KM:	Total number of kilometers driven obtained from the Department of Energy Mines and Resources (EMR), Ottawa. Kilometers driven were estimated by an EMR transportation model which was designed to account for changing fuel efficiencies over time.
MH:	Total number of male drivers under the age of 25. In Quebec the data were provided by the Régie (*Profile des Titulaires de Permis de Conduire*, 1984); and in Ontario from 1966 to 1980 were provided by Mr. Chester Orlowski, Ministry of Transportation and Communications (unpublished data); from 1980 in MTC *Ontario Road Safety Annual Report*.
NPDIR:	Personal disposable income in Ontario and Quebec — Statistics Canada (13-213), divided by the population sixteen years of age and over in the two provinces (Statistics Canada 91-511, 91-518, 91-520). This is divided by the Consumer Price Index (1981 base).
PD:	The number of reported property-damage-only accidents. Same sources as F.
RPG:	This is the real price of gasoline per kilometer driven. It was constructed using the department of Energy Mines and Resources' estimates of gasoline consumption per kilometer for passenger automobiles (which account for the changing fuel efficiency of vehicles over time). The "price" of gasoline used was the price charged at "full-service" stations for leaded gasoline in Montreal and Toronto (prices obtained from Statistics Canada).
V:	Total vehicles registered in Ontario and Quebec — Statistics Canada 53-219. This figure is adjusted from 1975 (1976 in Ontario) onwards to subtract the number of mopeds from the total figure since they had not been registered prior to this time.

Notes

1. One of the first analysts to set forth a coherent treatment of the goals of accident law from the law and economics perspective is Calabresi (1970).

2. The qualification *almost* is used in characterizing the Quebec environment since the problem with analyzing Quebec is that a number of important changes occurred at the same

time. Namely, the province switched to no-fault automobile insurance for bodily injury accidents, premiums became invariant to driver's characteristics as well as invariant to driving experience, and bodily injury insurance became publicly administered under the no-fault scheme. All three of these changes may influence the same driving variables.

3. There are fifteen no-fault states in the United States, all of which have some limitation on the right to sue in the event of an automobile accident. However, the threshold value in each state beyond which suits may arise is low. Of the 12 states that prescribe a specific dollar threshold, eight are below $800, two are $1,000, and the remaining two are $4,000 and $4,500. The other three no-fault states have verbal thresholds, which depend on the nature of the damages (commonly describing the type of bodily injury which would exceed the threshold) (United States 1985).

4. For an introduction to the now standard insurance model based on expected utility theory, see Ehrlich and Becker (1972). In contrast to their paper, however, this present model does not focus on the choice of whether or not to insure. Insurance is assumed to be compulsory — in keeping with the fact that every province in Canada (indeed, most jurisdictions in North America) has mandatory automobile insurance.

5. Notice that this specification of P_{ci} implies that $P_{ins}(x)$ — the insurance premium — does not vary with kilometers driven. This is a simplification of reality in that in Ontario and the old system of Quebec the number of kilometers driven to the place of employment is used as a risk-class separator. (However, the relationship between kilometers driven and insurance premium is generally not a direct one.)

6. Note that the same analysis may apply even when nonpecuniary losses are introduced; see Cook and Graham (1977).

7. The asterisk on K does not imply that the socially optimal amount of kilometers driven will be taken. In Fact, unless premiums are a function of K as well greater than socially optimal driving takes place.

8. See Boyer and Dionne (1987) for another analysis of the Quebec automobile insurance plan.

9. See the appendix for a description of the data used.

10. The LM test is designed to determine if certain variables ought to be included as explanatory variables in an equation. Essentially, a test statistic is constructed which is the product of the number of observations in the sample and the R-squared statistic, which results from regressing the errors from the original equation on the original independent variables *plus* the potentially omitted variable(s). The resulting statistic has a chi-squared distribution with the degrees of freedom equal to the number of potentially omitted variables in the equation.

11. The change in residual income results from the new insurance pricing regime. High-risk drivers experienced a significant decline in insurance premiums, hence their residual income (income net of fixed automobile costs) increased by 9%. The low-risk drivers, however, experienced a decrease in residual income of .23%. The coefficient on NPDIR (net real per capita income) is used to estimate the impact on accidents of this increase in high-risk drivers' residual income and the decrease in low-risk drivers' residual income (Devlin 1988). Note that two effects are present — the first is a distributional effect — the fact that high-risk drivers have more residual income and low-risk drivers have less. Secondly, average insurance premiums fell, hence, average residual income rises — resulting in an increase in kilometers driven (given that kilometers driven is a normal good).

12. Two factors are lumped together in this estimate: first, the "risk-composition" effect — the number of fatal accidents expected as a result of more high-risk drivers and fewer low-risk drivers on the road from the pooling of bodily-injury premiums. Second, there is

the "average residual income" effect, which arises since the overall average premium paid by the driving population declined after no-fault was introduced.

13. According to the Régie, the public insurance administer in Quebec, seatbelt legislation was loosely enforced until 1982 (RAAQ Annual Report, 1982–83, 29). Evidence on seatbelt usage suggests that it was immediately enforced in Ontario in 1976 (see Transport Canada 1987). Furthermore, a new Quebec highway code came into effect in April 1982, which contained stiffer penalties for a number of traffic offenses.

14. The variable that ought to be in the accident equation is one which captures the policing expenditures made towards road safety separately from changes in individuals' care decisions. CCDL, the number of criminal code traffic violations per licensed driver may increase because the former has increased *or* because the latter has decreased. Unfortunately, this work is unable to use the theoretically desirable measures of the expected cost of a traffic violation or of the amount of traffic enforcement in operation due to data availability constraints.

15. Once again a series of LM tests were performed on the fatal accident equation to determine if there were some obvious omitted variables in the equation. These tests checked if the no-fault dummy variable interacted with other variables in a statistically significant manner in the fatal accident equation. The possible inclusion of the per-capita consumption of alcohol (ALCN) was also tested to examine if it should be included in the fatal accident equation. The interactive variables tested were the product of the no-fault dummy variable and MH/DL, LMH/DL, KM, LKM, and CCDL. None of these additional variables had a test statistic which rejected the null hypothesis that it does not belong in the equation. (The LM statistics for each variable are: .0004 for MH/DL*NFQ, .0320 for LMH/DL*NFQ, 1.095 for KM*NFQ, .137 for LKM*NFQ, .012 for CCDL*NFQ, and 2.044 for ALCN. The critical value of the Chi-squared statistic necessary to reject the null hypothesis (that the variable should be omitted) is 3.84 at the 5% level of significance.)

16. Note that even thought the restrictions that the coefficients are the same across provinces were tested, given the small sample size the strength of these tests may not be great.

17. The estimated coefficients from the Quebec only equation are

$$1845.3 + 279.00*NFQ - 769.88*LMH/DL + 2360.0*MH/DL - 3.2165*LKM$$
$$(3.49) \quad\quad (1.81) \quad\quad\quad (.04) \quad\quad\quad\quad (.10) \quad\quad\quad\quad\quad (1.28)$$

$$+ 2.8807*KM - 46.356*SB - 58.344*SP + .1834*CCDL - 59.448*TIME$$
$$(1.68) \quad\quad\quad (.29) \quad\quad\quad (.20) \quad\quad\quad (.74) \quad\quad\quad\quad (1.74)$$

The *t*-statistics are in parentheses. First-order serial correlation is corrected using a rho value of −.8115. The final value of the Durban-Watson statistic is 3.11 which, given that there are only 13 observations (one observation is lost due to the IV procedure) and 10 explanatory variables, is well within the zone of ignorance for the DW statistic.

18. Total kilometers driven is the theoretically correct measure of driving activity, hence, even though they are measured with error, they are used in the accident equations. Furthermore, there are problems associated with the other two measures of activity — for instance, total vehicles or passenger cars on the road do not indicate the extent to which such vehicles are actually driven. Estimates of the fatal accident equation when other measures of driving activity are used are found in Devlin (1988). Essentially, the influence of the dummy variable (which captures the average care taken) yielded consistent results across the various measures of activity.

19. Gaudry (1991) estimates the direct care effect (from a no-fault dummy variable) as

resulting in a 4% increase in fatalities. He also suggests that other effects (resulting from imputing possible activity changes) will result in an additional 6% increase in fatalities. Gaudry also highlights the important fact that the new regime in Quebec results in insurance being unavoidable — and hence an additional moral hazard effect may result from this increased coverage (previously uninsured drivers now must insure). Unlike this present study, Gaudry uses a Canada-wide price index for the price of insurance before and after the introduction of the new regime. This study uses insurance price data obtained from an insurance company which was operating in both Ontario and Quebec over the period in question. (Recall that the insurance premium is used to calculate the fixed cost of motoring, and hence the residual income effect of the change in insurance pricing by each risk class. See footnote 11.)

20. Note that the Bartlett's M statistic for the BI and PD equations indicate that the errors of the Quebec and Ontario series are heteroscedastistic. This was corrected by weighing the regression by the inverse of the variances in each province.

21. Note that there is an additional explanatory variable in the estimation of PD which is REALMIN. This variable is the real dollar value of the mandated minimum dollar threshold above which an accident must be reported. The nominal dollar reporting amount changed three times over the sample for each of Ontario and Quebec: from 1960 to 1970 in Ontario and to 1971 in Quebec this amount was $100 whereupon it became $200 (RSO 1970 c202, s139(1); Government of Quebec, Ministére de Transports 1971). In 1978 it was increased to $400 in Ontario (RSO 1980 c198) and in 1979 to $250 in Quebec (Government of Quebec, Ministere de Transports 1979). Finally, in 1985 Ontario increased the limit to $700.

References

Boyer, M., and G. Dionne. (1989). "Moral Hazard and Experience Rating: An Empirical Analysis," *Review of Economics and Statistics* LXXI (1), 128–134.

Boyer, M., and G. Dionne. (1987). "Description and Analysis of the Quebec Automobile Insurance Plan," *Canadian Public Policy* XIII (2), 181–195.

Brown, J. P. (1973). "Toward an Economic Theory of Liability," *Journal Legal Studies* II (2), 323–349.

Calabresi, G. (1970). *The Costs of Accidents*. New Haven, CT: Yale University Press.

Cook, P. J., and D. A. Graham. (1977). "The Demand for Insurance Protection: The Case of Irreplaceable Commodities," *Quarterly Journal of Economics* XCI, 143–156.

Demsetz. H. (1972). "When Does the Rule of Liability Matter?" *Journal of Legal Studies* I (1), 13–28.

Devlin, R. A. (1988). *Liability Versus No-Fault Automobile Insurance Regimes: An Analysis of the Experience in Quebec*. Ph.D. Dissertation, Department of Economics, University of Toronto.

Diamond, P. (1974). "Single Activity Accidents," *Journal of Legal Studies* III (1), 107–164.

Ehrlich, I., and G. S. Becker. (1982). "Market Insurance, Self-Insurance and Self-Protection," *Journal of Political Economy* 80, 623–648.

Engle, R. F. (1982). "A General Approach to Lagrange Multiplier Model Diagnostics," *Journal of Econometrics* 20, 83–104.

Fluet, C., and P. Lefebvre. (1986). "L'Assurance Automobile au Québec: Bilan d'une Réforme," Government of Quebec, RAAQ.

Friedland, M., M. Trebilcock and K. Roach. (1987). "Regulating Traffic Safety: A Survey of Control Strategies," Law and Economics Workshop paper WS 1987–88-(2), University of Toronto.

Gaudry, M. (1991). "Measuring the Effects of the No-Fault 1978 Quebec Automobile Insurance Act with the DRAG Model," in G. Dionne, ed., *Contributions to Insurance Economics*. Norwell, MA: Kluwer Academic Publishers.

Green, J. (1976). "On the Optimal Structure of Liability Laws," *Bell Journal of Economics* 7 (2), 553–554.

Hoy, M. (1982). "Categorizing Risks in the Insurance Industry," *Quarterly Journal of Economics* 97, 321–336.

Johnston, J. (1960). *Econometric Methods*, 2d ed. New York: McGraw Hill Book Co.

Judge, G. (1980). *The Theory and Practice of Econometrics*. New York: John Wiley and Sons.

Kochanowski, P. S., and M. V. Young. (1985). "Deterrent Aspects of No-Fault Automobile Insurance: Some Empirical Findings," *Journal of Risk and Insurance* 52, 269–288.

Landes, E. M. (1982). "Insurance, Liability, and Accidents: A Theoretical and Empirical Investigation of the Effect of No-Fault Accidents," *Journal of Law and Economics* XXV (1), 49–65.

Quebec, Government of, Ministere des Transports, "Statistiques d'accidents de vehicles automobiles," 1970–1979.

Quebec, Government of, Regie de l'assurance Automobile du Quebec. *Annual Reports*, Direction de la Statistique, RAAQ, 1978–1986.

Quebec, RAAQ. (1984). *Profil des Titulaires de Permis de Conduire, 1970–1982.* mai, Direction de la Statistique.

Rea, S. A. (1982). "Nonpecuniary Loss and Breach of Contract," *Journal of Legal Studies* XI (1), 35–53.

Rea S. A. (1987). "The Economics of Comparative Negligence," *International Review of Law and Economics* 12, 149–162.

Rea, S. A. (1991). "Insurance Classifications and Social Welfare," in G. Dionne, ed., *Contributions to Insurance Economics*. Norwell, MA: Kluwer Academic Publishers.

Saffer, H., and M. Grossman. (1987) "Drinking Age Laws and Highway Mortality Rates: Cause and Effect," *Economic Inquiry* XXV (3), 403–417.

Shavell, S. (1987). *Economic Analysis of Accident Law*. Cambridge, MA: Harvard University Press.

Transport Canada. (1987). *Road Safety*. Leaflet TP2436.

Transport Canada. Undated mimeo, "Estimates of Seat Belt Use from National Surveys," mimeo of seat belt use and statistics, 1975 and 1977.

United States Department of Transportation. (1985). *Compensating Automobile Accident Victims, A Follow-up Report on No-Fault Automobile Insurance Experiences.*

Zador, P., and A. Lund. (1986). "Re-Analysis of the Effects of No-Fault Automobile Insurance on Fatal Crashes," *Journal of Risk and Insurance* LIII (3), 226–241.

Index